MASS VIOLENCE IN AMERICA

Advisory editors:

ROBERT M. FOGELSON   RICHARD E. RUBENSTEIN

MASS VIOLENCE IN AMERICA

WILD LIFE ON THE PLAINS

AND HORRORS OF INDIAN WARFARE

ARNO PRESS & THE NEW YORK TIMES

New York • 1969

Editorial Note

Nations, like men, are sometimes interested in burying the past.

In early 1968, after more than five years marked by political assassinations, racial uprisings, campus disorders, mass demonstrations and the violent suppression of protest, *The New York Times Magazine* asked a group of distinguished scholars to reply to the question, "Is America by nature a violent society?" In answer, University of Chicago anthropologist Clifford Geertz wrote:

> "We do not know very well what kind of society we live in, what kind of history we have had, what kind of people we are. We are just now beginning to find out, the hard way . . ."

The proposition was astonishing but correct: what was least understood about domestic political violence was its role in American history. It was common knowledge that the United States had had a Revolution, a Civil War, some trouble with the Indians and a period of labor-management conflict. But one could search the shelves of the nation's great libraries without discovering more than a handful of works on the subject of violence in American history, and these hopelessly out of date.

Historians had generally ignored or soft-pedaled the history of farmer uprisings, native vigilantism, labor-management struggles, ethnic conflicts and race riots; comparative work in the history of social conflict was particularly weak. Sociologists and political scientists in the grip of "consensus" theory tended to treat episodes of mass violence in America as insignificant or aberrational—temporary exceptions to the norm of peaceful progress. Psychologists and behavioral scientists discussed "mob violence" in terms which suggested that riots, revolts, insurrections and official violence were the products of individual or group pathology. All such interpretations had the effect not only of minimizing group violence in America, but of depriving it of political content—hence, of relevance to the present.

As a result, as late as 1968, the rich, multifarious and often terrifying history of domestic political violence was still largely *terra incognita*. So long as most Americans wished to keep certain skeletons locked away in their closets, few scholars would attempt to open doors. Conversely, once the American people, frightened yet emboldened by the sudden reappearance of intense social conflict, began to ask new questions about the past, so did the scholars.

Our purpose in helping Arno Press and *The New York Times* select and publish significant documents in the history of political violence has not been to compound past errors by overemphasizing the role of conflict in American history. On the contrary, our aim has been to provide materials which will aid in the search for an accurate perspective on the present. MASS VIOLENCE IN AMERICA includes eyewitness reports, government documents and other descriptive and analytic material relating to mass political violence in the United States. These documents not only provide information—they give the "feel" or "flavor" of past eras of civil disorder by evoking the emotional and political context in which revolts took place. Most of them have long been out of print and are obtainable, if at all, only in the nation's largest libraries.

The scope of this series is wide, ranging from accounts of Indian warfare to descriptions of labor-management violence, from narratives of colonial insurrections to reports on modern racial uprisings. It is not, however, limitless, nor were the constituent volumes carelessly selected. The principle of coherence which guided the selections is implicit in the phrase "mass political violence." "Mass" denotes activity engaged in by large groups rather than individuals acting alone; "political" suggests a relationship between such activity and competition among domestic groups for power, property and prestige; and "violence" is narrowly construed as resulting in physical damage to persons or property. In short, the materials reproduced herein are intended to illuminate the resort to violence by American groups seeking to change or to preserve the status quo. Although historical, they are of interest to any who wishes to understand the causes, nature and direction of domestic political violence, whether they be social scientists, historians or just interested Americans.

Of course, we are particularly hopeful that these volumes will prove useful to those now engaged in curriculum-revision and the teaching of high school and college courses in the area of American studies. What Christopher Jencks and David Reisman term "the Academic Revolution" has made difficult demands on all educators, not the least of which is the demand for courses which are both relevant to the condition of modern America and of the highest academic quality. These volumes are meant to provide raw material for such courses—primary source matter which will help both instructors and students to deepen and enrich their views of the American experience.

Most important, the editors and publisher recognize that these volumes appear during a national crisis which is also a crisis of the spirit, a time in which the public response to various manifestations of civil disorder is increasingly governed by anger, fear and hysteria. In such an atmosphere it is important to recognize that one is not alone in time—that such events have taken place before in America and, unless fundamental changes in our social and political life take place, will probably recur in the future. Our fondest hope is that this work, and others like it, will help to keep alive, in a time of growing unreason, the spirit of reasoned inquiry.

RICHARD E. RUBENSTEIN
The Adlai Stevenson Institute
Chicago, Illinois

ROBERT M. FOGELSON
Harvard-MIT Joint Center
for Urban Studies
Cambridge, Massachusetts

WILD LIFE ON THE PLAINS

AND HORRORS OF INDIAN WARFARE

SITTING BULL.

WILD LIFE ON THE PLAINS

AND

Horrors of Indian Warfare.

BY A CORPS OF COMPETENT AUTHORS AND ARTISTS.

BEING

A Complete History of Indian Life, Warfare and Adventure in America.

MAKING SPECIALLY PROMINENT THE

LATE INDIAN WAR,

WITH FULL DESCRIPTIONS OF

THE MESSIAH CRAZE, GHOST DANCE, LIFE OF SITTING BULL

THE WHOLE FORMS AN AUTHENTIC AND COMPLETE HISTORY OF THE SAVAGE
RACES IN AMERICA—THEIR ILLUSTRIOUS LEADERS, THEIR
BELIEFS, MANNERS AND CUSTOMS,

COMPRISING

Terrible Battles, Wonderful Escapes, Thrilling Tales of Heroism, Daring Exploits, Wonderful Fortitude, etc., etc.

SUPERBLY ILLUSTRATED.

PUBLISHED BY

CONTINENTAL PUBLISHING CO.,

SAINT LOUIS, MO.

CONTENTS.

(5)

CONTENTS.

CHAPTER IX.

CHAPTER X.

CHAPTER XI.

CHAPTER XIV.

CHAPTER XV.

CHAPTER XVI.

CHAPTER XXI.

CHAPTER XXII.

CHAPTER XXIII.

CHAPTER XXIV

CHAPTER XXV.

CHAPTER XXVI.

CHAPTER XXVII.

CHAPTER XXVIII.

CHAPTER XXIX.

Truly Yours
G. A. Custer

LIFE ON THE PLAINS.

I

AS a fitting introduction to some of the personal incidents and sketches which I shall hereafter present to the readers of this book, a brief description of the country in which these events transpired may not be deemed inappropriate.

It is but a few years ago that every schoolboy, supposed to possess the rudiments of a knowledge of the geography of the United States, could give the boundaries and a general description of the "Great American Desert." As to the boundary the knowledge seemed to be quite explicit: on the north bounded by the Upper Missouri, on the east by the Lower Missouri and Mississippi, on the south by Texas, and on the west by the Rocky Mountains. The boundaries on the northwest and south remained undisturbed, while on the east civilization, propelled and directed by Yankee enterprise, adopted the motto, "Westward the star of empire takes its way." Countless throngs of emigrants crossed the Mississippi and Missouri rivers, selecting homes in the rich and fertile territories lying beyond. Each year this tide of emigration, strengthened and increased by the flow from foreign shores, advanced toward the setting sun, slowly but surely narrowing the preconceived limits of the "Great American Desert," and correspondingly enlarging the limits of civilization. At last the geographical myth was dispelled. It was gradually discerned that the Great American Desert did not exist, that it had no abiding place, but that within its supposed limits, and instead of what had been regarded as a sterile and unfruitful tract of land, incapable of sustaining either man or beast, there existed the fairest and richest portion of the national domain, blessed with a climate pure, bracing, and healthful, while its undeveloped soil rivalled if it did not surpass the most productive portions of the Eastern, Middle, or Southern States.

Discarding the name "Great American Desert," this immense tract of country, with its eastern boundary moved back by civilization to a distance of nearly three hundred miles west of the Missouri river, is now known as "The Plains," and by this more appropriate title it shall be called when reference to it is necessary. The Indian tribes which have caused the Government most anxiety and whose depredations have been most serious against our frontier settlements and prominent lines of travel across the Plains, infest that portion of the Plains bounded on the north by the valley of the Platte river and its tributaries, on the east by a line running north and south between the 97th and 98th meridians, on the south by the valley of the Arkansas river, and west by the Rocky Mountains—although by treaty stipulations almost every tribe with which the Government has recently been at war is particularly debarred from entering or occupying any portion of this tract of country.

Of the many persons whom I have met on the Plains as transient visitors from the States or from Europe, there are few who have not expressed surprise that their original ideas concerning the appearance and characteristics of the country were so far from correct, or that the Plains in imagination, as described in books, tourists' letters, or reports of isolated scientific parties, differed so widely from the Plains as they actually exist and appear to the eye. Travellers writers of fiction, and journalists have spoken and written a great deal con-

13

cerning this immense territory, so unlike in all its qualities and characteristics to the settled and cultivated portion of the United States; but to a person familiar with the country the conclusion is forced, upon reading these published descriptions, either that the writers never visited but a limited portion of the country they aim to describe, or, as is most commonly the case at the present day, that the journey was made in a stage-coach or Pullman car, half of the distance travelled in the night time, and but occasional glimpses taken during the day. A journey by rail across the Plains is at best but ill adapted to a thorough or satisfactory examination of the general character of the country, for the reason that in selecting the route for railroads the valley of some stream is, if practicable, usually chosen to contain the road-bed. The valley being considerably lower than the adjacent country, the view of the tourist is correspondingly limited. Moreover, the vastness and varied character of this immense tract could not fairly be determined or judged of by a flying trip across one portion of it. One would scarcely expect an accurate opinion to be formed of the swamps of Florida from a railroad journey from New York to Niagara.

After indulging in criticisms on the written descriptions of the Plains, I might reasonably be expected to enter into what I conceive a correct description, but I forbear. Beyond a general outline embracing some of the peculiarities of this slightly known portion of our country, the limits and character of these sketches of Western life will not permit me to go.

The idea entertained by the greater number of people regarding the appearance of the Plains, while it is very incorrect so far as the latter are concerned, is quite accurate and truthful if applied to the prairies of the Western States. It is probable, too, that romance writers, and even tourists at an earlier day, mistook the prairies for the Plains, and in describing one imagined they were describing the other; whereas the two have little in common to the eye of the beholder, save the general absence of trees.

In proceeding from the Missouri river to the base of the Rocky Mountains, the ascent, although gradual, is quite rapid. For example, at Fort Riley, Kansas, the bed of the Kansas river is upward of 1,000 feet above the level of the sea, while Fort Hays, at a distance of nearly 150 miles further west, is about 1,500 feet above the level of the sea. Starting from almost any point near the central portion of the Plains, and moving in any direction, one seems to encounter a series of undulations at a more or less remote distance from each other, but constantly in view. Comparing the surface of the country to that of the ocean, a comparison often indulged in by those who have seen both, it does not require a very great stretch of the imagination, when viewing this boundless ocean of beautiful living verdure, to picture these successive undulations as gigantic waves, not wildly chasing each other to or from the shore, but standing silent and immovable, and by their silent immobility adding to the impressive grandeur of the scene. These undulations, varying in height from fifty to five hundred feet, are sometimes formed of a light sandy soil, but often of different varieties of rock, producing at a distance the most picturesque effect. The constant recurrence of these waves, if they may be so termed, is quite puzzling to the inexperienced plainsman. He imagines, and very naturally too, judging from appearances, that when he ascends to the crest he can overlook all the surrounding country. After a weary walk or ride of perhaps several miles, which appeared at starting not more than one or two, he finds himself at the desired point, but discovers that directly beyond, in the direction he desires to go, rises a second wave, but slightly higher than the first, and from the crest of which he must certainly be able to scan the country as far as the eye can reach. Thither he pursues his course, and after a ride of from five to ten miles, although the distance did not seem half so great before starting, he finds himself on the crest, or, as it is invariably termed, the "divide," but again only to discover that another and apparently a higher divide rises in his front, and at about the same distance. Hundreds, yes, thousands of miles may be journeyed over, and this same effect witnessed every few hours.

As you proceed toward the west from the Missouri, the size of the trees diminishes as well as the number of kinds. As you penetrate the borders of the Indian country, leaving civilization behind you, the sight of forests is no longer enjoyed, the only trees to be seen being scattered along the banks of the streams, these becoming smaller and more rare, finally disappearing altogether and giving place to a few scattering willows and osiers. The greater portion of the Plains may be said to be without timber of any kind. As to the cause of this absence scientific men disagree, some claiming that the high winds which prevail in unobstructed force prevent the growth and existence of not only trees but even the taller grasses. This theory is well supported by facts, as, unlike the Western prairies, where the grass often attains a height sufficient to conceal a man on horseback, the Plains are covered by a grass which rarely, and only under favorable circumstances, exceeds three inches in height. Another theory, also somewhat plausible, is that the entire Plains were at one time covered with timber more or less dense, but this timber, owing to various causes, was destroyed, and has since been prevented from growing or spreading over the Plains by the annual fires which the Indians regularly create, and which sweep over the entire country. These fires are built by the Indians in the fall to burn the dried grass and hasten the growth of the pasturage in the early spring. Favoring the theory that the Plains were at one time covered with forests, is the fact that entire trunks of large trees have been found in a state of petrifaction on elevated portions of the country, and far removed from streams of water.

While dwarfed specimens of almost all varieties of trees are found fringing the banks of some of the streams, the prevailing species are cottonwood and poplar trees (*Populus monilifera* and *Populus angulosa*). Intermingled with these are found clumps of osiers (*Salix longifolia*). In almost any other portion of the country the cottonwood would be the least desirable of trees; but to the Indian, and, in many instances which have fallen under my observation, to our troops, the cottonwood has performed a service for which no other tree has been found its equal, and that is as forage for horses and mules during the winter season, when the snow prevents even dried grass from being obtainable. During the winter campaign of 1868-'69 against the hostile tribes south of the Arkansas, it not unfrequently happened that my command while in pursuit of Indians exhausted its supply of forage, and the horses and mules were subsisted upon the young bark of the cottonwood tree. In routing the Indians from their winter villages, we invariably discovered them located upon that point of the stream promising the greatest supply of cottonwood bark, while the stream in the vicinity of the village was completely shorn of its supply of timber, and the village itself was strewn with the white branches of the cottonwood entirely stripped of their bark. It was somewhat amusing to observe an Indian pony feeding on cottonwood bark. The limb being usually cut into pieces about four feet in length and thrown upon the ground, the pony, accustomed to this kind of "long forage," would place one fore foot on the limb in the same maner as a dog secures a bone, and gnaw the bark from it. Although not affording anything like the amount of nutriment which either hay or grain does, yet our horses invariably preferred the bark to either, probably on account of its freshness.

The herbage to be found on the principal portion of the Plains is usually sparse and stunted in its growth. Along the banks of the streams and in the bottom lands there grows generally in rich abundance a species of grass often found in the States east of the Mississippi; but on the uplands is produced what is there known as the "buffalo grass," indigenous and peculiar in its character, differing in form and substance from all other grasses. The blade under favorable circumstances reaches a growth usually of from three to five inches, but instead of being straight, or approximately so, it assumes a curled or waving shape, the grass itself becoming densely matted, and giving to the foot, when walking upon it, a sensation similar to that produced by stepping upon moss or the most costly of velvet carpets.

Nearly all graminivorous animals inhabiting the Plains, except the elk and some species of the deer, prefer the buffalo grass to that of the lowland; and it is probable that even these exceptions would not prove good if it were not for the timber on the bottom land, which affords good cover to both the elk and the deer. Both are often found in large herds grazing upon the uplands, although the grass is far more luxuriant and plentiful on the lowlands. Our domestic animals invariably choose the buffalo grass, and experience demonstrates beyond question that it is the most nutritious of all varieties of wild grass.

The favorite range of the buffalo is contained in a belt of country running north and south, about two hundred miles wide, and extending from the Platte river on the north to the valley of the Upper Canadian on the south. In migrating, if not grazing or alarmed, the buffalo invariably moves in single file, the column generally being headed by a patriarch of the herd, who is not only familiar with the topography of the country, but whose prowess "in the field" entitles him to become the leader of his herd. He maintains this leadership only so long as his strength and courage enable him to remain the successful champion in the innumerable contests which he is called upon to maintain. The buffalo trails are always objects of interest and inquiry to the sight-seer on the Plains. These trails made by the herds in their migrating movements are so regular in their construction and course as to well excite curiosity. They vary but little from eight to ten inches in width, and are usually from two to four inches in depth; their course is almost as unvarying as that of the needle, running north and south. Of the thousands of buffalo trails which I have seen, I recollect none of which the general direction was not north and south. This may seem somewhat surprising at first thought, but it admits of a simple and satisfactory explanation.

The general direction of all streams, large and small, on the Plains, is from the west to the east, seeking as they do an entrance to the Mississippi. The habits of the buffalo incline him to graze and migrate from one stream to another, moving northward and crossing each in succession as he follows the young grass in the spring, and moving southward seeking the milder climate and open grazing in the fall and winter. Throughout the buffalo country are to be seen what are termed "buffalo wallows." The number of these is so great as to excite surprise; a moderate estimate would give from one to three to each acre of ground throughout this vast tract of country These wallows

THE BUFFALO RANGE.

are about eight feet in diameter and from six to eighteen inches in depth, and are made by the buffalo bulls in the spring when challenging a rival to combat for the favor of the opposite sex. The ground is broken by pawing—if an animal with a hoof can be said to paw—and if the challenge is accepted, as it usually is, the combat takes place; after which the one who comes off victorious remains in possession of the battle-field, and, occupying the "wallow" of fresh upturned earth, finds it produces a cooling sensation to his hot and gory sides. Sometimes the victory which gives possession of the battle-field and drives a hated antagonist away is purchased at a dear price. The carcass of the victor is often found in the wallow, where his brief triumph has soon terminated from the effects of his wounds. In the early spring, during the shedding season, the buffalo resorts to his "wallow" to aid in removing the old coat. These "wallows" have proven of no little benefit to man, as well as to animals other than the buffalo. After a heavy rain they become filled with water, the soil being of such a compact character as to retain it. It has not unfrequently been the case when making long marches that the streams would be found dry, while water in abundance could be obtained from the "wallows." True, it was not of the best quality, particularly if it had been standing long and the buffalo had patronized the wallows as "summer resorts"; but on the Plains a thirsty man or beast, far from any streams of water, does not parley long with these considerations.

Wherever water is found on the Plains, particularly if it is standing, innumerable gadflies and mosquitoes generally abound. To such an extent do these pests to the animal kingdom exist, that to our thinly-coated animals, such as the horse and mule, grazing is almost an impossibility, while the buffalo with his huge shaggy coat can browse undisturbed. The most sanguinary and determined of these troublesome insects are the "buffalo flies"; they move in myriads, and so violent and painful are their assaults upon horses that a herd of the latter has been known to stampede as the result of an attack from a swarm of these flies.

But here again is furnished what some reasoners would affirm is evidence of the "eternal fitness of things." In most localities where these flies are found in troublesome numbers, there are also found flocks of starlings, a species of blackbird; these, more, I presume, to obtain a livelihood than to become the defender of the helpless, perch themselves upon the backs of the animals when woe betide the hapless gadfly who ventures near, only to become a choice morsel for the starling. In this way I have seen our herds of cavalry horses grazing undisturbed, each horse of the many hundreds having perched upon his back from one to dozens of starlings, standing guard over him while he grazed.

One of the first subjects which addresses itself to the mind of the stranger on the Plains, particularly if he be of a philosophical or scientific turn of mind, is the mirage, which is here observed in all its perfection. Many a weary mile of the traveller has been whiled away in endeavors to account for the fitful and beautifully changing visions presented by the mirage. Sometimes the distortions are wonderful, and so natural as to deceive the most experienced eye. Upon one occasion I met a young officer who had spent several years on the Plains and in the Indian country. He was, on the occasion alluded to, in command of a detachment of cavalry in pursuit of a party of Indians who had been committing depredations on our frontier. While riding at the head of his command he suddenly discovered, as he thought, a party of Indians not more than

a mile distant. The latter seemed to be galloping toward him. The attention of his men was called to them, and they pronounced them Indians on
horseback. The "trot" was sounded, and the column moved forward to the
attack. The distance between the attacking party and the supposed foe was rapidly diminishing, the Indians appearing plainer to view each moment. The
charge was about to be sounded, when it was discovered that the supposed
party of Indians consisted of the decayed carcasses of half a dozen slain buffaloes, which number had been magnified by the mirage, while the peculiar motion imparted by the latter had given the appearance of Indians on horseback.

I have seen a train of government wagons with white canvas covers moving through a mirage which, by elevating the wagons to treble their height
and magnifying the size of the covers, presented the appearance of a line of
large sailing vessels under full sail, while the usual appearance of the mirage gave a correct likeness of an immense lake or sea. Sometimes the mirage has been the cause of frightful suffering and death by its deceptive appearance.

Trains of emigrants making their way to California and Oregon have, while
seeking water to quench their thirst and that of their animals, been induced to
depart from their course in the endeavor to reach the inviting lake of water
which the mirage displayed before their longing eyes. It is usually represented at a distance of from five to ten miles. Sometimes, if the nature of the
ground is favorable, it is dispelled by advancing toward it; at others it is like
an *ignis fatuus*, hovering in sight, but keeping beyond reach. Here and there
throughout this region are pointed out the graves of those who are said to have
been led astray by the mirage until their bodies were famished and they suc-
cumbed to thirst.

The routes usually chosen for travel across the Plains may be said to furnish,
upon an average, water every fifteen miles. In some instances, however, and
during the hot season of the year, it is necessary in places to go into what is
termed "a dry camp," that is, to encamp where there is no water. In such
emergencies, with a previous knowledge of the route, it is practicable to transport from the last camp a sufficient quantity to satisfy the demands of the people
composing the train, but the dumb brutes must trust to the little moisture
obtained from the night grazing to quench their thirst.

The animals inhabiting the Plains resemble in some respects the fashionable
society of some of our larger cities. During the extreme heat of the summer
they forsake their accustomed haunts and seek a more delightful retreat. For,
although the Plains are drained by streams of all sizes, from the navigable
river to the humblest of brooks, yet at certain seasons the supply of water in
many of them is of the most uncertain character. The pasturage, from the
excessive heat, the lack of sufficient moisture, and the withering hot winds
which sweep across from the south, becomes dried, withered, and burnt, and is
rendered incapable of sustaining life. Then it is that the animals usually
found on the Plains disappear for a short time, and await the return of a
milder season.

Having briefly grouped the prominent features of the central Plains, and as
some of the incidents connected with my service among the Indian tribes occurred far to the south of the localities already referred to, a hurried reference
to the country north of Texas, and in which the Wichita mountains are located,
a favorite resort of some of the tribes, is here made. To describe as one
would view it in journeying upon horseback over this beautiful and romantic
country, to picture with the pen those boundless solitude—so silent that their

silence alone increases their grandeur—to gather inspiration from nature and to attempt to paint the scene as my eye beheld it, is a task before which a much readier pen than mine might well hesitate.

It was a beautiful and ever-changing panorama which at one moment excited the beholder's highest admiration, at the next impressed him with speechless veneration. Approaching the Wichita mountains from the north, and after the eye has perhaps been wearied by the tameness and monotony of the un- broken Plains, one is gladdened by the relief which the sight of these pictur- esque and peculiarly beautiful mountains affords.

Here are to be seen all the varied colors which Bierstadt and Church en- deavor to represent in their mountain scenery. A journey across and around them on foot and upon horseback will well repay either the tourist or artist. The air is pure and fragrant, and as exhilarating as the purest of wine; the climate entrancingly mild; the sky clear, and blue as the most beautiful sap- phire, with here and there clouds of rarest loveliness, presenting to the eye the richest commingling of bright and varied colors; delightful odors are con- stantly being wafted by; while the forests, filled with the mocking bird, the colibri, the humming bird, and the thrush, constantly put forth a joyful chorus, and all combine to fill the soul with visions of delight and enhance the perfec- tion and glory of the creation. Strong indeed must be that unbelief which can here contemplate nature in all her purity and glory, and, unawed by the sub- limity of this closely-connected testimony, question either the Divine origin or purpose of the beautiful firmament.

Unlike most mountains, the Wichita cannot properly be termed a range or chain, but more correctly a collection or group, as many of the highest and most beautiful are detached, and stand on a level plain "solitary and alone." They are mainly composed of granite, the huge blocks of which exhibit numer- ous shades of beautiful colors, crimson, purple, yellow, and green predominat- ing. They are conical in shape, and seem to have but little resemblance to the soil upon which they are founded. They rise abruptly from a level sur- face—so level and unobstructed that it would be an easy matter to drive a car- riage to any point of the circumference at the base; and yet so steep and broken are the sides that it is only here and there that it is possible to ascend them. From the foot of almost every mountain pours a stream of limpid water, of almost icy coldness.

If the character given to the Indian by Cooper and other novelists, as well as by well-meaning but mistaken philanthropists of a later day, were the true one; if the Indian were the innocent, simple-minded being he is represented, more the crea. ure of romance than reality, imbued only with a deep veneration for the works of nature, freed from the passions and vices which must accom- pany a savage nature; if, in other words, he possessed all the virtues which his admirers and works of fiction ascribe to him, and were free from all the vices which those best qualified to judge assign to him, he would be just the character to complete the picture which is presented by the country embracing the Wi- chita mountains. Cooper, to whose writings more than to those of any other author are the people speaking the English language indebted for a false and ill-judged estimate of the Indian character, might well have laid the scenes of his fictitious stories in this beautiful and romantic country.

It is to be regretted that the character of the Indian as described in Coop- er's interesting novels is not the true one. But as, in emerging from childhood into the years of a maturer age, we are often compelled to cast aside many of our earlier illusions and replace them by beliefs less inviting but more real so we, as a people, with opportunities enlarged and facilities for obtaining knowledge increased, have been forced by a multiplicity of causes to study and endeavor to comprehend thoroughly the character of the red man. So intimately has he become associated with the Government as ward of the nation, and so prominent a place among the questions of national policy does the much mooted "Indian question" occupy, that it behooves us no longer to study this problem from works of fiction, but to deal with it as it exists in reality. Stripped of the beautiful romance with which we have been so long willing to envelop him, transferred from the inviting pages of the novelist to the localities where we are compelled to meet with him, in his native village, on the war path, and when raiding upon our frontier settlements and lines of travel, the Indian forfeits his claim to the appellation of the "*noble* red man." We see him as he is, and, so far as all knowledge goes, as he ever has been, a *savage* in every sense of the word; not worse, perhaps, than his white brother would be similarly born and bred, but one whose cruel and ferocious nature far exceeds that of any wild beast of the desert. That this is true no one who has been brought into intimate contact with the wild tribes will deny. Perhaps there are some who, as members of peace commissions or as wandering agents of some benevolent society, may have visited these tribes or attended with them at councils held for some pacific purpose, and who, by passing through the villages of the Indian while *at peace*, may imagine their opportunities for judging of the Indian nature all that could be desired. But the Indian, while he can seldom be accused of indulging in a great variety of wardrobe, can be said to have a character capable of adapting itself to almost every occasion. He has one character, perhaps his most serviceable one, which he preserves carefully, and only airs it when making his appeal to the Government or its agents for arms, ammunition, and license to employ them. This character is invariably paraded, and often with telling effect, when the motive is a peaceful one. Prominent chiefs invited to visit Washington invariably don this character, and in their "talks" with the "Great Father" and other less prominent personages they successfully contrive to exhibit but this one phase. Seeing them under these or similar circumstances only, it is not surprising that by many the Indian is looked upon as a simple-minded "son of nature," desiring nothing beyond the privilege of roaming and hunting over the vast unsettled wilds of the West, inheriting and asserting but few native rights, and never trespassing upon the rights of others. This view is equally erroneous with that which regards the Indian as a creature possessing the human form but divested of all other attributes of humanity, and whose traits of character, habits, modes of life, disposition, and savage customs disqualify him from the exercise of all rights and privileges, even those pertaining to life itself. Taking him as we find him, at peace or at war, at home or abroad, waiving all prejudices, and laying aside all partiality, we will discover in the Indian a subject for thoughtful study and investigation. In him we will find the representative of a race whose origin is, and promises to be, a subject forever wrapped in mystery; a race incapable of being judged by the rules or laws applicable to any other known race of men; one between which and civilization there seems to have existed from time immemorial a determined and unceasing warfare—a hostility so deep-seated and inbred with the Indian character, that in the exceptional instances where the modes and habits of civilization have been reluctantly adopted, it has been at the sacrifice of power and influence as a tribe, and the more serious loss of health, vigor, and courage as individuals.

II.

IF the character of the Indian is enveloped in mystery, how much more so is his origin. From his earliest history to the present time learned men have striven to unravel this mystery, and to trace the genealogy of the red man to its original source. But in spite of all study and the deepest research capable of being brought to bear on this subject, it is to-day surrounded by a darkness almost as deep and impenetrable as that which enfolded it centuries ago. Various writers of ability have attempted to prove that the Indians came from eastern Asia; others trace them to Africa, others to Phœnicia, while another class believes them to be autochthones. In favor of each of these beliefs strong circumstantial evidence can be produced. By closely studying the customs, costumes, faith, and religious traditions of the various tribes, a striking homogeneity is seen to exist. At the same time and from the same sources we are enabled to discover satisfactory resemblances between certain superstitions and religious rites practised among the Indian tribes and those which prevailed at one time among the ancient Persians, the Hebrews, and the Chaldeans. They who adhere to the belief of disparity of origin may readily adduce arguments in refutation of an opposite theory. The apparent similarity found to exist in the customs, dress, and religious rites of different tribes may be partially accounted for by their long intercourse under like circumstances, the effect of which would necessarily be an assimilation in beliefs and usages to a greater or less degree. The preponderance of facts inclines strongly in favor of that theory which does not ascribe unity of origin to the Indian tribes. Passing down the Mississippi to Mexico, and from Mexico to Peru, there once existed an un broken chain of tribes, which, either in a peaceful or warlike manner, maintained a connection and kept up an intercourse with each other. In various ways proofs have been discovered that at one time the most northern tribes must have held intercourse with the civilized nations of Peru and Mexico. These evidences have been seized upon by certain savants to support the theory that the Indian tribes of North America are descendants of the Aztecs and other kindred nations of the south—arriving at this conclusion from the fact of an apparent similarity in history, psychology, traditions, and customs. But by studying the migrations and tendencies of ancient nations, and making allowance for such modifications as climatic influences, intermarriage, contact with civilization, and an altered mode of living would necessarily produce upon any branch of the human race—remembering, too, that in the vast majority of cases relating to our subject we must be guided by tradition rather than history—it is not difficult to establish a strong typical likeness between the tribes of American Indians and some of the nations of most remote antiquity. When or in what exact manner they first reached this continent is a problem difficult of solution This theory necessarily involves the admission of emigration to this conti nent centuries before the landing of Columbus. Upon this point there is much that may be inferred, and not a little susceptible of strong proof.

When civilization made its first inroads within the borders of this continent, numerous tribes, each powerful in numbers, were found inhabiting it. Each tribe had its peculiar customs, whether of war, the chase, or religion They

exhibited some close resemblances as well as widely different traits of charao-
ter. That they sprang from different nations rather than from a single source
seems highly probable. It is said that when the Spaniards conquered Yucatan
a number of intelligent Indians declared that by traditions from their ancestors
they had learned that their country had been peopled by nations coming from
the east, whom God had delivered from their enemies by opening a road for
them across the sea.

Few persons will deny that the existence of America was believed in if not
positively known centuries before its discovery by Columbus. Even so far
back as the time of Alexander the Great, a historian named Theopompus, in
giving a dialogue that took place between Midas and Silenus, credits the latter
with saying that Europe, Asia, and Africa were only islands, but that a vast fertile continent existed beyond the sea. This continent was peopled by a race of
powerful men, and gold and silver were abundant on its surface. Hanno, eight
hundred years before Christ, made a voyage along the coast of Africa, and
sailed due west for thirty days. From the account which he afterward wrote
of his voyage, it is probable that he saw portions of America or some of the
West India islands. Reference is also made by Homer and Horace to the existence of islands at a long distance west of Europe and Africa. Diodo-
rus speaks of an immense island many days' sail to the west of Africa; immense rivers flowed from its shores; its inhabitants resided in beautiful man-
sions; its soil was fruitful and highly cultivated. The description corresponds
with that given of Mexico by the Spaniards who first discovered it. Aristotle
makes mention of it in the following terms: "It is said that the Carthaginians
have discovered beyond the Pillars of Hercules a very fertile island, but which
is without inhabitants, yet full of forests, of navigable rivers, and abounding in
fruit. It is situated many days' journey from the mainland." After the discovery of America Europeans were surprised to find in villages in Guatemala
inhabitants wearing the Arabian masculine costume and the Jewish feminine
costume. Travellers in South America have discovered Israelites among
the Indians. This discovery strengthens the theory given by Garcia, a Spanish
writer, that the Indians are the descendants of the tribes of Israel that were led
captive into Assyria. Many of the Indian customs and religious rites closely
resemble those of the Israelites. In many tribes the Indians offer the first
fruits of the earth and of the chase to the Great Spirit. They have also certain
ceremonies at stated periods. Their division of the year corresponds with the
Jewish festivals. In some tribes the brother of a deceased husband receives
the widow into his lodge as his legitimate wife. Some travellers claim to have
seen circumcision practised among certain tribes. Another analogy between
the Jews and the Indians is seen in their purifications, baths, anointings, fasts,
manner of praying, and abstaining from certain quadrupeds, birds, and reptiles
considered impure. In general Indians are only permitted to marry in their
own tribe. Some tribes are said to carry with them an ark similar to the one
mentioned in Holy Writ. I know that all tribes with which I have been brought
in contact carry with them a mysterious something which is regarded with the
utmost sacredness and veneration, and upon which the eye of no white man at
least is ever permitted to rest. Then again the "medicine man" of the tribe,
who is not, as his name implies, the physician, but stands in the character of high
priest, assumes a dress and manner corresponding to those of the Jewish high
priest. Mr. Adair, who spent forty years among the various northern tribes,
and who holds to the idea that the Indian is descended from the Hebrew, as-

INDIAN MEDICINE MAN.

serts that he discovered an unmistakable resemblance between various Indian words and the Hebrew intended to express the same idea. He further asserts that he once heard an Indian apply the following expression to a culprit: " *Tschi kaksit canaha* "—Thou art like unto a Canaanite sinner.

Numerous evidences and various authorities go to prove that prior to the discovery of America by Columbus a series of voyages had been made from the old to the new continent. The historical records of the Scandinavians, describing their migratory expeditions, fix not only the dates of such excursions, but also the exact points on the American coast at which landings were made and colonies established. In 1002, Thorwald Ericsson, following the example of his countrymen, began a voyage, during which he landed near Cape Cod. He was afterward slain in an encounter with the natives. Other expeditions were undertaken by the Scandinavians at subsequent periods down to the early part of the fifteenth century, when, owing to various causes of decline, including savage wars and disease, these early explorers lost their foothold on the American continent and disappeared from its limits. But from the ninth to the fifteenth century it is easily proved by their historical records and traditions that the American continent had been visited and occupied by pioneers from the Scandinavians. From the great number of inscriptions, antique utensils, arms, bones, and monuments discovered in the New England States, it is fair to presume that these adventurers had occupied a larger portion of the new continent than their manuscripts would lead us to suppose. At the same time the discoveries in the Western States and territories of mounds containing human bones, earthen vessels, and weapons whose form and structure prove that their original owners belonged to a different people from any with which we are acquainted at the present day, should be received as evidence strongly confirmatory of the early migrations claimed to have been made by the Scandinavians and other nations. Admitting that there are certain physiological attributes common to nearly all the Indian tribes, sufficiently decided and clear to enable them to be classed together as one branch of the human family, yet an intimate study of all the tribes of North America will develop physical diversities sufficiently ample to justify the belief that the various tribes may have sprung from different nationalities. We find them, although generally of a copper color, presenting all shades of complexion from a deep black to a shade of white. Some tribes are of powerful stature, others are dwarfed. So marked are these differences that a person accustomed to meeting the various tribes can at a glance distinguish the individuals of one from the other. Almost every tribe possesses a language peculiarly its own, and what seems remarkable is the fact that no matter how long or how intimately two tribes may be associated with each other, they each preserve and employ their own language, and individuals of the one tribe rarely become versed in the spoken language of the other, all intercommunication being carried on either by interpreters or in the universal sign language. This is noticeably true of Cheyennes and Arrapahoes, two tribes which for years have lived in close proximity to each other, and who are so strongly bound together, offensively and defensively, as to make common cause against the enemies of either, particularly against the white man. These tribes encamp together, hunt together, and make war together, yet but a comparatively small number of either can speak fluently the language of the other. I remember to have had an interview at one time with a number of prominent chiefs belonging to five different tribes, the Cheyennes, Kiowas, Osages, Kaws, and Apaches. In communicating with them it was necessary for my language to be interpreted into each of the five Indian tongues, no representatives of any two of the tribes being able to understand the language of each other; yet all of these tribes were accustomed to more or less intimate association. Between the tribes which inhabited the Eastern States and those originally found on the Plains a marked difference is seen to exist. They have but little in common, while a difference equally marked is discov ered between the Indians of the Plains and those of the mountain regions fur ther west, as well as the tribes of both Old and New Mexico.

Inseparable from the Indian character, wherever he is to be met with, is his remarkable taciturnity, his deep dissimulation, the perseverance with which he follows his plans of revenge or conquest, his concealment and apparent lack of curiosity, his stoical courage when in the power of his enemies, his cunning, his caution, and last, but not least, the wonderful power and subtlety of his senses. Of this last I have had most interesting proof, one instance of which will be noted when describing the Washita campaign. In studying the Indian char- acter, while shocked and disgusted by many of his traits and customs, I find much to be admired, and still more of deep and unvarying interest. To me In- dian life, with its attendant ceremonies, mysteries, and forms, is a book of un- ceasing interest. Grant that some of its pages are frightful, and, if possible, to be avoided, yet the attraction is none the weaker. Study him, fight him, civil- ize him if you can, he remains still the object of your curiosity, a type of man peculiar and undefined, subjecting himself to no known law of civilization, con- tending determinedly against all efforts to win him from his chosen mode of life. He stands in the group of nations solitary and reserved, seeking alliance with none, mistrusting and opposing the advances of all. Civilization may and should do much for him, but it can never civilize him. A few instances to the contrary may be quoted, but these are susceptible of explanation. No tribe enjoying its accustomed freedom has ever been induced to adopt a civilized mode of life, or, as they express it, to follow the white man's road. At various times certain tribes have forsaken the pleasures of the chase and the excitement of the war-path for the more quiet life to be found on the " reservation." Was this course adopted voluntarily and from preference? Was it because the Indian chose the ways of his white brother rather than those in which he had been born and bred?

In no single instance has this been true. What then, it may be asked, have been the reasons which influenced certain tribes to abandon their predatory, nomadic life, and to-day to influence others to pursue a similar course? The answer is clear, and as undeniable as it is clear. The gradual and steady de- crease in numbers, strength, and influence, occasioned by wars both with other tribes and with the white man, as well as losses brought about by diseases partly attributable to contact with civilization, have so lowered the standing and diminished the available fighting force of the tribe as to render it unable to cope with more powerful neighboring tribes with any prospect of success. The stronger tribes always assume an overbearing and dominant manner to- ward their weaker neighbors, forcing them to join in costly and bloody wars or themselves to be considered enemies. When a tribe falls from the position of a leading one, it is at the mercy of every tribe that chooses to make war, being forced to take sides, and at the termination of the war is generally sacrificed to the interests of the more powerful. To avoid these sacrifices, to avail itself of the protection of civilization and its armed forces, to escape from the ruin ing influences of its more warlike and powerful neighbors, it reluctantly ac-

SANTATAS' BOASTFUL HARANGUE BEFORE THE GENERAL.

cepts the situation, gives up its accustomed haunts, its wild mode of life, and nestles down under the protecting arm of its former enemy, the white man, and tries, however feebly, to adopt his manner of life. In making this change the Indian has to sacrifice all that is dear to his heart; he abandons the only mode of life in which he can be a warrior and win triumphs and honors worthy to be sought after; and in taking up the pursuits of the white man he does that which he has always been taught from his earliest infancy to regard as degrading to his manhood—to labor, to work for his daily bread, an avocation suitable only for squaws.

To those who advocate the application of the laws of civilization to the Indian, it might be a profitable study to investigate the effect which such application produces upon the strength of the tribe as expressed in numbers. Looking at him as the fearless hunter, the matchless horseman and warrior of the Plains, where Nature placed him, and contrasting him with the reservation Indian, who is supposed to be revelling in the delightful comforts and luxuries of an enlightened condition, but who in reality is grovelling in beggary, bereft of many of the qualities which in his wild state tended to render him noble, and heir to a combination of vices partly his own, partly bequeathed to him from the pale-face, one is forced, even against desire, to conclude that there is unending antagonism between the Indian nature and that with which his well-meaning white brother would endow him. Nature intended him for a savage state; every instinct, every impulse of his soul inclines him to it. The white race might fall into a barbarous state, and afterwards, subjected to the influence of civilization, be reclaimed and prosper. Not so the Indian. He cannot be himself and be civilized; he fades away and dies. Cultivation such as the white man would give him deprives him of his identity. Education, strange as it may appear, seems to weaken rather than strengthen his intellect. Where do we find any specimens of educated Indian eloquence comparing with that of such native, untutored orators as Tecumseh, Osceola, Red Jacket, and Logan; or, to select from those of more recent fame, Red Cloud of the Sioux, or Sa-tan-ta of the Kiowas? Unfortunately for the last-named chief, whose name has been such a terror to our frontier settlements, he will have to be judged for other qualities than that of eloquence. Attention has more recently been directed to him by his arrest by the military authorities near Fort Sill, Indian Territory, and his transportation to Texas for trial by civil court for various murders and depredations, alleged to have been committed by him near the Texas frontier. He has since had his trial, and, if public rumor is to be credited, has been sentenced to death. Reference will be made to this noted chief in succeeding pages. His eloquence and able arguments upon the Indian question in various councils to which he was called won for him the deserved title of "Orator of the Plains." In his boasting harangue before the General of the Army, which furnished the evidence of his connection with the murders for which he has been tried and sentenced, he stated as a justification for such outrages, or rather as the occasion of them, that they were in retaliation for his arrest and imprisonment by me some three years ago. As there are two sides to most questions, even if one be wrong, when the proper time arrives a brief account of Sa-tan-ta's arrest and imprisonment, with the causes leading thereto, will be given in these sketches. One of the favorite remarks of Sa-tan-ta in his orations, and one too which other chiefs often indulge in, being thrown out as a "glittering generality," meaning much or little as they may desire, but most often the latter, was that he was tired of making war and desired now "to follow the white man's road. It is scarcely to be presumed that

he found the gratification of this oft-expressed desire in recently following the
" white man's road " to Texas, under strong guard and heavily manacled, with
hanging, to the Indian the most dreaded of all deaths, plainly in the perspective.   Aside, however, from his character for restless barbarity, and activity in
conducting merciless forays against our exposed frontiers, Sa-tan-ta is a remarkable man—remarkable for his powers of oratory, his determined warfare
against the advances of civilization, and his opposition to the abandonment of
his accustomed mode of life, and its exchange for the quiet, unexciting, uneventful life of a reservation Indian.   If I were an Indian, I often think that I would
greatly prefer to cast my lot among those of my people who adhered to the free
open plains, rather than submit to the confined limits of a reservation, there to be
the recipient of the blessed benefits of civilization, with its vices thrown in
without stint or measure.   The Indian can never be permitted to view the question in this deliberate way.   He is neither a luxury nor necessary of life.   He
can hunt, roam, and camp when and wheresoever he pleases, provided always
that in so doing he does not run contrary to the requirements of civilization
in its advancing tread.   When the soil which he has claimed and hunted
over for so long a time is demanded by this to him insatiable monster, there
is no appeal; he must yield, or, like the car of Juggernaut, it will roll merci-
lessly over him, destroying as it advances.   Destiny seems to have so willed
it, and the world looks on and nods its approval.   At best the history of our
Indian tribes, no matter from what standpoint it is regarded, affords a melan-
choly picture of loss of life.   Two hundred years ago it required millions
to express in numbers the Indian population, while at the present time less
than half the number of thousands will suffice for the purpose.   Where and
why have they gone?   Ask the Saxon race, since whose introduction into and
occupation of the country these vast changes have been effected.

But little idea can be formed of the terrible inroads which diseases before
unknown to them have made upon their numbers.   War has contributed its
share, it is true, but disease alone has done much to depopulate many of the Indian tribes.   It is stated that the small-pox was first introduced among them by
the white man in 1837, and that in the short space of one month six tribes lost
by this disease alone twelve thousand persons.

Confusion sometimes arises from the division of the Indians into nations,
tribes, and bands.   A nation is generally a confederation of tribes which have
sprung from a common stock or origin.   The tribe is intended to embrace all
bands and villages claiming a common name, and is presided over by a head chief,
while each band or village is presided over by one or more subordinate chiefs,
but all acknowledging a certain allegiance to the head or main village.   This
division cannot always be accounted for.   It arises sometimes from necessity,
where the entire tribe is a large one, and it is difficult to procure game and
grazing in one locality sufficient for all.   In such cases the various bands are
not usually separated by any great distance, but regulate their movements so
as to be able to act in each other's behalf.   Sometimes a chief more warlike
than the others, who favors war and conquest at all times, and refuses to
make peace even when his tribe assents to it, will separate himself, with those
who choose to unite their fortunes with his, from the remainder of the tribe,
and act for the time independently.   Such a character produces endless trouble; his village becomes a shelter and rendezvous for all the restless spirits of
the tribe.   While the latter is or pretends to be at peace, this band continues
to make war, yet when pressed or pursued avails itself of the protection of
those who are supposed to be peaceable.

Having hurriedly sketched the country in which we shall find it necessary to go, and glanced at certain theories calculated to shed some light on the origin and destiny of the Indian tribes, the succeeding pages will be devoted to my personal experience on the Plains, commencing with the expedition of Major-General Hancock in the spring of 1867.

III.

" THERE are two classes of people who are always eager to get up an Indian war—the army and our frontiersmen."

I quote from an editorial on the Indian question, which not long since appeared in the columns of one of the leading New York daily newspapers. That this statement was honestly made I do not doubt, but that instead of being true it could not have been further from the truth I will attempt to show. I assert, and all candid persons familiar with the subject will sustain the assertion, that of all classes of our population the army and the people living on the frontier entertain the greatest dread of an Indian war, and are willing to make the greatest sacrifices to avoid its horrors. This is a proposition, the assertion of which almost carries its proof with it.

Under the most auspicious circumstances, and in time of peace with the Indians, the life of an army officer on the Plains or along our frontier is at best one involving no little personal discomfort, and demanding the sacrifice of many of the luxuries and benefits which he could obtain were he located within the limits of civilization. To many officers, service in the West amounts almost to social exile. Some can have their families with or near them. There is a limited opportunity for social intercourse; travel from the States, to and across the Plains, either for business or pleasure, is uninterrupted, and mail facilities with friends and relations in the States are maintained. An Indian war changes all this. The troops must prepare to take the field. Provided with but few comforts, necessarily limited in this respect by the amount of transportation, which on the Plains is narrowed down to the smallest practicable, the soldier bids adieu—often a final one—to the dear ones of home, and with his comrades in arms sets out, no matter how inclement the season, to seek what? fame and glory? How many military men have reaped laurels from their Indian campaigns? Does he strive to win the approving smile of his countrymen? That is indeed, in this particular instance, a difficult task. For let him act as he may in conducting or assisting in a campaign against the Indians, if he survives the campaign he can feel assured of this fact, that one-half of his fellow-citizens at home will revile him for his zeal and pronounce his success, if he achieves any, a massacre of poor, defenceless, harmless Indians; while the other half, if his efforts to chastise the common enemy are not crowned with satisfactory results, will cry "Down with him. Down with the regular army, and give us brave volunteers who can serve the Government in other ways besides eating rations and drawing pay."

An unsuccessful campaign, under which head nineteen out of twenty may reasonably be classed, satisfies no portion of the public, and greatly dissatisfies that portion of the Western population whose knowledge of the murders and depredations committed by the Indians is, unlike that of the people of the States further east, of too recent origin to be swept away by false notions of clemency. During the continuance of the campaign both officers and soldiers are generally cut off from all communication with the friends left behind. Couriers, sent as bearers of a few despatches and letters, are sometimes under cover of the night enabled to make their way back to the forts; but even these fail sometimes. I now recollect the circumstance of two trusty scouts being sent with despatches and a small mail, to make their way from the southern por-

FATE OF THE TWO TRUSTY SCOUTS

tion of Kansas to Fort Dodge on the Arkansas. When we saw them again we beheld their lifeless, mangled remains, their bodies pierced with numerous arrows, and mutilated almost beyond recognition—our letters scattered here and there by the savages, who had torn open the little canvas mail-bag in search of plunder. The Indians had surrounded these faithful fellows when within about ten miles of the end of their perilous journey. The numerous empty cartridge shells which lay around and near the bodies of the two men, proved how persistently and bravely they had struggled for their lives.

The opening of an Indian campaign is also the signal for the withdrawal of all privileges and enjoyments, such as leaves of absence, visits from Eastern friends, hunting and pleasure parties of all kinds. The reception from the East of all luxuries and delicacies for the table and of all current literature, such as the numerous railroads being constructed in the West, particularly the two Pacifics, render easy of procurement, ceases; and not only the private soldier but the officer is limited in his mess fare to an indifferent portion of the ordinary ration. Is it probable or reasonable that these objects and results, the principal ones generally, so far as the army as individuals is concerned, would be considered sufficient to render either officers or soldiers " eager to get up an Indian war "? I have yet to make the acquaintance of that officer of the army who, in time of undisturbed peace, desired a war with the Indians. On the contrary, the army is the Indian's best friend, so long as the latter desires to maintain friendship. It is pleasant at all times, and always interesting, to have a village of peaceable Indians locate their lodges near our frontier posts or camps. The daily visits of the Indians, from the most venerable chief to the strapped pappoose, their rude interchange of civilities, their barterings, races, dances, legends, strange customs, and fantastic ceremonies, all combine to render them far more agreeable as friendly neighbors than as crafty, bloodthirsty enemies.

As to the frontiersman, he has everything to lose, even to life, and nothing to gain by an Indian war. " His object is to procure a fat contract or a market for his produce," adds the journal from which the opening lines of this chapter are quoted. This seems plausible and likely enough. But does that journal, and do the people who believe on this question as it does, know that there are two reasons—more are not required—why its statement is a very great error? First, our frontier farmers, busily employed as they are in opening up their farms, never have any produce to dispose of, but consider themselves fortunate if they have sufficient for their personal wants. They are never brought in contact with the Indian except when the latter makes a raid or incursion of at least hundreds of miles, and attacks the settlements. It is another case of Mohammed and the mountain. The frontiersman never goes beyond the settlements. The Indian forsakes his accustomed hunting-grounds when ambitious of obtaining scalps or plunder, and visits the settlements. The only ground upon which the frontiersman can be accused of inspiring or inciting a war with the Indian is, that when applied to by the latter to surrender his life, family, and property, scalp thrown in, he stoutly refuses, and sometimes employs force to maintain this refusal. I have shown that this abused class of the pioneers of civilization have no hand in the fat contracts. Who are the fortunate parties? With but rare exceptions our most expensive expeditions against the Indians on the Plains have been supplied by contracts made with parties far inside the limits of civilization, who probably never saw a hostile Indian, and who never even visited the Indian country. The supplies are purchased far from the frontiers, in the rich and thickly settled portions of the States, then shipped by rail and boat to the most available military post, from which point they are generally drawn by huge trains of army wagons, or carried on pack animals.

Of the many important expeditions organized to operate in the Indian country, none, perhaps, of late years has excited more general and unfriendly comment, considering the slight loss of life inflicted upon the Indians, than the expedition organized and led in person by Major-General Hancock in the spring of 1867. The clique generally known as the " Indian ring" were particularly malevolent and bitter in their denunciations of General Hancock for precipitating, as they expressed it, an Indian war. This expedition was quite formidable in appearance, being made up of eight troops of cavalry, seven companies of infantry, and one battery of light artillery, numbering altogether about 1,400 men. As General Hancock at the time and since has been so often accused of causelessly bringing on an Indian war, a word in explanation may not be amiss.

Being in command of the cavalry connected with the expedition, I had ample and frequent opportunities for learning the true purposes and objects of the march into the heart of the Indian country. I know no better mode of explaining these than by quoting the following extract from letters written by General Hancock to the agents of the various tribes with which we expected to be brought in contact: " I have the honor to state for your information that I am at present preparing an expedition to the Plains, which will soon be ready to move. My object in doing so at this time is, to convince the Indians within the limits of this department that we are able to punish any of them who may molest travellers across the Plains, or who may commit other hostilities against the whites. We desire to avoid if possible any troubles with the Indians, and to treat them with justice, and according to the requirements of our treaties with them; and I wish especially in my dealings with them to act through the agents of the Indian Department as far as it is possible so to do. . . . . . . If you as their agent can arrange these matters satisfactorily with them, we will be pleased to defer the whole subject to you. In case of your inability to do so, I would be pleased to have you accompany me when I visit the country of your tribes, to show that the officers of the Government are acting in harmony. I will be pleased to talk with any of the chiefs whom we may meet."

Surely there was no hostile intent here expressed. In another communication to the agents of different tribes, General Hancock, in referring to certain murders which had been recently committed, and which had been traced to the tribes in question, said: " These cases will now be left entirely in the hands of the Indian Department, and I do not expect to make war against any of the Indians of your agency unless they commence war against us."

It may be asked, What had the Indians done to make this incursion necessary? They had been guilty of numerous thefts and murders during the preceding summer and fall, for none of which had they been called to account. They had attacked the stations of the overland mail route, killed the employees, burned the station, and captured the stock. Citizens had been murdered in their homes on the frontier of Kansas; murders had been committed on the Arkansas route. The principal perpetrators of these acts were the Cheyennes and Sioux. The agent of the former, if not a party to the murder on the Arkansas, knew who the guilty persons were, yet took no steps to bring the murderers to punishment. Such a course would have interfered with his trade and profits. It was not to punish for these sins of the past that the expedition was set on foot, but rather by its imposing appearance and its early presence in the

Indian country to check or intimidate the Indians from a repetition of their late conduct. This was deemed particularly necessary from the fact that the various tribes from which we had greatest cause to anticipate trouble had during the winter, through their leading chiefs and warriors, threatened that as soon as the grass was up in spring a combined outbreak would take place along our entire frontier, and especially against the main routes of travel. To assemble the tribes for the desired council, word was sent early in March to the agents of those tribes whom it was desirable to meet. The agents sent runner to the villages inviting them to meet us at some point near the Arkansas river.

General Hancock, with the artillery and six companies of infantry, reached Fort Riley, Kansas, from Fort Leavenworth by rail the last week in March; here he was joined by four companies of the Seventh Cavalry and an additional company of the Thirty-seventh Infantry. It was at this point that I joined the expedition. And as a very fair sample of the laurels which military men may win in an Indian campaign by a zealous discharge of what they deem their duty, I will here state, in parenthesis, that after engaging in the expedition, some of the events of which I am about to relate, and undergoing fatigue, privations, and dangers equal to those of a campaign during the Rebellion, I found myself at the termination of the campaign again at Fort Riley *in arrest.* This is not mentioned in a fault-finding spirit. I have no fault to find. It is said that blessings sometimes come in disguise. Such proved to be true in this instance, although I must say the disguise for some little time was most perfect.

From Fort Riley we marched to Fort Harker, a distance of ninety miles, where our force was strengthened by the addition of two more troops of cavalry. Halting only long enough to replenish our supplies, we next directed our march toward Fort Larned, near the Arkansas, about seventy miles to the southeast. A march from the 3d to the 7th of April brought us to Fort Larned The agent for the Comanches and Kiowas accompanied us. At Fort Larned we found the agent of the Cheyennes, Arapahoes, and Apaches; from the latter we learned that he had, as requested, sent runners to the chiefs of his agency inviting them to the council, and that they had agreed to assemble near Fort Larned on the 10th of the month, requesting that the expedition would remain there until that date. To this request General Hancock acceded.

On the 9th of April, while encamped awaiting the council, which was to be held the following day, a terrible snow-storm occurred, lasting all day until late in the evening. It was our good fortune to be in camp rather than on the march; had it been otherwise, we could not well have escaped without loss of life from the severe cold and blinding snow. The cavalry horses suffered seriously, and were only preserved by doubling their ration of oats, while to prevent their being frozen during the intensely cold night which followed, the guards were instructed to keep passing along the picket lines with a whip, and to keep the horses moving constantly. The snow was eight inches in depth. The council, which was to take place the next day, had to be postponed until the return of good weather. Now began the display of a kind of diplomacy for which the Indian is peculiar. The Cheyennes and a band of the Sioux were encamped on Pawnee Fork, about thirty miles above Fort Larned. They neither desired to move nearer to us nor have us approach nearer to them. On the morning of the 11th they sent us word that they had started to visit us, but discovering a large herd of buffalo near their camp, they had stopped to procure a supply of meat. This message was not received with much confidence, nor was a buffalo hunt deemed of sufficient importance to justify the Indians in breaking their engagement. General Hancock decided, however, to delay another day, when, if the Indians still failed to come in, he would move his command to the vicinity of their village and hold the conference there.

Orders were issued on the evening of the 12th for the march to be resumed on the following day. Later in the evening two chiefs of the " Dog Soldiers," a band composed of the most warlike and troublesome Indians on the Plains, chiefly made up of Cheyennes, visited our camp. They were accompanied by a dozen warriors, and expressed a desire to hold a conference with General Hancock, to which he assented. A large council fire was built in front of the General's tent, and all the officers of his command assembled there. A tent had been erected for the accommodation of the chiefs a short distance from the General's. Before they could feel equal to the occasion, and in order to obtain time to collect their thoughts, they desired that supper might be prepared for them, which was done. When finally ready they advanced from their tent to the council fire in single file, accompanied by their agent and an interpreter. Arrived at the fire, another brief delay ensued. No matter how pressing or momentous the occasion, an Indian invariably declines to engage in a council until he has filled his pipe and gone through with the important ceremony of a smoke. This attended to, the chiefs announced that they were ready " to talk." They were then introduced to the principal officers of the group, and seemed much struck with the flashy uniforms of the few artillery officers who were present in all the glory of red horsehair plumes, aigulets, etc. The chiefs seemed puzzled to determine whether these insignia designated chieftains or medicine men. General Hancock began the conference by a speech, in which he explained to the Indians his · purpose in coming to see them, and what he expected of them in the future. He particularly informed them that he was not there to make war, but to promote peace. Then expressing his regret that more of the chiefs had not visited him, he announced his intention of proceeding on the morrow with his command to the vicinity of their village and there holding a council with all of the chiefs. Tall Bull, a fine, warlike-looking chieftain, replied to General Hancock, but his speech contained nothing important, being made up of allusions to the growing scarcity of the buffalo, his love for the white man, and the usual hint that a donation in the way of refreshments would be highly acceptable; he added that he would have nothing new to say at the village.

Several years prior to the events referred to, our people had captured from the Indians two children. I believe they were survivors of the Chivington massacre at Sand Creek, Colorado. These children had been kindly cared for and were being taught to lead a civilized mode of life. Their relatives, however, made demands for them, and we by treaty stipulation agreed to deliver them up. One of them, a little girl, had been cared for kindly in a family living near Denver, Colorado; the other, a boy, had been carried East to the States, and it was with great difficulty that the Government was able to learn his whereabouts and obtain possession of him. He was finally discovered, however, and sent to General Hancock, to be by him delivered up to his tribe. He accompanied the expedition, and was quite a curiosity for the time being. He was dressed comfortably, in accordance with civilized custom; and, having been taken from his people at so early an age, was apparently satisfied with the life he led. The Indians who came to our camp expressed a great desire to see him, and when he was brought into their presence they exhibited no emotion such as white men under similar circumstances might be expected to show

They evidently were not pleased to see him clothed in the white man's dress. The little fellow, then some eight or ten years of age, seemed little disposed to go back to his people. I saw him the following year in the village of his tribe; he then had lost all trace of civilization, had forgotten his knowledge of the English language, and was as shy and suspicious of the white men as any of his dusky comrades. From older persons of the tribe we learned that their first act after obtaining possession of him was to deprive him of his "store clothes," and in their stead substitute the blanket and leggings.

Rightly concluding that the Indians did not intend to come to our camp as they had at first agreed to, it was decided to move nearer to their village. On the morning following the conference held with the two chiefs of the "Dog Soldiers," our entire force therefore marched from Fort Larned up Pawnee Fork in the direction of the main village, encamping the first night about twenty-one miles from the fort. Several parties of Indians were seen in our advance during the day, evidently watching our movements; while a heavy smoke, seen to rise in the direction of the Indian village, indicated that something more than usual was going on. This smoke we afterwards learned arose from the burning grass. The Indians, thinking to prevent us from encamping in their vicinity, had set fire to and burned all the grass for miles in the direction from which they expected us. Before we arrived at our camping-ground we were met by several chiefs and warriors belonging to the Cheyennes and Sioux. Among the chiefs were Pawnee Killer of the Sioux, and White Horse of the Cheyennes. It was arranged that these chiefs should accept our hospitality and remain with us during the night, and in the morning all the chiefs of the two tribes then in the village were to come to General Hancock's headquarters and hold a council. On the morning of the 14th Pawnee Killer left our camp at an early hour, for the purpose, as he said, of going to the village to bring in the other chiefs to the council. Nine o'clock had been agreed upon as the hour at which the council should assemble. The hour came, but the chiefs did not. Now an Indian council is not only often an important but always an interesting occasion. And, somewhat like a famous recipe for making a certain dish, the first thing necessary in holding an Indian council is to get the Indian. Half-past nine o'clock came, and still we were lacking this one important part of the council. At this juncture Bull Bear, an influential chief among the Cheyennes, came in and reported that the chiefs were on their way to our camp, but would not be able to reach it for some time. This was a mere artifice to secure delay. General Hancock informed Bull Bear that as the chiefs could not arrive for some time, he would move his forces up the stream nearer to the village, and the council could be held at our camp that night. To this proposition Bull Bear gave his assent.

At 11 A. M. we resumed the march, and had proceeded but a few miles when we witnessed one of the finest and most imposing military displays, prepared according to the Indian art of war, which it has ever been my lot to behold. It was nothing more nor less than an Indian line of battle drawn directly across our line of march; as if to say, Thus far and no further. Most of the Indians were mounted; all were bedecked in their brightest colors, their heads crowned with the brilliant war-bonnet, their lances bearing the crimson pennant, bows strung, and quivers full of barbed arrows. In addition to these weapons, which with the hunting-knife and tomahawk are considered as forming the armament of the warrior, each one was supplied with either a breech-loading rifle or revolver, sometimes with both—the latter obtained through the wise foresight and strong love of fair play which prevails in the

Indian Department, which, seeing that its wards are determined to fight, is equally determined that there shall be no advantage taken, but that the two sides shall be armed alike; proving, too, in this manner the wonderful liberality of our Government, which not only is able to furnish its soldiers with the latest improved style of breech-loaders to defend it and themselves, but is equally able and willing to give the same pattern of arms to their common foe. The only difference is, that the soldier, if he loses his weapon, is charged double price for it; while to avoid making any such charge against the Indian, his weapons are given him without conditions attached. In the line of battle before us there were several hundred Indians, while further to the rear and at different distances were other organized bodies acting apparently as reserves. Still further were small detachments who seemed to perform the duty of couriers, and were held in readiness to convey messages to the village. The ground beyond was favorable for an extended view, allowing the eye to sweep the plain for several miles. As far as the eye could reach small groups or individuals could be seen in the direction of the village; these were evidently parties of observation, whose sole object was to learn the result of our meeting with the main body and hasten with the news to the village.

For a few moments appearances seemed to foreshadow anything but a peaceful issue. The infantry was in the advance, followed closely by the artillery, while my command, the cavalry, was marching on the flank. General Hancock, who was riding with his staff at the head of the column, coming suddenly in view of the wild fantastic battle array, which extended far to our right and left and not more than half a mile in our front, hastily sent orders to the infantry, artillery, and cavalry to form line of battle, evidently determined that if war was intended we should be prepared. The cavalry, being the last to form on the right, came into line on a gallop, and, without waiting to align the ranks carefully, the command was given to "draw sabre." As the bright blades flashed from their scabbards into the morning sunlight, and the infantry brought their muskets to a carry, a most beautiful and wonderfully interesting sight was spread out before and around us, presenting a contrast which, to a military eye, could but be striking. Here in battle array, facing each other, were the representatives of civilized and barbarous warfare. The one, with but few modifications, stood clothed in the same rude style of dress, bearing the same patterned shield and weapon that his ancestors had borne centuries before; the other confronted him in the dress and supplied with the implements of war which the most advanced stage of civilization had pronounced the most perfect. Was the comparative superiority of these two classes to be subjected to the mere test of war here? Such seemed the prevailing impression on both sides. All was eager anxiety and expectation. Neither side seemed to comprehend the object or intentions of the other; each was waiting for the other to deliver the first blow. A more beautiful battle-ground could not have been chosen. Not a bush or even the slightest irregularity of ground intervened between the two lines which now stood frowning and facing each other. Chiefs could be seen riding along the line as if directing and exhorting their braves to deeds of heroism.

After a few moments of painful suspense, General Hancock, accompanied by General A. J. Smith and other officers, rode forward, and through an interpreter invited the chiefs to meet us midway, for the purpose of an interview In response to this invitation Roman Nose, bearing a white flag, accompanied by Bull Bear, White Horse, Gray Beard, and Medicine Wolf on the part of the Cheyennes, and Pawnee Küler, Bad Wound Tail Bear that Walks under the

BULL BEAR.

Ground, Left Hand, Little Bear, and Little Bull on the part of the Sioux, rode forward to the middle of the open space between the two lines. Here we shook hands with all of the chiefs, most of them exhibiting unmistakable signs of gratification at this apparently peaceful termination of our rencounter. General Hancock very naturally inquired the object of the hostile attitude displayed before us, saying to the chiefs that if war was their object we were ready then and there to participate. Their immediate answer was that they did not desire war, but were peacefully disposed. They were then told that we would continue our march toward the village, and encamp near it, but would establish such regulations that none of the soldiers would be permitted to approach or disturb them. An arrangement was then effected by which the chiefs were to assemble at General Hancock's headquarters as soon as our camp was pitched. The interview then terminated, and the Indians moved off in the direction of their village, we following leisurely in rear.

A march of a few miles brought us in sight of the village, which was situated in a beautiful grove on the banks of the stream up which we had been marching. The village consisted of upwards of three hundred lodges, a small fraction over half belonging to the Cheyennes, the remainder to the Sioux. Like all Indian encampments, the ground chosen was a most romantic spot, and at the same time fulfilled in every respect the requirements of a good camping-ground; wood, water, and grass were abundant. The village was placed on a wide, level plateau, while on the north and west, at a short distance off, rose high bluffs, which admirably served as a shelter against the cold winds which at that season of the year prevail from these directions. Our tents were pitched within half a mile of the village. Guards were placed between to prevent intrusion upon our part. A few of the Indian ponies found grazing near our camp were caught and returned to them, to show that our intentions were at least neighborly. We had scarcely pitched our tents when Roman Nose, Bull Bear, Gray Beard, and Medicine Wolf, all prominent chiefs of the Cheyennes, came into camp, with the information that upon our approach their women and children had all fled from the village, alarmed by the presence of so many soldiers, and imagining a second Chivington massacre to be intended. General Hancock insisted that they should all return, promising protection and good treatment to all; that if the camp was abandoned he would hold it responsible. The chiefs then stated their belief in their ability to recall the fugitives, could they be furnished with horses to overtake them. This was accordingly done, and two of them set out mounted on two of our horses. An agreement was also entered into at the same time that one of our interpreters, Ed. Gurrier, a half-breed Cheyenne who was in the employ of the Government, should remain in the village and report every two hours as to whether any Indians were leaving the village. This was about seven o'clock in the evening. At half past nine the half-breed returned to headquarters, with the intelligence that all the chiefs and warriors were saddling up to leave, under circumstances showing that they had no intention of returning, such as packing up such articles as could be carried with them, and cutting and destroying their lodges, this last being done to obtain small pieces for temporary shelter.

I had retired to my tent, which was located some few hundred yards from that of General Hancock, when a messenger from the latter awakened me with the information that General Hancock desired my presence at his tent. Imagining a movement on the part of the Indians, I made no delay in responding to the summons. General Hancock briefly stated the situation of affairs, and directed me to mount my command as quickly and as silently as possible, surround the Indian village, and prevent the departure of its inhabitants. Easily said, but not so easily done. Under ordinary circumstances, silence not being necessary, I could have returned to my camp, and by a few blasts from the trumpet placed every soldier in his saddle almost as quickly as it has taken time to write this sentence. No bugle calls must be sounded; we were to adopt some of the stealth of the Indian—how successfully remains to be seen. By this time every soldier, officers as well as men, was in his tent sound asleep. How to awaken them and impart to each the necessary order? First going to the tent of the adjutant and arousing him, I procured an experienced assistant in my labors. Next the captains of companies were awakened and orders imparted to them. They in turn transmitted the order to the first sergeant, who similarly aroused the men. It has often surprised me to observe the alacrity with which disciplined soldiers, experienced in campaigning, will hasten to prepare themselves for the march in an emergency like this. No questions are asked, no time is wasted. A soldier's toilet, on an Indian campaign, is a simple affair, and requires little time for arranging. His clothes are gathered up hurriedly, no matter how, so long as he retains possession of them. The first object is to get his horse saddled and bridled, and until this is done his own toilet is a matter of secondary importance, and one button or hook must do the duty of half a dozen. When his horse is ready for the mount the rider will be seen completing his own equipment; stray buttons will receive attention, arms be overhauled, spurs restrapped; then, if there still remain a few spare moments, the homely black pipe is filled and lighted, and the soldier's preparation is completed.

The night was all that could be desired for the success of our enterprise. The air was mild and pleasant; the moon, although nearly full, kept almost constantly behind the clouds, as if to screen us in our hazardous undertaking. I say hazardous, because there were none of us who imagined for one moment that if the Indians discovered us in our attempt to surround them and their village, we would escape without a fight—a fight, too, in which the Indians, sheltered behind the trunks of the stately forest trees under which their lodges were pitched, would possess all the advantage. General Hancock, anticipating that the Indians would discover our approach, and that a fight would ensue, ordered the artillery and infantry under arms, to await the result of our moonlight venture. My command was soon in the saddle, and silently making its way toward the village. Instructions had been given forbidding all conversation except in a whisper. Sabres were so disposed of as to prevent clanging. Taking a camp-fire which we could see in the village as our guiding point, we made a detour so as to place the village between ourselves and the infantry. Occasionally the moon would peep out from behind the clouds and enable us to catch a hasty glance at the village. Here and there under the thick foliage we could see the white, conical-shaped lodges. Were their inmates slumbering, unaware of our close proximity, or were their dusky defenders concealed, as well they might have been, along the banks of the Pawnee, quietly awaiting our approach, and prepared to greet us with their well-known war-whoop? These were questions that were probably suggested to the mind of each individual of my command. If we were discovered approaching in the stealthy, suspicious manner which characterized our movements, the hour being midnight, it would require a more confiding nature than that of the Indian to assign a friendly or peaceful motive to our conduct. The same flashes of moonlight which gave us hurried glimpses of the village enabled us to see our own column of horsemen stretching its silent length far into the dim darkness, and winding its course, like some huge anaconda about to envelop its victim.

The method by which it was determined to establish a cordon of armed troopers about the fated village, was to direct the march in a circle, with the village in the centre, the commanding officer of each rear troop halting his command at the proper point, and deploying his men similarly to a line of skirmishers—the entire circle, when thus formed, facing toward the village, and distant from it perhaps a few hundred yards. No sooner was our line completely formed than the moon, as if deeming darkness no longer essential to our success, appeared from behind her screen and lighted up the entire scene. And a beautiful scene it was. The great circle of troops, each individual of which sat on his steed silent as a statue, the beautiful and in some places dense foliage of the cotton trees sheltering and shading the bleached, skin-clad lodges of the red man, while in the midst of all murmured undisturbedly in its channel the little stream on whose banks the village was located, all combined to produce an artistic effect, as beautiful as it was interesting. But we were not there to study artistic effects. The next step was to determine whether we had captured an inhabited village, involving almost necessarily a fierce conflict with its savage occupants, or whether the red man had again proven too wily and crafty for his more civilized brothers.

Directing the entire line of troopers to remain mounted with carbines held at the "advance," I dismounted, and taking with me Gurrier, the half-breed, Dr. Coates, one of our medical staff, and Lieutenant Moylan, the adjutant, proceeded on our hands and knees toward the village. The prevailing opinion was that the Indians were still asleep. I desired to approach near enough to the lodges to enable the half-breed to hail the village in the Indian tongue, and if possible establish friendly relations at once. It became a question of prudence with us, which we discussed in whispers as we proceeded on our "Tramp, tramp, tramp, the boys are creeping," how far from our horses and how near to the village we dared to go. If so few of us were discovered entering the village in this questionable manner, it was more than probable that, like the returners of stolen property, we should be suitably rewarded and no questions asked. The opinions of Gurrier, the half-breed, were eagerly sought for and generally deferred to. His wife, a full-blooded Cheyenne, was a resident of the village. This with him was an additional reason for wishing a peaceful termination to our efforts. When we had passed over two-thirds of the distance between our horses and the village, it was deemed best to make our presence known. Thus far not a sound had been heard to disturb the stillness of the night. Gurrier called out at the top of his voice in the Cheyenne tongue. The only response came from the throats of a score or more of Indian dogs which set up a fierce barking. At the same time one or two of our party asserted that they saw figures moving beneath the trees. Gurrier repeated his summons, but with no better result than before.

A hurried consultation ensued. The presence of so many dogs in the village was regarded by the half-breed as almost positive assurance that the Indians were still there. Yet it was difficult to account for their silence. Gurrier in a loud tone repeated who he was, and that our mission was a friendly one. Still no answer. He then gave it as his opinion that the Indians were on the alert, and were probably waiting in the shadow of the trees for us to approach nearer, when they would pounce upon us. This comforting opinion induced another conference. We must ascertain the truth of the matter; our party could do this as well as a larger number, and to go back and send another party in our stead could not be thought of.

Forward was the verdict. Each one grasped his revolver, resolved to do nis best, whether it was in running or fighting. I think most of us would have preferred to take our own chances at running. We had approached near enough to see that some of the lodges were detached some distance from the main encampment. Selecting the nearest of these, we directed our advance on it. While all of us were full of the spirit of adventure, and were further encouraged with the idea that we were in the discharge of our duty, there was scarcely one of us who would not have felt more comfortable if we could have got back to our horses without loss of pride. Yet nothing, under the circumstances, but a positive order would have induced any one to withdraw. The doctor, who was a great wag, even in moments of greatest danger, could not restrain his propensities in this direction. When everything before us was being weighed and discussed in the most serious manner, he remarked: "General, this recalls to my mind those beautiful lines:

> Backward, turn backward, O Time, in thy flight,
> Make me a child again just for one night—

this night of all others."

We shall meet the doctor again before daylight, but under different circumstances.

CAUTIOUSLY approaching, on all fours, to within a few yards of the nearest lodge, occasionally halting and listening to discover evidence as to whether the village was deserted or not, we finally decided that the Indians had fled before the arrival of the cavalry, and that none but empty lodges were before us. This conclusion somewhat emboldened as well as accelerated our progress. Arriving at the first lodge, one of our party raised the curtain or mat which served as a door, and the doctor and myself entered. The interior of the lodge was dimly lighted by the decaying embers of a small fire built in the centre. All around us were to be seen the usual adornments and articles which constitute the household effects of an Indian family. Buffalo robes were spread like carpets over the floor; head-mats, used to recline upon, were arranged as if for the comfort of their owners; parfleches, a sort of Indian bandbox, with their contents apparently undisturbed, were to be found carefully stowed away under the edges or borders of the lodge. These, with the doormats, paint-bags, rawhide ropes, and other articles of Indian equipment, were left as if the owners had only absented themselves for a brief period. To complete the picture of an Indian lodge, over the fire hung a camp-kettle, in which, by means of the dim light of the fire, we could see what had been intended for the supper of the late occupants of the lodge. The doctor, ever on the alert to discover additional items of knowledge, whether pertaining to history or science, snuffed the savory odors which arose from the dark recesses of the mysterious kettle. Casting about the lodge for some instrument to aid him in his pursuit of knowledge, he found a horn spoon, with which he began his investigation of the contents, finally succeeding in getting possession of a fragment which might have been the half of a duck or rabbit, judging merely from its size. "Ah!" said the doctor, in his most complacent manner, "here is the opportunity I have long been waiting for. I have often desired to test and taste of the Indian mode of cooking. What do you suppose this is?" holding up the dripping morsel. Unable to obtain the desired information, the Doctor, whose naturally good appetite had been sensibly sharpened by his recent exercise à la quadrupède, set to with a will and ate heartily of the mysterious contents of the kettle. "What can this be?" again inquired the doctor. He was only satisfied on one point, that it was delicious—a dish fit for a king. Just then Guerrier, the half-breed, entered the lodge. He could solve the mystery, having spent years among the Indians. To him the doctor appealed for information. Fishing out a huge piece, and attacking it with the voracity of a hungry wolf, he was not long in determining what the doctor had supped so heartily upon. His first words settled the mystery: "Why, this is dog." I will not attempt to repeat the few but emphatic words uttered by the heartily disgusted member of the medical fraternity as he rushed from the lodge.

Other members of our small party had entered other lodges, only to find them, like the first, deserted. But little of the furniture belonging to the lodges had been taken, showing how urgent and hasty had been the flight of the owners. To aid in the examination of the village, reinforcements were added to our party, and an exploration of each lodge was determined upon. At the same time a messenger was despatched to General Hancock, informing him of the flight of the Indians. Some of the lodges were closed by having brush or timber piled up against the entrance, as if to preserve the contents. Others had huge pieces cut from their sides, these pieces evidently being carried away to furnish temporary shelter to the fugitives. In most of the lodges .the fires were still burning. I had entered several without discovering anything important. Finally, in company with the doctor, I arrived at one, the interior of which was quite dark, the fire having almost died out. Procuring a lighted fagot, I prepared to explore it, as I had done the others; but no sooner had I entered the lodge than my fagot failed me, leaving me in total darkness. Handing it out to the doctor to be relighted, I began feeling my way about the interior of the lodge. I had almost made the circuit when my hand came in contact with a human foot; at the same time a voice unmistakably Indian, and which evidently came from the owner of the foot, convinced me that I was not alone. My first impression was that in their hasty flight the Indians had gone off leaving this one asleep. My next, very naturally, related to myself. I would have gladly placed myself on the outside of the lodge, and there matured plans for interviewing its occupant; but unfortunately to reach the entrance of the lodge I must either pass over or around the owner of the before-mentioned foot and voice. Could I have been convinced that among *its* other possessions there was neither tomahawk nor scalping-knife, pistol nor war-club, or any similar article of the noble red man's toilet, I would have risked an attempt to escape through the low narrow opening of the lodge; but who ever saw an Indian without one or all of these interesting trinkets? Had I made the attempt, I should have expected to encounter either the keen edge of the scalping-knife or the blow of the tomahawk, and to have engaged in a questionable struggle for life. This would not do. I crouched in silence for a few moments, hoping the doctor would return with the lighted fagot. I need not say that each succeeding moment spent in the darkness of that lodge seemed like an age. I could hear a slight movement on the part of my unknown neighbor, which did not add to my comfort. Why does not the doctor return? At last I discovered the approach of a light on the outside. When it neared the entrance I called to the doctor and informed him that an Indian was in the lodge, and that he had better have his weapons ready for a conflict. I had, upon discovering the foot, drawn my hunting-knife from its scabbard, and now stood waiting the *dénouement*. With his lighted fagot in one hand and cocked revolver in the other, the doctor cautiously entered the lodge. And there, directly between us, wrapped in a buffalo robe, lay the cause of my anxiety—a little Indian girl, probably ten years old; not a full-blood, but a half-breed. She was terribly frightened at finding herself in our hands, with none of her people near. Why was she left behind in this manner? Guerrier, our half-breed interpreter, was called in. His inquiries were soon answered. The little girl, who at first was an object of our curiosity, became at once an object of pity. The Indians, an unusual thing for them to do toward their own blood, had wilfully deserted her; but this, alas! was the least of their injuries to her. After being shamefully abandoned by the entire village, a few of the young men of the tribe returned to the deserted lodge, and upon the person of this little girl committed outrages, the details of which are too sickening for these pages. She was carried to the fort and placed under the care of kind hands and warm hearts, where everything was done for her comfort that was possible. Other parties in exploring the deserted village found an old, decrepit Indian of the Sioux tribe, who also had been deserted, owing to his infirmities and inability to travel with the tribe. He also was kindly cared for by the authorities of the fort. Nothing was gleaned from our search of the village which might indicate the direction of the flight. General Hancock, on learning the situation of affairs, despatched some companies of infantry to the deserted village, with orders to replace the cavalry and protect the village and its contents from disturbance until its final disposition could be determined upon. Starting my command back to our camp near General Hancock's headquarters, I galloped on in advance to report the particulars to the General. It was then decided that with eight troops of cavalry I should start in pursuit of the Indians at early dawn on the following morning (April 15). There was no sleep for my command the remainder of the night, the time being fully occupied in preparation for the march, neither the extent nor direction of which was known.

Mess kits were overhauled, and fresh supplies of coffee, sugar, flour, and the other articles which go to supply the soldier's larder, were laid in. Blankets were carefully rolled so as to occupy as little space as possible; every useless pound of luggage was discarded, for in making a rapid pursuit after Indians, much of the success depends upon the lightness of the order of march. Saratoga trunks and their accompaniments are at a discount. Never was the old saying that in Rome one must do as Romans do more aptly illustrated than on an Indian campaign. The Indian, knowing that his safety either on offensive or defensive movements depends in a great measure upon the speed and endurance of his horse, takes advantage of every circumstance which will favor either the one or the other. To this end he divests himself of all superfluous dress and ornament when preparing for rapid movements. The white man, if he hopes for success, must adopt the same rule of action, and encumber his horse as little as possible. Something besides well-filled mess chests and carefully rolled blankets is necessary in preparing for an Indian campaign. Arms must be reëxamined, cartridge-boxes refilled, so that each man should carry about one hundred rounds of ammunition " on his person," while each troop commander must see that in the company wagon there are placed a few boxes of reserve ammunition. Then, when the equipment of the soldier has been attended to, his horse, without whose assistance he is helpless, must be looked after; loose shoes are tightened by the driving of an additional nail, and to accomplish this one may see the company blacksmith, a soldier, with the few simple tools of his kit on the ground beside him, hurriedly fastening the last shoe by the uncertain light of a candle held in the hands of the rider of the horse, their mutual labor being varied at times by queries as to " How long shall we be gone?" "I wonder if we will catch Mr. Lo?" "If we do, we'll make it lively for him." So energetic had everybody been that before daylight everything was in readiness for the start. In addition to the regularly organized companies of soldiers which made up the pursuing column, I had with me a detachment of white scouts or Plainsmen, and one of friendly Indians, the latter belonging to the tribe of Delawares, once so famous in Indian wars. Of the Indians one only could speak English; he acted as interpreter for the party. Among the white scouts were numbered some of the most noted of their class. The most prominent man among them was " Wild Bill," whose highly varied career was made the subject of an illustrated sketch in one of the popular monthly periodicals a few years ago. " Wild Bill " was a strange character, just the one which a novelist might gloat over. He was a Plainsman in every sense of the word, yet unlike any other of his class. In person he was about six feet one in height, straight as the straightest of the warriors whose implacable foe he was; broad shoulders, well-formed chest and limbs, and a face strikingly handsome; a sharp, clear, blue eye, which stared you straight in the face when in conversation; a finely-shaped nose, inclined to be aquiline; a well-turned mouth, with lips only partially concealed by a handsome moustache. His hair and complexion were those of the perfect blond. The former was worn in uncut ringlets falling carelessly over his powerfully formed shoulders. Add to this figure a costume blending the immaculate neatness of the dandy with the extravagant taste and style of the frontiersman, and you have Wild Bill, then as now the most famous scout on the Plains. Whether on foot or on horseback, he was one of the most perfect types of physical manhood I ever saw. Of his courage there could be no question; it had been brought to the test on too many occasions to admit of a doubt. His skill in the use of the rifle and pistol was unerring; while his deportment was exactly the opposite of what might be expected from a man of his surroundings. It was entirely free from all bluster or bravado. He seldom spoke of himself unless requested to do so. His conversation, strange to say, never bordered either on the vulgar or blasphemous. His influence among the frontiersmen was unbounded, his word was law; and many are the personal quarrels and disturbances which he has checked among his comrades by his simple announcement that " this has gone far enough," if need be followed by the ominous warning that when persisted in or renewed the quarreller " must settle it with me." " Wild Bill " is anything but a quarrelsome man; yet no one but himself can enumerate the many conflicts in which he has been engaged, and which have almost invariably resulted in the death of his adversary. I have a personal knowledge of at least half a dozen men whom he has at various times killed, one of these being at the time a member of my command. Others have been severely wounded, yet he always escapes unhurt. On the Plains every man openly carries his belt with its invariable appendages, knife and revolver often two of the latter. Wild Bill always carried two handsome ivory-handled revolvers of the large size; he was never seen without them. Where this is the common custom, brawls or personal difficulties are seldom if ever settled by blows. The quarrel is not from a word to a blow, but from a word to the revolver, and he who can draw and fire first is the best man. No civil law reaches him; none is applied for. In fact there is no law recognized beyond the frontier but that of " might makes right." Should death result from the quarrel, as it usually does, no coroner's jury is impanelled to learn the cause of death, and the survivor is not arrested. But instead of these old-fashioned proceedings, a meeting of citizens takes place, the survivor is *requested* to be present when the circumstances of the homicide are inquired into, and the unfailing verdict of " justifiable," " self-defence," etc., is pronounced, and the law stands vindicated. That justice is often deprived o a victim there is not a doubt. Yet in all of the many affairs of this kind in which " Wild Bill " has performed a part, and which have come to my knowledge, there is not a single instance in which the verdict of twelve fair-minded men would not be pronounced in his favor. That the even tenor of his way continues to be disturbed by little events of this description may be inferred from an item which has been floating lately through the columns of the press, and which states that " the funeral of ' Jim Bludso,' who was killed the other day by ' Wild Bill,' took place to-day." It then adds: " The funeral expenses were borne by ' Wild Bill.' " What could be more thoughtful than this? Not only to send a fellow mortal out of the world, but to pay the expenses of the transit. Guerrier, the half-breed, also accompanied the expedition as guide and interpreter.

Everything being in readiness to move, the column began its march, and reached the vicinity of the village before day had fully dawned. Here a brief halt was necessary, until the light was sufficient to enable our scouts to discover the trail of the Indians. When they finally set to discover this, their method was highly interesting, and resembled not a little the course of a thorough sportsman, who, with a well-trained pointer or setter, thoroughly ' ranges " and " beats " the ground in search of his coveted game. The Indians had set out on their flight soon after dark the preceding night; a heavy frost covered the ground and rendered it difficult to detect the trail from the many pony tracks which are always found in the vicinity of a village. We began to grow impatient at the delay, when one of the Indians gave the "halloo " as the signal that the trail was discovered, and again the column marched forward. Our order of march was for the Indian and white scouts to keep a few hundred paces in advance of the troops, so that momentary delays upon the part of those watching and following the trail should not extend to the troops. The Indians on leaving the village had anticipated pursuit and had adopted measures to mislead us. In order to prevent their trail from being easily recognizable, they had departed in as many detachments or parties almost as there were families or lodges in the village, each party taking a different direction from the others, having personally agreed, of course, upon the general direction and place of reuniting. Once being satisfied that we were on the right trail, no difficulty was found in following it as rapidly as our horses could walk. The Indians had nearly twelve hours the start of us, but being encumbered by their families, we hoped to overhaul them before many days. Our first obstacle was encountered when we struck Walnut creek, a small stream running east and west some thirty miles north of the Arkansas at that point. The banks were so high and abrupt that it was impossible to reach the water's edge, let alone clamber up the opposite bank. A few of the Indians had been able to accomplish this feat, as shown by the tracks on the opposite side; but the main band had moved up stream in search of a favorable crossing, and we were compelled to do likewise. Here we found that the Indians had called a halt, built fires, and cooked their breakfast. So rapidly had we gained upon them that the fires were burning freshly, and the departure of the Indians had been so abrupt that they left several ponies with their packs tied to trees. One of the packs belonged to a famous chief, " Roman Nose," who was one of those who met us at the grand gathering just before we reached their village a few days before. One of our Delawares who made the capture was very proud of the success, and was soon seen ornamenting his head-dress with the bright crimson feathers taken from the wardrobe of " Roman Nose." Encouraged by our progress, we continued the pursuit as rapidly as a due regard for our horses would permit. Thus far, neither myself nor any of the soldiers had caught sight of any Indians; but our Delaware scouts, who were constantly in the advance and on our flanks, taking advantage of the bluffs to reconnoitre, frequently reported that they saw small parties of Indians observing our movements from a distance. From positive evidences, familiar to those accustomed to the Plains, we were convinced that we were rapidly gaining upon the Indians. The earth upturned by the feet of their ponies and by the ends of the trailing lodge-poles, was almost as damp and fresh as that disturbed by the horses of the command. Soon we discovered additional signs of encouragement. The route now became strewn with various lodge-poles and other obstacles peculiar to an Indian's outfit, showing that they were " lightening up so as to facilitate their escape. So certain did we feel of our ability to out-trail them, that the only question now was one which has often determined the success of military operations. Would darkness intervene to disappoint us? We must imitate the example of the Indians, and disembarrass ourselves of everything tending to retard our speed. The troops would march much faster, if permitted to do so, than the rate at which our wagons had forced themselves along. It was determined to leave the wagons, under escort of one squadron, to follow our trail as rapidly as they could, while the other three squadrons pushed on in pursuit. Should darkness settle down before overtaking the Indians, the advantage was altogether against us, as we would be compelled to await daylight to enable us to follow the trail, while the Indians were free to continue their flight, sheltered and aided by the darkness. By three o'clock P. M. we felt that we were almost certain to accomplish our purpose. No obstacle seemed to stand in our way; the trail was broad and plain, and apparently as fresh as our own. A half hour, or an hour at furthest, seemed only necessary to enable us to dash in upon our wily enemy. Alas for human calculations! The Indians, by means of the small reconnoitring parties observed by our scouts, had kept themselves constantly informed regarding our movements and progress. They had first risked their safety upon the superior speed and endurance of their ponies—a safe reliance when favored by the grass season, but in winter this advantage was on our side. Failing in their first resource, they had a second and better method of eluding us. So long as they kept united and moved in one body, their trail was as plainly to be seen and as easily followed as if made by a heavily-laden wagon train. We were not called upon to employ time and great watchfulness on the part of our scouts to follow it. But when it was finally clear to be seen that, in the race as it was then being run, the white man was sure to win, the proverbial cunning of the red man came to his rescue and thwarted the plans of his pursuers. Again dividing his tribe, as when first setting out from the village, into numerous small parties, we were discouraged by seeing the broad well-beaten trail suddenly separate into hundreds of indistinct routes, leading fan-shape in as many different directions. What was to be done?

The general direction of the main trail, before dissolving into so many small ones, had been nearly north, showing that if undisturbed in their flight the Indians would strike the Smoky Hill overland route, cross it, then pursue their way northward to the headwaters of the Solomon or Republican river, or further still, to the Platte river. Selecting a central trail, we continued our pursuit, now being compelled often to halt and verify our course. The trail gradually grew smaller and smaller, until by five o'clock it had become so faint as to be followed with the greatest difficulty. We had been marching exactly twelve hours without halting, except to water our horses. Reluctantly we were forced to go into camp and await the assistance of daylight. The Delaware scouts continued the pursuit six miles further, but returned without accomplishing anything. The Indians, after dividing up into small parties, kept up communication with each other by means of columns of signal smoke. These signal smokes were to be seen to the west, north, and east of us, but none nearer than ten miles. They only proved to us that we were probably on the trail of the main body, as the fires were in front and on both sides of us. We had marched over thirty-five miles without a halt. The Delawares having determined the direction of the trail for six miles, we would be able next morning to continue that far at least unaided by daylight. Our wagons over took us a few hours after we reached camp. Reveille was sounded at two o'clock the next morning, and four o'clock found us again in the saddle, and following the guidance of our friendly Delawares. The direction of our march took us up the valley and almost dry bed of a small stream. The Delawares thought we might find where the Indians had encamped during the night, by following the upward course of the stream, but in this we were disappointed. The trail became more and more indistinct, until it was lost in the barren waste over which we were then moving. To add to our annoyance, the water-course had become entirely dry, and our guides were uncertain as to whether water could be procured in one day's march in any direction except that from which we had come. We were, therefore, forced to countermarch after reaching a point thirteen miles from our starting-place in the morning, and retrace our steps until the uncertain stream in whose valley we then were would give us water enough for our wants.

Here I will refer to an incident entirely personal, which came very near costing me my life. When leaving our camp that morning I felt satisfied that the Indians, having travelled at least a portion of the night, were then many miles in advance of us, and there was neither danger nor probability of encountering any of them near the column. We were then in a magnificent game country, buffalo, antelope, and smaller game being in abundance on all sides of us. Although an ardent sportsman, I had never hunted the buffalo up to this time, consequently was exceedingly desirous of tasting its excitement. I had several fine English greyhounds, whose speed I was anxious to test with that of the antelope, said to be—which I believe—the fleetest of animals. I was mounted on a fine large thoroughbred horse. Taking with me but one man, the chief bugler, and calling my dogs around me, I galloped ahead of the column as soon as it was daylight, for the purpose of having a chase after some antelope which could be seen grazing nearly two miles distant. That such a course was rashly imprudent I am ready to admit. A stirring gallop of a few minutes brought me near enough to the antelope, of which there were a dozen or more, to enable the dogs to catch sight of them. Then the chase began, the antelope running in a direction which took us away from the command. By availing myself of the turns in the course, I was able to keep well in view of the exciting chase, until it was evident that the antelope were in no danger of being caught by the dogs, which latter had become blown from want of proper exercise. I succeeded in calling them off, and was about to set out on my return to the column. The horse of the chief bugler, being a common-bred animal, failed early in the race, and his rider wisely concluded to regain the command, so that I was alone. How far I had travelled from the troops I was trying to determine, when I discovered a large, dark-looking animal grazing nearly a mile distant. As yet I had never seen a wild buffalo, but I at once recognized this as not only a buffalo, but a very large one. Here was my opportunity. A ravine near by would enable me to approach unseen until almost within pistol range of my game. Calling my dogs to follow me, I slowly pursued the course of the ravine, giving my horse opportunity to gather himself for the second run. When I emerged from the ravine I was still several hundred yards from the buffalo, which almost instantly discovered me, and set off as fast as his legs could carry him. Had my horse been fresh the race would have been a short one, but the preceding long run had not been with out effect. How long or how fast we flew in pursuit, the intense excitemen of the chase prevented me from knowing. I only knew that even the greyhounds were left behind, until finally my good steed placed himself and me close alongside the game. It may be because this was the first I had seen, but surely of the hundreds of thousands of buffaloes which I have since seen, none have corresponded with him in size and lofty grandeur. My horse was above the average size, yet the buffalo towered even above him. I had carried my revolver in my hand from the moment the race began. Repeatedly could I have placed the muzzle against the shaggy body of the huge beast, by whose side I fairly yelled with wild excitement and delight, yet each time would I withdrawn the weapon, as if to prolong the enjoyment of the race. It was a race for life or death, yet how different the award from what could be imagined. Still we sped over the springy turf, the high breeding and mettle of my horse being plainly visible over that of the huge beast that struggled by his side. Mile after mile was traversed in this way, until the rate and distance began to tell perceptibly on the bison, whose protruding tongue and labored breathing plainly betrayed his distress. Determined to end the chase and bring down my game, I again placed the muzzle of the revolver close to the body of the buffalo, when, as if divining my intention, and feeling his inability to escape by flight, he suddenly determined to fight, and at once wheeled, as only a buffalo can, to gore my horse. So sudden was this movement, and so sudden was the corresponding veering of my horse to avoid the attack, that to retain my control over him I hastily brought up my pistol hand to the assistance of the other. Unfortunately as I did so my finger, in the excitement of the occasion, pressed the trigger, discharged the pistol, and sent the fatal ball into the very brain of the noble animal I rode. Running at full speed he fell dead in the course of his leap. Quick as thought I disengaged myself from the stirrups and found myself whirling through the air over and beyond the head of my horse. My only thought, as I was describing this trajectory, and my first thought on reaching *terra firma*, was, "What will the buffalo do with me?" Although at first inclined to rush upon me, my strange procedure seemed to astonish him. Either that, or pity for the utter helplessness of my condition, inclined him to alter his course and leave me alone to my own bitter reflections.

In a moment the danger into which I had unluckily brought myself stood out in bold relief before me. Under ordinary circumstances the death of my horse would have been serious enough. I was strongly attached to him; had ridden him in battle during a portion of the late war; yet now his death, except in its consequences, was scarcely thought of. Here I was, alone in the heart of the Indian country, with warlike Indians known to be in the vicinity. I was not familiar with the country. How far I had travelled, or in what direction from the column, I was at a loss to know. In the excitement of the chase I had lost all reckoning. Indians were liable to pounce upon me at any moment. My command would not note my absence probably for hours. Two of my dogs overtook me, and with mute glances first at the dead steed, then at me, seemed to inquire the cause of this strange condition of affairs. Their instinct appeared to tell them that we were in misfortune. While I was deliberating what to do, the dogs became uneasy, whined piteously, and seemed eager to leave the spot. In this desire I sympathized with them, but whither should I go? I observed that their eyes were generally turned in one particular direction; this I accepted as my cue, and with one parting look at my horse, and grasping a revolver in each hand, I set out on my uncertain journey. As long as the body of my horse was visible above the horizon, I kept referring to it as my guiding point, and in this way contrived to preserve my direction. This resource soon failed me, and I then had recourse to weeds, buffalo skulls, or any two objects I could find on my line of march. Constantly my eyes kept scanning the horizon, each moment expecting, and with reason too, to find myself discovered by Indians.

I had travelled in this manner what seemed to me about three or four miles, when far ahead in the distance I saw a column of dust rising. A hasty examination soon convinced me that the dust was produced by one of three causes: white men, Indians, or buffalo. Two to one in my favor at any rate. Selecting a ravine where I could crawl away undiscovered should the approaching body prove to be Indians, I called my dogs to my side and concealed myself as well as I could to await developments. The object of my anxious solicitude was still several miles distant. Whatever it was, it was approaching in my direction, as was plainly discernible from the increasing columns of dust. Fortunately I had my field-glass slung across my shoulder, and if Indians I could discover them before they could possibly discover me. Soon I was able to see the heads of mounted men running in irregular order. This discovery shut out the probability of their being buffaloes, and simplified the question to white men or Indians. Never during the war did I scan an enemy's battery or approaching column with half the anxious care with which I watched the party then approaching me. For a long time nothing satisfactory could be determined, until my eye caught sight of an object which, high above the heads of the approaching riders, told me in unmistakable terms that friends were approaching. It was the cavalry guidon, and never was the sight of stars and stripes more welcome. My comrades were greatly surprised to find me seated on the ground alone and without my horse. A few words explained all. A detachment of my men, following my direction, found my horse and returned with the saddle and other equipments. Another horse, and Richard was himself again, plus a little valuable experience, and minus a valuable horse.

In retracing our steps later in the day, in search of water sufficient for camping purposes, we marched over nine miles of our morning route, and at two P. M. of April 16 we went into camp. From this point I wrote a despatch to General Hancock and sent it back by two of my scouts, who set out on their journey as soon as it was dark. It was determined to push on and reach the Smoky Hill route as soon as possible, and give the numerous stage stations along that route notice of the presence of warlike Indians. This was before the Pacific Railroad or its branches had crossed the Plains. Resting our animals from two until seven P. M., we were again in the saddle and setting out for a night march, our only guide being the north star. We hoped to strike the stage route near a point called Downie's Station. After riding all night we reached and crossed about daylight the Smoky Hill river, along whose valley the stage route runs. The stations were then from ten to fifteen miles apart; if Indians had crossed this line at any point the station men would be informed of it. To get information as to this, as well as to determine where we were, an officer with one company was at once despatched on this mission. This party had scarcely taken its departure and our pickets been posted, before the entire command of tired, sleepy cavalrymen, scouts, and Delawares had thrown themselves on the ground and were wrapped in the deepest slumber. We had slept perhaps an hour or more, yet it seemed but a few moments, when an alarm shot from the lookout and the startling cry of "Indians!" brought the entire command under arms.

V.

ALTHOUGH in search of Indians and supposed to be always piepared to encounter them, yet the warning shot of the sentry, followed as it was by his cry of "Indians!" could not but produce the greatest excitement in camp. Where all had been quiet before—men sleeping and resting after their long night march, animals grazing unsuspectingly in the midst of the wagons and tents which thickly dotted the Plain here and there—all was now bustle if not confusion. Herders and teamsters ran to their animals to conduct them inside the limits of camp. The troopers of one platoon of each company hastened to secure the cavalry horses and provide against a stampede, while those of the remaining platoons were rapidly marshalled under arms by their troop officers, and advanced in the direction from which the lookout reported the enemy to be approaching.

All this required but a few moments of time. Recovering from the first shock of surprise, we endeavored, one and all, to discover the number and purpose of the foes who had in so unceremonious a manner disturbed our much-needed slumbers.

Daylight had just dawned, but the sun was not yet high enough to render a satisfactory view of the country possible. This difficulty was aggravated, too, by a dull heavy mist, which hung like a curtain near the horizon. Yet in spite of all these obstructions we could clearly perceive, at a distance of perhaps a mile, the dim outlines of numerous figures—horsemen evidently—approaching our camp, not as if simply on the march, but in battle array. First came a deployed line of horsemen, followed in rear, as we could plainly see, by a reserve, also mounted and moving in compact order.

It required no practised eye to comprehend that be they who or what they might, the parties advancing in this precise and determined manner upon us were doing so with hostile purpose, and evidently intended to charge into our camp unless defeated in their purpose. No time was to be lost. Dispositions to meet the coming attack were rapidly made. To better observe the movements and determine the strength of the approaching parties, an officer ascended the knoll occupied by the lookout.

We had often heard of the high perfection of some of the Indian tribes in military evolutions and discipline, but here we saw evidences which went far to convince us that the red man was not far behind his more civilized brother in the art of war. Certainly no troops of my command could have advanced a skirmish line or moved a reserve more accurately than was done in our presence that morning.

As yet we had no means of determining to what tribe the attacking party belonged. We were satisfied they must be either Sioux or Cheyennes, or both; in either case we should encounter troublesome foes. But for the heavy mist we could have comprehended everything. Soon we began receiving reports from the officer who had ascended the lookout. First, there were not more than eighty horsemen to be seen. This number we could easily dispose of. Next, the attacking parties seemed to have changed their plan; a halt was ordered, and two or three horsemen seemed to be advancing to the front as if to parley, or reconnoitre our position. Then the skirmishers were suddenly withdrawn and united with the reserve, when the entire party wheeled about and began to move off. This was mystifying in the extreme, but a couple of young cavalry officers leaped into their saddles and taking a few mounted troopers with them dashed after our late enemies, determined to learn more about them than they seemed willing we should.

A brisk gallop soon cleared away the mystery, and furnished another proof of the deceptive effects produced by the atmosphere on the Plains. Those who have read the preceding article will remember that at the termination of the night march which brought us to our present camp, an officer was despatched with one troop of cavalry to find the nearest stage station on the overland route, near which we knew we must then be. Our camp lay on the Smoky Hill river. The stage route, better known as the "Smoky Hill route," was known to be but a few miles north of us. To determine our exact locality, as we had been marching by compass over a wild country and in the night-time, and to learn something regarding the Indians, this officer was sent out. He was selected for this service because of his professed experience on and knowledge of the Plains. He had set out from our camp an hour or more before daylight, but losing his bearings had marched his command in a semicircle until daylight found him on the side of our camp opposite that from which he had departed. The conical Sibley tent used in my command, resembling the Indian lodge from which it was taken, seen through the peculiar and uncertain morning atmosphere of that region, had presented to his eyes and to those of his men the appearance of an Indian village. The animals grazing about our camp might well have been taken for the ponies of the Indians. Besides, it was well known that large encampments of Indians were in the part of the country over which we were marching. The bewilderment of this detachment, then, was not surprising considering the attending circumstances. Had the officer in command been young and inexperienced, his mishap might have been credited to these causes; but here was an officer who had grown gray in the service, familiar with the Plains and with Indians, yet so completely misled by appearances as to mistake his camp, which he had left but an hour before, for an Indian village.

Few officers laboring under the same impression would have acted so creditably. He and his men imagined they had discovered the camp of the Indians whom we had been pursuing, and although believing their enemies outnumbered them ten to one, yet their zeal and earnestness prompted them, instead of sending to their main camp for reinforcements, thereby losing valuable time and probable opportunities to effect a surprise, to make a dash at once into the village. And it was only the increasing light of day that enabled them to discover their mistake and saved us from a charge from our own troopers. This little incident will show how necessary experienced professional guides are in connection with all military movements on the Plains. It was a long time before the officer who had been so unlucky as to lose his way heard the last of it from his brother officers.

The remainder of his mission was completed more successfully. Aided by daylight, and moving nearly due north, he soon struck the well-travelled overland route, and from the frightened employés at the nearest station he obtained intelligence which confirmed our worst fears as to the extent of the Indian outbreak. Stage stations at various points along the route had been attacked and burned, and the inmates driven off or murdered. All travel across the Plains was suspended, and an Indian war with all its barbarities had been forced upon the people of the frontier.

As soon as the officer ascertaining these facts had returned to camp and made his report, the entire command was again put in motion and started in the direction of the stage route, with the intention of clearing it of straggling bands of Indians, reopening the main line of travel across the Plains, and establishing if possible upon the proper tribes the responsibility for the numerous outrages recently committed. The stage stations were erected at points along the route distant from each other from ten to fifteen miles, and were used solely for the shelter and accommodation of the relays of drivers and horses employed on the stage route. We found, in passing over the route on our eastward march, that only about every fourth station was occupied, the occupants of the other three having congregated there for mutual defence against the Indians, the latter having burned the deserted stations.

From the employés of the company at various points we learned that for the few preceding days the Indians had been crossing the line, going toward the north in large bodies. In some places we saw the ruins of the burned stations, but it was not until we reached Lookout Station, a point about fifteen miles west of Fort Hays, that we came upon the first real evidences of an Indian outbreak. Riding some distance in advance of the command, I reached the station only to find it and the adjacent buildings in ashes, the ruins still smoking. Near by I discovered the bodies of the three station-keepers, so mangled and burned as to be scarcely recognizable as human beings. The Indians had evidently tortured them before putting an end to their sufferings. They were scalped and horribly disfigured. Their bodies were badly burned, but whether before or after death could not be determined. No arrow, or other article of Indian manufacuture, could be found to positively determine what particular tribe was the guilty one. The men at other stations had recognized some of the Indians passing as belonging to the Sioux and Cheyennes, the same we had passed from the village on Pawnee Fork.

Continuing our march, we reached Fort Hays, from which point I despatched a report to General Hancock, on the Arkansas, furnishing him all the information I had gained concerning the outrages and movements of the Indians. As it has been a question of considerable dispute between the respective advocates of the Indian peace and war policy, as to which party committed the first overt act of war, the Indians or General Hancock's command, I quote from a letter on the subject written by Major-General Hancock to General Grant, in reply to a letter of inquiry from the latter when commanding the armies of the United States. General Hancock says:

"When I learned from General Custer, who investigated these matters on the spot, that directly after they had abandoned the villages they attacked and burned a mail station on the Smoky Hill, killed the white men at it, disembowelled and burned them, fired into another station, endeavored to gain admittance to a third, fired on my expressmen both on the Smoky Hill and on their way to Larned, I concluded that this must be war, and therefore deemed it my duty to take the first opportunity which presented to resent these hostilities and outrages, and did so by destroying their villages."

The first paragraph of General Hancock's special field order directing the destruction of the Indian village read as follows:

"II. As a punishment for the bad faith practised by the Cheyennes and Sioux who occupied the Indian village at this place, and as a chastisement for murders and depredations committed since the arrival of the command at this point, by the people of these tribes, the village recently occupied by them, which is now in our hands, will be utterly destroyed."

From these extracts the question raised can be readily settled. This act of retribution on the part of General Hancock was the signal for an extensive pen and ink war, directed against him and his forces. This was to be expected. The pecuniary loss and deprivation of opportunities to speculate in Indian commodities, as practised by most Indian agents, were too great to be submitted to without a murmur. The Cheyennes, Arrapahoes, and Apaches had been united under one agency; the Kiowas and Comanches under another. As General Hancock's expedition had reference to all of these tribes, he had extended invitations to each of the two agents to accompany him into the Indian country, and be present at all interviews with the representatives of these respective tribes, for the purpose, as the invitation states, of showing the Indians "that the officers of the Government are acting in harmony."

These agents were both present at General Hancock's headquarters. Both admitted to General Hancock in conversation that Indians had been guilty of all the outrages charged against them, but each asserted the innocence of the particular tribes under his charge, and endeavored to lay their crimes at the door of their neighbors. The agent of the Kiowas and Comanches declared to the department commander that "the tribes of his agency had been grossly wronged by having been charged with various offences which had undoubtedly been committed by the Cheyennes, Arrapahoes, and Apaches, and that these tribes deserved severe and summary chastisement for their numerous misdeeds, very many of which had been laid at the doors of his innocent tribes."

Not to be outdone in the profuse use of fair words, however, the agent of the three tribes thus assailed informed General Hancock that his three tribes "were peacefully inclined, and rarely committed offences against the laws, but that most unfortunately they were charged in many instances with crimes which had been perpetrated by other tribes, and that in this respect they had suffered heavily from the Kiowas, who were the most turbulent Indians of the Plains, and deserved punishment more than any others."

Here was positive evidence from the agents themselves that the Indians against whom we were operating were guilty, and deserving of severe punishment. The only conflicting portion of the testimony was as to which tribe was most guilty. Subsequent events proved, however, that all of the five tribes named, as well as the Sioux, had combined for a general war throughout the Plains and along our frontier. Such a war had been threatened to our post commanders along the Arkansas on many occasions during the winter. The movement of the Sioux and Cheyennes toward the north indicated that the principal theatre of military operations during the summer would be between the Smoky Hill and Platte rivers. General Hancock accordingly assembled the principal chiefs of the Kiowas and Arrapahoes in council at Fort Dodge, hoping to induce them to remain at peace and observe their treaty obligations.

The most prominent chiefs in council were Satanta, Lone Wolf, and Kicking Bird of the Kiowas, and Little Raven and Yellow Bear of the Arrapahoes. During the council extravagant promises of future good conduct were made by these chiefs. So effective and convincing was the oratorical effort of Satanta, that at the termination of his address the department commander and staff presented him with the uniform coat, sash, and hat of a major-general. In return for this compliment Satanta, within a few weeks after, attacked the post at which the council was held, arrayed in his new uniform. This said chief had but recently headed an expedition to the frontier of Texas, where, among other murders committed by him and his band, was that known as the "Box massacre." The Box family consisted of the father, mother, and five children, the eldest a girl about eighteen, the youngest a babe. The entire family had been visiting at a neighbor's house, and were returning home in the evening, little dreaming of the terrible fate impending, when Satanta and his warriors dashed upon them, surrounded the wagon in which they were driving, and at the first fire killed the father and one of the children. The horses were hastily taken from the wagon, while the mother was informed by signs that she and her four surviving children must accompany their captors. Mounting their prisoners upon led horses, of which they had a great number stolen from the settlers, the Indians prepared to set out on their return to the village, then located hundreds of miles north. Before departing from the scene of the massacre, the savages scalped the father and child, who had fallen as their first victims. Far better would it have been had the remaining members of the family met their death in the first attack. From the mother, whom I met when released from her captivity, after living as a prisoner in the hands of the Indians for more than a year, I gathered the details of the sufferings of herself and children.

Fearing pursuit by the Texans, and desiring to place as long a distance as possible between themselves and their pursuers, they prepared for a night march. Mrs. Box and each of the three elder children were placed on separate horses and securely bound. This was to prevent escape in the darkness. The mother was at first permitted to carry the youngest child, a babe of a few months, in her arms, but the latter, becoming fretful during the tiresome night ride, began to cry. The Indians, fearing the sound of its voice might be heard by pursuers, snatched it from its mother's arms and dashed its brains out against a tree, then threw the lifeless remains to the ground and continued their flight. No halt was made for twenty-four hours, after which the march was conducted more deliberately. Each night the mother and three children were permitted to occupy one shelter, closely guarded by their watchful enemies.

After travelling for several days this war party arrived at the point where they rejoined their lodges. They were still a long distance from the main village, which was near the Arkansas. Each night the scalp of the father was hung up in the lodge occupied by the mother and children. A long and weary march over a wild and desolate country brought them to the main village. Here the captives found that their most serious troubles were to commence. In accordance with Indian custom, upon the return of a successful war party, a grand assembly of the tribe took place. The prisoners, captured horses, and scalps were brought forth, and the usual ceremonies, terminating in a scalp dance, followed. Then the division of the spoils was made. The captives were apportioned among the various bands composing the tribe, so that when the division was completed the mother fell to the possession of one chief, the eldest daughter to that of another, the second, a little girl of probably ten years, to another, and the youngest, a child of three years, to a fourth. No two members of the family were permitted to remain in the same band, but were each carried to separate villages, distant from each other several days' march. This was done partly to prevent escape.

No pen can describe the painful tortures of mind and body endured by this unfortunate family. They remained as captives in the hands of the Indians for more than a year, during which time the eldest daughter, a beautiful girl just ripening into womanhood, was exposed to a fate infinitely more dreadful than death itself. She first fell to one of the principal chiefs, who, after robbing her of that which was more precious than life, and forcing her to become

MISS BOX COMPELLED TO HELP DRESS BUFFALOES

the victim of his brutal lust, bartered her in return for two horses to another chief; he again, after wearying of her, traded her to a chief of a neighboring band; and in that way this unfortunate girl was passed from one to another of her savage captors, undergoing a life so horribly brutal that, when meeting her upon her release from captivity, one could only wonder how a young girl, nurtured in civilization and possessed of the natural refinement and delicacy of thought which she exhibited, could have survived such degrading treatment.

The mother and second daughter fared somewhat better. The youngest, however, separated from mother and sisters, and thrown among people totally devoid of all kind feeling, spent the time in shedding bitter tears. This so enraged the Indians that, as a punishment as well as preventive, the child was seized and the soles of its naked feet exposed to the flames of the lodge fire until every portion of the cuticle was burned therefrom. When I saw this little girl a year afterward, her feet were from this cause still in a painful and unhealed condition. These poor captives were reclaimed from their bondage through the efforts of officers of the army, and by the payment of a ransom amounting to many hundreds of dollars.

The facts relating to their cruel treatment were obtained by me directly from the mother and eldest daughter immediately after their release, which occurred a few months prior to the council held with Satanta and other chiefs. To prove something of the character of the Cheyennes, one of the principal tribes with which we were at war, I will give the following extract from an official communication addressed by me to General Hancock prior to the surrender of the little Indian boy of whom mention was made in a former article. My recommendation was not deemed practicable, as it had been promised by us in treaty stipulation to return the boy unconditionally.

" Having learned that a boy belonging to the Cheyenne tribe of Indians is in the possession of the military authorities, and that it is the intention of the Major-General commanding the department to deliver him up to the above-named tribe, I would respectfully state that a little white girl aged from four to seven years is held captive by the Cheyenne Indians, and is now in the possession of ' Cut Nose,' a chief of said tribe.

" The child referred to has been in the hands of the Indians a year or more. She was captured somewhere in the vicinity of Cache la Poudre, Colorado. The parents' name is Fletcher. The father escaped with a severe wound, the mother and two younger children being taken prisoners. The Indians killed one of the children outright, and the mother, after subjecting her to tortures too horrible to name.

" The child now held by the Indians was kept captive. An elder daughter made her escape and now resides in Iowa. The father resides in Salt Lake City. I have received several letters from the father and eldest daughter and from friends of both, requesting me to obtain the release of the little girl, if possible. I would therefore request that it be made a condition of the return of the Indian boy now in our possession, that the Cheyennes give up the white child referred to above."

This proposition failing in its object, and the war destroying all means of communication with the Indians and scattering the latter over the Plains, all trace of the little white girl was lost, and to this day nothing is known of her fate. At the breaking out of the Indian difficulty " Cut Nose " with his band was located along the Smoky Hill route in the vicinity of Monument Station. He frequently visited the stage stations for purposes of trade, and was invariably accompanied by his little captive. I never saw her, but those who did

5

represented her as strikingly beautiful; her complexion being fair, her eyes blue, and her hair of a bright golden hue, she presented a marked contrast to the Indian children who accompanied her. "Cut Nose," from the delicate light color of her hair, gave her an Indian name signifying "Little Silver Hair." He appeared to treat her with great affection, and always kept her clothed in the handsomest of Indian garments. All offers from individuals to ransom her proved unavailing. Although she had been with the Indians but a year, she spoke the Cheyenne language fluently, and seemed to have no knowledge of her mother tongue.

The treatment of the Box and Fletcher families is not given as isolated instances, but is referred to principally to show the character of the enemy with whom we were at war. Volume after volume might be filled in recounting the unprovoked and merciless atrocities committed upon the people of the frontier by their implacable foe, the red man. It will become necessary, however, in making a truthful record of the principal events which transpired under my personal observation, to make mention of Indian outrages surpassing if possible in savage cruelty any yet referred to.

As soon as General Hancock had terminated his council with the Kiowas and Arrapahoes, he marched with the remaining portion of the expedition across from the Arkansas to Fort Hays, where my command was then encamped, arriving there on the third of May. Here, owing to the neglect or delay of the officers of the Quartermaster's Department in forwarding the necessary stores, the cavalry was prevented from undertaking any extensive movement, but had to content itself for the time being in scouting the adjacent country.

The time, however, was well employed in the preparation of men and animals for the work which was to be assigned them. Unfortunately, desertions from the ranks became so frequent and extensive as to cause no little anxiety.

To produce these, several causes combined. Prominent among them was the insufficiency and inferior quality of the rations furnished the men. At times the latter were made the victims of fraud, and it was only by the zealous care and watchfulness of the officers immediately over them, that their wants were properly attended to.

Dishonest contractors at the receiving depots further east had been permitted to perpetrate gross frauds upon the Government, the result of which was to produce want and suffering among the men. For example, unbroken packages of provisions shipped from the main depot of supplies, and which it was impracticable to replace without loss of time, were when opened discovered to contain huge stones for which the Government had paid so much per pound according to contract price. Boxes of bread were shipped and issued to the soldiers of my command, the contents of which had been baked in 1861, yet this was in 1867. It is unnecessary to state that but little of this bread was eaten, yet there was none at hand of better quality to replace it. Bad provisions were a fruitful cause of bad health. Inactivity led to restlessness and dissatisfaction. Scurvy made its appearance, and cholera attacked neighboring stations. For all these evils desertion became the most popular antidote. To such an extent was this the case, that in one year one regiment lost by desertion alone more than half of its effective force.

General Hancock remained with us only a few days before setting out with the battery for his headquarters at Fort Leavenworth. Supplies were pushed out and every preparation made for resuming offensive movements against the Indians. To find employment for the few weeks which must ensue before

LITTLE SILVER HAIR.

breaking up camp was sometimes a difficult task. To break the monotony and give horses and men exercise, buffalo hunts were organized, in which officers and men joined heartily. I know of no better drill for perfecting men in the use of firearms on horseback, and thoroughly accustoming them to the saddle, than buffalo-hunting over a moderately rough country. No amount of riding under the best of drill-masters will give that confidence and security in the saddle, which will result from a few spirited charges into a buffalo herd.

The command, consisting of cavalry alone, was at last in readiness to move. Wagons had been loaded with reserve supplies, and we were only waiting the growth of the spring grass to set out on the long march which had previously been arranged. On the first of June, with about three hundred and fifty men and a train of twenty wagons, I left Fort Hays and directed our line of march toward Fort McPherson, on the Platte river, distant by the proposed route two hundred and twenty-five miles. The friendly Delawares accompanied us as scouts and trailers, but our guide was a young white man known on the Plains as "Will Comstock." No Indian knew the country more thoroughly than did Comstock. He was perfectly familiar with every divide, water-course, and strip of timber for hundreds of miles in either direction. He knew th) dress and peculiarities of every Indian tribe, and spoke the languages of many of them. Perfect in horsemanship, fearless in manner, a splendid hunter, and a gentleman by instinct, as modest and unassuming as he was brave, he was an interesting as well as valuable companion on a march such as was then before us. Many were the adventures and incidents of frontier life with which he was accustomed to entertain us when around the camp-fire or on the march. Little did he then imagine that his own life would soon be given as a sacrifice to his daring, and that he, with all his experience among the savages, would fall a victim of Indian treachery.

VI.

IT had been decided that my command should thoroughly scout the country from Fort Hays near the Smoky Hill river, to Fort McPherson, on the Platte; thence describe a semicircle to the southward, touching the head waters of the Republican, and again reach the Platte at or near Fort Sedgwick, at which post we would replenish our supplies; then move directly south to Fort Wallace, on the Smoky Hill, and from there march down the overland route to our starting-point at Fort Hays. This would involve a ride of upwards of one thousand miles.

As is usually the case, the first day's march was not to be a long one. The troops, under charge of the officer second in command, Colonel Wickliffe Cooper, left camp and marched up the valley of Big Creek a distance of eighteen miles, and there encamped. Two companies of cavalry and a small force of infantry were to constitute the garrison to remain behind. When the troops composing my command left, it became necessary to rearrange the camp and provide new dispositions for defence. My wife, who always accompanied me when in camp or on the march except when I was engaged in active pursuit of Indians, had rejoined me soon after my arrival at Fort Hays. She was accompanied by a young lady friend from the East, a schoolmate, who had been tempted by the novelties of wild Western life to make her a visit in camp. As there were other ladies in camp, wives of officers who were to remain with the garrison, my wife and friend decided to remain and await our return, rather than go back to the protection and luxuries of civilization. To arrange for their comfort and superintend the locating of their tents, I remained behind my command, intending to wait until after midnight, and then, guided by the moonlight, ride on and overtake my command before it should commence its second day's march. I retained with me two soldiers, one scout, and four of the Delawares.

As soon as the command moved, the portion to remain at Fort Hays was drawn in near the few buildings which constituted the fort. All of the cavalry and a portion of the infantry were to encamp in the valley and not far from the stream. For three-quarters of a mile on either side the valley consisted of a level unbroken plain; then a low bluff was encountered, succeeded by a second plain of less extent. This was bordered by a higher and more broken bluff than the first. Fortunately, in selecting the ground on which the tents intended for the ladies were to stand, I had chosen a little knoll, so small as to be scarcely perceptible, yet the only elevated ground to be found. It was within a few steps of the bank of the stream, while the main camp was located below and nearer the bluff. For safety a few soldiers were placed in camp a short distance above. In ordinary times the banks of Big Creek are at this point from twenty-five to forty feet above the water, and a person accustomed to the slow and gradual rise and fall which prevails along the beds of streams in the Eastern States, can with difficulty realize the suddenness with which the deep and narrow channels of watercourses on the Plains become filled to overflowing. In proportion to the surface of the country or the watersheds, the watercourses or channels are few, too few to accommodate the drainage necessities during the wet season. The bank on which the little knoll stood was, by actual measurement, thirty-six feet above ordinary water mark. The knoll was probably three or four feet above the level of the valley. Surely this location might be considered well enough protected naturally against the rainy season. So I thought, as I saw the working party putting the finishing touches to the bright white canvas house, which to all intents and purposes was to be to me, even in absence, my army home.

I confidently expected to return to this camp at the termination of my march. I will be pardoned if I anticipate events and terminate its history now. A few days after my command had marched, a heavy storm set in, the rain pouring down in a manner resembling a waterspout. The immediate effect of the heavy shower was not at once noticeable near the camp at Fort Hays, as the heaviest rainfall had occurred far above that point. But in the night-time, after the entire camp except the guards had long since retired and fallen asleep, the stream, overcharged by the rushing volumes from above, soon became transformed from a mild and murmuring brook into an irresistible, turbulent torrent. So sudden and unexpected had been the rise, that before the alarm could be given the thirty-six feet which had separated the surface of the water from the top of the banks had been overcome, and in addition the water began now sweeping over the entire plain. After overflowing the natural banks of the creek, the first new channel ran in such a manner as to surround the tents occupied by the ladies as well as that occupied by the few soldiers stationed up the stream, but still leaving communication open between the main camp and the bluff toward the mainland. The soldiers, as well as the officers and their families in the main camp, hastened to the bluff to escape being swept down before the huge torrent which each instant became more fearful.

To add to the embarrassment of the situation, the blackest darkness prevailed, only relieved at times by vivid gleams of lightning, while the deep sullen roar of the torrent, increasing each moment in depth and volume, was only drowned at intervals by the fierce and more deafening uproar of the thunder, which sounded like the applause of some huge fury watching this struggle between the elements.

When Mrs. Custer and her young lady companion were awakened by the storm, they discovered that their tents were surrounded by the new channel, and that all efforts to reach the main camp would prove unavailing. They had with them at this time only a colored female servant. They did not even know the fate of the other portion of the camp. In the midst of this fearful scene, they heard the cries of men in despair near their tent. The cries came from the soldiers who had been in camp above them, but were now being carried off in the darkness by the rising current. No assistance could reach them. It is doubtful if they could have been saved even had they been found by daylight. There were seven in all. One of them, as he was being swept by the tent, contrived, through accident no doubt, to grasp the branch of a small bush which grew on the bank. It was from him that the cries of distress principally proceeded Aided by the dim light of a camp lantern, the ladies were enabled to see this unfortunate man clinging, as it were, between life and death. With commendable presence of mind, considering the fate staring them in the face, a rope was procured, and after a few failures one end was thrown to the unfortunate man, and by the united strength of the two ladies and their servant he was pulled to shore and, for the time being at least, his life was saved. His six less fortunate companions were drowned.

Two of the officers, Brevet Major-General A. J. Smith, and his Adjutant-General, Colonel Weir, with a view to rescuing the ladies, had succeeded in making their way across the new channel made by the torrent to the knoll; but when attempting to return on horseback to the mainland, they found the current too deep and swift for them to succeed. They were compelled then to await their fate. The water continued to rise until the entire valley from the natural channel to the first bluff, a distance of a quarter of a mile, was covered by an unfordable river. The only point still free from water was the little knoll which I had been so fortunate as to select for the tents. But the rise in the water continued until it finally reached the edge of the tent. At this rate the tents themselves must soon be swept away. As a last resort, a Gatling gun which stood near the entrance of the tent, and which from its great weight would probably withstand the force of the current, was hauled closer to the tent and ropes securely attached to the wheels; by these ropes it was proposed to fasten the ladies and the servant to the gun, and in this way, should the streams not rise too high above the knoll, their lives might be saved.

The colored girl, Eliza, who was devoted to her mistress, and who had been amid scenes of great danger, was on this occasion invaluable. Eliza had quite a history before she visited the Plains. Formerly a slave, but set free by the war, she had accompanied me as cook during the last three years of the war. Twice taken prisoner by the Confederates, she each time made her escape and refound me. She was present at almost every prominent battle of the Army of the Potomac, accompanied my command on all the raids and winter marches, and upon more than one occasion during the progress of a battle Eliza might be seen near the front earnestly engaged in preparing a cup of coffee for the officers at headquarters, who but for her would have gone through the day dinnerless. I have seen her remain by her camp cook fire when the enemy's shells were bursting overhead, to such an extent that men who were similarly employed deserted their station and sought shelter in the rear. There were few officers or soldiers in the cavalry corps, from General Sheridan down, with whom Eliza was not a great favorite. All had a pleasant word for her, and few had not at some time or other cause to remember her kindness.

When the water finally approached close to the tent, Eliza marked its porgress from time to time by placing small stakes at the water line. How anxiously the gradual rise of the torrent must have been watched. At last, when all hope seemed almost exhausted, the waters were stayed in their progress, and soon, to the great joy of the little party besieged, began to recede. It was still dark, but so rapidly did the volume of water diminish—as rapidly as it had accumulated—that a few hours after daylight a safe passage was effected to the mainland. With the exception of those of the six soldiers, no lives were lost, although many narrow escapes were made.

In the morning, daylight showed the post hospital, a stone building, surrounded by an unfordable stream, the water rushing through the doors and windows. The patients had managed to climb upon the roof, and could be seen by the officers and men on the mainland. No boats were to be had, but no class of men are so full of expedients as soldiers. The beds of some government wagons were hastily removed, the canvas covers were stretched under the bottoms, and in this way a temporary kind of pontoon was constructed which answered the desired purpose, and by means of which the beleaguered patients were soon released.

The officer in command of the infantry, Major Merriam, was occupying a tent with his wife near the main camp. Finding himself cut off from the main land, but before the water had attained its greatest depth, he took his wife in his arms and forded the stream which ran between his tent and the bluff, and in this manner reached a point of safety. It is remarkable, however, that within two years from the date of this occurrence, this same officer with his wife and child encountered a similar freshet in Texas, hundreds of miles from this locality, and that the watery grave which was so narrowly avoided in Kansas awaited the mother and child in Texas. Of the circumstances of the storm at Fort Hays I was necessarily ignorant until weeks later.

Soon after midnight, everything being in readiness, and my little party having been refreshed by a cup of good army coffee, it only remained to say adieu to those who were to remain behind, and we were ready for our moonlight gallop.

But little was said as we made our way rapidly over the plain in the direction taken by the command. Occasionally, as we dashed across a ravine, we would suddenly come upon a herd of antelopes or a few scattering buffaloes, startling them from their repose and causing them to wonder what was the occasion and who the strange parties disturbing the peaceful quiet of the night in this unusual manner. On we sped, our good steeds snuffing the early morning air and pressing forward as eagerly as if they knew their companions were awaiting them in the advance.

Daylight had given us no evidence of its coming, when, after a ride of nearly twenty miles, we found ourselves descending into a valley in which we knew the command must be encamped. The moon had disappeared below the horizon, and we were left to make our way aided by such light as the stars twinkling in a clear sky afforded us. Our horses gave us unmistakable evidence that camp was near. To convince us beyond all doubt, the clear ringing notes of the bugle sounding the reveille greeted our ears, and directed by the sound we soon found ourselves in camp.

A cavalry camp immediately after reveille always presents an animated and most interesting scene. As soon as the rolls are called and the reports of absentees made to headquarters, the men of the companies, with the exception of the cooks, are employed in the care of the horses. The latter are fed, and while eating are thoroughly groomed by the men, under the superintendence of their officers. Nearly an hour is devoted to this important duty. In the meanwhile the company cooks, ten to each company, and the officers' servants, are busily engaged preparing breakfast, so that within a few minutes after the horses have received proper attention breakfast is ready, and being very simple it requires but little time to dispose of it. Immediately after breakfast the first bugle call indicative of the march is the "General," and is the signal for tents to be taken down and everything packed in readiness for moving. A few minutes later this is followed by the bugler at headquarters sounding "Boots and saddles," when horses are saddled up and the wagon train put in readiness for "pulling out." Five minutes later "To horse" is sounded, and the men of each company lead their horses into line, each trooper standing at the head of his horse. At the words "Prepare to mount," from the commanding officer, each trooper places his left foot in the stirrup; and at the command "Mount," every man rises on his stirrup and places himself in his saddle, the whole command presenting the appearance to the eye of a huge machine propelled by one power. Woe betide the unfortunate trooper who through carelessness or inattention fails to place himself in his saddle simultaneously with his companions. If he is not for this offence against military rule deprived of the services of his horse during the succeeding half day's march, he escapes luckily.

As soon as the command is mounted the "Advance" is sounded, and the troops, usually in "column of fours," move out. The company leading the advance one day march in rear the following day This successive changing gives each company an opportunity to march by regular turn in advance. Our average daily march, when not in immediate pursuit of the enemy, was about twenty-five miles. Upon reaching camp in the evening the horses were cared for as in the morning, opportunities being given them to graze before dark. Pickets were posted and every precaution adopted to guard against surprise.

Our second day's march brought us to the Saline river, where we encamped for the night. From our camp ground we could see on a knoll some two miles distant a platform or scaffold erected, which resembled somewhat one of our war signal stations. Curious to discover its purpose, I determined to visit it.

Taking with me Comstock and a few soldiers, I soon reached the point, and discovered that the object of my curiosity and surprise was an Indian grave. The body, instead of being consigned to mother earth, was placed on top of the platform. The latter was constructed of saplings, and was about twenty feet in height. From Comstock I learned that with some of the tribes this is the usual mode of disposing of the body after death. The prevailing belief of the Indian is that when done with this world the spirit of the deceased is transferred to the " happy hunting-ground," where he is permitted to engage in the same pleasures and pursuits which he preferred while on earth. To this end it is deemed essential that after death the departed must be supplied with the same equipment and ornaments considered necessary while in the flesh. In accordance with this belief a complete Indian outfit, depending in extent upon the rank and importance of the deceased, is prepared, and consigned with the body to the final resting-place.

The body found on this occasion must have been that of a son of some important chief; it was not full grown, but accompanied with all the arms and adornments usually owned by a warrior. There was the bow and quiver full of steel-pointed arrows, the tomahawk and scalping-knife, and a red clay pipe with a small bag full of tobacco. In order that the departed spirit should not be wholly dependent upon friends after his arrival at the happy hunting-ground, he had been supplied with provisions, consisting of small parcels containing coffee, sugar, and bread. Weapons of modern structure had also been furnished him, a revolver and rifle with powder and ball ammunition for each, and a saddle, bridle, and lariat for his pony. Added to these was a supply of wearing apparel, embracing every article known in an Indian's toilet, not excepting the various colored paints to be used in decorating himself for war. A handsome buckskin scalping-pocket, profusely ornamented with beads, completed the outfit But for fear that white women's scalps might not be readily obtainable, and desiring no doubt to be received at once as a warrior, who in his own country at least was not without renown, a white woman's scalp was also considered as a necessary accompaniment, a letter of introduction to the dusky warriors and chieftains who had gone before. As the Indian of the Plains is himself only when on horseback, provision must be made for mounting him properly in the Indian heaven. To accomplish this, the favorite war

INDIAN MODE OF FISHING.

pony is led beneath the platform on which the body of the warrior is placed at rest and there strangled to death.

No signs indicating the recent presence of Indians were discovered by our scouts until we neared the Republican river, where the trail of a small war party was discovered running down one of the tributaries of the Republican. After following it far enough to determine the futility of pursuit, the attempt was relinquished. Upon crossing the Republican we suddenly came in full view of about a hundred mounted warriors, who, without waiting for a parley of any kind, set off as fast as their horses could carry them. One squadron was sent in pursuit, but was unable to overhaul the Indians. From the tracks we learned that the Indians were mounted on horses stolen from the stage company. These horses were of a superior quality, and purchased by the company at a price about double that paid by the Government. This was the only occasion on which we saw Indians before reaching the Platte river.

One of our camps was pitched on the banks of a small stream which had been named Beaver Creek. Comstock informed us that here an opportunity could be had of killing a few beavers, as they were very numerous all along this stream, which had derived its name from that fact. We had gone into camp about 3 P. M. The numerous stumps and fallen trees, as well as the beaver dams, attested the accuracy of Comstock's statement. By his advice we waited until sundown before taking our stations on the bank, not far above the site of our camp, as at that time the beaver would be out and on shore.

Placing ourselves under Comstock's guidance, a small party proceeded to the ground selected, where we were distributed singly at stations along the stream and quietly awaited the appearance of the beaver. Whether the noise from the camp below or the passing of hunting parties of soldiers in the afternoon had frightened them, I know not. I remained at my station with my rifle in hand ready to fire at the first beaver which should offer itself as a sacrifice, until the sun had disappeared and darkness had begun to spread its heavy mantle over everything around me. No living thing had thus far disturbed my reveries. My station was on the immediate bank of the stream, on a path which had evidently been made by wild animals of some kind. The bank rose above me to a distance of nearly twenty feet. I was just on the point of leaving my station and giving up all hope of getting a shot, when I heard the rustling of the long dry grass a few yards lower down the stream. Cocking my rifle, I stood ready to deliver its contents into the approaching animal, which I presumed would be seen to be a beaver as soon as it should emerge from the tall grass. It did not make its appearance in the path in which I stood until within a few feet of me, when to my great surprise I beheld instead of a beaver an immense wildcat. It was difficult to say which of us was most surprised. Without delaying long to think, I took a hasty aim and fired. The next moment I heard a splash which relieved my mind as to which of us should retain the right of way on shore, the path being too narrow to admit of our passing each other. I had either wounded or killed the wildcat, and its body in the darkness had been carried down with the current, as the dogs which were soon attracted from the camp by my shot were unable to find the trail on either bank.

Nothing occurred to break the monotony of our march until we reached Fort McPherson, on the Platte river. The country over which we had marched had been quite varied in its character, and as we neared the Platte it became very broken and abrupt. It was only by availing ourselves of Comstock's superior knowledge of the country that we found an easy exit from the deep cañons and rough defiles which were encountered.

At Fort McPherson we refilled our wagons with supplies of rations and forage. At the same time, in accordance with my instructions, I reported by telegraph my arrival to General Sherman, who was then further west on the line of the Union Pacific road. He did not materially change my instructions, further than to direct me to remain near Fort McPherson until his arrival, which would be in the course of a few days.

Moving my command about twelve miles from the fort, I arranged for a council with Pawnee Killer and a few other Sioux chiefs, who had arrived at the Platte about the same time my command had. My object was, if possible, to induce Pawnee Killer and his band, with such other Indians as might choose to join them, to bring their lodges into the vicinity of the fort, and remain at peace with the whites. Pawnee Killer and his chiefs met me in council and the subject was discussed, but with no positive conclusions. While protesting strongly in favor of preserving peaceful relations with us, the subsequent conduct of the chiefs only confirmed the suspicion that they had arranged the council not to perfect a friendly agreement with us, but to spy out and discover, if possible, our future plans and movements. In this they were disappointed. Their numerous inquiries as to where we intended proceeding when we resumed the march were unavailing. Desiring to leave nothing undone to encourage a friendly attitude on their part, I gave the chiefs on parting with them liberal presents of coffee, sugar, and other articles gratifying to the taste of an Indian. They departed after giving utterance to the strongest expressions of their desire to live at peace with their "white brothers," and promised to collect their families and bring them in under protection of the fort, and thus avoid becoming entangled in the ravages of an Indian war which now promised to become general throughout the Plains. Pawnee Killer and his chiefs never attempted to keep their promises.

General Sherman arrived at my camp next day. He had no confidence in the faith of Pawnee Killer and his band, and desired that a party be sent in pursuit at once, and bring the chiefs back and retain a few of the prominent ones as hostages for the fulfilment of their agreement. This was decided to be impracticable. It was then judged best for me to move my command in a southwesterly direction to the forks of the Republican, a section of country usually infested by Indians, and there endeavor to find the village of Pawnee Killer, and compel him, if necessary, to move nearer to the fort, so that we might distinguish between those who were friendly and those who were not. Besides, it was known that the Cheyennes and Sioux, whom we had pursued from the Arkansas across the Smoky Hill river, had not crossed north of the Platte, and they were rightly supposed to be located somewhere near the forks of the Republican. I could reach this point in three days' marching after leaving the Platte river, on whose banks we were then encamped.

Owing to the rough and broken character of the bluffs which bound the valley of the Platte on the south side, it was determined to march up the men about fifteen miles from the fort and strike south through an opening in the bluffs known as Jack Morrow's cañon. General Sherman rode with us as far as this point, where, after commending the Cheyennes and Sioux to us in his expressive manner, he bade us good-by, and crossed the river to the railroad station on the north side. Thus far we had had no real Indian warfare. We were soon to experience it, attended by all its frightful barbarities.

VII.

BEFORE leaving the Platte I employed two additional interpreters who were familiar with the Sioux language. Both were white men, but, following the example of many frontiersmen, they had taken unto themselves Indian wives, and each had become the head of a considerable family of half-breeds.

Starting nearly due south from the Platte, and marching up the cañon, which forms a natural gateway through the otherwise almost impassable barrier of bluffs and deep ravines bordering the valley of the Platte river, we again set out in search of Indians. The latter are sought after so frequently and found so seldom, except when not wanted, that scouting parties, as a general thing, are not overburdened with confidence on beginning an expedition. Most of us, however, felt that we were destined to see Indians—an impression probably due to the fact that we had determined to accomplish our purpose, if hard riding and watchfulness could attain this result.

Our first day's march brought us to a small stream, a tributary of the Republican river, on whose banks we encamped for the night. Daylight the following morning found us in the saddle and ascending from the valley to the table-lands; we were still in the broken country. On reaching the plateau overlooking the valley we found ourselves enveloped in a dense fog, so dense that the sky was not visible, nor was an extended view of the country possible. Had the surface of the plain been, as usual, level and unbroken, we could have pursued our march guided by the unerring compass. But deep and impassable cañons divided the country in all directions and rendered our further progress impracticable. The sun, however, soon rose high enough to drive away the mist, and permitted us to proceed on what might be truly termed our winding way.

The afternoon of the fourth day we reached the forks of the Republican and there went into camp. We were then located about seventy-five miles southeast of Fort Sedgwick, and about the same distance northeast of Fort Wallace. Intending to scout the surrounding country thoroughly in search of Indians, we selected our camp with reference to a sojourn of several days, combining among its essentials wood, water, good grazing, and last, but not least, facilities for defence.

When I parted from General Sherman the understanding was, that after beating up the country thoroughly about the forks of the Republican river, I should march my command to Fort Sedgwick, and there I would either see General Sherman again or receive further instructions from him. Circumstances seemed to favor a modification of this plan, at least as to marching the entire command to Fort Sedgwick. It was therefore decided to send a trusty officer with a sufficient escort to Fort Sedgwick with my despatch, and to receive the despatches which might be intended for me. My proposed change of programme contemplated a continuous march, which might be prolonged twenty days or more. To this end additional supplies were necessary. The guides all agreed in the statement that we were then about equidistant from Fort Wallace on the south and Fort Sedgwick on the north, at either of which the required supplies could be obtained; but that while the country be-

79

tween our camp and the former was generally level and unbroken—favorable to the movement of our wagon train—that between us and Fort Sedgwick was almost impassable for heavily-laden wagons. The train then was to go to Fort Wallace under sufficient escort, be loaded with fresh supplies, and rejoin us in camp. At the same time the officer selected for that mission could proceed to Fort Sedgwick, obtain his despatch, and return.

Major Joel A. Elliot, a young officer of great courage and enterprise, was selected as bearer of despatches to Fort Sedgwick. As the errand was one involving considerable danger, requiring for the round trip a ride of almost two hundred miles, through a country which was not only almost unknown but infested by large numbers of hostile Indians, the Major was authorized to arrange the details in accordance with his own judgment.

Knowing that small detachments can move more rapidly than large ones, and that he was to depend upon celerity of movement rather than strength of numbers to evade the numerous war parties prowling in that vicinity, the Major limited the size of his escort to ten picked men and one of the guides, all mounted on fleet horses. To elude the watchful eyes of any parties that might be noting our movements, it was deemed advisable to set out from camp as soon as it was dark, and by making a rapid night ride get beyond the circle of danger. In this way the little party took its departure on the night of the 23d of June.

On the same day our train of wagons set out for Fort Wallace to obtain supplies. Colonel West with one full squadron of cavalry was ordered to escort the train to Beaver Creek, about midway, and there halt with one of his companies, while the train, under escort of one company commanded by Lieutenant Robbins, should proceed to the fort and return—Colonel West to employ the interval in scouting up and down Beaver Creek. The train was under the special management of Colonel Cook, who on this occasion was acting in the capacity of a staff officer.

While at Fort McPherson, and when under the impression that my command upon arriving at Fort Wallace, after terminating the scouting expedition we were then engaged upon, would remain in camp for several weeks, I wrote to my wife at Fort Hays, advising her to meet me at Fort Wallace, provided that travel between the two posts was considered safe. I expected her to reach Fort Wallace before the arrival of the train and escort from my camp, and under this impression I sent a letter to her by Colonel Cook, asking her to come to our camp on the Republican under escort of the Colonel, who was an intimate friend of the family. I am thus minute in giving these details, in order that the events of the succeeding few days may appear in their proper light.

After the departure of the two detachments, which left us in almost opposite directions, our camp settled down to the dull and unexciting monotony of waiting patiently for the time when we should welcome our comrades back again, and listen to such items of news as they might bring to us.

Little did we imagine that the monotony of idleness was so soon and so abruptly to be broken. That night our pickets were posted as usual; the horses and mules, after being allowed to graze in the evening, were brought in and securely tethered close to our tents, and the "stable guards" of the different troops had been assigned to their stations for the night. At half-past eight the bugler at headquarters sounded the signal for "taps," and before the last note had died away every light, in obedience to this command, disappeared, and nothing remained to the eye, except here and there a faint glimpse of a white tent, to indicate the presence of our camp.

It was just that uncertain period between darkness and daylight on the following morning, and I was lying in my tent deep in the enjoyment of that perfect repose which only camp life offers, when the sharp, clear crack of a carbine near by brought me to my feet. I knew in an instant that the shot came from the picket posted not far from the rear of my camp. At the same moment my brother, Colonel Custer, who on that occasion was officer of the day, and whose duties required him to be particularly on the alert, rushed past my tent, halting only long enough to show his face through the opening and shout, "They are here!"

Now I did not inquire who were referred to, or how many were included in the word "they," nor did my informant seem to think it necessary to explain. "They" referred to Indians, I knew full well. Had I doubted, the brisk fusillade which opened the next moment, and the wild war-whoop, were convincing evidences that in truth "they were here!"

Ordinarily, I must confess to having sufficient regard for the customs and courtesies of life to endeavor to appear in society suitably and appropriately dressed. But when the alarm of "Indians" was given, and in such a startling manner as to show they were almost in our midst, the question was not "What shall I wear?" but "What shall I do?" It has become so common—in fact, almost a law—to describe the costumes worn upon memorable occasions, that I may be pardoned if I indulge in a description which I will endeavor to make as brief as the costume itself. A modern Jenkins, if desiring to tell the truth, would probably express himself as follows: "General Custer on this occasion appeared in a beautiful crimson robe (red flannel *robe de nuit*), very becoming to his complexion. His hair was worn *au naturel*, and permitted to fall carelessly over his shoulders. In his hand he carried gracefully a handsome Spencer rifle. It is unnecessary to add that he became the observed of all observers."

My orderly, as was his custom, on my retiring had securely tied all the fastenings to my tent, and it was usually the work of several minutes to undo this unnecessary labor. I had no time to throw away in this manner. Leaping from my bed, I grasped my trusty Spencer, which was always at my side whether waking or sleeping, and with a single dash burst open the tent, and, hatless as well as shoeless, ran to the point where the attack seemed to be concentrated.

It was sufficiently light to see our enemies and be seen. The first shot had brought every man of my command from his tent, armed and equipped for battle. The Indians, numbering hundreds, were all around the camp, evidently intending to surround us, while a party of about fifty of their best mounted warriors had, by taking advantage of a ravine, contrived to approach quite close before being discovered. It was the intention of this party to dash through our camp, stampede all our horses, which were to be caught up by the parties surrounding us, and then finish us at their leisure.

The picket, however, discovered the approach of this party, and by firing gave timely warning, thus frustrating the plan of the Indians, who almost invariably base their hopes of success upon effecting a surprise.

My men opened on them such a brisk fire from their carbines that they were glad to withdraw beyond range. The picket who gave the alarm was shot down at his post by the Indians, the entire party galloping over his body, and being prevented from scalping him only by the fire from his comrades, who dashed out and recovered him. He was found to be badly though not mortally wounded by a rifle ball through the body.

The Indians, seeing that their attempt to surprise us and to stampede our horses had failed, then withdrew to a point but little over a mile from us, where they congregated, and seemed to hold a conference with each other. We did not fear any further attack at this time. They were satisfied with this attempt, and would await another opportunity.

It was desirable, however, that we should learn if possible to what tribe our enemies belonged. I directed one of our interpreters to advance midway between our camp and the Indians, and make the signal for holding a parley, and in this way ascertain who were the principal chiefs.

The ordinary manner of opening communication with parties known or supposed to be hostile, is to ride toward them in a zigzag manner or to ride in a circle. The interpreter gave the proper signal, and was soon answered by a small party advancing from the main body of the Indians to within hailing distance. It was then agreed that I, with six of the officers, should come to the bank of the river, which was about equidistant from my camp and from the point where the Indians had congregated, and there be met by an equal number of the leading chiefs. To guard against treachery, I placed most of my command under arms and arranged with the officer left in command that a blast from the bugle should bring assistance to me if required.

Six of the officers and myself, taking with us a bugler and an interpreter, proceeded on horseback to the designated point. Dismounting, we left our horses in charge of the bugler, who was instructed to watch every movement of the Indians, and upon the first appearance of violence or treachery to sound the "advance." Each of us took our revolvers from their leather cases and stuck them loosely in our belts.

Descending to the river bank, we awaited the arrival of the seven chiefs. On one side of the river the bank was level and covered with a beautiful green sward, while on the opposite side it was broken and thickly covered by willows and tall grass. The river itself was at this season of the year, and at this distance from its mouth, scarcely deserving of the name. The seven chiefs soon made their appearance on its opposite bank, and, after removing their leggings, waded across to where we stood. Imagine our surprise at recognizing as the head chief Pawnee Killer, our friend of the conference of the Platte, who on that occasion had overwhelmed us with the earnestness of his professions of peace, and who, after partaking of our hospitality under the guise of friendship, and leaving our camp laden with provisions and presents, returned to attack and murder us within a fortnight. This, too, without the slightest provocation, for surely we had not trespassed against any right of theirs since the exchange of friendly greetings near Fort McPherson.

Pawnee Killer and his chiefs met us as if they were quite willing to forgive us for interfering with the success of their intended surprise of our camp in the morning. I avoided all reference to what had occurred, desiring if possible to learn the locality of their village and their future movements. All attempts, however, to elicit information on these points were skilfully parried. The chiefs in turn were anxious to know our plans, but we declined to gratify them. Upon crossing to our side of the river, Pawnee Killer and his companions at once extended their hands, and saluted us with the familiar "How." Suspicious of their intentions, I kept one hand on my revolver during the continuance of our interview.

When we had about concluded our conference a young brave, completely armed, as were all the chiefs, emerged from the willows and tall grass on the opposite bank and waded across to where we were, greeting us as the others had done. Nothing was thought of this act until a few moments after another brave did the same, and so on until four had crossed over and joined our group. I then called Pawnee Killer's attention to the conditions under which we met, and told him he was violating his part of the contract. He endeavored to turn it off by saying that his young men felt well disposed toward us, and came over only to shake hands and say "How." He was told, however, that no more of his men must come. The conversation was then resumed and continued until another party of the warriors was seen preparing to cross from the other side. The conduct of these Indians in the morning, added to our opinions in general as regards treachery, convinced us that it would be in the highest degree imprudent to trust ourselves in their power. They already outnumbered us, eleven to seven, which were as heavy odds as we felt disposed to give. We all felt convinced that the coming over of these warriors, one by one, was but the execution of a preconceived plan whereof we were to become the victims as soon as their advantage in numbers should justify them in attacking us.

Again reminding Pawnee Killer of the stipulations of our agreement, and that while we had observed ours faithfully, he had disregarded his, I told him that not another warrior of his should cross the river to our side. And calling his attention to the bugler, who stood at a safe distance from us, I told him that I would then instruct the bugler to watch the Indians who were upon the opposite bank, and, upon any of them making a movement as if to cross, to sound the signal which would bring my entire command to my side in a few moments. This satisfied Pawnee Killer that any further attempt to play us false would only end in his own discomfiture. He at once signalled to the Indians on the other side to remain where they were.

Nothing definite could be gleaned from the replies of Pawnee Killer. I was satisfied that he and his tribe were contemplating mischief. Their previous declarations of peaceful intent went for naught. Their attack on our camp in the morning proved what they would do if able to accomplish their purpose. I was extremely anxious, however, to detain the chiefs near my camp, or induce them to locate their village near us, and keep up the semblance at least of friendship. I was particularly prompted to this desire by the fact that the two detachments which had left my command the previous day would necessarily continue absent several days, and I feared that they might become the victims of an attack from this band if steps were not taken to prevent it. Our anxiety was greatest regarding Major Elliot and his little party of eleven. Our only hope was that the Indians had not become aware of their departure. It was fortunate that the Major had chosen night as the most favorable time for setting out. As to the detachment that had gone with the train to Fort Wallace we felt less anxious, it being sufficiently powerful in numbers to defend itself, unless attacked after the detachment became divided at Beaver Creek.

Finding all efforts to induce Pawnee Killer to remain with us unavailing, I told him that we would march to his village with him. This did not seem satisfactory

Before terminating our interview, the chiefs requested me to make them presents of some sugar, coffee, and ammunition. Remembering the use they had made of the latter article in the morning, it will not appear strange if I declined to gratify them. Seeing that nothing was to be gained by prolonging the interview, we separated, the officers returning to our camp, and the Indians recrossing the river, mounting their ponies, and galloping off to the main body, which was then nearly two miles distant.

My command was in readiness to leap into their saddles, and I determined to attempt to follow the Indians, and, if possible, get near their village. They were prepared for this move on our part, and the moment we advanced toward them set off at the top of their speed. We followed as rapidly as our heavier horses could travel, but the speed of the Indian pony on this occasion, as on many others, was too great for that of our horses. A pursuit of a few hours proved our inability to overtake them, and we returned to camp.

Soon after arriving at camp a small party of Indians was reported in sight in a different direction. Captain Louis Hamilton, a lineal descendant of Alexander Hamilton, was immediately ordered to take his troop and learn something of their intentions. The Indians resorted to their usual tactics. There were not more than half a dozen to be seen—not enough to appear formidable. These were there as a decoy. Captain Hamilton marched his troop toward the hill on which the Indians had made their appearance, but on arriving at its crest found that they had retired to the next ridge beyond. This manœuvre was repeated several times, until the cavalry found itself several miles from camp. The Indians then appeared to separate into two parties, each going in different directions. Captain Hamilton divided his troop into two detachments, sending one detachment, under command of my brother, after one of the parties, while he with twenty-five men continued to follow the other.

When the two detachments had become so far separated as to be of no assistance to each other, the Indians developed their scheme. Suddenly dashing from a ravine, as if springing from the earth, forty-three Indian warriors burst out upon the cavalry, letting fly their arrows and filling the air with their wild war-whoops. Fortunately Captain Hamilton was an officer of great presence of mind as well as undaunted courage. The Indians began circling about the troops, throwing themselves upon the sides of their ponies and aiming their carbines and arrows over the necks of their well-trained war-steeds. Captain Hamilton formed his men in order to defend themselves against the assaults of their active enemies. The Indians displayed unusual boldness, sometimes dashing close up to the cavalry and sending in a perfect shower of bullets and arrows. Fortunately their aim, riding as they did at full speed, was necessarily inaccurate.

All this time we who had remained in camp were in ignorance of what was transpiring. Dr. Coates, whose acquaintance has been made before, had accompanied Captain Hamilton's command, but when the latter was divided the doctor joined the detachment of my brother. In some unexplained manner the doctor became separated from both parties, and remained so until the sound of the firing attracted him toward Captain Hamilton's party. When within half a mile of the latter, he saw what was transpiring; saw our men in the centre and the Indians charging and firing from the outside. His first impulse was to push on and endeavor to break through the line of savages, casting his lot with his struggling comrades. This impulse was suddenly nipped in the bud. The Indians, with their quick, watchful eyes, had discovered his presence, and half a dozen of their best mounted warriors at once galloped toward him.

TO THE RESCUE OF CAPT. HAMILTON.

Happily the doctor was in the direction of camp from Captain Hamilton's party, and, comprehending the peril of his situation at a glance, turned his horse's head toward camp, and applying the spur freely set out on a ride for life. The Indians saw this move, but were not disposed to be deprived of their victim in this way. They were better mounted than the doctor, his only advantage being in the start and the greater object to be attained. When the race began he was fully four miles from camp, the day was hot and sultry, the country rough and broken, and his horse somewhat jaded from the effects of the ride in the morning. These must have seemed immense obstacles in the eyes of a man who was riding for dear life. A false step, a broken girth, or almost any trifle, might decide his fate.

How often, if ever, the doctor looked back, I know not; his eyes more probably were strained to catch a glimpse of camp or of assistance accidentally coming to his relief. Neither the one nor the other appeared. His pursuers, knowing that their success must be gained soon if at all, pressed their fleet ponies forward until they seemed to skim over the surface of the green plain, and their shouts of exultation falling clearer and louder upon his ear told the doctor that they were surely gaining upon him. Fortunately our domestic horses, until accustomed to their presence, are as terrified by Indians as by a huge wild beast, and will fly from them if not restrained. The yells of the approaching Indians served no doubt to quicken the energies of the doctor's horse, and impelled him to greater efforts to escape.

So close had the Indians succeeded in approaching that they were almost within arrow range, and would soon have sent one flying through the doctor's body, when, to the great joy of the pursued and the corresponding grief of his pursuers, camp suddenly appeared in full view scarcely a mile distant. The ponies of the Indians had been ridden too hard to justify their riders in venturing near enough to provoke pursuit upon fresh animals. Sending a parting volley of bullets after the flying doctor, they turned about and disappeared. The doctor did not slacken his pace on this account, however; he knew that Captain Hamilton's party was in peril, and that assistance should reach him as soon as possible. Without tightening rein or sparing spur, he came dashing into camp, and the first we knew of his presence he had thrown himself from his almost breathless horse, and was lying on the ground unable, from sheer exhaustion and excitement, to utter a word.

The officers and men gathered about him in astonishment, eager and anxious to hear his story, for all knew that something far from any ordinary event had transpired to place the doctor in such a condition of mind and body. As soon as he had recovered sufficiently to speak, he told us that he had left Captain Hamilton surrounded by a superior force of Indians, and that he himself had been pursued almost to the borders of camp.

This was enough. The next moment the bugle rang out the signal "To horse," and in less time than would be required to describe it, horses were saddled and arms ready. Then "there was mounting in hot haste." A moment later the command set off at a brisk trot to attempt the rescue of their beleaguered comrades.

Persons unfamiliar with the cavalry service may mentally inquire why, in such an emergency as this, the intended reinforcements were not pushed forward at a rapid gallop? But in answer to this it need only be said that we had a ride of at least five miles before us in order to arrive at the point where Captain Hamilton and his command had last been seen, and it was absolutely ne-

cessary to so husband the powers of our horses as to save them for the real
work of conflict.

We had advanced in this manner probably two miles, when we discerned
in the distance the approach of Captain Hamilton's party. They were returning leisurely to camp, after having succeeded in driving off their assailants and
inflicting upon them a loss of two warriors killed and several wounded. The
Indians could only boast of having wounded a horse belonging to Captain
Hamilton's party.

This encounter with the Indians occurred in the direction taken by Major
Elliot's detachment on leaving camp, and the Indians, after this repulse by
Captain Hamilton, withdrew in that direction. This added to our anxiety concerning the safety of Major Elliot and his men. There was no doubt now that
all Indians infesting the broad belt of country between the Arkansas and Platte
rivers were on the war path, and would seek revenge from any party so unfortunate as to fall in their way. The loss of the two warriors slain in the fight.
and their wounded comrades, would be additional incentives to acts of hostility. If there had been any possible means of communicating with Major Elliot, and either strengthening or warning him, it would have been done. He
left us by no travelled or defined route, and it was by no means probable that
he would pass over the same trail in coming from Fort Sedgwick as in going
to that point; otherwise reinforcements could have been sent out over his trail
to meet him.

On the 27th our fears for the safety of the Major and his escort were dispelled by their safe return to camp, having accomplished a ride of nearly two
hundred miles through an enemy's country. They had concealed themselves
in ravines during the daytime and travelled at night, trusting to the faithful
compass and their guide to bring them safely back.

Now that the Major and his party had returned to us, our anxiety became
centred in the fate of the larger party which had proceeded with the train to
Fort Wallace for supplies. The fact that Major Elliot had made his trip unmolested by Indians, proved that the latter were most likely assembled south
of us, that is, between us and Fort Wallace. Wherever they were, their numbers were known to be large. It would be impossible for a considerable force,
let alone a wagon train, to pass from our camp to Fort Wallace and not be
seen by the Indian scouting parties. They had probably observed the departure of the train and escort at the time, and, divining the object which occasioned
the sending of the wagons, would permit them to go to the fort unmolested, but
would waylay them on their return, in the hope of obtaining the supplies they
contained. Under this supposition the Indians had probably watched the train
and escort during every mile of their progress; if so, they would not fail to discover that the larger portion of the escort halted at Beaver Creek, while the
wagons proceeded to the fort guarded by only forty-eight men; in which case
the Indians would combine their forces and attack the train at some point between Fort Wallace and Beaver Creek.

Looking at these probable events, I not only felt impelled to act promptly
to secure the safety of the train and its escort, but a deeper and stronger motive stirred me to leave nothing undone to circumvent the Indians. My wife,
who, in answer to my letter, I believed was then at Fort Wallace, would place
herself under the protection of the escort of the train and attempt to rejoin me
in camp. The mere thought of the danger to which she might be exposed
spurred me to decisive action. One full squadron, well mounted and armed,

under command of Lieutenant-Colonel Myers, an officer of great experience in Indian affairs, left our camp at dark on the evening of the day that Captain Hamilton had had his engagement with the Indians, and set out in the direction of Fort Wallace. His orders were to press forward as rapidly as practicable, following the trail made by the train. Written orders were sent in his care to Colonel West, who was in command of that portion of the escort which had halted at Beaver Creek, to join Colonel Myers's command with his own, and then to continue the march toward Fort Wallace until he should meet the returning train and escort. The Indians, however, were not to be deprived of this opportunity to secure scalps and plunder.

From our camp to Beaver Creek was nearly fifty miles. Colonel Myers marched his command without halting until he joined Colonel West at Beaver Creek. Here the two commands united, and under the direction of Colonel West, the senior officer of the party, proceeded toward Fort Wallace, following the trail left by the wagon train and escort. If the escort and Colonel West's forces could be united, they might confidently hope to repel any attack made upon them by Indians. Colonel West was an old Indian fighter, and too thoroughly accustomed to Indian tactics to permit his command to be surprised or defeated in any manner other than by a fair contest.

Let us leave them for a time and join the wagon train and its escort—the latter numbering, all told, as before stated, forty-eight men under the immediate command of Lieutenant Robbins. Colonel Cook, whose special duty connected him with the train and its supplies, could also be relied upon for material assistance with the troops, in case of actual conflict with the enemy. Comstock, the favorite scout, a host in himself, was sent to guide the party to and from Fort Wallace. In addition to these were the teamsters, who could not be expected to do more than control their teams should the train be attacked.

The march from camp to Beaver Creek was made without incident. Here the combined forces of Colonel West and Lieutenant Robbins encamped together during the night. Next morning at early dawn Lieutenant Robbins's party, having the train in charge, continued the march toward Fort Wallace, while Colonel West sent out scouting parties up and down the stream to search for Indians.

As yet none of their party were aware of the hostile attitude assumed by the Indians within the past few hours, and Colonel West's instructions contemplated a friendly meeting between his forces and the Indians should the latter be discovered. The march of the train and escort was made to Fort Wallace without interruption. The only incident worthy of remark was an observation of Comstock's, which proved how thoroughly he was familiar with the Indian and his customs.

The escort was moving over a beautifully level plateau. Not a mound or hillock disturbed the evenness of the surface for miles in either direction. To an unpractised eye there seemed no recess or obstruction in or behind which an enemy might be concealed, but everything appeared open to the view for miles and miles, look in what direction one might. Yet such was not the case. Ravines of greater or less extent, though not perceptible at a glance, might have been discovered if searched for, extending almost to the trail over which the party was moving. These ravines, if followed, would be found to grow deeper and deeper, until, after running their course for an indefinite extent, they would terminate in the valley of some running stream. These were the natural hiding-places of Indian war parties, waiting their opportunities to dash upon unsuspecting victims. These ravines serve the same purpose to the Indians of the timberless plains that the ambush did to those Indians of the Eastern States accustomed to fighting in the forests and everglades. Comstock's keen eyes took in all at a glance, and he remarked to Colonel Cook and Lieutenant Robbins, as the three rode together at the head of the column, that " If the Injuns strike us at all, it will be just about the time we are comin' along back over this very spot. Now mind what I tell ye all." We shall see how correct Comstock's prophecy was.

Arriving at the fort, no time was lost in loading up the wagons with fresh supplies, obtaining the mail intended for the command, and preparing to set out on the return to camp the following day. No late news regarding Indian movements was obtained. Fortunately, my letter from Fort McPherson to Mrs. Custer, asking her to come to Fort Wallace, miscarried, and she did not undertake a journey which in all probability would have imperilled her life, if not terminated it in a most tragic manner.

On the following morning Colonel Cook and Lieutenant Robbins began their return march. They had advanced one half the distance which separated them from Colonel West's camp without the slightest occurrence to disturb the monotony of their march, and had reached the point where, on passing before, Comstock had indulged in his prognostication regarding Indians; yet nothing had been seen to excite suspicion or alarm.

Comstock, always on the alert and with eyes as quick as those of an Indian, had been scanning the horizon in all directions. Suddenly he perceived, or thought he perceived, strange figures, resembling human heads, peering over the crest of a hill far away to the right. Hastily levelling his field-glass, he pronounced the strange figures, which were scarcely perceptible, to be neither more nor less than Indians. The officers brought into requisition their glasses, and were soon convinced of the correctness of Comstock's report. It was some time before the Indians perceived that they were discovered. Concealment then being no longer possible, they boldly rode to the crest and exposed themselves to full view. At first but twenty or thirty made their appearance; gradually their number became augmented, until about a hundred warriors could be seen.

It may readily be imagined that the appearance of so considerable a body of Indians produced no little excitement and speculation in the minds of the people with the train. The speculation was as to the intentions of the Indians, whether hostile or friendly. Upon this subject all doubts were soon dispelled. The Indians continued to receive accessions to their numbers, the reinforcements coming from beyond the crest of the hill on which their presence was first discovered. Finally, seeming confident in their superior numbers, the warriors, all of whom were mounted, advanced leisurely down the slope leading in the direction of the train and its escort. By the aid of field-glasses, Comstock and the two officers were able to determine fully the character of the party now approaching them. The last doubt was thus removed. It was clearly to be seen that the Indians were arrayed in full war costume, their heads adorned by the brilliantly colored war bonnets, their faces, arms, and bodies painted in various colors, rendering their naturally repulsive appearance even more hideous. As they approached nearer they assumed a certain order in the manner of their advance. Some were to be seen carrying the long glistening lance with its pennant of bright colors; while upon the

THE ATTACK UPON THE TRAIN.

left arm hung the round shield, almost bullet-proof, and ornamented with paint and feathers according to the taste of the wearer. Nearly all were armed with carbines and one or two revolvers, while many in addition to these weapons carried the bow and arrow.

When the entire band had defiled down the inclined slope, Comstock and the officers were able to estimate roughly the full strength of the party. They were astonished to perceive that between six and seven hundred warriors were bearing down upon them, and in a few minutes would undoubtedly commence the attack. Against such odds, and upon ground so favorable for the Indian mode of warfare, it seemed unreasonable to hope for a favorable result. Yet the entire escort, officers and men, entered upon their defence with the determination to sell their lives as dearly as possible.

As the coming engagement, so far as the cavalry was concerned, was to be purely a defensive one, Lieutenant Robbins at once set about preparing to receive his unwelcome visitors. Colonel Cook formed the train in two parallel columns, leaving ample space between for the horses of the cavalry. Lieutenant Robbins then dismounted his men and prepared to fight on foot. The led horses, under charge of the fourth trooper, were placed between the two columns of wagons, and were thus in a measure protected from the assaults which the officers had every reason to believe would be made for their capture. The dismounted cavalrymen were thus formed in a regular circle enclosing the train and horses. Colonel Cook took command of one flank, Lieutenant Robbins of the other, while Comstock, who as well as the two officers remained mounted, galloped from point to point wherever his presence was most valuable. These dispositions being perfected, the march was resumed in this order, and the attack of the savages calmly awaited.

The Indians, who were interested spectators of these preparations for their reception, continued to approach, but seemed willing to delay their attack until the plain became a little more favorable for their operations. Finally, the desired moment seemed to have arrived. The Indians had approached to within easy range, yet not a shot had been fired, the cavalrymen having been instructed by their officers to reserve their fire for close quarters. Suddenly, with a wild ringing war-whoop, the entire band of warriors bore down upon the train and its little party of defenders.

On came the savages, filling the air with their terrible yells. Their first object, evidently, was to stampede the horses and draught animals of the train; then, in the excitement and consternation which would follow, to massacre the escort and drivers. The wagon-master in immediate charge of the train had been ordered to keep his two columns of wagons constantly moving forward and well closed up. This last injunction was hardly necessary, as the frightened teamsters, glancing at the approaching warriors and hearing their savage shouts, were sufficiently anxious to keep well closed up upon their leaders.

The first onslaught of the Indians was made on the flank which was superintended by Colonel Cook. They rode boldly forward as if to dash over the mere handful of cavalrymen, who stood in skirmishing order in a circle about the train. Not a soldier faltered as the enemy came thundering upon them, but waiting until the Indians were within short rifle range of the train, the cavalrymen dropped upon their knees, and taking deliberate aim poured a volley from their Spencer carbines into the ranks of the savages, which seemed to put a sudden check upon the ardor of their movements and forced them to wheel off to the right. Several of the warriors were seen to reel in their saddles, while the ponies of others were brought down or wounded by the effectual fire of the cavalrymen.

Those of the savages who were shot from their saddles were scarcely permitted to fall to the ground before a score or more of their comrades dashed to their rescue and bore their bodies beyond the possible reach of our men. This is in accordance with the Indian custom in battle. They will risk the lives of a dozen of their best warriors to prevent the body of any one of their number from falling into the white man's possession. The reason for this is the belief, which generally prevails among all the tribes, that if a warrior loses his scalp he forfeits his hope of ever reaching the happy hunting-ground.

As the Indians were being driven back by the well-directed volley of the cavalrymen, the latter, overjoyed at their first success, became reassured, and sent up a cheer of exultation, while Comstock, who had not been idle in the fight, called out to the retreating Indians in their native tongue, taunting them with their unsuccessful assault.

The Indians withdrew to a point beyond the range of our carbines, and there seemed to engage in a parley. Comstock, who had closely watched every movement, remarked that "There's no sich good luck for us as to think them Injuns mean to give it up so. Six hundred red devils ain't agoin' to let fify men stop them from gettin' at the coffee and sugar that is in these wagons. And they ain't agoin' to be satisfied until they get some of our scalps to pay for the bucks we popped out of their saddles a bit ago."

It was probable that the Indians were satisfied that they could not dash through the train and stampede the animals. Their recent attempt had convinced them that some other method of attack must be resorted to. Nothing but their greater superiority in numbers had induced them to risk so much in a charge.

The officers passed along the line of skirmishers—for this in reality was all their line consisted of—and cautioned the men against wasting their ammunition. It was yet early in the afternoon, and should the conflict be prolonged until night, there was great danger of exhausting the supply of ammunition. The Indians seemed to have thought of this, and the change in their method of attack encouraged such a result.

But little time was spent at the parley. Again the entire band of warriors, except those already disabled, prepared to renew the attack, and advanced as before—this time, however, with greater caution, evidently desiring to avoid a reception similar to the first. When sufficiently near to the troops the Indians developed their new plan of attack. It was not to advance *en masse*, as before, but fight as individuals, each warrior selecting his own time and method of attack. This is the habitual manner of fighting among all Indians of the Plains, and is termed "circling." First the chiefs led off, followed at regular intervals by the warriors, until the entire six or seven hundred were to be seen riding in single file as rapidly as their fleet-footed ponies could carry them. Preserving this order, and keeping up their savage chorus of yells, war-whoops, and taunting epithets, this long line of mounted barbarians was guided in such manner as to envelop the train and escort, and make the latter appear like a small circle within a larger one.

The Indians gradually contracted their circle, although maintaining the full speed of their ponies, until sufficiently close to open fire upon the soldiers. At first the shots were scattering and wide of their mark; but, emboldened by the silence of their few but determined opponents, they rode nearer and fought with greater impetuosity. Forced now to defend themselves to the uttermost, the cavalrymen opened fire from their carbines, with most gratifying results. The Indians, however, moving at such a rapid gait and in single file, presented a most uncertain target. To add to this uncertainty, the savages availed themselves of their superior—almost marvellous—powers of horsemanship. Throwing themselves upon the sides of their well-trained ponies, they left no part of their persons exposed to the aim of the troopers except the head and one foot, and in this posture they were able to aim the weapons either over or under the necks of their ponies, thus using the bodies of the latter as an effective shield against the bullets of their adversaries.

At no time were the Indians able to force the train and its escort to come to a halt. The march was continued at an uninterrupted gait. This successful defence against the Indians was in a great measure due to the presence of the wagons, which, arranged in the order described, formed a complete barrier to the charges and assaults of the savages; and, as a last resort, the wagons could have been halted and used as a breastwork, behind which the cavalry, dismounted, would have been almost invincible against their more numerous enemies. There is nothing an Indian dislikes more in warfare than to attack a foe, however weak, behind breastworks of any kind. Any contrivance which is an obstacle to his pony is a most serious obstacle to the warrior.

The attack of the Indians, aggravated by their losses in warriors and ponies, as many of the latter had been shot down, was continued without cessation for three hours. The supply of ammunition of the cavalry was running low. The "fourth troopers," who had remained in charge of the led horses between the two columns of wagons, were now replaced from the skirmishers, and the former were added to the list of active combatants. If the Indians should maintain the fight much longer, there was serious ground for apprehension regarding the limited supply of ammunition.

If only night or reinforcements would come! was the prayerful hope of those who contended so gallantly against such heavy odds. Night was still too far off to promise much encouragement; while as to reinforcements, their coming would be purely accidental—at least so argued those most interested in their arrival. Yet reinforcements were at that moment striving to reach them. Comrades were in the saddle and spurring forward to their relief. The Indians, although apparently turning all their attention to the little band inside, had omitted no precaution to guard against interference from outside parties. In this instance, perhaps, they were more than ordinarily watchful, and had posted some of their keen-eyed warriors on the high line of bluffs which ran almost parallel to the trail over which the combatants moved. From these bluffs not only a good view of the fight could be obtained, but the country for miles in either direction was spread out beneath them, and enabled the scouts to discern the approach of any hostile party which might be advancing. Fortunate for the savages that this precaution had not been neglected, or the contest in which they were engaged might have become one of more equal numbers. To the careless eye nothing could have been seen to excite suspicion. But the warriors on the lookout were not long in discovering something which occasioned them no little anxiety. Dismounting from their ponies and concealing the latter in a ravine, they prepared to investigate more fully the cause of their alarm.

That which they saw was as yet but a faint dark line on the surface of the plain, almost against the horizon. So faint was it that no one but an Indian or practised frontiersman would have observed it. It was fully ten miles from them and directly in their line of march. The ordinary observer would have pronounced it a break or irregularity in the ground, or perhaps the shadow of a cloud, and its apparent permanency of location would have dispelled any fear as to its dangerous character. But was it stationary ? Apparently, yes. The Indians discovered otherwise. By close watching, the long faint line could be seen moving along, as if creeping stealthily upon an unconscious foe. Slowly it assumed a more definite shape, until what appeared to be a mere stationary dark line drawn upon the green surface of the plain, developed itself to the searching eyes of the red man into a column of cavalry moving at a rapid gait toward the very point they were then occupying.

Convinced of this fact, one of the scouts leaped upon his pony and flew with almost the speed of the wind to impart this knowledge to the chiefs in command on the plain below. True, the approaching cavalry, being still several miles distant, could not arrive for nearly two hours; but the question to be considered by the Indians was, whether it would be prudent for them to continue their attack on the train—their ponies already becoming exhausted by the three hours' hard riding given them—until the arrival of the fresh detachment of the enemy, whose horses might be in condition favorable to a rapid pursuit, and thereby enable them to overtake those of the Indians whose ponies were exhausted. Unwilling to incur this new risk, and seeing no prospect of overcoming their present adversaries by a sudden or combined dash, the chiefs decided to withdraw from the attack, and make their escape while the advantage was yet in their favor.

The surprise of the cavalrymen may be imagined at seeing the Indians, after pouring a shower of bullets and arrows into the train, withdraw to the bluffs, and immediately after continue their retreat until lost to view.

This victory for the troopers, although so unexpected, was none the less welcome. The Indians contrived to carry away with them their killed and wounded. Five of their bravest warriors were known to have been sent to the happy hunting-ground, while the list of their wounded was much larger.

After the Indians had withdrawn and left the cavalrymen masters of the field, our wounded, of whom there were comparatively few, received every possible care and attention. Those of the detachment who had escaped unharmed were busily engaged in exchanging congratulations and relating incidents of the fight.

In this manner nearly an hour had been whiled away, when far in the distance, in their immediate front, fresh cause for anxiety was discovered. At first the general opinion was that it was the Indians again, determined to contest their progress. Field-glasses were again called into requisition, and revealed, not Indians, but the familiar blue blouses of the cavalry. Never was the sight more welcome. The next moment Colonel Cook, with Comstock and a few troopers, applied spurs to their horses and were soon dashing forward to meet their comrades.

The approaching party was none other than Colonel West's detachment, hastening to the relief of the train and its gallant little escort. A few words explained all, and told the heroes of the recent fight.how it happened that reinforcements were sent to their assistance ; and then was explained why the Indians had so suddenly concluded to abandon their attack and seek safety in quietly withdrawing from the field.

VIII.

ON the morning of the 28th the train, with its escort, returned to the main camp on the Republican. All were proud of the conduct of those detachments of the command which had been brought into actual conflict with the Indians. The heroes of the late fights were congratulated heartily upon their good luck, while their comrades who had unavoidably remained in camp consoled themselves with the hope that the next opportunity might be theirs.

The despatches brought by Major Elliott from General Sherman directed me to continue my march, as had been suggested, up the North Republican, then strike northward and reach the Platte again at some point west of Fort Sedgwick, near Riverside Station. This programme was carried out. Leaving our camp on the Republican, we marched up the north fork of that river about sixty miles, then turned nearly due north, and marched for the valley of the Platte.

The only incident connected with this march was the painful journey under a burning July sun, of sixty-five miles, without a drop of water for our horses or draught animals. This march was necessarily effected in one day, and produced untold suffering among the poor dumb brutes. Many of the dogs accompanying the command died from thirst and exhaustion. When the sun went down we were still many miles from the Platte. The moon, which was nearly full at the time, lighted us on our weary way for some time; but even this was only an aggravation, as it enabled us from the high bluffs bordering the Platte valley to see the river flowing beneath us, yet many miles beyond our reach.

Taking Lieutenant Moylan, Dr. Coates, and one attendant with me, and leaving the command under temporary charge of Major Elliott, I pushed on, intending after arriving at the river to select as good camping ground as the darkness and circumstances would permit. We then imagined ourselves within four or five miles of the river, so near did it appear to us. Mile after mile was traversed by our tired horses, yet we apparently arrived no nearer our journey's end. At last, at about eleven o'clock, and after having ridden at a brisk rate for nearly fifteen miles, we reached the river bank. Our first act was to improve the opportunity to quench our thirst and that of our horses. Considering the lateness of the hour, and the distance we had ridden since leaving the command, it was idle to expect the latter to reach the river before daylight. Nothing was left to us but to bivouac for the night. This we did by selecting a beautiful piece of sward on the river bank for our couch, and taking our saddle blankets for covering and our saddles for pillows. Each of us attached his horse by the halter-strap to the hilt of his sabre, then forced the sabre firmly into the ground. Both horses and riders were weary as well as hungry. At first the horses grazed upon the fresh green pasture which grew luxuriantly on the river bank, but fatigue, more powerful than hunger, soon claimed the mastery, and in a few minutes our little group, horses and men, were wrapped in the sweetest of slumber.

Had we known that the Indians were then engaged in murdering men within a few minutes' ride of where we slept, and that when we awakened in the morning it would be to still find ourselves away from the command, our sleep would not have been so undisturbed.

Daylight was beginning to make its appearance in the east when our little party of slumbering troopers began to arouse themselves. Those unfortunate persons who have always been accustomed to the easy comforts of civilization, and who have never known what real fatigue or hunger is, cannot realize or appreciate the blissful luxury of a sleep which follows a day's ride in the saddle of half a hundred miles or more.

Being the first to awake, I rose to a sitting posture and took a hasty survey of our situation. Within a few feet of us flowed the Platte river. Our group, horses and men, presented an interesting subject for a painter. To my surprise I discovered that a heavy shower of rain had fallen during the night, but so deep had been our slumber that even the rain had failed to disturb us. Each one of the party had spread his saddle blanket on the ground to serve as his couch, while for covering we had called into requisition the india-rubber poncho or rubber blanket which invariably forms an important part of the plainsman's outfit. The rain, without awakening any of the party, had aroused them sufficiently to cause each one to pull his rubber blanket over his face, and, thus protected, he continued his repose. The appearance presented by this sombre-looking group of sleepers strongly reminded me of scenes during the war when, after a battle, the bodies of the slain had been collected for burial.

But this was no time to indulge in idle reveries. Arousing my comrades, we set about discovering the circumstances of our situation. First, the duties of a hasty toilet were attended to. Nothing, however, could be more simple. As we had slept in our clothes, top boots and all, we had so much less to attend to. The river flowing at our feet afforded a lavatory which, if not complete in its appointments, was sufficiently grand in its extent to satisfy every want.

It was now becoming sufficiently light to enable us to see indistinctly for almost a mile in either direction, yet our eyes failed to reveal to us any evidence of the presence of the command. Here was fresh cause for anxiety, not only as to our own situation, but as to the whereabouts of the troops. Saddling up our horses, each person acting as his own groom, we awaited the clearing away of the morning mist to seek the main body. We had not long to wait. The light was soon sufficient to enable us to scan the country with our field-glasses in all directions. Much to our joy we discovered the bivouac of the troops about three miles down the river. A brisk gallop soon placed us where we desired to be, and a few words explained how, in the darkness, the column had failed to follow us, but instead had headed for the river at a point below us, a portion not reaching the bank until near morning.

Breakfast disposed of, the next question was to ascertain our exact location and distance from the nearest telegraph station. Fortunately Riverside Station was near our camp, and from there we ascertained that we were then about fifty miles west of Fort Sedgwick. The party obtaining this information also learned that the Indians had attacked the nearest stage station west of camp the preceding evening, and killed three men. This station was only a few minutes' ride from the point on the river bank where myself and comrades had passed the night in such fancied security.

Believing that General Sherman must have sent later instructions for me to Fort Sedgwick than those last received from him, I sent a telegram to the officer in command at the fort, making inquiry to that effect. To my surprise I received a despatch saying that, the day after the departure of Major Elliott and his detachment from Fort Sedgwick with despatches, of which mention has been previously made, a second detachment of equal strength, viz., ten troopers of the Second United States Cavalry, under command of Lieutenant Kidder and guided by a famous Sioux chief Red Bead, had left Fort Sedgwick with important despatches for me from General Sherman, and that Lieutenant Kidder had been directed to proceed to my camp near the forks of the Republican, and failing to find me there he was to follow rapidly on my trail until he should overtake my command. I immediately telegraphed to Fort Sedgwick that nothing had been seen or heard of Lieutenant Kidder's detachment, and requested a copy of the despatches borne by him to be sent me by telegraph. This was done; the instructions of General Sherman were for me to march my command, as was at first contemplated, across the country from the Platte to the Smoky Hill river, striking the latter at Fort Wallace. Owing to the low state of my supplies, I determined to set out for Fort Wallace at daylight next morning.

Great anxiety prevailed throughout the command concerning Lieutenant Kidder and his party. True, he had precisely the same number of men that composed Major Elliott's detachment when the latter went upon a like mission, but the circumstances which would govern in the one case had changed when applied to the other. Major Elliott, an officer of experience and good judgment, had fixed the strength of his escort and performed the journey before it was positively known that the Indians in that section had entered upon the war path. Had the attack on the commands of Hamilton, Robbins, and Cook been made prior to Elliott's departure, the latter would have taken not less than fifty troopers as escort. After an informal interchange of opinions between the officers of my command regarding the whereabouts of Lieutenant Kidder and party, we endeavored to satisfy ourselves with the following explanation. Using the capital letter Y for illustration, let us locate Fort Sedgwick, from which post Lieutenant Kidder was sent with despatches, at the right upper point of the letter. The camp of my command at the forks of the Republican would be at the junction of the three branches of the letter. Fort Wallace relatively would be at the lower termination, and the point on the Platte at which my command was located the morning referred to would be at the upper termination of the left branch of the letter. Robbins and Cook, in going with the train to Wallace for supplies, had passed and returned over the lower branch. After their return and that of Major Elliott and his party, my entire command resumed the march for the Platte. We moved for two or three miles out on the heavy wagon trail of Robbins and Cook, then suddenly changed our direction to the right. It was supposed that Kidder and his party arrived at our deserted camp at the forks of the Republican about nightfall, but finding us gone had determined to avail themselves of the moonlit night and overtake us before we should break camp next morning. Riding rapidly in the dim light of evening, they had failed to observe the point at which we had diverged from the plainer trail of Robbins and Cook, and instead of following our trail had continued on the former in the direction of Fort Wallace. Such seemed to be a plausible if not the only solution capable of being given.

Anxiety for the fate of Kidder and his party was one of the reasons impelling me to set out promptly on my return. From our camp at the forks of the Republican to Fort Wallace was about eighty miles—but eighty miles of the most dangerous country infested by Indians. Remembering the terrible contest in which the command of Robbins and Cook had been engaged on this very route within a few days, and knowing that the Indians would in all probability maintain a strict watch over the trail to surprise any small party which might venture over it, I felt in the highest degree solicitous for the safety of Lieutenant Kidder and party. Even if he succeeded in reaching Fort Wallace unmolested, there was reason to apprehend that, impressed with the importance of delivering his despatches promptly, he would set out on his return at once and endeavor to find my command.

Let us leave him and his detachment for a brief interval, and return to events which were more immediately connected with my command, and which bear a somewhat tragic as well as personal interest.

In a previous chapter reference has been made to the state of dissatisfaction which had made its appearance among the enlisted men. This state of feeling had been principally superinduced by inferior and insufficient rations, a fault for which no one connected with the troops in the field was responsible, but which was chargeable to persons far removed from the theatre of our movements, persons connected with the supply departments of the army. Added to this internal source of disquiet, we were then on the main line of overland travel to some of our most valuable and lately discovered mining regions. The opportunity to obtain marvellous wages as miners and the prospect of amassing sudden wealth proved a temptation sufficiently strong to make many of the men forget their sworn obligations to their government and their duties as soldiers. Forgetting for the moment that the command to which they belonged was actually engaged in war, and was in a country infested with armed bodies of the enemy, and that the legal penalty of desertion under such circumstances was death, many of the men formed a combination to desert their colors and escape to the mines.

The first intimation received by any person in authority of the existence of this plot, was on the morning fixed for our departure from the Platte. Orders had been issued the previous evening for the command to march at daylight. Upwards of forty men were reported as having deserted during the night. There was no time to send parties in pursuit, or the capture and return of a portion of them might have been effected.

The command marched southward at daylight. At noon, having marched fifteen miles, we halted to rest and graze the horses for one hour. The men believed that the halt was made for the remainder of the day, and here a plan was perfected among the disaffected by which upwards of one third of the effective strength of the command was to seize their horses and arms during the night and escape to the mountains. Had the conspirators succeeded in putting this plan into execution, it would have been difficult to say how serious the consequences might be, or whether enough true men would remain to render the march to Fort Wallace practicable. Fortunately it was decided to continue the march some fifteen miles further before night. The necessary orders were given and everything was being repacked for the march, when attention was called to thirteen soldiers who were then to be seen rapidly leaving camp in the direction from which we had marched. Seven of these were mounted and were moving off at a rapid gallop; the remaining six were dismounted, not having been so fortunate as their fellows in procuring horses. The entire party were still within sound of the bugle, but no orders by bugle note or otherwise served to check or diminish their flight. The boldness of this attempt at desertion took every one by surprise. Such an occurrence as enlisted men deserting in broad daylight and under the immediate eyes of their officers had never been heard of. With the exception of the horses of the guard and a few belonging to the officers, all others were still grazing and unsaddled. The officer of the guard was directed to mount his command promptly, and if possible overtake the deserters. At the same time those of the officers whose horses were in readiness were also directed to join in the pursuit and leave no effort untried to prevent the escape of a single malcontent. In giving each party sent in pursuit instructions, there was no limit fixed to the measures which they were authorized to adopt in executing their orders. This, unfortunately, was an emergency which involved the safety of the entire command, and required treatment of the most summary character.

It was found impossible to overtake that portion of the party which was mounted, as it was afterwards learned that they had selected seven of the fleetest horses in the command. Those on foot, when discovering themselves pursued, increased their speed, but a chase of a couple of miles brought the pursuers within hailing distance.

Major Elliott, the senior officer participating in the pursuit, called out to the deserters to halt and surrender. This command was several times repeated, but without effect. Finally, seeing the hopelessness of further flight, the deserters came to bay, and to Major Elliott's renewed demand to throw down their arms and surrender, the ringleader drew up his carbine to fire upon his pursuers. This was the signal for the latter to open fire, which they did successfully, bringing down three of the deserters, although two of them were worse frightened than hurt.

Rejoining the command with their six captive deserters, the pursuing party reported their inability to overtake those who had deserted on horseback. The march was resumed and continued until near nightfall, by which time we had placed thirty miles between us and our last camp on the Platte. While on the march during the day, a trusty sergeant, one who had served as a soldier long and faithfully, imparted the first information which could be relied upon as to the plot which had been formed by the malcontents to desert in a body. The following night had been selected as the time for making the attempt. The best horses and arms in the command were to be seized and taken away. I believed that the summary action adopted during the day would intimidate any who might still be contemplating desertion, and was confident that another day's march would place us so far in a hostile and dangerous country, that the risk of encountering war parties of Indians would of itself serve to deter any but large numbers from attempting to make their way back to the settlements. To bridge the following night in safety was the next problem. While there was undoubtedly a large proportion of the men who could be fully relied upon to remain true to their obligations and to render any support to their officers which might be demanded, yet the great difficulty at this time, owing to the sudden development of the plot, was to determine who could be trusted.

This difficulty was solved by placing every officer in the command on guard during the entire night. The men were assembled as usual for roll-call at tattoo, and then notified that every man must be in his tent at the signal " taps," which would be sounded half an hour later; that their company officers, fully armed, would walk the company streets during the entire night, and any man appearing outside the limits of his tent between the hours of " taps " and reveille would do so at the risk of being fired upon after being once hailed.

The night passed without disturbance, and daylight found us in the saddle and pursuing our line of march toward Fort Wallace. It is proper to here record the fact that from that date onward desertion from that command during the continuance of the expedition was never attempted. It may become necessary in order "to perfect the record," borrowing a term from the War Department, to refer in a subsequent chapter to certain personal and official events which resulted partially from the foregoing occurrences.

Let us now turn our attention to Lieutenant Kidder and his detachment. The third night after leaving the Platte my command encamped in the vicinity of our former camp near the forks of the Republican. So far, nothing had been learned which would enable us to form any conclusion regarding the route taken by Kidder. Comstock, the guide, was frequently appealed to for an opinion which, from his great experience on the Plains, might give us some encouragement regarding Kidder's safety. But he was too cautious and careful a man, both in word and deed, to excite hopes which his reasoning could not justify. When thus appealed to he would usually give an ominous shake of the head and avoid a direct answer.

On the evening just referred to the officers and Comstock were grouped near headquarters discussing the subject which was then uppermost in the mind of every one in camp. Comstock had been quietly listening to the various theories and surmises advanced by different members of the group, but was finally pressed to state his ideas as to Kidder's chances of escaping harm.

"Well, gentle*men*," emphasizing the last syllable as was his manner, "before a man kin form any ijee as to how this thing is likely to end, thar are several things he ort to be acquainted with. For instance, now, no man need tell me any p'ints about Injuns. Ef I know anything, it's Injuns. I know jest how they'll do anything and when they'll take to do it; but that don't settle the question, and I'll tell you why. Ef I knowed this young lootenint—I mean Lootenint Kidder—ef I knowed what for sort of a man he is, I could tell you mighty near to a sartainty all you want to know; for you see Injun huntin' and Injun fightin' is a trade all by itself, and like any other bizness a man has to know what he's about, or ef he don't he can't make a livin' at it. I have lots uv confi*dence* in the fightin' sense of Red Bead the Sioux chief, who is guidin' the lootenint and his men, and ef that Injun kin have his own way thar is a fair show for his guidin' 'em through all right; but as I sed before, there lays the difficulty. Is this lootenint the kind of a man who is willin' to take advice, even ef it does cum from an Injun? My experience with you army folks has allus bin that the youngsters among ye think they know the most, and this is particularly true ef they hev just cum from West P'int. Ef some of them young fellars knowed half as much as they b'lieve they do, you couldn't tell them nothin'. As to rale book-larnin', why I 'spose they've got it all; but the fact uv the matter is, they couldn't tell the difference twixt the trail of a war party and one made by a huntin' party to save their necks. Half uv 'em when they first cum here can't tell a squaw from a buck, just because both ride straddle; but they soon larn. But that's neither here nor thar. I'm told that the lootenint we're talkin' about is a new-comer, and that this is his first scout. Ef that be the case, it puts a mighty onsartain look on the whole thing, and twixt you and me, gentle*men*, he'll be mighty lucky ef he gits through all right. To-morrow we'll strike the Wallace trail, and I kin mighty soon tell ef he has gone that way."

But little encouragement was to be derived from these expressions. The morrow would undoubtedly enable us, as Comstock had predicted, to determine whether or not the lieutenant and his party had missed our trail and taken that leading to Fort Wallace.

At daylight our column could have been seen stretching out in the direction of the Wallace trail. A march of a few miles brought us to the point of intersection. Comstock and the Delawares had galloped in advance, and were about concluding a thorough examination of the various tracks to be seen in the trail, when the head of the column overtook them. "Well, what do you find, Comstock?" was my first inquiry. "They've gone toward Fort Wallace, sure," was the reply; and in support of this opinion he added, "The trail shows that twelve American horses, shod all round, have passed at a walk, goin' in the direction of the fort; and when they went by this p'int they were all right, because their horses were movin' along easy, and there are no pony tracks behind 'em, as wouldn't be the case ef the Injuns had got an eye on 'em." He then remarked, as if in parenthesis, "It would be astonishin' ef that lootenint and his lay-out gits into the fort without a scrimmage. He may; but ef he does, it will be a scratch ef ever there was one, and I'll lose my confidence in Injuns."

The opinion expressed by Comstock as to the chances of Lieutenant Kidder and party making their way to the fort across eighty miles of danger unmolested, was the concurrent opinion of all the officers. And now that we had discovered their trail, our interest and anxiety became immeasurably increased as to their fate. The latter could not remain in doubt much longer, as two days' marching would take us to the fort. Alas! we were to solve the mystery without waiting so long.

Pursuing our way along the plain, heavy trail made by Robbins and Cook, and directing Comstock and the Delawares to watch closely that we did not lose that of Kidder and his party, we patiently but hopefully awaited further developments. How many miles we had thus passed over without incident worthy of mention, I do not now recall. The sun was high in the heavens, showing that our day's march was about half completed, when those of us who were riding at the head of the column discovered a strange-looking object lying directly in our path, and more than a mile distant. It was too large for a human being, yet in color and appearance, at that distance, resembled no animal frequenting the Plains with which any of us were familiar. Eager to determine its character, a dozen or more of our party, including Comstock and some of the Delawares, galloped in front.

Before riding the full distance the question was determined. The object seen was the body of a white horse. A closer examination showed that it had been shot within the past few days, while the brand, U. S., proved that it was a government animal. Major Elliott then remembered that while at Fort Sedgwick he had seen one company of cavalry mounted upon white horses. These and other circumstances went far to convince us that this was one of the horses belonging to Lieutenant Kidder's party. In fact there was no room to doubt that this was the case.

Almost the unanimous opinion of the command was that there had been a contest wi h Indians, and this only the first evidence we should have proving it. When the column reached the point where the slain horse lay, a halt was ordered, to enable Comstock and the Indian scouts to thoroughly examine the surrounding ground to discover, if possible, any additional evidence, such as empty cartridge shells, arrows, or articles of Indian equipment, showing that a fight had taken place. All the horse equipments, saddle, bridle, etc., had been carried away, but whether by friend or foe could not then be determined While the preponderance of circumstances favored the belief that the horse had been killed by Indians, there was still room to hope that he had been killed by Kidder's party and the equipments taken away by them; for it frequently happens on a march that a horse will be suddenly taken ill and be unable for the time being to proceed further. In such a case, rather than abandon him alive, with a prospect of his recovering and falling into the hands of the Indians to be employed against us, orders are given to kill him, and this might be the true way of accounting for the one referred to.

The scouts being unable to throw any additional light upon the question, we continued our march, closely observing the ground as we passed along. Comstock noticed that instead of the trail showing that Kidder's party was moving in regular order, as when at first discovered, there were but two or three tracks to be seen in the beaten trail, the rest being found on the grass on either side.

We had marched two miles perhaps from the point where the body of the slain horse had been discovered, when we came upon a second, this one, like the first, having been killed by a bullet, and all of his equipments taken away. Comstock's quick eyes were not long in detecting pony tracks in the vicinity, and we had no longer any but the one frightful solution to offer: Kidder and his party had been discovered by the Indians, probably the same powerful and bloodthirsty band which had been resisted so gallantly by the men under Robbins and Cook; and against such overwhelming odds the issue could not be doubtful.

We were then moving over a high and level plateau, unbroken either by ravines or divides, and just such a locality as would be usually chosen by the Indians for attacking a party of the strength of Kidder's. The Indians could here ride unobstructed and encircle their victims with a continuous line of armed and painted warriors, while the beleaguered party, from the even character of the surface of the plain, would be unable to find any break or depression from behind which they might make a successful defence. It was probably this relative condition of affairs which had induced Kidder and his doomed comrades to endeavor to push on in the hope of finding ground favorable to their making a stand against their barbarous foes.

The main trail no longer showed the footprints of Kidder's party, but instead Comstock discovered the tracks of shod horses on the grass, with here and there numerous tracks of ponies, all by their appearance proving that both horses and ponies had been moving at full speed. Kidder's party must have trusted their lives temporarily to the speed of their horses—a dangerous venture when contending with Indians. However, this fearful race for life must have been most gallantly contested, because we continued our march several miles further without discovering any evidence of the savages having gained any advantage.

How painfully, almost despairingly exciting must have been this ride for life! A mere handful of brave men struggling to escape the bloody clutches of the hundreds of red-visaged demons, who, mounted on their well-trained war ponies, were straining every nerve and muscle to reek their hands in the life-blood of their victims. It was not death alone that threatened this little band. They were not riding simply to preserve life. They rode, and doubtless prayed as they rode, that they might escape the savage tortures, the worse than death which threatened them. Would that their prayer had been granted

THE KIDDER MASSACRE.

We began leaving the high plateau and to descend into a valley, through which, at the distance of nearly two miles, meandered a small prairie stream known as Beaver Creek. The valley near the banks of this stream was covered with a dense growth of tall wild grass intermingled with clumps of osiers. At the point where the trail crossed the stream, we hoped to obtain more definite information regarding Kidder's party and their pursuers, but we were not required to wait so long. When within a mile of the stream I observed several large buzzards floating lazily in circles through the air, and but a short distance to the left of our trail. This, of itself, might not have attracted my attention seriously but for the rank stench which pervaded the atmosphere, reminding one of the horrible sensations experienced upon a battle-field when passing among the decaying bodies of the dead.

As if impelled by one thought, Comstock, the Delawares, and half-a-dozen officers, detached themselves from the column and, separating into squads of one or two, instituted a search for the cause of our horrible suspicions. After riding in all directions through the rushes and willows, and when about to relinquish the search as fruitless, one of the Delawares uttered a shout which attracted the attention of the entire command; at the same time he was seen to leap from his horse and assume a stooping posture, as if critically examining some object of interest. Hastening, in common with many others of the party, to his side, a sight met our gaze which even at this remote day makes my very blood curdle. Lying in irregular order, and within a very limited circle, were the mangled bodies of poor Kidder and his party, yet so brutally hacked and disfigured as to be beyond recognition save as human beings.

Every individual of the party had been scalped and his skull broken—the latter done by some weapon, probably a tomahawk—except the Sioux chief Red Bead, whose scalp had simply been removed from his head and then thrown down by his side. This, Comstock informed us, was in accordance with a custom which prohibits an Indian from bearing off the scalp of one of his own tribe. This circumstance, then, told us who the perpetrators of this deed were. They could be none other than the Sioux, led in all probability by Pawnee Killer.

Red Bead, being less disfigured and mutilated than the others, was the only individual capable of being recognized. Even the clothes of all the party had been carried away; some of the bodies were lying in beds of ashes, with partly burned fragments of wood near them, showing that the savages had put some of them to death by the terrible tortures of fire. The sinews of the arms and legs had been cut away, the nose of every man hacked off, and the features otherwise defaced so that it would have been scarcely possible for even a relative to recognize a single one of the unfortunate victims. We could not even distinguish the officer from his men. Each body was pierced by from twenty to fifty arrows, and the arrows were found as the savage demons had left them, bristling in the bodies. While the details of that fearful struggle will probably never be known, telling how long and gallantly this ill-fated little band contended for their lives, yet the surrounding circumstances of ground, empty cartridge shells, and distance from where the attack began, satisfied us that Kidder and his men fought as only brave men fight when the watchword is victory or death.

As the officer, his men, and his no less faithful Indian guide, had shared their final dangers together and had met the same dreadful fate at the hands of the same merciless foe, it was but fitting that their remains should be consigned to one common grave. This was accordingly done. A single trench was dug near the spot where they had rendered up their lives upon the altar of duty. Silently, mournfully, their comrades of a brother regiment consigned their mangled remains to mother earth, there to rest undisturbed, as we supposed, until the great day of final review. But this was not to be so; while the closest scrutiny on our part had been insufficient to enable us to detect the slightest evidence which would aid us or others in identifying the body of Lieutenant Kidder or any of his men, it will be seen hereafter how the marks of a mother's thoughtful affection were to be the means of identifying the remains of her murdered son, even though months had elapsed after his untimely death.

IX.

ON the evening of the day following that upon which we had consigned the remains of Lieutenant Kidder and his party to their humble resting-place, the command reached Fort Wallace on the Smoky Hill route. From the occupants of the fort we learned much that was interesting regarding events which had transpired during our isolation from all points of communication. The Indians had attacked the fort twice within the past few days, in both of which engagements men were killed on each side. The fighting on our side was principally under the command of Colonel Barnitz, whose forces were composed of detachments of the Seventh Cavalry. The fighting occurred on the level plain near the fort, where, owing to the favorable character of the ground, the Indians had ample opportunity to display their powers both as warriors and horsemen. One incident of the fight was related, which, its correctness being vouched for, is worthy of being here repeated. Both parties were mounted, and the fighting consisted principally of charges and counter-charges, the combatants of both sides becoming at times mingled with each other. During one of these attacks a bugler boy belonging to the cavalry was shot from his horse; before any of his comrades could reach him, a powerfully built warrior, superbly mounted on a war pony, was seen to dash at full speed toward the spot where the dying bugler lay. Scarcely checking the speed of his pony, who seemed to divine his rider's wishes, the warrior grasped the pony's mane with one hand and, stooping low as he neared the bugler, seized the latter with the other hand and lifted him from the earth, placing him across his pony in front of him. Still maintaining the full speed of his pony, he was seen to retain the body of the bugler but a moment, then cast it to the earth. The Indians being routed soon after and driven from the field, our troops, many of whom had witnessed the strange and daring action of the warrior, recovered possession of the dead, when the mystery became solved. The bugler had been scalped.

Our arrival at Fort Wallace was most welcome as well as opportune. The Indians had become so active and numerous that all travel over the Smoky Hill route had ceased; stages had been taken off the route, and many of the stage stations had been abandoned by the employees, the latter fearing a repetion of the Lookout Station massacre. No despatches or mail had been received at the fort for a considerable period, so that the occupants might well have been considered as undergoing a state of siege. Added to these embarrassments, which were partly unavoidable, an additional and under the circumstances a more frightful danger stared the troops in the face. We were over two hundred miles from the terminus of the railroad over which our supplies were drawn, and a still greater distance from the main dépôts of supplies. It was found that the reserve of stores at the post was well-nigh exhausted, and the commanding officer reported that he knew of no fresh supplies being on the way. It is difficult to account for such a condition of affairs. Some one must surely have been at fault; but it is not important here to determine who or where the parties were. The officer commanding the troops in my absence reported officially to headquarters that the bulk of the provisions issued to his men consisted of "rotten bacon" and "hard bread" that was "no better"

Cholera made its appearance among the men, and deaths occurred daily. The same officer, in officially commenting upon the character of the provisions issued to the troops, added: "The low state of vitality in the men, resulting from the long confinement to this scanty and unwholesome food, will, I think, account for the great mortality among the cholera cases; . . . and I believe that unless we can obtain a more abundant and better supply of rations than we have had, it will be impossible to check this fearful epidemic."

I decided to select upward of a hundred of the best mounted men in my command, and with this force open a way through to Fort Harker, a distance of two hundred miles, where I expected to obtain abundant supplies; from which point the latter could be conducted, well protected against Indians by my detachment, back to Fort Wallace. Owing to the severe marching of the past few weeks, the horses of the command were generally in an unfit condition for further service without rest. So that after selecting upward of a hundred of the best, the remainder might for the time be regarded as unserviceable; such they were in fact. There was no idea or probability that the portion of the command to remain in camp near Fort Wallace would be called upon to do anything but rest and recuperate from their late marches. It was certainly not expected that they would be molested or called out by Indians; nor were they. Regarding the duties to be performed by the picked detachment as being by far the most important, I chose to accompany it.

The immediate command of the detachment was given to Captain Hamilton, of whom mention has been previously made. He was assisted by two other officers. My intention was to push through from Fort Wallace to Fort Hays, a distance of about one hundred and fifty miles, as rapidly as was practicable; then, being beyond the most dangerous portion of the route, to make the remainder of the march to Fort Harker with half a dozen troopers, while Captain Hamilton with his command should follow leisurely. Under this arrangement I hoped to have a train loaded with supplies at Harker, and in readiness to start for Fort Wallace, by the time Captain Hamilton should arrive.

Leaving Fort Wallace about sunset on the evening of the 15th of July, we began our ride eastward, following the line of the overland stage route. At that date the Kansas Pacific Railway was only completed as far westward as Fort Harker. Between Forts Wallace and Harker we expected to find the stations of the overland stage company, at intervals of from ten to fifteen miles. In time of peace these stations are generally occupied by half a dozen employees of the route, embracing the stablemen and relays of drivers. They were well supplied with firearms and ammunition, and every facility for defending themselves against Indians. The stables were also the quarters for the men. They were usually built of stone, and one would naturally think that against Indians no better defensive work would be required. Yet such was not the case. The hay and other combustible material usually contained in them enabled the savages, by shooting prepared arrows, to easily set them on fire, and thus drive the occupants out to the open plain, where their fate would soon be settled. To guard against such an emergency, each station was ordinarily provided with what on the Plains is termed a "dug-out." The name implies the character and description of the work. The "dug-out" was commonly located but a few yards from one of the corners of the stable, and was prepared by excavating the earth so as to form an opening not unlike a cellar, which was usually about four feet in depth, and sufficiently roomy to accommodate at close quarters half a dozen persons. This opening was then covered with earth and loopholed on all sides at a height of a few inches above the original level of the ground. The earth was thrown on top until the "dug-out" resembled an ordinary mound of earth, some four or five feet in height. To the outside observer, no means apparently were provided for egress or ingress; yet such was not the case. If the entrance had been made above ground, rendering it necessary for the defenders to pass from the stable unprotected to their citadel, the Indians would have posted themselves accordingly, and picked them off one by one as they should emerge from the stable. To provide against this danger, an underground passage was constructed in each case, leading from the "dug-out" to the interior of the stable. With these arrangements for defence a few determined men could withstand the attacks of an entire tribe of savages. The recent depredations of the Indians had so demoralized the men at the various stations that many of the latter were found deserted, their former occupants having joined their forces with those of other stations. The Indians generally burned the deserted stations.

Marching by night was found to be attended with some disadvantages. The men located at the stations which were still occupied, having no notice of our coming, and having seen no human beings for several days except the war parties of savages who had attacked them from time to time, were in a chronic state of alarm, and held themselves in readiness for defence at a moment's notice. The consequence was, that as we pursued our way in the stillness of the night, and were not familiar with the location of the various stations, we generally rode into close proximity before discovering them. The station men, however, were generally on the alert, and, as they did not wait to challenge us or be challenged, but took it for granted that we were Indians, our first greeting would be a bullet whistling over our heads, sometimes followed by a perfect volley from the "dug-out." In such a case nothing was left for us to do but to withdraw the column to a place of security, and then for one of our number to creep up stealthily in the darkness to a point within hailing distance. Even this was an undertaking attended by no little danger, as by this time the little garrison of the "dug-out" would be thoroughly awake and every man at his post, his finger on the trigger of his trusty rifle, and straining both eye and ear to discover the approach of the hateful redskins, who alone were believed to be the cause of all this ill-timed disturbance of their slumbers. Huddled together, as they necessarily would be, in the contracted limits of their subterranean citadel, and all sounds from without being deadened and rendered indistinct by the heavy roof of earth and the few apertures leading to the inside, it is not strange that under the circumstances it would be difficult for the occupants to distinguish between the voice of an Indian and that of a white man. Such was in fact the case, and no sooner would the officer sent forward for that purpose hail the little garrison and endeavor to explain who we were, than, guided by the first sound of his voice, they would respond promptly with their rifles. In some instances we were in this manner put to considerable delay, and although this was at times most provoking, it was not a little amusing to hear the description given by the party sent forward of how closely he hugged the ground when endeavoring to establish friendly relations with the stage people. Finally, when successful, and in conversation with the latter, we inquired why they did not recognize us from the fact that we hailed them in unbroken English. They replied that the Indians resorted to so many tricks that they had determined not to be caught even by that one. They were somewhat justified in this idea, as we knew that among the Indians who were then on the war-path there was at least one full blood who had been educated within the limits of civilization, graduated at a popular institution of learning, and only exchanged his civilized mode of dress for the paint, blanket, and feathers of savage life after he had reached the years of manhood. Almost at every station we received intelligence of Indians having been seen in the vicinity within a few days of our arrival.

We felt satisfied they were watching our movements, although we saw no fresh signs of Indians until we arrived near Downer's station. Here, while stopping to rest our horses for a few minutes, a small party of our men, who had without authority halted some distance behind, came dashing into our midst and reported that twenty-five or thirty Indians had attacked them some five or six miles in rear, and had killed two of their number. As there was a detachment of infantry guarding the station, and time being important, we pushed on toward our destination. The two men reported killed were left to be buried by the troops on duty at the station. Frequent halts and brief rests were made along our line of march; occasionally we would halt long enough to indulge in a few hour's sleep. About three o'clock on the morning of the 18th we reached Fort Hays, having marched about one hundred and fifty miles in fifty-five hours, including all halts. Some may regard this as a rapid rate of marching; in fact, a few officers of the army who themselves have made many and long marches (principally in ambulances and railroad cars) are of the same opinion. It was far above the usual rate of a leisurely made march, but during the same season and with a larger command I marched sixty miles in fifteen hours. This was officially reported, but occasioned no remark. During the war, and at the time the enemy's cavalry under General J. E. B. Stuart made its famous raid around the Army of the Potomac in Maryland, a portion of our cavalry, accompanied by horse artillery, in attempting to overtake them, marched over ninety miles in twenty-four hours. A year subsequent to the events narrated in this chapter I marched a small detachment eighty miles in seventeen hours, every horse accompanying the detachment completing the march in as fresh condition apparently as when the march began.

Leaving Hamilton and his command to rest one day at Hays and then to follow on leisurely to Fort Harker, I continued my ride to the latter post, accompanied by Colonels Cook and Custer and two troopers. We reached Fort Harker at two o'clock that night, having made the ride of sixty miles without change of animals in less than twelve hours. As this was the first telegraph station, I immediately sent telegrams to headquarters and to Fort Sedgwick, announcing the fate of Kidder and his party. General A. J. Smith, who was in command of this military district, had his headquarters at Harker. I at once reported to him in person, and acquainted him with every incident worthy of mention which had occurred in connection with my command since leaving him weeks before. Arrangements were made for the arrival of Hamilton's party and for a train containing supplies to be sent back under their escort. Having made my report to General Smith as my next superior officer, and there being no occasion for my presence until the train and escort should be in readiness to return, I applied for and received authority to visit Fort Riley, about ninety miles east of Harker by rail, where my family was then located.

No movements against Indians of any marked importance occurred in General Hancock's department during the remainder of this year. Extensive preparations had been made to chastise the Indians, both in this department and in

FORT PHIL. KEARNY MASSACRE.

that of General Augur's on the north; but about the date at which this narrative has arrived, a determined struggle between the adherents of the Indian ring and those advocating stringent measures against the hostile tribes, resulted in the temporary ascendancy of the former. Owing to this ascendancy, the military authorities were so hampered and restricted by instructions from Washington as to be practically powerless to inaugurate or execute any decisive measures against the Indians. Their orders required them to simply act on the defensive. It may not be uninteresting to go back to the closing month of the preceding year. The great event in Indian affairs of that month and year was the Fort Phil Kearny massacre, which took place within a few miles of the fort bearing that name, and in which a detachment of troops, numbering in all ninety-four persons, were slain, and not one escaped or was spared to tell the tale. The alleged grievance of the Indians prompting them to this outbreak was the establishment by the Government of a new road of travel to Montana, and the locating of military posts along this line. They claimed that the building and use of this road would drive all the game out of their best hunting-grounds. When once war was determined upon by them, it was conducted with astonishing energy and marked success. Between the 26th of July and the 21st of December of the same year, the Indians opposing the establishment of this new road were known to have killed ninety-one enlisted men, five officers, and fifty-eight citizens, besides wounding twenty more and capturing and driving off several hundred head of valuable stock. And during this period of less than six months, they appeared before Fort Phil Kearny in hostile array on fifty-one separate occasions, and attacked every train and individual attempting to pass over the Montana road. It has been stated officially that at the three posts established for the defence of the Montana road, there were the following reduced amounts of ammunition: Fort C. F. Smith, ten rounds per man; Fort Phil Kearny, forty-five rounds per man, and Fort Reno, thirty rounds per man; and that there were but twelve officers on duty at the three posts, many of the enlisted men of which were raw recruits. The force being small, and the amount of labor necessary in building new posts being very great, but little opportunity could be had for drill or target practice. The consequence was, the troops were totally lacking in the necessary preparation to make a successful fight. As the massacre at Fort Phil Kearny was one of the most complete as well as terrible butcheries connected with our entire Indian history, some of the details, as subsequently made evident, are here given.

On the 6th of December the wood train was attacked by Indians about two miles from the fort. Colonel Fetterman, with about fifty mounted men, was sent to rescue the train. He succeeded in this, but only after a severe fight with the Indians and after suffering a loss of one officer (Lieutenant Bingham of the cavalry) and one sergeant, who were decoyed from the main body into an ambuscade. This affair seems to have given the Indians great encouragement, and induced them to form their plans for the extensive massacre which was to follow.

On the 21st the wood train was again assailed, and, as before, a party was sent out from the fort to its relief. The relieving party consisted of infantry and cavalry, principally the former, numbering in all ninety-one men with three officers—Captain Brown of the infantry, Lieutenant Grummond of the cavalry, and Colonel Fetterman of the infantry in command.

Colonel Fetterman sallied forth promptly with his command to the rescue of the train. He moved out rapidly, keeping to the right of the wood road, for the purpose, as is supposed, of getting in rear of the attacking party. As he advanced across the Piney a few Indians appeared on his front and flanks, and kept showing themselves just beyond rifle range until they finally disappeared beyond Lodge Trail ridge. When Colonel Fetterman reached Lodge Trail ridge the picket signalled the fort that the Indians had retreated, and that the train had moved toward the timber. About noon Colonel Fetterman's command, having thrown out skirmishers, disappeared over the crest of Lodge Trail ridge; firing at once commenced and was heard distinctly at the fort. From a few scattering shots it increased in rapidity until it became a continuous and rapid fire of musketry. A medical officer was sent from the post to join the detachment, but was unable to do so, Indians being encountered on the way. After the firing had become quite heavy, showing that a severe engagement was taking place, Colonel Carrington, the commander of the post, sent an officer and about seventy-five men to reinforce Colonel Fetterman's party. These reinforcements moved rapidly toward the point from which the sound of firing proceeded. The firing continued to be heard during their advance, diminishing in rapidity and number of shots until they had reached a high summit overlooking the battle-field, when one or two shots closed all sound of conflict. From this summit a full view could be obtained of the Peno valley beyond, in which Fetterman's command was known to be, but not a single individual of this ill-fated band could be seen. Instead, however, the valley was seen to be overrun by Indians, estimated to number fully three thousand warriors. Discovering the approach of the reinforcements, the Indians beckoned them to come on, but without awaiting their arrival commenced retreating. The troops then advanced to a point where the savages had been seen collected in a circle, and there found the dead naked bodies of Colonel Fetterman, Captain Brown, and about sixty-five of their men. All the bodies lay in a space not exceeding thirty-five feet in diameter A few American horses lay dead near by, all with their heads toward the fort. This spot was by the roadside and beyond the summit of a hill rising to the east of Peno creek. The road after ascending this hill follows the ridge for nearly three-quarters of a mile, and then descends abruptly to Peno valley About midway between the point where these bodies lay and that where the road begins to descend was the dead body of Lieutenant Grummond; and at the point where the road leaves the ridge to descend to the Peno valley were the dead bodies of three citizens and a few of the old, long-tried, and experienced soldiers. Around this little group were found a great number of empty cartridge shells; more than fifty were found near the body of a citizen who had used a Henry rifle; all going to show how stubbornly these men had fought, and that they had fought with telling effect on their enemies was evidenced by the fact that within a few hundred yards in front of their position ten Indian ponies lay dead, and near by them were sixty-five pools of dark and clotted blood. Among the records of the Indian Department in Washington there is on file a report of one of the Peace Commissioners sent to investigate the circumstances of this frightful slaughter. Among the conclusions given in this report, it is stated that the Indians were massed to resist Colonel Fetterman's advance along Peno creek on both sides of the road; that Colonel Fetterman formed his advanced lines on the summit of the hill overlooking the creek and valley, with a reserve near where the large number of dead bodies lay; that the Indians in large force attacked him vigorously in this position, and were successfully resisted for half an hour or more; that the command then being short of ammunition and seized with a

GENL. W. T. SHERMAN.

panic at this event and the great numerical superiority of the Indians, attempted to retreat toward the fort; that the mountaineers and old soldiers, who had learned that a movement from Indians in an engagement was equivalent to death, remained in their first position and were killed there; that immediately upon the commencement of the retreat the Indians charged upon and surrounded the party, who could not now be formed by their officers and were immediately killed. Only six men of the whole command were killed by balls, and two of these, Colonel Fetterman and Captain Brown, no doubt inflicted this death upon themselves, or each other, by their own hands, for both were shot through the left temple, and powder was burnt into the skin and flesh about the wound. These officers had often asserted that they would never be taken alive by Indians.

The difficulty, as further explained by this commissioner, was that the officer commanding the Phil Kearny district was furnished no more troops for a state of war than had been provided for a state of profound peace. " In regions where all was peace, as at Laramie in November, twelve companies were stationed; while in regions where all was war, as at Phil Kearny, there were only five companies allowed." The same criticism regarding the distribution of troops would be just if applied to a much later date.

The Indians invariably endeavored to conceal their exact losses, but they acknowledged afterwards to have suffered a loss of twelve killed on the field, sixty severely wounded, several of whom afterwards died, and many others permanently maimed. They also lost twelve horses killed outright, and fifty-six so badly wounded that they died within twenty-four hours.

The intelligence of this massacre was received throughout the country with universal horror, and awakened a bitter feeling toward the savage perpetrators. The Government was implored to inaugurate measures looking to their prompt punishment. This feeling seemed to be shared by all classes. The following despatch, sent by General Sherman to General Grant, immediately upon receipt of the news of the massacre, briefly but characteristically expresses the views of the Lieutenant-General of the Army·

St. Louis, Dec. 28, 1866.

GENERAL: Just arrived in time to attend the funeral of my Adjutant-General, Sawyer. I have given general instructions to General Cooke about the Sioux. I do not yet understand how the massacre of Colonel Fetterman's party could have been so complete. We must act with vindictive earnestness against the Sioux, even to their extermination, men, women, and children. Nothing less will reach the root of the case.

(Signed)   W. T. SHERMAN, Lieutenant-General.

The old trouble between the War and Interior Departments, as to which should retain control of the Indian question, was renewed with increased vigor. The Army accused the Indian Department, and justly too, of furnishing the Indians arms and ammunition. Prominent exponents of either side of the question were not slow in taking up their pens in advocacy of their respective views. In the succeeding chapter testimony will be offered from those high in authority, now the highest, showing that among those who had given the subject the most thoughtful attention the opinion was unanimous in favor of the " abolition of the civil Indian agents and licensed traders," and of the transfer of the Indian Bureau from the Interior Department back to the War Department, where it originally belonged.

X.

THE winter of 1867–'68 was a period of comparative id eness and quiet, so far as the troops guarding the military posts on the Plains and frontier were concerned. The Indians began their periodical depredations against the frontier settlers and overland emigrants and travellers early in the spring of 1868, and continued them with but little interruption or hindrance from any quarter until late in the summer and fall of that year.

General Sully, an officer of considerable reputation as an Indian fighter, was placed in command of the district of the Upper Arkansas, which embraced the Kansas frontier and those military posts on the central plains most intimately connected with the hostile tribes. General Sully concentrated a portion of the troops of his command, consisting of detachments of the Seventh and Tenth Cavalry and Third Infantry, at points on the Arkansas river, and set on foot various scouting expeditions, but all to no purpose. The Indians continued as usual not only to elude the military forces directed against them, but to keep up their depredations upon the settlers of the frontier.

Great excitement existed along the border settlements of Kansas and Colorado. The frequent massacres of the frontiersmen and utter destruction of their homes created a very bitter feeling on the part of the citizens of Kansas toward the savages, and from the Governor of the State down to its humblest citizen appeals were made to the authorities of the general government to give protection against the Indians, or else allow the people to take the matter into their own hands and pursue retaliatory measures against their hereditary enemies. General Sheridan, then in command of that military department, with headquarters at Fort Leavenworth, Kansas, was fully alive to the responsibilities of his position, and in his usual effective manner set about organizing victory.

As pretended but not disinterested friends of the Indians frequently acquit the latter of committing unprovoked attacks on helpless settlers and others, who have never in the slightest degree injured them, and often deny even that the Indians have been guilty of any hostile acts which justify the adoption of military measures to insure the protection and safety of our frontier settlements, the following tabular statement is here given. This statement is taken from official records on file at the headquarters Military Division of the Missouri, and, as it states, gives only those murders and other depredations which were officially reported, and the white people mentioned as killed are exclusive of those slain in warfare. I am particular in giving time, place, etc., of each occurrence, so that those who hitherto have believed the Indian to be a creature who could do no wrong may have ample opportunity to judge of the correctness of my statements. Many other murders by the Indians during this period no doubt occurred, but, occurring as they did over a wide and sparsely settled tract of country, were never reported to the military authorities.

The mass of the troops being concentrated and employed along the branches of the Upper Arkansas under General Sully, thus leaving the valleys of the Republican, Solomon, and Smoky Hill rivers comparatively without troops, and the valleys of the Upper Republican being, as we have in previous chapters learned, a favorite resort and camping-ground for the hostile tribes of the up-

TABULAR STATEMENT OF MURDERS, OUTRAGES, ROBBERIES, AND DEPREDATIONS COMMITTED BY INDIANS IN THE DEPARTMENT OF THE MISSOURI AND NORTHERN TEXAS, IN 1868 (EXCLUSIVE OF MILITARY ENGAGEMENTS), AND OFFICIALLY REPORTED TO HEADQUARTERS DEPARTMENT OF THE MISSOURI.

DATE	PLACE	White: Murdered	White: Wounded	White: Scalped	White: Scouts Murdered	White: Women outraged	Captured: Men	Captured: Women	Captured: Children	Live Stock: Horses and Mules	Live Stock: Stock Cattle	Houses attacked, burned, and plundered	Stage Coaches attacked and impeded	Wagon trains attacked and destroyed	Indians k'd (K.)	Indians w'd (W.)
1868.																
August 10	Saline Valley															
August 12	Settlements on Solomon River	15	2			4						6				
August 12	On Republican River	2				5				10		5				
August 12	Wright's Camp, near Dodge															
August 12	Pawnee Forks									2						
August 14	Granny Creek, on Republican	1	1			1				132						
August 22	Sheridan City											1				
August 23	Northern Texas	8									12					
August 23	Cheyenne Wells										300					
August 23	Two Butte Creek	3											1			
August 23	Pond Creek and Lake Station	2								25						
August 23	Bent's Fort											1	1			
August 24	Bent's Fort									15	4	1				
August 27	Fort Lyon	1													3	1
August 27	Cheyenne Wells												1			
August 27	Big Spring Station				1a											
August 28	Kiowa Station	3									50				1	
August 31	Kiowa Creek (near)									200	40		2			
September 1	West of Lake Station	2		2							30					
September 1	Reed's Springs	3	3													
September 1	Spanish Fort, Texas	4		8		3b				15						
September 2	Little Coon Creek		3													
September 3	Colorado City	4														
September 5	Hugo's Springs															
Sept. 6 and 7	Colorado Territory	25		20						5		1				
September 8	Turkey Creek, near Sheridan	2		2						76						
September 8	Cimmaron Crossing	17c								12	75		1			
September 9	Between Sheridan and Wallace	6											1			
September 10	Near Fort Wallace												1			
September 11	Lake Creek									81		1				
September 12	Bent's Old Fort									85		1				
September 17	Ella Station	1										1				
September 17	Fort Bascom	1	1							30						
September 19	Big Timber's Station											1				
September 29	Sharp's Creek	1					1d	1d	1d							
October 2	Fort Zarah	1										1				
October 2	Between Larned and Dodge	3	3							50						
October 4	Near Fort Dodge	2	1							68						
October 4	Asher Creek Settlement									7						
October 7	Purgatory Creek	1								38						
October 10	Fort Zarah									8						
October 13	Brown's Creek												1			
October 6	Sand Creek							1e	1e			1				
October 14	Prairie Dog Creek	1	1							26					1	
October 15	Fisher and Yocucy Creeks	4	1			1						1				
October 23	Fort Zarah	2											2			
October 30	Grinnell Station														1	
November 7	Coon Creek												1			
November 19	Little Coon Creek	1													5	
November 19	Fort Dodge	1												2		
November 20	Mulberry Creek				2f											
November 25	Indian Territory									20				2		
January*	Northern Texas‡	25		9					14g	20						
February*	Northern Texas‡	7							5h	50						
May†	Northern Texas‡								3i							
June†	Northern Texas‡	1														
July†	Brazos River, Texas‡	4														
	Total	154	16	41	3	14	1	4	24	669	958	24	11	4	11	1

a This scout was William Comstock.

b One of these three women was outraged by thirteen Indians, who afterward killed and scalped her, leaving a hatchet stuck in her head. They then killed her four little children.

c Fifteen of these persons were burned to death by the Indians, who attacked the train to which they belonged.

d These persons were Mr. Bassett, his wife, and child. The Indians having plundered and per plains, General Sheridan determined that, while devoting full attention to the Kiowas, Comanches, Apaches, Arapahoes, and Southern Cheyennes, to be found south of the Arkansas, he would also keep an eye out for the Sioux, Upper Cheyennes, and Arapahoes, and the "Dog Soldiers," usually infesting the valleys of the Upper Republican and Solomon rivers. The "Dog Soldiers" were a band of warriors principally composed of Cheyennes, but made up of the turbulent and uncontrollable spirits of all the tribes. Neither they nor their leaders had ever consented to the ratification of any of the treaties to which their brothers of the other tribes had agreed. Never satisfied except when at war with the white man, they were by far the most troublesome, daring, and war-like band to be found on the Plains. Their warriors were all fine-looking braves of magnificent physique, and in appearance and demeanor more nearly conformed to the ideal warrior than those of any other tribe. How they came by their name, the "Dog Soldiers," I never was able to learn satisfactorily. One explanation is, that they are principally members of the Cheyenne tribe, and were at first known as the Cheyenne soldiers. The name of the tribe "Cheyenne" was originally *Chien*, the French word for dog; hence the term "Dog Soldiers."

To operate effectually against these bands General Sheridan was without the necessary troops. Congress, however, had authorized the employment of detachments of frontier scouts to be recruited from among the daring spirits always to be met with on the border. It was upon a force raised from this class of our western population that General Sheridan relied for material assistance.

Having decided to employ frontiersmen to assist in punishing the Indians, the next question was the selection of a suitable leader. The choice, most fortunately, fell upon General George A. Forsyth ("Sandy"), then Acting Inspector-General of the Department of Missouri, who, eager to render his country an important service and not loath to share in the danger and excitement attendant upon such an enterprise, set himself energetically to work to raise and equip his command for the field. But little time was required, under Forsyth's stirring zeal, to raise the required number of men. It was wisely decided to limit the number of frontiersmen to fifty. This enabled Forsyth to choose only good men, and the size of the detachment, considering that they were to move without ordinary transportation—in fact were to almost adopt the Indian style of warfare—was as large as could be without being cumbersome. Last but not least, it was to be composed of men who, from their leader down, were intent on accomplishing an important purpose; they were not out on any holiday tour or pleasure excursion. Their object was to find Indians; a difficult matter for a large force to accomplish, because the Indians

burned Bassett's house, took the inmates captive; but Mrs. Bassett, being weak and unable to travel, was stripped, and, together with her child (two days old), left on the prairie. Mr. Bassett is supposed to have been murdered.

e Mrs. Blinn and child, afterward murdered by the Indians during Custer's attack on Black Kettle's camp.

f These scouts were Marshall and Davis.

g These fourteen children were afterward frozen to death while in captivity.

h Two of these children were given up to Colonel Leavenworth; the remaining three were taken to Kansas.

i These children belonged to Mr. McIlroy.

* Committed by Kiowa Indians.

† Committed by Comanche Indians.

‡ Additional murders and outrages committed by Indians, not heretofore enumerated, reported by P. McCusker, U. S. Interpreter, and S. T. Walkley, Acting Indian Agent.

are the first to discover their presence and take themselves out of the way; whereas with a small or moderate-sized detachment there is some chance, as Forsyth aftewards learned, of finding Indians.

Among all the officers of the army, old or young, no one could have been found better adapted to become the leader of an independent expedition, such as this was proposed to be, than General Forsyth. This is more particularly true considering the experiences which awaited this detachment. I had learned to know him well when we rode together in the Shenandoah valley, sometimes in one direction, and sometimes, but rarely, in the other; and afterwards in the closing struggle around Petersburg and Richmond, when his chief had been told to "press things," General Forsyth, "Sandy" as his comrades familiarly termed him, was an important member of the "press." In fact one of the best terms to describe him by is irrepressible; for, no matter how defeat or disaster might stare us in the face, and, as I have intimated, cause us to ride "the other" way, "Sandy" always contrived to be of good cheer and to be able to see the coming of a better day. This quality came in good play in the terrible encounter which I am about to describe.

The frontiersmen of the Kansas border, stirred up by numerous massacres committed in their midst by the savages, were only too eager and willing to join in an enterprise which promised to afford them an opportunity to visit just punishment upon their enemies.

Thirty selected men were procured at Fort Harker, Kansas, and twenty more at Fort Hays, sixty miles further west. In four days the command was armed, mounted, and equipped, and at once took the field. Lieutenant F. H. Beecher, of the Third Regular Infantry, a nephew of the distinguished divine of the same name, and one of the ablest and best young officers on the frontier, was second in command; and a surgeon was found in the person of Dr. John S. Movers, of Hays City, Kansas, a most competent man in his profession, and one who had had a large experience during the war of the rebellion as surgeon of one of the volunteer regiments from the State of New York. Sharpe Grover, one of the best guides and scouts the Plains afforded, was the guide of the expedition, while many of the men had at different times served in the regular and volunteer forces; for example, the man selected to perform the duties of First Sergeant of the detachment was Brevet Brigadier-General W. H. H. McCall, United States Volunteers, who commanded a brigade at the time the Confederate forces attempted to break the Federal lines at Fort Hell, in front of Petersburg, in the early spring of 1865, and was breveted for gallantry on that occasion. As a general thing the men composing the party were just the class eminently qualified to encounter the dangers which were soon to confront them. They were brave, active, hardy, and energetic, and, while they required a tight rein held over them, were when properly handled capable of accomplishing about all that any equal number of men could do under the same circumstances.

The party left Fort Hayes on the 29th day of August, 1868, and, under special instructions from Major-General Sheridan, commanding the department, took a north-westerly course, scouting the country to the north of the Saline river, crossed the south fork of the Solomon, Bow creek, north fork of the Solomon, Prairie Dog creek, and then well out toward the Republican river, and, swinging around in the direction of Fort Wallace, made that post on the eighth day from their departure. Nothing was met worthy of notice, but there were frequent indications of large camps of Indians which had evidently been abandoned only a few days or weeks before the arrival of the command.

Upon arriving at Fort Wallace, General Forsyth communicated with Gen eral Sheridan and proceeded to refit his command.

On the morning of September 10, a small war party of Indians attacked a train near Sheridan, a small railroad town some eighty miles beyond Fort Wallace, killed two teamsters and ran off a few cattle. As soon as information of this reached Fort Wallace, Forsyth started with his command for the town of Sheridan, where he took the trail of the Indians and followed it until dark. The next morning it was resumed, until the Indians finding themselves closely pursued, scattered in many directions and the trail became so obscure as to be lost. Determined, however, to find the Indians this time, if they were in the country, he pushed on to Short Nose creek, hoping to find them in that vicinity. Carefully scouting in every direction for the trail and still heading north as far as the Republican river, the command finally struck the trail of a small war party on the south bank of that stream, and followed it up to the forks of that river. This is familiar ground perhaps to some of my readers, as it was here Pawnee Killer and his band attacked our camp early one morning in the summer of '67, and hurried me from my tent without allowing me time to attend to my toilet. Continuing on the trail and crossing to the north bank, Forsyth found the trail growing constantly larger, as various smaller ones entered it from the south and north, and finally it developed into a broad and well-beaten road, along which large droves of cattle and horses had been driven. This trail led up the Arickaree fork of the Republican river, and constant indications of Indians, in the way of moccasins, jerked buffalo meat, and other articles, were found every few miles, but no Indians were seen. On the evening of the eighth day from Fort Wallace, the command halted about five o'clock in the afternoon and went into camp at or near a little island in the river, a mere sand-spit of earth formed by the stream dividing at a little rift of earth that was rather more gravelly than the sand in its immediate vicinity, and coming together again about a hundred yards further down the stream, which just here was about eight feet wide and two or three inches deep.

The watercourses in this part of the country in the dry season are mere threads of water meandering along the broad sandy bed of the river, which during the months of May and June is generally full to its banks, and at that time capable of floating an ordinary ship, while later in the season there is not enough water to float the smallest row-boat. In fact, in many places the stream sinks into the sand and disappears for a considerable distance, finally making its way up to the surface and flowing on until it again disappears and reappears many times in the course of a long day's journey.

Encamping upon the bank of the stream at this point—which at that time was supposed by the party to be Delaware creek, but which was afterwards discovered to be Arickaree fork of the Republican river—the command made the usual preparations for passing the night. This point was but a few marches from the scene of Kidder's massacre. Having already been out from Fort Wallace eight days, and not taking wagons with them, their supplies began to run low, although they had been husbanded with great care. During the last three days game had been very scarce, which fact convinced Forsyth and his party that the Indians whose trail they were following had scoured the country and driven off every kind of game by their hunting parties. The following day would see the command out of supplies of all kinds; but feeling assured that he was within striking distance of the Indians, Forsyth determined to push on until he found them, and fight them even if he could not whip them, in order that they might realize that their rendezvous was discovered, and that the Government was at last in earnest when it said that they were to be punished for their depredations on the settlements.

After posting their pickets and partaking of the plainest of suppers, Forsyth's little party disposed of themselves on the ground to sleep, little dreaming who was to sound their reveille in so unceremonious a manner.

At dawn on the following day, September 17, 1868, the guard gave the alarm "Indians." Instantly every man sprang to his feet and, with the true instinct of the frontiersman, grasped his rifle with one hand while with the other he seized his lariat, that the Indians might not stampede the horses. Six Indians dashed up toward the party, rattling bells, shaking buffalo robes, and firing their guns. The four pack mules belonging to the party broke away and were last seen galloping over the hills. Three other animals made their escape, as they had only been hobbled, in direct violation of the orders which directed that all the animals of the command should be regularly picketed to a stake or picket-pin, firmly driven into the ground. A few shots caused the Indians to sheer off and disappear in a gallop over the hills. Several of the men started in pursuit, but were instantly ordered to rejoin the command, which was ordered to saddle up with all possible haste, Forsyth feeling satisfied that the attempt to stampede the stock was but the prelude to a general and more determined attack. Scarcely were the saddles thrown on the horses and the girths tightened, when Grover, the guide, placing his hand on Forsyth's shoulder, gave vent to his astonishment as follows: " *O heavens, General, look at the Indians!* " Well might he be excited. From every direction they dashed toward the band. Over the hills, from the west and north, along the river, on the opposite bank, everywhere and in every direction they made their appearance. Finely mounted, in full war paint, their long scalp locks braided with eagles' feathers, and with all the paraphernalia of a barbarous war party—with wild whoops and exultant shouts, on they came.

There was but one thing to do. Realizing that they had fallen into a trap, Forsyth, who had faced danger too often to hesitate in an emergency, determined that if it came to a Fort Fetterman affair, described in a preceding chapter, he should at least make the enemy bear their share of the loss. He ordered his men to lead their horses to the island, tie them to the few bushes that were growing there in a circle, throw themselves upon the ground in the same form, and make the best fight they could for their lives. In less time than it takes to pen these words, the order was put into execution. Three of the best shots in the party took position in the grass under the bank of the river which covered the north end of the island; the others formed a circle inside of the line of animals, and throwing themselves upon the ground began to reply to the fire of the Indians, which soon became hot and galling in the extreme. Throwing themselves from their horses, the Indians crawled up to within a short distance of the island, and opened a steady and well-directed fire upon the party. Armed with the best quality of guns, many of them having the latest pattern breech-loaders with fixed ammunition (as proof of this many thousand empty shells of Spencer and Henry rifle ammunition were found on the ground occupied by the Indians after the fight), they soon made sad havoc among the men and horses. As it grew lighter, and the Indians could be distinguished, Grover expressed the greatest astonishment at the number of warriors, which he placed at nearly one thousand. Other members of the party estimated them at even a greater number. Forsyth expressed the opinion that there could not be more than four or five hundred, but in this it seems he was mistaken, as some of the Brulés, Sioux, and Cheyennes have since told him that their war party was nearly nine hundred strong, and was composed of Brulés, Sioux, Cheyennes, and Dog Soldiers; furthermore, that they had been watching him for five days previous to their attack, and had called in all the warriors they could get to their assistance. The men of Forsyth's party began covering themselves at once, by using case and pocket knives in the gravelly sand, and soon had thrown up quite a little earthwork consisting of detached mounds in the form of a circle. About this time Forsyth was wounded by a Minié ball, which, striking him in the right thigh, ranged upward, inflicting an exceedingly painful wound. Two of his men had been killed, and a number of others wounded. Leaning over to give directions to some of his men, who were firing too rapidly, and in fact becoming a little too nervous for their own good, Forsyth was again wounded, this time in the left leg, the ball breaking and badly shattering the bone midway between the knee and ankle. About the same time Dr. Movers, the surgeon of the party, who, owing to the hot fire of the Indians, was unable to render surgical aid to his wounded comrades, had seized his trusty rifle and was doing capital service, was hit in the temple by a bullet, and never spoke but one intelligible word again.

Matters were now becoming desperate, and nothing but cool, steady fighting would avail to mend them. The hills surrounding the immediate vicinity of the fight were filled with women and children, who were chanting war songs and filling the air with whoops and yells. The medicine men, a sort of high priests, and older warriors rode around outside of the combatants, being careful to keep out of range, and encouraged their young braves by beating a drum, shouting Indian chants, and using derisive words toward their adversaries, whom they cursed roundly for skulking like wolves, and dared to come out and fight like men.

Meantime the scouts were slowly but surely "counting game," and more than one Indian fell to the rear badly wounded by the rifles of the frontiersmen. Within an hour after the opening of the fight, the Indians were fairly frothing at the mouth with rage at the unexpected resistance they met, while the scouts had now settled down to earnest work, and obeyed to the letter the orders of Forsyth, whose oft reiterated command was, "Fire slowly, aim well, keep yourselves covered, and, above all, don't throw away a single cartridge."

Taken all in all, with a very few exceptions, the men behaved superbly. Obedient to every word of command, cool, plucky, determined, and fully realizing the character of their foes, they were a match for their enemies thus far at every point. About nine o'clock in the morning the last horse belonging to the scouts was killed, and one of the red skins was heard to exclaim in tolerably good English, "There goes the last damned horse anyhow;" a proof that some of the savages had at some time been intimate with the whites.

Shortly after nine o'clock a portion of the Indians began to form in a ravine just below the foot of the island, and soon about one hundred and twenty Dog Soldiers, the "banditti of the Plains," supported by some three hundred or more other mounted men, made their appearance, drawn up just beyond rifle shot below the island, and headed by the famous chief Roman Nose," prepared to charge the scouts. Superbly mounted, almost naked, although in full war dress, and painted in the most hideous manner, with their rifles in their hands, and formed with a front of about sixty men, they awaited the signal of their chief to charge, with apparently the greatest confidence. Roman

Nose addressed a few words to the mounted warriors, and almost immediately afterward the dismounted Indians surrounding the island poured a perfect shower of bullets into the midst of Forsyth's little party. Realizing that a crisis was at hand, and hot work was before him, Forsyth told his men to reload every rifle and to take and load the rifles of the killed and wounded of the party, and not to fire a shot until ordered to do so.

For a few moments the galling fire of the Indians rendered it impossible for any of the scouts to raise or expose any part of their persons. This was precisely the effect which the Indians desired to produce by the fire of their riflemen. It was this that the mounted warriors, under the leadership of Roman Nose, were waiting for. The Indians had planned their assault in a manner very similar to that usually adopted by civilized troops in assailing a fortified place. The fire of the Indian riflemen performed the part of the artillery on such occasions, in silencing the fire of the besieged and preparing the way for the assaulting column.

Seeing that the little garrison was stunned by the heavy fire of the dismounted Indians, and rightly judging that now, if ever, was the proper time to charge them, Roman Nose and his band of mounted warriors, with a wild, ringing war-whoop, echoed by the women and children on the hills, started forward. On they came, presenting even to the brave men awaiting the charge a most superb sight. Brandishing their guns, echoing back the cries of encouragement of their women and children on the surrounding hills, and confident of victory, they rode bravely and recklessly to the assault. Soon they were within the range of the rifles of their friends, and of course the dismounted Indians had to slacken their fire for fear of hitting their own warriors. This was the opportunity for the scouts, and they were not slow to seize it. "Now," shouted Forsyth. "Now," echoed Beecher, McCall, and Grover; and the scouts, springing to their knees, and casting their eyes coolly along the barrels of their rifles, opened on the advancing savages as deadly a fire as the same number of men ever yet sent forth from an equal number of rifles. Unchecked, undaunted, on dashed the warriors; steadily rang the clear, sharp reports of the rifles of the frontiersmen. Roman Nose, the chief, is seen to fall dead from his horse, then Medicine Man is killed, and for an instant the column of braves, now within ten feet of the scouts, hesitates—falters. A ringing cheer from the scouts, who perceive the effect of their well-directed fire, and the Indians begin to break and scatter in every direction, unwilling to rush to a hand-to-hand struggle with the men who, although outnumbered, yet knew how to make such effective use of their rifles. A few more shots from the frontiersmen and the Indians are forced back beyond range, and their first attack ends in defeat. Forsyth turns to Grover anxiously and inquires, "Can they do better than that, Grover?" "I have been on the Plains, General, since a boy, and never saw such a charge as that before. I think they have done their level best," was the reply. "All right," responds "Sandy"; "then we are good for them."

So close did the advance warriors of the attacking column come in the charge, that several of their dead bodies now lay within a few feet of the intrenchments. The scouts had also suffered a heavy loss in this attack. The greatest and most irreparable was that of Lieutenant Beecher, who was mortally wounded, and died at sunset of that day. He was one of the most reliable and efficient officers doing duty on the Plains. Modest, energetic, and ambitious in his profession, had he lived he undoubtedly would have had a brilliant future before him and had opportunity such as is offered by a great war ever have occurred, Lieutenant Beecher would have without doubt achieved great distinction.

The Indians still kept up a continuous fire from their dismounted warriors; but as the scouts by this time were well covered by their miniature earthworks, it did little execution. At two o'clock in the afternoon the savages again attempted to carry the island by a mounted charge, and again at sunset; but having been deprived of their best and most fearless leader by the fall of Roman Nose, they were not so daring or impulsive as in the first charge, and were both times repulsed with heavy losses. At dark they ceased firing, and withdrew their forces for the night. This gave the little garrison on the island an opportunity to take a breathing spell, and Forsyth to review the situation and sum up how he had fared. The result was not consoling. His trusted Lieutenant Beecher was lying dead by his side; his surgeon, Movers, was mortally wounded; two of his men killed, four mortally wounded, four severely, and ten slightly. Here, out of a total of fifty-one, were twenty-three killed and wounded. His own condition, his right thigh fearfully lacerated, and his left leg badly broken, only rendered the other discouraging circumstances doubly so. As before stated, the Indians' had killed all of his horses early in the fight. His supplies were exhausted, and there was no way of dressing the wounds of himself or comrades, as the medical stores had been captured by the Indians. He was about one hundred and ten miles from the nearest post, and savages were all around him. The outlook could scarcely have been less cheering. But Forsyth's disposition and pluck incline him to speculate more upon that which is, or may be gained, than to repine at that which is irrevocably lost. This predominant trait in his character now came in good play. In stead of wasting time in vain regrets over the advantages gained by his enemies, he quietly set about looking up the chances in his favor. And, let the subject be what it may, I will match " Sandy " " against an equal number " for making a favorable showing of the side which he espouses or advocates. To his credit account he congratulated himself and comrades, first upon the fact that they had beaten off their foes; second, water could be had inside their intrenchments by digging a few feet below the surface; then for food " horse and mule meat," to use Sandy's expression, " was lying around loose in any quantity; " and last, but most important of all, he had plenty of ammunition. Upon these circumstances and facts Forsyth built high hopes of successfully contending against any renewed assaults of the savages.

Two men, Trudeau and Stillwell, both good scouts, and familiar with the Plains, were selected to endeavor to make their way through the cordon of Indians and proceed to Fort Wallace, one hundred and ten miles distant, and report the condition of Forsyth and party, and act as guides to the troops which would be at once sent to the relief of the besieged scouts. It was a perilous mission, and called for the display of intrepid daring, cool judgment, and unflinching resolution, besides a thorough knowledge of the country, as much of their journey would necessarily be made during the darkness of night, to avoid discovery by wandering bands of Indians, who, no doubt, would be on the alert to intercept just such parties going for relief. Forsyth's selection of the two men named was a judicious one. Stillwell I afterwards knew well, having employed him as scout with my command for a long period. At the time referred to, however, he was a mere beardless boy of perhaps nineteen years, possessing a trim, lithe figure, which was set off to great advantage by the jaunty suit of buckskin which he wore cut and fringed according to the

THE SCOUTS DRIVEN BACK.

9

true style of the frontiersman. In his waist-belt he carried a large-sized revolver and a hunting knife. These, with his rifle, constituted his equipment. A capital shot whether afoot or on horseback, and a perfect horseman, this beardless boy on more than one occasion proved himself a dangerous foe to the wily red man. We shall not take final leave of Stillwell in this chapter.

These two men, Trudeau and Stillwell, after receiving Forsyth's instructions in regard to their dangerous errand, and being provided with his compass and map, started as soon as it was sufficiently dark on their long, weary tramp over a wild, desert country, thickly infested with deadly enemies. After their departure the wounded were brought in, the dead animals unsaddled, and the horse blankets used to make the wounded as comfortable as possible. The earthworks were strengthened by using the dead animals and saddles. A well was dug inside the intrenchments, and large quantities of horse and mule meat were cut off and buried in the sand to prevent it from putrefying. It began to rain, and the wounded were rendered less feverish by their involuntary but welcome bath.

As was expected, the night passed without incident or disturbance from the savages; but early the next morning the fight was renewed by the Indians again surrounding the island as before, and opening fire from the rifles of their dismounted warriors. They did not attempt to charge the island as they had done the previous day, when their attempts in this direction had cost them too dearly; but they were none the less determined and eager to overpower the little band which had been the cause of such heavy loss to them already The scouts, thanks to their efforts during the night, were now well protected, and suffered but little from the fire of the Indians, while the latter, being more exposed, paid the penalty whenever affording the scouts a chance with their rifles. The day was spent without any decided demonstration on the part of the red men, except to keep up as constant a fire as possible on the scouts, and to endeavor to provoke the latter to reply as often as possible, the object, no doubt, being to induce the frontiersmen to exhaust their supply of ammunition. But they were not to be led into this trap; each cartridge they estimated as worth to them one Indian, and nothing less would satisfy them.

On the night of the 18th two more men were selected to proceed to Fort Wallace, as it was not known whether Trudeau and Stillwell had made their way safely through the Indian lines or not. The last two selected, however, failed to elude the watchful eyes of the Indians, and were driven back to the island. This placed a gloomy look upon the probable fate of Trudeau and Stillwell, and left the little garrison in anxious doubt not only as to the safety of the two daring messengers, but as to their own final relief. On the morning of the 19th the Indians promptly renewed the conflict, but with less energy than before. They evidently did not desire or intend to come to close quarters again with their less numerous but more determined antagonists, but aimed as on the previous day to provoke a harmless fire from the scouts, and then, after exhausting their ammunition in this manner, overwhelm them by mass of numbers, and finish them with tomahawk and scalping knife. This style of tactics did not operate as desired. There is but little doubt that some of the Indians who had participated in the massacre of Fetterman and his party a few months before, when three officers and ninety-one men were killed outright, were also present and took part in the attack upon Forsyth and his party; and they must have been not a little surprised to witness the stubborn defence offered by this little party, which, even at the beginning, numbered but little over fifty men.

About noon the women and children, who had been constant and excited spectators of the fight from the neighboring hilltops, began to withdraw. It is rare indeed that in an attack by Indians their women and children are seen. They are usually sent to a place of safety until the result of the contest is known, but in this instance, with the overwhelming numbers of the savages and the recollection of the massacre of Fetterman and his party, there seemed to the Indians to be but one result to be expected, and that a complete, perhaps bloodless victory for them; and the women and children were permitted to gather as witnesses of their triumph, and perhaps at the close would be allowed to take part by torturing those of the white men who should be taken alive. The withdrawal of the women and children was regarded as a favorable sign by the scouts.

Soon after and as a last resort the Indians endeavored to hold a parley with Forsyth, by means of a white flag; but this device was too shallow and of too common adoption to entrap the frontiersman, the object simply being to accomplish by stratagem and perfidy what they had failed in by superior numbers and open warfare. Everything now seemed to indicate that the Indians had had enough of the fight, and during the night of the third day it was plainly evident that they had about decided to withdraw from the contest.

Forsyth now wrote the following despatch, and after nightfall confided it to two of his best men, Donovan and Plyley; and they, notwithstanding the discouraging result of the last attempt, set out to try and get through to Fort Wallace with it, which they successfully accomplished:

ON DELAWARE CREEK, REPUBLICAN RIVER, Sept. 19, 1868.

To Colonel Bankhead, or Commanding Officer, Fort Wallace.

I sent you two messengers on the night of the 17th instant, informing you of my critical condition. I tried to send two more last night, but they did not succeed in passing the Indian pickets, and returned. If the others have not arrived, then hasten at once to my assistance. I have eight badly wounded and ten slightly wounded men to take in, and every animal I had was killed save seven which the Indians stampeded. Lieutenant Beecher is dead, and Acting Assistant Surgeon Movers probably cannot live the night out. He was hit in the head Thursday, and has spoken but one rational word since. I am wounded in two places, in the right thigh and my left leg broken below the knee. The Cheyennes numbered 450 or more. Mr. Grover says they never fought so before. They were splendidly armed with Spencer and Henry rifles. We killed at least thirty-five of them and wounded many more, besides killing and wounding a quantity of their stock. They carried off most of their killed during the night, but three of their men fell into our hands. I am on a little island and have still plenty of ammunition left. We are living on mule and horse meat, and are entirely out of rations. If it was not for so many wounded, I would come in and take the chances of whipping them if attacked. They are evidently sick of their bargain.

I had two of the members of my company killed on the 17th, namely, William Wilson and George W. Calner. You had better start with not less than seventy-five men and bring all the wagons and ambulances you can spare. Bring a six-pound howitzer with you. I can hold out here for six days longer, *if absolutely necessary,* but please lose no time.

Very respectfully, your obedient servant,

(Signed) GEORGE A. FORSYTH,

U. S. Army, Commanding Co. Scouts

P. S. My surgeon having been mortally wounded, none of my wounded have had their wounds dressed yet, so please bring out a surgeon with you.

A small party of warriors remained in the vicinity watching the movements of the scouts; the main body, however, had departed.

The well men, relieved of the constant watching and fighting, were now able to give some attention to the wounded. Their injuries, which had grown very painful, were rudely dressed. Soup was made out of horse-flesh, and shelters were constructed protecting them from the heat, damp, and wind. On the sixth day the wounds of the men began to exhibit more decided and alarming signs of neglect. Maggots infested them and the first traces of gangrene had set in. To multiply the discomforts of their situation, the entire party was almost overpowered by the intolerable stench created by the decomposing bodies of the dead horses. Their supply was nearly exhausted. Under these trying circumstances Forsyth assembled his men. He told them " they knew their situation as well as he. There were those who were helpless, but aid must not be expected too soon. It might be difficult for the messengers to reach the fort, or there might be some delay by their losing their way. Those who wished to go should do so and leave the rest to take their chances." With one voice they resolved to stay, and, if all hope vanished, to die together.

At last the supply of jerked horse meat was exhausted, and the chances of getting more were gone. By this time the carcasses of the animals were a mass of corruption. There was no alternative—strips of putrid flesh were cut and eaten. The effect of this offensive diet was nauseating in the extreme. An experiment was made, with a view to improving the unpalatable flesh, of using gunpowder as salt, but to no purpose. The men allayed only their extreme cravings of hunger, trusting that succor might reach them before all was over.

On the morning of September 25, the sun rose upon Forsyth and his famished party with unusual splendor, and the bright colors of the morning horizon seemed like a rainbow of promise to their weary, longing spirits. Hope, grown faint with long waiting, gathered renewed strength from the brightness of nature. The solitary plain receding in all directions possessed a deeper interest than ever before, though it still showed no signs of life and presented the same monotonous expanse upon which the heroic band had gazed for so many trying days. Across the dim and indefinable distance which swept in all directions, the eye often wandered and wondered what might be the revelations of the next moment. Suddenly several dark figures appeared faintly on the horizon. The objects were moving. The question uppermost in the minds of all was, Are they savages or messengers of relief? As on such occasions of anxiety and suspense, time wore heavily, minutes seemed like hours, yet each moment brought the sufferers nearer the realization whether this was their doom or their escape therefrom. Over an hour had elapsed since the objects first came in sight, and yet the mystery remained unsolved. Slowly but surely they developed themselves, until finally they had approached sufficiently near for their character as friends or foes to be unmistakably established. To the joy of the weary watchers, the parties approaching proved to be troops; relief was at hand, the dangers and anxieties of the past few days were ended, and death either by starvation or torture at the hands of the savages no longer stared them in the face. The strong set up a shout such as men seldom utter. It was the unburdening of the heart of the weight of despair. The wounded lifted their fevered forms and fixed their glaring eyes upon the now rapidly approaching succor, and in their delirium involuntarily but feebly reiterated the acclamations of their comrades.

The troops arriving for their relief were a detachment from Fort Wallace under command of Colonel Carpenter of the regular cavalry, and had started from the fort promptly upon the arrival of Trudeau and Stillwell with intelligence of the condition and peril in which Forsyth and his party were.

When Colonel Carpenter and his men reached the island they found its defenders in a most pitiable condition, yet the survivors were determined to be plucky to the last. Forsyth himself, with rather indifferent success, affected to be reading an old novel that he had discovered in a saddlebag; but Colonel

Carpenter said his voice was a little unsteady and his eyes somewhat dim when he held out his hand to Carpenter and bade him welcome to "Beecher's Island," a name that has since been given to the battle-ground.

During the fight Forsyth counted thirty-two dead Indians within rifle range of the island. Twelve Indian bodies were subsequently discovered in one pit, and five in another. The Indians themselves confessed to a loss of seventy-five killed in action, and when their proclivity for concealing or diminishing the number of their slain in battle is considered, we can readily believe that their actual loss in this fight must have been much greater than they would have us believe.

Of the scouts, Lieutenant Beecher, Surgeon Movers, and six of the men were either killed outright or died of their wounds; eight more were disabled for life; of the remaining twelve who were wounded, nearly all recovered completely. During the fight innumerable interesting incidents occurred, some laughable and some serious. On the first day of the conflict a number of young Indian boys from fifteen to eighteen years of age crawled up and shot about fifty arrows into the circle in which the scouts lay. One of these arrows struck one of the men, Frank Herrington, full in the forehead. Not being able to pull it out, one of his companions, lying in the same hole with him, cut off the arrow with his knife, leaving the iron arrowhead sticking in his frontal bone; in a moment a bullet struck him in the side of the head, glanced across his forehead, impinged upon the arrowhead, and the two fastened together fell to the ground—a queer but successful piece of amateur surgery. Herrington wrapped a cloth around his head, which bled profusely, and continued fighting as if nothing had happened.

Howard Morton, another of the scouts, was struck in the head by a bullet which finally lodged in the rear of one of his eyes, completely destroying its sight forever; but Morton never faltered, but fought bravely until the savages finally withdrew. Hudson Farley, a young stripling of only eighteen, whose father was mortally wounded in the first day's fight, was shot through the shoulder, yet never mentioned the fact until dark, when the list of wounded was called for. McCall, the First Sergeant, Vilott, Clark, Farley the elder, and others who were wounded, continued to bear their full share of the fight, notwithstanding their great sufferings, until the Indians finally gave up and withdrew. These incidents, of which many similar ones might be told, only go to show the remarkable character of the men who composed Forsyth's party.

Considering this engagement in all its details and with all its attendant circumstances, remembering that Forsyth's party, including himself, numbered all told but fifty-one men, and that the Indians numbered about seventeen to one, this fight was one of the most remarkable and at the same time successful contests in which our forces on the Plains have ever been engaged; and the whole affair, from the moment the first shot was fired until the beleaguered party was finally relieved by Colonel Carpenter's command, was a wonderful exhibition of daring courage, stubborn bravery, and heroic endurance, under circumstances of greatest peril and exposure. In all probability there will never occur, in our future hostilities with the savage tribes of the West, a struggle the equal of that in which were engaged the heroic men who defended so bravely "Beecher's Island." Forsyth, the gallant leader, after a long period of suffering and leading the life of an invalid for nearly two years, finally recovered from the effects of his severe wounds, and is now, I am happy to say, as good as new, contentedly awaiting the next war to give him renewed excitement.

———

XI

THE winter of 1867–'68 found me comfortably quartered at Fort Leavenworth, Kansas, on the banks of the Missouri. A considerable portion of my regiment had been ordered to locate at that post in the fall, and make that their winter quarters. General Sheridan, then commanding that military department, had also established his headquarters there, so that the post became more than ever the favorite military station in the West. I had not been on duty with my regiment since my rapid ride from Fort Wallace to Fort Harker in July, nor was I destined to serve with it in the field for some time to come. This, at the time, seemed a great deprivation to me, but subsequent events proved most conclusively that it was all for the best, and the result could not have been to me more satisfactory than it was, showing as it did that the best laid plans of mice and men, etc. But I am anticipating.

Those who have read the tabulated list of depredations committed by the Indians, as given in the article describing General Forsyth's desperate fight on Arickaree Fork, may have noticed the name of William Comstock in the column of killed. Comstock was the favorite and best known scout on the central plains. Frequent reference has been made to him in preceding numbers, particularly in the description of the attack of the Indians on the detachment commanded by Robbins and Cook. Strange as it may seem, when his thorough knowledge of the Indian character is considered, he fell a victim to their treachery and barbarity. The Indians were encamped with their village not far from Big Spring station, in western Kansas, and were professedly at peace. Still, no one familiar with the deceit and bad faith invariably practised by the Indians when free to follow the bent of their inclinations, ought to have thought of trusting themselves in their power. Yet Comstock, with all his previous knowledge and experience, did that which he would certainly have disapproved in others. He left the camp of the troops, which was but a few miles from the Indian village, and with but a single companion rode to the latter, and spent several hours in friendly conversation with the chiefs. Nothing occurred during their visit to excite suspicion. The Indians assumed a most peaceable bearing toward them, and were profuse in their demonstrations of friendship. When the time came for Comstock and his comrade to take their departure, they were urged by the Indians to remain and spend the night in the village.

The invitation was declined, and after the usual salutations the two white men mounted their horses and set out to return to their camp. Comstock always carried in his belt a beautiful white-handled revolver, and wore it on this occasion. This had often attracted the covetous eyes of the savages, and while in the village propositions to barter for it had been made by more than one of the warriors. Comstock invariably refused all offers to exchange it, no matter how tempting. Months before, when riding together at the head of the column, in pursuit of Indians, Comstock, who had observed that I carried a revolver closely resembling his, remarked that I ought to have the pair, and then laughingly added that he would carry his until we found the Indians, and after giving them a sound whipping he would present me the revolver. Frequently during the campaign, when on the march and while sitting around the evening camp fire, Comstock would refer to his promise concerning the revolver. After hunting Indians all summer, but never finding them just when we desired them, Comstock was not unfrequently joked upon the conditions under which he was to part with his revolver, and fears were expressed that if he carried it until we caught and whipped the Indians, he might be forced to go armed for a long time. None of us imagined then that the revolver which was so often the subject of jest, and of which Comstock was so proud, would be the pretext for his massacre.

Comstock and his companion rode out of the village in the direction of their own camp, totally unconscious of coming danger, and least of all from those whose guests they had just been. They had proceeded about a mile from the village when they observed about a dozen of the young warriors galloping after them. Still suspecting no unfriendly design, they continued their ride until joined by the young warriors. The entire party then rode in company until, as was afterward apparent, the Indians succeeded in separating the two white men, the one riding in front, the other, Comstock, following in rear, each with Indians riding on either side of them. At a preconcerted signal a combined attack was made by the savages upon the two white men. Both the latter attempted to defend themselves, but the odds and the suddenness of the attack deprived them of all hope of saving their lives. Comstock was fatally wounded at the first onslaught, and soon after was shot from his horse. His companion, being finely mounted, wisely intrusted his life to the speed of his horse, and soon outstripped his pursuers, and reached camp with but a few slight wounds. The Indians did not seem disposed to press him as closely as is their usual custom, but seemed only anxious to secure Comstock. He, after falling to the ground severely wounded, was completely riddled by steel-pointed arrows, and nis scalp taken. The principal trophy, however, in the opinion of the savages, was the beautifully finished revolver with its white ivory handle, and, as they afterward confessed when peace was proclaimed with their tribe, it was to obtain this revolver that the party of young warriors left the village and followed Comstock to his death. Thoroughly reliable in his reports, brave, modest, and persevering in character, with a remarkable knowledge of the country and the savage tribes infesting it, he was the superior of all men who were scouts by profession with whom I have had any experience.

While sitting in my quarters one day at Fort Leavenworth, late in the fall of 1867, a gentleman was announced whose name recalled a sad and harrowing sight. It proved to be the father of Lieutenant Kidder, whose massacre, with that of his entire party of eleven men, was described in preceding pages. It will be remembered that the savages had hacked, mangled, and burned the bodies of Kidder and his men to such an extent that it was impossible to recognize the body of a single one of the party; even the clothing had been removed, so that we could not distinguish the officer from his men, or the men from each other, by any fragment of their uniform or insignia of their grade. Mr. Kidder, after introducing himself, announced the object of his visit; it was to ascertain the spot where the remains of his son lay buried, and, after procuring suitable military escort to proceed to the grave and disinter his son's remains preparatory to transferring them to a resting place in Dakota, of which territory he was at that time one of the judiciary. It was a painful task I had to perform when I communicated to the father the details of the killing of his son and followers. And equally harassing to the feelings was it to have to inform him that there was no possible chance of his being able to recognize his son's remains. "Was there not the faintest mark or fragment of his uni-

WILL COMSTOCK AND HIS COMPANION PURSUED BY INDIANS.

form by which he might be known?" inquired the anxious parent. "Not one," was the reluctant reply. "And yet, since I now recall the appearance of the mangled and disfigured remains, there was a mere trifle which attracted my attention, but it could not have been your son who wore it." "What was it?" eagerly inquired the father. "It was simply the collar-band of one of those ordinary check overshirts so commonly worn on the plains, the color being black and white; the remainder of the garment, as well as all other articles of dress, having been torn or burned from the body." Mr. Kidder then requested me to repeat the description of the collar and material of which it was made; happily I had some cloth of very similar appearance, and upon exhibiting this to Mr. Kidder, to show the kind I meant, he declared that the body I referred to could be no other than that of his murdered son. He went on to tell how his son had received his appointment in the army but a few weeks before his lamentable death, he only having reported for duty with his company a few days before being sent on the scout which terminated his life; and how, before leaving his home to engage in the military service, his mother, with that thoughtful care and tenderness which only a mother can feel, prepared some articles of wearing apparel, among others a few shirts made from the checked material already described. Mr. Kidder had been to Fort Sedgwick on the Platte, from which post his son had last departed, and there learned that on leaving the post he wore one of the checked shirts and put an extra one in his saddle pockets. Upon this trifling link of evidence Mr. Kidder proceeded four hundred miles west to Fort Wallace, and there being furnished with military escort visited the grave containing the bodies of the twelve massacred men. Upon disinterring the remains a body was found as I had described it, bearing the simple checked collar-band; the father recognized the remains of his son, and thus, as was stated at the close of a preceding chapter, was the evidence of a mother's love made the means by which her son's body was recognized and reclaimed, when all other had failed.

The winter and spring of 1868 were uneventful, so far as Indian hostilities or the movements of troops were concerned. To be on the ground when its services could be made available in case the Indians became troublesome, the Seventh Cavalry left its winter quarters at Fort Leavenworth in April, and marched two hundred and ninety miles west to a point near the present site of Fort Hays, where the troops established their summer rendezvous in camp. It not being my privilege to serve with the regiment at that time, I remained at Fort Leavenworth some time longer, and later in the summer repaired to my home in Michigan, there amid the society of friends to enjoy the cool breezes of Erie until the time came which would require me to go west.

In the mean time, until I can relate some of the scenes which were enacted under my own eye, and which were afterwards the subject of excited and angry comment, as well as of emphatic and authoritative approval, it will not be uninteresting to examine into some of the causes which led to the memorable winter campaign of 1868–'69, including the battle of the Washita; and the reader may also be enabled to judge as to what causes the people of the frontier are most indebted for the comparatively peaceable condition of the savage tribes of the plains during the past three years. The question may also arise as to what influence the wild nomadic tribes of the West are most likely to yield and become peaceably inclined toward their white neighbors, willing to forego their accustomed raids and attacks upon the frontier settlements, and content to no longer oppose the advance of civilization. Whether this desirable condition

of affairs can be permanently and best secured by the display and exercise of
a strong but just military power, or by the extension of the olive-branch or
one hand and government annuities on the other, or by a happy combination
of both, has long been one of the difficult problems whose solution has baffled
the judgment of our legislators from the formation of the government to the
present time. My firm conviction, based upon an intimate and thorough analysis of the habits, traits of character, and natural instinct of the Indian, and
strengthened and supported by the almost unanimous opinion of all persons
who have made the Indian problem a study, and have studied it, not from a
distance, but in immediate contact with all the facts bearing thereupon, is that
the Indian cannot be elevated to that great level where he can be induced to
adopt any policy or mode of life varying from those to which he has ever been
accustomed by any method of teaching, argument, reasoning, or coaxing
which is not preceded and followed closely in reserve by a superior physical
force. In other words, the Indian is capable of recognizing no controlling
influence but that of stern arbitrary power. To assume that he can be guided
by appeals to his ideas of moral right and wrong, independent of threatening or
final compulsion, is to place him far above his more civilized brothers of the
white race, who, in the most advanced stage of refinement and morality, still
find it necessary to employ force, sometimes resort to war, to exact justice from
a neighboring nation. And yet there are those who argue that the Indian·
with all his lack of moral privileges, is so superior to the white race as to be
capable of being controlled in his savage traits and customs, and induced to
lead a proper life, simply by being politely requested to do so. The campaign
of 1868–'69, under the direction of General Sheridan, who had entire command
of the country infested by the five troublesome and warlike tribes, the Cheyennes,
Arapahoes, Kiowas, Comanches, and Apaches, was fruitful in valuable results.
At the same time the opponents of a war policy raised the cry that the military
were making war on friendly Indians; one writer, an Indian agent, even asserting that the troops had attacked and killed Indians half civilized, who had
fought on the side of the Government during the war with the Confederate
States. It was claimed by the adherents of the peace party that the Indians
above named had been guilty of no depredations against the whites, and had
done nothing deserving of the exercise of military power. I believe it is a
rule in evidence that a party coming into court is not expected to impeach
his own witnesses. I propose to show by the official statements of the officers
of the Indian Department, including some of those who were loudest and
most determined in their assertions of the innocence of the Indians after
prompt punishment had been administered by the military, that the Indian
tribes whose names have been given were individually and collectively guilty
of unprovoked and barbarous assaults on the settlers of the frontier; that they
committed these depredations at the very time they were receiving arms and
other presents from the Government; and that no provocation had been offered
either by the Government or the defenceless citizens of the border. In other
words, by those advocating the Indian side of the dispute it will be clearly
established that a solemn treaty had been reluctantly entered into between the
Indians and the Government, by which the demands of the Indians were complied with, and the conditions embraced in the treaty afterwards faithfully carried out on the part of the Government; and at the very time that the leading
chiefs and old men of the tribes were pledging themselves and their people
that "they will not attack any persons at home or travelling, or disturb any

property belonging to the people of the United States, or to persons friendly therewith," and that "they will never capture or carry off from the settlements women or children, and they will never kill or scalp white men or attempt to do them harm," the young men and warriors of these same tribes, embracing the sons of the most prominent chiefs and signers of the treaty, were actually engaged in devastating the settlements on the Kansas frontier, murdering men, women, and children, and driving off the stock. Now to the evidence. First glance at the following brief summary of the terms of the treaty which was ratified between the Government and the Cheyennes and Arapahoes on the 19th of August, 1868, and signed and agreed to by all the chiefs of these two tribes known or claiming to be prominent, and men of influence among their own people. As the terms of the treaty are almost identical with those contained in most of the treaties made with other tribes, excepting the limits and location of reservations, it will be interesting for purposes of reference.

First. Peace and friendship shall forever continue.

Second. Whites or Indians committing wrongs to be punished according to law.

Third. The following district of country, to wit, "commencing at the point where the Arkansas river crosses the 37th parallel of north latitude; thence west on said parallel—the said line being the southern boundary of the State of Kansas—to the Cimarron river (sometimes called the Red fork of the Arkansas river); thence down said Cimarron river, in the middle of the main channel thereof, to the Arkansas river; thence up the Arkansas river in the middle of the main channel thereof to the place of beginning, is set apart for the Cheyenne and Arapahoe Indians."

Fourth. The said Indians shall have the right to hunt on the unoccupied lands of the United States so long as game may be found thereon, and so long as peace subsists among the whites and Indians on the border of the hunting districts.

Fifth. Is a provision for the selection and occupation of lands for those of said Indians who desire to commence farming on said reserve, and for expenditures for their benefit.

Sixth. The United States further provides for an annual distribution of clothing for a term of years.

The treaty with the Kiowa, Comanche, and Apache tribes, ratified August 25, 1868, embraced substantially the same provisions as those just quoted, excepting that relating to their reservation, which was as follows: "Commencing at a point where the Washita river crosses the 98th meridian west from Greenwich, thence up the Washita river, in the middle of the main channel thereof, to a point thirty miles west of Fort Cobb, as now established; thence due west to the north fork of Red river, provided said line strikes said river east of the 100th meridian of west longitude; if not, then only to said meridian line, and thence south on said meridian line to the said north fork of Red river thence down said north fork, in the middle of the main channel thereof, from the point where it may be first intersected by the lines above described, to the main Red river; thence down said river, in the main channel thereof, to its intersection with the 98th meridian of longitude west from Greenwich; thence north on said meridian line to the place of beginning."

To those who propose to follow the movements of the troops during the winter campaign of 1868–'69, it will be well to bear in mind the limits of the last named reservation, as the charge was made by the Indian agent that the military had attacked the Indians when the latter were peacefully located within the limits of their reservation.

To show that the Government through its civil agents was doing everything required of it to satisfy the Indians, and that the agent of the Cheyennes and Arapahoes was firmly of the opinion that every promise of the Government had not only been faithfully carried out, but that the Indians themselves had no complaint to make, the following letter from the agent to the Superintendent of Indian Affairs is submitted:

> FORT LARNED, KANSAS, August 10, 1868.
>
> SIR: I have the honor to inform you that I yesterday made the whole issue of annuity goods, arms, and ammunition to the Cheyenne chiefs [the Arapahoes and Apaches had received their portion in July. G. A. C.] and people of their nation; they were delighted at receiving the goods, particularly the arms and ammunition, and never before have I known them to be better satisfied and express themselves as being so well contented previous to the issue. I made them a long speech, following your late instructions with reference to what I said to them. They have now left for their hunting-grounds, and *I am perfectly satisfied that there will be no trouble with them this season, and consequently with no Indians of my agency.*
>
> I have the honor to be, with much respect, your obedient servant,
>
> E. W. WYNKOOP, United States Indian Agent.
>
> Hon. THOMAS MURPHY, Superintendent Indian Affairs.

The italics are mine, but I desire to invite attention to the confidence and strong reliance placed in these Indians by a man who was intimately associated with them, interested in their welfare, and supposed to be able to speak authoritatively as to their character and intentions. If they could deceive him, it is not surprising that other equally well-meaning persons further east should be equally misled. The above letter is dated August 10, 1868. The following extract is from a letter written by the same party and to the Superintendent of Indian Affairs, dated at same place on the 10th of September, 1868, exactly one month after his positive declaration that the Cheyennes " were perfectly satisfied, and there will be no trouble with them this season."

Here is the extract referred to: " Subsequently I received permission from the Department to issue to them their arms and ammunition, which I accordingly did. But a short time before the issue was made a war party had started north from the Cheyenne village, on the war path against the Pawnees; and they, not knowing of the issue and smarting under their *supposed* wrongs, committed the outrages on the Saline river which have led to the present unfortunate aspect of affairs. The United States troops are now south of the Arkansas river in hot pursuit of the Cheyennes, the effect of which I think will be to plunge other tribes into difficulty and finally culminate in a general Indian war." It will be observed that no justification is offered for the guilty Indians except that had they been aware of the wise and beneficent intention of the Government to issue them a fresh supply of arms, they might have delayed their murderous raid against the defenceless settlers until after the issue. Fears are also expressed that other tribes may be plunged into difficulty, but by the same witness and others it is easily established that the other tribes referred to were represented prominently in the war party which had devastated the settlements on the Saline. First I will submit an extract of a letter dated Fort Larned, August 1, 1868, from Thomas Murphy, Superintendent of Indian Affairs, to the Hon. N. G. Taylor, Commissioner of Indian Affairs, Washington, D. C.:

> SIR: I have the honor to inform you that I held a council to-day with the Arapahoes and Apache Indians, at which I explained to them why their arms and ammunition had been with

UNDER GOVERNMENT PROTECTION.

neld; that the white settlers were now well armed and determined that no more raids should be made through their country by large bodies of Indians; and that while the whites were friendly and well disposed toward the Indians, yet if the Indians attempted another raid such as they recently made on the Kaw reservation, I feared themselves and the whites would have a fight, and that it would bring on war.

The head chief of the Arapahoes, Little Raven, replied " that no more trips would be made by his people into the settlements: that their hearts were good toward the whites, and they wished to remain at peace with them." I told him I would now give them their arms and ammunition; that I hoped they would use them for the sole purpose of securing food for themselves and families, and that in no case would I ever hear of their using these arms against their white brethren. Little Raven and the other chiefs then promised that these arms should never be used against the whites, and Agent Wynkoop then delivered to the Arapahoes one hundred pistols, eighty Lancaster rifles, twelve kegs of powder, one and one-half kegs of lead, and fifteen thousand caps; and to the Apaches he gave forty pistols, twenty Lancaster rifles, three kegs of powder, one-half keg of lead, and five thousand caps, for which they seemed much pleased. . . . I would have remained here to see the Cheyennes did I deem it important to do so. From what I can learn there will be no trouble whatever with them. They will come here, get their ammunition and leave immediately to hunt buffalo. They are well and peacefully disposed toward the whites, and, unless some unlooked-for event should transpire to change their present feelings, they will keep their treaty pledges.

This certainly reads well, and at Washington or further east would be regarded as a favorable indication of the desire for peace on the part of the Indians. The reader is asked to remember that the foregoing letters and extracts are from professed friends of the Indian and advocates of what is known as the peace policy. The letter of Superintendent Murphy was written the day of council, August 1. Mark his words of advice to Little Raven as to how the arms were to be used, and note Little Raven's reply containing his strong promises of maintaining friendly relations with the whites. Yet the second night following the issue of arms, a combined war party of Cheyennes and Arapahoes, numbering over two hundred warriors, almost the exact number of pistols issued at the council, left the Indian village to inaugurate a bloody raid in the Kansas settlements; and among the Arapahoes was the son of Little Raven. By reading the speech made by this chief in the council referred to by Mr. Murphy, a marked resemblance will be detected to the stereotyped responses delivered by Indian chiefs visiting the authorities at Washington, or when imposing upon the credulous and kind-hearted people who assemble at Cooper Institute periodically to listen to these untutored orators of the plains. The statements and promises uttered in the one instance are fully as reliable as those listened to so breathlessly in the others. Regarding the raid made by the Cheyennes and Arapahoes, it will be considered sufficient perhaps when I base my statements upon the following " Report of an interview between Colonel E. W. Wynkoop, United States Indian Agent, and Little Rock, a Cheyenne chief, held at Fort Larned, Kansas, August 19, 1868, in the presence of Lieutenant S. M. Robbins, Seventh United States Cavalry, John S. Smith, United States interpreter, and James Morrison, scout for Indian agency."

Question by Colonel Wynkoop: " Six nights ago I spoke to you in regard to depredations committed on the Saline. I told you to go and find out by whom these depredations were committed and to bring me straight news. What news do you bring?"

Little Rock: " I took your advice and went there. I am now here to tell you all I know. This war party of Cheyennes which left the camp of these tribes above the forks of Walnut creek about the 2d or 3d of August, went out against the Pawnees, crossed the Smoky Hill about Fort Hays, and thence proceeded to the Saline, where there were ten lodges of Sioux in the Cheyenne camp when this war party left, and about twenty men of them and four Ara-

10

pahoes accompanied the party. The Cheyennes numbered about two hun dred; nearly all the young men in the village went; *Little Raven's son was one of the four Arapahoes.* When the party reached the Saline they turned down the stream, with the exception of twenty, who, being fearful of de predations being committed against the whites by the party going in the direction of the settlements, kept on north toward the Pawnees. The main party continued down the Saline until they came in sight of the settlement; they then camped there. A Cheyenne named Oh-e-ah-mo-he-a, a brother of White Antelope, who was killed at Sand Creek, and another named Red Nose, proceeded to the first house; they afterwards returned to the camp and with them a woman captive. The main party was surprised at this ac- tion, and forcibly took possession of her, and returned her to her house. The two Indians had outraged the woman before they brought her to the camp. After the outrage had been committed, the parties left the Saline and went north toward the settlement of the south fork of the Solomon, *where they were kindly received and fed by the white people.* They left the settlements on the south fork and proceeded toward the settlements on the north fork. When in sight of these settlements, they came upon a body of armed settlers, who fired upon them; they avoided the party, went around them, and approached a house some distance off. In the vicinity of the house they came upon a white man alone upon the prairie. Big Head's son * rode at him and knocked him down with a club. The Indian who had committed the outrage upon the white woman, known as White Antelope's brother, then fired upon the white man without effect, while the third Indian rode up and killed him. Soon after they killed a white man, and, close by, a woman—all in the same settlement. At the time these people were killed, the party was divided in feeling, the ma- jority being opposed to any outrages being committed; but finding it useless to contend against these outrages being committed without bringing on a strife among themselves, they gave way and all went in together. They then went to another house in the same settlement, and there killed two men and took two little girls prisoners; this on the same day. After committing this last outrage the party turned south toward the Saline, where they came upon a body of mounted troops; the troops immediately charged the Indians, and the pursuit was continued a long time. The Indians having the two chil- dren, their horses becoming fatigued, dropped the children without hurting them. Soon after the children were dropped the pursuit ceased; but the In- dians continued on up the Saline. A portion of the Indians afterward re- turned to look for the children, but they were unable to find them. After they had proceeded some distance up the Saline, the party divided, the majority going north toward the settlements on the Solomon, but thirty of them started toward their village, supposed to be some-distance northwest of Fort Larned. *Another small party returned to Black Kettle's village,* from which party I got this information.† I am fearful that before this time the party that started north had committed a great many depredations."

Question by Colonel Wynkoop: "Do you know the names of the principal men of this party that committed the depredations, besides White Antelope's brother?"

---

* Afterward captured by my command and killed in a difficulty with the guard at Fort Hays, Kansas, in the summer of 1869.

† Little Rock was a chief of Black Kettle's band of Cheyennes, and second in rank to Black Kettle.

RED NOSE CAPTURES A WOMAN.

Answer by Little Rock: "There were Medicine Arrow's oldest son, named Tall Wolf; Red Nose, who was one of the men who outraged the woman, Big Head's son named Porcupine Bear; and Sand Hill's brother, known as the Bear that Goes Ahead."

Question by Colonel Wynkoop: "You told me your nation wants peace; will you, in accordance with your treaty stipulations, deliver up the men whom you have named as being the leaders of the party who committed the outrages named?"

Answer by Little Rock: "I think that the only men who ought to suffer and be responsible for these outrages are White Antelope's brother and Red Nose, the men who ravished the woman; and when I return to the Cheyenne camp and assemble the chiefs and head men, I think those two men will be delivered up to you."

Question by Colonel Wynkoop: "I consider the whole party guilty; but it being impossible to punish all of them, I hold the principal men, whom you mentioned, responsible for all. They had no right to be led and governed by two men. If no depredations had been committed after the outrage on the woman, the two men whom you have mentioned alone would have been guilty."

Answer by Little Rock: "After your explanation, I think your demand for the men is right. I am willing to deliver them up, and will go back to the tribe and use my best endeavors to have them surrendered. I am but one man, and cannot answer for the entire nation."

Other questions and answers of similar import followed.

The terms of the interview between Colonel Wynkoop and Little Rock were carefully noted down and transmitted regularly to his next superior officer, Superintendent Murphy, who but a few days previous, and within the same month, had officially reported to the Indian Commissioner at Washington that peace and good will reigned undisturbed between the Indians under his charge and the whites. Even he, with his strong leaning toward the adoption of morbid measures of a peaceful character, and his disinclination to believe the Indians could meditate evil toward their white neighbors, was forced, as his next letter shows, to alter his views.

OFFICE SUPERINTENDENT INDIAN AFFAIRS, ATCHISON, KANSAS, August 22, 1868.

SIR : I have the honor herewith to transmit a letter of the 19th inst. from Agent Wynkoop, enclosing report of a talk which he had with Little Rock, a Cheyenne chief, whom he had sent to ascertain the facts relative to the recent troubles on the Solomon and Saline rivers, in this State. The agent's letter and report are full, and explain themselves. I fully concur in the views expressed by the agent that the innocent Indians, who are trying to keep, in good faith, their treaty pledges, be protected in the manner indicated by him, while I earnestly recommend that the Indians who have committed these gross outrages be turned over to the military, and that they be severely punished. When I reflect that at the very time these Indians were making such loud professions of friendship at Larned, receiving their annuities, etc., they were then contemplating and planning this campaign, I can no longer have confidence in what they say or promise. War is surely upon us, and in view of the importance of the case, I earnestly recommend that Agent Wynkoop be furnished promptly with the views of the Department, and that full instructions be given him for his future action.

Very respectfully, your obedient servant,

(Signed) THOMAS MURPHY, Superintendent Indian Affairs.
Hon. C. E. MIX, Acting Commissioner of Indian Affairs, Washington, D. C.

What were the recommendations of Agent Wynkoop referred to in Mr. Murphy's letter? They were as follows: "Let me take those Indians whom I know to be guiltless and desirous of remaining at peace, and locate them with their lodges and families at some good place that I may select in the vicinity of this post (Larned); and let those Indians be entirely subsisted by the Government until this trouble is over, and be kept within certain bounds; and let me be furnished with a small battalion of United States troops, for the purpose of protecting them from their own people, and from being forced by them into war; let those who refuse to respond to my call and come within the bounds prescribed, be considered at war, and let them be properly punished. By this means, if war takes place—which I consider inevitable—we can be able to discriminate between those who deserve punishment and those who do not; otherwise it will be a matter of impossibility."

This proposition seems, from its wording, to be not only a feasible one, but based on principles of justice to all concerned, and no doubt would be so interpreted by the theorizers on the Indian question who study its merits from afar. Before acting upon Colonel Wynkoop's plan, it was in the regular order referred to General Sherman, at that time commanding the Military Division of the Missouri, in which the Indians referred to were located. His indorsement in reply briefly disposed of the proposition by exposing its absurdity:

HEADQUARTERS MILITARY DIVISION OF THE MISSOURI, ST. LOUIS, MISSOURI, }
September 19, 1868. }

I now regard the Cheyennes and Arapahoes at war, and that it will be impossible for our troops to discriminate between the well-disposed and the warlike parts of these bands, unless an absolute separation be made. I prefer that the agents collect all of the former and conduct them to their reservation within the Indian territory south of Kansas, there to be provided for under their supervision, say about old Fort Cobb. I cannot consent to their being collected and held near Fort Larned. So long as Agent Wynkoop remains at Fort Larned the vagabond part of the Indians will cluster about him for support, and to beg of the military. The vital part of these tribes are committing murders and robberies from Kansas to Colorado, and it is an excess of generosity on our part to be feeding and supplying the old, young, and feeble, while their young men are at war.

I do not pretend to say what should be done with these, but it will simplify our game of war, already complicated enough, by removing them well away from our field of operations.

I have the honor to be, your obedient servant,

(Signed)   W. T. SHERMAN, Lieutenant-General, commanding.

Again, on the 26th of the same month, General Sherman, in a letter to General Schofield, then Secretary of War, writes: "The annuity goods for these Indians, Kiowas and Comanches, should be sent to Fort Cobb, and the Indian agent for these Indians should go there at once. And if the Secretary of the Interior has any contingent fund out of which he could provide food, or if he could use a part of the regular appropriation for food instead of clothing, it may keep these Indians from joining the hostile Cheyennes and Arapahoes. The latter should receive nothing, and now that they are at war, I propose to give them enough of it to satisfy them to their hearts' content, and General Sheridan will not relax his efforts till the winter will put them at our mercy. He reports that he can already account for about seventy dead Indians, and his forces are right in among these hostile Indians on the Upper Republican, and on the head of the Canadian south of Fort Dodge."

Still another letter from General Sherman to the Secretary of War argues the case as follows: "All the Cheyennes and Arapahoes are now at war. Admitting that some of them have not done acts of murder, rape, etc., still they have not restrained those who have, nor have they on demand given up the criminals as they agreed to do. The treaty made at Medicine Lodge is, therefore, already broken by them, and the War Department should ask the concurrence of the Indian Department, or invoke the superior orders of the President against any goods whatever, even clothing, going to any part of the tribes named, until this matter is settled. As military commander I have the right, unless restrained by superior orders, to prevent the issue of any goods whatever to Indians outside of these reservations; and if the agency for the Cheyennes and Arapahoes be established at or near old Fort Cobb, the agent should if possible be able to provide for and feed such as may go there of their own volition, or who may be driven there by our military movements. . . . I have despatched General Hazen to the frontier, with a limited amount of money wherewith to aid the said agents to provide for the peaceful parts of those tribes this winter, while en route to and after their arrival at their new homes No better time could be possibly chosen than the present for destroying or humiliating those bands that have so outrageously violated their treaties and begun a devastating war without one particle of provocation; and after a reasonable time given for the innocent to withdraw, I will solicit an order from the President declaring all Indians who remain outside of their lawful reservations to be outlaws, and commanding all people, soldiers and citizens, to proceed against them as such. We have never heretofore been in a condition to adopt this course, because until now we could not clearly point out to these Indians where they may rightfully go to escape the consequences of the hostile acts of their fellows. The right to hunt buffaloes, secured by the treaties, could also be regulated so as to require all parties desiring to hunt to procure from the agent a permit, which permit should be indorsed by the commanding officer of the nearest military post; but I think, the treaty having been clearly violated by the Indians themselves, this hunting right is entirely lost to them, if we so declare it."

The foregoing extracts from letters and official correspondence which passed between high dignitaries of the Government, who were supposed not only to be thoroughly conversant with Indian affairs, but to represent the civil and military phase of the question, will, when read in connection with the statements of the superintendent and agent of the Indians, and that of the chief, Little Rock, give the reader some idea of the origin and character of the difficulties between the whites and Indians in the summer and fall of 1868. The tabulated list of depredations by Indians, accompanying the chapter descriptive of General Forsyth's campaign, will give more extended information in a condensed form.

While Forsyth was moving his detachment of scouts through the valleys of the Republican, in the northwestern portion of Kansas, General Sheridan had also arranged to have a well-equipped force operating south of the Arkansas river, and in this way to cause the two favorite haunts of the Indians to be overrun simultaneously, and thus prevent them when driven from one haunt from fleeing in safety and unmolested to another. The expedition intended to operate south of the Arkansas was composed of the principal portion of the Seventh Cavalry and a few companies of the Third Regular Infantry, the entire force under command of Brigadier-General Alfred Sully, an officer of long experience among the Indians, and one who had in times gone by achieved no little distinction as an Indian fighter, and at a later date became a partial advocate of the adoption of the peace policy. General Sully's expedition, after being thoroughly equipped and supplied, under his personal supervision, with everything needful in a campaign such as was about to be undertaken, crossed the Arkansas river about the 1st of September, at Fort Dodge, and marching a little west of south struck the Cimarron river, where they first encountered

Indians. From the Cimarron the troops moved in a southeasterly direction, one day's march to Beaver creek, the savages opposing and fighting them during the entire day. That night the Indians came close enough to fire into the camp, an unusual proceeding in Indian warfare, as they rarely molest troops during the hours of night. The next day General Sully directed his march down the valley of the Beaver; but just as his troops were breaking camp, the long wagon train having already "pulled out," and the rear guard of the troops having barely got into their saddles, a party of between two and three hundred warriors, who had evidently in some inexplicable manner contrived to conceal their approach until the proper moment, dashed into the deserted camp within a few yards of the rear of the troops, and succeeded in cutting off a few led horses and two of the cavalrymen who, as is so often the case, had lingered a moment behind the column. General Sully and staff were at that moment near the head of the column, a mile or more from camp. The General, as was his custom on the march, being comfortably stowed away in his ambulance, of course it was impossible that he or his staff, from their great distance from the scene of actual attack, could give the necessary orders in the case.

Fortunately, the acting adjutant of the cavalry, Brevet Captain A. E. Smith, was riding at the rear of the column and witnessed the attack of the Indians. Captain Hamilton of the cavalry was also present in command of the rear guard. Wheeling his guard to the right about, he at once prepared to charge the Indians and to attempt the rescue of the two troopers who were being carried off as prisoners before his very eyes. At the same time Captain Smith, as representative of the commanding officer of the cavalry, promptly took the responsibility of directing a squadron of cavalry to wheel out of column and advance in support of Captain Hamilton's guard. With this hastily formed detachment, the Indians, still within pistol range, but moving off with their prisoners, were gallantly charged and so closely pressed that they were forced to relinquish possession of one of their prisoners, but not before shooting him through the body and leaving him on the ground, as they supposed, mortally wounded. The troops continued to charge the retreating Indians, upon whom they were gaining, determined if possible to effect the rescue of their remaining comrade. They were advancing down one slope while the Indians just across a ravine were endeavoring to escape with their prisoner up the opposite ascent, when a peremptory order reached the officers commanding the pursuing force to withdraw their men and reform the column at once. Delaying only long enough for an ambulance to arrive from the train in which to transport their wounded comrade, the order was obeyed. Upon rejoining the column the two officers named were summoned before the officer commanding their regiment, and, after a second-hand reprimand, were ordered in arrest and their sabres taken from them, for leaving the column without orders—the attempted and half successful rescue of their comrades and the repulse of the Indians to the contrary notwithstanding. Fortunately wiser and better-natured counsels prevailed in a few hours, and their regimental commander was authorized to release these two officers from their brief durance, their sabres were restored to them, and they became, as they deserved, the recipients of numerous complimentary expressions from their brother officers. The terrible fate awaiting the unfortunate trooper carried off by the Indians spread a deep gloom throughout the command. All were too familiar with the horrid customs of the savages to hope for a moment that the captive would be reserved for aught but a slow lingering death, from torture the most horrible and painful which savage, bloodthirsty minds could suggest. Such was in truth his sad fate, as we learned afterwards when peace (?) was established with the tribes then engaged in war. Never shall I forget the consummate coolness and particularity of detail with which some of the Indians engaged in the affair related to myself and party the exact process by which the captured trooper was tortured to death; how he was tied to a stake, strips of flesh cut from his body, arms, and legs, burning brands thrust into the bleeding wounds, the nose, lips, and ears cut off, and finally, when from loss of blood, excessive pain, and anguish, the poor, bleeding, almost senseless mortal fell to the ground exhausted, the younger Indians were permitted to rush in and despatch him with their knives.

The expedition proceeded on down the valley of Beaver creek, the Indians contesting every step of the way. In the afternoon, about three o'clock, the troops arrived at a ridge of sand-hills, a few miles southeast of the present site of "Camp Supply," where quite a determined engagement took place with the savages, the three tribes, Cheyennes, Arapahoes and Kiowas, being the assailants. The Indians seemed to have reserved their strongest efforts until the troops and train had advanced well into the sand-hills, when a most obstinate and well-conducted resistance was offered to the further advance of the troops It was evident to many of the officers, and no doubt to the men, that the troops were probably nearing the location of the Indian villages, and that this last display of opposition to their further advance was to save the villages. The character of the country immediately about the troops was not favorable to the operations of cavalry; the surface of the rolling plain was cut up by irregular and closely located sand-hills, too steep and sandy to allow cavalry to move with freedom, yet capable of being easily cleared of savages by troops fighting on foot. The Indians took post on the hill-tops and began a harassing fire on the troops and train. Had the infantry been unloaded from the wagons promptly, instead of adding to the great weight, sinking the wheels sometimes almost in to the axles, and had they, with the assistance of a few of the dismounted cavalry, been deployed on both sides of the train, the latter could have been safely conducted through what was then decided to be impassable sand-hills, but which were a short time afterward proved to be perfectly practicable. And once beyond the range of sand-hills but a short distance, the villages of the attacking warriors would have been found exposed to an easy and important capture, probably terminating the campaign by compelling a satisfactory peace. Captain Yates, with his single troop of cavalry, was ordered forward to drive the Indians away. This was a proceeding which did not seem to meet with favor from the savages. Captain Yates could drive them wherever he encountered them, but it was only to cause the redskins to appear in increased numbers at some other threatened point. After contending in this non-effective manner for a couple of hours, the impression arose in the minds of some that the train could not be conducted through the sand-hills in the face of the strong opposition offered by the Indians. The order was issued to turn about and withdraw. This order was executed, and the troop and train, followed by the exultant Indians, retired a few miles to the Beaver, and encamped for the night on the ground now known as "Camp Supply."

Captain Yates had caused to be brought off the field, when his troop was ordered to retire, the body of one of his men who had been slain in the fight by the Indians. As the troops were to continue their backward movement next day, and it was impossible to transport the dead body further, Captain

Yates ordered preparations made for interring it in camp that night; but knowing that the Indians would thoroughly search the deserted camp-ground almost before the troops should get out of sight, and would be quick with their watchful eyes to detect a grave, and if successful in discovering it would unearth the body in order to obtain the scalp, directions were given to prepare the grave after nightfall, and the spot selected would have baffled the eye of any one but that of an Indian. The grave was dug under the picket line to which the seventy or eighty horses of the troops would be tethered during the night, so that their constant tramping and pawing should completely cover up and obliterate all traces of the grave containing the body of the dead trooper. The following morning even those who had performed the sad rites of burial to their fallen comrade could scarcely have been able to indicate the exact location of the grave. Yet when we returned to that point a few weeks afterward it was discovered that the wily savages had found the grave, unearthed the body, and removed the scalp of their victim, on the day following the interment.

Early on the morning succeeding the fight in the sand-hills General Sully resumed his march toward Fort Dodge, the Indians following and harassing the movements of the troops until about two o'clock in the afternoon, when, apparently satisfied with their success in forcing the expedition back, thus relieving their villages and themselves from the danger which had threatened them, they fired their parting shots and rode off in triumph. That night the troops camped on Bluff creek, from which point General Sully proceeded to Fort Dodge, on the Arkansas, leaving the main portion of the command in camp on Bluff creek, where we shall see them again.

XII.

IN a late chapter I promised to submit testimony from those high in authority, now the highest, showing that among those who had given the subject the most thoughtful attention, the opinion was unanimous in favor of the
"abolition of the civil Indian agents and licensed traders," and the transfer of
the Indian Bureau back to the War Department, where it originally belonged.
The question as to which cabinet minister, the Secretary of War or the
Secretary of the Interior, should retain control of the bureau regulating Indian affairs, has long been and still is one of unending discussion, and is of far
more importance to the country than the casual observer might imagine. The
army as a unit, and from motives of peace and justice, favors giving this control to the Secretary of War. Opposed to this view is a large, powerful, and
at times unscrupulous party, many of whose strongest adherents are dependent upon the fraudulent practices and profits of which the Indian is the victim
for the acquirement of dishonest wealth—practices and profits which only exist so long as the Indian Bureau is under the supervision of the Interior Department. The reasons in favor of the War Department having the control of the
government of the Indians exist at all times. But the struggle for this control seems to make its appearance, like an epidemic, at certain periods, and for
a brief time will attract considerable comment and discussion both in and out
of Congress, then disappear from public view. To a candid, impartial mind I
believe the reasons why the Indians should be controlled by the Department
of War, the department which must assume the reins of power when any real
control is exercised, are convincing. It may be asked, Then why, if the reasons are so convincing, are not proper representations made to the authorities
at Washington and the transfer secured? This inquiry seems natural enough.
But the explanation is sufficiently simple. The army officers, particularly
those stationed on the frontier, have but little opportunity, even had they the
desire, to submit their views or recommendations to Congress as a body or to
members individually. When impressed with ideas whose adoption is deemed
essential to the Government, the usual and recognized mode of presenting
them for consideration is by written communications forwarded through the
intermediate and superior commanders until laid before the Secretary of War,
by whom, if considered sufficiently important, they are submitted to the President, and by him to Congress. Having made this recommendation and furnished the Department with his reasons therefor, an officer considers that he
has discharged his duty in the premises, and the responsibility of the adoption
or rejection of his ideas then rests with a superior power. Beyond the con-
scientious discharge of his duty he has no interest, certainly none of a pecuniary nature, to serve. In the periodical contests which prevail between
the military and civil aspirants for the control of the Indian Bureau, the military content themselves as above stated with a brief and unbiassed presenta-
tion of their views, and having submitted their argument to the proper tribu-
nal, no further steps are taken to influence the decision. Not so with those
advocating the claims of the civil agents and traders to public recognition.
The preponderance of testimony and the best of the argument rest with the
military. But there are many ways of illustrating that the battle is not always

155

to the strong nor the race to the swift. The ways of Congress are sometimes peculiar—not to employ a more expressive term.

Under the Constitution of the United States there are but two houses of Congress, the Senate and the House of Representatives, and most people residing within the jurisdiction of its laws suppose this to be the extent of the legislative body; but to those acquainted with the internal working of that important branch of the Government, there is still a third house of Congress, better known as the lobby. True, its existence is neither provided for nor recognized by law; yet it exists nevertheless, and so powerful, although somewhat hidden, is its influence upon the other branches of Congress, that almost any measure it is interested in becomes a law. It is somewhat remarkable that those measures which are plainly intended to promote the public interests are seldom agitated or advocated in the third house, while those measures of doubtful propriety or honesty usually secure the almost undivided support of the lobby. There are few prominent questions connected with the feeble policy of the Government which can and do assemble so powerful and determined a lobby as a proposed interference with the system of civilian superintendents, agents, and traders for the Indians. Let but some member of Congress propose to inquire into the workings of the management of the Indians, or propose a transfer of the bureau to the War Department, and the leaders of the combination opposed raise a cry which is as effective in rallying their supporters as was the signal of Roderick Dhu. From almost every State and territory the retainers of the bureau flock to the national capital. Why this rallying of the clans? Is there any principle involved? With the few, yes; with the many, no. Then what is the mighty influence which brings together this hungry host? Why this determined opposition to any interference with the management of the Indians? I remember making this inquiry years ago, and the answer then, which is equally applicable now, was: "There is too much money in the Indian question to allow it to pass into other hands." This I believe to be the true solution of our difficulties with the Indians at the present day. It seems almost incredible that a policy which is claimed and represented to be based on sympathy for the red man and a desire to secure to him his rights, is shaped in reality and manipulated behind the scenes with the distinct and sole object of reaping a rich harvest by plundering both the Government and the Indians. To do away with the vast army of agents, traders, and civilian employees which is a necessary appendage of the civilian policy, would be to deprive many members of Congress of a vast deal of patronage which they now enjoy. There are few, if any, more comfortable or desirable places of disposing of a friend who has rendered valuable political service or electioneering aid, than to secure for him the appointment of Indian agent. The salary of an agent is comparatively small. Men without means, however, eagerly accept the position; and in a few years, at furthest, they almost invariably retire in wealth. Who ever heard of a retired Indian agent or trader in limited circumstances? How do they realize fortunes upon so small a salary? In the disposition of the annuities provided for the Indians by the Government, the agent is usually the distributing medium. Between himself and the Indian there is no system of accountability, no vouchers given or received, no books kept, in fact no record except the statement which the agent chooses to forward to his superintendent.

The Indian has no means of knowing how much in value or how many presents of any particular kind the Government, the "Great Father" as he

INDIAN POST TRADER.

terms it, has sent him. For knowledge on this point he must accept the statement of the agent. The goods sent by the Government are generally those which would most please an Indian's fancy. The Indian trader usually keeps goods of a similar character. The trader is most frequently a particular friend of the agent, often associated with him in business, and in many instances holds his position of trader at the instance of the agent. They are always located near each other. The trader is usually present at the distribution of annuities. If the agent, instead of distributing to the Indians all of the goods intended for them by the Government, only distributes one half and retains the other half, who is to be the wiser? Not the Indian, defrauded though he may be, for he is ignorant of how much is coming to him. The word of the agent is his only guide. He may complain a little, express some disappointment at the limited amount of presents, and intimate that the "Great Father" has dealt out the annuities with a sparing hand; but the agent explains it by referring to some depredations which he knows the tribe to have been guilty of in times past; or if he is not aware of any particular instance of guilt, he charges them generally with having committed such acts, knowing one can scarcely go amiss in accusing a tribe of occasionally slaying a white man, and ends up his charge by informing them that the "Great Father," learning of these little irregularities in their conduct and being pained greatly thereat, felt compelled to reduce their allowance of blankets, sugar, coffee, etc., when at the same time the missing portion of said allowance is safely secured in the storehouse of the agent near by. Well, but how can he enrich himself in this manner? it may be asked. By simply, and unseen by the Indians, transferring the unissued portion of the annuities from his government storehouse to the trading establishment of his friend the trader. There the boxes are unpacked and their contents spread out for barter with the Indians. The latter, in gratifying their wants, are forced to purchase from the trader at prices which are scores of times the value of the article offered. I have seen Indians dispose of buffalo robes to traders, which were worth from fifteen to twenty dollars each, and get in return only ten to twenty cups of brown sugar, the entire value of which did not exceed two or three dollars. This is one of the many ways agents and traders have of amassing sudden wealth. I have known the head chiefs of a tribe to rise in a council in the presence of other chiefs and of officers of the army, and accuse his agent, then present, of these or similar dishonest practices. Is it to be wondered at that the position of agent or trader among the Indians is greatly sought after by men determined to become rich, but not particular as to the manner of doing so? Or is it to be wondered at that army officers, who are often made aware of the injustice done the Indian yet are powerless to prevent it, and who trace many of our difficulties with the Indians to these causes, should urge the abolishment of a system which has proven itself so fruitful in fraud and dishonest dealing toward those whose interests it should be their duty to protect?

In offering the testimony which follows, and which to those at all interested in the subject of our dealings with the Indian must have no little weight, I have given that of men whose interest in the matter could only spring from experience and a supposed thorough knowledge of the Indian character, and a desire to do justice to him as well as to the Government. At the present writing a heavy cloud portending a general Indian war along our entire frontier, from the British possessions on the north to the Mexican border on the south, hangs threateningly over us. Whether it will really result in war or in isolated acts of barbarity remains to be seen. But enough is known to prove that the day has not yet arrived when the lawless savage of the plains is prepared or willing to abandon his favorite pastime of war and depredation upon the defenceless frontier, and instead to settle quietly down and study the arts and callings of a quiet and peaceful life. It is impossible for the Indian to comprehend the force of any law or regulation which is not backed up by a power sufficiently strong to compel its observance. This is not surprising, as a large proportion of their white brethren are equally obtuse. Lieutenant-General Sheridan showed his thorough appreciation of the Indian character, in an endorsement recently written by him upon a complaint relating to Indian depredations, forwarded from one of his subordinates to the War Department. General Sheridan writes, "We can never stop the wild Indians from murdering and stealing until we punish them. If a white man in this country commits a murder, we hang him; if he steals a horse, we put him in the penitentiary. If an Indian commits these crimes, we give him better fare and more blankets. I think I may say with reason, that under this policy the civilization of the wild red man will progress slowly."

As might naturally be expected, a massacre like that at Fort Phil Kearny, in which ninety-one enlisted men and three officers were slain outright, and no one left to tell the tale, excited discussion and comment throughout the land, and raised inquiry as to who was responsible for this lamentable affair. The military laid the blame at the door of the Indian Bureau with its host of civil agents and traders, and accused the latter of supplying the Indians with the arms and ammunition which were afterward turned against the whites. The supporters of the Indian Bureau not only did not deny the accusation, but went so far as to claim that all our difficulties with the Indians could be traced to the fact that the military commanders, particularly Generals Hancock and Cooke, had forbidden the traders from furnishing the Indians with arms and ammunition. This was the official statement of the Commissioner of Indian Affairs in the spring of 1867. It was rather a queer complaint upon which to justify a war that, because the Government would not furnish the savages with implements for murdering its subjects in approved modern method, these same savages would therefore be reluctantly forced to murder and scalp such settlers and travellers as fell in their paths, in the old-fashioned tomahawk, bow and arrow style. The Commissioner of Indian Affairs, in his report to the Secretary of the Interior in the spring of 1867, labored hard to find a justification for the Indians in their recent outbreak at Fort Phil Kearny. The withholding of arms and ammunition from the Indians seemed to be the principal grievance. As the views of the Commissioner find many supporters in quarters remote from the scene of Indian depredations, and among persons who still cling to the traditional Indian, as wrought by the pen of Cooper, as their ideal red man, I quote the Commissioner's words: "An order issued by General Cooke at Omaha on the 31st of July last, in relation to arms and ammunition, has had a very bad effect. I am satisfied that such orders are not only unwise but really cruel, and therefore calculated to produce the very worst effect. Indians are men, and when hungry will like others resort to any means to obtain food; and as the chase is their only means of subsistence, if you deprive them of the power of procuring it, you certainly produce great dissatisfaction. If it were true that arms and ammunition could be accumulated by them to war against us, it would certainly be unwise to give it to them, but this is not the fact. No Indian will buy two guns. One he absolutely needs; and as he has no means of taking care of powder, he necessarily will take, when offered to him, but a very limited quantity. It is true that formerly they hunted with bows and arrows, killing buffalo, antelope, and deer with the same; but to hunt successfully with bow and arrows requires horses, and as the valleys of that country are now more or less filled with white men prospecting for gold and silver, their means of subsisting their horses have passed away, and they now have but few horses. I mention these facts so as to place before the country, as briefly as possible, the condition as well as the wants of the Indians."

Unfortunately for the Commissioner, his premises were entirely wrong, and his conclusions necessarily so. It is a difficult task to prove that men whose habits, instincts, and training incline them to deeds of murder, will be less apt to commit those deeds, provided we place in their hands every implement and facility for their commission; yet such in effect was the reasoning of the Commissioner. Where or from whom he could have obtained the opinions he expressed, it is difficult to understand. He certainly derived no such ideas from a personal knowledge of the Indians themselves. How well his statements bear examination: "If it were true that arms and ammunition could be accumulated by them to war against us, it would certainly be worse to give it to them, but this is not the fact. No Indian will buy two guns."

On the contrary, every person at all familiar with the conduct of the Indians knows that there is no plan or idea which they study more persistently than that of accumulating arms and ammunition, and in the successful execution of this plan they have collected, and are to-day collecting arms and ammunition of the latest and most approved pattern. This supply of arms and ammunition is not obtained for purposes of hunting, for no matter how bountifully the Indian may be supplied with firearms, his favorite and most successful mode of killing the buffalo, his principal article of food, is with the bow and arrow. It is, at the same time, the most economical mode, as the arrows, after being lodged in the bodies of the buffalo, may be recovered unimpaired, and be used repeatedly. "No Indian will buy two guns!" If the honorable Commissioner had added the words, provided he can steal them, his statement would be heartily concurred in. From a knowledge of the facts, I venture the assertion that there is scarcely an Indian on the plains, no matter how fully armed and equipped, but will gladly barter almost anything he owns, of proper value, in exchange for good arms and ammunition. Even if his personal wants in this respect are satisfied, the Indian is too shrewd at driving a bargain to throw away any opportunity of possessing himself of arms or ammunition, as among his comrades he is aware that no other articles of trade command the prices that are paid for implements of war. An Indian may not desire two guns for his own use, but he will buy or procure one gun and one or more revolvers as a part of his equipment for war, and there are few of the chiefs and warriors of the plains who to-day are not the possessors of at least one breech-loading rifle or carbine, and from one to two revolvers. This can be vouched for by any officer who has been brought in contact with the hostile Indians of late years. As to the Indian not having proper means to take care of his ammunition, experience has shown that when he goes into action he carries a greater number of rounds of ammunition than do our soldiers, and in time of peace he exercises far better care of his supply than do our men. The army declared itself almost unanimously against the issue of arms to the Indians, while the traders, who were looking to the profits, and others of the Indian Bureau.

11

proclaimed loudly in favor of the issue, unlimited and unrestrained. General Hancock, commanding at that time one of the most important and extensive of the Indian departments, issued orders to his subordinates throughout the Indian country, similar to the order referred to of General Cooke. The order simply required post commanders and other officers to prevent the issue or sale of arms and ammunition to any Indians of the plains. As we were then engaged in hostilities with nearly all the tribes, it would have been simply assisting our enemies not to adopt this course. A spontaneous outcry came from the traders who were to be affected by this order—an outcry that did not cease until it resounded in Washington. General Hancock reported his action in the matter to his next superior officer, at that time Lieutenant-General Sherman. General Sherman at once sent the following letter to General Hancock, emphatically approving the course of the latter, and reiterating the order:

HEADQUARTERS MILITARY DIVISION OF THE MISSOURI, }
ST. LOUIS, MISSOURI, January 26, 1867. }

GENERAL : I have this moment received your letter of January 22, about the sale of arms and ammunition to Indians by traders and agents. We, the military, are held responsible for the peace of the frontier, and it is an absurdity to attempt it if Indian agents and traders can legalize and encourage so dangerous a traffic. I regard the paper enclosed, addressed to Mr. D. A. Butterfield, and signed by Charles Bogy, W. R. Irwin, J. H. Leavenworth, and others, as an outrage upon our rights and supervision of the matter, and I now authorize you to disregard that paper, and at once stop the practice, keeping the issues and sales of arms and ammunition under the rigid control and supervision of the commanding officers of the posts and districts near which the Indians are.

If the Indian agents may, without limit, supply the Indians with arms, I would not expose our troops and trains to them at all, but would withdraw our soldiers, who already have a herculean task on their hands.

This order is made for this immediate time, but I will, with all expedition, send these papers, with a copy of this, to General Grant, in the hope that he will lay it before the President, who alone can control both War and Indian Departments, under whom, at present, this mixed control of the Indian question now rests in law and practice.

Your obedient servant,
W. T. SHERMAN, Lieutenant-General Commanding.

General W. S. HANCOCK. commanding Department of the Missouri.

This was before the peace policy had become supreme, or the appointment of agents from the Society of Friends had been discovered as a supposed panacea for all our Indian difficulties.

General Sherman, as stated in his letter, forwarded all the papers relating to the arms question to the headquarters of the army. General Grant, then in command of the army, forwarded them to the Secretary of War, accompanied by the following letter, which clearly expresses the views he then held:

HEADQUARTERS ARMIES OF THE UNITED STATES, }
WASHINGTON, D. C., February 1, 1867. }

SIR : The enclosed papers, just received from General Sherman, are respectfully forwarded, and your special attention invited. They show the urgent necessity for an immediate transfer of the Indian Bureau to the War Department, and the abolition of the civil agents and licensed traders. If the present practice is to be continued, I do not see that any course is left open to us but to withdraw our troops to the settlements and call upon Congress to provide means and troops to carry on formidable hostilities against the Indians, until all the Indians or all the whites on the great plains, and between the settlements on the Missouri and the Pacific slope, are exterminated. The course General Sherman has pursued in this matter, in disregarding the permits of Mr. Bogy and others, is just right. I will instruct him to enforce his order until it is countermanded by the President or yourself. I would also respectfully ask that this matter be placed before the President, and his disapproval of licensing the sale of arms to Indians asked. We have treaties with all tribes of Indians from time to time. If the rule is to be followed that all tribes with which we have treaties, and pay annuities, can procure such articles without stint or limit, it will not be long before the matter becomes perfectly understood by the Indians, and they avail themselves of it to

GENL. U. S. GRANT.

equip themselves for war. They will get the arms either by making treaties themselves or through tribes who have such treaties.

I would respectfully recommend that copies of the enclosed communications be furnished to the Military Committee of each house of Congress.

Very respectfully, your obedient servant,

U. S. GRANT, General.

Hon. E. M. STANTON, Secretary of War.

In response to a request from General Grant to furnish the Department with a statement of his views on the question of a transfer of the Indian Bureau from the Interior to the War Department, General John Pope, whose great experience among and knowledge of the Indians of the plains eminently qualified him to judge of the real merits of the question, wrote an able letter, briefly stating the prominent reasons favoring the proposed change. As the question of the transfer of the Indian Bureau from the control of the Interior to that of the War Department is constantly being brought up, and after the failure of the present policy is most likely to be raised again, the arguments advanced by General Pope, being those generally maintained by the army, and still having full force, are here given:

WASHINGTON, D. C., January 25, 1867.

GENERAL : In compliance with your suggestions, I have the honor to submit the following leading reasons why the Indian Bureau should be retransferred to the War Department. The views which I shall submit are by no means original, but are well-settled opinions of every officer of the army who has had experience on the subject, and are and have been entertained for years by nearly every citizen of the territories not directly or indirectly connected with the present system of Indian management.

Under present circumstances there is a divided jurisdiction over Indian affairs. While the Indians are officially at peace, according to treaties negotiated with them by the civil officers of the Indian Bureau, the military forces stationed in the Indian country have no jurisdiction over the Indians, and of consequence no certain knowledge of their feelings or purposes, and no power to take any action, either of a precautionary or aggressive character. The first that is known of Indian hostilities is a sudden report that the Indians have commenced a war, and have devastated many miles of settlements or massacred parties of emigrants or travellers. By the time such information reaches the military commander, the worst has been accomplished, and the Indians have escaped from the scene of outrage. Nothing is left to the military except pursuit, and generally unavailing pursuit. The Indian agents are careful never to locate their agencies at the military posts, for reasons very well understood. It is not in human nature that two sets of officials, responsible to different heads, and not in accord either in opinion or purpose, should act together harmoniously ; and instead of combined, there is very certain to be conflicting action. The results are what might be expected. It would be far better to devolve the whole management of Indian affairs upon one or the other department, so as to secure at least consistent and uniform policy. At war the Indians are under the control of the military, at peace under the control of the civil officers. Exactly what constitutes Indian hostilities is not agreed on ; and, besides this, as soon as the military forces, after a hard campaign, conducted with great hardship and at large expense, have succeeded in forcing the Indians into such a position that punishment is possible, the Indian, seeing the result and the impossibility of avoiding it, immediately proclaims his wish to make peace. The Indian agent, anxious, for manifest reasons, to negotiate a treaty, at once interferes " to protect " (as he expresses it) the Indians from the troops, and arrests the further prosecution of the military expedition just at the moment when results are to be obtained by it, and the whole labor and cost of the campaign are lost. The Indian makes a treaty to avoid immediate danger by the troops, without the slightest purpose of keeping it, and the agent knows very well that the Indian does not intend to observe it. While the army is fighting the Indians at one end of the line, Indian agents are making treaties and furnishing supplies at the other end, which supplies are at once used to keep up the conflict. With this divided jurisdiction and responsibility it is impossible to avoid these unfortunate transactions. If the Indian department, as at present constituted, were given sole jurisdiction of the Indians, and the troops removed, it is certain that a better condition of things would be obtained than now exists, since the whole responsibility of Indian wars, and their results to unprotected citizens, would belong to the Indian Bureau alone, without the power of shifting the responsibility of consequences upon others. The military officer is the representative of force, a logic which the Indian understands, and with which he does not invest the Indian agent. It is a fact which can be easily authenticated, that the Indians, in mass, prefer to deal entirely with military commanders, and would unanimously vote for the transfer of the Indian department to the War Department. In this they are mainly influenced by the knowledge that they can rely upon what the military commander tells or promises them, as they see he has power to fulfil his promise.

The first and great interest of the army officer is to preserve peace with the Indians. His home during his life is to be at some military post in the Indian country, and aside from the obligations of duty, his own comfort and quiet, and the possibility of escaping arduous and harassing field service against Indians at all seasons of the year, accompanied by frequent changes of station, which render it impossible for him to have his family with him, render a state of peace with Indians the most desirable of all things to him. He therefore omits no proper precautions, and does not fail to use all proper means, by just treatment, honest distribution of annuities, and fair dealing, to secure quiet and friendly relations with the Indian tribes in his neighborhood. His honest distribution of the annuities appropriated to the Indians is further secured by his life commission in the army, and the odium which would blast his life and character by any dishonest act. If dismissed from the service for such malfeasance, he would be publicly branded by his own profession, and would be powerless to attribute his removal from office to any but the true cause. The Indian agent, on the other hand, accepts his office for a limited time and for a specific purpose, and he finds it easy when he has secured his ends (the rapid acquisition of money) to account for his removal from office on political grounds or the personal enmity of some other official of his department superior in rank to himself. The eagerness to secure an appointment as Indian agent, on a small salary, manifested by many persons of superior ability, ought of itself to be a warning to Congress as to the objects sought by it. It is a common saying in the West that next to, if not indeed before, the consulship to Liverpool, an Indian agency is the most desirable office in the gift of the Government. Of course the more treaties an Indian agent can negotiate, the larger the appropriation of money and goods which passes through his hands, and the more valuable his office. An Indian war on every other day, with treaty-making on intermediate days, would be therefore the condition of affairs most satisfactory to such Indian agents. I by no means say that all Indian agents are dishonest. In truth I know some who are very sincere and honorable men, who try to administer their offices with fidelity to the Government; but that the mass of Indian agents on the frontier are true only to their personal and pecuniary interests, I am very sure no one familiar with the subject will dispute. I repeat, then, that a condition of peace with the Indians is above all things desirable to the military officer stationed in their country: something very like the reverse to the Indian agent.

The transfer of the Indian Bureau to the War Department would at once eliminate from our Indian system the formidable army of Indian superintendents, agents, sub-agents, special agents, jobbers, contractors, and hangers-on, who now infest the frontier States and territories, and save to the Government annually a sum of money which I will not venture to estimate. The army officers detailed to perform duty in their places would receive no compensation in addition to their army pay. Previous to the creation of the Interior Department and the transfer of the Indian Bureau to that department, army officers performed well and honestly the duties of Indian agents, and it is only necessary to refer to our past history to demonstrate that our relations at that time with the Indians were far more friendly and satisfactory than they have been since. . . . The military are absolutely necessary in the Indian country to protect the lives and property of our citizens. Indian agents and superintendents are not necessary, since their duties have been and can still be faithfully and efficiently performed by the army officers stationed with the troops. Harmonious and concerted action can never be secured while both parties are retained. The military are necessary—the civil officers are not; and as it is essential that the one or the other be displaced, I cannot see what doubt exists as to which party must give way. These are only the general reasons for the retransfer of the Indian Bureau to the War Department—reasons which are well understood by every one familiar with the subject. . . . In order that any policy whatever may be consistently and efficiently pursued, a change in our present administration of Indian affairs is absolutely essential. The retransfer of the Indian Bureau to the War Department is believed to be the first step toward a reformation, and until that step is taken it is useless to expect any improvement in the present condition of our Indian relations.

I am, General, respectfully your obedient servant,

JOHN POPE, Brevet Major-General U. S. Army.

GENERAL U. S. GRANT, General-in-Chief, Washington, D. C.

General Grant was at that time so impressed with the importance of General Pope's letter that he forwarded it to the Secretary of War, with the request that it might be laid before both branches of Congress.

It might be urged that the above letters and statements are furnished by officers of the army, who are exponents of but one side of the question. Fortunately it is possible to go outside the military circle and introduce testimony which should be considered impartial and free from bias. At this particular period in the discussion of the Indian question, Colonel E. S. Parker, a highly educated and thoroughly cultivated gentleman, was asked to submit a plan for the establishment of a permanent and perpetual peace, and for settling all matters of difference between the United States and the various Indian tribes.

Colonel Parker is well known as a distinguished chief of the once powerful Six Nations, and since the time referred to has been better known as Commissioner of Indian Affairs during the early part of the present administration. Being an Indian, his sympathies must be supposed to have been on the side of his own people, and in his endeavor to establish a permanent peace he would recommend no conditions prejudicial or unjust to their interests. He recommended: "First, the transfer of the Indian Bureau from the Interior Department back to the War Department, or military branch of the Government, where it originally belonged, until within the last few years. The condition and disposition of all the Indians west of the Mississippi river, as developed in consequence of the great and rapid influx of immigration by reason of the discovery of the precious metals throughout the entire West, renders it of the utmost importance that military supervision should be extended over the Indians. Treaties have been made with a very large number of the tribes, and generally reservations have been provided as homes for them. Agents, appointed from civil life, have generally been provided to protect their lives and property, and to attend to the prompt and faithful observance of treaty stipulations. But as the hardy pioneer and adventurous miner advanced into the inhospitable regions occupied by the Indians, in search of the precious metals, they found no rights possessed by the Indians that they were bound to respect. The faith of treaties solemnly entered into was totally disregarded, and Indian territory wantonly violated. If any tribe remonstrated against the violation of their natural and treaty rights, members of the tribe were inhumanly shot down, and the whole treated as mere dogs. Retaliation generally followed, and bloody Indian wars have been the consequence, costing many lives and much treasure. In all troubles arising in this manner, the civil agents have been totally powerless to avert the consequences, and when too late the military have been called in to protect the whites and punish the Indians, when if, in the beginning, the military had had the supervision of the Indians, their rights would not have been improperly molested, or if disturbed in their quietude by any lawless whites, a prompt and summary check to any further aggression could have been given. In cases where the Government promises the Indians the quiet and peaceable possession of a reservation, and precious metals are discovered or found to exist upon it, the military alone can give the Indians the needed protection, and keep the adventurous miner from encroaching upon the Indians until the Government has come to some understanding with them. In such cases the civil agent is absolutely powerless.

"Most of the Indian treaties contain stipulations for the payment to Indians of annuities, either in money or goods, or both, and agents are appointed to make these payments whenever Government furnishes them the means. I know of no reason why officers of the army could not make all these payments as well as civilians. The expense of agencies would be saved, and I think the Indians would be more honestly dealt by. An officer's honor and interest are at stake, which impels him to discharge his duty honestly and faithfully, while civil agents have none of these incentives, the ruling passion with them being generally to avoid all trouble and responsibility and to make as much money as possible out of their offices. In the retransfer of this bureau, I would provide for the complete abolishment of the system of Indian traders, which, in my opinion, is a great evil to Indian communities. I would make Government the purchaser of all articles usually brought in by Indians, giving them a fair equivalent for the same in money, or goods at cost prices. In this way it would be an easy matter to regulate the sale or issue of arms and ammunition to Indians, a question which of late has agitated the minds of the civil and military authorities. If the entry of large numbers of Indians to any military post is objectionable, it can easily be arranged that only limited numbers shall be admitted daily."

Colonel Parker next quotes from messages of Washington and Jefferson, showing that they had favored the exclusion of civil agents and traders. His recommendation then proceeds: "It is greatly to be regretted that this beneficent and humane policy had not been adhered to, for it is a fact not to be denied, that at this day Indian trading licenses are very much sought after, and when once obtained, although it may be for a limited period, the lucky possessor is considered as having already made his fortune. The eagerness also with which Indian agencies are sought after, and large fortunes made by the agents in a few years, notwithstanding the inadequate salary given, is presumptive evidence of frauds against the Indians and the Government. Many other reasons might be suggested why the Indian department should altogether be under military control, but a familiar knowledge of the practical working of the present system would seem to be the most convincing proof of the propriety of the measure. It is pretty generally advocated by those most familiar with our Indian relations, and, so far as I know, the Indians themselves desire it. Civil officers are not usually respected by the tribes, but they fear and regard the military, and will submit to their counsels, advice, and dictation, when they would not listen to a civil agent."

In discussing the establishment of reservations, and the locating of the Indians upon them, Colonel Parker says: "It may be imagined that a serious obstacle would be presented to the removal of the Indians from their homes on account of the love they bear for the graves of their ancestors. This, indeed, would be the least and last objection that would be raised by any tribe. Much is said in the books about the reverence paid by Indians to the dead, and their antipathy to deserting their ancestral graves. Whatever may have been the customs for the dead in ages gone by, and whatever pilgrimages may have been made to the graves of their loved and distinguished dead, none of any consequence exist at the present day. They leave their dead without any painful regrets, or the shedding of tears. And how could it be otherwise with a people who have such indefinite and vague ideas of a future state of existence? And to my mind it is unnatural to assume or suppose that the wild or untutored Indian can have more attachment for his home, or love for the graves of his ancestors, than the civilized and enlightened Christian."

I regret that I cannot, in this brief space, give all the suggestions and recommendations submitted by this eminent representative of the red man, displaying as they do sound judgment and thorough mastery of his subject. In regard to the expense of his plan he says: "I believe it to be more economical than any other plan that could be suggested. A whole army of Indian agents, traders, contractors, jobbers, and hangers-on would be dispensed with, and from them would come the strongest opposition to the adoption of this plan, as it would effectually close to them the corrupt sources of their wealth."

General Grant, then commanding the army, must have approved at that time of the views of the distinguished Indian; for a few years later, on entering upon the duties of President of the United States, he appointed him Commissioner of Indian Affairs, thus giving Colonel Parker an opportunity to inaugurate the system which he had urged as being most conducive to the welfare of his people and tending to restrain them from acts of war. The influences brought to bear by the exponents of the peace policy, as it was termed, were too powerful to be successfully resisted, and Colonel Parker felt himself forced to resign his position, for the reason, as stated by him, that the influences operating against him were so great that he was unable to give effect to the principles which he believed should prevail in administering the affairs of his important bureau.

The latter part of the summer and fall of 1867 was not characterized by active operations either upon the part of the troops or that of the Indians. A general council of all the tribes infesting the southern plains was called to assemble on "Medicine Lodge creek." This council was called in furtherance of a plan of pacification proposed by Congress with a view to uniting and locating all the tribes referred to on a reservation to be agreed upon. Congress provided that the tribes invited to the council should be met by a peace commission on the part of the Government, composed of members of each house of Congress, distinguished civilians, and officers of the army of high rank. At this council all the southern tribes assembled; presents in profusion were distributed among the Indians, the rule of distribution, I believe, being as usual that the worst Indians received the greatest number of valuable presents; an agreement was entered into between the Indians and the representatives of the Government; reservations embracing a large extent of the finest portions of the public lands were fixed upon, to the apparent satisfaction of all concerned, and the promise of the Indians to occupy them and to keep away from the settlements and lines of travel was made without hesitation. This was the beginning of the promised era of peace. The lion and the lamb had agreed to lie down together, but the sequel proved that when they got up again 'the lamb was missing."

XIII.

Comrades, leave me here a little, while as yet 'tis early morn;
Leave me here, and when you want me, sound upon the bugle horn.

IN this instance, however, the bugle whose summoning notes I was supposed to be listening for was one of peculiar structure, and its tones could only be rendered effective when prompted by the will of the director at Washington. In other words, I was living in involuntary but unregretful retirement from active service. I had spent the winter of 1867–'68 most agreeably with many of my comrades at Fort Leavenworth, but in the spring was forced to see them set out for their summer rendezvous for operations against the Indians, and myself compelled by superior authority, or rather by "circumstances over which I had no control," to remain in the rear, a non-combatant in every sense of the word; so much so that I might have been eligible to election as honorary member of some one of those preponderous departments referred to by General Hazen in "The School and the Army," as "holding military rank, wearing the uniform," but living in complete "official separation from the line," except that I was not "divided from it in heart and sympathy." It is a happy disposition that can content itself in all phases of fortune by the saying that "that which cannot be cured must be endured." I had frequent recourse to this and similar consoling expressions, in the endeavor to reconcile myself to the separation from my command. For fear some of my readers may not comprehend my situation at the time, I will briefly remark in parenthesis, and by way of note of explanation, that for precisely what I have described in some of the preceding chapters, the exact details of which would be out of place here, it had apparently been deemed necessary that my connection with certain events and transactions, every one of which has been fully referred to heretofore, should be submitted to an official examination in order to determine if each and every one of my acts had been performed with a due regard to the customs of war in like cases. To enter into a review of the proceedings which followed, would be to introduce into these pages matters of too personal a character to interest the general reader. It will suffice to say that I was placed in temporary retirement from active duty, and this result seemed satisfactory to those parties most intimately concerned in the matter. When, in the spring of 1868, the time arrived for the troops to leave their winter quarters, and march westward to the Plains, the command with which I had been associated during the preceding year left its station at Fort Leavenworth, Kansas, and marched westward about three hundred miles, there to engage in operations against the Indians. While they, under command of General Sully, were attempting to kill Indians, I was studying the problem of how to kill time in the most agreeable manner. My campaign was a decided success. I established my base of operations in a most beautiful little town on the western shores of Lake Erie, from which I projected various hunting, fishing, and boating expeditions. With abundance of friends and companions, and ample success, time passed pleasantly enough; yet withal there was a constant longing to be with my comrades in arms in the far West, even while aware of the fact that their campaign was not resulting in any material advantage. I had no reason to believe that I would be permitted to rejoin them until the following winter. It was on the evening of the 24th of September, and when about to "break bread" at the house of a friend in the little town referred to that I received the following telegram:

HEADQUARTERS DEPARTMENT OF THE MISSOURI,
IN THE FIELD, FORT HAYS, KANSAS, September 24, 1868.

General G. A. CUSTER, Monroe, Michigan:

Generals Sherman, Sully, and myself, and nearly all the officers of your regiment, have asked for you, and I hope the application will be successful. Can you come at once? Eleven compa nies of your regiment will move about the 1st of October against the hostile Indians, from Medi cine Lodge creek toward the Wichita mountains.

(Signed) P. H. SHERIDAN, Major General Commanding.

The reception of this despatch was a source of unbounded gratification to me, not only because I saw the opportunity of being actively and usefully employed opened before me, but there were personal considerations inseparable from the proposed manner of my return, which in themselves were in the highest degree agreeable; so much so that I felt quite forbearing toward each and every one who, whether intentionally or not, had been a party to my retirement, and was almost disposed to favor them with a copy of the preceding despatch, accompanied by an expression of my hearty thanks for the unintentional favor they had thrown in my way.

Knowing that the application of Generals Sherman and Sheridan and the other officers referred to would meet with a favorable reply from the authorities at Washington, I at once telegraphed to General Sheridan that I would start to join him by the next train, not intending to wait the official order which I knew would be issued by the War Department. The following day found me on a railway train hastening to the plains as fast as the iron horse could carry me. The expected order from Washington overtook me that day in the shape of an official telegram from the Adjutant General of the Army, directing me to proceed at once and report for duty to General Sheridan.

At Fort Leavenworth I halted in my journey long enough to cause my horses to be shipped by rail to Fort Hays. Nor must I omit two other faithful companions of my subsequent marches and campaigns, named Blucher and Maida, two splendid specimens of the Scotch staghound, who were destined to share the dangers of an Indian campaign and finally meet death in a tragic manner—the one by the hand of the savage, the other by an ill-directed bullet from a friendly carbine. Arriving at Fort Hays on the morning of the 30th, I found General Sheridan, who had transferred his headquarters temporarily from Fort Leavenworth to that point in order to be nearer the field of operations, and better able to give his personal attention to the conduct of the coming campaign. My regiment was at that time on or near the Arkansas river in the vicinity of Fort Dodge, and about three easy marches from Fort Hays. After remaining at General Sheridan's headquarters one day and receiving his instructions, I set out with a small escort across the country to Fort Dodge to resume command of my regiment. Arriving at Fort Dodge without incident, I found General Sully, who at that time was in command of the district in which my regiment was serving. With the exception of a few detachments, the main body of the regiment was encamped on Bluff creek, a small tributary of the Arkansas, the camp being some thirty miles southeast from Fort Dodge. Taking with me the detachment at the fort, I proceeded to the main camp, arriving there in the afternoon. I had scarcely assumed command when a band of Indians dashed close up to our camp and fired upon us. This was getting into active service quite rapidly. I was in the act of taking my seat for dinner, my ride having given me a splendid relish for the repast, when the shouts and firing of the savages informed me that more serious duties were at hand. Every man flew to arms and almost without command rushed to oppose the enemy. Officers and men provided themselves with rifles or carbines, and soon began delivering a deliberate but ineffective fire against the Indians. The latter, as usual, were merely practising their ordinary *ruse de guerre*, which was to display a very small venturesome force in the expectation of tempting pursuit by an equal or slightly superior force, and, after having led the pursuing force well away from the main body, to surround and destroy it by the aid of overwhelming numbers, previously concealed in a ravine or ambush until the proper moment. On this occasion the stratagem did not succeed. The Indians, being mounted on their fleetest ponies, would charge in single file past our camp, often riding within easy carbine range of our men, displaying great boldness and unsurpassable horsemanship. The soldiers, unaccustomed to firing at such rapidly moving objects, were rarely able to inflict serious damage upon their enemies. Occasionally a pony would be struck and brought to the ground, but the rider always succeeded in being carried away upon the pony of a comrade. It was interesting to witness their marvellous abilities as horsemen; at the same time one could not but admire the courage they displayed. The ground was level, open, and unobstructed; the troops were formed in an irregular line of skirmishers dismounted, the line extending a distance of perhaps two hundred yards. The Indians had a rendezvous behind a hillock on the right, which prevented them from being seen or disturbed by the soldiers. Starting out singly, or by twos and threes, the warriors would suddenly leave the cover of the hillock, and with war whoops and taunts dash over the plain in a line parallel to that occupied by the soldiers, and within easy carbine range of the latter. The pony seemed possessed of the designs and wishes of his dusky rider, as he seemed to fly unguided by bridle, rein, or spur. The warrior would fire and load and fire again as often as he was able to do, while dashing along through the shower of leaden bullets fired above, beneath, in front, and behind him by the excited troopers, until finally, when the aim of the latter improved and the leaden messengers whistled uncomfortably close, the warrior would be seen to cast himself over on the opposite side of his pony, until his foot on the back and his face under the neck of the pony were all that could be seen, the rest of his person being completely covered by the body of the pony. This manœuvre would frequently deceive the recruits among the soldiers; having fired probably about the time the warrior was seen to disappear, the recruit would shout exultingly and call the attention of his comrades to his lucky shot. The old soldiers, however, were not so easily deceived, and often afterwards would remind their less experienced companion of the terrible fatality of his shots.

After finding that their plan to induce a small party to pursue them did not succeed, the Indians withdrew their forces, and, concealment being no longer necessary, we were enabled to see their full numbers as that portion of them which had hitherto remained hidden behind a bluff rode boldly out on the open plain. Being beyond rifle range, they contented themselves with taunts and gestures of defiance, then rode away. From the officers of the camp I learned that the performance of the Indians which had occupied our attention on this afternoon was of almost daily occurrence, and that the savages, from having been allowed to continue in their course unmolested, had almost reduced the camp to a state of siege; so true had this become that at no hour of the day was it safe for individuals to pass beyond the chain of sentinels which enveloped the immediate limits of the camp. Before it became known that the Indians were so watchful and daring, many narrow escapes were made, and many laughable although serious incidents occurred—laughable, however, only to those who were not the parties most interested. Two of these serio-comic affairs now recur to me. There was a beautiful clear stream of water, named Bluff creek, running through camp, which supplied bathing facilities to the officers and men, a privilege which but few allowed to pass unimproved. Whether to avoid the publicity attending localities near camp, or to seek a point in the bed of the stream where the water was fresh and undisturbed, or from a motive different from either of these, two of our young officers mounted their horses one day without saddles and rode down the valley of the stream perhaps a mile or more in search of a bathing place. Discovering one to their taste, they dismounted, secured their horses, and, after disposing of their apparel on the greensward covering the banks, were soon floating and floundering in the water like a pair of young porpoises. How long they had been enjoying this healthful recreation, or how much longer they might have remained, is not necessary to the story. One of them happening to glance toward their horses observed the latter in a state of great trepidation. Hastening from the water to the bank, he discovered the cause of the strange conduct on the part of the horses, which was nothing more nor less than a party of about thirty Indian warriors, mounted, and stealthily making their way toward the bathing party, evidently having their eyes on the latter, and intent upon their capture. Here was a condition of affairs that was at least as unexpected as it was unwelcome. Quickly calling out to his companion, who was still in the water unconscious of approaching danger, the one on shore made haste to unfasten their horses and prepare for flight. Fortunately the Indians, who were now within a few hundred yards of the two officers, were coming from the direction opposite camp, leaving the line of retreat of the officers open. No sooner did the warriors find that their approach was discovered than they put their ponies to their best speed, hoping to capture the officers before the latter could have time to mount and get their horses under headway. The two officers in the meanwhile were far from idle; no flesh brushes or bathing towels were required to restore a healthy circulation, nor was time wasted in an idle attempt to make a toilet. If they had sought their bathing ground from motives of retirement or delicacy, no such sentiments were exhibited now, for, catching up their wardrobe from the ground in one hand and seizing the bridle rein with the other, one leap and they were on their horses' backs and riding toward camp for dear life. They were not exactly in the condition of Flora McFlimsy with nothing to wear, but to all intents and purposes might as well have been so. Then followed a race which, but for the risk incurred by two of the riders, might well be compared to that of John Gilpin. Both of the officers were experienced horsemen; but what experienced horseman would willingly care to be thrust upon the bare back of a flying steed, minus all apparel, neither boots, breeches, nor saddle, not even the spurs and shirt collar which are said to constitute the full uniform of a Georgian colonel, and when so disposed of, to have three or four score of hideously painted and feathered savages, well mounted and near at hand, straining every nerve and urging their fleet-footed war ponies to their highest speed in order that the scalps of the experienced horsemen might be added to the other human trophies which grace their lodges? Truly this was one of the occasions when personal appearance is nothing, and "a man's a man for a' that," so at least thought our amateur Mazeppas as they came dashing toward camp, ever and anon casting anxious glances over their shoulders at their pursuers, who, despite every exertion of the former, were surely overhauling their pale-faced brothers. To the pursued, camp seemed a long way in the distance, while the shouts of the warriors, each time seeming nearer than before, warned them to urge their steeds to their fastest pace. In a few moments the occupants of camp discovered the approach of this strangely appearing party. It was an easy matter to recognize the warriors, but who could name the two who rode at the front? The pursuing warriors, seeing that they were not likely to overtake and capture the two knights of the bath, slackened their pace and sent a volley of arrows after them. A few moments later and the two officers were safe inside the lines, where they lost no time in making their way to their tents to attend to certain matters relating to their toilet which the sudden appearance of their dusky visitors had prevented. It was a long time before they ceased to hear allusions made by their comrades to the cut and style of their riding suit.

The other affair to which I have alluded occurred about the same time, but in a different direction from camp. One of the officers, who was commanding a troop, concluded one day that it would be safe to grant permission to a part of his command to leave camp for the purpose of hunting buffalo and obtaining fresh meat for the men. The hunting party, being strong enough to protect itself against almost any ordinary war party of Indians that might present itself, left camp at an early hour in the morning and set out in the direction in which the buffalo were reported to be. The forenoon passed away, noon came, and still no signs of the return of the hunters. The small hours of the afternoon began to come and go, and still no tidings from the hunters, who were expected to return to camp after an absence of two or three hours. The officer to whose troop they belonged, and who was of an exceedingly nervous temperament, began to regret having accorded them permission to leave camp, knowing that Indians had been seen in the vicinity. The hunting party had gone by a route across the open country which carried them up a long but very gradual ascent of perhaps two miles, beyond which, on the level plain, the buffalo were supposed to be herding in large numbers. Anxious to learn something concerning the whereabouts of his men, and believing he could obtain a view of the country beyond which might prove satisfactory, the officer, whose suspense was constantly increasing, determined to mount his horse and ride to the summit of the ridge beyond which his men had disappeared in the morning. Taking no escort with him, he leisurely rode off, guided by the trail made by the hunters. The distance to the crest proved much further than it had seemed to the eye before starting. A ride of over two miles had to be made before the highest point was reached, but once there the officer felt well repaid for his exertion, for in the dim deceptions of a beautiful mirage he saw what to him was his hunting party leisurely returning toward camp. Thinking they were still a long distance from him and would not reach him for a considerable time, he did what every prudent cavalryman would have done under similar circumstances—dismounted to allow his horse an opportunity to rest. At the same time he began studying the extended scenery, which from his exalted position lay spread in all directions beneath him. The camp, seen nestling along the banks of the creek at the base of the ridge, appeared as a pleasant relief to the monotony of the view, which otherwise was undisturbed. Having scanned the horizon in all directions, he turned to watch the approach of his men; when, behold! instead of his own trusty troopers returning laden with the fruits of the chase, the mirage had disappeared, and he saw a dozen well-mounted warriors riding directly toward him at full speed. They were still far enough away to enable him to mount his horse and have more than an even chance to outstrip them in the race to camp. But no time was to be thrown away; the beauties of natural scenery had, for the time at least, lost their attraction. Camp never seemed so inviting before. Heading his horse toward camp and gathering the reins in one hand and holding his revolver in the other, the officer set out to make his escape. Judgment had to be employed in riding this race, for the distance being fully two miles before a place of safety could be reached, his horse, not being high-bred and accustomed to going such a distance at full speed, might, if forced too rapidly at first, fail before reaching camp. Acting upon this idea, a tight rein was held and as much speed kept in reserve as safety would permit. This enabled the Indians to gain on the officer, but at no time did he feel that he could not elude his pursuers. His principal anxiety was confined to the character of the ground, care being taken to avoid the rough and broken places. A single misstep or a stumble on the part of his horse, and his pursuers would be upon him before he could rise. The sensations he experienced during that flying ride could not have been enviable. Soon the men in camp discerned his situation, and seizing their carbines hastened out to his assistance. The Indians were soon driven away and the officer again found himself among his friends. The hunters also made their appearance shortly after, well supplied with game. They had not found the buffalo as near camp as they had expected, and after finding them were carried by a long pursuit in a different direction from that taken by them in the morning. Hence their delay in returning to camp.

These and similar occurrences, added to the attack made by the Indians on the camp the afternoon I joined, proved that unless we were to consider ourselves as actually besieged and were willing to accept the situation, some decisive course must be adopted to punish the Indians for their temerity. No offensive measures had been attempted since the infantry and cavalry forces of General Sully had marched up the hill and then, like the forces of the king of France, had marched down again. The effect of this movement, in which the Indians gained a decided advantage, was to encourage them in their attempts to annoy and disturb the troops, not only by prowling about camp in considerable numbers and rendering it unsafe, as has been seen, to venture beyond the chain of sentinels, but by waylaying and intercepting all parties passing between camp and the base of supplies at Fort Dodge. Knowing, from my recent interview with General Sheridan, that activity was to characterize the future operations of the troops, particularly those of the cavalry, and that the sooner a little activity was exhibited on our part the sooner perhaps might we be freed from the aggressions of the Indians, I returned from the afternoon skirmish to my tent and decided to begin offensive movements that same night, as soon as darkness should conceal the march of the troops. It was reasonable to infer that the war parties which had become so troublesome in the vicinity of camp, and made their appearance almost daily, had a hiding place or rendezvous on some of the many small streams which flowed within a distance of twenty miles of the point occupied by the troops; and it was barely possible that if a simultaneous movement was made by several well-conducted parties with a view of scouting up and down the various streams referred to, the hiding place of the Indians might be discovered and their forays in the future broken up. It was deemed most prudent, and to promise greatest chance of success, to make these movements at night, as during the hours of daylight the Indians no doubt kept close watch over everything transpiring in the vicinity of camp, and no scouting party could have taken its departure in daylight unobserved by the watchful eyes of the savages. Four separate detachments were at once ordered to be in readiness to move immediately after dark. Each detachment numbered about one hundred cavalry well mounted and well armed. Guides who knew the country well were assigned to each, and each party was commanded and accompanied by zealous and efficient officers. The country was divided into four sections, and to each detachment was assigned one of the sections, with orders to thoroughly scout the streams running through it. It was hoped that some one of these parties might, if in no other way, stumble upon a camp-fire or other indication of the rendezvous of the Indians; but subsequent experience only confirmed me in the opinion that Indians seldom, if ever, permit hostile parties to stumble upon them unless the stumblers are the weaker party. Before proceeding further in my narrative I will introduce to the reader a personage who is destined to appear at different intervals, and upon interesting occasions, as the campaign proceeds. It is usual on the plains, and particularly during time of active hostilities, for every detachment of troops to be accompanied by one or more professional scouts or guides. These guides are employed by the government at a rate of compensation far in excess of that paid to the soldiers, some of the most experienced receiving pay about equal to that of a subaltern in the line. They constitute a most interesting as well as useful and necessary portion of our frontier population. Who they are, whence they come or whither they go, their names even, except such as they choose to adopt or which may be given them, are all questions which none but themselves can answer. As their usefulness to the service depends not upon the unravelling of either of these mysteries, but little thought is bestowed upon them. Do you know the country thoroughly? and can you speak any of the Indian languages? constitute the only examination which civil or uncivil service reform demands on the plains. If the evidence on these two important points is satisfactory, the applicant for a vacancy in the corps of scouts may consider his position as secured, and the door to congenial employment, most often leading to a terrible death, opens before him. They are almost invariably men of very superior judgment or common sense, with education generally better than that of the average frontiersman. Their most striking characteristics are love of adventure, a natural and cultivated knowledge of the country without recourse to maps, deep hatred of the Indian, and an intimate acquaintance with all the habits and customs of the latter, whether pertaining to peace or war, and last but most necessary to their calling, skill in the use of firearms and in the management of a horse. The possessor of these qualifications, and more than the ordinary amount of courage, may feel equal to discharge the dangerous and trying duties of a scout. In concentrating the cavalry which had hitherto been operating in small bodies, it was found that each detachment brought with it the scouts who had been serving with them. When I joined the command I found quite a number of these scouts attached to various portions of the cavalry, but each acting separately. For the purposes of organization it was deemed best to unite them into a separate detachment under command of one of their own number. Being unacquainted personally with the merits or demerits of any of them, the selection of a chief had necessarily to be made somewhat at random. There was one among their number whose appearance would have attracted the notice of any casual observer. He was a man about forty years of age, perhaps older, over six feet in height, and possessing a well-proportioned frame. His head was covered with a luxuriant crop of long, almost black hair, strongly inclined to curl, and so long as to fall carelessly over his shoulders. His face, at least so much of it as was not concealed by the long, waving brown beard and moustache, was full of intelligence and pleasant to look upon. His eye was undoubtedly handsome, black and lustrous, with an expression of kindness and mildness combined. On his head was generally to be seen, whether asleep or awake, a huge sombrero or black slouch hat. A soldier's overcoat with its large circular cape, a pair of trousers with the legs tucked in the top of his long boots, usually constituted the outside make-up of the man whom I selected as chief scout. He was known by the euphonious title of " California Joe ", no other name seemed ever to have been given him, and no other name ever seemed necessary. His military armament consisted of a long breech-loading Springfield musket, from which he was inseparable, and a revolver and hunting-knife, both the latter being carried in his waist-belt. His mount completed his equipment for the field, being instead of a horse a finely-formed mule, in whose speed and endurance he had every confidence. Scouts usually prefer a good mule to a horse, and wisely too, for the reason that in making their perilous journeys, either singly or by twos or threes, celerity is one principal condition to success. The object with the scout is not to outrun or overwhelm the Indians, but to avoid both by secrecy and caution in his movements. On the plains at most seasons of the year the horse is incapable of performing long or rapid journeys without being supplied with forage on the route. This must be transported, and in the case of scouts would necessarily be transported on the back of the horse, thereby adding materially to the weight which must be carried. The mule will perform a rapid and continuous march without forage, being able to subsist on the grazing to be obtained in nearly all the valleys on the plains during the greater portion of the year. California Joe was an inveterate smoker, and was rarely seen without his stubby, dingy-looking brierwood pipe in full blast. The endurance of his smoking powers was only surpassed by his loquacity. His pipe frequently became exhausted and required refilling, but California Joe seemed never to lack for material or disposition to carry on a conversation, principally composed of personal adventures among the Indians, episodes in mining life, or experience in overland journeying before the days of steam engines and palace cars rendered a trip across the plains a comparatively uneventful one. It was evident from the scraps of information volunteered from time to time, that there was but little of the Western country from the Pacific to the Missouri river with which California Joe was not intimately acquainted. He had lived in Oregon years before, and had become acquainted from time to time with most of the officers who had served on the plains or on the Pacific coast. I once inquired of him if he had ever seen General Sheridan? "What, Gineral Shuridun? Why, bless my soul, I knowed Shuridun way up in Oregon more'n fifteen years ago, an' he wuz only a second lootenant uv infantry. He wuz quartermaster of the foot or something uv that sort, an' I hed the contract uv furnishin' wood to the post, and, would ye b'leve it? I hed a kind of a sneakin' notion then that he'd hurt somebody ef they'd ever turn him loose. Lord, but ain't he old lightnin'?" This was the man whom upon a short acquaintance I decided to appoint as chief of the scouts. This thrust of professional greatness, as the sequel will prove, was more than California Joe aspired to, or, considering some of his undeveloped traits, was equal to; but I am anticipating.

As the four detachments already referred to were to move as soon as it was dark, it was desirable that the scouts should be at once organized and assigned. So, sending for California Joe, I informed him of his promotion and what was expected of him and his men. After this official portion of the interview had been completed, it seemed proper to Joe's mind that a more intimate acquaintance between us should be cultivated, as we had never met before. His first interrogatory, addressed to me in furtherance of this idea, was frankly put as follows: "See hyar, Gineral, in order that we hev no misonderstandin', I'd jest like to ask ye a few questions." Seeing that I had somewhat of a character to deal with, I signified my perfect willingness to be interviewed by him. "Are you an ambulance man ur a hoss man?" Preter ling not to discover his meaning, I requested him to explain. "I mean do you b'leve in catchin' Injuns in ambulances or on hossback?" Still assuming ignorance, I replied, "Well, Joe, I believe in catching Indians wherever we can find them, whether they are found in ambulances or on horseback." This did not satisfy him. "That ain't what I'm drivin' at. S'pose you're after Injuns and really want to hev a tussle with 'em, would ye start after 'em on hossback, or would ye climb into an ambulance and be haulded after 'em? That's the pint I'm headin' fur." I answered that "I would prefer the method on horseback provided I really desired to catch the Indians; but if I wished them to catch me, I would adopt the ambulance system of attack." This reply seemed to give him complete satisfaction. "You've hit the nail squar on the hed. I've bin with 'em on the plains whar they started out after the Injuns on wheels, jist as ef they war goin' to a town funeral in the States, an' they stood 'bout as many chances uv catchin' Injuns az a six-mule team wud uv catchin' a pack of thievin' Ki-o-tees, jist as much. Why that sort uv work is only fun fur the Injuns; they don't want anything better. Ye ort to've seen how they peppered it to us, an' we a doin' nuthin' a' the time. Sum uv 'em wuz 'fraid the mules war goin' to stampede and run off with the train an' all our forage and grub, but that wuz impossible; fur besides the big loads uv corn an' bacon an' baggage the wagons hed in them, thar war from eight to a dozen infantry men piled into them besides. Ye ort to hev heard the quartermaster in charge uv the train tryin' to drive the infantry men out of the wagons and git them into the fight. I 'spect he wuz an Irishman by his talk, fur he sed to them, 'Git out uv thim wagons, git out uv thim wagons; yez 'll hev me tried fur disobadience uv ordhers fur marchin' tin min in a wagon whin I've ordhers but fur ait!'"

How long I might have been detained listening to California Joe's recita' of incidents of first campaigns, sandwiched here and there by his peculiar but generally correct ideas of how to conduct an Indian campaign properly, I do not know; time was limited, and I had to remind him of the fact to induce him to shorten the conversation. It was only deferred, however, as on every occasion thereafter California Joe would take his place at the head of the column on the march, and his nearest companion was made the receptacle of a fresh instalment of Joe's facts and opinions. His career as "chief scout" was of the briefest nature. Everything being in readiness, the

CALIFORNIA JOE.

four scouting columns, the men having removed their sabres to prevent clanging and detection, quietly moved out of camp as soon as it was sufficiently dark, and set out in different directions. California Joe accompanied that detachment whose prospects seemed best of encountering the Indians. The rest of the camp soon afterward returned to their canvas shelter, indulging in all manner of surmises and conjectures as to the likelihood of either or all of the scouting parties meeting with success. As no tidings would probably be received in camp until a late hour of the following day, taps, the usual signal from the bugle for "lights out," found the main camp in almost complete darkness, with only here and there a stray glimmering of light from the candle of some officer's tent, who was probably reckoning in his own mind how much he was losing or perhaps gaining by not accompanying one of the scouting parties. What were the chances of success to the four detachments which had departed on this all night's ride? Next to nothing. Still, even if no Indians could be found, the expeditions would accomplish this much: they would leave their fresh trails all over the country within a circuit of twenty miles of our camp, trails which the practised eyes of the Indians would be certain to fall upon in daylight, and inform them for the first time that an effort was being made to disturb them if nothing more.

Three of the scouting columns can be disposed of now by the simple statement that they discovered no Indians, nor the remains of any camps or lodging places indicating the recent presence of a war party on any of the streams visited by them. The fourth detachment was that one which California Joe had accompanied as scout. What a feather it would be in his cap if, after the failure of the scouts accompanying the other columns to discover Indians, the party guided by him should pounce upon the savages, and by a handsome fight settle a few of the old scores charged against them!

The night was passing away uninterrupted by any such event, and but a few hours more intervened before daylight would make its appearance. The troops had been marching constantly since leaving camp; some were almost asleep in their saddles when the column was halted, and word was passed along from man to man that the advance guard had discovered signs indicating the existence of Indians near at hand. Nothing more was necessary to dispel all sensations of sleep, and to place every member of the command on the alert. It was difficult to ascertain from the advance guard, consisting of a non-commissioned officer and a few privates, precisely what they had seen. It seemed that in the valley beyond, into which the command was about to descend, and which could be overlooked from the position the troops then held, something unusual had been seen by the leading troopers just as they had reached the crest. What this mysterious something was, or how produced, no one could tell; it appeared simply for a moment, and then only as a bright flash of light of varied colors; how far away it was impossible to determine in the heavy darkness of the night. A hasty consultation of the officers took place at the head of the column, when it was decided that in the darkness which then reigned it would be unwise to move to the attack of an enemy until something more was known of the numbers and position of the foe. As the moon would soon rise and dispel one of the obstacles to conducting a careful attack, it was determined to hold the troops in readiness to act upon a moment's notice, and at the same time send a picked party of men, under guidance of California Joe, to crawl as close to the supposed position of the Indians as possible, and gather all the information available. But where was California Joe all this time? Why was he not at the front where his services would be most likely to be in demand? Search was quietly made for him all along both flanks of the column, but on careful inquiry it seemed that he had not been seen for some hours, and then at a point many miles from that at which the halt had been ordered. This was somewhat remarkable, and admitted of no explanation—unless, perhaps, California Joe had fallen asleep during the march and been carried away from the column; but this theory gained no supporters. His absence at this particular time, when his advice and services might prove so invaluable, was regarded as most unfortunate. However, the party to approach the Indian camp was being selected when a rifle shot broke upon the stillness of the scene, sounding in the direction of the mysterious appearance which had first attracted the attention of the advanced troopers. Another moment, and the most powerful yells and screams rose in the same direction, as if a terrible conflict was taking place. Every carbine was advanced ready for action, each trigger was carefully sought, no one as yet being able to divine the cause of this sudden outcry, when in a moment who should come charging wildly up to the column, now dimly visible by the first rays of the moon, but California Joe, shouting and striking wildly to the right and left as if beset by a whole tribe of warriors. Here, then, was the solution of the mystery. Not then, but in a few hours, everything was rendered clear. Among the other traits or peculiarities of his character, California Joe numbered an uncontrollable fondness for strong drink; it was his one great weakness—a weakness to which he could only be kept from yielding by keeping all intoxicating drink beyond his reach. It seemed, from an after development of the affair, that the sudden elevation of California Joe, unsought and unexpected as it was, to the position of chief scout, was rather too much good fortune to be borne by him in a quiet or undemonstrative manner. Such a profusion of greatness had not been thrust upon him so often as to render him secure from being affected by his preferment. At any rate he deemed the event deserving of celebration—professional duties to the contrary notwithstanding—and before proceeding on the night expedition had filled his canteen with a bountiful supply of the worst brand of whiskey, such as is only attainable on the frontier. He, perhaps, did not intend to indulge to that extent which might disable him from properly performing his duties; but in this, like many other good men whose appetites are stronger than their resolutions, he failed in his reckoning. As the liquor which he imbibed from time to time after leaving camp began to produce the natural or unnatural effect, Joe's independence greatly increased until the only part of the expedition which he recognized as at all important was California Joe. His mule, no longer restrained by his hand, gradually carried him away from the troops, until the latter were left far in the rear. This was the relative position when the halt was ordered. California Joe, having indulged in drink sufficiently for the time being, concluded that the next best thing would be a smoke; nothing would be better to cheer him on his lonely night ride. Filling his ever present brierwood with tobacco, he next proceeded to strike a light, employing for this purpose a storm or tempest match; it was the bright and flashing colors of this which had so suddenly attracted the attention of the advance guard. No sooner was his pipe lighted than the measure of his happiness was complete, his imagination picturing him to himself, perhaps, as leading in a grand Indian fight. His mule by this time had turned toward the troops, and when California Joe set up his unearthly howls, and began his imaginary charge into an Indian village, he was carried at full speed straight to the column, where his good fortune alone prevented him from receiving a volley before he was recognized as not an Indian

His blood was up, and all efforts to quiet or suppress him proved unavailing, until finally the officer in command was forced to bind him hand and foot, and in this condition secured him on the back of his faithful mule. In this sorry plight the chief scout continued until the return of the troops to camp, when he was transferred to the tender mercies of the guard as a prisoner for misconduct. Thus ended California Joe's career as chief scout. Another was appointed in his stead, but we must not banish him from our good opinion yet. As a scout, responsible only for himself, he will reappear in these pages with a record which redounds to his credit.

Nothing was accomplished by the four scouting parties except, perhaps, to inspire the troops with the idea that they were no longer to be kept acting merely on the defensive, while the Indians, no doubt, learned the same fact, and at the same time. The cavalry had been lying idle, except when attacked by the Indians, for upward of a month. It was reported that the war parties, which had been so troublesome for some time, came from the direction of Medicine Lodge creek, a stream running in the same general direction as Bluff creek, and about two marches from the latter in a northeasterly direction. It was on this stream—Medicine Lodge creek—that the great peace council had been held with all the southern tribes with whom we had been and were then at war, the Government being represented at the council by Senators and other members of Congress, officers high in rank in the army, and prominent gentlemen selected from the walks of civil life. The next move, after the unsuccessful attempt in which California Joe created the leading sensation, was to transfer the troops across from Bluff creek to Medicine Lodge creek, and to send scouting parties up and down the latter in search of our enemies. This movement was made soon after the return of the four scouting expeditions sent out from Bluff creek. As our first day's march was to be a short one, we did not break camp on Bluff creek until a late hour in the morning. Soon everything was in readiness for the march, and like a travelling village of Bedouins, the troopers and their train of supplies stretched out into column. First came the cavalry, moving in column of fours; next came the immense wagon train, containing the tents, forage, rations, and extra ammunition of the command, a very necessary but unwieldy portion of a mounted military force. Last of all came the rear guard, usually consisting of about one company. On this occasion it was the company commanded by the officer whose narrow escape from the Indians while in search of a party of his men who had gone buffalo hunting, has been already described in this chapter. The conduct of the Indians on this occasion proved that they had been keeping an unseen but constant watch on everything transpiring in or about camp. The column had scarcely straightened itself out in commencing the march, and the rear guard had barely crossed the limits of the deserted camp, when out from a ravine near by dashed a war party of fully fifty well-mounted, well-armed warriors. Their first onslaught was directed against the rear guard, and a determined effort was made to drive them from the train, and thus place the latter at their mercy, to be plundered of its contents. After disposing of flankers, for the purpose of resisting any efforts which might be made to attack the train from either flank, I rode back to where the rear guard were engaged, to ascertain if they required reinforcements. At the same time orders were given for the column of troops and train to continue the march, as it was not intended that so small a party as that attacking us should delay our march by any vain effort on our part to ride them down, or overhaul them, when we knew they could outstrip us if the contest was to be decided by a race. Joining the rear guard, I had an opportunity to witness the Indian mode of fighting in all its perfection. Surely no race of men, not even the famous Cossacks, could display more wonderful skill in feats of horsemanship than the Indian warrior on his native plains, mounted on his well-trained war pony, voluntarily running the gauntlet of his foes, drawing and receiving the fire of hundreds of rifles, and in return sending back a perfect shower of arrows, or, more likely still, well-directed shots from some souvenir of a peace commission, in the shape of an improved breech-loader. The Indian warrior is capable of assuming positions on his pony, the latter at full speed, which no one but an Indian could maintain for a single moment without being thrown to the ground. The pony, of course, is perfectly trained, and seems possessed of the spirit of his rider. An Indian's wealth is most generally expressed by the number of his ponies. No warrior or chief is of any importance or distinction who is not the owner of a herd of ponies numbering from twenty to many hundreds. He has for each special purpose a certain number of ponies, those that are kept as pack animals being the most inferior in quality and value; then the ordinary riding ponies used on the march or about camp, or when visiting neighboring villages; next in consideration is the "buffalo pony," trained to the hunt, and only employed when dashing into the midst of the huge buffalo herds, when the object is either food from the flesh or clothing and shelter for the lodges. to be made from the buffalo hide; last, or rather first, considering its value and importance, is the "war pony," the favorite of the herd, fleet of foot, quick in intelligence, and full of courage. It may be safely asserted that the first place in the heart of the warrior is held by his faithful and obedient war pony.

Indians are extremely fond of bartering, and are not behindhand in catching the points of a good bargain. They will sign treaties relinquishing their lands, and agree to forsake the burial ground of their forefathers; they will part, for due consideration, with their bow and arrows, and their accompanying quiver, handsomely wrought in dressed furs; their lodges even may be purchased at not an unfair valuation, and it is not an unusual thing for a chief or warrior to offer to exchange his wife or daughter for some article which may have taken his fancy. This is no exaggeration; but no Indian of the plains has ever been known to trade, sell, or barter away his favorite "war pony." To the warrior his battle horse is as the apple of his eye. Neither love nor money can induce him to part with it. To see them in battle, and to witness how the one almost becomes a part of the other, one might well apply to the warrior the lines—

> But this gallant
> Had witchcraft in 't; he grew into his seat,
> And to such wondrous doing brought his horse,
> As he had been encorps'd and demi-natur'd
> With the brave beast; so far he passed my thought
> That I, in forgery of shapes and tricks,
> Come short of what he did.

The officer in command of the rear guard expressed the opinion that he could resist successfully the attacks of the savages until a little later, when it was seen that the latter were receiving accessions to their strength and were becoming correspondingly bolder and more difficult to repulse, when a second troop of cavalry was brought from the column, as a support to the rear guard. These last were ordered to fight on foot, their horses, in charge of every fourth trooper, being led near the train. The men being able to fire so much more

THE INDIAN AND HIS WAR PONY.

accurately when on foot, compelled the Indians to observe greater caution in their manner of attack. Once a warrior was seen to dash out from the rest in the peculiar act of "circling," which was simply to dash along in front of the line of troopers, receiving their fire and firing in return. Suddenly his pony. while at full speed, was seen to fall to the ground, showing that the aim of at least one of the soldiers had been effective. The warrior was thrown over and beyond the pony's head, and his capture by the cavalry seemed a sure and easy matter to be accomplished. I saw him fall, and called to the officer commanding the troop which had remained mounted to gallop forward and secure the Indian. The troop advanced rapidly, but the comrades of the fallen Indian had also witnessed his mishap, and were rushing to his rescue. He was on his feet in a moment, and the next moment another warrior, mounted on the fleetest of ponies, was at his side, and with one leap the dismounted warrior placed himself astride the pony of his companion; and thus doubly burdened, the gallant little steed, with his no less gallant riders, galloped lightly away, with about eighty cavalrymen, mounted on strong domestic horses, in full cry after them. There is no doubt but that by all the laws of chance the cavalry should have been able to soon overhaul and capture the Indians in so unequal a race; but whether from lack of zeal on the part of the officer commanding the pursuit, or from the confusion created by the diversion attempted by the remaining Indians, the pony, doubly weighted as he was, distanced his pursuers and landed his burden in a place of safety. Although chagrined at the failure of the pursuing party to accomplish the capture of the Indians, I could not wholly suppress a feeling of satisfaction, if not gladness, that for once the Indian had eluded the white man. I need not add that any temporary tenderness of feeling toward the two Indians was prompted by their individual daring and the heroic display of comradeship in the successful attempt to render assistance to a friend in need.

Without being able to delay our march, yet it required the combined strength and resistance of two full troops of cavalry to defend the train from the vigorous and dashing attacks of the Indians. At last, finding that the command was not to be diverted from its purpose, or hindered in completing its regular march, the Indians withdrew, leaving us to proceed unmolested. These contests with the Indians, while apparently yielding the troops no decided advantage, were of the greatest value in view of future and more extensive operations against the savages. Many of the men and horses were far from being familiar with actual warfare, particularly of this irregular character. Some of the troopers were quite inexperienced as horsemen, and still more inexpert in the use of their weapons, as their inaccuracy of fire when attempting to bring down an Indian within easy range clearly proved. Their experience, resulting from these daily contests with the red men, was to prove of incalculable benefit, and fit them for the duties of the coming campaign. Our march was completed to Medicine Lodge creek, where a temporary camp was established, while scouting parties were sent both up and down the stream as far as there was the least probability of finding Indians. The party, consisting of three troops, which scouted down the valley of Medicine Lodge creek, proceeded down to the point where was located and then standing the famous "medicine lodge," an immense structure erected by the Indians, and used by them as a council house, where once in each year the various tribes of the southern plains were wont to assemble in mysterious conclave to consult the Great Spirit as to the future, and to offer up rude sacrifices and engage in imposing ceremonies, such as were believed to be appeasing and satisfactory

to the Indian Deity. In the conduct of these strange and interesting incantations, the presiding or directing personages are known among the Indians as
"medicine men." They are the high priests of the red man's religion, and in
their peculiar sphere are superior in influence and authority to all others in the
tribe, not excepting the head chief. No important step is proposed or put in
execution, whether relating to war or peace, even the probable success of a
contemplated hunt, but is first submitted to the powers of divination confidently believed to be possessed by the medicine man of the tribe. He, after a
series of enchantments, returns the answer supposed to be prompted by the
Great Spirit, as to whether the proposed step is well advised and promises
success or not. The decisions given by the medicine men are supreme, and
admit of no appeal. The medicine lodge just referred to had been used as
the place of assembly of the grand council held between the warlike tribes and
the representatives of the Government, referred to in preceding pages. The
medicine lodge was found in a deserted but well-preserved condition. Here
and there, hanging overhead, were collected various kinds of herbs and plants,
vegetable offerings no doubt to the Great Spirit; while, in strange contrast
to these peaceful specimens of the fruits of the earth, were trophies of the war
path and the chase, the latter being represented by the horns and dressed skins
of animals killed in the hunt, some of the skins being beautifully ornamented
in the most fantastic of styles peculiar to the Indian idea of art. Of the trophies relating to war, the most prominent were human scalps, representing all
ages and sexes of the white race. These scalps, according to the barbarous
custom, were not composed of the entire covering of the head, but of a small
surface surrounding the crown, and usually from three to four inches in diameter, constituting what is termed the scalp lock. To preserve the scalp from
decay, a small hoop of about double the diameter of the scalp is prepared
from a small withe, which grows on the banks of some of the streams in the
West. The scalp is placed inside the hoop, and properly stretched by a net-
work of thread connecting the edges of the scalp with the circumference of the
hoop. After being properly cured, the dried fleshy portion of the scalp is ornamented in bright colors, according to the taste of the captor, sometimes the
addition of beads of bright and varied colors being made to heighten the effect.
In other instances the hair is dyed, either to a beautiful yellow or golden, or to
crimson. Several of these horrible evidences of past depredations upon the defenceless inhabitants of the frontier, or overland emigrants, were brought back
by the troopers on their return from their scout. Old trails of small parties of
Indians were discovered, but none indicating the recent presence of war parties in that valley were observable. The command was then marched back to
near its former camp on Bluff creek, from whence, after a sojourn of three or
four days, it marched to a point on the north bank of the Arkansas river,
about ten miles below Fort Dodge, there to engage in earnest preparation and
reorganization for the winter campaign, which was soon to be inaugurated, and
in which the Seventh Cavalry was to bear so prominent a part. We pitched
our tents on the banks of the Arkansas on the 21st of October, 1868, there to
remain usefully employed until the 12th of the following month, when we
mounted our horses, bade adieu to the luxuries of civilization, and turned our
faces toward the Wichita mountains in the endeavor to drive from their winter hiding places the savages who had during the past summer waged such
ruthless and cruel war upon our exposed settlers on the border. How far and
in what way we were successful in this effort, will be learned in the following
chapter

XIV.

IN concluding to go into camp for a brief period on the banks of the Arkansas, two important objects were in view: first, to devote the time to refitting, reorganizing, and renovating generally that portion of the command which was destined to continue active operations during the inclement winter season; second, to defer our movement against the hostile tribes until the last traces of the fall season had disappeared, and winter in all its bitter force should be upon us. We had crossed weapons with the Indians time and again during the mild summer months, when the rich verdure of the valleys served as bountiful and inexhaustible granaries in supplying forage to their ponies, and the immense herds of buffalo and other varieties of game roaming undisturbed over the Plains supplied all the food that was necessary to subsist the war parties, and at the same time allow their villages to move freely from point to point; and the experience of both officers and men went to prove that in attempting to fight Indians in the summer season we were yielding to them the advantages of climate and supplies—we were meeting them on ground of their own selection, and at a time when every natural circumstance controlling the result of a campaign was wholly in their favor; and as a just consequence the troops, in nearly all these contests with the red men, had come off second best. During the grass season nearly all Indian villages are migratory, seldom remaining longer than a few weeks at most in any one locality, depending entirely upon the supply of grass; when this becomes exhausted the lodges are taken down, and the entire tribe or band moves to some other point, chosen with reference to the supply of grass, water, wood, and game. The distance to the new location is usually but a few miles. During the fall, when the buffaloes are in the best condition to furnish food, and the hides are suitable to be dressed as robes, or to furnish covering for the lodges, the grand annual hunts of the tribes take place, by which the supply of meat for the winter is procured. This being done, the chiefs determine upon the points at which the village shall be located; if the tribe is a large one, the village is often subdivided, one portion or band remaining at one point, other portions choosing localities within a circuit of thirty or forty miles. Except during seasons of the most perfect peace, and when it is the firm intention of the chiefs to remain on friendly terms with the whites at least during the winter and early spring months, the localities selected for their winter resorts are remote from the military posts and frontier settlements, and the knowledge which might lead to them carefully withheld from every white man. Even during a moderate winter season, it is barely possible for the Indians to obtain sufficient food for their ponies to keep the latter in anything above a starving condition. Many of the ponies actually die from want of forage, while the remaining ones become so weak and attenuated that it requires several weeks of good grazing in the spring to fit them for service—particularly such service as is required from the war ponies. Guided by these facts, it was evident that if we chose to avail ourselves of the assistance of so exacting and terrible an ally as the frosts of winter—an ally who would be almost as uninviting to friends as to foes—we might deprive our enemy of his points of advantage, and force him to engage in a combat in which we should do for him what he had hitherto done for us;

compel him to fight upon ground and under circumstances of our own selection. To decide upon making a winter campaign against the Indians was certainly in accordance with that maxim in the art of war which directs one to do that which the enemy neither expects nor desires to be done. At the same time it would dispel the old-fogy idea, which was not without supporters in the army, and which was confidently relied on by the Indians themselves, that the winter season was an insurmountable barrier to the prosecution of a successful campaign. But aside from the delay which was necessary to be submitted to before the forces of winter should produce their natural but desired effect upon our enemies, there was much to be done on our part before we could be ready to coöperate in an offensive movement.

The Seventh Cavalry, which was to operate in one body during the coming campaign, was a comparatively new regiment, dating its existence as an organization from July, 1866. The officers and companies had not served together before with much over half their full force. A large number of fresh horses were required and obtained; these had to be drilled. All the horses in the command were to be newly shod, and an extra fore and hind shoe fitted to each horse; these, with the necessary nails, were to be carried by each trooper in the saddle pocket. It has been seen that the men lacked accuracy in the use of their carbines. To correct this, two drills in target practice were ordered each day. The companies were marched separately to the ground where the targets had been erected, and, under the supervision of the troop officers, were practised daily in firing at targets placed one hundred, two hundred, and three hundred yards distant. The men had been previously informed that out of the eight hundred men composing the command, a picked corps of sharpshooters would be selected, numbering forty men, and made up of the forty best marksmen in the regiment. As an incentive to induce every enlisted man, whether non-commissioned officer or private, to strive for appointment in the sharpshooters, it was given out from headquarters that the men so chosen would be regarded, as they really would deserve to be, as the *élite* of the command; not only regarded as such, but treated with corresponding consideration. For example, they were to be marched as a separate organization, independently of the column, a matter which in itself is not so trifling as it may seem to those who have never participated in a long and wearisome march. Then again no guard or picket duty was to be required of the sharpshooters, which alone was enough to encourage every trooper to excel as a marksman. Besides these considerations, it was known that, should we encounter the enemy, the sharpshooters would be most likely to be assigned a post of honor, and would have superior opportunities for acquiring distinction and rendering good service. The most generous as well as earnest rivalry at once sprung up, not only between the various companies, as to which should secure the largest representation among the sharpshooters, but the rivalry extended to individuals of the same company, each of whom seemed desirous of the honor of being considered as "one of the best shots."

To be able to determine the matter correctly, a record of every shot fired by each man of the command, throughout a period of upwards of one month, was carefully kept. It was surprising to observe the marked and rapid improvement in the accuracy of aim attained by the men generally during this period. Two drills at target practice each day, and allowing each man an opportunity at every drill to become familiar with the handling of his carbine and in judging of the distances of the different targets, worked a most satisfactory improvement in the average accuracy of fire; so that at the end of the period named, by taking the record of each trooper's target practice, I was enabled to select forty marksmen in whose ability to bring down any warrior, whether mounted or not, who might challenge us, as we had often been challenged before, I felt every confidence. They were a superb body of men, and felt the greatest pride in their distinction. A sufficient number of non-commissioned officers, who had proven their skill as marksmen, were included in the organization—among them, fortunately, a first sergeant, whose expertness in the use of any firearm was well established throughout the command. I remember having seen him, while riding at full speed, bring down four buffaloes by four consecutive shots from his revolver. When it is remembered that even experienced hunters are usually compelled to fire half a dozen shots or more to secure a single buffalo, this statement will appear the more remarkable. The forty sharpshooters being supplied with their complement of sergeants and corporals, and thus constituting an organization by themselves, only lacked one important element, a suitable commander—a leader who, aside from being a thorough soldier, should possess traits of character which would not only enable him to employ skilfully the superior abilities of those who were to constitute his command, but at the same time feel that *esprit de corps* which is so necessary to both officers and soldiers when success is to be achieved. Fortunately, in my command were a considerable number of young officers, nearly all of whom were full of soldierly ambition, and eager to grasp any opportunity which opened the way to honorable preferment. The difficulty was not in finding an officer properly qualified in every way to command the sharpshooters, but, among so many who I felt confident would render a good account of themselves if assigned to that position, to designate a leader *par excellence*. The choice fell upon Colonel Cook, a young officer whose acquaintance the reader will remember to have made in connection with the plucky fight he had with the Indians near Fort Wallace the preceding summer. Colonel Cook, at the breaking out of the rebellion, although then but a lad of sixteen years, entered one of the New York cavalry regiments, commencing at the foot of the ladder. He served in the cavalry arm of the service throughout the war, participating in Sheridan's closing battles near Richmond, his services and gallantry resulting in his promotion to the rank of lieutenant-colonel. While there were many of the young officers who would have been pleased if they instead of another had been chosen, there was no one in the command, perhaps, who did not regard the selection as a most judicious one. Future events only confirmed this judgment.

After everything in the way of reorganization and refitting which might be considered as actually necessary had been ordered, another step, bordering on the ornamental perhaps, although in itself useful, was taken. This was what is termed in the cavalry " coloring the horses," which does not imply, as might be inferred from the expression, that we actually changed the color of our horses, but merely classified or arranged them throughout the different squadrons and troops according to the color. Hitherto the horses had been distributed to the various companies of the regiment indiscriminately, regardless of color, so that in each company and squadron horses were found of every color For uniformity of appearance it was decided to devote one afternoon to a gen eral exchange of horses. The troop commanders were assembled at head-quarters and allowed, in the order of their rank, to select the color they preferred. This being done, every public horse in the command was led out and placed in line: the grays collected at one point, the bays—of which there was a great preponderance in numbers—at another, the blacks at another, the sorrels by themselves; then the chestnuts, the blacks, the browns; and last of all came what were jocularly designated the "brindles," being the odds and ends so far as colors were concerned—roans and other mixed colors—the junior troop commander of course becoming the reluctant recipient of these last, valuable enough except as to color. The exchanges having been completed, the men of each troop led away to their respective picket or stable lines their newly-acquired chargers. Arriving upon their company grounds, another assignment in detail was made by the troop commanders. First, the non-commissioned officers were permitted to select their horses in the order of their rank; then the remaining horses were distributed among the troopers generally, giving to the best soldiers the best horses. It was surprising to witness what a great improvement in the handsome appearance of the command was effected by this measure. The change when first proposed had not been greeted with much favor by many of the troopers who by long service and association in times of danger had become warmly attached to their horses; but the same reasons which had endeared the steed to the soldier in the one instance, soon operate in the same manner to render the new acquaintances fast friends.

Among the other measures adopted for carrying the war to our enemy's doors, and in a manner "fight the devil with fire," was the employment of Indian allies. These were to be procured from the "reservation Indians," tribes who, from engaging in long and devastating wars with the whites and with other hostile bands, had become so reduced in power as to be glad to avail themselves of the protection and means of subsistence offered by the reservation plan. These tribes were most generally the objects of hatred in the eyes of their more powerful and independent neighbors of the Plains, and the latter, when making their raids and bloody incursions upon the white settlements of the frontiers, did not hesitate to visit their wrath equally upon whites and reservation Indians. To these smaller tribes it was a welcome opportunity to be permitted to ally themselves to the forces of the Government, and endeavor to obtain that satisfaction which acting alone they were powerless to secure. The tribes against which we proposed to operate during the approaching campaign had been particularly cruel and relentless in their wanton attacks upon the Osages and Kaws, two tribes living peaceably and contentedly on well-chosen reservations in southwestern Kansas and the northern portion of the Indian Territory. No assistance in fighting the hostile tribes was desired, but it was believed, and correctly too, that in finding the enemy and in discovering the location of his winter hiding-places, the experience and natural tact and cunning of the Indians would be a powerful auxiliary if we could enlist them in our cause. An officer was sent to the village of the Osages to negotiate with the head chiefs, and was successful in his mission, returning with a delegation consisting of the second chief in rank of the Osage tribe, named "Little Beaver," "Hard Rope," the counsellor or wise man of his people, and eleven warriors, with an interpreter. In addition to the monthly rate of compensation which the Government agreed to give them, they were also to be armed, clothed, and mounted at Government expense.

Advices from General Sheridan's headquarters, then at Fort Hays, Kansas, were received early in November, informing us that the time for resuming active operations was near at hand, and urging the early completion of all preliminaries looking to that end. Fort Dodge, on the Arkansas river, was the extreme post south in the direction proposed to be taken by us, until the Red river should be crossed and the northwestern posts of Texas could be reached, which were further south than our movements would probably carry us. To use Fort Dodge as our base of supplies, and keep open to that point our long line of communications, would have been, considering the character of the country and that of the enemy to be encountered, an impracticable matter with our force. To remedy this a temporary base was decided upon, to be established about one hundred miles south of Fort Dodge, at some point yet to be determined, from which we could obtain our supplies during the winter. With this object in view an immense train, consisting of about four hundred army wagons, was loaded with forage, rations, and clothing, for the supply of the troops composing the expedition. A guard composed of a few companies of infantry was detailed to accompany the trains and to garrison the point which was to be selected as the new base of supplies. Everything being in readiness, the cavalry moved from its camp on the north bank of the Arkansas on the morning of the 12th of November, and after fording the river began its march toward the Indian Territory. That night we encamped on Mulberry creek, where we were joined by the infantry and the supply train. General Sully, commanding the district, here took active command of the combined forces. Much anxiety existed in the minds of some of the officers, remembering no doubt their late experience, lest the Indians should attack us while on the march, when, hampered as we should be in the protection of so large a train of wagons, we might fare badly. The country over which we were to march was favorable to us, as we were able to move our trains in four parallel columns formed close together. This arrangement shortened our flanks and rendered them less exposed to attack. The following morning after reaching Mulberry creek the march was resumed soon after daylight, the usual order being: the four hundred wagons of the supply train and those belonging to the troops formed in four equal columns; in advance of the wagons at a proper distance rode the advance guard of cavalry; a corresponding cavalry force formed the rear guard. The remainder of the cavalry was divided into two equal parts, and these parts again divided into three equal detachments; these six detachments were disposed of along the flanks of the column, three on a side, maintaining a distance between themselves and the train of from a quarter to half a mile, while each of them had flanking parties thrown out opposite the train, rendering it impossible for an enemy to appear in any direction without timely notice being received. The infantry on beginning the march in the morning were distributed throughout the train in such manner that should the enemy attack, their services could be rendered most effective. Unaccustomed, however, to field service, particularly marching, the infantry apparently were only able to march for a few hours in the early part of the day, when, becoming weary, they would straggle from their companies and climb into the covered wagons, from which there was no determined effort to rout them. In the afternoon there would be little evidence perceptible to the eye that infantry formed any portion of the expedition, save here and there the butt of a musket or point of a bayonet peeping out from under the canvas wagon-covers, or perhaps an officer of infantry "treading alone his native heath," or better still mounted on an Indian pony, the result of some barter with the Indians when times were a little more peaceable, and neither wars nor rumors of wars disturbed the monotony of garrison life. Nothing occurred giving us any clue

13

to the whereabouts of Indians until we had been marching several days and were moving down the valley of Beaver creek, when our Indian guides discovered the trail of an Indian war party, numbering, according to their estimate, from one hundred to one hundred and fifty warriors, mounted and moving in a northeasterly direction. The trail was not over twenty-four hours old, and by following it to the point where it crossed Beaver creek, almost the exact numbers and character of the party could be determined from the fresh signs at the crossing. Everything indicated that it was a war party sent from the very tribes we were in search of, and the object, judging from the direction they had been moving, and other circumstances, was to make a raid on the settlements in Western Kansas. As soon as we had reached camp for the night, which was but a short distance from the point at which we crossed the Indian trail, I addressed a communication to the senior officer, who was commanding the expedition, and, after stating the facts learned in connection with the trail, requested that I might be permitted to take the cavalry belonging to the expedition, leaving the trains to be guarded by the infantry, whose numbers were ample for this purpose, and with the Indian scouts as trailers set out early the next morning, following the trail of the war party, not in the direction taken by them, as this would be an idle attempt, but in the direction from which they came, expressing the conviction that such a course would in all probability lead us direct to the villages of the marauders, which was the ultimate object of the movement we were thus engaged in. By so doing we might be able to strike a prompt blow against our enemies, and visit swift punishment upon the war party, whose hostile purposes were but too evident. In these views I was sustained by the opinions of our Indian allies, who expressed confidence in their ability to take the trail and follow it back to the villages. The officer to whom my application was submitted, and whose sanction was necessary before I could be authorized to execute my proposed plan, returned an elaborate argument attempting to prove that no successful results could possibly attend the undertaking I had suggested, and ended with the remark that it was absurd to suppose for one moment that a large military force such as ours was, and accompanied by such an immense train of wagons, could move into the heart of the Indian country and their presence remain undiscovered by the watchful savages for even a single day. This specious reasoning sounded well—read well—but it gave no satisfaction to the men and officers of the cavalry, all of whom thought they saw a fine opportunity neglected. However, we shall strike this trail again, but on different ground and under different circumstances. Great as was our temporary disappointment at being restrained, the result satisfied all of us that, for very different reasons from those adduced to withhold us from making the proposed movement, all, as the sequel proved, was for the best. On the sixth day after leaving our camp on the north bank of the Arkansas the expedition arrived at the point which was chosen as our future base, where the infantry were to remain and erect quarters for themselves and storehouses for the military supplies. The point selected—which was then given the name it now bears, Camp Supply—was in the angle formed by Wolf and Beaver creeks, about one mile above the junction of these two streams. These streams by their union form the north fork of the Canadian river. The exact geographical location of the point referred to is lat. 36 deg. 30 min., long. 99 deg. 30 min., being in the neighborhood of one hundred miles in a southerly direction from Fort Dodge on the Arkansas. We of the cavalry knew that our detention at this point would be but brief. Within two or three days of our arrival the hearts of the entire command were gladdened by the sudden appearance in our midst of strong reinforcements. These reinforcements consisted of General Sheridan and staff. Hearing of his near approach, I mounted my horse and was soon galloping beyond the limits of camp to meet him. If there were any persons in the command who hitherto had been in doubt as to whether the proposed winter campaign was to be a reality or otherwise, such persons soon had cause to dispel all mistrust on this point. Selecting from the train a sufficient number of the best teams and wagons to transport our supplies of rations and forage, enough to subsist the command upon for a period of thirty days, our arrangements were soon completed by which the cavalry, consisting of eleven companies and numbering between eight and nine hundred men, were ready to resume the march. In addition we were to be accompanied by a detachment of scouts, among the number being California Joe; also our Indian allies from the Osage tribe, headed by Little Beaver and Hard Rope. As the country in which we were to operate was beyond the limits of the district which constituted the command of General Sully, that officer was relieved from further duty with the troops composing the expedition, and in accordance with his instructions withdrew from Camp Supply and returned to his headquarters at Fort Harker, Kansas, accompanied by Colonel Keogh, Seventh Cavalry, then holding the position of staff officer at district headquarters.

After remaining at Camp Supply six days, nothing was required but the formal order directing the movement to commence. This came in the shape of a brief letter of instructions from Department headquarters. Of course, as nothing was known positively as to the exact whereabouts of the Indian villages, the instructions had to be general in terms. In substance, I was to march my command in search of the winter hiding-places of the hostile Indians, and wherever found to administer such punishment for past depredations as my force was able to. On the evening of November 22d, orders were issued to be in readiness to move promptly at daylight the following morning. That night, in the midst of other final preparations for a long separation from all means of communication with absent friends, most of us found time to hastily pen a few parting lines, informing them of our proposed expedition, and the uncertainties with which it was surrounded, as none of us knew when or where we should be heard from again once we bade adieu to the bleak hospitalities of Camp Supply. Alas! some of our number were destined never to return. It began snowing the evening of the 22d, and continued all night, so that when the shrill notes of the bugle broke the stillness of the morning air at reveille on the 23d, we awoke at four o'clock to find the ground covered with snow to a depth of over one foot, and the storm still raging in full force. Surely this was anything but an inviting prospect as we stepped from our frail canvas shelters and found ourselves standing in the constantly and rapidly increasing depth of snow which appeared in every direction. "How will this do for a winter campaign?" was the half sarcastic query of the adjutant, as he came trudging back to the tent through a field of snow extending almost to the top of his tall troop boots, after having received the reports of the different companies at reveille. "Just what we want," was the reply. Little grooming did the shivering horses receive from the equally uncomfortable troopers that morning. Breakfast was served and disposed of more as a matter of form and regulation than to satisfy the appetite; for who, I might inquire, could rally much of an appetite at five o'clock in the morning, and when standing around a camp fire almost up to the knees in snow? The signal, "The general," for tents to be taken down and wagons packed for the march, gave every one employment. Upon the principle that a short horse is soon curried, and as we were going to take but little with us in the way of baggage of any description, the duties of packing up were soon performed. It still lacked some minutes of daylight when the various commanders reported their commands in readiness to move, save the final act of saddling the horses, which only arrested the signal sounds of the chief bugler at headquarters. "Boots and saddles" rang forth, and each trooper grasped his saddle, and the next moment was busily engaged arranging and disposing of the few buckles and straps upon which the safety of his seat and the comfort of his horse depended. While they were thus employed, my horse being already saddled and held near by, by the orderly, I improved the time to gallop through the darkness across the narrow plain to the tents of General Sheridan, and say good-by. I found the headquarter tents wrapped in silence, and at first imagined that no one was yet stirring except the sentinel in front of the General's tent, who kept up his lonely tread, apparently indifferent to the beating storm. But I had no sooner given the bridle-rein to my orderly than the familiar tones of the General called out, letting me know that he was awake, and had been an attentive listener to our notes of preparation. His first greeting was to ask what I thought about the snow and the storm. To which I replied that nothing could be more to our purpose. We could move and the Indian villages could not. If the snow only remained on the ground one week, I promised to bring the General satisfactory evidences that my command had met the Indians. With an earnest injunction from my chief to keep him informed, if possible, should anything important occur, and many hearty wishes for a successful issue to the campaign, I bade him adieu. After I had mounted my horse, and had started to rejoin my command, a staff officer of the General, a particular friend, having just been awakened by the conversation, called out, while standing in the door of his tent enveloped in the comfortable folds of a huge buffalo robe, "Goodby, old fellow; take care of yourself!" and in these brief sentences the usual farewell greetings between brother officers separating for service took place. By the time I rejoined my men they had saddled their horses and were in readiness for the march. "To horse" was sounded, and each trooper stood at his horse's head. Then followed the commands "Prepare to mount" and "Mount," when nothing but the signal "Advance" was required to put the column in motion. The band took its place at the head of the column, preceded by the guides and scouts, and when the march began it was to the familiar notes of that famous old marching tune, "The girl I left behind me."

If we had entered into solemn compact with the clerk of the weather—this being before the reign of "Old Probabilities"—to be treated to winter in its severest aspect, we could have claimed no forfeiture on account of non-fulfilment of contract. We could not refer to the oldest inhabitant, that mythical personage in most neighborhoods, to attest to the fact that this was a storm unparalleled in severity in that section of country. The snow continued to descend in almost blinding clouds. Even the appearance of daylight aided us but little in determining the direction of our march. So dense and heavy were the falling lines of snow, that all view of the surface of the surrounding country, upon which the guides depended to enable them to run their course, was cut off. To such an extent was this true that it became unsafe for a person to wander from the column a distance equal to twice the width of Broadway, as in that short space all view of the column was prevented by the storm. **None** of the command except the Indian guides had ever visited the route we desired to follow, and they were forced to confess that until the storm abated sufficiently to permit them to catch glimpses of the landmarks of the country, they could not undertake to guide the troops to the point where we desired to camp that night. Here was a serious obstacle encountered quite early in the campaign.

The point at which we proposed to encamp for the night was on Wolf creek, only some twelve or fifteen miles from Camp Supply, it not being intended that our first day's progress should be very great. We had started, however, and notwithstanding the discouraging statements of our guides it would never do to succumb to opposition so readily. There was but one course to pursue now that the guides could no longer conduct us with certainty and that was to be guided—like the mariner in mid-ocean—by the never-failing compass. There are few cavalry officers but what carry a compass in some more or less simple form. Mine was soon in my hand, and having determined as accurately as practicable, from my knowledge of the map of the country, the direction in which we ought to move in order to strike Wolf creek at the desired camping ground, I became for the time guide to the column, and after marching until about two P. M. reached the valley of Wolf creek, where a resting place for the night was soon determined upon. There was still no sign of abatement on the part of the weather. Timber was found along the banks of· the creek in ample quantity to furnish us with fuel, but so imbedded in snow as to render the prospect of a camp fire very remote and uncertain. Our march of fifteen miles through the deep snow and blinding storm had been more fatiguing to our horses than an ordinary march of thirty miles would have been. Our wagons were still far in rear. While they were coming up every man in the command, officers as well as enlisted men, set briskly to work in gathering a good supply of wood, as our personal comfort in camp in such weather would be largely dependent on the quality and quantity of our firewood. Fallen and partly seasoned trees were in great demand, and, when discovered in the huge beds of snow, were soon transformed, under the vigorous blows of a score of axes, into available fuel. It was surprising as well as gratifying to witness the contentment and general good humor everywhere prevailing throughout the command. Even the chill of winter and the bitterest of storms were insufficient to produce a feeling of gloom, or to suppress the occasional ebullition of mirthful feeling which ever and anon would break forth from some Celtic or Teutonic disciple of Mars. Fires were soon blazing upon the grounds assigned to the different troops, and upon the arrival of the wagons, which occurred soon after, the company cooks were quickly engaged in preparing the troopers' dinner, while the servants of the officers were employed in a similar manner for the benefit of the latter. While the cooks were so engaged, officers and men were busily occupied in pitching the tents, an operation which under the circumstances was most difficult to perform satisfactorily, for the reason that before erecting the tent it was desirable, almost necessary, to remove the snow from the surface of the ground intended to form the floor of the tent; otherwise the snow, as soon as a fire should be started within the tent, would melt and reduce the ground to a very muddy condition. But so rapidly did the large flakes continue to fall that the most energetic efforts of two persons were insufficient to keep the ground properly clear; such at least was the experience of Lieutenant Moylan, the adjutant, and myself, in our earnest endeavors to render our temporary abiding place a fit habitation for the night. Tents up at last, dinner was not long in being prepared, and even less time employed in disposing of it. A good cup of strong coffee went far toward reconciling us to everything that had but a few moments before appeared somewhat uninviting. By this time a cheerful fire was blazing in the centre of our tent; my comfortable bed of buffalo robes was prepared on a framework of strong boughs, and with my ever-faithful dogs lying near me, I was soon reclining in a state of comparative comfort, watching the smoke as it ascended through the narrow apex of the tent, there to mingle with the descending flakes of snow. In regard to the storm still prevailing outside, and which in itself or its effects we were to encounter the following morning and for an indefinite period thereafter, I consoled myself with the reflection that to us it was as an unpleasant remedy for the removal of a still more unpleasant disease. If the storm seemed terrible to us, I believed it would prove to be even more terrible to our enemies, the Indians. Promptly at the appointed hour, four o'clock the following morning, camp was bustling and active in response to the bugle notes of reveille. The storm had abated, the snow had ceased falling, but that which had fallen during the previous twenty-four hours now covered the ground to a depth of upward of eighteen inches. The sky was clear, however, or, to adopt the expressive language of California Joe, "the travellin' was good overhead." It is always a difficult matter, the first few days of a march, to inculcate upon the minds of the necessary hangers-on of a camp, such as teamsters, wagon-masters, etc., the absolute necessity of promptness and strict obedience to orders, particularly orders governing the time and manner of marching; and one or two days usually are required to be devoted to disciplining these unruly characters. When the hour arrived which had been previously designated as the one at which the command would begin the second day's march, the military portion were in complete readiness to "move out," but it was found that several of the teams were still unharnessed and the tents of the wagon-masters still standing. This was a matter requiring a prompt cure. The officer of the day was directed to proceed with his guard, and, after hastening the unfinished preparations for the march, to arrest the wagon-masters and most dilatory of the teamsters, and compel them to march on foot as a punishment for their tardiness. This was no slight matter, considering the great depth of the snow. So effective was this measure that not many hours had elapsed before the deposed drivers and their equally unfortunate superiors sent through the officer of the guard a humble request that they be permitted to resume their places in the train, promising at the same time never to give renewed cause for complaints of tardiness to be made against them. Their request was granted, and their promise most faithfully observed during the remainder of the campaign.

All of the second day we continued to march up the valley of the stream we had chosen as our first camping ground. The second night we encamped under circumstances very similar to those which attended us the first night, except that the storm no longer disturbed us. The snow did not add to our discomfort particularly, save by increasing the difficulty of obtaining good and sufficient fuel. Our purpose was to strike the Canadian river in the vicinity of "Antelope Hills," which are famous and prominent landmarks in that region, and then be governed in our future course by circumstances. Resuming the march at daylight on the morning of the third day, our route still kept us in the valley of Wolf creek, on whose banks we were to encamp for the third time. Nothing was particularly worthy of notice during our third day's march, except the immense quantities of game to be seen seeking the weak shelter from the storm offered by the little strips of timber extending along the valleys of Wolf creek and its tributaries. Even the buffalo, with their huge, shaggy coats—sufficient, one would imagine, to render the wearer indifferent to the blasts of winter—were frequently found huddled together in the timber, and so drowsy or benumbed from the effects of the cold as to not discover our approach until we were within easy pistol range, when the Indian guides and our white scouts who rode in advance would single out those appearing in best condition, and by deliberate aim bring them down. Details of a few troopers from each company were left at these points to cut up the butchered game and see to its being loaded in the company wagons as the trains came along. In this way a bountiful supply of good fresh meat was laid in, the weather favoring the keeping of the meat for an indefinite period. Occasionally we would discover a herd of buffaloes on the bluffs overlooking the stream. Then would occur some rare scenes of winter sport: a few of the officers and men would obtain permission to lead the column and join in the chase—an indulgence that could be safely granted, as no fears were entertained that hostile Indians were in our immediate vicinity. The deep snow was a serious obstacle to exhibiting speed either in the buffalo or his pursuers. It was most laughable to witness the desperate and awkward efforts of buffalo, horse, and rider, in the frantic endeavor to make rapid headway through the immense fields of snow. Occasionally an unseen hole or ditch or ravine covered up by the snow would be encountered, when the buffalo or his pursuer, or perhaps all three— horse, rider, and buffalo—would disappear in one grand tumble in the depths of the snowdrifts, and when seen to emerge therefrom it was difficult to determine which of the three was most badly frightened. Fortunately no accidents occurred to mar the pleasure of the excitement. Seeing a fine herd of young buffaloes a short distance in the advance, I determined to test the courage of my stag-hounds "Blucher" and "Maida." Approaching as near the herd as possible before giving them the alarm, I managed to single out and cut off from the main herd a fine yearling bull. My horse, a trained hunter, was soon alongside, but I was unable to use my pistol to bring the young buffalo down, as both the dogs were running close to either side, and by resolutely attacking him endeavoring to pull him down. It was a new experience to them; a stag they could easily have mastered, but a lusty young buffalo bull was an antagonist of different calibre. So determined had the dogs become, their determination strengthened no doubt by the occasional vigorous blows received from the ready hoofs of the buffalo, that I could not call them off; neither could I render them assistance from my pistol, for fear of injuring them. There was nothing left for me to do but to become a silent although far from disinterested participant in the chase. The immense drifts of snow through which we were struggling at our best pace would soon vanquish one or the other of the party; it became a question of endurance simply, and the buffalo was the first to come to grief. Finding escape by running impossible, he boldly came to bay and faced his pursuers; in a moment both dogs had grappled with him as if he had been a deer. Blucher seized him by the throat, Maida endeavored to secure a firm hold on the shoulders. The result was that Blucher found himself well trampled in snow, and but for the latter would have been crushed to death. Fearing for the safety of my dogs, I leaped from my horse, who I knew would not leave me, and ran to the assistance of the stag-hounds. Drawing my hunting-knife and watching a favorable opportunity, I succeeded in cutting the hamstrings of the buffalo, which had the effect to tumble him over in the snow, when I was enabled to despatch him with my pistol.

On that afternoon we again encamped in the same valley up which we had been moving during the past three days. The next morning, following the lead of our Indian guides, who had been directed to conduct us to a point on the Canadian river near the Antelope Hills, our course, which so far had been westerly, now bore off almost due south. After ascending gradually for some hours to the crest or divide which sloped on the north down to the valley of the stream we had just left, we reached the highest line and soon began to gradually descend again, indicating that we were approaching a second valley; this the Indians assured us was the valley of the Canadian. Delayed in our progress by the deep snow and the difficulty from the same cause always experienced by our guides in selecting a practicable route, darkness overtook us before the entire command arrived at the point chosen for our camp on the north bank of the Canadian. As there is little or no timber found along the immediate banks of that river as far up as we then were, we pitched our tents about one mile from the river, and near a small fresh-water tributary whose valley was abundantly supplied with wood. If any prowling bands or war parties belonging to either of the tribes with which we were at war were moving across the Canadian in either direction, it was more than probable that their crossing would be made at some point above us, and not more than ten or fifteen miles distant. The season was rather far advanced to expect any of these parties to be absent from the village, but the trail of the war party, discovered by our Indian guides just before the expedition reached Camp Supply, was not forgotten, and the heavy storm of the past few days would be apt to drive them away from the settlements and hasten their return to their village. We had every reason to believe that the latter was located somewhere south of the Canadian. After discussing the matter with Little Beaver and Hard Rope, and listening to the suggestions of California Joe and his confrères, I decided to start a strong force up the valley of the Canadian at daybreak the following morning, to examine the banks and discover, if possible, if Indians had been in the vicinity since the snow had fallen. Three full troops of cavalry under Major Joel H. Elliot, 7th Cavalry, were ordered to move without wagons or *otro impedimiento*, each trooper to carry one hundred rounds of ammunition, one day's rations and forage. Their instructions were to proceed up the north bank of the Canadian a distance of fifteen miles. If any trail of Indians was discovered, pursuit was to be taken up at once, at the same time sending information of the fact back to the main command, indicating the number and character of the Indians as determined by their trail, and particularly the direction in which they were moving, in order that the main body of the troops might endeavor if possible to intercept the Indians, or at least strike the trail by a shorter route than by following the first detachment. A few of our Indian trailers were designated to accompany the party, as well as some of the white scouts. The latter were to be employed in carrying despatches back to the main command, should anything be discovered of sufficient importance to be reported. In the mean time I informed Major Elliot that as soon as it was fairly daylight I would commence crossing the main command over the Canadian—an operation which could not be performed hastily, as the banks were almost overflowing, the current being very rapid and the water filled with floating snow and ice. After making the cross ing I would, in the absence of any reports from him, march up the bluffs forming Antelope Hills and strike nearly due south, aiming to encamp that night on some one of the small streams forming the headwaters of the Washita river, where we would again unite the two portions of the command and continue our march to the south.

Major Elliot was a very zealous officer, and daylight found him and his command on the march in the execution of the duty to which they had been assigned. Those of us who remained behind were soon busily occupied in making preparations to effect a crossing of the Canadian. California Joe had been engaged since early dawn searching for a ford which would be practicable for our wagons; the troopers and horses could cross almost anywhere. A safe fording place barely practicable was soon reported, and the cavalry and wagon train began moving over. It was a tedious process; sometimes the treacherous quicksand would yield beneath the heavily laden wagons, and double the usual number of mules would be required to extricate the load. In less than three hours the last wagon and the rear guard of the cavalry had made a successful crossing. Looming up in our front like towering battlements were the Antelope Hills. These prominent landmarks, which can be seen from a distance of over twenty miles in all directions, are situated near the south bank of the Canadian, and at 100 deg. W. longitude. The Antelope Hills form a group of five separate hillocks, and are sometimes called Boundary Mounts. They vary in height above the average level of the plains between one hundred and fifty and three hundred feet. Two of the hills are conical and the others oblong; they are composed of porous sandstone, and are crowned with white and regular terraces about six yards in depth. From the summit of these terraces one enjoys a most commanding view. On the left is to be seen the red bed of the Canadian, whose tortuous windings, coming from the southwest, direct their course for a while northwards, and finally disappear in a distant easterly direction. The horizon is but an immense circle of snowy whiteness, of which the centre is the point of observation. Here and there a few acclivities rise above the plains, divided by rows of stunted trees, indicating a ravine, or more frequently a humble brook such as that on whose banks we camped the night previous to crossing the Canadian. It never occurred to any of us, when folding our tents that bleak winter morning on the bank of the Canadian, that there were those among our number who had bidden a last and final adieu to the friendly shelter of their canvas-covered homes; that for some of us, some who could but sadly be spared, the last reveille had sounded, and that when sleep again closed their eyes it would be that sleep from which there is no awakening. But I am anticipating.

One by one the huge army wagons, with their immense white covers, began the long ascent which was necessary to be overcome before attaining the level of the plains. As fast as they reached the high ground the leading wagons were halted and parked to await the arrival of the last to cross the river. In the mean time the cavalry had closed up and dismounted, except the rear guard, which was just then to be seen approaching from the river, indicating that "everything was closed up." I was about to direct the chief bugler to sound "To horse," when far in the distance, on the white surface of the snow, I descried a horseman approaching us as rapidly as his tired steed could carry him. The direction was that in which Elliot's command was supposed to be, and the horseman approaching could be none other than a messenger from Elliot. What tidings would he bring? was my first thought. Perhaps Elliot could not find a ford by which to cross the Canadian, and simply desired instructions as to what his course should be. Perhaps he has discovered an Indian trail—a fresh one; but it must be fresh if one at all; as the snow is scarcely three days old. If a trail has been discovered, then woe unto the luckless Indians whose footprints are discoverable in the snow; for so long as that remains and the endurance of men and horses holds out, just so long will we follow that trail, until the pursuer and pursued are brought face to face, or the one or the other succumbs to the fatigues and exhaustion of the race. These and a host of kindred thoughts flashed in rapid succession through my mind as soon as I had discovered the distant approach of the scout, for a scout I knew it must be. As yet none of the command had observed his coming, not being on as high ground as where I stood. By means of my field glass I was able to make out the familiar form of " Corbin," one of the scouts. After due waiting, when minutes seemed like hours, the scout galloped up to where I was waiting, and in a few hurried, almost breathless words, informed me that Elliot's command, after moving up the north bank of the Canadian about twelve miles, had discovered the trail of an Indian war party numbering upwards of one hundred and fifty strong; that the trail was not twenty-four hours old, and the party had crossed the Canadian and taken a course a little east of south. Elliot had crossed his command, and at once taken up the pursuit as rapidly as his horses could travel. Here was news, and of a desirable character. I asked the scout if he could overtake Elliot if furnished with a fresh horse. He thought he could. A horse was at once supplied him, and he was told to rejoin Elliot as soon as possible, with instructions to continue the pursuit with all possible vigor, and I would move with the main command in such direction as to strike his trail about dark. If the Indians changed their general direction, he was to inform me of the fact; and if I could not overtake him by eight o'clock that night, Elliot was to halt his command and await my arrival, when the combined force would move as circumstances might determine. My resolution was formed in a moment, and as quickly put in train of execution. The bugle summoned all the officers to report at once. There was no tardiness on their part, for while they had not heard the report brought in by the scout, they had witnessed his unexpected arrival and his equally sudden departure—circumstances which told them plainer than mere words that something unusual was in the air. The moment they were all assembled about me I acquainted them with the intelligence received from Elliot, and at the same time informed them that we would at once set out to join in the pursuit—a pursuit which could and would only end when we overtook our enemies. And in order that we should not be trammelled in our movements, it was my intention then and there to abandon our train of wagons, taking with us only such supplies as we could carry on our persons and strapped to our saddles. The train would be left under the protection of about eighty men detailed from the different troops, and under command of one officer, to whom orders would be given to follow us with the train as rapidly as the character of our route would permit. Each trooper was to carry with him one hundred rounds of ammunition, a small amount of coffee and hard bread, and on his saddle an equally small allowance of forage for his horse. Tents and extra blankets were to be left with the wagons. We were to move in light marching order as far as this was practicable. Then taking out my watch, the officers were notified that in twenty minutes from that time " the advance " would be sounded and the march in pursuit begun—

CORBIN THE SCOUT.

the intervening time to be devoted to carrying out the instructions just given. In a moment every man and officer in the command was vigorously at work preparing to set out for a rough ride, the extent or result of which no one could foresee. Wagons were emptied, mess chests called upon to contribute from their stores, ammunition chests opened and their contents distributed to the troopers. The most inferior of the horses were selected to fill up the detail of eighty cavalry which was to remain and escort the train; an extra amount of clothing was donned by some who realized that when the bitter, freezing hours of night came we would not have the comforts of tents and camp-fire to sustain us. If we had looked with proper dread upon the discomforts of the past three days, the severity of the storm, the deep snow, and our limited facilities for withstanding the inclemencies of midwinter even when provided with shelter, food, and fire, what was the prospect now opened before us when we proposed to relinquish even the few comforts we had at command, and start out on a mission not only full of danger, but where food would be very limited, and then only of the plainest kind? Shelterless we should be in the midst of the wide, open plains, where the winds blow with greater force, and owing to our proximity to the Indians even fires would be too costly an aid to our comfort to be allowed. Yet these thoughts scarcely found a place in the minds of any members of the command. All felt that a great opportunity was before us, and to improve it only required determination and firmness on our part. How thoroughly and manfully every demand of this kind was responded to by my command, I will endeavor to relate in the next chapter.

XV.

BEFORE proceeding to narrate the incidents of the pursuit which led us to the battle of the Washita, I will refer to the completion of our hasty preparations to detach ourselves from the encumbrance of our immense wagon train. In the last chapter it has been seen that the train was to be left behind under the protection of an officer and eighty cavalrymen, with orders to push after us, following our trail in the snow as rapidly as the teams could move. Where or when it would again join us no one could foretell; in all probability, however, not until the pursuit had terminated and we had met and vanquished our savage foes, or had been defeated by them. Under existing orders the guard for the protection of our train was each day under the command of the officer of the day, the tour of duty of the latter continuing twenty-four hours, beginning in the morning. On that day the duties of officer of the day fell in regular routine upon Captain Louis McLane Hamilton, Seventh Cavalry, a grandson of Alexander Hamilton. Of course this detail would require him to remain behind with the train while his squadron, one of the finest in the command, would move forward to battle under charge of another. To a soldier of Hamilton's pride and ambition, to be left behind in this inglorious manner was galling in the extreme. He foresaw the situation at once, and the moment that intelligence of the proposed movement reached him he came galloping up from the rear in search of me. I was busily engaged at the time superintending the hurried arrangements for commencing the pursuit. Coming up to me, with a countenance depicting the most earnest anxiety, his first words were to frame an inquiry as to whether I intended him to remain behind. Fully appreciating his anxious desire to share with his comrades the perils of the approaching conflict, and yet unable to substitute, without injustice, another officer for him unless with the consent of the former, I could not give him the encouragement he desired. The moment that the plans for pursuit were being formed, I remembered that the accidents of service were to deprive the pursuing column of the presence and aid of one whose assistance in such an emergency could always be confidently relied upon. Some of his brother officers had bethought themselves of the same, and at once came to me with the remark that " we ought to have Hamilton with us." My only reply was that while my desires were all one way my duty prescribed that Hamilton should remain with the guard and train, it being his detail, and it also being necessary that some officer should remain upon this important duty. I answered his repeated request, that while I desired him in command of his squadron, particularly then of all times, I was powerless to have it so without being unjust to some other officer. While forced to admit this to be true, he added, " It seems hard that I must remain." Finally I said to him that all I could do would be to allow him to get some other officer to willingly take his place with the train, adding that some officer might be found in the command who, from indisposition or other causes, did not feel able to undertake a rapid and tiresome pursuit such as we would probably have, and under such circumstances I would gladly order the change He at once departed in search of some one who would assume his duties with the train and leave him free to resume his post at the head of his splendid squadron—that squadron in whose organization and equipment he had displayed such energy and forethought, and whose superior excellency and efficiency long bore the impress of his hand. I am thus minute in detailing these circumstances affecting the transfer of Captain Hamilton from one duty to another, as the sad sequel will show how intimately connected the destiny of one of the parties was with the slight matter of this change. Hamilton had been absent but a few minutes when he returned overflowing with joy, and remarked that an officer had been found who consented to take his place, ending with the question, " Shall I join my squadron?" To this I gladly assented, and he galloped to another part of the field, where his men were, to hasten and superintend their preparations for the coming struggle. The officer who had consented to take Hamilton's place with the train had that day been affected with partial snow-blindness, and felt himself disqualified and unable to join in the pursuit, and it was exceedingly proper for him under the circumstances to agree to the proposed change.

During all this time Elliot with his three companies of calvary was following hard and fast upon the trail left by the Indians in the deep snow. By being informed, as we were, of the direction in which the trail was leading, and that direction being favorable to our position, the main command by moving due south would strike the trail of the Indians, and of Elliot also, at some point not far in rear perhaps of Elliot's party. Everything being in readiness to set out at the expiration of the allotted twenty minutes, "the advance" was sounded and the pursuit on our part began. Our route carried us across the broad, open plains, the snow over a foot in depth, with surface of course unbroken. This rendered it exceedingly fatiguing to the horses moving in the advance, and changes were frequently rendered necessary. The weather, which during the past few days had been so bitterly cold, moderated on that day sufficiently to melt the upper surface of the snow. After leaving the wagon train, we continued our march rapidly during the remaining hours of the forenoon and until the middle of the afternoon. Still no tidings from Elliot's party nor any sign of a trail. No halt was made during the day either for rest or refreshment. Toward evening we began to feel anxious concerning Elliot's detachment. Could it be that the Indians had discovered that they were pursued, and had broken up into smaller parties or changed the direction of their trail? If so, could Elliot's messengers reach us in time to make the information valuable to us? We had hurried along, our interest increasing with each mile passed over, until the sun was not more than one hour high above the western horizon; and still, strain our eyes as we would, and scan the white surface of the plains in every direction in our front, the snow seemed unbroken and undisturbed as far as the eye could reach. Our scouts and Indian guides were kept far out in front and on the proper flank, to discover, if possible, the trail. At last one of the scouts gave the signal that the trail had been discovered, and in a few moments the command had reached it, and we were now moving with lighter and less anxious hearts. After studying the trail our Osage warriors informed us that the Indians whose trail we were pursuing were undoubtedly a war party, and had certainly passed where we then were during the forenoon. This was encouraging, and a free rein was given to our horses as we hastened along through the snow. The object now was to overtake as soon as practicable the party of Elliot, which from the heavy trail we could see was in advance of us. The almost level and unbroken character of the country enabled us to see for miles in all directions, and in this way we knew that Elliot must be many miles ahead of our party At the same time I could see that we were gradually descending into a valley, probably of some stream, and far in advance appeared the dim outline of timber, such as usually fringes the banks of many of the Western streams. Selecting a few well-mounted troopers and some of the scouts, I directed them to set out at a moderate gallop to overtake Elliot, with orders to the latter to halt at the first favorable point where wood and water could be obtained, and await our arrival, informing him at the same time that after allowing the men an hour to prepare a cup of coffee and to feed and rest their horses, it was my intention to continue the pursuit during the night—a measure to which I felt urged by the slight thawing of the snow that day, which might result in our failure if we permitted the Indians to elude us until the snow had disappeared. Satisfied now that we were on the right course, our anxiety lessened, but our interest increased. Soon after dark we reached the valley whose timbered surface we had caught faint glimpses of hours before. Down this valley and through this sparse timber the trail led us. Hour after hour we struggled on, hoping to overtake the three troops in advance, for hunger, unappeased since before daylight, began to assert its demands in the strongest terms. Our faithful horses were likewise in great need of both food and water, as well as rest, as neither had been offered them since four o'clock in the morning. So far had Elliot pushed his pursuit that our scouts were a long time in reaching him, and it was nine o'clock at night when the main command arrived at the point where he and his three troops were found halted. A stream of good water with comparatively deep banks ran near by, while the valley at this point was quite heavily timbered.

To enable the men to prepare a cup of coffee, and at the same time give no evidence of our presence to the Indians, who, for all we knew, might be not far from us, advantage was taken of the deep banks of the creek, and by building small fires down under the edge of the bank, they were prevented from being seen, except at a small distance. At the same time the horses were relieved of their saddles and unbitted, and a good feed of oats distributed to each. Officers and men were glad to partake of the same quality of simple fare that night, consisting only of a most welcome and refreshing cup of good strong coffee and a handful of army crackers—"hard tack." By waiting an hour we not only gained by rest and refreshment, but the light of the moon would then probably be sufficient to guide us on our night ride. When the hour had nearly expired, we began our preparations in the most quiet manner to resume the pursuit. No bugle calls were permitted, as in this peculiar country sound travels a long distance, and we knew not but that our wily foes were located near by. Before starting I conferred with our Indian allies, all of whom were firmly convinced that our enemy's village was probably not far away, and most likely was in the valley in which we then were, as the trail for some miles had led us down the stream on whose banks we halted. "Little Beaver," who acted as spokesman for the Osages, seemed confident that we could overtake and surprise the Indians we had been pursuing, and most probably follow them direct to their village; but, much to my surprise, Little Beaver strongly advised that we delay further pursuit until daylight, remaining concealed in the timber as we were at the time. When asked for his reasons for favoring such a course, he could give none of a satisfactory nature. I then concluded that his disinclination to continue pursuit that night arose from the natural reluctance, shared by all Indians, to attack an unseen foe, whether con-

THE OSAGE SCOUTS.

14

cealed by darkness or other natural or artificial means of shelter. Indians rarely attack between the hours of dark and daylight, although their stealthy movements through the country, either in search of an enemy or when attempting to elude them, are often executed under cover of night.

As soon as each troop was in readiness to resume the pursuit, the troop commander reported the fact at headquarters. Ten o'clock came and found us in our saddles. Silently the command stretched out its long length as the troopers filed off four abreast. First came two of our Osage scouts on foot; these were to follow the trail and lead the command; they were our guides, and the panther, creeping upon its prey, could not have advanced more cautiously or quietly than did these friendly Indians, as they seemed to glide rather than walk over the snow-clad surface. To prevent the possibility of the command coming precipitately upon our enemies, the two scouts were directed to keep three or four hundred yards in advance of all others; then came, in single file, the remainder of our Osage guides and the white scouts—among the rest California Joe. With these I rode, that I might be as near the advance guard as possible. The cavalry followed in rear, at the distance of a quarter or half a mile; this precaution was necessary, from the fact that the snow, which had thawed slightly during the day, was then freezing, forming a crust which, broken by the tread of so many hundreds of feet, produced a noise capable of being heard at a long distance. Orders were given prohibiting even a word being uttered above a whisper. No one was permitted to strike a match or light a pipe—the latter a great deprivation to the soldier. In this silent manner we rode mile after mile. Occasionally an officer would ride by my side and whisper some inquiry or suggestion, but aside from this our march was unbroken by sound or deed. At last we discovered that our two guides in front had halted, and were awaiting my arrival. Word was quietly sent to halt the column until inquiry in front could be made. Upon coming up with the two Osages we were furnished an example of the wonderful and peculiar powers of the Indian. One of them could speak broken English, and in answer to my question as to "What is the matter?" he replied, "Me don't know, but me smell fire." By this time several of the officers had quietly ridden up, and upon being informed of the Osage's remark, each endeavored, by sniffing the air, to verify or disprove the report. All united in saying that our guide was mistaken. Some said he was probably frightened, but we were unable to shake the confidence of the Osage warrior in his first opinion. I then directed him and his companion to advance even more cautiously than before, and the column, keeping up the interval, resumed its march. After proceeding about half a mile, perhaps further, again our guides halted, and upon coming up with them I was greeted with the remark, uttered in a whisper, "Me told you so;" and sure enough, looking in the direction indicated, were to be seen the embers of a wasted fire, scarcely a handful, yet enough to prove that our guide was right, and to cause us to feel the greater confidence in him. The discovery of these few coals of fire produced almost breathless excitement. The distance from where we stood was from seventy-five to a hundred yards, not in the line of our march, but directly to our left, in the edge of the timber. We knew at once that none but Indians, and they hostile, had built that fire. Where were they at that moment? Perhaps sleeping in the vicinity of the fire.

It was almost certain to our minds that the Indians we had been pursuing were the builders of the fire. Were they still there and asleep? We were too near already to attempt to withdraw undiscovered. Our only course was to determine the facts at once, and be prepared for the worst. I called for a few volunteers to quietly approach the fire and discover whether there were Indians in the vicinity; if not, to gather such information as was obtainable, as to their numbers and departure. All the Osages and a few of the scouts quickly dismounted, and with rifles in readiness and fingers on the triggers silently made their way to the nearest point of the timber, Little Beaver and Hard Rope leading the way. After they had disappeared in the timber they still had to pass over more than half the distance before reaching the fire. These moments seemed like hours, and those of us who were left sitting on our horses, in the open moonlight, and within easy range from the spot where the fire was located, felt anything but comfortable during this suspense. If Indians, as then seemed highly probable, were sleeping around the fire, our scouts would arouse them and we would be in fair way to be picked off without being in a position to defend ourselves. The matter was soon determined. Our scouts soon arrived at the fire, and discovered it to be deserted. Again did the skill and knowledge of our Indian allies come in play. Had they not been with us we should undoubtedly have assumed that the Indians who had had occasion to build the fire and those we were pursuing constituted one party. From examining the fire and observing the great number of pony tracks in the snow, the Osages arrived at a different conclusion, and were convinced that we were then on the ground used by the Indians for grazing their herds of ponies. The fire had been kindled by the Indian boys, who attend to the herding, to warm themselves by, and in all probability we were then within two or three miles of the village. I will not endeavor to describe the renewed hope and excitement that sprung up. Again we set out, this time more cautiously if possible than before, the command and scouts moving at a greater distance in rear.

In order to judge of the situation more correctly, I this time accompanied the two Osages. Silently we advanced, I mounted, they on foot, keeping at the head of my horse. Upon nearing the crest of each hill, as is invariably the Indian custom, one of the guides would hasten a few steps in advance and peer cautiously over the hill. Accustomed to this, I was not struck by observing it until once, when the same one who discovered the fire advanced cautiously to the crest and looked carefully into the valley beyond. I saw him place his hand above his eyes as if looking intently at some object, then crouch down and come creeping back to where I waited for him. "What is it?" I inquired as soon as he reached my horse's side. "Heaps Injuns down there," pointing in the direction from which he had just come. Quickly dismounting and giving the reins to the other guide, I accompanied the Osage to the crest, both of us crouching low so as not to be seen in the moonlight against the horizon. Looking in the direction indicated, I could indistinctly recognize the presence of a large body of animals of some kind in the valley below, and at a distance which then seemed not more than half a mile. I looked at them long and anxiously, the guide uttering not a word, but was unable to discover anything in their appearance different from what might be presented by a herd of buffalo under similar circumstances. Turning to the Osage, I inquired in a low tone why he thought there were Indians there. "Me heard dog bark," was the satisfactory reply. Indians are noted for the large number of dogs always found in their villages, but never accompanying their war parties. I waited quietly to be convinced; I was assured, but wanted to be doubly so. I was rewarded in a moment by hearing the barking of a dog in the heavy timber off to the right of the herd, and soon after I heard the tinkling of a

THE BATTLE OF THE WASHITA.

small bell; this convinced me that it was really the Indian herd I then saw, the bell being one worn around the neck of some pony who was probably the leader of the herd. I turned to retrace my steps when another sound was borne to my ear through the cold, clear atmosphere of the valley—it was the distant cry of an infant; and savages though they were, and justly outlawed y the number and atrocity of their recent murders and depredations on the helpless settlers of the frontier, I could not but regret that in a war such as we were forced to engage in, the mode and circumstances of battle woul possibly prevent discrimination.

Leaving the two Osages to keep a careful lookout, I hastened back until I met the main party of the scouts and Osages. They were halted and a message sent back to halt the cavalry, enjoining complete silence, and directing every officer to ride to the point we then occupied. The hour was then past midnight. Soon they came, and after dismounting and collecting in a little circle, I informed them of what I had seen and heard; and in order that they might individually learn as much as possible of the character of the ground and the location of the village, I proposed that all should remove their sabres, that their clanking might make no noise, and proceed gently to the crest and there obtain a view of the valley beyond. This was done; not a word was spoken until we crouched together and cast our eyes in the direction of the herd and village. In whispers I briefly pointed out everything that was to be seen, then motioned all to return to where we had left our sabres; then, standing in a group upon the ground or crust of snow, the plan of the attack was explained to all and each assigned his part. The general plan was to employ the hours between then and daylight to completely surround the village, and, at daybreak, or as soon as it was barely light enough for the purpose, to attack the Indians from all sides. The command, numbering, as has been stated, about eight hundred mounted men, was divided into four nearly equal detachments. Two of them set out at once, as they had each to make a circuitous march of several miles in order to arrive at the points assigned them from which to make their attack. The third detachment moved to its position about an hour before day, and until that time remained with the main or fourth column. This last, whose movements I accompanied, was to make the attack from the point from which we had first discovered the herd and village. Major Elliot commanded the column embracing G, H, and M troops, Seventh Cavalry, which moved around from our left to a position almost in rear of the village; while Colonel Thompson commanded the one consisting of B and F troops, which moved in a corresponding manner from our right to a position which was to connect with that of Major Elliot. Colonel Myers commanded the third column, composed of E and I troops, which was to take position in the valley and timber a little less than a mile to my right. By this disposition it was hoped to prevent the escape of every inmate of the village. That portion of the command which I proposed to accompany consisted of A, C, D, and K troops, Seventh Cavalry, the Osages and scouts, and Colonel Cook with his forty sharpshooters. Captain Hamilton commanded one of the squadrons, Colonel West the other. After the first two columns had departed for their posts—it was still four hours before the hour of attack—the men of the other two columns were permitted to dismount, but much intense suffering was unavoidably sustained. The night grew extremely cold towards morning; no fires of course could be permitted, and the men were even ordered to desist from stamping their feet and walking back and forth to keep warm, as the crushing of the snow beneath produced so much noise that it might give the alarm to our wily enemies.

During all these long weary hours of this terribly cold and comfortless night each man sat, stood, or lay on the snow by his horse, holding to the rein of the latter. The officers, buttoning their huge overcoats closely about them, collected in knots of four or five, and, seated or reclining upon the snow's hard crust, discussed the probabilities of the coming battle—for battle we knew it would be, and we could not hope to conquer or kill the warriors of an entire village without suffering in return more or less injury. Some, wrapping their capes about their heads, spread themselves at full length upon the snow and were apparently soon wrapt in deep slumber. After being satisfied that all necessary arrangements were made for the attack, I imitated the example of some of my comrades, and gathering the cavalry cape of my greatcoat about my head lay down and slept soundly for perhaps an hour. At the end of that time I awoke, and on consulting my watch found there remained nearly two hours before we would move to the attack. Walking about among the horses and troopers, I found the latter generally huddled at the feet of the former in squads of three and four, in the endeavor to keep warm. Occasionally I would find a small group engaged in conversation, the muttered tones and voices strangely reminding me of those heard in the death-chamber. The officers had disposed of themselves in similar but various ways; here at one place were several stretched out together upon the snow, the body of one being used by the others as a pillow. Nearly all were silent; conversation had ceased, and those who were prevented by the severe cold from obtaining sleep were no doubt fully occupied in their minds with thoughts upon the morrow and the fate that might be in store for them. Seeing a small group collected under the low branches of a tree which stood a little distance from the ground occupied by the troops, I made my way there to find the Osage warriors with their chiefs Little Beaver and Hard Rope. They were wrapped up in their blankets sitting in a circle, and had evidently made no effort to sleep during the night. It was plain to be seen that they regarded the occasion as a momentous one, and that the coming battle had been the sole subject of their conference. What the views expressed by them were I did not learn until after the engagement was fought, when they told me what ideas they had entertained regarding the manner in which the white men would probably conduct and terminate the struggle next day. After the success of the day was decided, the Osages told me that, with the suspicion so natural and peculiar to the Indian nature, they had, in discussing the proposed attack upon the Indian village, concluded that we would be outnumbered by the occupants of the village, who of course would fight with the utmost desperation in defence of their lives and lodges, and to prevent a complete defeat of our forces or to secure a drawn battle, we might be induced to engage in a parley with the hostile tribe, and on coming to an agreement we would probably, to save ourselves, offer to yield up our Osage allies as a compromise measure between our enemies and ourselves. They also mistrusted the ability of the whites to make a successful attack upon a hostile village, located—as this one was known to be—in heavy timber, and aided by the natural banks of the stream. Disaster seemed certain in the minds of the Osages to follow us, if we attacked a force of unknown strength and numbers; and the question with them was to secure such a position in the attack as to be able promptly to detect any move disadvantageous to them. With this purpose they came to the conclusion that standard-bearer was a very important personage, and neither he nor his standard would be carried into danger or exposed to the bullets of the enemy. They determined therefore to take their station immediately behind my stand-ard-bearer when the lines became formed for attack, to follow him during the action, and thus be able to watch our movements, and if we were successful over our foes to aid us; if the battle should go against us, then they, being in a safe position, could take advantage of circumstances and save themselves as best they might.

Turning from our Osage friends, who were, unknown to us, entertaining such doubtful opinions as to our fidelity to them, I joined another group near by, consisting of most of the white scouts. Here were California Joe and several of his companions. One of the latter deserves a passing notice. He was a low, heavy-set Mexican, with features resembling somewhat those of the Ethiopian— thick lips, depressed nose, and low forehead. He was quite a young man, probably not more than twenty-five years of age, but had passed the greater portion of his life with the Indians, had adopted their habits of life and modes of dress, and had married among them. Familiar with the language of the Cheyennes and other neighboring tribes, he was invaluable both as a scout and interpreter. His real name was Romero, but some of the officers of the command, with whom he was a sort of favorite, had dubbed him Romeo, and by this name he was always known, a sobriquet to which he responded as readily as if he had been christened under it; never protesting, like the ori-ginal Romeo,

> Tut, I have lost myself; I am not here;
> This is not Romeo, he's some other where.

The scouts, like nearly all the other members of the command, had been interchanging opinions as to the result of the movements of the following day. Not sharing the mistrust and suspicion of the Osage guides, yet the present experience was in many respects new to them, and to some the issue seemed at least shrouded in uncertainty. Addressing the group, I began the conversa-tion with the question as to what they thought of the prospect of our having a fight. "Fight!" responded California Joe; "I havn't nary doubt concernin' that part uv the business; what I've been tryin' to get through my topknot all night is whether we'll run aginst more than we bargain fur." "Then you do not think the Indians will run away, Joe?" "Run away! How in creation can Injuns or anybody else run away when we'll have 'em clean surrounded afore daylight?" "Well, suppose then that we succeed in surrounding the village, do you think we can hold our own against the Indians?" "That's the very pint that's been botherin' me ever since we planted ourselves down here, and the only conclusion I kin come at is that it's purty apt to be one thing or t'other; if we pump these Injuns at daylight, we're either goin' to make a spoon or spile a horn, an' that's my candid judgment, sure. One thing's certain, ef them Injuns doesn't har anything uv us till we open on 'em at day-light, they'll be the most powerful 'stonished redskins that's been in these parts lately—they will, sure. An' ef we git the bulge on 'em, and keep puttin' it to 'em sort a lively like, we'll sweep the platter—thar won't be nary trick left for 'em. As the deal stands now, we hold the keerds and are holdin' over 'em; they've got to straddle our blind or throw up their hands. Howsomever, thar's a mighty sight in the draw."

California Joe continued in this strain, and, by a prolific use of terms con-nected with other transactions besides fighting Indians, did not fail to impress his hearers that his opinion in substance was that our attack in the morning was to result in overwhelming success to us, or that we would be utterly routed and dispersed—that there would be no drawn battle.

The night passed in quiet. I anxiously watched the opening signs of dawn in order to put the column in motion. We were only a few hundred yards from the point from which we were to attack. The moon disappeared about two hours before dawn, and left us enshrouded in thick and utter darkness, making the time seem to drag even slower than before.

At last faint signs of approaching day were visible, and I proceeded to collect the officers, awakening those who slept. We were standing in a group near the head of the column, when suddenly our attention was attracted by a remarkable sight, and for a time we felt that the Indians had discovered our presence. Directly beyond the crest of the hill which separated us from the village, and in a line with the supposed location of the latter, we saw rising slowly but perceptibly, as we thought, up from the village, and appearing in bold relief against the dark sky as a background, something which we could only compare to a signal rocket, except that its motion was slow and regular. All eyes were turned to it in blank astonishment, and but one idea seemed to be entertained, and that was that one or both of the two attacking columns under Elliot or Thompson had encountered a portion of the village, and this that we saw was the signal to other portions of the band near at hand. Slowly and majestically it continued to rise above the crest of the hill, first appearing as a small brilliant flaming globe of bright golden hue. As it ascended still higher it seemed to increase in size, to move more slowly, while its colors rapidly changed from one to the other, exhibiting in turn the most beautiful combinations of prismatic tints. There seemed to be not the shadow of doubt that we were discovered. The strange apparition in the heavens maintained its steady course upward. One anxious spectator, observing it apparently at a standstill, exclaimed, "How long it hangs fire! why don't it explode?" still keeping the idea of a signal rocket in mind. It had risen perhaps to the height of half a degree above the horizon as observed from our position, when, lo! the mystery was dispelled. Rising above the mystifying influences of the atmosphere, that which had appeared so suddenly before us, and excited our greatest apprehensions, developed into the brightest and most beautiful of morning stars. Often since that memorable morning have I heard officers remind each other of the strange appearance which had so excited our anxiety and alarm. In less perilous moments we probably would have regarded it as a beautiful phenomenon of nature, of which so many are to be witnessed through the pure atmosphere of the plains.

All were ordered to get ready to advance; not a word to officer or men was spoken above undertone. It began growing lighter in the east, and we moved forward toward the crest of the hill. Up to this time two of the officers and one of the Osages had remained on the hill overlooking the valley beyond, so as to detect any attempt at a movement on the part of the occupants of the village below. These now rejoined the troops. Colonel West's squadron was formed in line on the right, Captain Hamilton's squadron in line on the left, while Colonel Cook with his forty sharpshooters was formed in advance of the left, dismounted. Although the early morning air was freezingly cold, the men were directed to remove their overcoats and haversacks, so as to render them free in their movements. Before advancing beyond the crest of the hill, strict orders were issued prohibiting the firing of a single shot until the signal to attack should be made. The other three detachments had been informed before setting out that the main column would attack promptly at daylight, without waiting to ascertain whether they were in position or not. In fact it would be impracticable to communicate with either of the first two until the attack began. The plan was for each party to approach as closely to the village as possible without being discovered, and there await the approach of daylight. The regimental band was to move with my detachment, and it was understood that the band should strike up the instant the attack opened. Colonel Myers, commanding the third party, was also directed to move one-half his detachment dismounted. In this order we began to descend the slope leading down to the village. The distance to the timber in the valley proved greater than it had appeared to the eye in the darkness of the night. We soon reached the outskirts of the herd of ponies. The latter seemed to recognize us as hostile parties and moved quickly away. The light of day was each minute growing stronger, and we feared discovery before we could approach near enough to charge the village. The movement of our horses over the crusted snow produced considerable noise, and would doubtless have led to our detection but for the fact that the Indians, if they heard it at all, presumed it was occasioned by their herd of ponies. I would have given much at that moment to know the whereabouts of the first two columns sent out. Had they reached their assigned positions, or had unseen and unknown obstacles delayed or misled them? These were questions which could not then be answered. We had now reached the level of the valley, and began advancing in line toward the heavy timber in which and close at hand we knew the village was situated.

Immediately in rear of my horse came the band, all mounted, and each with his instrument in readiness to begin playing the moment their leader, who rode at their head, and who kept his cornet to his lips, should receive the signal. I had previously told him to play "Garry Owen" as the opening piece. We had approached near enough to the village now to plainly catch a view here and there of the tall white lodges as they stood in irregular order among the trees. From the openings at the top of some of them we could perceive faint columns of smoke ascending, the occupants no doubt having kept up their feeble fires during the entire night. We had approached so near the village that from the dead silence which reigned I feared the lodges were deserted, the Indians having fled before we advanced. I was about to turn in my saddle and direct the signal for attack to be given—still anxious as to where the other detachments were—when a single rifle shot rang sharp and clear on the far side of the village from where we were. Quickly turning to the band leader, I directed him to give us "Garry Owen." At once the rollicking notes of that familiar marching and fighting air sounded forth through the valley, and in a moment were reëchoed back from the opposite sides by the loud and continued cheers of the men of the other detachments, who, true to their orders, were there and in readiness to pounce upon the Indians the moment the attack began. In this manner the battle of the Washita commenced. The bugles sounded the charge, and the entire command dashed rapidly into the village. The Indians were caught napping; but realizing at once the dangers of their situation, they quickly overcame their first surprise and in an instant seized their rifles, bows, and arrows, and sprang behind the nearest trees, while some leaped into the stream, nearly waist deep, and using the bank as a rifle-pit, began a vigorous and determined defence. Mingled with the exultant cheers of my men could be heard the defiant war-whoop of the warriors, who from the first fought with a desperation and courage which no race of men could surpass. Actual possession of the village and its lodges was ours within a few moments after the charge was made, but this was an empty victory unless we could vanquish the late occupants, who were then pouring in a rapid and well-directed fire from their stations behind trees and banks. At the first onset a considerable number of the Indians rushed from the village in the direction from which Elliot's party had attacked. Some broke through the lines, while others came in contact with the mounted troopers, and were killed or captured.

Before engaging in the fight, orders had been given to prevent the killing of any but the fighting strength of the village; but in a struggle of this character it is impossible at all times to discriminate, particularly when, in a hand-to-hand conflict, such as the one the troops were then engaged in, the squaws are as dangerous adversaries as the warriors, while Indian boys between ten and fifteen years of age were found as expert and determined in the use of the pistol and bow and arrow as the older warriors. Of these facts we had numerous illustrations. Major Benteen, in leading the attack of his squadron through the timber below the village, encountered an Indian boy, scarcely fourteen years of age; he was well mounted, and was endeavoring to make his way through the lines. The object these Indians had in attempting this movement we were then ignorant of, but soon learned to our sorrow. This boy rode boldly toward the Major, seeming to invite a contest. His youthful bearing, and not being looked upon as a combatant, induced Major Benteen to endeavor to save him by making "peace signs" to him and obtaining his surrender, when he could be placed in a position of safety until the battle was terminated; but the young savage desired and would accept no such friendly concessions. He regarded himself as a warrior, and the son of a warrior, and as such he purposed to do a warrior's part. With revolver in hand he dashed at the Major, who still could not regard him as anything but a harmless lad. Levelling his weapon as he rode, he fired, but either from excitement or the changing positions of both parties, his aim was defective and the shot whistled harmlessly by Major Benteen's head. Another followed in quick succession, but with no better effect. All this time the dusky little chieftain boldly advanced, to lessen the distance between himself and his adversary. A third bullet was sped on its errand, and this time to some purpose, as it passed through the neck of the Major's horse, close to the shoulder. Making a final but ineffectual appeal to him to surrender, and seeing him still preparing to fire again, the Major was forced in self-defence to level his revolver and despatch him, although as he did so it was with admiration for the plucky spirit exhibited by the lad, and regret often expressed that no other course under the circumstances was left him. Attached to the saddle bow of the young Indian hung a beautifully wrought pair of small moccasins, elaborately ornamented with beads. One of the Major's troopers afterward secured these and presented them to him. These furnished the link of evidence by which we subsequently ascertained who the young chieftain was—a title which was justly his, both by blood and bearing.

We had gained the centre of the village, and were in the midst of the lodges, while on all sides could be heard the sharp crack of the Indian rifles and the heavy responses from the carbines of the troopers. After disposing of the smaller and scattering parties of warriors, who had attempted a move ment down the valley, and in which some were successful, there was but little opportunity left for the successful employment of mounted troops. As the Indians by this time had taken cover behind logs and trees, and under the banks of the stream which flowed through the centre of the village, from which stronghold it was impracticable to dislodge them by the use of mounted men, a large portion of the command was at once ordered to fight on foot, and the men were instructed to take advantage of the trees and other natural means of cover, and fight the Indians in their own style. Cook's sharpshooters had adopted this method from the first, and with telling effect. Slowly but steadily the Indians were driven from behind the trees, and those who escaped the carbine bullets posted themselves with their companions who were already firing from the banks. One party of troopers came upon a squaw endeavoring to make her escape, leading by the hand a little white boy, a prisoner in the hands of the Indians, and who doubtless had been captured by some of their war parties during a raid upon the settlements. Who or where his parents were, or whether still alive or murdered by the Indians, will never be known, as the squaw, finding herself and prisoner about to be surrounded by the troops, and her escape cut off, determined, with savage malignity, that the triumph of the latter should not embrace the rescue of the white boy. Casting her eyes quickly in all directions, to convince herself that escape was impossible, she drew from beneath her blanket a huge knife and plunged it into the almost naked body of her captive. The next moment retributive justice reached her in the shape of a well-directed bullet from one of the troopers' carbines. Before the men could reach them life was extinct in the bodies of both the squaw and her unknown captive.

The desperation with which the Indians fought may be inferred from the following: Seventeen warriors had posted themselves in a depression in the ground, which enabled them to protect their bodies completely from the fire of our men, and it was only when the Indians raised their heads to fire that the troopers could aim with any prospect of success. All efforts to drive the warriors from this point proved abortive, and resulted in severe loss to our side. They were only vanquished at last by our men securing positions under cover and picking them off by sharpshooting as they exposed themselves to get a shot at the troopers. Finally the last one was despatched in this manner. In a deep ravine near the suburbs of the village the dead bodies of thirty-eight warriors were reported after the fight terminated. Many of the squaws and children had very prudently not attempted to leave the village when we attacked it, but remained concealed inside their lodges. All these escaped injury, although when surrounded by the din and wild excitement of the fight, and in close proximity to the contending parties, their fears overcame some of them, and they gave vent to their despair by singing the death song, a combination of weird-like sounds which were suggestive of anything but musical tones. As soon as we had driven the warriors from the village, and the fighting was pushed to the country outside, I directed "Romeo," the interpreter, to go around to all the lodges and assure the squaws and children remaining in them that they would be unharmed and kindly cared for; at the same time he was to assemble them in the large lodges designated for that purpose, which were standing near the centre of the village. This was quite a delicate mission, as it was difficult to convince the squaws and children that they had any thing but death to expect at our hands.

It was perhaps ten o'clock in the forenoon, and the fight was still raging, when to our surprise we saw a small party of Indians collected on a knoll a little over a mile below the village, and in the direction taken by those Indians who had effected an escape through our lines at the commencement of the attack. My surprise was not so great at first, as I imagined that the Indians we saw were those who had contrived to escape, and having procured their ponies from the herd had mounted them and were then anxious spectators of the fight, which they felt themselves too weak in numbers to participate in. In the mean time the herds of ponies belonging to the village, on being alarmed by the firing and shouts of the contestants, had, from a sense of imagined security or custom, rushed into the village, where details of troopers were made to receive them. California Joe, who had been moving about in a promiscuous and independent manner, came galloping into the village, and reported that a large herd of ponies was to be seen near by, and requested authority and some men to bring them in. The men were otherwise employed just then, but he was authorized to collect and drive in the herd if practicable. He departed on his errand, and I had forgotten all about him and the ponies, when in the course of half an hour I saw a herd of nearly three hundred ponies coming on the gallop toward the village, driven by a couple of squaws, who were mounted, and had been concealed near by, no doubt; while bringing up the rear was California Joe, riding his favorite mule, and whirling about his head a long lariat, using it as a whip in urging the herd forward. He had captured the squaws while endeavoring to secure the ponies, and very wisely had employed his captives to assist in driving the herd. By this time the group of Indians already discovered outside our lines had increased until it numbered upwards of a hundred. Examining them through my field glass, I could plainly perceive that they were all mounted warriors; not only that, but they were armed and caparisoned in full war costume, nearly all wearing the bright-colored war-bonnets and floating their lance pennants. Constant accessions to their numbers were to be seen arriving from beyond the hill on which they stood. All this seemed inexplicable. A few Indians might have escaped through our lines when the attack on the village began, but only a few, and even these must have gone with little or nothing in their possession save their rifles and perhaps a blanket. Who could these new parties be, and from whence came they? To solve these troublesome questions I sent for "Romeo," and taking him with me to one of the lodges occupied by the squaws, I interrogated one of the latter as to who were the Indians to be seen assembling on the hill below the village. She informed me, to a surprise on my part almost equal to that of the Indians at our sudden appearance at daylight, that just below the village we then occupied, and which was a part of the Cheyenne tribe, were located in succession the winter villages of all the hostile tribes of the southern plains with which we were at war, including the Arrapahoes, Kiowas, the remaining band of Cheyennes, the Comanches, and a portion of the Apaches; that the nearest village was about two miles distant, and the others stretched along through the timbered valley to the one furthest off, which was not over ten miles.

What was to be done?—for I needed no one to tell me that we were certain to be attacked, and that, too, by greatly superior numbers, just as soon as the Indians below could make their arrangements to do so; and they had probably been busily employed at these arrangements ever since the sound of firing had reached them in the early morning, and been reported from village to village. Fortunately, affairs took a favorable turn in the combat in which we were then engaged, and the firing had almost died away. Only here and there where some warrior still maintained his position was the fight continued. Leaving as few men as possible to look out for these, I hastily collected and reformed my command, and posted them in readiness for the attack which we all felt was soon to be made; for already at different points and in more than one direction we could see more than enough warriors to outnumber us, and we knew they were only waiting the arrival of the chiefs and warriors from the lower villages before making any move against us. In the meanwhile our temporary hospital had been established in the centre of the village, where the wounded were receiving such surgical care as circumstances would permit. Our losses had been severe; indeed we were not then aware how great they had been. Hamilton, who rode at my side as we entered the village, and whose soldierly tones I heard for the last time as he calmly cautioned his squadron, " Now, men, keep cool, fire low, and not too rapidly," was among the first victims of the opening charge, having been shot from his saddle by a bullet from an Indian rifle. He died instantly. His lifeless remains were tenderly carried by some of his troopers to the vicinity of the hospital. Soon afterwards I saw four troopers coming from the front bearing between them, in a blanket, a wounded soldier; galloping to them, I discovered Colonel Barnitz, another troop commander, who was almost in a dying condition, having been shot by a rifle bullet directly through the body in the vicinity of the heart. Of Major Elliot, the officer second in rank, nothing had been seen since the attack at daylight, when he rode with his detachment into the village. He, too had evidently been killed, but as yet we knew not where or how he had fallen. Two other officers had received wounds, while the casualties among the enlisted men were also large. The sergeant-major of the regiment, who was with me when the first shot was heard, had not been seen since that moment. We were not in as effective condition by far as when the attack was made, yet we were soon to be called upon to contend against a force immensely superior to the one with which we had been engaged during the early hours of the day. The captured herds of ponies were carefully collected inside our lines, and so guarded as to prevent their stampede or recapture by the Indians. Our wounded, and the immense amount of captured property in the way of ponies, lodges, etc., as well as our prisoners, were obstacles in the way of our attempting an offensive movement against the lower villages. To have done this would have compelled us to divide our forces, when it was far from certain that we could muster strength enough united to repel the attacks of the combined tribes. On all sides of us the Indians could now be seen in considerable numbers, so that from being the surrounding party, as we had been in the morning, we now found ourselves surrounded and occupying the position of defenders of the village. Fortunately for us, as the men had been expending a great many rounds, Major Bell, the quartermaster, who with a small escort was endeavoring to reach us with a fresh supply of ammunition, had by constant exertion and hard marching succeeded in doing so, and now appeared on the ground with several thousand rounds of carbine ammunition, a reinforcement greatly needed. He had no sooner arrived safely than the Indians attacked from the direction from which he came. How he had managed to elude their watchful eyes I never could comprehend, unless their attention had been so completely absorbed in watching our movements inside as to prevent them from keeping an eye out to discover what might be transpiring elsewhere.

Issuing a fresh supply of ammunition to those most in want of it, the fight soon began generally at all points of the circle. For such in reality had our line of battle become—a continuous and unbroken circle of which the village was about the centre. Notwithstanding the great superiority in numbers of the Indians, they fought with excessive prudence and a lack of that confident manner which they usually manifest when encountering greatly inferior numbers—a result due, no doubt, to the fate which had overwhelmed our first opponents. Besides, the timber and the configuration of the ground enabled us to keep our men concealed until their services were actually required. It seemed to be the design and wish of our antagonists to draw us away from the village; but in this they were foiled. Seeing that they did not intend to press the attack just then, about two hundred of my men were ordered to pull down the lodges in the village and collect the captured property in huge piles preparatory to burning. This was done in the most effectual manner. When everything had been collected the torch was applied, and all that was left of the village were a few heaps of blackened ashes. Whether enraged at the sight of this destruction or from other cause, the attack soon became general along our entire line, and pressed with so much vigor and audacity that every available trooper was required to aid in meeting these assaults. The Indians would push a party of well-mounted warriors close up to our lines in the endeavor to find a weak point through which they might venture, but in every attempt were driven back. I now concluded, as the village was off our hands and our wounded had been collected, that offensive measures might be adopted. To this end several of the squadrons were mounted and ordered to advance and attack the enemy wherever force sufficient was exposed to be a proper object of attack, but at the same time to be cautious as to ambuscades. Colonel Weir, who had succeeded to the command of Hamilton's squadron, Colonels Benteen and Myers with their respective squadrons, all mounted, advanced and engaged the enemy. The Indians resisted every step taken by the troops, while every charge made by the latter was met or followed by a charge from the Indians, who continued to appear in large numbers at unexpected times and places. The squadrons acting in support of each other, and the men in each being kept well in hand, were soon able to force the line held by the Indians to yield at any point assailed. This being followed up promptly, the Indians were driven at every point and forced to abandon the field to us. Yet they would go no further than they were actually driven. It was now about three o'clock in the afternoon. I knew that the officer left in charge of the train and eighty men would push after us, follow our trail, and endeavor to reach us at the earliest practicable moment. From the tops of some of the highest peaks or round hills in the vicinity of the village I knew the Indians could reconnoitre the country for miles in all directions. I feared if we remained as we were then until the following day, the Indians might in this manner discover the approach of our train and detach a sufficient body of warriors to attack and capture it; and its loss to us, aside from that of its guard, would have proven most serious, leaving us in the heart of the enemy's country, in midwinter, totally out of supplies for both men and horses.

By actual count we had in our possession eight hundred and seventy-five captured ponies, so wild and unused to white men that it was difficult to herd them. What we were to do with them was puzzling, as they could not have been led had we been possessed of the means of doing this; neither could we drive them as the Indians were accustomed to do. And even if we could take them with us, either the one way or the other, it was anything but wise or desirable on our part to do so, as such a large herd of ponies, constituting so much wealth in the eyes of the Indians, would have been too tempting a prize to the warriors who had been fighting us all the afternoon, and to effect their recapture they would have followed and waylaid us day and night, with every prospect of success, until we should have arrived at a place of safety. Besides, we had upwards of sixty prisoners in our hands, to say nothing of our wounded, to embarrass our movements. We had achieved a great and important success over the hostile tribes; the problem now was how to retain our advantage and steer safely through the difficulties which seemed to surround our position. The Indians had suffered a telling defeat, involving great losses in life and valuable property. Could they succeed, however, in depriving us of the train and supplies, and in doing this accomplish the killing or capture of the escort, it would go far to offset the damage we had been able to inflict upon them and render our victory an empty one

As I deliberated on these points in the endeavor to conclude upon that which would be our wisest course, I could look in nearly all directions and see the warriors at a distance collected in groups on the tops of the highest hills, apparently waiting and watching our next move that they might act accordingly. To guide my command safely out of the difficulties which seemed just then to beset them, I again had recourse to that maxim in war which teaches a commander to do that which his enemy neither expects nor desires him to do.

XVI.

THE close of the last article left my command on the Washita, still surrounded by a superior but badly defeated force of Indians. We were burdened with a considerable number of prisoners and quite a number of our own and the enemy's wounded, and had in our possession nearly nine hundred ponies which we had just captured from the enemy. We were far away—just how far we did not know—from our train of supplies, and the latter with its escort was in danger of capture and destruction by the savages if we did not act to prevent it. We felt convinced that we could not, in the presence of so large a body of hostile Indians, hope to make a long march through their country, the latter favorable to the Indian mode of attack by surprise and ambush, and keep with us the immense herd of captured ponies. Such a course would only encourage attack under circumstances which would almost insure defeat and unnecessary loss to us. We did not need the ponies, while the Indians did. If we retained them they might conclude that one object of our expedition against them was to secure plunder, an object thoroughly consistent with the red man's idea of war. Instead, it was our desire to impress upon his uncultured mind that our every act and purpose had been simply to inflict deserved punishment upon him for the many murders and other depredations committed by him in and around the homes of the defenceless settlers on the frontier. Impelled by these motives, I decided neither to attempt to take the ponies with us nor to abandon them to the Indians, but to adopt the only measure left—to kill them. To accomplish this seemingly—like most measures of war—cruel but necessary act, four companies of cavalrymen were detailed dismounted, as a firing party. Before they reluctantly engaged in this uninviting work, I took Romeo, the interpreter, and proceeded to the few lodges near the centre of the village which we had reserved from destruction, and in which were collected the prisoners, consisting of upward of sixty squaws and children. Romeo was directed to assemble the prisoners in one body, as I desired to assure them of kind treatment at our hands, a subject about which they were greatly wrought up; also to tell them what we should expect of them, and to inform them of our intention to march probably all that night, directing them at the same time to proceed to the herd and select therefrom a suitable number of ponies to carry the prisoners on the march. When Romeo had collected them in a single group, he, acting as interpreter, acquainted them with my purpose in calling them together, at the same time assuring them that they could rely confidently upon the fulfilment of any promises I made them, as I was the "big chief." The Indians refer to all officers of a command as "chiefs," while the officer in command is designated as the "big chief." After I had concluded what I desired to say to them, they signified their approval and satisfaction by gathering around me and going through an extensive series of hand-shaking. One of the middle-aged squaws then informed Romeo that she wished to speak on behalf of herself and companions. Assent having been given to this, she began the delivery of an address which for wisdom of sentiment, and easy, natural, but impassioned delivery might have been heard with intense interest by an audience of cultivated refinement. From her remarks, interpreted by Romeo, I gathered much—in fact, the first reliable information as to what band we had attacked at daylight, which chiefs commanded, and many interesting scraps of information. She began by saying that now she and the women and children about her were in the condition of captivity, which for a long time she had prophesied would be theirs sooner or later. She claimed to speak not as a squaw, but as the sister of the head chief of her band, Black Kettle, who had fallen that morning almost the moment the attack was made. He it was who was the first to hear our advance, and leaping forth from his lodge with rifle in hand, uttered the first war-whoop and fired the first shot as a rally signal to his warriors, and was almost immediately after shot down by the opening volley of the cavalry. Often had she warned her brother of the danger the village, with its women and children, was exposed to, owing to the frequent raiding and war parties which from time to time had been permitted to go forth and depredate upon the settlements of the white men. In the end it was sure to lead to detection and punishment, and now her words had only proven too true. Not a chief or warrior of the village in her belief survived the battle of the forenoon. And what was to become of all these women and children, bereft of everything and of every friend? True, it was just. The warriors had brought this fate upon themselves and their families by their unprovoked attacks upon the white man. Black Kettle, the head chief and the once trusted friend of the white man, had fallen. Little Rock, the chief second in rank in the village, had also met his death while attempting to defend his home against his enemies; others were named in the order of their rank or prowess as warriors, but all had gone the same way. Who was left to care for the women and children who still lived? Only last night, she continued, did the last war party return from the settlements, and it was to rejoice over their achievements that the entire village were engaged until a late hour dancing and singing. This was why their enemies were able to ride almost into their lodges before they were aroused by the noise of the attack. For several minutes she continued to speak, first upbraiding in the bitterest terms the chiefs and warriors who had been the cause of their capture, then bewailing in the most plaintive manner their sad and helpless condition. Turning to me she added, " You claim to be a chief. This man " (pointing to Romeo) " says you are the big chief. If this be true and you are what he claims, show that you can act like a great chief and secure for us that treatment which the helpless are entitled to."

After the delivery of this strongly melodramatic harangue there was introduced a little by-play, in which I was unconsciously made to assume a more prominent part than either my inclinations or the laws of society might approve. Black Kettle's sister, whose name was Mah-wis-sa, and whose address had just received the hearty approval of her companions by their earnest expression of " Ugh!" the Indian word intended for applause, then stepped into the group of squaws, and after looking earnestly at the face of each for a moment, approached a young Indian girl—probably seventeen years of age—and taking her by the hand conducted her to where I was standing. Placing the hand of the young girl in mine, she proceeded in the Indian tongue to the delivery of what I, in my ignorance of the language, presumed was a form of administering a benediction, as her manner and gestures corresponded with this idea. Never dreaming of her purpose, but remembering how sensitive and suspicious the Indian nature was, and that any seeming act of inattention or disrespect on my part might be misunderstood, I stood a passive participant in the strange ceremony then being enacted.   After concluding the main portion of the formalities, she engaged in what seemed an invocation of the Great Spirit, casting her eyes reverently upward, at the same time moving her hands slowly down over the faces of the young squaw and myself.   By this time my curiosity got the better of my silence, and turning to Romeo, who stood near me, and who I knew was familiar with Indian customs, I quietly inquired, "What is this woman doing, Romeo?"   With a broad grin on his swarthy face he replied, "Why, she's marryin' you to that young squaw!"   Although never claimed as an exponent of the peace policy about which so much has been said and written, yet I entertained the most peaceable sentiments toward all Indians who were in a condition to do no harm nor violate any law.   And while cherishing these friendly feelings and desiring to do all in my power to render our captives comfortable and free from anxiety regarding their future treatment at our hands, I think even the most strenuous and ardent advocate of that peace policy which teaches that the Indian should be left free and unmolested in the gratification of his simple tastes and habits, will at least not wholly condemn me when they learn that this last touching and unmistakable proof of confidence and esteem, offered by Mah-wis-sa and gracefully if not blushingly acquiesced in by the Indian maiden, was firmly but respectfully declined.   The few reasons which forced me to deny myself the advantages of this tempting alliance were certain circumstances over which I then had no control, among which was a previous and already solemnized ceremony of this character, which might have a tendency to render the second somewhat invalid.   Then, again, I had not been consulted in regard to my choice in this matter—a trifling consideration, but still having its due influence.   I had not had opportunities to become acquainted with the family of the young damsel who thus proposed to link her worldly fate with mine.   Her father's bank account might or might not be in a favorable condition.   No opportunity had been given me to study the tastes, disposition, or character of the young lady—whether she was fond of music, literature, or domestic duties. All these were questions with which I was not sufficiently familiar to justify me in taking the important step before me.   I did not, however, like certain candidates for office, thrice decline by standing up, and with my hand pressed to my heart say, "Your husband I cannot be"; but through the intermediation of Romeo, the interpreter, who from the first had been highly entertained by what he saw was an excellent joke on the big chief, and wondering in his own mind how I would extricate myself without giving offence, I explained to Mah-wis-sa my due appreciation of the kindness intended by herself and her young friend, but that according to the white man's laws I was debarred from availing myself of the offer, at the same time assuring them of my high consideration, etc.   Glad to get away to duties that called me elsewhere, I left with Romeo.   As soon as we had turned our backs on the group, I inquired of Romeo what object could have been in view which induced Black Kettle's sister to play the part she did.   "That's easy enough to understand; she knows they are in your power, and her object is to make friends with you as far as possible.   But you don't believe anything she tells you, do you?   Why, that squaw—give her the chance, and she'd lift your or my scalp for us and never wink.   Lord, I've heerd 'em talk fine too often to be catched so easy.   To hear her talk and abuse old Black Kettle and the rest that I hope we've done for, you'd think that squaw never had had a hand in torturin' to death many a poor devil who's been picked up by them.   But it's a fact, 'taint no two ways 'bout it. I've lived with them people too long not to know 'em—root and branch. When she was talkin' all that palaver to you 'bout protectin' 'em and all that sort of stuff, if she could 'a know'd that minute that these outside Injuns was 'bout to gobble us up she'd 'a been the very fust one to ram a knife smack into ye. That's the way they allus talk when they want anythin'. Do you know her game in wantin' to marry that young squaw to you? Well, I'll tell ye; ef you'd 'a married that squaw, then she'd 'a told ye that all the rest of 'em were her kinfolks, and as a nateral sort of a thing you'd 'a been expected to kind o' provide and take keer of your wife's relations. That's jist as I tell it to you—fur don't I know? Didn't I marry a young Cheyenne squaw and give her old father two of my best ponies for her, and it wasn't a week till every tarnal Injun in the village, old and young, came to my lodge, and my squaw tried to make me b'lieve they were all relations of hern, and that I ought to give 'em some grub; but I didn't do nothin' of the sort." "Well, how did you get out of it, Romeo?" "Get out of it? Why, I got out by jist takin' my ponies and traps, and the first good chance I lit out; that's how I got out. I was satisfied to marry one or two of 'em, but when it come to marryin' an intire tribe, 'scuse me."

At this point Romeo was interrupted by the officer in command of the men detailed to kill the ponies. The firing party was all ready to proceed with its work, and was only waiting until the squaws should secure a sufficient number of ponies to transport all the prisoners on the march. The troopers had endeavored to catch the ponies, but they were too wild and unaccustomed to white men to permit them to approach. When the squaws entered the herd they had no difficulty in selecting and bridling the requisite number. These being taken off by themselves, the work of destruction began on the remainder, and was continued until nearly eight hundred ponies were thus disposed of. All this time the Indians who had been fighting us from the outside covered the hills in the distance, deeply interested spectators of this to them strange proceeding. The loss of so many animals of value was a severe blow to the tribe, as nothing so completely impairs the war-making facilities for the Indians of the Plains as the deprivation or disabling of their ponies.

In the description of the opening of the battle in the preceding chapter, I spoke of the men having removed their overcoats and haversacks when about to charge the village. These had been disposed of carefully on the ground, and one man from each company left to guard them, this number being deemed sufficient, as they would be within rifle-shot of the main command; besides, the enemy as was then supposed would be inside our lines and sufficiently employed in taking care of himself to prevent any meddling on his part with the overcoats and haversacks. This was partly true, but we had not calculated upon Indians appearing in force and surrounding us. When this did occur, however, their first success was in effecting the capture of the overcoats and rations of the men, the guard barely escaping to the village. This was a most serious loss, as the men were destined to suffer great discomfort from the cold; and their rations being in the haversacks, and it being uncertain when we should rejoin our train, they were compelled to endure both cold and hunger. It was when the Indians discovered our overcoats and galloped to their capture, that one of my staghounds, Blucher, seeing them riding and yelling as if engaged in the chase, dashed from the village and joined the Indians, who no sooner saw him than they shot him through with an arrow.

Several months afterward I discovered his remains on the ground near where the overcoats had been deposited on that eventful morning.

Many noteworthy incidents were observed or reported during the fight. Before the battle began, our Osage allies, in accordance with the Indian custom, dressed in their war costume, painting their faces in all imaginable colors, except one tall, fine-looking warrior, who retained his ordinary dress. Upon inquiring of the chief, Little Beaver, why this one did not array himself as the others had done, he informed me that it was in obedience to a law among all the tribes, under which any chief or warrior who has had a near relative killed by an enemy belonging to another tribe, is not permitted to don the war costume or put on war paint until he has avenged the murder by taking a scalp from some member of the hostile tribe. A war party of the Cheyennes had visited the Osage village the preceding summer, under friendly pretences. They had been hospitably entertained at the lodge of the warrior referred to by his squaw, he being absent on a hunt. When ready to depart they killed his squaw and destroyed his lodge, and until he could secure a scalp he must go on the war path unadorned by feathers or paint. After the battle had been waged for a couple of hours in the morning, I saw this warrior approaching, his horse urged to his highest speed; in his hand I saw waving wildly overhead something I could not distinguish until he halted by my side, when I perceived that it was an entire scalp, fresh and bleeding. His vengeance had been complete, and he was again restored to the full privileges of a warrior—a right he was not long in exercising, as the next time I saw him on the field his face was completely hidden under the stripes of yellow, black, and vermilion, the colors being so arranged apparently as to give him the most hideous visage imaginable.

Riding in the vicinity of the hospital, I saw a little bugler boy sitting on a bundle of dressed robes, near where the surgeon was dressing and caring for the wounded. His face was completely covered with blood, which was trickling down over his cheek from a wound in his forehead. At first glance I thought a pistol bullet had entered his skull, but on stopping to inquire of him the nature of his injury, he informed me that an Indian had shot him in the head with a steel-pointed arrow. The arrow had struck him just above the eye, and upon encountering the skull had glanced under the covering of the latter, coming out near the ear, giving the appearance of having passed through the head. There the arrow remained until the bugler arrived at the hospital, when he received prompt attention. The arrow being barbed could not be withdrawn at once, but by cutting off the steel point the surgeon was able to withdraw the wooden shaft without difficulty. The little fellow bore his suffering manfully. I asked him if he saw the Indian who wounded him. Without replying at once, he shoved his hand deep down into his capacious trousers pocket and fished up nothing more nor less than the scalp of an Indian, adding in a nonchalant manner, "If anybody thinks I didn't see him, I want them to take a look at that." He had killed the Indian with his revolver after receiving the arrow wound in his head.

After driving off the Indians who had attacked us from the outside, so as to prevent them from interfering with our operations in the vicinity of the village, parties were sent here and there to look up the dead and wounded of both sides. In spite of the most thorough search, there were still undiscovered Major Elliott and nineteen enlisted men, including the sergeant-major, for whose absence we were unable to satisfactorily account. Officers and men of the various commands were examined, but nothing was elicited from them except that Major Elliott had been seen about daylight charging with his command into the village. I had previously given him up as killed, but was surprised that so many of the men should be missing, and none of their comrades be able to account for them. All the ground inside of the advanced lines held by the Indians who attacked us after our capture of the village was closely and carefully examined, in the hope of finding the bodies of some if not all the absentees, but with no success. It was then evident that when the other bands attempted to reinforce our opponents of the early morning, they had closed their lines about us in such manner as to cut off Elliott and nineteen of our men. What had been the fate of this party after leaving the main command? This was a question to be answered only in surmises; and few of these were favorable to the escape of our comrades. At last one of the scouts reported that soon after the attack on the village began he had seen a few warriors escaping, mounted, from the village, through a gap that existed in our line between the commands of Elliott and Thompson, and that Elliott and a small party of troopers were in close pursuit; that a short time after he had heard very sharp firing in the direction taken by the Indians and Elliott's party, but that as the firing had continued for only a few minutes, he had thought nothing more of it until the prolonged absence of our men recalled it to his mind. Parties were sent in the direction indicated by the scout, he accompanying them; but after a search extending nearly two miles, all the parties returned, reporting their efforts to discover some trace of Elliott and his men fruitless. As it was now lacking but an hour of night, we had to make an effort to get rid of the Indians, who still loitered in strong force on the hills, within plain view of our position. Our main desire was to draw them off from the direction in which our train might be approaching, and thus render it secure from attack until under the protection of the entire command, when we could defy any force our enemies could muster against us. The last lodge having been destroyed, and all the ponies except those required for the pursuit having been killed, the command was drawn in and united near the village. Making dispositions to overcome any resistance which might be offered to our advance, by throwing out a strong force of skirmishers, we set out down the valley in the direction where the other villages had been reported, and toward the hills on which were collected the greatest number of Indians. The column moved forward in one body, with colors flying and band playing, while our prisoners, all mounted on captured ponies, were under sufficient guard immediately in rear of the advanced troops. For a few moments after our march began the Indians on the hills remained silent spectators, evidently at a loss at first to comprehend our intentions in thus setting out at that hour of the evening, and directing our course as if another night march was contemplated; and more than all, in the direction of their villages, where all that they possessed was supposed to be. This aroused them to action, as we could plainly see considerable commotion among them—chiefs riding hither and thither, as if in anxious consultation with each other as to the course to be adopted. Whether the fact that they could not fire upon our advance without endangering the lives of their own people, who were prisoners in our hands, or some other reason prevailed with them, they never offered to fire a shot or retard our movements in any manner, but instead assembled their outlying detachments as rapidly as possible, and began a precipitate movement down the valley in advance of us, fully impressed with the idea no doubt that our purpose was to overtake their flying

people and herds and administer the same treatment to them that the occu
pants of the upper village had received.   This was exactly the effect I desired,
and our march was conducted with such appearance of determination and ra
pidity that this conclusion on their part was a most natural one.   Leaving a
few of their warriors to hover along our flanks and watch our progress, the
main body of the Indians, able to travel much faster than the troops, soon disappeared from our sight in front.   We still pushed on in the same direction.
and continued our march in this manner until long after dark, by which time
we reached the deserted villages, the occupants—at least the non-combatants
and herds—having fled in the morning when news of our attack on Black Kettle's village reached them.   We had now reached a point several miles below
the site of Black Kettle's village, and the darkness was sufficient to cover our
movements from the watchful eyes of the Indian scouts, who had dogged our
march as long as the light favored them.

Facing the command about, it was at once put in motion to reach our
train, not only as a measure of safety and protection to the latter, but as a ne
cessary movement to relieve the wants of the command, particularly that por
tion whose haversacks and overcoats had fallen into the hands of the Indians
early in the morning.   By ten o'clock we reached the battle ground, but without halting pushed on, following the trail we had made in striking the village.
The march was continued at a brisk gait until about two o'clock in the morning, when I concluded it would be prudent to allow the main command to halt
and bivouac until daylight, sending one squadron forward without delay, to reinforce the guard with the train.   Colonel West's squadron was detailed upon
this duty.   The main body of the troops was halted, and permitted to build
nuge fires, fuel being obtainable in abundance from the timber which lined the
valley of the Washita—our march still leading us up the course of this stream.

At daylight the next morning we were again in our saddles and wending
our way hopefully toward the train.   The location of the latter we did not
know, presuming that it had been pushing after us since we had taken our
abrupt departure from it.   Great was our joy and satisfaction, about ten
o'clock, to discover the train safely in camp.   The teams were at once har-
nessed and hitched to the wagons, and without halting even to prepare breakfast, the march was resumed, I being anxious to encamp at a certain point
that night from where I intended sending scouts through with despatches to
General Sheridan.   Early in the afternoon this camp was reached; it was near
the point where we had first struck the timbered valley, at the time not knowing that it was the valley of the Washita.   Here men and horses were given
the first opportunity to procure a satisfactory meal since the few hasty morsels
obtained by them during the brief halt made between nine and ten o'clock the
night we arrived in the vicinity of the village.   After posting our pickets and
rendering the camp secure from surprise by the enemy, horses were unsaddled, tents pitched, and every means taken to obtain as comfortable a night as
the limited means at our disposal and the severities of the season would permit.   After partaking of a satisfactory dinner, I began writing my report to
General Sheridan.   First I sent for California Joe, and informed him that I
desired to send a despatch to General Sheridan that night, and would have it
ready by dark, so that the bearer could at once set out as soon as it was sufficiently dark to conceal his movements from the scouts of the enemy, who no
doubt were still following and watching us.   I told California Joe that I had
selected him as the bearer of the despatch, and he was at liberty to name the

number of men he desired to accompany him, as it was a most perilous mission on which he was going. The exact distance he would have to ride in order to reach General Sheridan's headquarters at Camp Supply could not be determined. The command had occupied four days in accomplishing it, but California Joe, with his thorough knowledge of the country, and the experience of our march, would be able to follow a much more direct route than a large command moving with a train.

He did not seem in the least disturbed when told of his selection for this errand, so full of danger. When informed that he might name the number of men to accompany him, I supposed he would say about twelve or more, under command of a good non-commissioned officer. Very few persons in or out of the military service would have cared to undertake the journey with much less than ten times that force, but he contented himself by informing me that before answering that question he would walk down to where the scouts were in camp and consult his "pardner." He soon returned saying, "I've just been talkin' the matter over with my pardner, and him and me both concludes that as safe and sure a way as any is for him and me to take a few extra rounds of ammunition and strike out from here together the very minnit it's dark. As for any more men, we don't want 'em, because yer see in a case of this 'ere kind thar's more to be made by dodgin' an' runnin' than thar is by fightin', an' two spright men kin do better at that than twenty; they can't be seen half as fur. Besides, two won't leave as much of a trail for the Injuns to find. If my pardner an' me kin git away from here as soon as it is plum dark, we'll be so fur from here by daylight to-morrer mornin' the Injuns never couldn't tetch hide nor har of us. Besides, I don't reckon the pesky varmints 'll be so overly keen in meddlin' with our business, seein' as how they've got their han's tolerable full settin' things to rights at home, owin' to the little visit we've jist made 'em. I rather s'pect, all things considerin', them Injuns would be powerful glad to call it quits for a spell any way, an' if I ain't off the trail mightily, some of them 'ere head chiefs as ain't killed will be headin' for the nighest Peace Commissioner before they git the war paint clean off their faces. This thing of pumpin' 'em when the snow's a foot deep, and no grass for their ponies, puts a new wrinkle in these Injuns' scalp, an' they ain't goin' to git over it in a minnit either. Wal, I'm goin' back to the boys to see if I can borrer a little smokin' tobacker. I may want to take a smoke on the way. Whenever you git yer dockiments ready jist send your orderly down thar, and me and my pardner will be ready. I'm mighty glad I'm goin' to-night, for I know Gineral Sheridan 'll be monstrous glad to see me back so soon. Did I tell yer I used to know the Gineral when he was second or third lootenant and post quartermaster in Oregon? That must 'a been afore your time."

Leaving California Joe to procure his "tobacker," I assembled all the officers of the command and informed them that as there was but an hour or two in which I was to write my report of the battle of the Washita, I would not have time, as I should have preferred to do, to send to them for regular and formally written reports of their share in the engagement; but in order that I might have the benefit of their combined knowledge of the battle and its results, each officer in response to my request gave me a brief summary of some of the important points which his report would have contained if submitted in writing. With this information in my possession, I sat down in my tent and penned, in as brief manner as possible, a report to General Sheridan detailing our movements from the time Elliott, with his three companies, discovered the trail, up to the point from which my despatch was written, giving particularly the main facts of our discovery, attack, and complete destruction of the village of Black Kettle. It was just about dark when I finished this despatch and was about to send for California Joe, when that loquacious personage appeared at the door of my tent. "I'm not so anxious to leave yer all here, but the fact is, the sooner me and pardner are off, I reckon the better it'll be in the end. I want to put at least fifty miles 'tween me and this place by daylight to-morrer mornin', so if yer'll jest hurry up yer papers, it'll be a lift for us."

On going outside the tent I saw that the "pardner" was the scout Jack Corbin, the same who had first brought the intelligence of Elliott's discovery of the trail to us at Antelope Hills. He was almost the antipodes of California Joe in regard to many points of character, seldom indulging in a remark or suggestion unless prompted by a question. These two scouts recalled to my mind an amicable arrangement said to exist between a harmonious married pair, in which one was willing to do all the talking and the other was perfectly willing he should. The two scouts, who were about to set out to accomplish a long journey through an enemy's country, with no guides save the stars, neither ever having passed over the route they proposed to take, and much of the ride to be executed during the darkness of night, apparently felt no greater, if as great, anxiety as to the result of their hazardous mission than one ordinarily feels in contemplating a journey of a few hours by rail or steamboat. California Joe was dressed and equipped as usual. About his waist and underneath his cavalry greatcoat and cape he wore a belt containing a Colt revolver and hunting knife; these, with his inseparable companion, a long Springfield breech-loading rifle, composed his defensive armament. His "pardner," Jack Corbin, was very similarly arrayed except in equipment, his belt containing two revolvers instead of one, while a Sharps carbine supplied the place of a rifle, being more readily carried and handled on horseback. The mounts of the two men were as different as their characters, California Joe confiding his safety to the transporting powers of his favorite mule, while Corbin was placing his reliance upon a fine gray charger. Acquainting the men with the probable route we should pursue in our onward march toward Camp Supply, so that, if desirable, they might be able to rejoin us, I delivered my report to General Sheridan into the keeping of California Joe, who, after unbuttoning numerous coats, blouses, and vests, consigned the package to one of the numerous capacious inner pockets with which each garment seemed supplied, with the remark, "I reckon it'll keep dry thar in case of rain or accident." Both men having mounted, I shook hands with them, wishing them God-speed and a successful journey. As they rode off in the darkness California Joe, irrepressible to the last, called out, "Wal, I hope an' trust yer won't have any scrimmage while I'm gone, because I'd hate mightily now to miss anything of the sort, seein' I've stuck to yer this fur."

After enjoying a most grateful and comparatively satisfactory night's rest, the demands of hunger on the part of man and beast having been bountifully supplied from the stores contained in our train, while a due supply of blankets and robes, with the assistance of huge camp-fires, enabled the men to protect themselves against the intense cold of midwinter, our march was resumed at daylight in the direction of Camp Supply. Our wounded had received every possible care and attention that a skilful and kind-hearted medical officer could suggest. Strange to add, and greatly to our surprise as well as joy, Colonel Barnitz, who had been carried into the village shot through the body,

CALIFORNIA JOE HIDING HIS TRAIL.

and, as all supposed, mortally wounded, with apparently but a few minutes to live, had not only survived the rough jostling of the night march made after leaving the village, but the surgeon, Dr. Lippincott, who was unceasing in his attentions to the wounded, reported indications favorable to a prolongation of life if not a complete recovery. This was cheering news to all the comrades of Colonel Barnitz. I well remember how, when the Colonel was first carried by four of his men, in the folds of an army blanket, into the village, his face wore that pale deathly aspect so common and peculiar to those mortally wounded. He, as well as all who saw him, believed his end near at hand. But like a brave soldier, as he was and had proven himself to be, death had no terrors for him. When asked by me, as I knelt at the side of the litter on which he was gasping for breath, whether he had any messages to send to absent friends, he realized the perils of his situation, and in half-finished sentences, mingled with regrets, delivered, as he and all of us supposed, his farewell messages to be transmitted to dear ones at home. And yet, despite the absence of that care and quiet, not to mention little delicacies and luxuries, regarded as so essential, and which would have been obtainable under almost any other circumstances, Colonel Barnitz continued to improve, and before many weeks his attendant medical officer was able to pronounce him out of danger, although to this day he is, and for the remainder of life will be, disabled from further active duty, the ball by which he was wounded having severed one of his ribs in such a manner as to render either riding or the wearing of a sabre or revolver too painful to be endured. By easy marches we gradually neared Camp Supply, and had begun to descend the long slope leading down to the valley of Wolf creek, the stream on which we had encamped three nights when we first set out from Camp Supply in search of Indians.

With two or three of the Osage guides and as many of the officers, I was riding some distance in advance of the column of troops, and could indistinctly see the timber fringing the valley in the distance, when the attention of our little party was attracted to three horsemen who were to be seen riding slowly along near the edge of the timber. As yet they evidently had not observed us, the troops behind us not having appeared in view. We were greatly at a loss to determine who the three horsemen might be; they were yet too distant to be plainly visible to the eye, and the orderly with my field glass was still in rear. While we were halting and watching their movements we saw that they also had discovered us, one of their number riding up to a small elevation near by from which to get a better view of our group. After studying us for a few moments he returned at a gallop to his two companions, when all three turned their horses toward the timber and moved rapidly in that direction. We were still unable to determine whether they were Indians or white men, the distance being so great between us, when my orderly arrived with my field glass, by which I was able to catch a glimpse of them just as they were disappearing in the timber, when whose familiar form should be revealed but that of California Joe, urging his mule to its greatest speed in order to reach the timber before we should discover them. They had evidently taken us for Indians, and well they might, considering that two of our party were Osages and the others were dressed in anything but the regulation uniform. To relieve the anxious minds of California Joe and his companions, I put spurs to my horse and was soon bounding down the plains leading into the valley to join him. I had not proceeded over half way when the scouts rode cautiously out from the timber, and California Joe, after shading his eyes with his hand and looking for a few moments, raised his huge sombrero from his matted head, and waving it above him as a signal of recognition, pressed his great Mexican spurs deep into the sides of his humble-looking steed, if a mule may receive such an appellation, and the three scouts were soon galloping toward us.

The joy at the meeting was great on both sides, only dampened somewhat on the part of California Joe by the fact that he and his comrades had taken to the timber so promptly when first they discovered us; but he explained it by saying, "I counted on it bein' you all the time when I fust got my eye on yer, until I saw two Injuns in the squad, an' forgettin' all about them Osages we had along, I jumped at the conclusion that if thar war any Injuns around, the comfortablest place I knowed for us three was to make fur the timber, and there make a stand. We war gettin' ready to give it to yer if it turned out yer war all Injuns. Wal, I'm powerful glad to see yer agin, an' that's sure."

From his further conversation we were informed that Jack Corbin and himself had made their trip to General Sheridan's headquarters without hindrance or obstacle being encountered on their way, and that after delivering the despatches and being well entertained in the mean time, they, with one other scout, had been sent by the General to endeavor to meet us, bringing from him a package of orders and letters.

While the column was overtaking us, and while California Joe, now in his element, was entertaining the attentive group of officers, scouts, and Osages who gathered around him to hear him relate in his quaint manner what he saw, heard, and told at General Sheridan's headquarters, I withdrew to one side and opened the large official envelope in which were contained both official and personal despatches. These were eagerly read, and while the satisfaction derived from the perusal of some of the letters of a private and congratulatory nature from personal friends at Camp Supply was beyond expression, the climax of satisfaction was reached when my eye came to an official-looking document bearing the date and heading which indicated department headquarters as its source. We had but little further to go before going into camp for that night, and as the command had now overtaken us, we moved down to the timber and there encamped; and in order that the approving words of our chief should be transmitted promptly to every individual of the command, the line was formed and the following order announced to the officers and men:

HEADQUARTERS DEPARTMENT OF THE MISSOURI, IN THE FIELD, DEPOT ON THE NORTH CANADIAN, AT THE JUNCTION OF BEAVER CREEK, INDIAN TERRITORY,
November 29, 1868.

GENERAL FIELD ORDERS No. 6.—The Major General commanding announces to this command the defeat, by the Seventh regiment of cavalry, of a large force of Cheyenne Indians, under the celebrated chief Black Kettle, reënforced by the Arrapahoes under Little Raven, and the Kiowas under Satanta, on the morning of the 27th instant, on the Washita river, near the Antelope Hills, Indian Territory, resulting in a loss to the savages of one hundred and three warriors killed, including Black Kettle, the capture of fifty-three squaws and children, eight hundred and seventy-five ponies, eleven hundred and twenty-three buffalo robes and skins, five hundred and thirty-five pounds of powder, one thousand and fifty pounds of lead, four thousand arrows, seven hundred pounds of tobacco, besides rifles, pistols, saddles, bows, lariats, and immense quantities of dried meat and other winter provisions, the complete destruction of their village, and almost total annihilation of this Indian band.

The loss to the Seventh Cavalry was two officers killed, Major Joel H. Elliott and Captain Louis McL. Hamilton, and nineteen enlisted men; three officers wounded, Brevet Lieutenant-Colonel Albert Barnitz (badly), Brevet Lieutenant-Colonel T. W. Custer, and Second Lieutenant T. Z. March (slightly), and eleven enlisted men.

The energy and rapidity shown during one of the heaviest snow-storms that has visited this section of the country, with the temperature below freezing point, and the gallantry and bravory displayed, resulting in such signal success, reflect the highest credit upon both the officers and men of the Seventh Cavalry; and the Major-General commanding, while regretting the loss of such gallant officers as Major Elliott and Captain Hamilton, who fell while gallantly leading their men, desires to express his thanks to the officers and men engaged in the battle of the Washita, and his special congratulations are tendered to their distinguished commander, Brevet Major-General George A. Custer, for the efficient and gallant services rendered, which have characterized the opening of the campaign against hostile Indians south of the Arkansas.

By command of

Major-General P. H. SHERIDAN.

(Signed)   J. SCHUYLER CROSBY, Brevet Lieutenant-Colonel, A. D. C., A. A. A. General.

This order, containing as it did the grateful words of approval from our revered commander, went far to drown the remembrance of the hunger, cold, and danger encountered by the command, in the resolute and united effort made by it to thoroughly discharge its duty.

Words like these, emanating from the source they did, and upon an occasion such as this was, were immeasurably more welcome, gratifying, and satisfactory to the pride of officers and men than would have been the reception of a budget of brevets, worded in the regular stereotyped form and distributed in a promiscuous manner, having but little regard to whether the recipient had bravely imperilled his life on the battle-field in behalf of his country, or had taken particular care to preserve that life upon some field far removed from battle.

The last camp before we reached Camp Supply was on Wolf creek, about ten miles from General Sheridan's headquarters. The weather had now moderated to the mildest winter temperature, the snow having melted and disappeared.

From this point I sent a courier to General Sheridan soon after going into camp, informing him of our whereabouts and the distance from his camp, and that we would reach the latter at such an hour in the forenoon, when the officers and men of my command would be pleased to march in review before him and his staff as we finished our return march from the opening of the winter campaign. Officers and men, in view of this, prepared to put on their best appearance. At the appointed hour on the morning of December 2, the command moved out of camp and began its last day's march toward Camp Supply. Considering the hard and trying character of the duty they had been engaged in since leaving Camp Supply, the appearance of officers, men, and horses was far better than might naturally have been expected of them. When we arrived within a couple of miles of General Sheridan's headquarters, we were met by one of his staff officers with a message from the General, that it would give him great pleasure to review the Seventh Cavalry as proposed, and that he and his staff would be mounted, and take up a favorable position for the review near headquarters. In approaching Camp Supply by the route we were marching, a view of the camp and depot is first gained from the point where the high level plain begins to descend gradually, to form the valley in the middle of which Camp Supply is located; so that by having a man on the lookout, to report when the troops should first make their appearance on the heights overlooking Beaver creek, the General was enabled not only to receive timely notice of our approach, but to take position with his staff to witness our march down the long gradual slope leading into the valley. The day was all we could wish—a bright sun overhead, and favorable ground for the manœuvring of troops.

I had taken the precaution to establish the formation of the marching column before we should appear in view from General Sheridan's camp, so that after our march began down the beautifully descending slope to the valley, no change was made. In many respects the column we formed was unique in appearance. First rode our Osage guides and trailers, dressed and painted in the extremest fashions of war according to their rude customs and ideas. As we advanced these warriors chanted their war songs, fired their guns in triumph, and at intervals gave utterance to their shrill war-whoops. Next came the scouts riding abreast, with California Joe astride his faithful mule bringing up the right, but unable, even during this ceremonious and formal occasion, to dispense with his pipe. Immediately in rear of the scouts rode the Indian prisoners under guard, all mounted on Indian ponies, and in their dress, conspicuous by its bright colors, many of them wearing the scarlet blanket so popular with the wild tribes, presenting quite a contrast to the dull and motley colors worn by the scouts. Some little distance in rear came the troops formed in column of platoons, the leading platoon, preceded by the band playing " Garry Owen," being composed of the sharpshooters under Colonel Cook, followed in succession by the squadrons in the regular order of march. In this order and arrangement we marched proudly in front of our chief, who, as the officers rode by giving him the military salute with the sabre, returned their forma. courtesy by a graceful lifting of his cap and a pleased look of recognition from his eye, which spoke his approbation in language far more powerful than studied words could have done. In speaking of the review afterwards, General Sheridan said the appearance of the troops, with the bright rays of the sun reflected from their burnished arms and equipments, as they advanced in beautiful order and precision down the slope, the band playing, and the blue of the soldiers' uniforms slightly relieved by the gaudy colors of the Indians, both captives and Osages, the strangely fantastic part played by the Osage guides, their shouts, chanting their war songs, and firing their guns in air, all combined to render the scene one of the most beautiful and highly interesting he remembered ever having witnessed.

After marching in review, the troops were conducted across the plain to the border of Beaver creek, about a quarter of a mile from General Sheridan's camp, where we pitched our tents and prepared to enjoy a brief period of rest.

We had brought with us on our return march from the battle-ground of the Washita the remains of our slain comrade, Captain Louis McLane Hamilton. Arrangements were at once made, upon our arrival at Camp Supply, to offer the last formal tribute of respect and affection which we as his surviving comrades could pay. As he had died a soldier's death, so like a soldier he should be buried. On the evening of the day after our arrival at Camp Supply the funeral took place. A little knoll not far from camp was chosen as the resting-place to which we were to consign the remains of our departed comrade. In the arrangements for the conduct of the funeral ceremonies, no preliminary or important detail had been omitted to render the occasion not only one of imposing solemnity, but deeply expressive of the high esteem in which the deceased had been held by every member of the command. In addition to the eleven companies of the Seventh Cavalry, the regular garrison of Camp Supply, numbering several companies of the Third Regular Infantry, the regiment in which Captain Hamilton had first entered the regular service, was also in attendance. The body of the deceased was carried in an ambulance as a hearse, and covered with a large American flag. The ambulance was preceded by Captain Hamilton's squadron, commanded by Brevet Lieutenant-Colonel T. B. Weir, and was followed by his horse, covered with a mourning sheet and bearing on the saddle—the same in which Captain Hamilton was seated when he received his death wound—the sabre and belt and the reversed top-boots of the deceased. The pall-bearers were Major-General Sheridan, Brevet Lieutenant-Colonels J. Schuyler Crosby, W. W. Cook, and T. W. Custer. Brevet Major W. W. Beebe, Lieutenant Joseph Hall, and myself.

Our sojourn at Camp Supply was to be brief. We arrived there on the 2d of December, and in less than one week we were to be in the saddle with our numbers more than doubled by reinforcements, and again wending our way southward over the route we had so lately passed over.

Before setting out on the last expedition, I had stated to the officers in a casual manner that all parties engaged in the conduct of the contemplated campaign against the Indians must reconcile themselves in advance—no matter how the expedition might result—to becoming the recipients of censure and unbounded criticism; that if we failed to engage and whip the Indians—labor as we might to accomplish this—the people in the West, particularly along and near the frontier, those who had been victims of the assaults made by Indians, would denounce us in unmeasured terms as being inefficient or lukewarm in the performance of our duty; whereas if we should find and punish the Indians as they deserved, a wail would rise up from the horrified humanitarians throughout the country, and we would be accused of attacking and killing friendly and defenceless Indians. My predictions proved true; no sooner was the intelligence of the battle of the Washita flashed over the country than the anticipated cry was raised. In many instances it emanated from a class of persons truly good in themselves and in their intentions, but who were familiar to only a very limited degree with the dark side of the Indian question, and whose ideas were of the sentimental order. There was another class, however, equally loud in their utterances of pretended horror, who were actuated by pecuniary motives alone, and who, from their supposed or real intimate knowledge of Indian character and of the true merits of the contest between the Indians and the Government, were able to give some weight to their expressed opinions and assertions of alleged facts. Some of these last described actually went so far as to assert not only that the village we had attacked and destroyed was that of Indians who had always been friendly and peaceable toward the whites, but that many of the warriors and chiefs were partially civilized and had actually borne arms in the Union army during the war of rebellion. The most astonishing fact connected with these assertions was not that they were uttered, but that many well-informed people believed them.

The Government, however, was in earnest in its determination to administer proper and deserved punishment to the guilty; and as a mark of approval of the opening event of the winter campaign, the following telegram from the Secretary of War was transmitted to us at Camp Supply:

LIEUTENANT-GENERAL SHERMAN, St. Louis, Mo.

WAR DEPARTMENT, WASHINGTON CITY, December 2, 1868.

I congratulate you, Sheridan, and Custer on the splendid success with which your campaign is begun. Ask Sheridan to send forward the names of officers and men deserving of special mention. (Signed) J. M. SCHOFIELD, Secretary of War.

It was impracticable to comply with the request contained in the closing portion of the despatch from the Secretary of War, for the gratifying reason that every officer and man belonging to the expedition had performed his full part in rendering the movement against the hostile tribes a complete success

16

XVII.

THE close of the last chapter left my command in camp near General Sheridan's headquarters, at the point now known as Camp Supply, Indian Territory. We had returned on the 30th of November from the campaign of the Washita, well satisfied with the result of our labors and exposures; but we were not to sit quietly in our tents or winter quarters, and give way to mutual congratulations upon the success which had already rewarded our efforts. The same spirit who, in the Shenandoah Valley campaign of 1864, had so successfully inaugurated the "whirling" movement, was now present, and it was determined that upon a slightly modified principle, reinforced by the biting frosts of winter, we should continue to "press things" until our savage enemies should not only be completely humbled, but be forced by the combined perils of war and winter to beg for peace, and settle quietly down within the limits of their reservation.

Such was the import of the closing sentences in the "Congratulatory Order" published by General Sheridan to the Seventh Cavalry and quoted in the preceding chapter. "The *opening* of the campaign against hostile Indians south of Arkansas," were the words used. We have seen the "opening;" if the reader will accompany me, I will endeavor to relate that which followed, introducing the principal events which, in connection with the battle of the Washita, resulted in forcing all the "hostile Indians south of the Arkansas" to a condition of comparative peace, and gave peace and protection to that portion of our frontier which had so long suffered from their murderous and thieving raids.

In less than one week from the date of our arrival at Camp Supply, we were to be again in the saddle and wending our way southward toward the supposed winter haunts of our enemies—this time, however, with more than double our former numbers. So long had the thrifty and enterprising settlers upon the frontier of Kansas, particularly those who had selected homes in the fertile valleys of the Saline, Solomon, and Republican rivers, been subjected to the depredations of the Cheyennes, Arrapahoes, Apaches, Kiowas, and Sioux, and so frequent had the murder and capture of settlers by these Indians become, that the citizens and the officials of the State felt forced to take measures in their own defence, and for the purpose of uniting with the forces of the General Government, in the attempt to give quiet and protection to life and property to the inhabitants of the border settlements. The last needed impulse to this movement on the part of the people of Kansas was given when the Indians, late in the preceding summer, made two raids upon the settlements in the Saline, Solomon, and Republican valleys, and, after murdering many of the men and children, burning houses, and destroying or capturing a vast amount of stock, carried off into captivity two young women or girls, both belonging to highly respected families residing on the exposed border of the State. Although one of the captives was married, her marriage to a farmer having been celebrated less than one month prior to the day of her unfortunate capture by the Indians, yet neither of them could scarcely be said to have passed the line which separates girlhood from womanhood. Mrs. Morgan, the bride, was but nineteen, while her companion in misfortune, Miss

White, was still her junior by a year or more. As they played no unimportant part in subsequent operations against the Indians, the principal events attending their capture may not be out of place. Neither knew the other, nor had they ever seen each other until they met as captives in an Indian village hundreds of miles from their frontier homes. One can readily imagine with what deep interest and mutual sympathy the acquaintance of these two helpless girls began. Miss White had been captured and carried to the Indian village about one month before the capture of Mrs. Morgan occurred. The brief story of the capture of the former is soon told. One day, her father being at work in the field, she and a younger sister were engaged in the garden, when she saw four Indians entering the house where her mother and the younger children of the family were. Her first impulse was to fly, but seeing an Indian on the opposite side of the garden she turned and entered the house. One or two of the Indians could speak broken English; all of them assumed a most friendly demeanor and requested something to eat. This request was met by a most prompt and willing response upon the part of Mrs. White and her children. With true Western hospitality they prepared for their unbidden guests as bountifully as the condition of the larder would permit. No depredations had been committed in that vicinity for some time, and as it was not an unusual occurrence for small parties of Indians when engaged on hunting excursions to visit the settlements, where they invariably met with kind treatment at the hands of the settlers, it was hoped that after obtaining the desired meal the party would quietly withdraw without committing any depredations. Such, however, was not the intention of the savages. Already on that day their hands had been dipped in the white man's blood, and the peaceful procurement of something to appease their hunger was merely the dropping of the curtain between two acts of a terrible drama. Having satisfied the demands of their appetites, it was then time for them to throw aside the guise of friendship, under which they had entered the house and been treated as favored guests, and to reveal the true object of their visit. Two stalwart warriors grasped Miss White in their arms and rushed toward the door. Neither her shrieks nor the feeble resistance she was able to offer retarded their movements. As she found herself being rapidly carried from the house the last glimpse she obtained of those within revealed her mother engaged in an unequal struggle with a powerful warrior, while another of the savages had felled a younger sister to the floor and was then engaged in destroying such articles of furniture or table ware as he could lay hands upon. Her two captors hurried her from the house, hastened to the spot where they had left their ponies, and after binding their captive upon the back of one of their ponies, and being joined by the others of the party, began their flight from the settlements, well knowing that the alarm would soon be given, and pursuit by the enraged settlers would be the result. Amid the terrible surroundings of her own situation, the anxieties of the fair captive to know the fate of the dear ones left behind must have been unspeakable. I can scarcely imagine a more deplorable fate than that to which this defenceless girl had become the victim. Torn from her home amid scenes of heartrending atrocities, distracted with anxious thoughts as to the fate which had befallen her mother and sisters, she now found herself a helpless prisoner in the hands of the most cruel, heartless, and barbarous of human enemies. Unable to utter or comprehend a word of the Indian language, and her captors only being able to express the most ordinary words in broken English, her condition was rendered the more forlorn, if possible, by her inability to communicate with those in whose power she found herself.

With war parties returning from a foray upon the settlements, the first object is to place as long a distance as possible between themselves and any party which may be in pursuit. To accomplish this, as soon as they have completed the destruction and havoc of which the settlers are the victims, the entire party, usually numbering from fifty to one hundred warriors, collect at a point near the settlements previously agreed upon, and at once begin their flight toward their village, probably located at least two hundred miles from the scene of their attack. Being mounted, as all war parties are, upon the fleetest of Indian ponies with extra animals driven along, little or no rest for either pony or rider is taken during the first twenty-four hours, by which time it is no unusual feat for a war party to traverse a distance of one hundred miles.

During the early part of the flight every precaution is adopted to prevent leaving a heavy trail, or one easily to be followed; to this end, instead of moving, as is customary, in single file, thereby leaving a clearly defined path, each warrior moves independently of his fellows, until all danger from pursuit is safely passed, when the party falls into single file, and, with the chief at the head, moves along in almost unbroken silence. If during an attack upon the frontier settlements the Indians should encounter unexpected and successful resistance, necessitating a premature withdrawal and flight on their part, they still resort to stratagem in order to secure their safety. In accordance with a plan previously formed and understood by each member of the party, and specially provided for an emergency, the war party finding themselves about to encounter successful resistance on the part of the frontiersmen beat a hasty retreat; but instead of taking their flight in a single direction and in one party, thereby leaving an unmistakable clue for their pursuers, the entire party breaks up into numerous smaller bands, each apparently fleeing in an independent direction, a few of the best mounted usually falling behind to attract the attention of the pursuers and give time to those of the party who are burdened with prisoners and captured stock to make good their escape. In such an emergency as this, a rendezvous for the entire party has been previously fixed upon. Its location is usually upon or near some water-course or prominent landmark, distant perhaps thirty or forty miles; thither all smaller parties direct their course, each by a separate and usually a circuitous course. Should either of these smaller parties find themselves closely pursued, or their trail being followed and all efforts to throw the pursuers off prove unavailing, they relinquish the plan of uniting with the others at the established rendezvous, as that would imperil the safety of their comrades, and select a new route leading neither in the direction of the rendezvous nor of the village, in order not only to elude but mislead their pursuers. Then ensues a long and tiresome flight, until, having worn out or outwitted their pursuers, of whose movements they keep themselves thoroughly informed, they make their way in safety to the village. At the latter, lookouts are constantly kept on some prominent hill to watch the coming of the absent warriors, and give notice of their approach. A war party returning from a successful raid into the settlements, and bringing with them prisoners and captured stock, is an event of the greatest importance to every occupant of the village. Having arrived within a few miles of the village, and feeling safe from all danger from pursuit, the chief in command of the war party causes a signal smoke to be sent up from some high point along the line of march, well knowing that watchful eyes near the village are on the alert and will not fail to observe the signal and understand its meaning.

It is wonderful to what a state of perfection the Indian has carried this simple mode of telegraphing. Scattered over a great portion of the plains, from
British America in the north almost to the Mexican border on the south, are
to be found isolated hills, or, as they are usually termed, "buttes," which can
be seen a distance of from twenty to more than fifty miles. These peaks are
selected as the telegraphic stations. By varying the number of the columns of
smoke different meanings are conveyed by the messages. The most simple as
well as most easily varied mode, and resembling somewhat the ordinary alpha-
bet employed in the magnetic telegraph, is arranged by building a small fire
which is not allowed to blaze; then, by placing an armful of partially green
grass or weeds over the fire, as if to smother it, a dense white smoke is created,
which ordinarily will ascend in a continuous vertical column for hundreds of
feet. This column of smoke is to the Indian mode of telegraphing what the
current of electricity is to the system employed by the white man; the alpha-
bet so far as it goes is almost identical, consisting as it does of long lines and
short lines or dots. But how formed? is perhaps the query of the reader.
By the simplest of methods. Having his current of smoke established, the Indian operator simply takes his blanket and by spreading it over the small pile
of weeds or grass from which the column of smoke takes its source, and properly controlling the edges and corners of the blanket, he confines the smoke,
and is in this way able to retain it for several moments. By rapidly displac-
ing the blanket, the operator is enabled to cause a dense volume of smoke to
rise, the length or shortness of which, as well as the number and frequency
of the columns, he can regulate perfectly, simply by the proper use of the
blanket. For the transmission of brief messages, previously determined
upon, no more simple method could easily be adopted. As soon as the lookout near the village discerns the approach in the distance of the expected
war party, the intelligence is at once published to the occupants of the village
through the stentorian tones of the village crier, the duties of which office are
usually performed by some superannuated or deposed chief. Runners mounted
upon fleet ponies are at once despatched to meet the returning warriors and
gather the particulars of the expedition—whether successful or otherwise;
whether they are returning laden with scalps and plunder or come empty-
handed. Have they brought prisoners and captured horses? and are their
own numbers unbroken, or do their losses exceed their gains? These
and similar questions are speedily solved, when the runners hasten back to
the village and announce the result, whereupon the occupants of the entire
village, old and young, sally forth to meet the returning warriors. If the
latter have been successful and have suffered no loss, they become the recipients of all the triumph which a barbarous and excited people are capable of
heaping upon them. They advance toward the village painted and dressed in
full war costume, singing their war songs, discharging their fire-arms, and
uttering ever and anon the war-whoop peculiar to their tribe. Added to this,
every soul in the village capable of uttering a sound joins in the general re
joicing, and for a time the entire population is wild with excitement. If, however, instead of returning in triumph, the war party has met with disaster and
suffered the loss of one or more warriors, the scene witnessed upon their arrival at the village is as boisterous as the other, but even more horrible. The
party is met as before by all the inhabitants of the village, but in a widely dif-
erent manner; instead of the shouts and songs of victory which greet the successful warriors, only the screams and wails of an afflicted people are to be heard

the war paint and bright colors give way to a deep black with which all the mourners and friends of the fallen warriors besmear their faces, while the members of the immediate family begin hacking and scarifying their faces, arms, and bodies with knives, and give way to lamentations the most piercing and horrible in sound. A not infrequent mode of disfiguring themselves, and one which I have often seen, is for the mourner, particularly if the one mourned is a wife or husband, to cut off the first joint of the little finger. This of course is done without the slightest regard for the rules of surgery, of which the Indians generally are wofully ignorant. The operation is simply performed by taking a knife, often of questionable sharpness, and cutting through the flesh and first joint of the little finger, leaving no "flap" of flesh to cover the exposed bone. As a result, in healing the flesh withdraws from the mutilated portion of the finger, and usually leaves nearly an inch of bone exposed, presenting of course a most revolting appearance.

The village to which Miss White's captors belonged was located at that time south of the Arkansas river, and distant from her home at least three hundred miles. How many girls of eighteen years of age possess the physical ability to survive a journey such as lay before this lonely captive? Unprovided with a saddle of any description, she was mounted upon an Indian pony, and probably required to accomplish nearly, if not quite, one hundred miles within the first twenty-four hours, and thus to continue the tiresome journey with but little rest or nourishment. Added to the discomforts and great fatigue of the journey was something more terrible and exhausting than either. The young captive, although a mere girl, was yet sufficiently versed in the perils attending frontier life to fully comprehend that upon her arrival at the village a fate awaited her more dreadful than death itself. She realized that if her life had been spared by her savage captors it was due to no sentiment of mercy or kindness on their part, but simply that she might be reserved for a doom far more fearful and more to be dreaded than death.

The capture of Mrs. Morgan occurred about one month later, and in the same section of country, and the story of her capture is in its incidents almost a repetition of that of Miss White. Her young husband was engaged at work in a field, not far from the house, when the crack of a rifle from the woods near by summoned her to the door. She barely had time to see her husband fall to the ground when she discovered several Indians rushing toward the house. Her first impulse was to seek safety in flight, but already the Indians had surrounded the house, and upon her attempting to escape one of the savages felled her to the ground by a blow from his war club, and she lost all consciousness. When she recovered her senses it was only to find herself bound upon the back of a pony which was being led by a mounted warrior, while another warrior rode behind and urged the pony she was mounted upon to keep up the trot. There were about fifty warriors in the party, nearly all belonging to the Cheyenne tribe, the others belonging to the Sioux and Arrapahoes. As in the case of the capture of Miss White, a rapid flight immediately followed the capture.

It was the story oft repeated of outrages like these, but particularly of these two, that finally forced the people of Kansas to take up arms in their own defence. Authority was obtained from the General Government to raise a regiment of cavalry, whose services were to be accepted for a period of six months. So earnest and enthusiastic had the people of the frontier become in their determination to reclaim the two captives, as well as administer justly-merited punishment, that people of all classes and callings were eager to abandon their professions and take up arms against the traditional enemy of the frontier. The Governor of the State, Hon. S. J. Crawford, resigned the duties of the Executive of the State into the hands of the Lieutenant-Governor, and placed himself at the head of the regiment, which was then being organized and equipped for service during the winter campaign. After the return of the Seventh Cavalry from the Washita campaign, we were simply waiting the arrival at Camp Supply of the Kansas volunteers before again setting out to continue the campaign, whose opening had begun so auspiciously. Severe storms delayed the arrival of the Kansas troops beyond the expected time. They reached Camp Supply, however, in time for the 7th of December to be fixed upon as the date of our departure. My command, as thus increased, consisted of eleven companies of the Seventh United States Cavalry; ten companies of the Nineteenth Kansas volunteer Cavalry, Colonel S. J. Crawford commanding; a detachment of scouts under Lieutenant Silas Pepoon, Tenth Cavalry; and between twenty and thirty whites, Osage and Kaw Indians, as guides and trailers. As our ultimate destination was Fort Cobb, Indian Territory, where we would obtain a renewal of our supplies after the termination of our proposed march, and as General Sheridan desired to transfer his headquarters " in the field " to that point, he decided to accompany my command, but generously declined to exercise any command of the expedition, merely desiring to avail himself of this opportunity of an escort without rendering a detachment for that purpose necessary; and, as he remarked when announcing his intention to accompany us, he simply wished to be regarded as a " passenger."

The day prior to our departure I was standing in front of my tent, when a young man, probably twenty-one or two years of age, accosted me and began a conversation by inquiring when I expected the expedition would move. Any person who has had much to do with expeditions in the Indian country knows how many and how frequent are the applications made to the commanding officer to obtain employment as scouts or guides. Probably one in fifty of the applicants is deserving of attention, and if employed would prove " worthy of his hire." Taking but a glance at the young man who addressed me, and believing him to be one of the numerous applicants for employment, my attention being at the time absorbed with other matters, I was in no mood to carry on a conversation which I believed would terminate in an offer of services not desired. I was disposed to be somewhat abrupt in my answers, but there was something in the young man's earnest manner, the eagerness with which he seemed to await my answers, that attracted and interested me. After a few questions on his part as to what portion of the country I expected to march through, what tribes I might encounter, and others of a similar nature, he suddenly said, " General, I want to go along with you." This only confirmed my first impression, although from his conversation I soon discovered that he was not one of the professional applicants for employment as a scout or guide, but more likely had been seized with a spirit of wild romance, and imagined the proper field for its display would be discovered by accompanying an expedition against the Indians. Many instances of this kind had previously fallen under my observation, and I classed this as one of them; so I simply informed him that I had already employed as many scouts and guides as were required, and that no position of that character, or any other in fact, was open to him. Not in the least discouraged by this decided refusal, he replied: " But you do not understand me; I do not desire employment in your command, nor any position requiring pay. I only ask permission to accompany your expedition. I have neither arms nor horse; if you will furnish me these, and permit me to go with you, I will serve you in any capacity I can, and will expect no pay."

My curiosity was now excited; I therefore pressed him to explain his motive in desiring to accompany the expedition.

" Well, I'll tell you; it's a sad story. About four months ago the Indians attacked my home, and carried off my only sister, a girl nineteen years of age. Since that day I have heard not a word as to what has become of her. I know not whether she is among the living or dead; but when I think of what must be her fate if among the living, I am almost tempted to wish she was quietly resting among the dead. I do not even know what tribe was engaged in her capture, but hearing of your expedition I thought it might afford me the means of getting some clue to my sister's fate. You may have a council with some of the chiefs, or some of the prisoners you captured at the battle of the Washita may tell me something of her; or if I can only learn where she is, perhaps you can exchange some of your prisoners for her; at any rate, the only chance I have to learn anything concerning her is by being permitted to accompany your expedition."

Of course he was permitted to accompany the expedition; not only that, but he was provided with a horse and arms, and appointed to a remunerative position. I asked him why he had not informed me at first as to his object in desiring to go with us. He replied that he feared that if it was known that he was in search of a lost sister, and we should afterward have interviews with the Indians, as we certainly would at Fort Cobb, he might not be as successful in obtaining information as if the object of his mission was unknown.

The name of this young man was Brewster, and the lost sister in whose search he was so earnestly engaged was Mrs. Morgan, whose capture has already been described. From him I learned that Mrs. Morgan's husband, although shot down at the first fire of the Indians, was in a fair way to recover, although crippled probably for life. But for his wounds, he too would have joined the brother in a search for the sister and for his bride, whose honeymoon had met with such a tragic interruption. Young Brewster remained with my command during the entire winter, accompanying it, and every detachment made from it, in the eager hope to learn something of the fate of his sister. In his continued efforts to discover some clue leading to her he displayed more genuine courage, perseverance, and physical endurance, and a greater degree of true brotherly love and devotion, than I have ever seen combined in one person. We will hear from him as the story progresses.

It was decided to send the captives taken at the Washita to Fort Hays, Kansas, where they could not only be safely guarded, but be made far more comfortable than at Camp Supply. Before the expedition moved I suggested to General Sheridan that I should take with the expedition three of the squaws who were prisoners in our hands, with a view to rendering their services available in establishing communication with the hostile villages, if at any time this should become a desirable object. General Sheridan approved of the suggestion, and I selected three of the captives who were to accompany us. The first was Mah-wis-sa, the sister of Black Kettle, whose acquaintance the reader may have formed in the preceding chapter; the second was a Sioux squaw, probably fifty years of age, whom Mah-wis-sa expressed a desire to have accompany her, and who at times was disposed to be extremely com municative in regard to the winter resorts of the various tribes, and other mat ters connected with the purposes of the expedition. The third was the daughter of Little Rock, the chief second in rank to Black Kettle, who had been killed at the battle of the Washita. Little Rock's daughter was an ex ceedingly comely squaw, possessing a bright, cheery face, a countenance beam ing with intelligence, and a disposition more inclined to be merry than one usually finds among the Indians. She was probably rather under than over twenty years of age. Added to bright, laughing eyes, a set of pearly teeth, and a rich complexion, her well-shaped head was crowned with a luxuriant growth of the most beautiful silken tresses, rivalling in color the blackness of the raven, and extending, when allowed to fall loosely over her shoulders, to below her waist. Her name was Mo-nah-se-tah, which, anglicized, means "The young grass that shoots in the spring." Mo-nah-se-tah, although yet a maiden in years and appearance, had been given in marriage, or, more prop erly speaking, she had been traded in marriage, as an Indian maiden who should be so unfortunate as to be "given" away would not be looked upon as a very desirable match. In addition to her handsome appearance, both in form and feature, and to any other personal attraction which might be con sidered peculiarly her own, Mo-nah-se-tah, being the daughter of a chief high in rank, was justly considered as belonging to the cream of the aristocracy, if not to royalty itself; consequently the suitors who hoped to gain her hand must be prepared, according to the Indian custom, to pay handsomely for an alliance so noble. Little Rock, while represented as having been a kind and affectionate father, yet did not propose that the hand of his favorite daugh ter should be disposed of without the return of a due equivalent.

Among the young warriors of the tribe there were many who would have been proud to call Mo-nah-se-tah to preside over the domestic destinies of their lodge, but the price to be paid for so distinguished an alliance was beyond the means of most of them. Among the number of young braves who aspired to the honor of her hand was one who, so far as worldly wealth was concerned, was eligible. Unfortunately, however, he had placed too much reliance upon this fact, and had not thought that while obtaining the consent of paterfamilias it would be well also to win the heart of the maiden; or per haps he had, in seeking her hand, also attempted to gain her heart, but not meeting with the desired encouragement from the maiden of his choice, was willing to trust to time to accomplish the latter, provided only he could secure the first. According to Indian customs the consent of the bride to a proposed marriage, while it may be ever so desirable, is not deemed essential. All that is considered absolutely essential is, that the bridegroom shall be accept able to the father of the bride, and shall transfer to the possession of the latter ponies or other articles of barter, in sufficient number and value to be consid ered a fair equivalent for the hand of the daughter. When it is stated that from two to four ponies are considered as the price of the average squaw, and that the price for the hand of Mo-nah-se-tah, as finally arranged, was eleven ponies, some idea can be formed of the high opinion entertained of her.

It proved, however, so far as the young warrior was concerned, an unsat isfactory investment. The ponies were transferred to Little Rock, and all the formalities were duly executed which, by Indian law and custom, were necessary to constitute Mo-nah-se-tah the wife of the young brave. She was forced to take up her abode in his lodge, but refused to acknowledge him as her husband, or to render him that obedience and menial service which the Indian husband exacts from his wife. Time failed to soften her heart, or to cause her to look kindly upon her self-constituted but unrecognized lord and master.

Here was a clear case of "incompatibility of disposition"; and within the jurisdiction of some of our State laws a divorce would have been granted almost unquestioned. The patience of the young husband having become exhausted, and he having unsuccessfully resorted to every measure of kindness deemed likely to win the love and obedience of his wife, he determined to have recourse to harsher measures—if necessary, to employ force. Again he mistook the character of her upon whose apparently obdurate heart neither threats nor promises had produced the faintest effect. Mo-nah-se-tah had probably been anticipating such a decision, and had prepared herself accordingly. Like most Indian women, she was as skilful in the handling and use of weapons as most warriors are; and when her husband, or rather the husband who had been assigned to her, attempted to establish by force an authority which she had persistently refused to recognize, she reminded him that she was the daughter of a great chief, and rather than submit to the indignities which he was thus attempting to heap upon her, she would resist even to the taking of life; and suiting the action to the word, she levelled a small pistol which she had carried concealed beneath her blanket and fired, wounding him in the knee and disabling him for life.

Little Rock, learning of what had occurred, and finding upon investigation that his daughter had not been to blame, concluded to cancel the marriage—to grant a divorce—which was accomplished simply by returning to the unfortunate husband the eleven ponies which had been paid for the hand of Mo-nan-se-tah. What an improvement upon the method prescribed in the civilized world! No lawyer's fees, no publicity nor scandal; all tedious delays are avoided, and the result is as nearly satisfactory to all parties as is possible.

Having sent a messenger to ask the three Indian women referred to to come to my tent, I acquainted them with my intention of taking them with the expedition when we moved in search of the hostile villages. To my surprise they evinced great delight at the idea, and explained it by saying that if they accompanied us they might be able to see or communicate with some of their people, while by remaining with the other prisoners, and becoming further separated from their own country and hunting-grounds, they could entertain little or no hope of learning anything concerning the fate of other portions of their tribe. They gladly acceded to the proposition to accompany the troops. I then inquired of them in which mode they preferred to travel, mounted upon ponies, as was their custom, or in an ambulance. Much to my surprise, remembering how loath the Indian is to adopt any contrivance of the white man, they chose the ambulance, and wisely too, as the season was that of midwinter, and the interior of a closely covered ambulance was a much less exposed position than that to be found on the back of a pony.

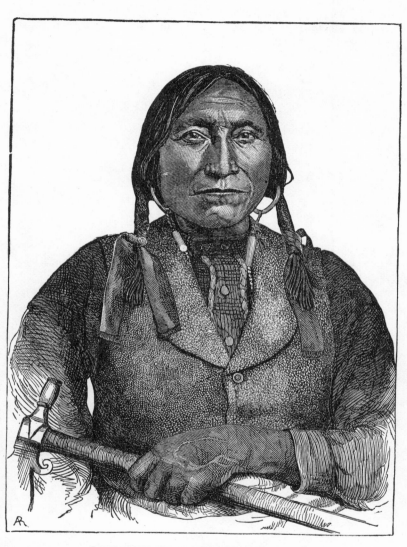

LONE WOLF, HEAD CHIEF OF THE KIOWAS.

XVIII.

FORAGE for the horses and mules, and rations for the men, sufficient of both to last thirty days, having been loaded on the wagons, the entire command, composed as previously stated, and accompanied by General Sheridan and staff, left Camp Supply early on the morning of December 7, and turning our horses' heads southward, we marched in the direction of the battle-ground of the Washita. Our march to the Washita was quiet and uneventful, if we except the loquacity of California Joe, who, now that we were once more in the saddle with the prospect of stirring times before us, seemed completely in his element, and gave vent to his satisfaction by indulging in a connected series of remarks and queries, always supplying the answer to the latter himself if none of his listeners evinced a disposition to do so for him. His principal delight seemed to be in speculating audibly as to what would be the impression produced on the minds of the Indians when they discovered us returning with increased numbers both of men and wagons.

" I'd jist like to see the streaked count'nances of Satanta, Medicine Arrow, Lone Wolf, and a few others of 'em, when they ketch the fust glimpse of the outfit. They'll think we're comin' to spend an evenin' with 'em sure, and hev brought our knittin' with us. One look 'll satisfy 'em thar 'll be sum of the durndest kickin' out over these plains that ever war heern tell uv. One good thing, it's goin' to cum as nigh killin' uv 'em to start 'em out this time uv year as ef we hed an out an' out scrummage with 'em. The way I looks at it they hev jist this preference: them as don't like bein' shot to deth kin take ther chances at freezin'." In this interminable manner California Joe would pursue his semi-soliloquies, only too delighted if some one exhibited interest sufficient to propound an occasional question.

As our proposed route bore to the southeast after reaching the battle-field, our course was so chosen as to carry us to the Washita river a few miles below, at which point we encamped early in the day. General Sheridan desired to ride over the battle-ground, and we hoped by a careful examination of the surrounding country to discover the remains of Major Elliott and his little party, of whose fate there could no longer be the faintest doubt. With one hundred men of the Seventh Cavalry, under command of Captain Yates, we proceeded to the scene of the battle, and from there dispersed in small parties in all directions, with orders to make a thorough search for our lost comrades. We found the evidences of the late engagement

253

much as we had left them.   Here were the bodies, now frozen, of the seven hundred ponies which we had slain after the battle; here and there, scattered in and about the site of the former village of Black Kettle, lay the bodies of many of the Indians who fell during the struggle.   Many of the bodies, however, particularly those of Black Kettle and Little Rock, had been removed by their friends.   Why any had been allowed to remain uncared for, could only be explained upon the supposition that the hasty flight of the other villages prevented the Indians from carrying away any except the bodies of the most prominent chiefs or warriors, although most of those remaining on the battle-ground were found wrapped in blankets and bound with lariats preparatory to removal and burial.   Even some of the Indian dogs were found loitering in the vicinity of the places where the lodges of their former masters stood; but, like the Indians themselves, they were suspicious of the white man, and could hardly be induced to establish friendly relations.   Some of the soldiers, however, managed to secure possession of a few young puppies; these were carefully brought up, and to this day they, or some of their descendants, are in the possession of members of the command.

After riding over the ground in the immediate vicinity of the village, I joined one of the parties engaged in the search for the bodies of Major Elliott and his men.   In describing the search and its result, I cannot do better than transcribe from my official report, made soon after to General Sheridan:

"After marching a distance of two miles in the direction in which Major Elliott and his little party were last seen, we suddenly came upon the stark, stiff, naked, and horribly mutilated bodies of our dead comrades.   No words were needed to tell how desperate had been the struggle before they were finally overpowered.   At a short distance from where the bodies lay, could be seen the carcasses of some of the horses of the party, which had probably been killed early in the fight.   Seeing the hopelessness of breaking through the line which surrounded them, and which undoubtedly numbered more than one hundred to one, Elliott dismounted his men, tied their horses together, and prepared to sell their lives as dearly as possible.   It may not be improper to add that in describing, as far as possible, the details of Elliott's fight, I rely not only upon a critical and personal examination of the ground and attendant circumstances, but am sustained by the statements of Indian chiefs and warriors who witnessed and participated in the fight, and who have since been forced to enter our lines and surrender themselves up, under circumstances which will be made to appear in other portions of this report.

"The bodies of Elliott and his little band, with but a single exception, were found lying within a circle not exceeding twenty yards in diameter.   We found them exactly as they fell, except that their barbarous foes had stripped and mutilated the bodies in the most savage manner.

"All the bodies were carried to camp.   The latter was reached after dark. It being the intention to resume the march before daylight the following day, a grave was hastily prepared on a little knoll near our camp, and, with the exception of that of Major Elliott, whose remains were carried with us for interment at Fort Arbuckle, the bodies of the entire party, under the dim light of a few torches held by of sorrowing comrades, were consigned to one common resting place.   No funeral note sounded to measure their passage to the grave.   No volley was fired to tell us a comrade was receiving the last sad rites of burial, that the fresh earth had closed over some of our truest and most daring soldiers.

" Before interment, I caused a complete examination of each body to be made by Dr. Lippincott, chief medical officer of the expedition. with direction to report on the character and number of wounds received by each, as well as to mutilations to which they had been subjected. The following extracts are taken from Dr. Lippincott's report:

" Major Joel H. Elliott, two bullet holes in head, one in left cheek, right hand cut off, left foot almost cut off, ... deep gash in right groin, deep gashes in calves of both legs, little finger of left hand cut off, and throat cut.

" Sergeant-Major Walter Kennedy, bullet hole in right temple, head partly cut off, seventeen bullet holes in back, and two in legs.

" Corporal Harry Mercer, Troop E, bullet hole in right axilla, one in region of heart, three in back, eight arrow wounds in back, right ear cut off, head scalped, and skull fractured, deep gashes in both legs, and throat cut.

" Private Thomas Christer, Troop E, bullet hole in head, right foot cut off, bullet hole in abdomen, and throat cut.

" Corporal William Carrick, Troop H, bullet hole in right parietal bone, both feet cut off throat cut, left arm broken.

" Private Eugene Clover, Troop H, head cut off, arrow wound in right side, both legs terribly mutilated.

" Private William Milligan, Troop H, bullet hole in left side of head, deep gashes in right leg, ... left arm deeply gashed, head scalped, and throat cut.

" Corporal James F. Williams, Troop I, bullet hole in back; head and both arms cut off, many and deep gashes in back. . . . .

" Private Thomas Dooney, Troop I, arrow hole in region of stomach, thorax cut open, head cut off, and right shoulder cut by a tomahawk.

" Farrier Thomas Fitzpatrick, Troop M, bullet hole in left parietal bone, head scalped, arm broken, ... throat cut.

" Private John Myres, Troop M, several bullet holes in head, scalped, nineteen bullet holes in body, ... throat cut.

" Private Cal. Sharpe, Troop M, two bullet holes in right side, throat cut, one bullet hole in left side of head, one arrow hole in left side, ... left arm broken.

" Unknown, head cut off, body partially destroyed by wolves.

" Unknown, head and right hand cut off, ... three bullet and nine arrow holes in back.

" Unknown, scalped, skull fractured, six bullet and thirteen arrow holes in back, and three bullet holes in chest."

I have quoted these extracts in order to give the reader an insight of the treatment invariably meted out to white men who are so unfortunate as to fall within the scope of the red man's bloodthirsty and insatiable vengeance. The report to General Sheridan then continues as follows:

" In addition to the wounds and barbarities reported by Dr. Lippincott, I saw a portion of the stock of a Lancaster rifle protruding from the side of one of the men; the stock had been broken off near the barrel, and the butt of it, probably twelve inches in length, had been driven into the man's side a distance of eight inches. The forest along the banks of the Washita, from the battle-ground a distance of twelve miles, was found to have been one continuous Indian village. Black Kettle's band of Cheyennes was above; then came other hostile tribes camped in the following order: Arrapahoes under Little Raven; Kiowas under Satanta and Lone Wolf; the remaining bands of Cheyennes, Comanches, and Apaches. Nothing could exceed the disorder and haste with which these tribes had fled from their camping grounds. They had abandoned thousands of lodge poles, some of which were still standing, as when last used. Immense numbers of camp kettles, cooking utensils, coffee-mills, axes, and several hundred buffalo robes were found in the abandoned camps adjacent to Black Kettle s village, but which had not been visited before by our troops. By actual examination, it was computed that over six hundred lodges had been standing along the Washita during the battle, and within five miles of the battle-ground, and it was from these villages, and others still lower down the stream, that the immense number of warriors came who, after our rout and destruction of Black Kettle and his band, surrounded my command and fought until defeated by the Seventh Cavalry about 3 P. M. on the 27th ult. . . . In the deserted camp, lately occupied by Satanta with the Kiowas, my men discovered the bodies of a young white woman and child, the former apparently about twenty-three years of age, the latter probably eighteen months old. They were evidently mother and child, and had not long been in captivity, as the woman still retained several articles of her wardrobe about her person—among others a pair of cloth gaiters but little worn, everything indicating that she had been but recently captured, and upon our attacking and routing Black Kettle's camp her captors, fearing she might be recaptured by us and her testimony used against them, had deliberately murdered her and her child in cold blood. The woman had received a shot in the forehead, her entire scalp had been removed, and her skull horribly crushed. The child also bore numerous marks of violence."

At daylight on the following morning the entire command started on the trail of the Indian villages, nearly all of which had moved down the Washita toward Fort Cobb, where they had good reason to believe they would receive protection. The Arrapahoes and remaining band of Cheyennes left the Washita valley and moved across in the direction of Red river. After following the trail of the Kiowas and other hostile Indians for seven days, over an almost impassable country, where it was necessary to keep two or three hundred men almost constantly at work with picks, axes, and spades, before being able to advance with our immense train, my Osage scouts came galloping back on the morning of the 17th of December, and reported a party of Indians in our front bearing a flag of truce.

It is to this day such a common occurrence for Indian agents to assert in positive terms that the particular Indians of their agency have not been absent from their reservation, nor engaged in making war upon the white men, when the contrary is well known to be true, that I deem it proper to introduce one of the many instances of this kind which have fallen under my observation, as an illustration not only of how the public in distant sections of the country may be misled and deceived as to the acts and intentions of the Indians, but also of the extent to which the Indian agents themselves will proceed in attempting to shield and defend the Indians of their particular agency. Sometimes, of course, the agent is the victim of deception, and no doubt conscientiously proclaims that which he firmly believes; but I am forced by long experience to the opinion that instances of this kind are rare, being the exception rather than the rule. In the example to which I refer, the high character and distinction as well as the deservedly national reputation achieved by the official then in charge of the Indians against whom we were operating, will at once absolve me from the imputation of intentionally reflecting upon the integrity of his action in the matter. The only point to occasion surprise is how an officer possessing the knowledge of the Indian character, derived from an extensive experience on the frontier, which General Hazen could justly lay claim to, should be so far misled as to give the certificate of good conduct which follows. General Hazen had not only had superior opportunities for studying the Indian character, but had participated in Indian wars, and at the very time he penned the following note he was partially disabled from the effects of an Indian wound. The Government had selected him from the large number of intelligent officers of high rank whose services were available for the position, and had assigned him with plenary powers to the superintendency of the Southern Indian District, a position in which almost the entire control of all the southern tribes was vested in the occupant. If gentlemen of the experience and military education of General Hazen, occupying the intimate and official relation to the Indians which he did, could be so readily and completely deceived as to their real character, it is not strange that the mass of the people living far from the scene of operations, and only possessing such information as reaches them in scraps through the public press, and generally colored by interested parties, should at times entertain extremely erroneous impressions regarding the much-vexed Indian question. Now to the case in point:

With the Osage scouts who came back from the advance with the intelligence that a party of Indians were in front, also came a scout who stated that he was from Fort Cobb, and delivered to me a despatch, which read as follows:

HEADQUARTERS SOUTHERN INDIAN DISTRICT, FORT COBB, 9 P. M. December 16, 1868.

To the Officer, commanding troops in the Field.

Indians have just brought in word that our troops to-day reached the Washita some twenty miles above here. I send this to say that all the camps this side of the point reported to have been reached are friendly, and have not been on the war path this season. If this reaches you, it would be well to communicate at once with Satanta or Black Eagle, chiefs of the Kiowas, near where you now are, who will readily inform you of the position of the Cheyennes and Arrapahoes, also of my camp. Respectfully,

(Signed) W. B. HAZEN, Brevet Major-General.

This scout at the same time informed me that a large party of Kiowa warriors, under Lone Wolf, Satanta, and other leading chiefs, were within less than a mile of my advance, and notwithstanding the above certificate regarding their friendly character, they had seized a scout who accompanied the bearer of the despatch, disarmed him, and held him a prisoner of war. Taking a small party with me, I proceeded beyond our lines to meet the flag of truce. I was met by several of the leading chiefs of the Kiowas, including those above named. Large parties of their warriors could be seen posted in the neighboring ravines and upon the surrounding hilltops. All were painted and plumed for war, and nearly all were armed with one rifle, two revolvers, bow and arrow, some of their bows being strung, and their whole appearance and conduct plainly indicating that they had come for war. Their declarations to some of my guides and friendly Indians proved the same thing, and they were only deterred from hostile acts by discovering our strength to be far greater than they had imagined, and our scouts on the alert. Aside, however, from the question as to what their present or future intentions were at that time, how deserving were those Indians of the certificate of good behavior which they had been shrewd enough to obtain? The certificate was dated De-

17

cember 16, and stated that the camps had not been on the war path "this sea-son."

What were the facts? On the 27th of November, only twenty-one days prior to the date of the certificate, the same Indians, whose peaceable charac-ter was vouched for so strongly, had engaged in battle with my command by attacking it during the fight with Black Kettle. It was in their camp that the bodies of the murdered mother and child were found, and we had followed day by day the trail of the Kiowas and other tribes, leading us directly from the dead and mangled bodies of our comrades, slain by them a few days pre-vious, until we were about to overtake and punish the guilty parties, when the above communication was received, some forty or fifty miles from Fort Cobb, in the direction of the Washita battle-ground.

This, of itself, was conclusive evidence of the character of the tribes we were dealing with; but aside from these incontrovertible facts, had additional evidence been needed of the openly hostile conduct of the Kiowas and Co-manches, and of their active participation in the battle of the Washita, it is only necessary to refer to the collected testimony of Black Eagle and other leading chiefs. This testimony was written, and was then in the hands of the agents of the Indian Bureau. It was given voluntarily by the Indian chiefs referred to, and was taken down at the time by the Indian agents, not for the army, or with a view of furnishing it to officers of the army, but simply for the benefit and information of the Indian Bureau. This testimony, making due allowance for the concealment of much that would be prejudicial to the interests of the Indians, plainly states that the Kiowas and Comanches took part in the battle of the Washita: that the former constituted a portion of the war party whose trail I followed, and which led my command into Black Kettle's village: and that some of the Kiowas remained in Black Kettle's vil-lage until the morning of the battle.

This evidence is all contained in a report made to the Superintendent of Indian Affairs, by one Philip McCuskey, United States interpreter for the Kiowa and Comanche tribes. This report was dated Fort Cobb, December 3, while the communication from General Hazen, certifying to the friendly disposition and conduct of these tribes, was dated at the same place thirteen days later. Mah-wis-sa also confirmed these statements, and pointed out to me, when near the battle-ground, the location of Satanta's village. It was from her, too, that I learned that it was in Satanta's village that the bodies of the white woman and child were found. As I pen these lines, the daily press contains frequent allusions to the negotiations which are being conducted between the Governor of Texas and the General Government, looking to the release of Satanta from the Texas penitentiary, to which institution Satanta, after a trial before the civil authorities for numerous murders committed on the Texas frontier, was sent three or four years ago to serve out a life sentence.

After meeting the chiefs, who with their bands had approached our ad-vance under flag of truce, and compelling the release of the scout whom they had seized and held prisoner, we continued our march toward Fort Cobb, the chiefs agreeing to ride with us and accompany my command to that place. Every assurance was given me that the villages to which these various chiefs belonged would at once move to Fort Cobb, and there encamp, thus separat-ing themselves from the hostile tribes, or those who preferred to decline this proposition of peace, and to continue to wage war; and as an evidence of the sincerity of their purpose, some eighteen or twenty of the most prominent chiefs, generally Kiowas, voluntarily proposed to accompany us during the march of that day and the next, by which time it was expected that the command would reach Fort Cobb. The chiefs only requested that they might send one of their number, mounted on a fleet pony, to the villages, in order to hasten their movement to Fort Cobb. How eager for peace were these poor, confiding sons of the forest is the mental ejaculation of some of my readers, particularly if they are inclined to be converts to the humanitarian doctrines supposed to be applicable in the government of Indians. If I am addressing any of this class, for whose kindness of heart I have the utmost regard, I regret to be compelled to disturb the illusion.

Peace was not included among the purposes which governed the chiefs who so freely and unhesitatingly proffered their company during our march to Fort Cobb. Nor had they the faintest intention of either accompanying us or directing their villages to proceed to the fort. The messenger whom they seemed so anxious to despatch to the village was not sent to hasten the movement of their villages toward Fort Cobb, as claimed by them, but to hasten their movement in a precisely opposite direction, viz., towards the head waters of Red river, near the northwestern limits of Texas. This sudden effusion of friendly sentiments rather excited my suspicions, but I was unable at first to divine the real intents and purposes of the chiefs. Nothing was to be done but to act so as to avoid exciting their suspicion, and trust to time to unravel the scheme. When we arrived at our camping ground, on the evening of that day, the chiefs requested permission to despatch another messenger to their people to inform them where we were encamped. To this proposition no objection was made. That evening I caused an abundant supply of provisions, consisting principally of beef, bread, coffee, and sugar, to be distributed among them. In posting my pickets that night for the protection of the camp, I arranged to have the reserve stationed within a short distance of the spot on which the chiefs were to encamp during the night, which point was but a few paces from my headquarters. Before retiring, I took Romeo, the interpreter, and strolled down to pay a visit to the chiefs. The latter, after the substantial meal in which they had just indulged, were seated, Indian fashion, around a small fire, enjoying such comfort as was to be derived from the occasional whiffs of smoke which each in proper turn inhaled from the long-stemmed pipe of red clay that was kept passing from right to left around the circle. Their greeting of me was cordial in the extreme, but, as in the play—of "Richelieu," I believe—they "bowed too low." Through Romeo I chatted on indifferent subjects with the various chiefs, and from nearly all of them received assurances of their firmly fixed resolution to abandon forever the dangers and risks of the war path, to live no longer at variance with their white brothers, to eschew henceforth all such unfriendly customs as scalp-taking, murdering defenceless women and children, and stealing stock from the settlers of the frontier. All this was to be changed in the future. It seemed strange, listening to these apparently "artless sons of nature," that men entertaining the ardent desire for repose which they professed, had not turned their backs on the war path long ago, and settled down to the quiet enjoyment of the blessings of peace. But better that this conclusion should be arrived at late than not at all. The curtain had fallen from their eyes, and they were enabled to see everything in its proper light. To adopt their own language, "their hearts had become good," "their tongues had become straight," they had cast aside the bad ways in which they had so long struggled unsuccessfully, and had now resolved to follow the white man's road, to adopt his mode of dress, till the soil, and establish schools for the education of their children, until in time the white man and the red man would not only be brothers in name, but would be found travelling the same road with interests in common.

Had I been a latter-day Peace Commissioner, I should have felt in duty bound to send a despatch to the chief of the proper bureau at Washington, in terms somewhat as follows:

Hon John Smith, Secretary of the ——— Department.

I have just concluded a most satisfactory council with the Kiowa and other tribes, certain members of which have lately been accused of being more or less connected with the troubles lately occurring upon our frontier. All the prominent chiefs met me in council, and after a free interchange and expression of opinions, I am happy to inform the Department that these chiefs, representing as they do one of the most powerful and important of the southern tribes, have voluntarily and solemnly agreed to cease all hostile acts against the white men, to prevent raids or war parties from being organized among their young men, to abandon for all future time the war path, and to come within the limits of their reservation, there to engage in the peaceful pursuits of civilized life. They express a warm desire to have educational facilities extended them for the benefit of their children. As the season is far advanced, rendering it too late for them to successfully cultivate a crop the present year, they ask, and I recommend, that provisions sufficient for their subsistence the present season be issued them. They also request that, owing to the scarcity of game, a few breech-loading arms be furnished them, say one rifle and one revolver to each male over fourteen years of age. I am satisfied that this is a most reasonable request, and that the granting of it would go far to restore confidence in the good intentions of the Government, as I am forced to remark that some of the recent acts of the military, such as the occurrence on the Washita, have done much to produce an unsettled feeling on the part of these untutored wards of the nation. No further anxiety need be felt as to the complete pacification of this tribe. I wish you might have shared with me the pleasure of listening to these untaught chieftains, begging for such assistance and guidance as would lead them in the paths of peace. I leave here on the —th, to visit the neighboring tribes, provided the military commander at this point will furnish me a suitable escort.

I have the honor to be your obedient servant,

JOHN JONES, Indian Agent.

P. S.—I have thought that if we could confer the ballot upon those of the chiefs and warriors who show the greatest aptitude and desire for peace, it might be a great step toward completing their civilization. Of course some line of distinction or qualification would have to be drawn; for example, confer the right of ballot upon all those who faithfully accept their rations from the Government for a period of six months. I merely throw this out for the consideration of the Department.

J. J.

Not being an orthodox Peace Commissioner, in good standing in that fraternity, I did not send a despatch of this character. What I did, however, answered every purpose. I went to the station of the guard near by and directed the non-commissioned officer in charge to have his men keep a watch ful eye upon those same "untutored sons of the forest," as I felt confident their plans boded us no good. Romeo was also told to inform the chiefs that after the camp had quieted down for the night, it would not be prudent for them to wander far from their camp fire, as the sentries might mistake them for enemies and fire upon them. This I knew would make them hug their fire closely until morning. Before daylight we were again in the saddle and commencing the last march necessary to take us to Fort Cobb. Again did it become important, in the opinion of the chiefs, to despatch another of their number to hurry up the people of their villages, in order, as they said, that the villages might arrive at Fort Cobb at the same time we did. As the march progressed these applications became more frequent, until most of the chiefs had been sent away as messengers. I noticed, however, that in selecting those to be sent, the chiefs lowest in rank and importance were first chosen, so that those who remained were the highest. When their numbers had dwindled down to less than half the original party, I saw that instead of acting in good faith this party of chiefs was solely engaged in the effort to withdraw our attention from the villages, and, by an apparent offer on their part to accompany us to Fort Cobb, where we were encouraged to believe the villages would meet us, prevent us from watching and following the trail made by the lodges, which had already diverged from the direct route to Fort Cobb, the one the villages would have pursued had that fort been their destination. It became palpably evident that the Indians were resorting, as usual, to stratagem to accomplish their purpose, which of course involved our deception. Fortunately their purpose was divined in time to thwart it. As no haste was necessary, I permitted the remaining chiefs to continue the march with us, without giving them any grounds to suppose that we strongly doubted their oft-repeated assertions that their hearts were good and their tongues were straight. Finally, as our march for that day neared its termination and we were soon to reach our destination, the party of chiefs, which at first embraced upwards of twenty, had become reduced until none remained except the two head chiefs, Lone Wolf and Satanta, and these no doubt were laughing in their sleeves, if an Indian may be supposed to possess that article of apparel, at the happy and highly successful manner in which they had hoodwinked their white brethren. But had they known all that had been transpiring they would not have felt so self-satisfied. As usual, quite a number of officers and orderlies rode at the head of the column, including a few of General Sheridan's staff.

As soon as the scheme of the Indians was discovered, I determined to seize the most prominent chiefs as hostages for the fulfilment of their promises regarding the coming on of the villages; but as for this purpose two hostages were as valuable as twenty, I allowed all but this number to take their departure apparently unnoticed. Finally, when none but Lone Wolf and Satanta remained, and they no doubt were prepared with a plausible excuse to bid us in the most improved Kiowa *au revoir*, the officers just referred to, at a given signal, drew their revolvers, and Lone Wolf and Satanta were informed through Romeo that they were prisoners.

XIX

NOT even the proverbial stoicism of the red man was sufficient to conceal the chagrin and disappointment recognizable in every lineament of the countenances of both Satanta and Lone Wolf when they discovered that all their efforts at deception had not only failed, but left them prisoners in our hands. Had we been in doubt as to whether their intention had really been to leave us in the lurch or not, all doubt would have been dispelled by a slight circumstance which soon after transpired. As I before stated, we had almost reached Fort Cobb, which was our destination for the time being. The chiefs who had already made their escape now became anxious in regard to the non-arrival in their midst of Satanta and Lone Wolf. The delay of the last two could not be satisfactorily accounted for. Something must have gone amiss.

Again was stratagem resorted to. We were marching along without interruption or incident to disturb our progress, such of us as were at the head of the column keeping watchful eyes upon our two swarthy prisoners, who rode sullenly at our sides, and whose past career justified us in attributing to them the nerve and daring necessary to induce an effort to secure their liberty should there be the slightest probability of success. Suddenly a mounted Indian appeared far away to our right, and approached us at a gallop until almost within rifle range, when halting his well-trained pony upon a little hillock which answered his purpose, he gracefully detached the scarlet blanket he wore, and began waving it in a peculiar but regular manner. Both chiefs looked anxiously in the direction of the warrior, then merely glanced toward me as if to see if I had also observed this last arrival; but too proud to speak or prefer a request, they rode silently on, apparently indifferent to what might follow. Turning to Romeo, who rode in rear, I directed him to inquire of the chiefs the meaning of the signals which the warrior was evidently endeavoring to convey to them. Satanta acted as spokesman, and replied that the warrior in sight was his son, and that the latter was signalling to him that he had something important to communicate, and desired Satanta to ride out and join him.

To have seen the innocent and artless expression of countenance with which Satanta made this announcement, one would not have imagined that the son had been sent as a decoy to cover the escape of the father, and that the latter had been aware of this fact from the first   However, I pretended to humor Satanta. Of course there was no objection to his galloping out to where his son awaited him, because, as he said, that son was, and for good reason perhaps, unwilling to gallop in to where his father was. But if Satanta was so eager to see and communicate with his son, there should be no objection to the presence of a small escort—not that there existed doubts in my mind as to Satanta's intention to return to us, because no such doubt existed. I was positively convinced that once safely beyond our reach, the place at the head of the column, which had known him for a few brief hours, would know him no more forever. I told Romeo to say to Satanta that he might ride across the plain to where his son was, and not only that, but several of us would do ourselves the honor to volunteer as his escort.

SATANTA.

The most careless observer would have detected the air of vexation with which Satanta turned his pony's head, and taking me at my word started to meet his son. A brisk gallop soon brought us to the little hillock upon which Satanta's son awaited us. He was there, a tall, trimly built, warrior-like young fellow of perhaps twenty, and bore himself while in our presence as if he would have us to understand he was not only the son of a mighty chief, but some day would wear that title himself. What was intended to be gained by the interview did not become evident, as the presence of Romeo prevented any conversation between father and son looking to the formation of plans for escape. Questions were asked and answered as to where the village was, and in regard to its future movements, but nothing satisfactory either to Satanta or his captors was learned from the young warrior. Finally, I suggested to Satanta that as we only intended to proceed a few miles further, being then in the near vicinity of Fort Cobb, and would there encamp for an indefinite period, his son had better accompany us to camp, where Lone Wolf and Satanta would be informed what was to be required of them and their people, and then, after conferring with each other, the two chiefs could send Satanta's son to the village with any message which they might desire to transmit to their people. At the same time I promised the young warrior good treatment, with permission to go and come as he chose, and in no manner to be regarded or treated as a prisoner.

This proposition seemed to strike the Indians favorably, and much to my surprise, knowing the natural suspicion of the Indian, the young warrior readily consented to the plan, and at once placed himself in our power. Turning our horses' heads, we soon resumed our places at the head of the column, the three Indians riding in silence, brooding, no doubt, over plans looking to their freedom.

By way of a slight digression from the main narrative, I will here remark that during the prolonged imprisonment of the two chiefs, Satanta's son became a regular visitor to our camp, frequently becoming the bearer of important messages from the chiefs to their villages, and in time he and I, apparently, became firm friends. He was an excellent shot with the rifle. Satanta said he was the best in the tribe, and frequently, when time hung heavily on my hands, and I felt a desire for recreation, he and I took our rifles, and, after passing beyond the limits of camp, engaged in a friendly match at target practice, a much more agreeable mode of testing our skill as marksmen than by using each other as a target.

Satanta had exhibited no little gratification when I first engaged to shoot with his son, and as the lodge in which he was kept a closely guarded prisoner was on my route in returning from target practice to my tent, I usually stopped a few moments in his lodge to exchange passing remarks. He was evidently disappointed when informed as to the result of the first trial with our rifles, that his son had come off only second best; and numerous were the explanations which his fertile mind suggested as the causes leading to this result—a result which in the eyes of the Indian assumed far greater importance than would ordinarily be attached to it by white men. As we had agreed to have frequent contests of this kind, Satanta assured me that his son would yet prove himself the better man. Each meeting, however, only resulted as the first, although by varying the distance every opportunity was given for a fair test. Finally, when all other explanations had failed, Satanta thought he had discovered the real obstacle to the success of his son, by ascribing superior qualities to my rifle as compared with the one used by him. Fairness on my part then required that I should offer the young warrior the use of my rifle, and that I should use his in the next match; a proposition which was at once accepted, and, as if to be better prepared to make an excellent score, my rifle was soon in his hands and undergoing the critical inspection and manipulation of trigger, sights, etc., which always suggest themselves the moment an experienced marksman finds a new rifle in his hands. The following day we engaged as usual in rifle practice, he with my rifle, I with his. I frankly confess that having entered into the contest from the first with as much zest and rivalry as even my dusky competitor could lay claim to, and having come off victor in the preceding contests, I was not entirely free from anxiety lest the change in rifles might also change the result, and detract, in the eyes of the Indians at least, from my former successes. On this occasion, as on all previous ones, we were alone, and consequently we were our own judges, umpire, and referee. Greatly to my satisfaction, my good fortune enabled me to make a better score than did my opponent, and this result seemed to settle his opinion finally as to our relative merits as marksmen. I attached no little importance to these frequent and friendly meetings between Satanta's son and myself. Any superiority in the handling or use of weapons, in horseback exercises, or in any of the recognized manly sports, is a sure stepping-stone in obtaining for the possessor the highest regard of the red man.

Upon our arrival at Fort Cobb, the day of the seizure of the two chiefs, Lone Wolf and Satanta, we selected a camp with a view of remaining at that point during the negotiations which were to be conducted with the various tribes who were still on the war path. So far as some of the tribes were concerned, they were occupying that equivocal position which enabled them to class themselves as friendly and at the same time engage in hostilities. This may sound ambiguous, but is easily explained. The chiefs and old men, with the women and children of the tribe, were permitted to assemble regularly at the agency near Fort Cobb, and as regularly were bountifully supplied with food and clothing sufficient for all their wants; at the same time the young men, warriors, and war chiefs of the tribe were almost continually engaged in making war upon the frontier of northern Texas and southeastern Kansas. Indeed, we established the fact, while at or near Fort Cobb, that while my command was engaged in fighting the warriors and chiefs of certain tribes at the battle of the Washita, the families of these same warriors and chiefs were being clothed and fed by the agent of the Government then stationed at Fort Cobb.

Surprising as this may seem, it is not an unusual occurrence. The same system has prevailed during the past year. While my command was resisting the attacks of a large body of warriors on the Yellowstone river last summer, the families of many of these warriors, the latter representing seven tribes or bands, were subsisting upon provisions and clothed in garments issued to them at the regular Indian agencies by the Government. But of this more anon.

The three tribes which became at that time the special objects of our attention, and with whom we were particularly anxious to establish such relations as would prevent in the future a repetition of the murders and outrages of which they had so long been guilty, were the Kiowas, Cheyennes, and Arapahoes; the object being to complete our work by placing these three tribes upon reservations where they might be cared for, and at the same time be kept under proper surveillance. The Washita campaign had duly impressed them with the power and purpose of the Government to inflict punishment upon all

INDIANS COMMITTING OUTRAGES, WHILE THE GOVERNMENT FEEDS THEIR FAMILIES.

who chose to make war; and each tribe, dreading a repetition of the blow upon themselves, had removed their villages to remote points where they deemed themselves secure from further chastisement. Having Lone Wolf and Satanta, the two leading chiefs of the Kiowas, in our hands, we thought that through them the Kiowas could be forced to a compliance with the just and reasonable demands of the Government, and with the terms of their treaty providing for the reservation system.

All demands upon the Kiowas were communicated by me to Lone Wolf and Satanta, under the instructions of General Sheridan, who, although on the ground, declined to treat directly with the faithless chiefs. The Kiowas were informed that unless the entire tribe repaired to the vicinity of the agency, then located not far from Fort Cobb, the war, which had been inaugurated with such vigor and effect at the Washita, would be renewed and continued until the terms of their treaty had been complied with. This proposition was imparted to Lone Wolf and Satanta, and by them transmitted to their tribe, through the son of the latter, who acted as a sort of diplomatic courier between the Kiowa village and our camp.

The Kiowas, while sending messages apparently in accord with the proposition, and seeming to manifest a willingness to come in and locate themselves upon their reservation, continued, after the manner of Indian diplomacy, to defer from time to time the promised movement. There was every reason to believe that, finding the military disposed to temporarily suspend active operations, and resort to negotiation, the Kiowas had located their village within a short distance of our camp, as Satanta's son, in going and coming with messages from one to the other, easily made the round journey in a single day; so that had they been so disposed, the Kiowas could have transferred their village to our immediate vicinity, as desired by the military authorities, in one day. The truth was, however, that while manifesting an apparent desire to conform to this requirement, as a precedent to final peace, they had not intended at any time to keep faith with the Government, but, by a pretended acquiescence in the proposed arrangement, secure the release of the two head chiefs, Lone Wolf and Satanta, and then hasten, with the entire village, to join forces with the other two tribes, the Cheyennes and Arapahoes, who were then represented as being located somewhere near the source of Red river, and on the border of the Llano Estacado, or Staked Plain, a region of country supposed to be impenetrable by civilized man. Every promise of the Kiowas to come in was always made conditional upon the prior release of Lone Wolf and Satanta.

Their efforts to procrastinate or evade a fulfilment of their part of the agreement finally exhausted the forbearance which thus far had prompted none but the mildest measures on the part of the military authorities, in the efforts of the latter to bring about a peaceful solution of existing difficulties. It had become evident that, instead of intending to establish relations of permanent peace and friendship with the whites, the majority of the tribe were only waiting the release of Lone Wolf and Satanta to resume hostilities, or at least to more firmly ally themselves with the extremely hostile tribes then occupying the head waters of Red river.

Spring was approaching, when the grass would enable the Indians to recuperate their ponies, which, after the famished condition to which winter usually reduced them, would soon be fleet and strong, ready to do duty on the war path. It was therefore indispensable that there should be no further delay in the negotiations, which had been needlessly prolonged through several weeks,

General Sheridan promptly decided upon the terms of his ultimatum. Like most of the utterances of that officer, they were brief and to the point. I remember the day and the circumstances under which they were given. The General and myself were standing upon opposite sides of a rude enclosure which surrounded the space immediately about his tent, composed of a single line of rough poles, erected by the unskilled labor of some of the soldiers. The day was one of those bright, warm, sunshiny days so frequent in the Indian Territory, even in winter. I had left my tent, which was but a few paces from that of General Sheridan, to step over and report, as I did almost daily, the latest message from the Kiowas as to their intention to make peace. On this occasion, as on all former ones, there was a palpable purpose to postpone further action until Lone Wolf and Satanta should be released by us. After hearing the oft-repeated excuses of the Kiowas, General Sheridan communicated his resolve to me in substance as follows: "Well, Custer, these Kiowas are endeavoring to play us false. Their object is to occupy us with promises until the grass enables them to go where they please and make war if they choose. We have given them every opportunity to come in and enjoy the protection of the Government, if they so desired. They are among the worst Indians we have to deal with, and have been guilty of untold murders and outrages, at the same time they were being fed and clothed by the Government. These two chiefs, Lone Wolf and Satanta, have forfeited their lives over and over again. They could now induce their people to come in and become friendly if they chose to exert their influence in that direction. This matter has gone on long enough, and must be stopped, as we have to look after the other tribes before spring overtakes us. You can inform Lone Wolf and Satanta that we shall wait until sundown to-morrow for their tribe to come in; if by that time the village is not here, Lone Wolf and Satanta will be hung, and the troops sent in pursuit of the village."

This might be regarded as bringing matters to a crisis. I proceeded directly to the lodge in which Lone Wolf and Satanta were prisoners, accompanied by Romeo as interpreter. I found the two chiefs reclining lazily upon their comfortable, if not luxurious couches of robes. Satanta's son was also present. After a few preliminary remarks, I introduced the subject which was the occasion of my visit, by informing the chiefs that I had just returned from General Sheridan's tent, where the question of the failure of the Kiowas to comply with their oft-repeated promises had been discussed, and that I had been directed to acquaint them with the determination which had been formed in regard to them and their people. At this announcement I could see that both chiefs became instantly and unmistakably interested in what was being said.

I had so often heard of the proverbial stoicism of the Indian character, that it occurred to me that this was a favorable moment for judging how far this trait affects their conduct. For it will be readily acknowledged that the communication which I was about to make to them was one likely, at all events, to overturn any self-imposed stolidity which was not deeply impregnated in their nature. After going over the subject of the continued absence of the Kiowas from their reservation, their oft-made promises, made only to be violated, I told them that they were regarded, as they had a right to be, as the two leading and most influential chiefs of the tribe; that although they were prisoners, yet so powerful were they among the people of their own tribe, that their influence, even while prisoners, was greater than that of all the other chiefs combined; hence all negotiations with the Kiowas had been conducted through them, and although they had it in their power, by a single command, to cause a satisfactory settlement of existing difficulties to be made, yet so far they had failed utterly to exert an influence for peace between their people and the Government. The announcement then to be made to them must be regarded as final, and it remained with them alone to decide by their action what the result should be. In as few words as possible I then communicated to them the fate which undoubtedly awaited them in the event of the non-appearance of their tribe. Until sunset of the following day seemed a very brief period, yet I failed to detect the slightest change in the countenance of either when told that that would be the extent of their lives if their tribe failed to come in. Not a muscle of their warrior-like faces moved. Their eyes neither brightened nor quailed; nothing in their actions or appearance gave token that anything unusual had been communicated to them. Satanta's son alone of the three seemed to realize that matters were becoming serious, as could readily be told by watching his anxious glances, first at his father, then at Lone Wolf; but neither spoke.

Realizing the importance of time, and anxious to bring about a peaceful as well as satisfactory termination of our difficulties with the Kiowas, and at the same time to afford every facility to the two captive chiefs to save their oft-forfeited lives—for all familiar with their bloody and cruel career would grant that they merited death—I urged upon them the necessity of prompt action in communicating with their tribe, and pointed to Satanta's son, who could be employed for this purpose. Quickly springing to his feet, and not waiting to hear the opinions of the two chiefs, the young warrior rushed from the lodge, and was soon busily engaged in tightening the girths of his Indian saddle, preparatory to a rapid gallop on his fleet pony.

In the mean time Lone Wolf and Satanta began exchanging utterances, at first slow and measured, in tones scarcely audible. Gradually they seemed to realize how desperate was the situation they were in, and how much depended upon themselves. Then laying aside the formality which had up to that moment characterized their deportment, they no longer appeared as the dignified, reserved, almost sullen chiefs, but acted and spoke as would be expected of men situated as they were. In less time than I have taken to describe the action, Satanta's handsome son appeared at the entrance of the lodge, mounted and in readiness for his ride. Although he seemed by his manner to incline toward his father as the one who should give him his instructions, yet it was soon apparent that a more correct understanding existed between the two captives. Lone Wolf was the head chief of their tribe, Satanta the second in rank. The occasion was too important to leave anything to chance. A message from Satanta might receive prompt attention; a command from the head chief could not be disregarded; hence it was that Satanta stood aside, and Lone Wolf stepped forward and addressed a few hasty but apparently emphatic sentences to the young courier, who was all eagerness to depart on his mission. As Lone Wolf concluded his instructions, and the young warrior was gathering up his reins and lariat, and turning his pony from the lodge in the direction of the village, Satanta simply added, in an energetic tone, "Hoodle-teh, hoodle-teh" (make haste, make haste); an injunction scarcely needed, as the young Indian and his pony were the next moment flying across the level plain.

I then reëntered the lodge with Lone Wolf and Satanta, accompanied by Romeo. Through the latter Lone Wolf informed me that he had sent orders to the Kiowa village, which was not a day's travel from us, to pack up and come in as soon as the courier should reach them.   At the same time he informed them of what depended upon their coming.   He had also sent for Black Eagle, the third chief in rank, to come in advance of the village, bringing with him a dozen or more of the prominent chiefs.   I inquired if he felt confident that his people would arrive by the appointed time?   He almost smiled at the question, and assured me that an Indian would risk everything to save a comrade, leaving me to infer that to save their two highest chiefs nothing would be permitted to stand in the way.   Seeing, perhaps, a look of doubt on my face, he pointed to that locality in the heavens which the sun would occupy at two o'clock, and said, "Before that time Black Eagle and the other chiefs accompanying him will be here; and by that time," indicating in a similar manner sunset, "the village will arrive."

No general commanding an army, who had transmitted his orders to his corps commanders, directing a movement at daylight the following morning, could have exhibited more confidence in the belief that his orders would be executed, than did this captive chief in the belief that, although a prisoner in the hands of his traditional enemies, his lodge closely guarded on all sides by watchful sentinels, his commands to his people would meet with a prompt and willing compliance.   After a little further conversation with the two chiefs, I was preparing to leave the lodge, when Lone Wolf, true to the Indian custom, under which an opportunity to beg for something to eat is never permitted to pass unimproved, called me back, and said that the next day his principal chiefs would visit him, and although he was a prisoner, yet he would be glad to be able to entertain them in a manner befitting his rank and importance in the tribe, and therefore I was appealed to to furnish the provisions necessary to provide a feast for a dozen or more hungry chiefs and their retainers; in reply to which modest request I made the heart of Lone Wolf glad, and called forth, in his most emphatic as well as delighted manner, the universal word of approval, "How," by informing him that the feast should certainly be prepared if he only would supply the guests.

The next day was one of no little interest, and to none more than to the two chiefs, who expected to see the first step taken by their people which would terminate in their release from a captivity which had certainly become exceedingly irksome, not to mention the new danger which stared them in the face.   Lone Wolf, however, maintained his confidence, and repeatedly assured me during the forenoon that Black Eagle and the other chiefs, whom he had sent for by name, would arrive not later than two o'clock that day.   His confidence proved not to be misplaced.   The sun had hardly marked the hour of one in the heavens, when a small cavalcade was seen approaching in the distance from the direction of the Kiowa village.   The quick eye of Satanta was the first to discover it.   A smile of haughty triumph lighted up the countenance of Lone Wolf when his attention was called to the approaching party, his look indicating that he felt it could not be otherwise: had he not ordered it?

On they came, first about a dozen chiefs, riding at a deliberate and dignified pace, they and their ponies richly caparisoned in the most fantastic manner.   The chiefs wore blankets of bright colors, scarlet predominating, with here and there a bright green.   Each face was painted in brilliant colors, yellow, blue, green, red, black, and combinations of all of them, no two faces being ornamented alike, and each new face seeming more horrible than its predecessor.   The ponies had not been neglected, so far as their outward make-up was concerned, eagle feathers and pieces of gaudy cloth being interwoven in their manes and tails.   Following the chiefs rode a second line, only less ornamented than the chiefs themselves. These were warriors and confidential friends and advisers of the chiefs in whose train they rode. In rear of all rode a few meek-looking squaws, whose part in this imposing pageant became evident when the chiefs and warriors dismounted, giving the reins of their ponies to the squaws, who at once busied themselves in picketing the ponies of their lords, and, in every sense of the word, masters, wherever the grazing seemed freshest and most abundant. This being done, their part was performed, and they waited, near the ponies, the return of the chiefs and warriors. The latter, after forming in one group, and in similar order to that in which they rode, advanced toward the lodge outside of which, but within the chain of sentinels, stood Lone Wolf and Satanta. The meeting between the captive chiefs and their more fortunate comrades occasioned an exhibition of more feeling and sensibility than is generally accredited to the Indian. A bevy of school girls could not have embraced each other, after a twenty-four hours' separation, with greater enthusiasm and demonstrations of apparent joy than did these chieftains, whose sole delight is supposed to be connected with scenes of bloodshed and cruelty. I trust no gentle-minded reader, imbued with great kindness of heart, will let this little scene determine his estimate of the Indian character; for be it understood, not one of the chiefs who formed the group of which I am writing but had participated in acts of the most barbarous and wanton cruelty. It was a portion of these chiefs who had led and encouraged the band that had subjected the Box family to such a horrible fate, of which Major-General Hancock made full report at the time.

Immediately after greetings had been exchanged between the captives and their friends, I was requested, by a message from Lone Wolf, to repair to his lodge in order to hear what his friends had to say. As I entered the lodge the entire party of chiefs advanced to meet me, and began a series of hand-shaking and universal "Hows," which in outward earnestness made up for any lack of real sincerity, and to an inexperienced observer or a tender-hearted peace commissioner might well have appeared as an exhibition of indubitable friendship if not affection. After all were seated, and the ever-present long red clay pipe had passed and repassed around the circle, each chief indulging in a few silent whiffs, Black Eagle arose, and after shaking hands with me, proceeded, after the manner of an oration, to inform me, what I had had reason to expect, and what the reader no doubt has also anticipated, that the entire Kiowa village was at that moment on the march, and would arrive in the vicinity of our camp before dark. No reference was made to the fact that this general movement on their part was one of compulsion, but on the contrary, to have heard Black Eagle, who was an impressive orator, one might well have believed that, no longer able to endure the separation from their brothers, the white men, who, as Black Eagle said, like themselves were all descended from one father, the Kiowas had voluntarily resolved to pack up their lodges, and when they next should put them down it would be alongside the tents of their white friends.

In nothing that was said did it appear that the impending execution of Lone Wolf and Satanta had aught to do with hastening the arrival of their people. At the termination of the conference, however, Black Eagle intimated that as the tribe was about to locate near us, it would be highly agreeable to them if their two head chiefs could be granted their liberty and permitted to resume their places among their own people.

That evening the Kiowa village, true to the prediction of Lone Wolf, ar-

18

rived, and was located a short distance from our camp. The next morning the family or families of Satanta appeared in front of headquarters and made known their desire to see Satanta, to which, of course, no objection was made, and the guards were instructed to permit them to pass the lines. Satanta's home circle was organized somewhat on the quadrilateral plan; that is, he had four wives. They came together, and, so far as outward appearances enabled one to judge, they constituted a happy family. They were all young and buxom, and each was sufficiently like the others in appearance to have enabled the lot to pass as sisters; and, by the way, it is quite customary among the Indians for one man to marry an entire family of daughters as rapidly as they reach the proper age. To those who dread a multiplicity of mothers-in-law this custom possesses advantages. To add in a material as well as maternal way to the striking similarity in appearance presented by Satanta's dusky spouses, each bore on her back, encased in the capacious folds of a scarlet blanket, a pledge of affection in the shape of a papoose, the difference in the extreme ages of the four miniature warriors, or warriors' sisters, being too slight to be perceptible. In single file the four partners of Satanta's joys approached his lodge, and in the same order gained admittance. Satanta was seated on a buffalo robe when they entered. He did not rise—perhaps that would have been deemed unwarriorlike—but each of his wives advanced to him, when, instead of going through the ordinary form of embracing, with its usual accompaniments, on such occasions considered proper, the papoose was unslung—I know of no better term to describe the dexterous manner in which the mother transferred her offspring from its cosey resting-place on her back to her arms—and handed to the outstretched arms of the father, who kissed it repeatedly, with every exhibition of paternal affection, scarcely deigning to bestow a single glance on the mother, who stood by meekly, contenting herself with stroking Satanta's face and shoulders gently, at the same time muttering almost inaudible expressions of Indian endearment. This touching little scene lasted for a few moments, when Satanta, after bestowing a kiss upon the soft, cherry lips of his child, transferred it back to its mother, who passed on and quietly took a seat by Satanta's side. The second wife then approached, when precisely the same exhibition was gone through with, not being varied from the first in the slightest particular. This being ended, the third took the place of the second, the latter passing along with her babe and seating herself next to the first, and so on, until the fourth wife had presented her babe, received it back, and quietly seated herself by the side of the third; not a word being spoken to or by Satanta from the beginning to the end of this strange meeting.

The Kiowas were now all located on their reservation except a single band of the tribe, led by a very wicked and troublesome chief, named Woman Heart, although his conduct and character were anything but in keeping with the gentleness of his name. He had taken his band and moved in the direction of the Staked Plains, far to the west of the Kiowa reservation.

However, the Indian question, so far as the Kiowas were concerned, was regarded as settled, at least for the time being, and it became our next study how to effect a similar settlement with the Cheyennes and Arapahoes, who had fled after the battle of the Washita, and were then supposed to be somewhere between the Witchita mountains and the western border of Texas, north of the head waters of Red river. It was finally decided to send one of the friendly chiefs of the Apaches, whose village was then near the present site of Fort Sill, and one of the three captive squaws whom we had brought with us.

All the chiefs of that region who were interested in promoting peace between the whites and Indians were assembled at my headquarters, when I informed them of the proposed peace embassy, and asked that some chief of prominence should volunteer as bearer of a friendly message to the Cheyennes and Arapahoes. A well-known chief of the Apaches, named Iron Shirt, promptly offered himself as a messenger in the cause of peace. In reply to my inquiry, he said he could be ready to depart upon his commendable errand the following day, and estimated the distance such that it would be necessary to take provision sufficient to last him and his companion three weeks. Having arranged all the details of the journey, the assemblage of chiefs dispersed, the next step being to decide which of the three squaws should accompany Iron Shirt to her tribe. I concluded to state the case to them, and make the selection a matter for them to decide. Summoning Mah-wis-sa, Mo-nah-see-tah, and the Sioux squaw, their companion, to my tent, I, through Romeo, acquainted them with the desire of the Government to establish peace with their people and with the Arapahoes, and in order to accomplish this we intended despatching a friendly message to the absent tribes, which must be carried by some of their own people. After conferring with each other a few minutes, they concluded that Mah-wis-sa, the sister of Black Kettle, should return to her people. Every arrangement was provided, looking to the comfort of the two Indians who were to undertake this long journey. A bountiful supply of provisions was carefully provided in convenient packages, an extra amount of clothing and blankets being given to Mah-wis-sa in order that she should not return to her people empty-handed. To transport their provisions and blankets a mule was given them to be used as a pack-animal. It was quite an event, sufficient to disturb the monotony of camp, when the hour arrived for the departure of the two peace commissioners. I had told Iron Shirt what he was to say to the chiefs of the tribes who still remained hostile, which was in effect that we were anxious for peace, and to that end invited them to come at once and place themselves and their people on the reservations, where we would meet and regard them as friends, and all present hostilities, as well as reckoning for past differences, should cease; but if this friendly proffer was not accepted favorably and at once, we would be forced to regard it as indicating their desire to prolong the war, in which event the troops would be sent against them as soon as practicable. I relied not a little on the good influence of Mah-wis-sa, who, as I have before stated, was a woman of superior intelligence, and was strongly impressed with a desire to aid in establishing a peace between her people and the white men. Quite a group, composed of officers, soldiers, teamsters, guards, and scouts, assembled to witness the departure of Iron Shirt and Mah-wis-sa, and to wish them God-speed in their mission.

After Iron Shirt and Mah-wis-sa had seated themselves upon their ponies and were about to set out, Mah-wis-sa, suddenly placing her hand on the neat belt which secured her blanket about her, indicated that she was unprovided with that most essential companion of frontier life, a *mutch-ka* as she expressed it, meaning a hunting-knife. Only those who have lived on the plains can appreciate the unpurchasable convenience of a hunting-knife. Whether it is to carve a buffalo or a mountain trout, mend horse equipments, or close up a rent in the tent, there is a constant demand for the services of a good hunting-knife. Mah-wis-sa smiled at the forgetfulness which had made her fail to discern this omission sooner, but I relieved her anxiety by taking from my belt the hunting-knife which hung at my side and giving it to her, adding as I did so that I expected her to return it to me before the change in the moon, that being fixed as the extreme limit of their absence. When all was ready for the start, Iron Shirt rode first, followed by the pack-mule, which he led, while Mah-wis-sa, acting as a driver to the latter and well mounted, brought up the rear.

As they rode away amid the shower of good wishes which was bestowed upon them and their mission, many were the queries as to the probable extent of their journey, their return, and whether they would be successful. For upon the success or failure of these two Indians depended in a great measure the question whether or not we were to be forced to continue the war; and among the hundreds who watched the departing bearers of the olive branch, there was not one but hoped earnestly that the mission would prove successful, and we be spared the barbarities which a further prosecution of the war would necessarily entail. Yet there are those who would have the public believe that the army is at all times clamorous for an Indian war. I have yet to meet the officer or man belonging to the army, who, when the question of war or peace with the Indians was being agitated, did not cast the weight of his influence, the prayers of his heart, in behalf of peace. When I next called Mah-wis-sa's attention to the *mutch-ka* (knife), it was far from the locality we then occupied, and under very different circumstances.

After the departure of Iron Shirt and Mah-wis-sa, we were forced to settle down to the dullest routine of camp life, as nothing could be done until their return. It was full three weeks before the interest in camp received a fresh impetus, by the tidings, which flew from tent to tent, that Iron Shirt had returned. He did return, but Mah-wis-sa did not return with him. His story was brief. He and Mah-wis-sa, after leaving us and travelling for several days westward, had arrived at the Cheyenne and Arapaho villages. They delivered their messages to the chiefs of the two tribes, who were assembled in council to hear them, and after due deliberation thereon, Iron Shirt was informed that the distance was too great, the ponies in too poor condition, to permit the villages to return. In other words, these two tribes had virtually decided that rather than return to their reservation they preferred the chances of war. When asked to account for Mah-wis-sa's failure to accompany him back, Iron Shirt stated that she had desired to fulfil her promise and return with him, but the chiefs of her tribe would not permit her to do so.

The only encouragement derived from Iron Shirt was in his statement that Little Robe, a prominent chief of the Cheyennes, and Yellow Bear, the second chief of the Arapahoes, were both extremely anxious to effect a permanent peace between their people and the Government, and both had promised Iron Shirt that they would leave their villages soon after his departure and visit us, with a view to prevent a continuation of the war. Iron Shirt was rewarded for his journey by bountiful presents of provisions for himself and his people. True to their promises made to Iron Shirt, it was but a short time before Little Robe and Yellow Bear arrived at our camp and were well received.

They reported that their villages had had under consideration the question of accepting our invitation to come in and live at peace in the future, and that many of their people were strongly in favor of adopting this course, but for the present it was uncertain whether or not the two tribes would come in. The two tribes would probably act in concert, and if they intended coming, would make their determination known by despatching couriers to us in a few days. In spite of the sincerity of the motives of Little Robe and Yellow Bear, whom I have always regarded as two of the most upright and peaceably inclined Indians I have ever known, and who have since that time paid a visit to the President at Washington, it was evident that the Cheyennes and Arapahoes, while endeavoring to occupy us with promises and pretences, were only interested in delaying our movements until the return of spring, when the young grass would enable them to recruit the strength of their winter-famished ponies and move when and where they pleased.

After waiting many long weary days for the arrival of the promised couriers from the two tribes, until even Little Robe and Yellow Bear were forced to acknowledge that there was no longer any reason to expect their coming, it occurred to me that there was but one expedient yet untried which furnished even a doubtful chance of averting war. This could only be resorted to with the approval of General Sheridan, whose tent had been pitched in our midst during the entire winter, and who evidently proposed to remain on the ground until the Indian question in that locality should be disposed of. My plan was as follows:

We had some fifteen hundred troops, a force ample to cope with all the Indians which could then, or since, be combined at any one point on the plains. But in the state of feeling existing among those Indians at that time, consequent upon the punishment which they had received at and since the Washita campaign, it would have been an extremely difficult if not impracticable matter to attempt to move so large a body of troops near their villages, and retain the latter in their places, so fearful were they of receiving punishment for their past offences. It would also have been impracticable to move upon them stealthily, as they were then, for causes already given, more than ever on the alert, and were no doubt kept thoroughly informed in regard to our every movement.

It was thus considered out of the question to employ my entire command of fifteen hundred men in what I proposed should be purely a peaceful effort to bring about a termination of the war, as so large a force would surely intimidate the Indians, and cause them to avoid our presence.

I believed that if I could see the leading chiefs of the two hostile tribes and convince them of the friendly desire of the Government, they might be induced to relinquish the war and return to their reservation. I have endeavored to show that I could not go among them with my entire command, neither was I sufficiently orthodox as a peace commissioner to believe what so many of that order preach, but fail to practise, that I could take an olive branch in one hand, the plan of a school-house in the other, and, unaccompanied by force, visit the Indian villages in safety. My life would certainly have been the price of such temerity. Too imposing a force would repel the Indians; too small a force would tempt them to murder us, even though our mission was a friendly one.

After weighing the matter carefully in my own mind, I decided that with General Sheridan's approval I would select from my command forty men, two officers, and a medical officer, and, accompanied by the two chiefs, Little Robe and Yellow Bear, who regarded my proposition with favor, I would set out in search of the hostile camp, there being but little doubt that with the assistance of the chiefs I would have little difficulty in discovering the whereabouts of the villages; while the smallness of my party would prevent unnecessary alarm or suspicion as to our intentions. From my tent to General Sheridan's was but a few steps, and I soon submitted my proposition to the General, who

from the first was inclined to lend his approval to my project. After discussing it fully, he gave his assent by saying that the character of the proposed
expedition was such that he would not order me to proceed upon it, but if I
volunteered to go, he would give me the full sanction of his authority and
every possible assistance to render the mission a successful one; in conclusion
urging me to exercise the greatest caution against the stratagems or treachery
of the Indians, who no doubt would be but too glad to massacre my party in
revenge for their recent well-merited chastisement. Returning to my tent, I
at once set about making preparations for my journey, the extent or result of
which now became interesting subjects for deliberation. The first thing necessary was to make up the party which was to accompany me.

As the number of men was to be limited to forty, too much care could not
be exercised in their selection. I chose the great majority of them from the
sharpshooters, men who, in addition to being cool and brave, were experienced and skilful marksmen. My standard-bearer, a well-tried sergeant, was
selected as the senior non-commissioned officer of the party. The officers
who were to accompany me were my brother Colonel Custer, Captain Robbins, and Dr. Renick, Acting Assistant Surgeon U. S. Army. As guide I had
Ne-va, a Blackfoot Indian, who had accompanied General Fremont in his ex-
plorations, and who could speak a little English. Little Robe and Yellow
Bear were also to be relied upon as guides, while Romeo accompanied us as
interpreter. Young Brewster, determined to miss no opportunity of discovering his lost sister, had requested and been granted permission to become one
of the party. This completed the *personnel* of the expedition. All were well
armed and well mounted. We were to take no wagons or tents; our extra
supplies were to be transported on pack-mules. We were to start on the evening of the second day, the intervening time being necessary to complete our
preparations. It was decided that our first march should be a short one, sufficient merely to enable us to reach a village of friendly Apaches, located a few
miles from our camp, where we would spend the first night and be joined
by Little Robe and Yellow Bear, who at that time were guests of the Apaches.
I need not say that in the opinion of many of our comrades our mission was
regarded as closely bordering on the imprudent, to qualify it by no stronger
term.

So confident did one of the most prudent officers of my command feel in
regard to our annihilation by the Indians, that in bidding me good-by he contrived to slip into my hand a small pocket Derringer pistol, loaded, with the
simple remark, " You had better take it, General; it may prove useful to you."
As I was amply provided with arms, both revolvers and rifle, and as a pocket
Derringer may not impress the reader as being a very formidable weapon to
use in Indian warfare, the purpose of my friend in giving me the small pocket
weapon may not seem clear. It was given me under the firm conviction that
the Indians would overwhelm and massacre my entire party; and to prevent
my being captured, disarmed, and reserved for torture, that little pistol was
given me in order that at the last moment I might become my own execution-
er—an office I was not seeking, nor did I share in my friend's opinion.

Everything being ready for our departure, we swung into our saddles,
waved our adieus to the comrades who were to remain in camp, and the next
moment we turned our horses' heads westward and were moving in the direction of the Apache village.

XX.

THE Apache village had been represented as located only five or six miles from our camp, but we found the distance nearly twice as great; and although we rode rapidly, our horses being fresh, yet it was quite dark before we reached the first lodge, the location of the rest of the village being tolerably well defined by the apparently countless dogs, whose barking at our approach called forth most of the inhabitants of the village.

As our coming had been previously announced by Little Robe and Yellow Bear, our arrival occasioned no surprise. Inquiring of the first we saw where the stream of water was, as an Indian village is invariably placed in close proximity to water, we were soon on our camp ground, which was almost within the limits of the village. Our horses were soon unsaddled and picketed out to graze, fires were started by the men preparatory to the enjoyment of a cup of coffee, and every preliminary made for a good night's rest, and early start in the morning. But here the officers of the party encountered their first drawback. From some unexplained cause the pack-mule which carried our blankets had with his attendant failed thus far to put in an appearance. His head leader had probably fallen behind, and in the darkness lost the party. The bugler was sent to a neighboring eminence to sound signals with his bugle, in the hope that the absent man with his mule might make his way to us, but all to no purpose. We were soon forced to relinquish all hope of seeing either man, mule, or blankets until daylight, and consequently the prospect of enjoying a comfortable rest was exceedingly limited. Saddle blankets were in great demand, but I was even more fortunate. A large number of the Apaches had come from their lodges out of mere curiosity to see us, hoping no doubt too that they might secure something to eat. Among them was one with whom I was acquainted, and to whom I made known the temporary loss of my blankets. By promising him a pint of sugar and an equal amount of coffee on my return to my camp, he agreed to loan me a buffalo robe until morning. With this wrapped around me and the aid of a bright blazing camp fire, I passed a most comfortable night among my less fortunate companions, as we all lay stretched out on the ground, using our saddles for pillows.

Early next morning (our pack animals having come up in the night) we were in our saddles, and on our way ready and eager for whatever might be in store for us. The route taken by the guides led us along the northern border of the Witchita Mountains, our general direction being nearly due west. A brief description of these mountains and of the surrounding scenery is contained in the first chapter of " Life on the Plains." As soon as it had become known in the main camp that the expedition of which I now write was contemplated, young Brewster, who had never relinquished his efforts or inquiries to determine the fate of his lost sister, came to me with an earnest request to be taken as one of the party—a request which I was only too glad to comply with. No person who has not lived on the frontier and in an Indian country, can correctly realize or thoroughly appreciate the extent to which a frontiersman becomes familiar with, and apparently indifferent to the accustomed dangers which surround him on every side. It is but another verification of the truth of the old saying, " Familiarity breeds contempt."

After getting well on our way I began, through Romeo, conversing with the two chiefs Little Robe and Yellow Bear, who rode at my side, upon the topic which was uppermost in the minds of the entire party: When and where should we probably find their people? Before our departure they had given me to understand that the villages might be found on some one of the small streams flowing in a southerly direction past the western span of the Witchita mountains, a distance from our main camp not exceeding sixty or seventy miles; but I could easily perceive that neither of the chiefs spoke with a great degree of confidence. They explained this by stating that the villages would not remain long in one place, and it was difficult to say positively in what locality or upon what stream we should find them; but that when we reached the last peak of the Witchita mountains, which commanded an unlimited view of the plains beyond, they would send up signal smoke, and perhaps be able to obtain a reply from the village.

In the evening we reached a beautiful stream of water, with abundance of wood in the vicinity; here we halted for the night. Our horses were fastened to the trees, while the officers and men spread their blankets on the ground, and in groups of twos and threes prepared for the enjoyment of a good night's rest. One sentry remained awake during the night, and in order that the loss of sleep should be as little as might be consistent with our safety, the relief, instead of being composed of three men, each of whom would have to remain on duty two hours for every four hours of rest, was increased in number so that each member thereof was required to remain on post but a single hour during the night. While I felt confidence in the good intentions of the two chiefs, I did not neglect to advise the guards to keep a watchful eye upon them, as we could not afford to run any avoidable risks. Long after we had sought the solace of our blankets, and I had dropped into a comfortable doze, I was awakened by an Indian song. There was, of course, no occasion for alarm from this incident, yet it was sufficient to induce me to get up and make my way to the small fire, around which I knew the three Indians and Romeo to be lying, and from the vicinity of which the singing evidently came. As I approached the fire I found Neva, the Blackfoot, replenishing the small flame with a few dried twigs, while Romeo and Yellow Bear were sitting near by enjoying some well-broiled beef ribs. Little Robe was reclining, in a half-sitting position, against a tree, and, apparently oblivious to the presence of his companions, was singing or chanting an Indian melody, the general tenor of which seemed to indicate a lightness of spirits. Young Brewster —unable, perhaps, to sleep, owing to thoughts of his lost sister—had joined the group, and appeared an interested observer of what was going on. I inquired of Romeo why Little Robe had selected such an unreasonable hour to indulge in his wild melodies. Romeo repeated the inquiry to Little Robe, who replied that he had been away from his lodge for a long time, and the thought of soon returning, and of being with his people once more, had filled his heart with a gladness which could only find utterance in song.

Taking a seat on the ground by the side of young Brewster, I joined the group. As neither Little Robe nor Yellow Bear could understand a word of English, and Neva was busily engaged with his culinary operations, young Brewster, with unconcealed delight, informed me that from conversations with Little Robe, who appeared in a more communicative mood than usual, he felt cheered by the belief that at last he was in a fair way to discover the whereabouts of his captive sister. He then briefly detailed how Little Robe, little dreaming that his listener was so deeply interested in his words, had admitted that the Cheyennes had two white girls as prisoners, the date of the capture of one of them and the personal description given by Little Robe closely answering to that of Brewster's sister. In the hope of gleaning other valuable information from time to time, I advised the young man not to acquaint the Indians with the fact that he had lost a sister by capture; else, becoming suspicious, the supply of information might be cut off.

The tidings in regard to the captured girls were most encouraging, and spurred us to leave no effort untried to release them from the horrors of their situation. Before daylight the following morning we had breakfasted, and as soon as it was sufficiently light to enable us to renew our march we set out, still keeping almost due west. In the afternoon of that day we reached the last prominent peak of the Witchita mountains, from which point Little Robe and Yellow Bear had said they would send up a signal smoke.

I had often during an Indian campaign seen these signal smokes, on my front, on my right and left—everywhere, in fact—but could never catch a glimpse of the Indians who were engaged in making them, nor did I comprehend at the time the precise import of the signals. I was glad, therefore, to have an opportunity to stand behind the scenes, as it were, and not only witness the *modus operandi*, but understand the purpose of the actors.

Arriving at the base of the mountain or peak, the height of which did not exceed one thousand feet, we dismounted, and leaving our horses on the plain below, owing to the rough and rocky character of the ascent, a small portion of our party, including of course, the two chiefs, climbed to the summit. After sweeping the broad horizon which spread out before us, and failing to discover any evidence of the presence of an Indian village anywhere within the scope of our vision, the two chiefs set about to make preparations necessary to enable them to " call to the village," as they expressed it.

I have alluded in a former article to the perfect system of signals in use among the Indians of the plains. That which I am about to describe briefly was but one of many employed by them. First gathering an armful of dried grass and weeds, this was carried and placed upon the highest point of the peak, where, everything being in readiness, the match was applied close to the ground; but the blaze was no sooner well lighted and about to envelop the entire amount of grass collected, than Little Robe began smothering it with the unlighted portion. This accomplished, a slender column of gray smoke began to ascend in a perpendicular column. This, however, was not enough, as such a signal, or the appearance of such, might be created by white men, or might rise from a simple camp fire. Little Robe now took his scarlet blanket from his shoulders, and with a graceful wave threw it so as to cover the smouldering grass, when, assisted by Yellow Bear, he held the corners and sides so closely to the ground as to almost completely confine and cut off the column of smoke. Waiting but for a few moments, and until he saw the smoke beginning to escape from beneath, he suddenly threw the blanket aside, and a beautiful balloon shaped column puffed upward, like the white cloud of smoke which attends the discharge of a field piece.

Again casting the blanket on the pile of grass, the column was interrupted as before, and again in due time released, so that a succession of elongated, egg-shaped puffs of smoke kept ascending toward the sky in the most regular manner. This beadlike column of smoke, considering the height from which it began to ascend, was visible from points on the level plain fifty miles distant.

The sight of these two Indian chiefs so intently engaged in this simple but effective mode of telegraphing was to me full of interest, and this incident was vividly recalled when I came across Stanley's painting of "The Signal," in which two chiefs or warriors are standing upon a large rock, with lighted torch in hand, while far in the distance is to be seen the answering column, as it ascends above the tops of the trees, from the valley where no doubt the village is pleasantly located. In our case, however, the picture was not so complete in its results. For strain our eager eyes as we might in every direction, no responsive signal could be discovered, and finally the chiefs were reluctantly forced to acknowledge that the villages were not where they expected to find them, and that to reach them would probably involve a longer journey than we had anticipated. Descending from the mountain, we continued our journey, still directing our course nearly due west, as the two chiefs felt confident the villages were in that direction. That day and the next passed without further incident.

After arriving at camp on the second evening, a conversation with the two Indian chiefs made it seem probable that our journey would have to be prolonged several days beyond the time which was deemed necessary when we left the main camp. And as our supply of provisions was limited to our supposed wants during the shorter journey, it was necessary to adopt measures for obtaining fresh supplies. This was the more imperative as the country through which we were then passing was almost devoid of game. Our party was so small in number that our safety would be greatly imperilled by any serious reduction, yet it was a measure of necessity that a message should be sent back to General Sheridan, informing him of our changed plans and providing for a renewal of our stores.

I acquainted the men of my command with my desire, and it was not long before a soldierly young trooper announced that he would volunteer to carry a despatch safely through. The gallant offer was accepted, and I was soon seated on the ground, pencil in hand, writing to General Sheridan a hurried account of our progress thus far and our plans for the future, with a request to forward to us a supply of provisions; adding that the party escorting them could follow on our trail, and I would arrange to find them when required. I also requested that Colonel Cook, who commanded the sharpshooters, should be detailed to command the escort, and that California Joe might also be sent with the party.

It was decided that the despatch bearer should remain in camp with us until dark and then set out on his return to the main camp. Being well mounted, well armed, and a cool, daring young fellow, I felt but little anxiety as to his success. Leaving him to make his solitary journey guided by the light of the stars, and concealing himself during the day, we will continue our search after what then seemed to us the two lost tribes.

Daylight as usual found us in our saddles, the country continuing interesting but less rolling, and (we judge by appearances) less productive. We saw but little game along our line of march, and the importance of time rendered delays of all kinds undesirable. The countenances of Little Robe and Yellow Bear wore an anxious look, and I could see that they began to doubt their ability to determine positively the locality of the villages. Neva, the Blackfoot, was full of stories connected with his experiences under General Fremont, and appeared more hopeful than the two chiefs. He claimed to be a son-in-law of Kit Carson, his wife, a half-breed, being deceased. Carson, it appeared, had always regarded Neva with favor, and often made him and his family handsome presents. I afterwards saw a son of Neva, an extremely handsome boy of fourteen, whose comely face and features clearly betrayed the mixture of blood indicated by Neva.

Yellow Bear finally encouraged us by stating that by noon the following day we would arrive at a stream, on whose banks he expected to find the Arapaho village, and perhaps that of the Cheyennes. This gave us renewed hope, and furnished us a topic of conversation after we had reached our camp that night. Nothing occurred worthy of note until about noon next day, when Yellow Bear informed me that we were within a few miles of the stream to which he had referred the day before, and added that if the village was there his people would have a lookout posted on a little knoll which we would find about a mile from the village in our direction; and as the appearance of our entire force might give alarm, Yellow Bear suggested that he, with Little Robe, Romeo, Neva, myself, and two or three others, should ride some distance in advance.

Remembering the proneness of the Indians to stratagem, I was yet impressed not only with the apparent sincerity of Yellow Bear thus far, but by the soundness of the reasons he gave for our moving in advance. I assented to his proposition, but my confidence was not sufficiently great to prevent me from quietly slipping a fresh cartridge in my rifle, as it lay in front of me across my saddle-bow, nor from unbuttoning the strap which held my revolver in place by my side. Fortunately, however, nothing occurred to make it necessary to displace either rifle or revolver.

After riding in advance for a couple of miles, Yellow Bear pointed out in the distance the little mound at which he predicted we would see something posted in the way of information concerning his tribe. If the latter was not in the vicinity a letter would no doubt be found at the mound, which now became an object of interest to all of us, each striving to be the first to discover the confirmation of Yellow Bear's prediction.

In this way we continued to approach the mound until not more than a mile of level plain separated us from it, and still nothing could be seen to encourage us, when, owing to my reason being quickened by the excitement of the occasion, thus giving me an advantage over the chiefs, or from other causes, I caught sight of what would ordinarily have been taken for two half-round stones or small bowlders, just visible above the upper circle of the mound, as projected against the sky beyond. A second glance convinced me that instead of the stones which they so closely resembled, they were neither more nor less than the upper parts of the heads of two Indians, who were no doubt studying our movements with a view of determining whether we were a friendly or war party.

Reassuring myself by the aid of my field-glass, I announced my discovery to the chiefs and the rest of the party. Yellow Bear immediately cantered his pony a few yards to the front, when, freeing his scarlet blanket from his shoulders, he waved it twice or thrice in a mysterious manner, and waited anxiously the response. In a moment the two Indians, the tops of whose heads had alone been visible, rode boldly to the crest of the mound and answered the signal of Yellow Bear, who uttered a quick, oft-repeated whoop, and, at my suggestion, galloped in advance, to inform his people who we were, and our object in visiting them. By the time we reached the mound all necessary explanations had been made, and the two Indians advanced at Yellow

Bear's bidding and shook hands with me, afterward going through the same ceremony with the other officers. Yellow Bear then despatched one of the Indians to the village, less than two miles distant, to give news of our approach.

It seemed that they had scarcely had time to reach the village, before young and old began flocking out to meet us, some on ponies, others on mules, and occasionally two full-grown Indians would be seen mounted on one diminutive pony. If any of our party had feared that our errand was attended with risk, their minds probably underwent a change when they looked around, and upon all sides saw armed warriors, whose numbers exceeded ours more than ten to one, and whose entire bearing and demeanor toward us gave promise of any but hostile feelings.

Not deeming it best to allow them to encircle us too closely, I requested Yellow Bear, in whose peaceable desires I had confidence, to direct his people to remain at some distance from us, so as not to impede our progress; at the same time to inform them that it was our purpose to pitch our camp immediately alongside of theirs, when full opportunity would be given for interchange of visits. This proposition seemed to meet with favor, and our route was left unobstructed. A short ride brought us to the village, the lodges composing which were dotted in a picturesque manner along the left branch of Mulberry creek, one of the tributaries of Red river.

I decided to cross the creek and bivouac on the right bank, opposite the lower end of the village, and within easy pistol range of the nearest lodge. This location may strike the reader with some surprise, and may suggest the inquiry why we did not locate ourselves at some point further removed from the village. It must be remembered that in undertaking to penetrate the Indian country with so small a force, I acted throughout upon the belief that if proper precautions were adopted, the Indians would not molest us. Indians contemplating a battle, either offensive or defensive, are always anxious to have their women and children removed from all danger thereof. By our watchfulness we intended to let the Indians see that there would be no opportunity for them to take us by surprise, but that if fighting was intended, it should not be all on one side. For this reason I decided to locate our camp as close as convenient to the village, knowing that the close proximity of their women and children, and their necessary exposure in case of conflict, would operate as a powerful argument in favor of peace, when the question of peace or war came to be discussed.

But right here I will do the Arapahoes justice, by asserting that after the first council, which took place in my camp the same evening, and after they had had an opportunity to learn the exact character and object of our mission, as told to them by me, and confirmed by the earnest addresses of Yellow Bear and Little Robe, they evinced toward us nothing but friendly feeling, and exhibited a ready willingness to conform to the only demand we made of them, which was that they should proceed at once, with their entire village, to our main camp, within their reservation, and then report to General Sheridan.

Little Raven, the head chief, spoke for his people, and expressed their gratification at the reports brought to them by Yellow Bear and Little Robe. They accepted with gladness the offer of peace, and promised to set out in three days to proceed to our main camp, near the site of Fort Sill. As it was quite late before the council concluded the discussion of questions pertaining to the Arapahoes, no reference was made to the Cheyennes; besides, I knew

LITTLE RAVEN, HEAD CHIEF OF THE ARAPAHOES.

that Little Robe would be able to gather all possible information concerning them.

Little Raven invited me to visit him the following day in his village, an invitation I promised to accept. Before the chiefs separated, I requested Little Raven to give notice through them to all his people, that after it became dark it would no longer be safe for any of them to approach our camp, as, according to our invariable custom, guards would be posted about camp during the entire night; and as we could not distinguish friends from foes in the darkness, the sentries would be ordered to fire on every object seen approaching our camp. To this Little Raven and his chiefs promised assent. I then further informed him that during our stay near them we should always be glad, during the hours of daylight, to receive visits from him or from any of his people, but to prevent confusion or misunderstanding, not more than twenty Indians would be permitted to visit our camp at one time. This also was agreed to, and the chiefs, after shaking hands and uttering the customary "How," departed to their village. Yellow Bear remained only long enough to say that, his family being in the village, he preferred, of course, to be with them, but assured us that his people were sincere in their protestations of peace, and that we might sleep as soundly as if we were back among our comrades, in the main camp, with no fears of unfriendly interruption.

After tethering our horses and pack mules securely in our midst, and posting the guards for the night, each one of our little party, first satisfying himself that his firearms were in good order and loaded, spread his blanket on the ground, and, with his saddle for a pillow, the sky unobscured by tent or roof above him, was soon reposing comfortably on the broad bosom of mother earth, where, banishing from the mind as quickly as possible all visions of Indians, peace commissioners, etc., sleep soon came to the relief of each, and we all, except the guards, rested as peacefully and comfortably as if at home under our mother's roof; and yet we all, in seeking our lowly couches that night, felt that the chances were about even whether or not we should be awakened by the war whoop of our dusky neighbors. Nothing occurred, however, to disturb our dreams or break our slumber, save, perhaps, in my own case. From a greater sense of responsibility, perhaps, than rested on my comrades, but not greater danger, I awoke at different hours during the night, and to assure myself that all was well, rose up to a sitting posture on the ground, and, aided by the clear sky and bright starlight, looked about me, only to see, however, the dim outlines of my sleeping comrades as they lay in all manner of attitudes around me, wrapped in their blankets of gray, while our faithful horses, picketed in the midst of their sleeping riders, were variously disposed, some lying down, resting from the fatigues of the march, others nibbling the few tufts of grass which the shortness of their tether enabled them to reach. That which gave me strongest assurance of safety, however, as I glanced across the little stream, and beheld the conical forms of the white lodges of the Indians, was the silent picture of the sentry as he paced his lonely post within a few feet of where I lay. And when to my inquiry, in subdued tones, if all had been quiet during the night, came the prompt, soldierly response, "All quiet, sir," I felt renewed confidence, and again sought the solace of my equestrian pillow.

Breakfasting before the stars bade us good night, or rather good morning, daylight found us ready for the duties of the day. As soon as the Indians were prepared for my visit, Yellow Bear came to inform me of the fact, and to escort me to Little Raven's lodge. Romeo and Neva accompanied me, the former as interpreter. I directed Captain Robbins, the officer next in rank, to cause all men to remain closely in camp during my absence, and to be careful not to permit more than the authorized number of Indians to enter; also to watch well the Indian village, not that I believed there would be an attempt at stratagem, but deemed it well to be on guard. To convince the Indians of my own sincerity, I left my rifle and revolver with my men, a measure of not such great significance as it might at first seem, as the question of arms or no arms would have exercised but little influence in determining my fate had the Indians, as I never for a moment believed, intended treachery.

Arrived at Little Raven's lodge, I found him surrounded by all his principal chiefs, a place being reserved by his side for me. After the usual smoke and the preliminary moments of silence, which strongly reminded me of the deep silence which is the prelude to religious services in some of our churches, Little Raven began a speech, which was mainly a review of what had been agreed upon the evening before, and closed with the statement that his people were highly pleased to see white men among them as friends, and that the idea of complying with my demand in regard to proceeding to our main camp had been discussed with great favor by all of his people, who were delighted with this opportunity of terminating the war. All questions affecting the Arapahoes being satisfactorily disposed of, I now introduced the subject of the whereabouts of the Cheyenne village, stating that my purpose was to extend to them the same terms as had been accepted by the Arapahoes.

To this I could obtain no decisive or satisfactory reply. The Cheyennes were represented to be moving constantly, hence the difficulty in informing me accurately as to their location; but all agreed that the Cheyennes were a long distance west of where we then were. Finally I obtained a promise from Little Raven that he would select two of his active young warriors, who would accompany me in my search for the Cheyenne village, and whose knowledge of the country and acquaintance with the Cheyennes would be of incalculable service to me. As the limited amount of provisions on hand would not justify us in continuing our search for the Cheyennes, I decided to await the arrival of Colonel Cook, who, I felt confident, would reach us in a few days.

In the meanwhile the day fixed for the departure of the Arapahoes came, and the village was all commotion and activity, lodges being taken down and packed on ponies and mules; the activity, I might mention, being confined, however, to the squaws, the noble lords of the forest sitting unconcernedly by, quietly smoking their long red clay pipes. I was sorry to lose the services of Yellow Bear, but it was necessary for him to accompany his people, particularly as he represented the peace element. I gave him a letter to General Sheridan, in which I informed the latter of our meeting with the Arapahoes, the council, and the final agreement. In view of the further extension of our journey, I requested a second detachment to be sent on our trail, with supplies, to meet us on our return. Everything being in readiness, the chiefs, commencing with Little Raven, gathered around me, and bade me good-by, Yellow Bear being the last to take his leave. This being ended, the entire village was put in motion, and soon stretched itself into a long, irregular column.

The chiefs formed the advance; next came the squaws and children and the old men, followed by the pack animals bearing the lodges and household goods; after these came the herd, consisting of hundreds of loose ponies and mules, driven by squaws; while on the outskirts of the entire cavalcade rode the young men and boys, performing the part of assistants to the herders, but more important as flankers or videttes in case of danger or attack. Nor must I omit another important element in estimating the population of an Indian village, the dogs. These were without number, and of all colors and sizes. It was difficult to determine which outnumbered the other, the dogs or their owners. Some of the former were mere puppies, unable to travel; these were carefully stowed away in a comfortable sort of basket, made of willows, and securely attached to the back of one of the pack animals, the mother of the interesting family trotting along contentedly by the side of the latter.

After the excitement attending the departure of the Indians had passed, and the last glimpse of the departing village had been had, our little party seemed lonely enough, as we stood huddled together on the bank of Mulberry creek. There was nothing to be done until the arrival of our expected supplies. Little Robe, impatient at the proposed delay, concluded to start at once in quest of his people, and if possible persuade them to meet us instead of awaiting our arrival. He evidently was anxious to have peace concluded with the Cheyennes, and thus enable his people to be placed on the same secure footing with the Arapahoes. Instead of opposing, I encouraged him in the execution of his plan, although loath to part with him. The two young Arapahoes were to remain with me, however, and by concert of plan between them and Little Robe we would be able to follow the trail.

It was agreed that if Little Robe should come up with his people and be able to induce them to return, he was to send up smoke signals each morning and evening, in order that we might receive notice of their approach and be able to regulate our march accordingly. Giving him a sufficient supply of coffee, sugar, and hard bread, we saw Little Robe set out on his solitary journey in the character of a veritable peace commissioner.

I might fill several pages in describing the various expedients to which our little party resorted in order to dispose of our time while waiting the arrival of our supplies. How Romeo, by the promise of a small reward in case he was successful, was induced to attempt to ride a beautiful Indian pony, which we had caught on the plains, and which was still as wild and unbroken as if he had never felt the hand of man. The ground selected was a broad border of deep sand, extending up and down the valley. Two long lariats were securely fastened to the halter. At the end of one was my brother. I officiated at the end of the other, with the pony standing midway between us, some twenty feet from either, and up to his fetlocks in sand, an anxious spectator of what was going on. Everything being in readiness, Romeo, with never a fear or doubt as to the result, stepped quietly up to the side of the pony, who, turning his head somewhat inquiringly, uttered a few snorts indicative of anything but gentleness. Romeo, who was as active as a cat, succeeded in placing his hands on the pony's back, and with an injunction to us to keep firm hold on the lariats, he sprang lightly upon the back of the pony and seized the mane. I have seen trained mules, the delight of boys who attend the circus, and sometimes of persons of more advanced age, and have witnessed the laughable efforts of the youngsters who vainly endeavor to ride the contumacious quadruped once around the ring; but I remember nothing of this description to equal or resemble the frantic plunges of the Indian pony in his untrained efforts to free his back from its burden, nor the equally frantic and earnest efforts of the rider to maintain his position. Fortunately for the holders of the lariats, they exceeded the length of the pony's legs, or his

19

heels, which were being elevated in all directions, and almost at the same time, would have compelled us to relinquish our hold, and leave Romeo to his fate. As both pony and rider seemed to redouble their efforts for the mastery, the scenebecame more ludicrous, while the hearty and prolonged shouts of laughter from the bystanders on all sides seemed only to add intensity to the contest.

This may strike the reader as a not very dignified proceeding, particularly upon the part of one of the lariat holders; but we were not studying how to appear dignified, but how to amuse ourselves. So exhausted did I become with unrestrained laughter, as I beheld Romeo in his lofty gyrations about a centre which belonged to the movable order, that a much further prolongation of the sport would have forced me to relinquish my hold on the lariat. But I was spared this result. The pony, as if studying the problem, had indulged in almost every conceivable form of leaping, and now, rising almost perpendicularly on his hind legs, stood erect, pawing the air with his fore legs, and compelling Romeo, in order to prevent himself from sliding off, to clasp him about the neck with both arms. The pony seemed almost as if waiting this situation, as with the utmost quickness, and before Romeo could resume his seat, he descended from his elevated attitude, and the next moment his head was almost touching the ground, and his heels occupied the space just vacated by his head in mid air. This sudden change was too much for Romeo, and as if projected from an ancient catapult, he departed from his place on the back of the pony, and landed on the deep, soft sand, many feet in advance of his late opponent. Three times was this repeated, with almost the same result, until finally Romeo, as he brushed the sand from his matted locks, expressed it as his opinion that no one but an Indian could ride that pony. As Romeo was half Indian, the distinction seemed finely drawn.

Innumerable were the tricks played on each other by one and all; everything seemed legitimate sport which tended to kill time. Three days after the departure of the Arapaho village, the lookout reported that parties were in sight some three or four miles in the direction taken by the village. This created no little excitement in camp. Field-glasses were brought into immediate requisition, and after a careful examination of the parties, who could be plainly seen approaching us in the distance, we all came to the conclusion that what we saw must be the escort with our supplies. A few horses were soon saddled, and two of the officers, with some of the men, galloped out to meet the advancing party. It proved to be Colonel Cook, with California Joe and a dozen men, bringing with them several pack animals loaded with fresh supplies.

I need not say how we welcomed their arrival. It was too late in the day to make it desirable for us to set out on the trail of Little Robe, as it was necessary to unpack and issue rations and repack the remainder; so that it was concluded to remain until next morning, an additional reason in favor of this resolution being that the horses of Colonel Cook's party would have the benefit of rest. The account given by Colonel Cook and California Joe concerning their march was exceedingly interesting. It will be remembered that it was the expectation that we would find the Arapaho village nearer our main camp than we afterward did, and in my letter to General Sheridan I had intimated that Colonel Cook would probably overtake us at a point not far from the termination of the Witchita mountains.

Colonel Cook arrived at the designated point, but we, of course, had gone, and not finding any letter or signal at our deserted camp, he became, not un-naturally, anxious as to where we had gone. This will not be wondered at when it is remembered that he had but thirteen men with him, and was then in a hostile country, and far from all support. However, he had nothing to do but to continue on our trail. That night will no doubt live long in the memory of Colonel Cook.

After reaching camp with his little party, in a small piece of timber, he, as he afterward related to me, began taking a mental survey of his situation. For fear of misleading the reader, I will here remark, as I have indicated in previous chapters, that fear, or a lack of the highest order of personal courage, was not numbered among the traits of character possessed by this officer. After seeing that the animals were properly secured for the night, and his men made comfortable, he sat down by the camp fire awaiting the pre-paration of his evening meal. In the mean time California Joe found him, and entered into a discussion as to the probabilities of overtaking us soon, and in a kind of Jack Bunsby style suggested, if not, why not?

The more Colonel Cook looked at the matter, the more trying seemed his position. Had he known, as we then knew, that the Arapahoes had been found, and a peaceful agreement entered into, it would have solved all his difficulty. Of this he of course was ignorant, and thoughts ran through his mind that perhaps my little party had been led on only to be massacred, and his would follow blindly to the same fate. This recalled all former Indian atrocities with which he was familiar, while prominent above them all rose before him the fate of young Kidder and party, whose fate is recorded in a former chapter.

In thinking of this, Colonel Cook was struck by a coincidence. Kidder's party consisted of almost the identical number which composed his own. Kid-der had a guide, and Cook had California Joe; all of which, without attach-ing any importance to his words, the latter took pains to remind Colonel Cook of. By the time supper was prepared Colonel Cook felt the responsibilities of his position too strongly to have any appetite for food, so that when supper was commenced he simply declined it, and invited California Joe to help himself—an invitation the latter was not slow in accepting. Posting his guards for the night, Colonel Cook felt that to sleep was impossible. He took his seat by the camp fire, and with his arms by his side impatiently waited the coming of dawn.

California Joe, who regarded the present as of far more importance than the future, and whose slumber would have been little disturbed even had he known that hostile Indians were soon to be encountered, disposed of Colonel Cook's supper, and then, wrapping himself up in his blanket, stretched himself under a tree near the fire, and was soon sleeping soundly. His brief account of the enjoyment he derediv from Colonel Cook's supper was characteristic: "Thar I sot an' sot a eatin' uv that young man's wittles, while he in his cavalry boots, with his pistols in his belt, stood a lookin' inter the fire."

Early next morning, as soon as the light was sufficient to enable them to follow our trail, Colonel Cook and his party were on their way. About noon, as they were passing over a low ridge, yet sufficiently high to enable them to see for miles beyond, the eyes of one of the party caught a view of a long line of dark-looking objects miles in advance, yet directly in their path. Each moment the objects became more distinct, until finally Colonel Cook, who was studying them intently through his glass, pronounced the simple word, "Indians." "Ef that is so, Colonel, thar's a many one uv 'em," was the sober response of California Joe, who rode at his side.

By this time the Indians could be plainly seen, although numbers of them continued to gallop up from the rear. It was evident from their movements that they had discovered Colonel Cook's party almost as soon as he had seen them, and that the entire body of Indians was directing its march toward the little eminence from which the white men were now watching their movements. "What do yer think about it now, Colonel?" said California Joe, at last breaking the silence. "Well, Joe, we must do the best we can; there is no use in running." "You're right," replied Joe; "an Injun 'll beat a white man runnin' every time, so I 'spect our best holt is fitin', but, Lor' a' mercy! look at 'em; thar ain't enuff uv us to go half round!"

Getting his little party collected in good order, and speaking words of encouragement to all, Colonel Cook quietly awaited further developments. His thoughts in the meanwhile must have been such as he probably never wishes to indulge in again. All sorts of terrible visions and ideas flashed through his mind; the most prominent as well as plausible being that the Indians had made away with my party, and from Little Robe and Yellow Bear had learned of the expected supplies, with their small escort, and were now in search of the latter. Whatever varied thoughts of this character chased each other through his brain, he at once came to the firm resolve that whatever fate was in store for him, he would meet it like a soldier, and if the worst came he would fight to the last.

By this time it was seen that a single Indian was galloping in advance of the rest, as if hastening to reach the white men. "That's a queer dodge," remarked California Joe; but the mystery was soon cleared away, as the Indian began to draw near to the party without slackening his pace. Colonel Cook and California Joe instinctively advanced to meet him, when to their great joy and surprise it proved to be none other than the faithful Yellow Bear, who, realizing the situation, had ridden in advance of his people in order to assure the whites of their friendly character. His coming no doubt caused the hearts of Colonel Cook and his party to beat lighter. Or, as California Joe expressed it: "When I seed it wuz Yaller Bar I knowed we wuz all right." From Yellow Bear Colonel Cook learned where he might expect to find us, and thus another cause of anxiety was lifted from his mind.

The morning after my party had been reinforced by the arrival just described, we set out under guidance of Neva and the two young Arapaho warriors, and followed the direction in which Little Robe had gone. It being one of the winter months, the Indian ponies were still in unfit condition to make long or rapid marches; for this reason the two Arapahoes had left their ponies with the village, and were accompanying or rather preceding us on foot; an undertaking which they seemed to have no difficulty in accomplishing. The grazing became more indifferent each day as we journeyed toward the west, until finally we ceased to rely upon it, but as a substitute fed our horses upon the bark of the young cottonwood trees which are generally found fringing the borders of the streams. In spite, however, of our utmost care, our horses and pack animals, having exhausted their supply of forage, began to fail in strength and condition under their cottonwood bark diet.

After reaching and crossing Red river at a point west of that at which the survey of Marcy and McClellan crossed it, and failing to discover any indication of the recent occupation of the ground by Indians, I had fears that if I pro-

YELLOW BEAR, SECOND CHIEF OF THE ARAPAHOES.

longed my journey much further our animals would not be able to reach the main camp, so famished had they become in the last few days. I therefore, after consultation with Neva and the two Arapahoes, decided to recross to the north bank of Red river, and follow up its course until we should reach a small tributary coming in from the northwest, and which Neva informed me would furnish a good camp ground. In the meanwhile Neva, who was well mounted on a hardy, active mule, was to take with him the two young Arapahoes, and push on in advance in search of the Cheyenne village, the understanding being that I should follow in his direction until the stream referred to was reached, where I would await his return for three days. Should he fail to rejoin us in that time, we would commence our return march to the main camp.

When it was known that this plan had been definitely settled upon, young Brewster, who never for a moment had become discouraged as to his final success in discovering his lost sister, came to me, and in the most earnest manner asked permission to accompany Neva in his search for the Cheyenne village. I did everything I could to dissuade him from so dangerous a project.

No arguments were of any avail. He felt satisfied that his sister was a prisoner in the Cheyenne village, and this his last and only opportunity to gain a knowledge of the fact; and even with the chances of death or torture staring him in the face he preferred to risk all, and learn the truth, rather than live longer in a state of horrible uncertainty. Against my judgment in the matter, I was forced by his importunate manner to grant him permission to accompany Neva.

Taking a suitable amount of supplies with them, the three Indians and young Brewster set out, Neva being the only one of the party mounted. After they had left us we moved in the same direction, with the intention of halting on the stream indicated by Neva, there to await their return. While the reader is also waiting their return, I will refer to an incident which should have appeared in an earlier part of this chapter. It was neither more nor less than what might, among fashionable notices in the Indian press—provided they had one—have been termed an elopement in high life.

One evening after we had gone into camp, many long weary miles from our point of starting, and when we supposed we had left all the Kiowas safely in camp awaiting the release of their two chiefs, Lone Wolf and Satanta, we were all surprised to see a young and handsome Kiowa warrior gallop into our midst accompanied by a young squaw, who certainly could not have reached the age which distinguishes the woman from the girl. In a few moments our little party gathered about these two wayfarers, eager to learn the cause of their sudden and unexpected visit. The girl was possessed of almost marvellous beauty, a beauty so remarkable that my companions of that march refer to her to this day as the most beautiful squaw they have ever seen. Her graceful and well-rounded form, her clearly-cut features, her dark expressive eyes, fringed with long silken lashes, cheeks rich with the color of youth, teeth of pearly whiteness occasionally peeping from between her full, rosy lips, added withal to a most bewitching manner, required not the romance of her story to make her an object of deep interest in the eyes of the gallants of our party. But to their story.

She was the daughter of Black Eagle, at that time the acting head chief of the Kiowas. The young warrior who rode at her side was somewhat of a young Lochinvar in disposition. It was the old, old story, only to be repeated again by these representatives of the red man—mutual and determined love on the part of the youngsters, opposition equally determined upon the part of Black Eagle; not that the young warrior was objectionable, but unfortunately, as is but too often the case, he was poor, and could not offer in exchange for the hand of a chief's daughter the proper number of ponies. Black Eagle was inexorable—the lovers, constancy itself. There was but one thing for them to do, and they did it.

Aware of our proposed expedition in search of the Cheyennes and Arapahoes, they timed their affairs accordingly. Giving us time to get two days the start, they slipped away from their village at dusk the evening of the second day after our departure, and hastening unperceived to a thicket near by, where the lover had taken the precaution to conceal two of the fleetest ponies of the village already saddled, they were soon in their saddles and galloping for love and life away from the Kiowa village. I say galloping for life, for by the Indian law, if the father or relatives of the girl could overtake the lovers within twenty-four hours, the life of the young woman would pay the forfeit.

They followed our trail in order to avail themselves of our protection by travelling with us as far as our course might lead them in the direction of the Staked Plains, on the borders of which a straggling band of Kiowas, under the chief Woman Heart, was supposed to be, and which the lovers intended to join, at least until the rage of *paterfamilias* should subside and they be invited to return. This in brief was their story. I need not add that they found a hearty welcome in our midst, and were assured that they need no longer fear pursuit.

That evening, after the camp fires were lighted, the officers of our party, with Romeo as interpreter, gathered about the camp fire of the bridal couple and passed a pleasant hour in conversation. Their happiness and exultation at their success in escaping from their village were too powerful to be restrained, and in many delicate little ways the bride—for by Indian law twenty-four hours' absence from the village with her lover made her a bride—plainly betrayed her exceeding fondness for him who had risked all to claim her as his own.

After my return to the main camp I met Black Eagle, and informed him that his daughter and her husband had been companions of our march. "Yes. Why did you not kill him?" was his reply, which upon inquiry he explained by saying that if some person had kindly put an end to the life of his son-in-law, it would have benefited him to the value of several ponies; his difficulty seeming to be in overcoming the loss of the ponies which should have been paid for his daughter's hand. I afterwards learned, however, that the haughty chief became reconciled to the wilful lovers, and invited them to return to his lodge, an invitation they were not tardy in accepting.

We pitched our camp at the point agreed upon between Neva and myself, and prepared to await the return of his party. Neva had been informed that our delay could not extend beyond three days, as our store of provisions and forage was almost exhausted, and this fact alone would force us to retrace our steps. I had hoped that during the time we were to spend in camp, hunting parties might be able to bring in a sufficient amount of game to satisfy our wants; but although parties were despatched in all directions, not an animal or bird could be found. So barren was the country as to offer no inducements that would attract game of any species.

Our last ounce of meat had been eaten, and the men, after one day's deprivation of this essential part of their rations, were almost ravenous. Our horses had several days since eaten their last ration of grain, and the grass was so sparse and indifferent as to furnish insufficient diet to sustain life. Resort was had to cottonwood bark, to obtain which we cut down large numbers of the trees, and fed our horses upon the young bark of the branches. Knowing that in answer to my second request supplies of provisions both for men and horses must be on their way and probably near to us, I determined to begin our return march one day sooner than I had expected when Neva and his companions left us, as they would be able on finding our camp to follow our trail and overtake us.

We moved only a few miles, but even this short distance was sufficient to demonstrated how weak and famished our horses had become, one of them dying from starvation before we reached camp, the first day of our return march. This circumstance, however, was turned to our advantage. Much has been said and written in praise of the savoriness of horseflesh as a diet. Our necessities compelled us to put this question to practical test, and the animal had scarcely fallen, unable to rise again, when it was decided to prepare his carcass for food. That evening the men treated themselves to a bountiful repast made up of roasts, steaks, and broils, all from the flesh of the poor animal, whose death was attributable to starvation alone. Judging, however, from the jolly laughter which rang through camp at supper time, the introduction of this new article of diet met with a cordial reception.

Soon after finishing our supper, we discovered in the distance and following in our trail a horseman. We at once concluded that this must be Neva, a fact rendered conclusive by the aid of a field-glass. Various were the surmises indulged in by the different members of our party as to the success of Neva's mission. What had become of his companions, particularly young Brewster? These and many other inquiries suggested themselves as we watched his approach. We could almost read the answer on Neva's face when he reached us as to the success of his search for the Cheyennes. Disappointment, hunger, and fatigue were plainly marked in his features as he dismounted and shook hands with us. Knowing that one of the characteristics of the Indian is to talk but little until the wants of the inner man have been fully attended to, I at once ordered him a steak. One of the party, however, fearing that if he knew the exact character of the diet offered him he might from some superstitious cause decline it, suggested that Neva be asked if he would like a nice buffalo steak, a deception which seemed somewhat justifiable under the circumstances. To this Neva returned a hearty affirmative, when one of the men placed before him a raw steak, whose dimensions would have amply gratified the appetites of an ordinary family of half a dozen. Having held the steak over the blazing fire until sufficiently done to suit his taste, Neva seated himself on the ground near by and began helping himself liberally to the dripping morsel. After he had indulged for some time in this pleasing entertainment, and having made no remark, one of the officers inquired of him if he was hungry.

"Yes," was his reply, but added in his very indifferent English, "Poor buffano, poor buffano." None of us ever informed him of the little deception which had been practised upon him.

His account of his journey was brief. He had travelled nearly due west, accompanied by Brewster and the two young Arapahoes, and had discovered a trail of the Cheyenne village some two weeks old, leading still further to the west, and under circumstances which induced him to believe the village had moved far away. Under these circumstances there was no course left to him but to return. The Arapahoes decided to follow on and join the Cheyenne village. Neva and young Brewster began their return together, but the latter, being unable to travel as fast as Neva, fell behind. Neva, anxious to keep his promise and rejoin us at the time and place indicated, pushed forward as rapidly as possible. Young Brewster, however, manfully struggled along, and reached our camp a few hours after Neva's arrival.

The next morning we set out on our homeward or return march. During the night one of our horses strayed away from camp, and as one of the men thought he could find it before we made our start in the morning, he left camp with that purpose. Failing to rejoin us at the proper time, I sent parties in search of him, but they returned unsuccessful. We were compelled by our necessities to move without further delay. Weeks and months elapsed, and no tidings of the lost trooper reached us, when one day, while encamped near Fort Hays, Kansas, hundreds of miles from the locality of which I am now writing, who should step up to my tent but the man who was lost from us in northwestern Texas. He had become bewildered after losing sight of our camp, took the wrong direction, and was never able thereafter during his wanderings to determine his course. Fortunately he took a southerly route, and after nearly two months of solitary roaming over the plains of northern Texas, he arrived at a military post south of Red river in Texas, and by way of Galveston, the Gulf of Mexico, the Mississippi and Missouri rivers, rejoined his regiment in Kansas.

As we gained the crest of the hill from which we obtained a view of the white tents which formed our camp, there was no one of our little party who did not enjoy a deep feeling of gratitude and thankfulness that our long and trying journey was about to end under happier auspices than many might have supposed when we began it. We had found the Arapahoes, and succeeded in placing them on their reservation, where, from that date to the present time, they have remained, never engaging as a tribe in making war or committing depredations on the whites, so far as my knowledge extends.

We did not succeed so well with the Cheyennes, but we established facts regarding their location, disposition, and intentions as to peace, which were of invaluable service to us in determining future operations looking to the establishment of peace with them.

Our arrival in camp created a sensation among our comrades, who had seen us depart upon what they might well have considered an errand of questionable prudence. Leaving my companions of the march to answer the many queries of those who had not accompanied us, I galloped across the narrow plain which separated General Sheridan's tents from my camp, and was soon greeted by the General and staff in terms of hearty welcome. Repairing to the General's tent, I soon recounted the principal incidents of my expedition, with most of which the reader has been already made acquainted. I found that the Arapahoes had kept their promise, made to me while I was in their village, and that the village was then located near our main camp. It might be proper here to remark that, although a period of several years has elapsed since the Arapahoes were induced to accept the offer of peace made to them, and promised to relinquish in the future their predatory mode of life, yet to this day, so far as I know, they as a tribe have remained at peace with the white men.

This remark may not, and probably does not, apply to particular individuals of the tribe, but it is due to the tribe to state that their conduct, since the events related in the preceding chapter, has been greatly to their credit, as well as to the peace and comfort of the settlers of the frontier; results wholly due to the Washita campaign and the subsequent events with which the reader of these articles is familiar.

The conduct of the Cheyennes, however, in declining our proffers of peace, left the Indian question in that section of country still unsettled; but this only rendered new plans necessary, plans which were quickly determined upon. Other events of great public importance rendered General Sheridan's presence necessary elsewhere at an early day.

It was therefore decided that he, accompanied by his escort of scouts under Lieutenant Pepoon, should proceed northward to Camp Supply, while I, with the Seventh Regulars and the Nineteenth Kansas Cavalry, and my Osage scouts, a force numbering about fifteen hundred men, should move westward in quest of the recalcitrant Cheyennes, and administer to them such treatment as their past conduct might merit and existing circumstances demanded. Satanta and Lone Wolf were still prisoners in our hands, a portion of their tribe having failed thus far to comply with the terms of the agreement by which they were to settle down peaceably on their reservation. As the greater portion of the tribe, however, was then encamped near us, and as both Satanta and Lone Wolf were loud in their protestations of peace, it was decided to release them. Accordingly, after conference with General Sheridan, I went to the lodge in which I kept the two chiefs closely guarded as prisoners, and informed them of the decision which had been arrived at in their behalf, the only response being a most hearty and emphatic "How" from the two robust chieftains.

General Sheridan had up to this time declined all their requests for an interview, but now deemed it best to see them and speak a few words of warning and caution as to their future conduct. No peace commissioners were ever entertained by promises of good behavior, peaceable intentions, and regrets for past offences, which smacked of greater earnestness and sincerity than those volunteered by Lone Wolf and Satanta when informed that they were free to rejoin their people. According to their voluntary representations, their love for their white brothers was unbounded; their desire for peace, their hatred of war, ungovernable; and nothing would satisfy them in future but to be permitted to lead their people "the white man's road," by cultivating the soil, building schoolhouses and churches, and forever eschewing a predatory or warlike life.

Alas, the instability of human resolutions—particularly of the human in an Indian! and the resolutions are expressed—not formed—simply to obtain a certain advantage, or, as is most usually the case, to tickle the fanciful imagination of some thoroughly well-meaning but utterly impractical peace commissioner, whose favorable influence is believed by the Indian to be allpotent in securing fresh invoices of new blankets, breech-loading arms, and provisions. Neither blankets, breech-loading arms, nor an unnecessary amount of provisions were distributed by the military among the adherents of Satanta and Lone Wolf.

Scarcely one year had elapsed, however, before Satanta defiantly informed the General of the Army, then on a visit to Fort Sill, that he had just returned from an expedition to Texas, during which he and his party had murdered and robbed several white men. It was this confession which led to Satanta's trial, conviction, and sentence to death by the civil authorities of Texas. Through the intercession of the General Government, the Executive of Texas was induced to commute the punishment of Satanta from hanging to imprisonment for life, a step which all familiar with Indians and Indian management knew would result sooner or later in his release, and that of his confederate, Big Tree.

Importuned constantly by the tender-hearted representations of the peace commissioners, who could not be induced to look upon Satanta and Big Tree as murderers, the Governor of Texas very unwisely yielded to their persistent appeals, and upon the strength of promises solemnly made by the peace commissioners, according to which not only Satanta and Big Tree were to abstain from acts of bloodshed and murder in the future, but their entire tribe was also to remain at peace and within their reservation limits, the two chiefs who had unfortunately escaped the halter were again turned loose to engage in acts of hostility against the whites; an opportunity they and their treacherous people have not been slow to improve from that day to this.

The winter of 1868–'69 was rapidly terminating, acting as a forcible reminder to us that if we hoped to operate in the field with any advantage over the Cheyennes, the movement must be made before the spring grass should make its appearance for the benefit of the Indian ponies. Accordingly, as soon as our arrangements were perfected, our camp at the present site of Fort Sill, Indian Territory, was broken up, and General Sheridan, accompanied by his staff and escort, set out for Camp Supply in the north, while my command faced westward and began its search for the Cheyennes, passing along the southern base of the Witchita mountains, on the afternoon of inauguration day, at old Camp Radziminsky, a station which had been occupied by our troops prior to the war between the Northern and Southern States, and whose name, no doubt, will recall pleasant reminiscences to many who afterwards wore the blue or the gray.

On the morning of the first day after leaving the Witchita mountains behind us, no little excitement was created throughout the command by the discovery of a column of smoke directly on our course, and apparently about fifteen or twenty miles in front of us. That Indians had originated the fire was beyond a doubt, as we all knew that beyond us, in the direction of the smoke, the country was inhabited by no human beings save hostile Indians. I at once decided to push on with the command to the point from which the smoke was ascending, and discover if possible some trace of the Indians. Be it understood that neither I nor any members of my command supposed for one moment that when we arrived at the desired point we would find the Indians there awaiting our arrival, but we did hope to discover their trail. Of the many experienced frontiermen embraced in the command, including of course California Joe, there were none who judged the distance which separated us from the smoke as greater than could be easily passed over by us before three or four o'clock that afternoon.

It was evidently not a signal smoke—ascending from a single point and regulated by human control—but appeared from our standpoint more like a fire communicated to the prairie grass from an abandoned or neglected camp fire. Pushing on as rapidly as our horses could travel, we were again reminded from time to time of the deceptive character of the plains as regards distances. When three o'clock arrived, and we had been marching steadily for nine hours, the dense and changing columns of deep gray smoke, which had been our guiding point all day, seemed as far distant as when our march began in the morning. Except to water our animals, and once to enable the men to prepare a cup of coffee, no halts were made from six o'clock in the morning until we finally reached the desired locality—not at three or four o'clock in the afternoon, but at two o'clock that night.

Our surmises proved correct. The fire had evidently been communicated to the dry winter grass from some Indian camp fire. The Indians of course had gone; but where? As this was a question that could not be solved until daylight, and as all of us were glad enough of an opportunity to get a few hours' repose, the troops bivouacked in promiscuous order as they arrived.

Only those who have enjoyed similar experiences know how brief the preparation required for sleep. As for myself, as soon as the necessary directions had been given relating to the command, I unsaddled my horse, arranged my saddle for my pillow, tethered my horse within easy reach, and in less time than has been required to write these few lines, I was enjoying one of those slumbers which only come as the reward of a day of earnest activity in the saddle.

As soon as it was light enough for our purpose, we were in the saddle and searching in all directions for the trail left by the Indians who had fired the prairie. Our Osage scouts were not long in making the desired discovery. The trail led westward, following the general course of a small valley in which it was first discovered. The party was evidently a small one, numbering not more than fifteen persons, but the direction in which they were moving led me to hope that by following them carefully and with due caution to prevent discovery of our pursuit, we might be led to the main village.

All that day our Osage scouts clung to the trail with the pertinacity of sleuth hounds. The course led us up and across several different streams of beautiful, clear water; but to our great disappointment, and to that of our horses as well, we discovered, upon attempting to quench our thirst at different times, that every stream was impregnated to the fullest degree with salt.

Later in the day this became a serious matter, and had we not been on an Indian trail, I should have entertained earnest apprehensions as to whether or not we were destined to find pure water by continuing further in the direction we were then moving; but I felt confident that the Indians we were pursuing were familiar with the country, and would no doubt lead us, unintentionally of course, to streams of fresh water.

One of the streams we crossed was so strongly impregnated with salt that the edges near the banks were covered with a border of pure white salt, resembling the borders of ice often seen along rivulets in winter. This border was from one to three feet in width, and sufficiently thick to support the weight of a horse. Fortunately the Indian trail, as I had anticipated, led us to a refreshing spring of pure, cold water near by. Here we halted to prepare a cup of coffee before continuing the pursuit.

While halted at this point I observed a trooper approaching with an armful of huge cakes of pure white salt, gathered from the salt stream just described, and which flowed at the foot of the hill from which also bubbled forth the spring of fresh water to which we were indebted for the means of preparing our first meal on that day. Salt was not an abundant article with us at that time, and the trooper referred to, aware of this fact, had, in behalf of himself and comrades, collected from the literal "salt of the earth" a quantity ample for all present need. After conveying his valuable load to the vicinity of the cook fire, he broke the cakes of salt into small particles with an axe, and then passing the fragments through a coffee-mill, he was in possession of table salt whose quality would have satisfied a more exacting epicure than a hungry cavalryman.

Finishing our meal, which not only was our breakfast for that day, but a late dinner as well, we resumed the pursuit, observing before doing so that the Indians had also made a brief halt at the same point, and had built a fire and prepared their meal, as we had done after them.

Crossing a high ridge, or divide, the trail led us down into a beautiful open valley. After following up the course of the latter several miles, the freshness of the trail indicated that the Indians had passed over it that same day. As it was not our purpose to overtake them, but to follow as closely as prudence would allow, I determined to go into camp until the following morning. Soon after resuming the pursuit next day rain began to fall, at first slowly, but later in the day in copious showers. I knew the Indians would not travel in the rain if they could avoid it, unless they knew they were pursued, and of this fact I had reason to believe they were still ignorant, as evidences found all along the trail indicated that they were moving very leisurely.

To avoid placing ourselves in too close proximity to them, I ordered a halt about noon, and began preparation for camping for the night. Our wagons were still in rear. In the mean time the horses were all unsaddled and picketed out in the usual manner to graze. As was my usual custom upon halting for the night, I had directed the Osage scouts, instead of halting and unsaddling, to advance in the direction we were to follow next day, and examine the country for a distance of a few miles. We had barely completed the unsaddling of our horses and disposed of them over the grazing ground, when I discovered the Osage scouts returning over the ridge in front of us as fast as their ponies could carry them. Their story was soon told. Disliking to travel in the rain, the Indians whom we were pursuing had gone into camp also, and the Osage scouts had discovered them not more than a mile from us, the ridge referred to preventing the Indians from seeing us or being seen by us.

Quickly the words " Saddle up " flew from mouth to mouth, and in a marvellously brief time officers and men were in the saddle and, under the guidance of the Osage scouts, were moving stealthily to surprise the Indian camp. Passing around a little spur of the dividing ridge, there before us, at a distance of but a few hundred yards, stood the half-erected lodges of the Indians, while scattered here and there in the immediate vicinity were to be seen the Indian ponies and pack animals, grazing in apparent unconsciousness of the close proximity of an enemy. At a given signal the cavalry put spurs to their steeds, drew their revolvers, and in a few moments were in possession of the Indian camp, ponies and all—no, not all, for not a single Indian could be discovered.

The troops were deployed at a gallop in all directions, but failed to find the trace of an Indian. Our capture was apparently an empty one. How the occupants of the Indian camp had first discovered our presence and afterwards contrived to elude us was a mystery which even puzzled our Osage scouts. This mystery was afterwards explained, and in order to avoid detaining the reader, I will anticipate sufficiently to state that in the course of subsequent events we came face to face, under a flag of truce, with the late occupants of the Indian camp, and learned from them that in this instance history had reproduced itself. Rome was saved by the cackling of geese: the Indians owed their safety to the barking of dogs—not the barking of dogs belonging to their own camp, but to ours.

It seemed that during the haste and excitement attendant upon the discovery of the close proximity of the Indian camp to ours, two of our dogs, whether or not sharing in the bellicose humor of their masters, engaged in a quarrel, the noise of which reached the quick ears of the Indians nearly one mile distant. Comprehending the situation at once, the Indians, realizing the danger of delay, abandoned their camp and ponies and fled on foot, the better to effect concealment and elude pursuit.

On the following day we resumed the march. There being no longer any trail for us to follow, we continued in the same direction, believing that the small party we had been pursuing had been directing their course toward the location of the main village, which was somewhere to the westward of us. Day after day we travelled in this direction, hoping to discover some sign or trail which might give us a clue to the whereabouts of the Cheyenne village. We had left the Indian Territory far behind us, and had advanced into Texas well toward the 102d meridian of longitude. Nearly all hope of discovering the Indians had vanished from the minds of the officers and men, when late in the afternoon the trail of a single lodge was discovered, leading in a southwesterly direction. The trail was nearly if not quite one month old; hence it did not give great encouragement. To the surprise of most of the command, I changed the direction of our march at once, and put the Osages on the trail, having decided to follow it.

This may seem to the reader an ill-advised move, but the idea under which the decision was made was, that the owner of the lodge the trail of which we had discovered had probably been absent from the main village in search of game, as is customary for small parties of Indians at that season of the year. In the spring, however, the entire tribe assembles at one point and determines its plans and movements for the summer, whether relating to war or hunting. There was a chance—a slight one, it is true—that the trail of the single lodge just discovered might lead us to the rendezvous of the tribe. I deemed it worthy of our attention, and a pursuit of a few days at furthest would determine the matter.

Following our faithful Osages, who experienced no difficulty in keeping the trail, we marched until near sundown, when we arrived at the banks of a small stream upon which, and near a cool, bubbling spring, we discovered the evidences of an Indian camp, which must have not only included the lodge whose trail we had been following, but about a dozen others. Here was a speedier confirmation of my hopes than I had anticipated. Here I determined to encamp until morning, and while the cavalry were unsaddling and pitching their tents, I asked Mo-nah-see-tah to examine the Indian camp minutely and to tell me how long a time had elapsed since its occupation by the Indians, how many constituted the party, and the character and probable indications of the latter.

No detective could have set about the proposed examination with greater thoroughness than did this Indian girl. The ashes of the camp fires were raked carefully away and examined with all the scrutiny of a chemical analysis. Bits of cloth or fragments of the skins of animals found within the limits of the camp were lifted from their resting-places as tenderly as if they were articles of greatest value. Here and there were to be seen the bones of deer or antelope which had been obtained by the Indians as food. These Mo-nah-see-tah examined carefully; then, shattering them between two stones, the condition of the marrow seemed a point of particular importance to her as tending to determine the length of time the bones had been lying on the camp. After many minutes spent in this examination, during which I accompanied her, a silent but far from disinterested spectator, she, apparently like a judge who had been carefully reviewing all the evidence, gave me her conclusions, communicating with me, through the medium of the sign language, with a grace characteristic of the Indian race, and which added to the interest of her statements.

Briefly summed up her conclusions were as follows: twelve lodges had encamped at that point, probably constituting the band of some petty chief, the different members of which, like the one whose trail we had that day discovered, had been separated for purposes of hunting, but had been called together at that point preparatory to joining the main village. The lodges had left this camp not to exceed two weeks previous to that date, and in all probability had moved to the rendezvous appointed for the main tribe, which would without doubt be found by other small bands from time to time, until the village would all be assembled at one point. Moving in this manner and at this early season of the year, when grass was scarce and no enemy known to be in the country, the Indians would make very short moves each day, passing merely from one stream to another, not accomplishing in one day a greater distance, probably, than the cavalry would in two or three hours.

This intelligence, of course, was most gratifying, and for encouragement was soon communicated to the individual members of the command. The trail was found to lead almost in a northerly direction, slightly inclining to the east. Perhaps no one of the command experienced such a feeling of hope and anxious suspense as the new discoveries gave rise to in the breast of young Brewster, who now more than ever believed, and with reason too, that he was soon to unravel or forever seal the fate of his lost sister, whose discovery and release had been the governing impulses of his life for months past.

With renewed interest the cavalry resumed the pursuit at daylight the following morning. We had marched but a few miles before we reached a second camping ground, which had been occupied not only by those whose trail we were then following, but the number of fires showed that the strength of the Indians had been increased by about twenty-five lodges, thus verifying the correctness of the surmises advanced by Mo-nah-see-tah.

Continuing our progress, we had the satisfaction of seeing still further accessions to the trail, until it was evident that at least one hundred lodges had united and passed in one body on the trail. As we marched in one day over the distance passed over in three by the Indians, and as the latter were moving unsuspicious of the presence of an enemy in that section of the country, the trail was becoming freshened as we advanced.

That night we encamped with every precaution calculated to conceal our presence from the Indians. No fires were permitted until after dark, and then but small ones, for fear the quick and watchful eye of the Indian might detect the ascending columns of smoke. As soon as the men had prepared their suppers the fires were put out. In the morning breakfast was prepared before daylight, and the fires at once smothered by heaping damp earth over them.

Resuming the pursuit as soon as it was sufficiently light to follow the trail, we soon arrived at the camp vacated by the Indians the previous day, the extent of which showed that from three to four hundred lodges of Indians had occupied the ground. In many places the decayed embers of the lodge fires were still glowing; while the immense quantity of young cottonwood timber found cut and lying throughout the camp stripped of its young bark, showed that the Indian ponies were being mainly subsisted on cottonwood bark, the spring grass not being sufficiently advanced to answer the purpose. Nothing indicated that the Indians had departed in a precipitate manner, or that they had discovered our approach. It was reasonable, therefore, to suppose that we would come in contact with them that day, if not actually reach the village.

All our plans were made accordingly. The Osages, as usual, were kept in the advance, that their quick eyes might the sooner discover the Indians should they appear in our front. In order to avail myself of the earliest information, I, with Colonel Cook, accompanied the Osages. Two of the latter kept in advance of all, and as they neared a ridge or commanding piece of ground they would cautiously approach the crest on foot and peer beyond, to ascertain whether an enemy was in sight before exposing our party to discovery. This proceeding, a customary one with Indians, did not excite unusual attention upon the part of Colonel Cook and myself, until once we saw Hard Rope, the head warrior, who was in advance, slowly ascend a slight eminence in our front, and, after casting one glimpse beyond, descend the hill and return to us as rapidly as his pony could carry him. We almost anticipated his report, so confident was everybody in the command that we were going to overtake the village.

In a few words Hard Rope informed us that less than a mile beyond the hill from which he had obtained a view, there was in plain sight a large herd of Indian ponies grazing, being herded and driven by a few Indian boys. As yet they had not seen us, but were liable to discover the column of troops further to the rear. To judge of the situation I dismounted, and, conducted by Hard Rope, advanced to the crest of the hill in front and looked beyond; there I saw in plain view the herd of ponies, numbering perhaps two hundred, and being driven in the opposite direction toward what seemed the valley of a stream, as I could see the tops of the forest trees which usually border the water courses.

The ponies and their protectors soon disappeared from view, but whether they had discovered us yet or not I was unable to determine. Sending a messenger back as rapidly as his horse could carry him, I directed the troops to push to the front, and to come prepared for action. I knew the village must be near at hand, probably in the vicinity of the trees seen in the distance. As the country was perfectly open, free from either ravines or timber capable of affording concealment to Indians, I took my orderly with me and galloped in advance in the direction taken by the Indians, leaving Colonel Cook to hasten and direct the troops as the latter should arrive.

After advancing about half way to the bluff overlooking the valley I saw about half a dozen Indian heads peering over the crest, evidently watching my movements; this number was soon increased to upwards of fifty. I was extremely anxious to satisfy myself as to the tribe whose village was evidently near at hand. There was but little doubt that it was the Cheyennes, for whom we had been searching. If this should prove true, the two white girls whose discovery and release from captivity had been one of the objects of the expedition, must be held prisoners in the village which we were ap

20

proaching; and to effect their release unharmed then became my study, for I remembered the fate of the white woman and child held captive by a band of this same tribe at the battle of the Washita. I knew that the first shot fired on either side would be the signal for the murder of the two white girls. While knowing the Cheyennes to be deserving of castigation, and feeling assured that they were almost in our power, I did not dare to imperil the lives of the two white captives by making an attack on the village, although never before or since have we seen so favorable an opportunity for administering well-merited punishment to one of the strongest and most troublesome of the hostile tribes. Desiring to establish a truce with the Indians before the troops should arrive, I began making signals inviting a conference. This was done by simply riding in a circle, and occasionally advancing toward the Indians on the bluff in a zigzag manner. Immediately there appeared on the bluffs about twenty mounted Indians; from this group three advanced toward me at a gallop, soon followed by the others of the party. I cast my eyes behind me to see if the troops were near, but the head of the column was still a mile or more in rear. My orderly was near me, and I could see Colonel Cook rapidly approaching about midway between the column and my position.

Directing the orderly to remain stationary, I advanced toward the Indians a few paces, and as soon as they were sufficiently near made signs to them to halt, and then for but one of their number to advance midway and meet me. This was assented to, and I advanced with my revolver in my left hand, while my right hand was held aloft as a token that I was inclined to be friendly. The Indian met me as agreed upon, and in response to my offer exchanged friendly greetings, and shook hands. From him I learned that the village of the entire Cheyenne tribe was located on the streams in front of us, and that Medicine Arrow, the head chief of the Cheyennes, was in the group of Indians then in view from where we stood. Little Robe, with his band numbering about forty lodges, was a short distance further down the stream. I asked the Indian to send for Medicine Arrow, as I desired to talk with the head chief. Calling to one of his companions, who had halted within hailing distance, the latter was directed to convey to Medicine Arrow my message, to do which he set off at a gallop.

At this juncture I perceived that the Indians, to the number of twenty or more, had approached quite near, while some of the party seemed disposed to advance to where I was. To this I had decided objections, and so indicated to the Indian who was with me. He complied with my wishes, and directed his companions to remain where they were. As a precaution of safety, I took good care to keep the person of the Indian between me and his friends. Medicine Arrow soon came galloping up accompanied by a chief.

While engaged in shaking hands with him and his companions, and exchanging the usual salutation, "How," with the new arrivals, I observed that the Indians who had been occupying a retired position had joined the group, and I found myself in the midst of about twenty chiefs and warriors. Medicine Arrow exhibited the most earnest desire to learn from me the number of troops following me. Whether this question was prompted by any contemplated act of treachery, in case my followers were few in number, or not, I do not know. But if treachery was thought of, the idea was abandoned when I informed him that my followers numbered fifteen hundred men, the advance guard being then in sight. Medicine Arrow then informed me that his vilage was near by, and that the women and children would be greatly excited and

MEDICINE ARROW AND HIS SQUAW.

ala/med by the approach of so large a body of troops. To give assurance to them he urged me to accompany him to his village in advance of the troops, and by my presence satisfy his people that no attack upon them would be made. This I consented to do.

By this time Colonel Cook had again joined me, also Dr. Lippincott. Leaving the doctor with directions for the troops, and taking Colonel Cook with me, I started with Medicine Arrow and a considerable party of his warriors to the village, Medicine Arrow urging us to put our horses to the gallop. The reader may regard this movement on my part as having been anything but prudent, and I will admit that viewed in the ordinary light it might seem to partake somewhat of a foolhardy errand. But I can assure them that no one could be more thoroughly convinced of the treachery and bloodthirsty disposition of the Indian than I am, nor would I ever trust life in their hands except it was to their interest to preserve that life; for no class of beings act so much from self-interest as the Indian, and on this occasion I knew, before accepting the proposal of the chief to enter his village, that he and every member of his band felt it to be to their interest not only to protect me from harm, but treat me with every consideration, as the near approach of the troops and the formidable number of the latter would deter the Indians from any act of hostility, knowing as they did that in case of an outbreak of any kind it would be impossible for a great portion of the village, particularly the women and children, to escape. I considered all this before proceeding to the village.

As we were turning our horses' heads in the direction of the village, I caught sight of a familiar face in the group of Indians about me; it was that of Mah-wis-sa, the squaw whom I had sent as peace commissioner from our camp near Fort Sill, and who had failed to return. She recognized me at once, and laughed when I uttered the word "Mutah-ka," referring to the hunting-knife I had loaned her as she was about to depart on her errand of peace. A brisk gallop soon brought us to the village, which was located beneath the trees on the bank of a beautiful stream of clear running water. The name of the latter I found to be the Sweetwater; it is one of the tributaries of Red river, and is indicated on the map as crossing the 100th meridian not far south of the Canadian river.

Medicine Arrow hurried me to his lodge, which was located almost in the centre of the village, the latter being the most extensive I had ever seen. As soon as I had entered the lodge I was invited to a seat on one of the many buffalo robes spread on the ground about the inner circumference of the lodge. By Medicine Arrow's direction the village crier, in a loud tone of voice, began calling the chiefs together in council. No delay occurred in their assembling. One by one they approached and entered the lodge, until fifteen of the leading chiefs had taken their seats in the circle within the lodge in the order of their rank. I was assigned the post of honor, being seated on the right of Medicine Arrow, while on my immediate right sat the medicine man of the tribe, an official scarcely second in influence to the head chief.

The squaw of Medicine Arrow built a huge fire in the centre of the lodge. As soon as all the chiefs had assembled, the ceremonies, which were different from any I ever witnessed before or since, began. The chiefs sat in silence while the medicine man drew forth from a capacious buckskin tobacco pouch, profusely ornamented with beads and porcupine quills, a large red clay pipe, with a stem about the size of an ordinary walking-stick. From another buckskin pouch which hung at his girdle he drew forth a handful of kinnikinic, and placed it on a cloth spread on the ground before him; to this he added, in various amounts, dried leaves and herbs, with which he seemed well supplied. After thoroughly mixing these ingredients, he proceeded with solemn ceremony to fill the pipe with the mixture, muttering at times certain incantations, by which no doubt it was intended to neutralize any power or proclivity for harm I may have been supposed to possess.

To all of this I was a silent but far from disinterested spectator. My interest perceptibly increased when the medicine man, who was sitting close to me, extended his left hand and grasped my right, pressing it strongly against his body over the region of his heart, at the same time, and with complete devoutness of manner, engaging in what seemed to me a petition or prayer to the Great Spirit; the other chiefs from time to time ejaculating, in the most earnest manner, their responses, the latter being made simultaneously. To the Indians it was a most solemn occasion, and scarcely less impressive to me, who could only judge of what was transpiring by catching an occasional word, and by closely following their signs.

After the conclusion of the address or prayer by the medicine man, the latter released my hand, which up to this time had been tightly grasped in his, and taking the long clay pipe in both hands, it likewise was apparently placed under an imaginary potent spell, by a ceremony almost as long as that which I have just described. This being ended, the medicine man, first pointing slowly with the stem of the pipe to each of the four points of the compass, turned to me, and without even so much as saying, " Smoke, sir? " placed the mouthpiece of the long stem in my mouth, still holding the bowl of the pipe in his hand.

Again taking my right hand in his left, the favor or protecting influence of the Great Spirit was again invoked in the most earnest and solemn manner, the other chiefs joining at regular intervals with their responses. Finally, releasing my hand, the medicine man lighted a match, and applying it to the pipe made signs to me to smoke. A desire to conform as far as practicable to the wishes of the Indians, and a curiosity to study a new and interesting phase of the Indian character, prompted me to obey the direction of the medicine man, and I accordingly began puffing away with as great a degree of nonchalance as a man unaccustomed to smoking could well assume. Now being, as I have just stated, one of that class which does not number smoking among its accomplishments, I took the first few whiffs with a degree of confidence which I felt justified in assuming, as I imagined the smoking portion of the ceremony was to be the same as usually observed among Indians so devoted to the practice, in which each individual takes the pipe, enjoys half a dozen whiffs, and passes it to his next neighbor on his left. That much I felt equal to; but when, after blowing away the first half dozen puffs of smoke from my face, the medicine man still retained his hold of the pipe, with an evident desire that I should continue the enjoyment of this Indian luxury, I proceeded more deliberately, although no such rule of restraint seemed to govern the volubility of the medicine man, whose invocation and chants continued with unabated vigor and rapidity.

When the first minute had added to itself four more, and still I was expected to make a miniature volcano of myself, minus the ashes, I began to grow solicitous as to what might be the effect if I was subjected to this course of treatment. I pictured to myself the commander of an important **expedition seated** in solemn council with a **score and a half** of dusky chieftains, the pipe of peace being passed, and before it had left the hands of the aforesaid commander, he becoming deathly sick, owing to lack of familiarity with the noxious weed or its substitutes. I imagined the sudden termination of the council, the absurdity of the figure cut, and the contempt of the chiefs for one who must, under the circumstances, appear so deficient in manly accomplishments. These and a hundred similar ideas flashed through my mind as I kept pulling vigorously at the pipe, and wondering when this thing would terminate.

Fortunately for my peace of body as well as of mind, after a period which seemed to me equal to a quarter of an hour at least, I felt relieved by the medicine man taking the pipe from my mouth, and, after refilling it, handing it to the head chief, sitting on my left, who, drawing three or four long, silent whiffs, passed it to his next neighbor on his left; and in similar manner it made the circle of the chiefs, until it finally returned to the medicine man, who, after taking a few final whiffs, laid it aside, much to my relief, as I feared the consequences of a repetition of my former effort.

Romeo, the interpreter, having been mounted upon an indifferent animal, had fallen to the rear of the column during the march that day, and I was deprived of his services during my interview with the chief. Colonel Cook, during this time, was in an adjoining lodge, each moment naturally becoming more solicitous lest upon the arrival of the troops there should be a collision between the Indians and the excited volunteers. To the inquiries of the chiefs I explained the object of our march, without alluding to the two captive girls, the time not having arrived for discussing that subject. Having resolved to obtain the release of the captives, all other purposes were necessarily laid aside; and as I knew that the captives could not be released should hostilities once occur between the troops and Indians, I became for the time being an ardent advocate of peace measures, and informed the chiefs that such was my purpose at the time. I also requested them to inform me where I would find the most suitable camping ground in the vicinity of the village, to which request Medicine Arrow replied that he would accompany me in person and point out the desired ground.

When this offer was made I accepted it as a kindness, but when the chief conducted me to a camp ground separated from the village, and from all view of the latter, I had reason to modify my opinion of his pretended kindness, particularly when coupled with his subsequent conduct. My command soon came up, and was conducted to the camp ground indicated by Medicine Arrow, the distance between the camp and the village not exceeding three-fourths of a mile. I was still uncertain as to whether there were any grounds to doubt that the two white girls were captives in Medicine Arrow's village. I anxiously awaited the arrival of Mo-nah-see-tah, who could and would solve this question. She came with the main body of the troops, and I at once informed her whose village it was alongside of which we were located.

To my inquiry as to whether the two white girls were prisoners in Medicine Arrow's village, she promptly replied in the affirmative, and at the same time exhibited a desire to aid as far as possible in effecting their release. It was still early in the afternoon, and I did not deem it necessary, or even advisable, to proceed with undue haste in the negotiations by which I expected to bring about the release of the two captives. Although our camp, as already explained, was cut off from a view of the village, yet I had provided

against either surprise or strategem, by posting some of my men on prominent points near by, from which they obtained a full view of both our camp
and the village, and thus rendered it impossible for any important movement to take place in the latter without being seen. I felt confident that
as soon as it was dark the entire village would probably steal away, and
leave us in the lurch; but I proposed to make my demand for the surrender
of the captives long before darkness should aid the Indians in eluding us.

From fifty to one hundred chiefs, warriors, and young men were assembled at my headquarters, or about the camp fire built in front of headquarters. Apparently they were there from motives of mere curiosity, but
later developments proved they had another object in view. Finally Medicine Arrow came to my camp, accompanied by some of his head men, and
after shaking hands with apparent cordiality, stated that some of his young
men, desirous of manifesting their friendship for us, would visit our camp
in a few minutes, and entertain us by a serenade. This idea was a novel
one to me, and I awaited the arrival of the serenaders with no little curiosity.

Before their arrival, however, my lookouts reported unusual commotion
and activity in the Indian village. The herd of the latter had been called in,
and officers sent by me to investigate this matter confirmed the report, and
added that everything indicated a contemplated flight on the part of the Indians. I began then to comprehend the object of the proposed serenade;
it was to occupy our attention while the village could pack up and take
flight. Pretending ignorance of what was transpiring in the village, I continued to converse, through Romeo, with the chiefs, until the arrival of the
Indian musicians. These, numbering about a dozen young men, were
mounted on ponies which, like themselves, were ornamented in the highest degree, according to Indian fashion. The musicians were feathered
and painted in the most horrible as well as fantastic manner. Their in-
struments consisted of reeds, the sounds from which more nearly resembled those of the fife than any other, although there was a total lack of harmony between the various pieces. As soon as the musicians arrived they began riding in a gallop in a small circle, of which circle our little group,
composed of a few officers and the chiefs, composed the centre. The display of horsemanship was superb, and made amends for the discordant sounds
given forth as music.

During all this time reports continued to come in, leaving no room to
doubt that the entire village was preparing to decamp. To have opposed
this movement by a display of force on the part of the troops would have
only precipitated a terrible conflict, for which I was not yet prepared, keeping
in mind the rescue of the white girls. I did not propose, however, to relinquish the advantage we then had by our close proximity to the village, and
permit the latter to place several miles between us.

Knowing that the musicians would soon depart, and with them perhaps
the chiefs and warriors then grouped about my camp fire, I determined to
seize the principal chiefs then present, permit the village to depart if necessary, and hold the captured chiefs as hostages for the surrender of the white girls
and the future good behavior of the tribe. This was a move requiring not
only promptness but most delicate and careful handling, in order to avoid
bloodshed. Quietly passing the word to a few of the officers who sat near
me around the camp fire, I directed them to leave the group one by one,

and, in such manner as not to attract the attention of the Indians, proceed to their companies and select quickly some of their most reliable men, instructing the latter to assemble around and near my camp fire, well armed, as if merely attracted there by the Indian serenade. The men thus selected were to come singly, appear as unconcerned as possible, and be in readiness to act promptly, but to do nothing without orders from me.

In this manner about one hundred of my men were, in an inconceivably short space of time, mingled with the Indians, who, to the number of forty or more, sat or stood about my camp fire, laughing in their sleeves (had they not been minus these appendages), no doubt, at the clever dodge by which they were entertaining the white men while their village was hastening preparations for a speedy flight. When the musicians had apparently exhausted their programme, they took their departure, informing us that later in the evening they would return and repeat the performance; they might have added, "with an entire change of programme."

After their departure the conversation continued with the chiefs until, by glancing about me, I saw that a sufficient number of my men had mingled with the Indians to answer my purpose. Of the forty or more Indians in the group, there were but few chiefs, the majority being young men or boys. My attention was devoted to the chiefs, and acting upon the principle that for the purposes desired half a dozen would be as valuable as half a hundred, I determined to seize the principal chiefs then present, and permit the others to depart. To do this without taking or losing life now became the problem. Indicating in a quiet manner to some of my men who were nearest to me to be ready to prevent the escape of three or four of the Indians whom I pointed out, I then directed Romeo to command silence on the part of the Indians, and to inform them that I was about to communicate something of great importance to them. This was sufficient to attract their undivided attention. I then rose from my seat near the fire, and unbuckling my revolver from my waist asked the Indians to observe that I threw my weapons upon the ground, as an evidence that in what I was about to do I did not desire or propose to shed blood unless forced to do so. I then asked the chiefs to look about them and count the armed men whom I had posted among and around them, completely cutting off every avenue of escape. They had attempted, under pretence of a friendly visit to my camp, to deceive me, in order that their village might elude us, but their designs had been frustrated, and they were now in our power. I asked them to quietly submit to what was now inevitable, and promised them that if they and their people responded in the proper manner to the reasonable demands which I intended to make, all would be well, and they would be restored to their people.

The reader must not imagine that this was listened to in tame silence by the thoroughly excited Indians, old and young. Upon the first intimation from me regarding the armed men, and before I could explain their purpose, every Indian who was dismounted sprang instantly to his feet, while those who were mounted gathered the reins of their ponies; all drew their revolvers or strung their bows, and for a few moments it seemed as if nothing could avert a collision, which could only terminate in the annihilation of the Indians, and an equal or perhaps greater loss on our part. A single shot fired, an indiscreet word uttered, would have been the signal to commence. My men behaved admirably, taking their positions in such manner that each Indian was confronted by at least two men. All this time the Indians were gesticulating and talking in the most excited manner; the boys and young men counselling resistance, the older men and chiefs urging prudence until an understanding could be had.

The powers of Romeo as interpreter were employed without stint, in repeating to the chiefs my urgent appeals to restrain their young men and avoid bloodshed. Even at this date I recall no more exciting experience with Indians than the occasion of which I now write. Near me stood a tall, grayhaired chief, who, while entreating his people to be discreet, kept his cocked revolver in his hand ready for use, should the emergency demand it. He was one of the few whom I had determined to hold. Near him stood another, a most powerful and forbidding-looking warrior, who was without firearms, but who was armed with a bow, already strung, and a quiver full of iron-pointed arrows. His coolness during this scene of danger and excitement was often the subject of remark afterward between the officers whose attention had been drawn to him. He stood apparently unaffected by the excitement about him, but not unmindful of the surrounding danger. Holding his bow in one hand, with the other he continued to draw from his quiver arrow after arrow. Each one he would examine as coolly as if he expected to engage in target practice. First he would cast his eye along the shaft of the arrow, to see if it was perfectly straight and true. Then he would with thumb and finger gently feel the point and edge of the barbed head, returning to the quiver each one whose condition did not satisfy him.

In this manner he continued until he had selected perhaps half a dozen arrows, with which he seemed satisfied, and which he retained in his hand, while his quick eye did not permit a single incident about him to escape unnoticed. The noise of voices and the excitement increased until a movement began on the part of the Indians who were mounted, principally the young men and boys. If the latter could be allowed to escape and the chiefs be retained, the desired object would be gained. Suddenly a rush was made. But for the fact that my men were ordered not to fire, the attempt of the Indians would not have been successful. I, as well as the other officers near me, called upon the men not to fire. The result was that all but four broke through the lines and made their escape. The four detained, however, were those desired, being chiefs and warriors of prominence.

Forming my men about them in such impassable ranks that a glance was sufficient to show how futile all further efforts to escape would prove, I then explained to the four captive Indians that I knew the design under which they had visited our camp; that I also knew that in their village were held as captives two white girls, whose release the troops were there to enforce, and to effect their release, as well as to compel the Cheyennes to abandon the war path and return to their reservation, I had seized the four Indians as hostages. To prove my sincerity and earnest desire to arrange these matters amicably, and without resort to force, the Indians were told they might select one of their number, whom I would release and send as a messenger of peace to the village, the latter having left in indiscriminate flight as soon as the seizure of the chiefs was made.

It became a matter of great difficulty, without the employment of forces to induce the four Indians to give up their arms. I explained to them that they were prisoners, and it was one of our customs to disarm all men held as prisoners. Should they be released, however, I assured them their arms would be restored to them. No argument could prevail upon them to relinquish their arms until I stated to them that a persistence in their refusal would compel me to summon a sufficient number of men to take the arms by force; and it was even necessary to parade the men in front of them before the arms were finally given up. After a lengthy conference with each other, they announced that they had agreed upon one of their number who, in accordance with my promise, should be released and sent to the tribe as bearer of my demands, and of any messages they might desire to send to their people.

I accordingly caused bountiful presents of coffee and sugar to be given the one so chosen, returned to him his pony and arms, and intrusted him with verbal messages to his tribe, the substance of which was as follows: First, I demanded the unconditional surrender of the two white girls held captive in the village; hitherto surrenders of white captives by Indians had only been made on payment of heavy ransom. Second, I required the Cheyenne village, as an evidence of peaceable intentions and good faith on their part, to proceed at once to their reservation, and to locate near Camp Supply, reporting to the military commander at that station. Third, I sent a friendly message to Little Robe, inviting him to visit me with a view to the speedy settlement of the questions at issue, promising him unmolested transit coming and returning for him and as many of his people as chose to visit me. In case of failure to comply with the first two of my demands, hostilities would be continued, and my command would at once commence the pursuit of the village, which, considering its size and the poor condition of the ponies at that early season of the year, would be unable to escape from the cavalry.

The Indian who was to go as bearer of these demands was also invited to return, assured that whether the response of his people should prove favorable or not, he should be granted a safe-conduct between the camp and the village. Inwardly congratulating himself, no doubt, upon the good fortune which gave him his liberty, the messenger of peace or war, as his tribe might elect, took his departure for his village. With him went the earnest wishes for success of every inmate of the camp; but if this was the feeling of the command generally, who can realize the intense interest and anxiety with which young Brewster now awaited the result of this effort to secure the freedom of his sister? And if the two forlorn, helpless girls knew of the presence of troops of their own race, what must have been the bitter despondency, the painful relinquishment of all hope as they saw the village and its occupants commencing a hasty flight, and no apparent effort upon the part of the troops to effect their release?

What comfort it would have been to these ill-fated maidens could they have known, before being hurried from the village, of the steps already taken to restore them to home and friends, or better still, if one of them could have known that almost within the sound of her voice, a brother was patiently but determinedly biding the time that should restore his sister to his arms.

Relying upon the influence which I believed Little Robe would exert upon his people, and knowing the pressure we were able to bring to bear through the three chiefs we held as hostages, I felt confident that sooner or later the Cheyennes would be forced to release the two white girls from their captivity. Placing a strong guard over the three chiefs, and warning them not to attempt to escape if they valued their lives, I returned to my tent after having ordered every comfort possible to be provided for our prisoners consistent with their position.

It was perhaps an hour or more after dark when an Indian voice was heard calling from one of the hillocks overlooking the camp. I proceeded to the guard fire near which the three chiefs were still seated engaged in conversation, and through Romeo inquired who the parties were whose voices we heard, and their object. They informed me that the voices were those of some of their young men who were anxious to ascertain if their friends the captives were still alive. Anxious that they should not only see that their friends were alive, but well treated, I desired to induce them to come within our lines and visit the captive chiefs. This was communicated to them through the chiefs, who called to them in tones capable of being heard far beyond the point at which the young Indians were posted. But this did not satisfy their suspicious natures; they imagined some trap, and declined to accept the invitation. Romeo, the only one who could converse freely in the Indian tongue, might have been able to persuade them to come in, but it was not safe for him to venture beyond the line of our pickets and trust himself in the power of the young Indians.

In this emergency I thought of Mo-nah-see-tah, in whom I had every confidence, and who I believed might be successful in inducing her friends to come in. Sending for her, I soon acquainted her with my plan, to which she gave her ready assent, only expressing an apprehension that in passing our own chain of sentries in the darkness, they might mistake her for an enemy and fire upon her. This difficulty I removed by offering to escort her safely through the line of pickets, and there await her return. Starting at once in the darkness, she clinging to my hand with the natural timidity of a girl, we proceeded to the picket station nearest to the point from which the sound of voices had come, and after explaining to the sentry our purpose, passed beyond as far as it was prudent to do, and then, bidding Mo-nah-see-tah to proceed on her mission, I halted to await her return. A few moments later I heard her voice in the darkness calling to her friends beyond; back came the quick response, and soon after I could distinguish the tones of the assembled group as Mo-nah-see-tah endeavored to convince them of their security in trusting to the promises made them.

Her arguments finally prevailed over their suspicions, and in the dim light of the stars I could see her returning, accompanied by four or five others. Not caring to tempt them by meeting them alone so far from support, I slowly retired until I was near the picket post. Here the Indians found me, and after the form of an introduction by Mo-nah see-tah and a general hand-shaking, the entire party proceeded without hesitation to the guard fire, where they joined their less fortunate chiefs.

It may strike the reader with some surprise that Mo-nah-see-tah, herself a captive in our hands, should have voluntarily returned to us that night after once being safely beyond our lines. But she only confirmed the confidence that was placed in her. During her imprisonment, if her stay in our camp without a guard may be termed imprisonment, she had become a great favorite with the entire command; not only this, but she believed she would in due time be given up to her own people, and that until then she would receive kind treatment at our hands and be exposed to less personal danger and suffering during hostilities than if with her village.

The visit of the young men to our camp that night could not but have a beneficial influence upon the tribe, as they were enabled to see that the three chiefs were being treated with the utmost consideration, and were being held, as informed at first, simply as hostages, to enforce compliance with demands which even an Indian's ideas of right and wrong must pronounce just. After a lengthy conversation between the captives and their friends, the latter took their departure, charged with messages to the village, both from the captive chiefs and me, similar to those transmitted through the chief who had been released for that purpose.

The following day was passed without incident in awaiting the arrival of tidings from the village. Early in the afternoon the pickets reported a small body of Indians in sight. Upon a nearer approach the party appeared to consist of about fifty mounted Indians. They rode steadily in the direction of the camp, with no apparent wish to conceal their movements, thus indicating that they were on an errand of peace. When within half a mile or less of camp the entire party dismounted, and after picketing their ponies out to graze, advanced on foot directly toward camp. So strange a proceeding, and at a time when the excitement regarding our relations with the Indians ran high, was sufficient to assemble nearly all the occupants of camp to watch the approach of this delegation of Indians. The latter were apparelled in their best and most highly colored clothes. As they came near, it was perceived that several paces in advance of the main group strode two chiefs, evidently leaders of the party; both advanced with uncovered heads. Suddenly I thought I detected a familiar face and form in the taller of the two chiefs in front, and on more careful scrutiny I recognized my former friend and guest Little Robe, who had thus quickly responded to my invitation to cast aside all doubts and come and visit me, with a view to bringing about more friendly relations between his people and the whites.

As soon as I recognized him I advanced to meet him. He grasped my hand and embraced me with what seemed to me real cordiality. Waiting until the other members of his party came up, I shook hands with each individual, and then invited them to my tent. As the tent would not accommodate the entire party, Little Robe designated about a dozen of the most important, who entered, while the others remained outside. I soon found that in Little Robe I had a hearty coadjutor in the work before me. He admitted that the white girls were held as captives in the Cheyenne village, which was the first positive evidence received of this fact. He also stated, what I had no reason to doubt, that he had at various times attempted to purchase them, with a view, if successful, of returning them to the nearest military post; but his efforts in this direction had always failed. He admitted the justice of my demands upon his people, and assured me that to bring about a satisfactory condition of affairs he would use every exertion and employ all the influence at his command. It was to assure me of this desire on his part that he had hastened to visit me.

Knowing that the surest and speediest way to establish a state of good feeling in an Indian is to provide liberally for the wants of his stomach, I ordered a beef to be killed and distributed among the followers of Little Robe; with this also were distributed the usual supplies of coffee, sugar, flour, etc., so that the recipients were not only prepared to regard us as at least very kindly disposed, but I knew the effect on the village, when the result of the visit, and the treatment extended to our guests was described, would materially aid us in our negotiations with the tribe.

Little Robe, while earnest in his desire to see the white girls returned to us, frankly admitted that his influence was not supreme, and there were those who would object to their release, at least without compensation; and it might be that a satisfactory settlement of the question might be delayed for many days.

After partaking of a bountiful repast, Little Robe and his party set out for the village, promising to send me word the following day as to his success. Another day was passed in waiting, when the chief who had accompanied Little Robe the previous day again visited us, but brought no decisive or satisfactory reply. The substance of the reply was that the Cheyennes desired us to release the three chiefs then held by us as hostages, after which they would be prepared to consider the question of the release of the two white girls. To this I sent back a reply that we would remain in the camp we then occupied until the following day, when, if a favorable answer should not have been received, we would follow on their trail and encamp nearer to the village, the great distance then separating us, about twelve miles, being a hindrance in the way of transmitting messages promptly from one to the other.

I knew that the village was in no condition for a rapid or extended flight, and could be overhauled by the cavalry whenever desired; at the same time, to allow as much freedom in their deliberations as possible, I had not been unwilling that a few miles should separate us. No reply was received; consequently we packed up and marched down the Sweetwater, on the trail of the village, about ten miles, and went into camp. Here I received another visit from the chief who had previously acted as diplomatic courier between the camp and village, but the response of the Cheyennes was still unsatisfactory, and exhibited a disinclination on their part to make any decided promises respecting the release of the captive white girls. They insisted as preliminary to such decision that the three chiefs held by us should be restored to liberty, after which we might discuss the question relating to the release of the girls.

I will not weary the reader by describing the various subterfuges resorted to by the Indians, by which they strove to avoid or delay the surrender of the white girls without first, as had been customary, receiving a ransom. Finally, after I had almost exhausted the patience of the troops, particularly of the Kansas regiment which had been raised and organized mainly to effect the recapture of the white girls, or else avenge the outrage of which they had been the victims, I determined to force matters to an issue without further quibbling on the part of the Indians.

I sent for a delegation of chiefs from the Cheyenne village to receive my ultimatum. They came, and upon their arrival I assembled them in my tent, the three captured chiefs being also permitted to be present, as the conference, as will be seen, was to be of deep interest to them. After recounting to the chiefs the incidents of our pursuit of the village, their surprise at being overtaken, the stratagems by which they hoped to elude us, the steps we had already taken to obtain the release of the white girls, and the delays interposed by the Indians, I stated that I had but one other message to send to the village; and upon the chiefs of the latter would rest the responsibility of peace or war. Further delay would not be submitted to on our part. We knew they had two of our race captives in the village, and we were there to demand and enforce the demand for their release, cost what it might. I then informed them that if by sunset the following day the two white girls were not restored to our hands unharmed, the lives of the three chiefs would be forfeited, and the troops would resume active hostilities. At the same time I called attention to the fact that in the famished condition of their ponies they could not expect to escape the pursuit of the cavalry. Every argument which might have weight in influencing a favorable decision was stated to them. The conference then broke up, and the three chiefs were remanded to the custody of the guard. The delegation from the village, after a brief interview with their captive comrades, took a hasty departure, and set out upon their return to the village, deeply impressed, apparently, with the importance of promptness in communicating to the chiefs at the village the decision which had been arrived at regarding the captives.

The terms given to the Indians soon became known to every individual in the command, and naturally excited the deepest interest. All hoped for a favorable issue, but no one regarded the events then transpiring with the intense interest and anxiety felt by young Brewster, who now saw that his long-cherished hope to recover his sister was either about to be realized, or forever sealed in disappointment.

The captive chiefs did not pretend to conceal their solicitude as to the part they were involuntarily made to play in the events then transpiring. I did not expect prompt action on the part of the chiefs in the village. I knew they would practise every delay conceivable before complying with our demands; but when the question was forced upon them as to whether they preferred to deliver up the white girls to us or to force by their refusal the execution of the three chiefs, their decision would be in favor of their people.

Three o'clock arrived, and no tidings from the village. By this time the officers and men of the command had assembled near headquarters, and upon the small eminences near by, eagerly watching the horizon in the direction of the village, to catch the first glimpse of the messengers who must soon arrive to avert the execution of the three chiefs. Even the three chiefs became despondent as the sun slowly but surely approached the horizon, and no tidings from the village reached them. Finally Romeo came to me and stated that the three chiefs desired to see me. I repaired to their place of confinement at once, and was asked by the younger of the three if it was my firm purpose to make good my words in the event of the failure of their people to release the white girls. I replied in the affirmative. The chief then attempted a little Indian diplomacy, by assuring me that in the village and among his own people he was a man of great consequence, and could exert a wide influence; for this reason he requested me to release him, and he would hasten to the village, obtain the release of the two girls, and return in time to save his two companions.

When this proposition was first made I attributed it to fear that the chiefs in the village might decline to restore the two girls to liberty, and the lives of the three chiefs would be sacrificed thereby; but subsequent events proved that while this consideration may have had its influence, the principal motive which prompted the proposition was a desire to escape from our hands before the white girls should be restored to us, as the chief referred to had been a party to their capture and to the subsequent ill treatment they had received.

I replied to his proposal, that if he was of such importance in his tribe as he claimed to be, he was the most proper person for me to retain possession of, as his people would be more likely to accede to my demands to save his life than that of a person of less consequence.

The sun was perhaps an hour high when the dim outlines of about twenty mounted figures were discerned against the horizon, on a high hill, two or three miles to the west of us. Instantly all eyes were directed to the party, but the distance was too great to enable any of us to clearly define either the number or character of the group. The eyes of the three chiefs perceptibly brightened with hope. Securing my field glass, I carefully scanned the party on the hill. Every one about me waited in anxious suspense the result of my examination. Gradually, under the magnifying powers of the glass, I was able to make out the figures in sight. I could only determine at first that the group was, as might be imagined, composed of Indians, and began counting them audibly, when I discovered two figures mounted upon the same pony.

As soon as this was announced several of my companions at once exclaimed, "Can they be the girls?" I could detect nothing, however, in their appearance warranting such a conclusion, their dress apparently being the same as that of the other individuals of the group. While endeavoring to make out something more definite in regard to the party, I saw the two figures descend from the pony, and, leaving the rest of the group, advance toward us on foot. All this I reported to the anxious bystanders, who became now more than ever convinced that the two figures approaching must be the two girls. I began describing the appearance of the two as well as I could, with the aid of the glass: "One seems to have a short, heavy figure; the other is considerably taller and more slender." Young Brewster, who stood at my side, immediately responded, "The last one must be my sister; she is quite tall. Let me go and meet them; this anxiety is more than I can endure." But this I declined, fearing that should one of the two now approaching us prove to be his sister, seeing her in the forlorn condition in which she must be might provoke young Brewster beyond control, and induce him to attempt to obtain revenge in a manner not governed by either prudence or propriety. So I reluctantly declined to permit him to advance beyond our lines. But by this time the two figures had approached near enough to enable me clearly to determine that they were really of white complexion, and undoubtedly the two girls whose release we were so impatiently waiting for.

As the Kansas volunteers had left their homes and various occupations in civil life to accomplish, among other results, the release of the two girls who had been abducted from the frontier of their State, I deemed it appropriate that that regiment should be the first to welcome the two released captives to friends and freedom. Accordingly the three senior officers of the regiment were designated to proceed beyond our lines and conduct the two girls to camp —a duty whose performance carried its pleasure with it. The three officers advanced to meet the two figures (I use the term figures, as the dress was of that nondescript pattern which renders this term most appropriate). They had passed one fourth of the distance, perhaps, when young Brewster, whom I had detained at my side with difficulty, bounded away, and the next moment was running at full speed to greet his long-lost sister. Dashing past the three officers, he clasped in his arms the taller of the two girls. This told us all we had hoped for. We awaited their approach, and as they drew near to the little brook which flowed just beyond the point occupied by the group of officers around me, I stepped forward, and extending my hands to the two girls, bade them a hearty welcome to liberty. In a moment officers and men were struggling about them upon all sides, eager to take them by the hand, and testify the great joy felt at their deliverance from a life of captivity.

Men whom I have seen face death without quailing found their eyes filled with tears, unable to restrain the deep emotion produced by this joyful event. The appearance of the two girls was sufficient to excite our deepest sympathy. Miss White, the younger of the two, though not beautiful, possessed a most interesting face. Her companion would have been pronounced beautiful by the

THE TWO GIRLS ATTEMPT TO ESCAPE.

21

most critical judge, being of such a type as one might imagine Maud Müller to be.

Their joy at their deliverance, however, could not hide the evidences of privation and suffering to which they had been subjected by their cruel captors. They were clothed in dresses made from flour sacks, the brand of the mills being plainly seen on each dress; showing that the Indians who had held them in captivity had obtained their provisions from the Government at some agency. The entire dress of the two girls was as nearly like the Indian mode as possible; both wore leggings and moccasins; both wore their hair in two long braids, and as if to propitiate us, the Indians, before releasing them, had added to the wardrobe of the two girls various rude ornaments, such as are worn by squaws. About their wrists they wore coils of brass wire; on their fingers had been placed numerous rings, and about their necks strings of variously colored beads. Almost the first remark I heard young Brewster make after the arrival of the two girls was, "Sister, do take those hateful things off."

Fortunately they were not the only white women in camp. I had a white woman as cook, and to enable the two girls to improve their wardrobe a little before relating to us the history of their capture and captivity, they were conducted to the tent of the white woman referred to, from whose limited wardrobe they were able to obtain enough to replace the dresses made of flour sacks, and in a few minutes reappeared presenting a much more civilized appearance than when they first entered camp.

In a previous chapter I have given the main incidents of their capture. The story of their captivity was that of hundreds of other women and girls whose husbands, fathers, or brothers take their lives in their hands and seek homes on the frontier. There was much in their story not appropriate for these pages. They described how great their joy was at encountering each other for the first time as prisoners in the hands of the Indians. They had been traded repeatedly from the hands of one chief to those of another, the last transfer having been effected only two weeks prior to their release. Soon after their first meeting, it was their good fortune, comparatively, to become the property of one chief. This threw them into each other's society, and tended to lighten the horrors of their captivity. While thrown together in this manner, they planned an escape. Their plan, it seems, was more the result of desperation than of careful deliberation, as they had no idea as to what state or territory the village was then in, nor in what direction to travel should they escape from the village. Indeed, one of their first questions on entering our lines was to ask in what part of the country we were.

Determining at all hazards, however, to flee from their captors at the first opportunity, and trust to chance to lead them to the settlements or to some military post, they escaped from the village one night and travelled for several hours in a northerly direction. During this attempt to regain their liberty, they reached a wagon road, over which wagons and horses had passed recently, and were congratulating themselves upon the success of their effort, when a bullet whistled past them, and in close proximity to them. Casting an anxious look, they saw, to their horror and disappointment, their late captor or owner riding at full speed in pursuit. Escape was impossible. Nothing remained but to await the arrival of the chief, who came up excited with savage rage at the idea of their attempt to escape him. Marching back on foot to the village, they became the recipients of renewed insults and taunts. Nor did it end here. The squaws of the village, always jealous of white women when captives, took this opportunity to treat them with the greatest severity for their attempt to regain their liberty. The old chief, also, decided upon a change of programme. He had invested several ponies when he became the possessor of the two girls, and he did not propose to risk the loss of this property. So he determined to separate the two girls by selling one of them; and the two friends in misfortune were torn from each other. Miss White, in consideration of three ponies given in exchange, passed into the hands of another chief, whose lodge was generally located some miles from that of her late master.

The story of the two girls, containing accounts of wrongs and ill treatment sufficient to have ended the existence of less determined persons, is too long to be given here. Besides indignities and insults far more terrible than death itself, the physical suffering to which the two girls were subjected was too great almost to be believed. They were required to transport huge burdens on their backs, large enough to have made a load for a beast of burden. They were limited to barely enough food to sustain life; sometimes a small morsel of mule meat, not more than an inch square, was their allowance of food for twenty-four hours. The squaws beat them unmercifully with clubs whenever the men were not present. Upon one occasion one of the girls was felled to the ground by a blow from a club in the hands of one of the squaws. Their joy therefore at regaining their freedom after a captivity of nearly a year can be better imagined than described; while that of the brother who had struggled so long and determinedly to regain his sister could not be expressed in words.

After the momentary excitement consequent upon the safe arrival of the girls in camp had subsided, officers, particularly of the Kansas volunteers, came to me with the remark that when we first overtook the Cheyenne village and I failed to order an attack when all the chances were in our favor, they mentally condemned my decision as a mistake; but with the results accomplished afterwards they found ample reason to amend their first judgment, and frankly and cordially admit that the release of the two captives was far more gratifying than any victory over the Indians could have been if purchased by the sacrifice of their lives.

With this happy termination of this much of our negotiations with the Indians, I determined to march in the morning for Camp Supply, Indian Territory, satisfied that with the three chiefs in our possession, and the squaws and children captured at the Washita still held as prisoners at Fort Hays, Kansas, we could compel the Cheyennes to abandon the war path and return to their reservation. The three chiefs begged to be released, upon the ground that their people had delivered up the two girls; but this I told them was but one of the two conditions imposed; the other required the tribe to return to their reservation, and until this was done they need not hope for freedom; but in the mean while I assured them of kind treatment at our hands.

Before dark a delegation of chiefs from the village visited camp to likewise urge the release of the three chiefs. My reply to them was the same as that I had given to the captives. I assured them, however, that upon complying with their treaty obligations, and returning to their reservation, the three chiefs would be restored to their people, and we would return to them also the women and children captured at the Washita. Seeing that no modification of these terms could be obtained, they finally promised to accede to them, saying that their ponies, as I knew to be the fact, were in no condition to travel, but as soon as practicable they would surely proceed with their entire village to Camp Supply, and abandon the war path forever; a promise which, as a tribe, they have adhered to, from that day to this, with strict faith, so far as my knowledge extends.

I had not heard from General Sheridan since we separated at Fort Sill; he to set out for Camp Supply, and I with my command to begin my present movement. But when near Camp Supply a courier met me with despatches from General Sheridan—who had been meanwhile summoned to Washington —informing me in regard to the arrangements made for my command upon its arrival at Camp Supply. The Kansas volunteers were to march to Fort Hays, and there be mustered out of the service. The Seventh Cavalry was also to proceed to the same point, and there await further orders, as the General in his note stated that he had concluded to draw in the Seventh, and end the campaign.

In reply to my letter, written subsequently from Camp Supply, giving him a detailed account of our operations, including the release of the two white girls, I received a letter of warm encouragement from the General, written from Chicago, where he had just established his present headquarters. In that letter he wrote: " I am very much rejoiced at the success of your expedition, and feel proud of our winter's operations and of the officers and men who have borne its privations and hardships so manfully. . . . Give my kind regards to the officers, and say how happy I should be to see them should any of them come this way on leave." These words of hearty sympathy and approval, from one who had not only shared but appreciated at their true worth our " privations and hardships," were far more cheering and valued than the empty honor contained in half a dozen brevets bestowed grudgingly, and recalled in a moment of pique.

Making a brief halt at Camp Supply to rest our animals and replenish our stores, my command continued its march to Fort Hays, crossing the Arkansas river at Fort Dodge, Kansas. Upon our arrival at Fort Hays we were met by the husband of young Brewster's sister, who had learned of her restoration to liberty from the published despatches which had preceded us to Fort Hays. He was still lame from the effects of the bullet wound received at the time the Indians carried off his bride, whom he had given up as dead or lost to him forever. The joy of their meeting went far to smooth over their late sorrow. They could not find language to express their gratitude to the troops for their efforts in restoring them to each other. As the Indians had robbed them of everything at the time of the attack, a collection was taken up among the troops for their benefit, which resulted in the accumulation of several hundred dollars, to be divided between the two captives. The time came for our guests to leave us, and rejoin their people, or such of them as had survived the attack of the Indians. Good-bys were spoken, and the two girls, so lately victims of the most heartless and cruel captivity, departed, with husband, brother, and friends, for their frontier homes, bearing with them the warm sympathies and cordial good wishes of every soldier in the command.

Mo-nah-see-tah was anxious to visit her friends who were now captives at Fort Hays, and who were kept in a large stockade at the post, our camp being placed some two or three miles below the post. Accordingly she repaired to the stockade, and spent several hours, relating, no doubt, the story of our march since they had separated from each other. She preferred to live in the cavalry camp, where she was allowed to roam without the restraint of a guard; but it was deemed advisable soon after to place her with the other women and children inside the stockade. The three captive chiefs were also transferred to the same place for safe keeping. Here a most unfortunate misunderstanding arose. The chiefs had been confined inside the same enclosure with the women and children, but in separate tents. The commanding officer of the post decided to remove them to rooms in the guardhouse, adjoining the stockade. This was decided upon as a measure of security. There was no interpreter kept at the post; consequently there was no way of communicating with the Indians except by rude signs, and even this method was but indifferently understood by the infantry soldiers constituting the garrison of the post. From accounts given me by the Indians afterwards, it seems the men of the guard, in the execution of the order to transfer the three chiefs, entered the stockade muskets in hand, and upon the failure of the chiefs to comprehend what was required of them, the soldiers attempted to push the chiefs from the stockade by force, pointing with their bayonets to the outside. The chiefs, failing to understand a word spoken to them, and with the natural suspicion of their race, imagined that they were being led or driven forth to execution, and determined to die there and then. An attack was at once made upon the guard with knives which they carried beneath their blankets. The sergeant of the guard received a stab in the back which almost proved mortal. This was the signal for a determined fight between the three chiefs and the guard, the latter having the decided advantage in numbers and weapons. The result could not be long doubtful. One of the chiefs, Big Head, the young man who had proposed to proceed to the village and obtain the release of the two white girls, fell dead at the first fire of the guard. The oldest of the three, Dull Knife, received a bayonet wound through the body which proved fatal in a few days. The third, Fat Bear, was felled by a blow from the butt of a musket, but did not receive serious injury.

Knowing that I could converse with the Indians, and from my acquaintance with them might be able to quiet the excitement among the remaining prisoners, the commanding officer of the post sent to me for assistance. Upon repairing to the stockade, I found the women and children in a state of great excitement and huddled together inside their tents. Entering the stockade, I soon learned their version of the affair, which did not vary materially from that just given. Mo-nah-see-tah pointed to a bullet-hole in her blanket, the effect of a stray shot fired during the mêlée. The affair was a source of deep regret to all.

The Cheyennes, in accordance with their promise made to me, returned to their reservation; and having thus far complied with the terms of the agreement then made, it devolved upon the military authorities to return to them their people whom we had, up to that time and since the battle of the Washita, retained as prisoners of war. An order was accordingly issued releasing the only surviving chief, Fat Bear, and the women and children then held at Fort Hays. Wagons and subsistence were furnished them from Fort Hays to Camp Supply, and a squadron of the Seventh Cavalry escorted them to the latter point, where they were received by their own people. Monah-see-tah, although gladdened by the prospect of being restored to her people, exhibited marked feelings of regret when the time for her departure arrived. She had grown quite accustomed to the easy, idle life she had led among the troops, as compared with that mere existence of toil and drudgery to which all tribes of Indians consign their squaws.

ROMERO THE INTERPRETER AND HIS WIFE.

Romeo, who had accompanied us throughout the events described in these pages as interpreter, took unto himself a wife from the Cheyenne village, and thereafter became a sort of trader between the whites and Indians. I believe he is still acting in that capacity. Lone Wolf is still the leading chief of the Kiowas; but if public and private advices are to be relied upon, he has acted with extremely bad faith toward the Government, and even as these lines are being penned is reported as absent from his reservation, leading a war party of his people in committing depredations upon the people of the Texas frontier. Satanta, since his release from the Texas State prison, has led a comparatively quiet and uneventful life. How much of this is due to his incarceration in prison for a short term of years can only be inferred. Little Raven continues to exercise the powers of head chief of the Arapahoes, although he is too old and infirm to exercise active command. My former friend and companion, Yellow Bear, is the second chief in rank to Little Raven, and probably will succeed to the dignities of the latter ere many years have rolled around. Little Robe, of the Cheyennes, whose acts and words were always on the side of peace, died some three years ago.

A few words in regard to one other character with whom the reader of these sketches has been made acquainted, and I shall have disposed of the principal personages, not included in the military, whom the reader has encountered from time to time. California Joe accompanied my command to Fort Hays, Kansas, on the Kansas Pacific railroad, when the troops were partially disbanded and sent to different stations. California Joe had never seen a railroad nor a locomotive, and here determined to improve his first opportunity in these respects, and to take a trip in the cars to Leavenworth, distant about four hundred miles. A few days afterward an officer of my command, happening to be called to Leavenworth, thought he recognized a familiar form and face in front of the leading hotel of the city. A closer scrutiny showed that the party recognized was none other than California Joe. But how changed! Under the manipulations of the barber, and through the aid of the proprietor of a gentleman's furnishing store, the long, curly locks and beard of California Joe, both of which had avoided contact with comb, brush, or razor for many years, had undergone a complete metamorphosis. His hair and beard were neatly trimmed and combed, while his figure, a very commanding one, had discarded the rough suit of the frontiersman, and was now adorned by the latest efforts of fashion. If the reader imagines, however, that these changes were in keeping with the taste of California Joe, the impression is wholly incorrect. He had effected them simply for a sensation. The following day he took the cars for the West, satisfied with the faint glimpse of civilization he had had.

As I soon after left that portion of the plains in which these scenes are laid, I saw no more of California Joe; but I often wondered what had become of my loquacious friend, whose droll sayings and quaint remarks had often served to relieve the tedium of the march or to enliven the group about the camp-fire. I had begun, after a few years had passed without trace or tidings from Joe, to fear that he had perhaps gone to that happy hunting ground to which he no doubt had sent more than one dusky enemy, when a few weeks ago I was most agreeably surprised to receive indubitable evidence that California Joe was still in the land of the living, but exactly where I could not determine, as his letter was simply dated "Sierre Nevade Mountains, California." Now as this range of mountains extends through the entire length and embraces a considerable portion of the State of California, Joe's address could not be definitely determined. But as his letter is so characteristic of the man, I here introduce it as the valedictory of California Joe:

SIERRE NEVADE MOUNTAINS, CALEFORNIA, March 16, 1874.

Dear General after my respets to you and Lady i thought that i tell you that i am still on top of land yit i hev been in the rockey mountain the most of the time sence last I seen you but i got on the railroad and started west and the first thing I knew I landed in san Francisco so I could not go any further except goin by water and salt water at that so i turned back and headed for the mountains once more resolved never to go railroading no more i drifted up with the tide to sacramento city and i landed my boat so i took up through town they say thar is 20 thousand people living thar but it looks to me like to be 10ꝰ thousand counting chinaman and all i cant describe my wolfish feeling but i think that i look just like i did when we was chasing Buffalo on the cimarone so i struck up through town and i come to a large fine building crowded with people so　bulged in to see what was going on and when i got in to the counsil house i took a look around at the crowd and i seen the most of them had bald heads so i thought to myself i struck it now that they are indian peace commissioners so i look to see if i would know any of them but not one so after while the smartess lookin one got up and said gentlemen i introduce a bill to have speckle mountain trout and fish eggs imported to california to be put in the american Bear and yuba rivers—those rivers is so muddy that a tadpole could not live in them caused by mining—did any body ever hear of speckle trout living in muddy water and the next thing was the game law and that was very near as bad as the Fish for they aint no game in the country as big as mawking bird i heard some fellow behind me ask how long is the legislaturs been in session then i dropt on myself it wuzent Indian commissioners after all so i slid out took across to chinatown and they smelt like a kiowa camp in August with plenty buffalo meat around – it was gettin late so no place to go not got a red cent so i happen to think of an old friend back of town that i knowed 25 years ago so i lit out and sure enough he was thar just as i left him 25 years ago baching [leading the life of bachelor—G. A. C.] so i got a few seads i going to plant in a few days give my respects to the 7th calvery and except the same yoursly

CALIFORNIA JOE.

The events described in this chapter terminated my service in the field on what is known as the southern and middle plains, embracing all that portion of the plains south of the Platte river. From and after the Washita campaign the frontiers of Kansas have enjoyed comparative peace and immunity from Indian depredations. No general Indian war has prevailed in that part of the country, nor is it probable that anything more serious in this way than occasional acts of horse-stealing will occur hereafter. Many of my friends have expressed surprise that I have not included in "Life on the Plains" some of the hunting scenes and adventures which have formed a part of my experience; but I feared the introduction of this new feature, although probably the pleasantest and in many respects most interesting of my recollections of border life, might prolong the series of articles far beyond the length originally assigned to them. I hope, however, at an early day to relate some of my experiences with the large game so abundant on the plains, and in this way fill up a blank in these articles which my friends who are lovers of sport have not failed to observe.

As I pen these lines, I am in the midst of scenes of bustle and busy preparation attendant upon the organization and equipment of a large party for an important exploring expedition, on which I shall start before these pages reach the publishers' hands. During my absence I expect to visit a region of country as yet unseen by human eyes, except those of the Indian—a country described by the latter as abounding in game of all varieties, rich in scientific interest, and of surpassing beauty in natural scenery. Bidding adieu to civilization for the next few months, I also now take leave of my readers, who I trust, in accompanying me through my retrospect, have been enabled to gain a true insight into a cavalryman's "Life on the Plains."

XXI.

While we were seated around the camp fire one pleasant evening, a young corporal asked California Joe what was the narrowest escape he ever had from Indians.

"What wur the clusset 'scape I iver hed from the Injuns? Wall, young feller, I reckon thur's so mony on 'em, its mighty hard to purtickilurize, like. Did I iver tell ye 'bout the time I got away frum the Crows, upon the Yallerstun? Didn't? Wall, thet wur clost enuf, I kin tell ye.

" 'Twur nigh onto thirty years ago thet I wur trappin' round Chimley Rock, all alone by myself. I wur a mighty ventursome lad them days, an' thort nuthin' at all 'bout the risk, 's long 's beaver wur plenty, — an' 'pears to me I never see game so thick as 'twas that year.

"I'd made myself a camp on a little island in the river, and was hevin' the best of luck — didn't see a Injun, or the sign o' one for nigh two months, an' got careless, like.

"Wall, in visitin' my traps one arternoon, I seen bar signs. Not a grizzly, I know too much to go arter one o' them fellers 'ithout a kumrade, — no, this wur a thunderin' big black bar, from his tracks, an' I made up my mind to trail him in the mornin'.

"I started out soon arter sunup, an' followed the trail till late in the arternoon, an' I lost it in the shingle. 'Twur gittin' late, an' I concluded to go back to camp. As near's I could jedge, I wur about eight miles frum camp, but not more 'n a mile frum the river, fur the trail hed run kinder parallel to it, ye see.

"Thur wur a spring clost by whur I left the trail, an' I stopped to git a drink afore startin'. I wur jest risin' up frum the water, when I heerd a twig snap; an' lookin' up, I see five durned red niggers a comin' right to'rd me, an' not more 'n thirty rod off, either.

"I lit out o' that mighty suddint, you can bet, an', in course, the minute they seen they wur diskivered, they give a yell an' come tearin' arter me. My jints was a blamed sight more supple them days than they be now, an' the way I legged it wasn't slow, I reckon. I made fur the river, thinkin' mebbe I cud give 'em the slip an' git across, an' then I knew I could fool 'em and throw 'em of the trail among the rocks on that side.

"When I got down to the river bank 'twur dark, an' gittin'

darker every minute, bein' as thur wur a fog risin' from the water.

" I cudn't hear nothin' of the Injuns, an, I begun to think mebbe they'd lost the trail. I hed a notion that they mought hev a canoe *cached* thur, so I kimmenced lookin' fur it. All to onct I heerd the niggers comin' down the bank. They'd struck the river a little above me.

" I wur badly skeered, I tell ye, fur thur wur no place to hide, an' I knowed well enough 'twan't no use strikin' back into the timber.

" ' I'm a gone case,' thinks I, ' wiped out, sure ! ' when jest as I come to that conclusion I spied a thunderin' big log, or, rather, a hull tree, thet had been brought down by the spring floods, an' jest lodged by one eend on the bank, t'other eend reachin' out into the stream.

" Wall, I wa'n't long in gittin' out to the far eend of the log, which wur partly under water, but afloat. I straddled the log, with my legs in the water, and held my rifle acrost it in front of me, an' then bowed myself down an' hugged the bark like a possum.

" Jist as I got settled, an' wur a thinkin' what a durned nice thing it 'ud be if the stick 'd only float off, down come the red-skins to the edge of the bank and stood thar, within fifty feet of me, a peerin' 'round, kinder puzzled like, as if they wur won-derin' whar on airth I'd got to.

" ' Wall,' thinks I, ' if they diskiver me now, they'll lift my har, to a sartinty.' They spoke to one another; but I couldn't make out what they wur sayin', though I knowed thur lingo tolla-ble well. D'reckly one on 'em spoke a little louder, and my ears wur sharp enough to catch the words. He 'peared to be the head buck of the party, and said to t'other niggers : —

" ' Whar is the canoe? It must be close by ; step on the log and find it. '

" One of 'em handed his gun to the next one, and, steppin' on to the log, began to walk to'rd me. P'r'aps I didn't hug bark and hold my breath as he stooped down a'most over me, and kimmenced feelin' fur the canoe.

" He didn't 'pear to find it quick enough to suit the fellers on the bank, and another of 'em jumped onto the log to help him. The jar sent the durned thing afloat, an' splash it cum right into the river, chuckin' the two red niggers into the water. 'Twa'n't no time fur laughin', but I wur fit to bust when I seed how the old log throwed 'em cawallup into the water.

CALIFORNIA JOE'S NARROW ESCAPE.

" Hows'ever, they mighty quick got hold of the log again, and, in a minute more, thur wur three of us sittin' straddle of it, and a-floatin' down-stream with a right smart current.

" Thet wur a durned purty purdickerment, wurn't it, young feller, floatin' down the Yallerstun straddle of a log, 'long with two pison-sarpents of Injuns?

" The fellers on shore, when they fust seed the fix we were in, set up a laugh, 's if they thort it wur a mighty good joke; but 'twarn't no laughin' matter — leastways, to me — and my *ship-mates* 'peared to be of the same 'pinion. They called to thur kumrades on the bank to hurry up and git the canoe and take 'em off.

" Meanwhile we had floated two or three hundred yards down-stream, an' I wur a-sittin' straddle o' the small eend, jist as quiet as a deer listenin' fur the hounds, an' wonderin' how I wur goin' to get out of the scrape.

"All to onct, one of the Injuns, in tryin' to shift his position on the log, rolled the thing part way over, and come durned near spillin' me into the water. In tryin' to save myself, I must 'a made considerable noise, fur, when I got fixed again, I cud hear 'em mutterin' to each other, an' seed thet they knowed thur wur somebody or sumthing onto the log beside themselves.

" How the Injuns looked I cudn't tell, fur it wur so dark I cudn't see thur faces, but they must hev been wuss skeered than I was, fur *I* knowed who *they* wur, but *they* didn't know who *I* wur.

" They kept on jabberin' to each other, and at first I thort mebbe they wur goin' to quit the float and streak it, but d'reckly they stopped talkin' and began peepin' t'rd whar I wur *cached*, like a couple of cock-turkeys lookin' fur worms.

" Then one of 'em said, ' Don't you see something? '

" ' Yes,' answered the other, ' dark lump — bear, perhaps.'

"And the first speaker calls out, ' Who's there? '

" I hed nothin' to say, an' I growed small so fast, tryin' to squeeze myself out of sight, that my skin hung as loose as a Mackinaw blanket on a lodge-pole. They kept peepin' at me, an' finally I heerd one say, ' It's no bar — it's a man. Look at his head ! '

" Jist about then I wur so mad at myself fur gittin' into such a durned fix, that I wished my head wur under the log, or any-where else 'cept on my shoulders; but I sot up straight, fur I knew they seen me, an' I thort it wa'n't no use to play 'possum no longer.

"Wall, when I straightened up, the Injun nearest me calls out again, 'Who's thar?' '*I* am here,' says I, speakin' in thur own language. The minute I opened my meat-trap he laughed an' says to the other nigger, 'He's a pale-face.' The reesin he knowed thet so quick wur bekase I cudn't speak thur durned jaw-breakin' lingo 'zactly right. Then he turned to'rd me agin an' said, 'What are you doin' there? 'Sittin' down straddle of the small eend,' says I. Then they both gave an unearthly war-whoop.

"I tell you, young feller, it made me feel skeery, fur it did seem as if I wur scooped sure. Then they told the other red-skins on shore to get the canoe an' be quick. The others answered 'em, an' ran down the shore, laughing an tryin' to find the canoe. I kinder made up my mind that something had got to be done mighty quick, an' my dander begun to rise. 'Come here,' says one of the Injuns on the log, beckonin' to me — 'come quick, before the others come. I want your scalp.'

"Wall, when he said thet, I cudn't stand it no longer. My har wa'n't a-goin' to hang in no Injun's lodge — not ef I cud help it; so I throwed up my rifle, took aim at the red nigger, an' blazed away. He gave a yell, jumped up like a buck, an' fell splash in the water. As soon as I fired, the Injuns on the bank screamed out the war-whoop, and the other redskin on the log yelled out to 'em to come quick and bring his gun. I jumped up and crawled to him; he gathered himself up and stood his ground. The fust thing I knowed, he cum down on me all of a heap, breakin' an old limb into a dozen pieces over my head and shoulders — lucky fur me the limb wur rotten. His blow staggered me for a minute, but I soon rekivered myself, and, catching my rifle with both hands, I give him a side-wipe with the bar'l that knocked him off inter the water. As he cum up, I grabbed him by the har, an' as he tried to git up on the log, I jest held him under water.

"Bein' on the log an' he in the river, I ruther had him in a fix, and I jest kept bobbin' his head under. At first the bubbles cum up like I wur fillin' a bottle with water. You know when a bottle is full it won't bubble; then I jedged he war full of water, so I let him go, an' he went down to the bottom, an' I didn't *see* no more of *him*.

SHAM BATTLE BEFORE DUKE ALEXIS.

" I was jest tryin' to load my rifle when I heerd the Injuns push off their canoe, and the splashin' of the water as they paddled to'rd me. 'Twur too late to load, an' I knowed I cudn't kill more'n one of 'em anyway. An idee kim inter my noddle that mayhap I mought fool 'em agin, so I shoved my rifle under the log and made it fast with a piece of a lariat I had fur a sling. Then I chucked away my coonskin cap, and crawlin' clean to the eend of the log, eased myself off inter the water, leavin' nothin' outer water 'cept my head. Thar wur a small limb stickin' out from the under side of the log, an' I jest kep' holt of it with both hands and never stirred a muscle.

" 'Twarn't more'n a minit arter I got fixed, 'fore the canoe run aginst the log. The Injuns looked fur their kumrades, and called 'em by name ; but they didn't find 'em, not very much. Then one on 'em got on the log and crawled to'rd the eend whur I wur *cached*. Soon's he got near me, I sunk altogether an' held my breath. Bein' the small eend of the log, it began to sink, an' the redskin crawled back agin faster'n he came.

" I heerd 'em jabberin' to one another, an' one says, ' They must have killed him,' and another said, ' They are all gone.'

" They wur agood deal puzzled, an' pretty mad, too, I reckon, but 'twur no use — they cudn't make nothin' of it, so arter a while they paddled back to the shore, an' I cud hear 'em movin' up an' down the bank an' callin' to each other, like they wur lookin' fur their kumrades. I cud 'a told 'em whar to look fur the durned niggers, but 'twurn't none o' my funeral, so I crawled up onto the log agin an' floated away quite comfortable like.

" A little arter sun-up the current kerried the log on a p'int stickin' out inter the river, jest whar the Big Horn empties inter it. Thar I landed, stiff an' cramped, I kin tell ye, but hevin' my skelp all right, an' two more nicks fur to ornament the stock of the old shootin'-iron. I concluded I hedn't no more bizness in that air kentry jest then, so I jest legged it fur Fort Bertholt, an' got in thar in about ten days, safe an' sound.

" 'Bout two months later, I went back up the Yallerstun with ' Wild Bill,' — you know him, young feller? He wur a young trapper them days, an' we found my traps and peltries jist where I'd *cached* 'em, so, ye see, I didn't lose much by the operation. An' now ye've heerd the yarn out, I reckon we'd better turn in, if we 'spect to git arter them Indians termorrer ! ''

The final submission of the Cheyennes completed the work of

Custer in the Southwest, and stamped him as an " Indian fighter " of acknowledged merit. The close of this campaign allowed Gen. Custer a rest that was needed and well earned. During the entire campaign he had been separated from his faithful wife, and now they were again united. The Seventh Cavalry was stationed at Big Creek, near Fort Hays, during the entire summer of 1869, and here the entire command enjoyed " Wild Life on the Plains " to perfection. We pass over Gen. Custer's literary efforts during this period of inactivity, as also the years he was stationed in Louisville, Kentucky, and hasten to his campaign on the Yellowstone. An incident occurred in the winter of 1872 that is worthy of a place in this work. It was the year that the Russian Grand Duke Alexis came to America on a tour; and it was decided by those in charge to show him how the buffalo was hunted.

Lieutenant-General Sheridan was in command of the great western division, and it was he who selected Gen. Custer and the renowned scout, William Cody ("Buffalo Bill"), ordering them to report at Omaha, Nebraska. Here they met the royal guests, who were introduced to them.

The party, now consisting of the Grand Duke Alexis and his suite, Gen. Custer, Buffalo Bill, a company of cavalry under the command of Capt. Eagan, and a party of friendly Indians, proceeded southward across the South Platte to the broad plains, in search of buffalo.

Buffalo Bill thus quaintly describes this hunt: —

" General Custer, who was one of the hunting party, carried on a mild flirtation with one of Spotted Tail's daughters, who had accompanied her father thither, and it was noticed also that the Duke Alexis paid considerable attention to another handsome redskin maiden. The night passed pleasantly, and all retired with great expectations of having a most enjoyable and successful hunt. The Duke Alexis asked me a great many questions as to how we shot buffaloes, and what kind of a gun or pistol we used, and if he was going to have a good horse. I told him that he was to have my celebrated buffalo horse, Buckskin Joe, and when we went into a buffalo herd all he would have to do was to sit on the horse's back and fire away.

"At nine o'clock the next morning we were all in our saddles, and in a few minutes were galloping over the prairies in search of a buffalo herd. We had not gone far before we observed a

KILLING BUFFALO WITH ARROWS AND SPEARS.

herd some distance ahead of us crossing our way; after that we proceeded cautiously, so as to keep out of sight until we were ready to make the charge.

"Of course, the main thing was to give Alexis the first chance and the best shot at the buffaloes, and when all was in readiness we dashed over a little knoll that had hidden us from view, and in a few minutes we were among them. Alexis at first preferred to use his pistol instead of a gun. He fired six shots from this weapon at the buffaloes, only twenty feet away from him, but as he shot wildly, not one of his bullets took effect. Riding up to his side and observing that his weapon was empty, I exchanged pistols with him. He again fired six shots without dropping a buffalo.

"Seeing that the animals were bound to make their escape without his killing one of them, unless he had a better weapon, I rode up to him, gave him my old reliable 'Lucretia,' and told him to urge his horse close to the buffaloes, and I would then give him the word when to shoot; at the same time I gave old Buckskin Joe a blow with my whip, and with a few jumps the horse carried the Grand Duke to within about ten feet of a big buffalo bull.

"'Now is your time,' said I. He fired, and down went the bull. The Grand Duke stopped his horse, dropped his gun on the ground, and waved his hat aloft. When his suit came galloping up, he began talking to them in a tongue which I could not understand. Presently General Sheridan joined the group, and the ambulances were brought up. Very soon the corks began to fly from the champagne bottles, in honor of the Grand Duke Alexis, who had killed the first buffalo.

"It was thought that we had had sport enough for one day, and accordingly I was directed by General Sheridan to guide the party back to camp, and we were soon on our way thither. Several of the party, however, concluded to have a little hunt on their own account, and presently we saw them galloping over the prairie in different directions in pursuit of buffaloes.

"While we were crossing a deep ravine, on our way to camp, we ran into a small drove of buffaloes that had been frightened by some of the hunters. As they rushed past us, not more than thirty yards distant, Alexis raised his pistol, fired, and killed a buffalo cow. It was either an extraordinary good shot or a 'scratch,' — probably the latter, for it surprised the Grand Duke as well as everybody else. We gave him three cheers, and when the ambulance came up we took a pull at the champagne in honor of the Grand Duke's success. I was in hopes he would kill five or six more buffaloes before we reached camp, especially if a basket of champagne was to be opened every time he dropped one.

" General Sheridan directed me to take care of the hides and heads of the buffaloes which Alexis had killed, as the Duke wished to keep them as souvenirs of the hunt. I also cut out the choice meat from the cow and brought it into camp, and that night at supper Alexis had the pleasure of partaking of broiled buffalo steak obtained from the animal shot by himself.

" We remained at this camp two or three days, during which we hunted most of the time, the Grand Duke himself killing eight buffaloes."

One day Alexis desired to see how the Indians hunted buffaloes and killed them with bow and arrow. Spotted Tail, selecting some of his best hunters, had them surround a herd, and bring the animals down, not only with arrows, but with lances. The Grand Duke was told to follow upon the heels of one celebrated hunter whose name was " Two Lance," and watch him bring down the game; for this chief had the reputation of sending an arrow through and through the body of a buffalo.

Upon this occasion he did not belie his reputation, for he sent an arrow *through* a buffalo, which fell dead at the shot, and the arrow was given to Alexis as a souvenir of his hunt on the American plains.

That night the Indians gave a grand war-dance for the entertainment of the Grand Duke and suite, and two warriors gave a very interesting sham duel on horseback.

The chase over, the Duke insisted that Custer accompany him on his further trip through the West, which the latter did, returning with Alexis to Louisville. Here they were joined by Mrs. Custer, and the party visited the Mammoth Cave, and finally started on a regular trip through the South, which terminated in March, 1872, at New Orleans, where the Grand Duke and suite took ship for Russia.

Early in 1873 the Seventh Cavalry were again ordered into active service, their destination this time being Dakota.

Custer was, of course, delighted to be once more upon the plains. The life of quiet inactivity he had been leading was dis-

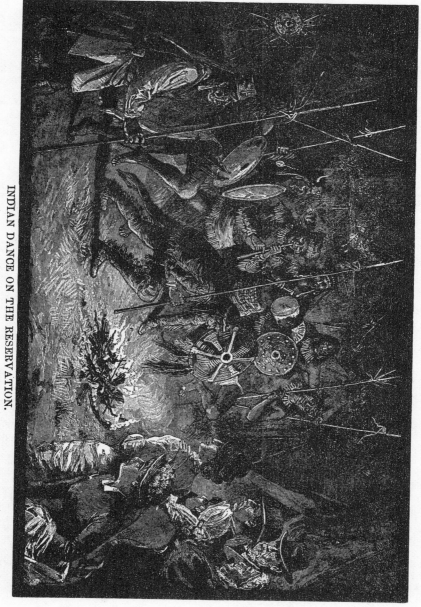

INDIAN DANCE ON THE RESERVATION.

tasteful to him. He desired nothing better than being well mounted and leading his brave command after the treacherous and hostile Indians. The Southwest having been conquered, it now became necessary to turn attention to the Northwest. General Custer received orders at Louisville to proceed with the two companies under his command and join the main body of the regiment at Memphis. From Memphis the regiment proceeded to Yankton by steamboat; and by the middle of April were again fully organized and prepared to chastise the rebellious hostiles.

From here the brave Seventh Cavalry and their gallant commander marched to Fort Rice, some six hundred miles from Yankton, where they arrived in safety in about six weeks. The ladies who were with the command were Mrs. Custer, Mrs. Calhoun, Mrs. Yates, Mrs. Smith, and several more whose names are not remembered. They passed through the Cheyenne, Brule, Yanktonnais and Standing Rock agencies, seeing for the first time the Northern Indians, and finally went into camp at Fort Rice late in May.

The regiment received orders here, to accompany the Yellowstone expedition, and the ladies were compelled to turn back. General Custer says: —

" Omitting the incidents of the march from our starting point, Fort Rice, on the Missouri, we come to the time when we found ourselves on the east bank of the beautiful and swift-flowing Yellowstone, about a hundred miles from its mouth. At this point the expedition was met by a steamer, sent for that purpose up the Missouri, hundreds of miles above Fort Rice, then up the Yellowstone to the point of junction. From it fresh supplies of forage and subsistence stores were obtained. This being done, the entire expedition, save a small detachment left at this point to guard our surplus stores, intended for our return march, was ferried by the steamer across the Yellowstone River. Our course for several days carried us up that stream; our tents at night being usually pitched on or near the river bank.

" The country, however, soon became so rough and broken in places, that we encountered serious delays at times, in finding a practicable route for our long and heavily laden wagon-trains, over rocks and through canons hitherto unexplored by white men. So serious did these embarrassments become, and so much time was lost in accomplishing our daily marches, that I suggested to General Stanley that I should take with me each day a couple of companies of cavalry and a few of the Indian scouts, and seek out and prepare a practicable road in advance, thereby preventing detention of the main command. This proposition being acceded to, it was my custom thereafter to push rapidly forward in the early morning, gaining an advance of several miles upon the main expedition, and by locating the route, relieving the troops and trains in the rear of a great amount of fatigue, and many tedious detentions. One result of this system was that my little party, who were acting as pioneers, and myself, usually arrived at the termination of our day's march, our camp-ground for the night, at an early hour in the day, several hours in advance of the main body.

"On the morning of August 4th, with two companies of the Seventh Cavalry, commanded by Captain Moylen and Colonel Custer, — who, with my adjutant, Lieutenant Calhoun, and Lieutenant Varnum, comprised the officers of the party, — and guided by my favorite scout, Bloody Knife, a young Arickaree warrior, the entire party numbering eighty-six men and five officers, I left camp at five o'clock in the morning, and set out as usual to explore the country and find a practicable route for the main column. Soon after we left camp, Bloody Knife's watchful eyes discovered fresh signs of Indians. Halting long enough to allow him to examine the trail, Bloody Knife was soon able to gather all the information attainable. A party of Indians had been prowling about our camp the previous night, and had gone away, travelling in the direction in which we were then marching.

"This intelligence occasioned no particular surprise, as we had been expecting to discover the presence of Indians for several days. Bloody Knife's information produced no change in our plans. The hostile party of whose presence we had become aware numbered nineteen; our party numbered over ninety.

"Over rock-ribbed hills, down timbered dells, and across open, grassy plains, we wended our way without unusual interest, except at intervals of a few miles, to discover the trail of the nineteen prowling visitors of the previous night, showing that our course, which was intended to lead us again to the Yellowstone, was in the same direction as theirs. Bloody Knife interpreted this as indicating that the village from which the nineteen had probably been sent to reconnoiter and report our movements, was located somewhere above us in the Yellowstone Valley. About ten o'clock we reached the crest of the high line of bluffs bordering the Yellowstone Valley, from which we obtained a fine view of the river and valley extending above and beyond us as far as the eye could reach.

" After halting upon the crest of the bluffs long enough to take in the pleasures of the scene, and admire the beautiful valley spread out like an exquisite carpet at our feet, we descended to the valley and directed our horses' heads toward a particularly attractive and inviting cluster of shade trees standing on the river bank, and distant from the crest of the bluffs nearly two miles. First allowing our thirsty horses to drink from the clear, crystal waters of the Yellowstone, which ran murmuringly by in its long, tortuous course to the Missouri, we then picketed them out to graze.

" Precautionary and necessary measures having been attended to, looking to the security of our horses, the next important and equally necessary step was to post half a dozen pickets in the open plain beyond, to give timely warning in the event of the approach of the hostile Indians. This being done, the remainder of our party busied themselves in arranging each for his individual comfort, disposing themselves in the grass beneath the shade of the wide-spreading branches of the cottonwoods that grew close to the river bank. For myself, so oblivious was I to the prospect of immediate danger, that after selecting a most inviting spot for my noon-day nap, and arranging my saddle and buckskin coat in the form of a comfortable pillow, I removed my boots, untied my cravat, and opened my collar, prepared to enjoy to the fullest extent the delights of the out-door siesta.

" I did not omit, however, to place my trusty Remington rifle within easy grasp — more from habit, it must be confessed, than from anticipation of danger. Near me, and stretched on the ground sheltered by the shade of the same tree, was my brother, the Colonel, divested of his hat, coat, and boots; while close at hand, wrapped in deep slumber, lay the other three officers, Moylan, Calhoun, and Varnum. Sleep had taken possession of us all — officers and men — excepting, of course, the watchful pickets into whose keeping the safety of our little detachment was for the time entrusted. How long we slept I scarcely know — perhaps an hour — when the cry of ' Indians! Indians!'

quickly followed by the sharp, ringing crack of the picket's carbines, aroused and brought us — officers and men — to our feet. There was neither time nor occasion for questions to be asked or answered. Catching up my rifle, and without waiting to don hat or boots, I glanced through the grove of trees to the open plain or valley beyond, and saw a small party of Indians bearing down toward us as fast as their ponies could carry them.

" 'Run to your horses, men! Run to your horses!' I fairly yelled, as I saw that the first move of the Indians was intended to·stampede our animals and leave us to be attended to afterward.

" At the same time the pickets opened fire upon our disturbers, who had already emptied their rifles at us as they advanced, as if boldly intending to ride us down. As yet we could see but half a dozen warriors, but those who were familiar with stratagems knew full well that so small a party of savages unsupported would not venture to disturb in open day a force the size of ours. Quicker than I could pen the description, each trooper, with rifle in hand, rushed to secure his horse, and men and horses were soon withdrawn from the open plain and concealed behind the clump of trees beneath whose shade we were but a few minutes before quietly sleeping. The firing of the pickets, the latter having been reinforced by a score of their comrades, checked the advance of the Indians, and enabled us to saddle our horses and be prepared for whatever might be in store for us.

" A few moments found us in our saddles and sallying forth from the timber to try conclusions with the daring intruders. We could only see half a dozen Sioux warriors galloping up and down in our front, boldly challenging us by their manner to attempt their capture or death. Of course it was an easy matter to drive them away, but as we advanced it became noticeable that they retired, and when we halted or diminished our speed they did likewise. It was apparent from the first that the Indians were resorting to stratagem to accomplish that which they could not do by an open attack. Taking twenty troopers with me headed by Colonels Custer and Calhoun, and directing Moylan to keep within supporting distance with the remainder, I followed the retreating Sioux up the valley, but with no prospect of overtaking them, as they were mounted upon the fleetest of ponies. Thinking to tempt them within our grasp, I, being mounted on a Kentucky thoroughbred in whose speed and

endurance I had confidence, directed Colonel Custer to allow
me to approach the Indians, accompanied only by my orderly,
who was also well mounted; at the same time to follow us cautiously at a distance of a couple of hundred yards. The wily
redskins were not to be caught by any such artifice. They were
perfectly willing that my orderly and myself should approach
them, but they at the same time carefully watched the advance
of the cavalry following me, and permitted no advantage. We
had by this time arrived almost abreast of an immense tract
of timber growing in the valley and extending to the water's
edge, but distant from our resting-place, from which we had so
rudely been aroused, about two miles.

" The route taken by the Indians, and which they evidently
intended us to follow, led past this timber, but not through it.
When we had arrived almost opposite the nearest point, I signalled to the cavalry to halt, which was no sooner done than the
Indians also came to a halt. I then made the sign to the latter
for a parley, which was done simply by riding my horse in a circle. To this the savages only responded by looking on in silence
for a few moments, then turning their ponies and moving off
slowly, as if to say, ' Catch us if you can.' My suspicions were
now more than ever aroused, and I sent my orderly back to tell
Colonel Custer to keep a sharp eye upon the heavy bushes on
our left, and scarcely three hundred yards distant from where I
sat on my horse. The orderly had delivered his message, and
had almost rejoined me, when, judging from our halt that we intended to pursue no further, the real design and purpose of the
savages was made evident. The small party in front had faced
toward us, and were advancing as if to attack. I could scarcely
credit the evidence of my eyes, but my astonishment had only
begun, when, turning to the wood on my left, I beheld, bursting
from their concealment, between three and four hundred Sioux
warriors, mounted and caparisoned with all the flaming adornments of paint and feathers which go to make up the Indian war
costume. When I first obtained a glimpse of them — and a
single glance was sufficient — they were dashing from the timber
at full speed, yelling and whooping as only Indians can. At the
same time, they moved in perfect line, and with as seeming good
order and alignment as the best drilled cavalry.

" To understand our relative positions the reader has only to
imagine a triangle whose sides are almost equal ; their length, in

this particular instance, being from three to four hundred yards; the three angles being occupied by Colonel Custer and his detachment, the Indians, and myself. Whatever advantage there was in length of sides fell to my lot, and I lost no time in availing myself of it. Wheeling my horse suddenly around, and driving the spurs into his sides, I rode as only a man rides for his life, to reach Colonel Custer and his men, not only in advance of the Indians, but before any of them could cut me off. Moylan, with his reserve, was still too far in the rear to render any assistance available in repelling the shock of the Indians' first attack. Realizing the great superiority of our enemies, not only in numbers, but in their ability to handle their arms and horses in a fight, and fearing they might dash through and disperse Colonel Custer's small party of twenty men, and having once broken the formation of the latter, dispatch them in detail, I shouted to Colonel Custer, at almost each bound of my horse, ' Dismount your men ! Dismount your men ! ' but the distance which separated us, and the excitement of the occasion, prevented him from hearing me.

" Fortunately, however, this was not the first time he had been called upon to contend against the sudden and unforeseen onslaught of savages ; and, although failing to hear my suggestion, he realized instantly that the safety of his little band of troopers depended upon the adoption of prompt means of defence.

" Scarcely had the long line of splendidly mounted warriors rushed from their hiding-place, before Colonel Custer's voice rang out, sharp and clear, ' Prepare to fight on foot.' This order required three out of four troopers to leap from their saddles and take their positions on the ground, where, by more deliberate aim, and being freed from the management of their horses, a more effective resistance could be opposed to the rapidly approaching warriors. The fourth trooper in each group of ' fours ' remained on his horse, holding the reins of the horses of his three comrades.

" Quicker than words can describe, the fifteen cavalrymen, now on foot and acting as infantry, rushed forward a few paces in advance of the horses, deployed into open order, and dropping on one or both knees in the low grass, waited with loaded carbines — and finger gently pressing the trigger — the approach of the Sioux, who rode boldly down as if apparently unconscious

CUSTER RIDES FOR LIFE.

23

that the small group of troopers were in their front. ' Don't fire, men, till I give the word, and when you *do* fire, *aim low*," was the quiet injunction given his men by their young commander, as he sat on his horse intently watching the advancing foe.

" Swiftly over the grassy plain leaped my noble steed, each bound bearing me nearer to both friends and foes. Had the race been confined to the Indians and myself, the closeness of the result would have satisfied an admirer even of the Derby. Nearer and nearer our paths approached each other, making it appear almost as if I were one of the line of warriors, as the latter bore down to accomplish the destruction of the little group of troopers in front. Swifter seem to fly our mettled steeds, the one to save, the other to destroy, until the common goal has been almost reached — a few more bounds, and friends and foes will meet — will form one contending mass.

"The victory was almost within the grasp of the red skins. It seemed that but a moment more, and they would be trampling the kneeling troopers beneath the feet of their lithe-limbed ponies. ' Now, men, let them have it ! ' was the signal for a well-directed volley, as fifteen cavalry carbines poured their contents into the ranks of the shrieking savages. Before the latter could recover from the surprise and confusion which followed, the carbines—thanks to the invention of breech-loaders—were almost instantly loaded, and a second carefully aimed discharge went whistling on its deadly errand. Several warriors were seen to reel in their saddles, and were only saved from falling by the quickly extended arms of their comrades. Ponies were tumbled over like butchered bullocks, their riders glad to find themselves escaping with less serious injuries. The effect of the rapid firing of the troopers, and the firm, determined stand, showing that they thought neither of flight nor surrender, was to compel the savages first to slacken their speed, then to lose their daring and confidence in their ability to trample down the little group of defenders in the front. Death to many of their number stared them in the face. Besides, if the small party of troopers in the front was able to oppose such plucky and destructive resistance to their attacks, what might not be expected should the main party under Moylan, now swiftly approaching to the rescue, also take part in the struggle? But more quickly than my sluggish pen has been able to record the description of the scene, the battle line of the warriors exhibited signs of faltering which soon degenerated into an absolute repulse. In a moment their attack was transformed into flight, in which each seemed only anxious to secure his individual safety. A triumphant cheer from the cavalrymen as they send a third instalment of leaden messengers whistling about the ears of the fleeing redskins served to spur both pony and rider to their utmost speed. Moylan by this time had reached the ground and had united the entire force. The Indians in the meantime had plunged out of sight into the recesses of the jungle from which they first made their attack. We knew too well that their absence would be brief, and that they would resume the attack, but not in the manner of the first.

"We knew that we had inflicted no little loss upon them — dead and wounded ponies could be seen on the ground passed over by the Indians. The latter would not be satisfied without determined efforts to get revenge. Of this we were well aware.

"A moment's hurried consultation between the officers and myself, and we decided that as we would be forced to act entirely upon the defensive against a vastly superior force, it would be better if we relieve ourselves as far as possible of the care of our horses, and take our chances in the fight which was yet to come, on foot. At tL same time, we were then so far out in the open plain and from the river bank, that the Indians, could surround us. We must get nearer to the river, conceal our horses or shelter them from fire, then with every available man form a line or semi-circle, with our backs to the river, and defend ourselves until the arrival of the main body of the expedition, an event we could not expect for several hours. As if divining our intentions and desiring to prevent their execution, the Indians now begun their demonstrations looking to a renewal of the fight.

"Of course it was easy to see what had been the original plan by which the Indians hoped to kill or capture our entire party. Stratagem, of course, was to play a prominent part in the quarrel. The few young warriors first sent to arouse us from our midday slumber came as a decoy to tempt us to pursue them beyond the ambush in which lay concealed the main body of the savages; the latter were to dash from their hiding place, intercept our retreat, and dispose of us after the most approved manner of barbarous warfare.

"The next move on our part was to fight our way back to the

little clump of bushes from which we had been so rudely startled. To do this Captain Moylan, having united his force to that of Colonel Custer, gave the order, ' Prepare to fight on foot.' This was quickly obeyed. Three-fourths of the fighting force were now on foot, armed with carbines only. These were deployed in somewhat of a circular skirmish line, of which the horses formed the centre: the circle having a diameter of several hundred yards. In this order we made our way back to the timber, the Indians whooping, yelling, and firing their rifles as they dashed madly by on their fleet war ponies. That the fire of these rifles should be effective under these circumstances could scarcely be expected; neither could the most careful aim of the cavalrymen produce much better results. It forced the savages to keep at a respectful distance, however, and enabled us to make our retrograde movement. A few of our horses were shot by the Indians in this irregular skirmish, none fatally, however. As we were falling back, contesting each foot of ground we passed over, I heard a sudden sharp cry of pain from one of the men in charge of our horses; the next moment I saw his arm hanging helplessly at his side, while a crimson current flowing near his shoulder told that the aim of the Indians had not been entirely in vain. The gallant fellow kept his seat in the saddle, however, and conducted the horses under his charge safely with the rest to the timber. Once concealed by the trees, and no longer requiring the horses to be moved, the number of horse-holders was reduced so as to allow but one trooper to eight horses, the remainder being required on the skirmish line. The redskins had followed us closely, step by step, to the timber, tempted in part by their great desire to obtain possession of our horses. If successful in this, they believed, no doubt, that flight on our part being no longer possible, we must be either killed or captured.

" Taking advantage of a natural terrace or embankment extending almost like a semi-circle in front of the little grove in which we had taken refuge, and at a distance of but a few hundred yards from the latter, I determined, by driving the Indians beyond, to adopt it as our breastwork or line of defence. This was soon accomplished, and we found ourselves deployed behind a natural parapet, or bulwark, from which the troopers could deliver a carefully directed fire upon their enemies, and, at the same time, be protected largely from the bullets of the latter.

The Indians made repeated and desperate efforts to dislodge us and force us to the level plateau. Every effort of this kind proved unavailing.

"Rather a remarkable exhibition of rifle-shooting took place in the early part of the contest. I was standing in a group of troopers, and with them was busily firing at such of our enemies as exposed themselves. Bloody Knife was with us, his handsome face lighted up by the fire of battle and the desire to avenge the many wrongs suffered by his people at the hands of the ruthless Sioux. All of us had had our attention drawn more than once to a Sioux warrior who, seeming more bold than his fellows, dashed rapidly along the front of our lines, scarcely two hundred yards distant ; and, although the troopers had singled him out, he had thus far escaped untouched by their bullets. Encouraged by his success, perhaps, he concluded to taunt us again, and at the same time exhibit his own daring, by riding along the lines at full speed, but nearer than before. We saw him coming. Bloody Knife, with his Henry rifle poised gracefully in his hands, watched his coming, saying he intended to make this his enemy's last ride — he would send him to the happy hunting-ground. I told the interpreter to tell Bloody Knife that at the moment the warrior reached a designated point directly opposite to us he (Bloody Knife) should fire at the rider, and I, at the same instant, would fire at the pony.

"A smile of approval passed over the swarthy features of the friendly scout as he nodded assent. I held in my hand my well-tried Remington. Resting on one knee and glancing along the barrel, at the same time seeing that Bloody Knife was also squatting low in the grass with rifle levelled, I awaited the approach of the warrior to the designated point. On he came, brandishing his weapons, and flaunting his shield in our faces, defying us by his taunts to come out and fight like men. Swiftly sped the gallant little steed that bore him, scarcely needing the guiding rein. Nearer and nearer both horse and rider approached the fatal spot, when, sharp and clear, and so simultaneous as to sound as one, rang forth the reports of the two rifles. The distance was less than two hundred yards. The Indian was seen to throw up his arms and reel in his saddle, while the pony made one final leap, and both fell to the ground. A shout rose from the group of troopers, in which Bloody Knife and I joined. The next moment a few of the comrades of the fallen warrior rushed to his rescue, and without dismounting from their ponies, or scarcely pulling rein, clutched up the body, and the next moment disappeared from view.

" Foiled in their repeated attempts to dislodge us, the Indians withdrew to a point beyond the range of our rifles for the apparent purpose of devising a new plan of attack. Of this we soon became convinced. Hastily returning to a renewal of the struggle, we saw our adversaries arrange themselves in groups along our entire front. They were seen to dismount, and the quick eyes of Bloody Knife detected them making their way toward us by crawling through the grass. We were at a loss to comprehend their designs, as we could not believe they intended to attempt to storm our position on foot. We were not left long in doubt. Suddenly, and almost as if by magic, we beheld numerous small columns of smoke shooting up all along our front.

" Calling Bloody Knife and the interpreter to my side, I inquired the meaning of what I saw. ' They are setting fire to the long grass, and intend to burn us out,' was the scout's reply, at the same time keeping his eyes intently bent on the constantly increasing columns of smoke. His features wore a most solemn look; anxiety was plainly depicted there. Looking to him for suggestions and advice in this new phase of our danger, I saw his face gradually unbend and a scornful smile part his lips. ' The Great Spirit will not help our enemies,' was his muttered reply to my question. ' See,' he continued, ' the grass refuses to burn.' Casting my eyes along the line formed by the columns of smoke, I saw Bloody Knife had spoken truly when he said, ' The grass refuses to burn.'

" This was easily accounted for. It was early in the month of August; the grass had not ripened or matured sufficiently to burn readily. A month later, and the flames would have swept us back to the river as if we had been surrounded by a growth of tinder. In a few moments the anxiety caused by the threatening of this new danger was dispelled. While the greatest activity was maintained in our front by our enemies, my attention was called to a single warrior who, mounted on his pony, had deliberately, and as I thought, rashly, passed around our left flank — our diminished numbers preventing us from extending our line close to the river — and was then in the rear of our skirmishers, riding slowly along the crest of the low river bank with as apparent unconcern as if in the midst of his friends instead of being almost in the power of his enemies. I imagine that his object was to get nearer to the grove in which our horses were concealed, and toward which he was moving slowly, to reconnoitre and ascertain how much force we held in reserve. At the same time, as I never can see an Indian engaged in an unexplained act without conceiving treachery or stratagem to be at the bottom of it, I called Lieut. Varnum, who commanded on the left, to take a few men and endeavor to cut the wily interloper off. This might have been done but for the excessive zeal of some of Varnum's men, who acted with lack of caution, and enabled the Indian to discover their approach and make his escape by a hurried gallop up the river. The men were at a loss even then to comprehend his strange manœuvre, but after the fight had ended, and we obtained an opportunity to ride over and examine the ground, all was made clear, and we learned how narrowly we had escaped a most serious, if not fatal, disaster.

"The river bank in our rear was from twenty to thirty feet high. At its base, and along the water's edge, ran a narrow, pebbly beach. The redskins had hit upon a novel, but to us most dangerous scheme, for capturing our horses, and at the same time throwing a large force of warriors in our rear. They had found a pathway beyond our rear, leading from the large tract of timber in which they were first concealed through a cut or ravine in the river bank. By this they were enabled to reach the water's edge, from which point they could move down the river, following the pebbly beach referred to, the height of the river bank protecting them perfectly from our observation. Thus they would have placed themselves almost in the midst of our horses before we could have become aware of their designs. Had they been willing, as white men would have been, to assume greater risks, their success would have been assured. But they feared that we might discover their movements and catch them while strung out along the narrow beach, with no opportunity to escape, A few men on the bank could have shot down a vastly superior force. In this case the Indians had sent on this errand about one hundred warriors. After the discovery of this attack and its failure, the battle languished for awhile, and we were surprised to notice, not very long after, a general withdrawal from in front of our right, and a concentration of their forces opposite our left. The reason for this was soon made clear to us. Looking far to the right, and over the crest of the hills already described, we could see an immense cloud of dust rising and rapidly approaching. We could not be mistaken; we could not see the cause producing this dust; but there was not one of us who did not say to himself, 'Relief is at hand.' A few moments later a shout arose from the men. All eyes were turned to the bluffs in the distance, and there were to be seen, coming almost with the speed of the wind, four separate squadron's of Uncle Sam's best cavalry, with banners flying, horses' manes and tails floating on the breeze, and comrades spurring forward in generous emulation as to which squadron should land its colors first in the fight. It was a grand and welcome sight, but we waited not to enjoy it. Confident of support, and wearied from fighting in the defensive, now was our time to mount our steeds and force our enemies to seek safety in flight, or to battle on more even terms. In a moment we were in our saddles and dashing after the foe. The only satisfaction we had was to drive at full speed for several miles a force outnumbering us five to one. In this pursuit we picked up a few ponies which the Indians were compelled to abandon on account of wounds or exhaustion. Their wounded, of whom there were quite a number, and their killed, as afterwards acknowledged by them when they returned to the agency to receive the provisions and fresh supplies of ammunition which a sentimental government, manipulated and directed by corrupt combinations, insists upon distributing annually, were sent to the rear before the flight of the main body. The number of Indians and ponies killed and wounded in this engagement, as shown by their subsequent admission, almost equalled that of half our entire force engaged.

" That night the forces of the expedition encamped on the battle-ground, which was nearly opposite the mouth of Tongue River. My tent was pitched under the hill from which I had been so unceremoniously disturbed at the commencement of the fight; while under the wide-spreading branches of a neighboring cottonwood, guarded and watched over by sorrowing comrades who kept up their lonely vigils through the night, lay the mangled bodies of two of our companions of the march, who, although not present, nor participating in the fight, had fallen victims to the cruelty of our foes."

Thus closes Custer's account of this, his first fight with the Northern Indians. In it will be noticed the same coolness and studied recklessness which made him so succesful an Indian fighter.   This was the first intimation that the Sioux were on the war path against the whites.

In the last sentence of Custer's account of this action, which closes his published articles on the plains, he mentions two victims of Indian cruelty.   It is necessary to explain the allusion, because these two men were remotely the cause of Custer's own death three years later.

They were both unarmed men, the veterinary surgeon and the sutler of the Seventh Cavalry.   Dr. Houzinger, the first, was a corpulent old man, of the quietest and most inoffensive habits, and a great favorite with the regiment.   Mr. Baliran, the sutler, was also an elderly man, and a great friend of Dr. Houzinger. The two were in the habit of straying off from the main body of the command, picking up natural curosities, and so far had experienced no trouble.   On the day of Custer's fight, these two quiet old men were somewhere about two miles behind his party, and ahead of the main body.   Their bodies were found by the advance of the main expedition, where they had been pounced upon and killed by the Indians.   Dr. Houzinger's skull was fractured as with some blunt instrument, but neither body was mutilated.   Who killed them was, of course, not known then.   It came to light in a very strange manner two years after, as we shall see in its place.

Another man, a soldier of company F, Seventh Cavalry, was also found killed, where he had been surprised at a spring, and it was the discovery of these bodies, together with the reports of scouts and stragglers that the Indians were up, that had induced General Stanley to send on help to Custer, arriving in time as it did.   Stanley mentions this fight in very handsome terms in his report.

For the next three days after the fight, Indians were to be seen hovering round the column, and on the 8th of August the appearance was explained.   A lodge pole trail, evidently belonging to a very large village, was found leading up the Yellowstone, and Custer was sent out with all the cavalry and scouts to pursue it, starting at nine that night.   The trail was followed for thirty-six hours, and on the 10th of August, it was found that the Indians had crossed the Yellowstone on " bull boats," the old trapper name for the wicker coracle, covered with a bull's hide, which is the transport of the plains' Indians.   Custer tried all the day to **cross after them**, but in vain; the American horses would not

ON THE RESERVATION.

swim the river. Next morning, he was attacked by the Indians, who had been watching his discomfiture. Some came down and fired at him across the river, while another body, probably from a second village, came down behind him, firing from the rear. The place where they now were, was on the north bank of the Yellowstone, three miles below the mouth of the Big Horn. Then, as now, the valley of the Upper Yellowstone, especially the southern bank, was the headquarters of the hostile Indians, and Sitting Bull was undoubtedly their leader.

The Indians, some fifteen hundred strong, having recrossed the river, commenced an attack at a distance. General Custer ordered out two companies of the regiment as skirmishers, and they were joined by companies C, I, F, and K, of the Twenty-Second Infantry. These troops followed the hostiles some nine or ten miles, when the Indians reached the hills and scattered.

No further trouble was experienced, and Custer returned at the close of the trip to Fort Rice, late in September. From thence he was ordered to Chicago to report to General Sheridan, with whom he went to Toledo to the reunion of the Army of the Tennessee, and thence to Monroe, where he again met his faithful little wife.

He was now granted a leave, part of which he spent at Chicago. At the close of his leave, Custer was ordered to assume command of the post at which he spent the remaining years of his life, Fort Abraham Lincoln, on the right bank of the Missouri River, opposite the little town of Bismarck. He started with Mrs. Custer and all his belongings, and went through to Bismarck on the very last train that ran that year. The next day winter set in and Custer and his little post were cut off from the rest of the world till the following spring.

XXII.

It will be remembered that in a previous chapter we recorded the murder of two inoffensive old men — Dr. Houzinger and Mr. Baliran — on the Yellowstone expedition. They were killed, it was supposed, by hostiles; but the discovery of agency property on the field of battle subsequently revealed that among these hostiles were some, so-called, "good Indians," who drew rations at the agencies, and received property from the government.

No hope was felt that the names of the Indians who killed the two unarmed old men would be found out. During the winter of 1875, however, their identity came out in a very strange manner.

Charley Reynolds, one of Custer's scouts, who afterwards was killed at the Little Horn battle, happened to be at Standing Rock Agency, a place some seventy miles below Fort Lincoln, where the Indians were drawing rations. As usual at their rejoicings, they were having "a dance." The Indians appear to signalize every great event by a dance, and this dance is always made the occasion of boasting about all the valiant deeds they ever have done. In the course of this dance, Charley Reynolds heard one of the Indians boasting how he had killed two men at a time, white men, too; and the savage went on with his pantomime dance, and described how he did it; how one of them was a fat old man, and how he fell from his horse; how he (the Indian) finished him off by smashing his skull with a big stone, and then shot the other white man, and took all they had. Then he proudly exhibited articles that Charley knew belonged to Dr. Houzinger; and the scout knew that he had found the murderer. That Indian was named "Rain-in-the-Face."

The rest of his story was written at the time (January, 1875), by Mrs. Custer, and she shall tell it to the reader in her own words:—

"I have been so much interested," says the dear little lady, "in the capture and present imprisonment of an Indian murderer, I cannot but think that the story might entertain others. Since so many of the 'ready writers' of the present day make up their histories of Indian life and incidents, thousands of miles

366

FINDING THE BODIES.

from the actual scene, I do not wonder that the true impression of the real wild Indian is confined mostly to those who live either with or near them. I must go back for a moment to the Yellowstone expedition under General Stanley, in the summer of 1873. Attached to the cavalry accompanying the expedition were two civilians, who rode a great part of the time together. They were not obliged to submit to the regulation that compels soldiers to keep the ranks, and so they daily guided their horses where they chose. One day, they stopped to water their steeds, and the main column was scarcely out of sight, hidden by a divide, before the two were surrounded and instantly murdered by Indians. A portion of the cavalry under General Custer, had, at the same time been surrounded, and were fighting, but unable, of course, to go to the relief of the two poor victims. Dr. Houzinger was an honest, kind-hearted, old man, who had followed the fortunes of the Seventh Cavalry for some years, as its veterinary surgeon. Mr. Baliran was the sutler for the cavalry. Both were favorites with the command, and were much regretted.

" It is now over a year and a half since their death. A few weeks since, reliable information came from the Indian agency below here on the river, that the murderer of Dr. Houzinger and Mr. Baliran was at the agency, drawing his rations, blankets, ammunition, etc., from the government, and boasting of his foul deed of the two summers preceding.

" This piece of news at once created the most intense excitement in our garrison, largely composed, as it is, of members of the Yellowstone expedition and friends of the slaughtered men. It really seemed too aggravating to endure the knowledge of the fact that the government should feed, clothe, and equip Indians to go out and fight and kill soldiers and others who were working to protect the frontier. So, after the excitement had somewhat lulled, a detachment was quickly prepared to march to the agency. No one knew the object of their trip. Most persons supposed it was to capture another Indian murderer, belonging to the agency, who had killed a citizen on Red River of the North, last summer. Four officers and a hundred men left this post, one cold, windy day, under sealed orders. The orders directed them to capture and bring back an Uncpapa Indian, called ' Rain-in-the-Face,' the assassin of Dr. Houzinger and Mr. Baliran. Our next post is twenty miles distant, and had the orders not been sealed, General Custer knew that the Sioux scouts em-

24

ployed by government at Fort Rice, as soon as the troops arrived there and told their errand, would send out a runner to the agency below and inform the Indians of the intended arrest, giving time for the murderer to escape. So the orders were not opened until Fort Rice was left behind twenty miles. As the troops neared the agency it was found necessary to observe the greatest care, to prevent the Indians from finding out the object of the visit.

" It was the day for our red brethren to draw beef from their generous Uncle Sam. Hundreds of them were there at the agency, of course armed to the teeth, as they always are. In the face of hundreds of fully armed Indians, though on the reservation, still most of them full of hate toward the white man, it seemed a very venturesome deed to appear in their midst and claim one of their number. The reservation Indians are constantly told that they will be fed, clothed, and armed, if they will consent never to make war on the white man, but if they do they must submit to the penalties of the law. But in the instance of this murderer, he dared everything to prove his courage. He had been frequently to the agency, boasting of his base deed. One party of troops had been down to capture him earlier in the winter, but he had hidden and escaped them. So Captain Yates, who had charge of the troops, sent one of the lieutentants, with forty men, to the Indian camp ten miles below, to make inquiries for three Indians who had murdered citizens on Red River, last summer.

" This ruse succeeded in deceiving the Indians as to the real object of their presence among them. As the trader's store is the great place of resort for the Indians, it was presumed that, in the course of the day, Rain-in-the-Face would be there. Colonel Custer (brother of the general) was directed to take five picked men, and go to the store and capture the murderer, should the latter put in an appearance. He remained in the store for several hours. The day was cold, and the Indians kept their blankets drawn about their heads, thus rendering it almost impossible to distinguish one from the other. At last one of them loosened his blanket, and Colonel Custer identified him as Rain-in-the-Face. Coming suddenly behind him, he threw his arms around him and seized the Winchester rifle that the Indian attempted in an instant to cock. The murderer was taken entirely by surprise. Stolid as their faces usually are, his, in this moment of

RAIN IN THE FACE.

amaze, was a study. No fear to be seen, but other emotions showed themselves with lightning rapidity on his countenance. Surprise, hate, revenge, then the final determination that he would show his brother warriors he was not afraid to die. He had been considered brave beyond precedent, to even enter the agency store and encounter this risk of arrest.

"As soon as Rain-in-the-Face was actually captured and his hands tied, an old Indian orator of the tribe began exhorting the Indians, who had assembled in the store to the number of thirty or more, to recapture their comrade. He spoke in the key assumed by the Indian warrior, high and loud, but with no rising or falling inflections. The most intense excitement prevailed among the braves. The instant Rain-in-the-Face was arrested, Captain Yates, who had remained outside a close observer of affairs, gave the signal, and rallied his entire force in the immediate vicinity of the trader's store, prepared to repel any attempt to rescue the prisoner. These precautions were adopted none too quickly, for no sooner had news of the capture of Rain-in-the-Face been conveyed to the numerous groups of Indians to be seen in the vicinity of the agency, than a mass of armed warriors, estimated at over five hundred in number, rushed to the trader's store, and in loud, threatening, and excited tones, demanded the instant release of their comrade. The occasion was one requiring the exercise of the utmost prudence as well as the most determined courage upon the part of the little group of officers and men who stood, with weapons in their hands, about the prisoner. Determined to resist to the very death any attempt at a rescue, Captain Yates, presenting a bold front to the Indians, enraged as they were, prevented the immediate recapture of his prisoner. By means of an interpreter, he then briefly explained to the Indians the cause of the arrest, and announced the determination of himself and men to maintain their hold over their captive. He at the same time urged the chiefs to withdraw with their followers, and thus avoid a collision that would only result in loss of life on both sides, without accomplishing any purpose. Seeing they could not carry out their end by intimidation or the display of greatly superior numbers, the Indians then resorted to parley and offers of compromise. They offered, through an interpreter, to sacrifice two Indians of the tribe, if Rain-in-the-Face could be released. He is a great warrior among them. He has five brothers at the agency, one of whom, Iron Horn, is a chief of influential standing in the tribe. It was not expected that Indians of any notoriety or rank would be offered as a sacrifice; only some who had not distinguished themselves in any way; and the selections were to be made by the great moguls of the tribe. These offers were, of course, refused, and Rain-in-the-Face was taken to the camp of the cavalry. In an incredibly short time not an Indian was to be seen at the agency. All went to their camp, ten miles below. Later in the day, a party of fifty mounted Indians dashed by the agency on the road to be taken by our troops on the return. Of course, our officers expected to be attacked by this party the next morning, but they were unmolested, and reached here after a march of three days, through cold and snow and winds such as only Dakota can furnish. It was explained to us afterward, that the party of fifty, seen passing the agency were on their way to the camp of the chief ' Two Bears,' to try and induce him to urge his young braves to combine with them in the release of Rain-in-the-Face. But Two Bears is an old chief, and he opposed the attack. He has been a friend to the whites for a long time, but his age would induce one to think the motive of his friendship was policy.

"After the officers had reported, General Custer sent for Rain-in-the-Face to interview him. He is a young man with an impenetrable countenance. This is as we saw him, but in a subsequent interview, when General Custer locked himself alone in a room with him, he showed some signs of agitation. After a time when they had talked by signs as far as it was possible, the interpreter was admitted, and for hours General Custer attempted by ever clever question he could invent, to induce Rain-in-the-Face to confess his crime. At last he succeeded in getting his account of the murder, and the next day, in the presence of a number of the officers, Rain-in-the-Face made a full confession of his crime. He called Dr. Houzinger, the old man, and says he shot him, but he rode some distance before falling from his horse. Mr. Baliran, he described as being among some trees, and signalling to them by holding up his hands as an overture of peace. He says that Baliran gave them his hat when they reached him, but they shot him at once, first with a gun, then with arrows. One of the arrows entered his back, and he tried to pull it through, but failed. They did not scalp their **victims**. Dr. Houzinger was bald, and Mr. Baliran had his hair closely cut. Neither of these gentlemen were armed when attacked by the Indians. This short but cruel story made our blood boil when we afterward learned that Rain-in-the-Face had confessed.

" The brother of the prisoner, ' Iron Horn,' and one other Indian, had followed the cavalry up from the agency and asked to see the captive before they went home. General Custer sent for Rain-in-the-Face, and he met his brother and had council with him. They expected it was a farewell interview as the Indians all believed Rain-in-the-Face would be hung.

" During the council, which was very solemn, Iron Horn took off his beautiful beaded blanket and put it on his brother, taking his common one in place of it. He also exchanged pipes with him, giving his highly ornamented one to Rain-in-the-Face, to present to General Custer. He charged his brother most solemnly not to try to escape ; that should he get back to the reservation he would be recaptured, and he believed he would be kindly treated while a captive. He hoped the Great Father would not hang him, and, perhaps, General Custer would intercede in his favor. The Great Father rarely hung Indians. Asking him not to lose his spirits, they took a farewell smoke and he departed.

" In about ten days he returned, bringing a party of Indians with him. Another interview with General Custer was obtained. After all the guests were seated, Rain-in-the-Face came over from the guard-house and entered, having been sent for at the request of the Indians. He came into the room, trying not show his pleasure at seeing his friends, nor his grief at his imprisonment and his evidently expected death; but these emotions passed over his face in quick succession, and then came the look of settled indifference that the Indian constantly tries to wear. His brother rose at once and went to Rain-in-the-Face, and, to the intense amazement of the few privileged spectators, General Custer had allowed to enter, he kissed him. An Indian kiss to be sure; the lips were laid quietly on his cheek, with no sound or motion; but it was a solemn caress, and one never seen before, with one single exception, by the oldest Indian fighter here. Several of the ranking Indians stepped solemnly to the prisoner and gave him the same dignified salute. Then one of the old men of the tribe walked in front of him, and lifting his hand above his head and raising his eyes, said a few words in prayer to the Great Spirit for this unfortunate brother. Rain-in-the-Face hung his head low on his breast, to hide the emotion he thought would ill-become a warrior as brave as he really is.

After a long speech by Iron Horn, delivered in the usual high, monotonous key, the next in rank rose, and so on, till half a dozen had spoken. Iron Horn thanked General Custer for his care of Rain-in-the-Face, and asked permission to visit him again, begged him to talk again to the Great Father and intercede for the life of their brother; and then, taking off the buckskin shirt he wore, he presented the highly ornamented garment to the General. Then came such a singular request. It was the story of Damon and Pythias among uncivilized warriors. Two shy young braves, sitting near the end of the circle among the untitled, asked, through Iron Horn, the privilege of sharing the captivity of Rain-in-the-Face. Not many murderers or felons in the States find friends who, in the hour of arrest or capture, ask to share the prison with them. Consent was given to this request, if the friends would be willing to be locked in the prison till the hour came for them to go home.''

They rested in the guard-house with their friend for a day and night, and then returned to the agency. The imprisonment of Rain-in-the-Face continued for several months, till the following occurrence gave him his liberty: —

General Custer had arrested several persons suspected of stealing from the government. Among these were two particularly hard cases who had been caught driving wagons loaded with hay off the government lands. These persons were all confined in the guard-house with Rain-in-the-Face.

'' The guard-house,'' says Mrs. Custer, '' was only a poorly built wooden building, quite insecure, and these prisoners had in one night cut a hole in the side of the rear wall, large enough to creep through. Two crept safely out, and Rain-in-the-Face, seeing the opening after they had gone, quickly made his escape. We found afterwards that he went at once to the hostile camp, and last spring he sent word by agency Indians that he had joined Sitting Bull, and was awaiting his revenge for his imprisonment.''

That he took it, all the world now knows; and they can see in his portrait, taken from an excellent photograph, what sort of a man this desperado is. Truly he looks soft enough, and as innocent as a lamb, but for all that he is well known as one of the bravest men of his nation. The tribe were particularly proud of him for one thing, — his extraordinary fortitude against physical pain. He was said to have hung for four hours in the " sun dance."

SITTING BULL.

While the retreat of 1868 had pacified most of the Sioux, and especially the great chiefs Red Cloud and Spotted Tail, with their bands, there was a small portion of the Sioux nation which remained implacable in its enmity to the whites, and kept to its original habits of life, out in the wilderness. This portion was generally known by the title of " the hostiles," and the most powerful chief of the different bands was and is known by the title of Sitting Bull. To explain to the general reader the meaning of the words " nation," " tribe," and " band," a short sketch of Indian polity is here necessary.

The Indian tribes of the plains bear a strong likeness, in their modes of government, to the Arabs and Tartars. Abstractly it may be termed patriarchal; but actually, it is nearly a pure republic. Every member of a band does just about what he pleases, and obeys his chief when it pleases him, subject always to the verdict of popular opinion and the physical ability of the chief to thrash him. While the dignity of his chieftainship appears to be hereditary, it is subject to so many checks, and depends so much on personal ability to persuade one's followers to pursue a certain line of conduct, that it may be called a mere delusion, in the hands of any but a great warrior; and prowess in war is the only sure road to real power among Indians. While the Indians, as a mass, are thus independent of all but persuasive influences, the patriarchal element so far prevails that the family is the basis of the organization for war and peace. The members of a family, in all its ramifications of brothers and cousins, uncles and nephews, generally travel together, hunt together, and fight together, agglomerating in time, with their connections by marriage, into a " band," varying from two to twenty or thirty lodges. These " bands " have a remoter connection, by blood ties, with other bands, and constitute together a " tribe," which may number from two to thirty or forty " bands." These tribes, again, have a still more remote blood connection with other tribes, constituting a " nation," such as the Sioux Nation, which comprises the

Yankton, Brule, Teton, Uncpapa, and several other tribes, each tribe in its turn embracing several bands.

The "hostiles," so-called, are formed of bands differently composed. The patriarchal ties noticeable in other bands are replaced here by a mere alliance of convenience. Every Indian who feels discontented at the agencies joins the "hostiles" and attaches himself to the band of Sitting Bull or Crazy Horse, the only two great chiefs who were, at the time we write of, avowedly "hostile." Thus their bands, originally numbering perhaps twenty lodges apiece, with a fighting force of a hundred warriors to each band, were swelled by the arrival of discontented families to many more.

The village of Crazy Horse, at the close of the winter of 1875, was found to contain one hundred and five lodges, which, at the ordinary rate of five or six warriors to a lodge, or "tepee," furnished a force of about five hundred warriors. Sitting Bull's band probably then numbered at least one hundred and fifty lodges, he being a more famous chief than Crazy Horse. During the summer time, the forces of both received constant additions from the agency Indians, who came out for a summer's hunt, provided with plenty of breech-loading and magazine guns and ammunition.

The position of the "hostiles" was very well selected, near the head of the Yellowstone, in a country surrounded by "bad lands," which prevented the whites from near approach, except on great and protracted expeditions, like that led by Stanley. To form an idea of the "bad lands" the Eastern reader can use a familiar illustration : You have all, no doubt, seen a clay-field after a long and hot drought in summer, how it is seamed over with innumerable cracks, perfectly perpendicular, leaving miniature chasms between. Such, magnified by a hundred, are the "bad lands" of the Northwest. They are patches of clay soil, baked by the long and intense droughts of that climate into chasms four our five feet wide, and, perhaps, twenty feet deep, absolutely impassable for wagons where they occur, — quagmires in the early spring freshets, a labyrinth of ravines in the summer. These bad lands surrounded the country of the hostiles in 1873, and surround them now.

So much for the natural advantage of Sitting Bull's position, considered in a defensive point of view; but a greater advantage accrues to him from the strategic lines of the country and the existence of the Indian agencies.   The Missouri River describes nearly a perfect circle around the country of the " hostiles," and all the Indian agencies are on this river.   If you will get a map of this region and examine it, you will begin to realize what is meant by the " strategic advantages " of Sitting Bull. Beginning at the mouth of the Cheyenne River, there are Cheyenne Agency, Brule Agency, Grand River Agency, Standing Rock Agency, Fort Berthold and Fort Peck, and several other places, all full of friendly Indians, supported by government, and ready to join the hostiles in the summer, bringing arms and ammunition with them.   To give an idea of the supplies of the latter, let us take what went through in the spring of 1876 alone, for distribution to Indians.   Our evidence is contained in the private letter of an officer on the spot.   This officer has investigated the matter, and finds that the following shipments were made by river steamer to these agencies, and to Forts Benton, McCloud and Claggett (also agencies), on the 21st of May, 20th of June, 6th and 30th of July, 1876, while the war was actually raging : —

No less than fifty-six *cases of arms*, or 1,120 *Winchester and Remington rifles*, and 413,000 *rounds of patent ammunition*, went there on these steamers, besides large quantities of loose powder, lead and primers.   These shipments were all *for issue to Indians, through the Indian agents, or for sale through Indian traders*.   The country to which they were sent contains only Indians, soldiers, and Indian traders or agents.   These shipments, moreover, were as nothing to those of previous years, and especially those of the summer of 1875, when more than a million rounds of ammunition and several thousand stands of arms were sent through.

Now, perhaps, Sitting Bull's chief advantage can be seen, as first shown in the Yellowstone expedition of 1873.   This expedition started from Fort Rice in the summer of 1873, and moved off at a leisurely pace, due west.   Indian runners at the same time started off up and down the Missouri to carry the news. Many of them travelled luxuriously by the steamers the government was kind enough to supply, to carry stores to the agencies, for the use of the Indians.   By the time Stanley had reached the Little Missouri, every agency all along the line of the river was informed of his movements, and parties of warriors on their war ponies, with no burdens save arms, ammunition, and food, were starting from the *circumference of the quarter circle* to find Sitting Bull and have a little fun.

All those from the *upper agencies* had a shorter distance to travel than Stanley and knew the county better. No wonder they arrived before him. The trail which Stanley struck on the Yellowstone was in all probability that of the real acknowledged " hostiles," the village of Sitting Bull, with a force of some eight hundred braves, but the reinforcements which afterwards swelled his numbers to fifteen hundred in the fight near Pompey's Pillar, must have come from the northern agencies, and Stanley says so in his report, specifying Fort Peck as " the centre of all villainy of the Indian Department."

Thus, in carrying on war with the United States War Department, Sitting Bull had great and peculiar advantages from the nature of his position, and these advantages it was which had made him constantly triumphant. It may have seemed strange to many that Custer should have been able, alone, to have beaten the Indians of the Southern Plains, while the Sioux of the north had overcome all successive combinations against them, compelling the government to pacify them by giving them up all they asked for, in the treaty of 1868.

The War Department had made a gallant struggle to hold this country, but Sitting Bull and the hostiles had beaten them. Look again on the map at the sites of old Fort Reno and old Fort Phil Kearney. The last is right at the edge of Sitting Bull's stronghold. It was the scene of the fearful massacre of 1868, when almost the whole garrison was annihilated. It was difficult to keep this fort supplied. Everything had to come by wagon train from Fort Fetterman on the south, while Sitting Bull drew all his supplies of ammunition from Fort Peck and a dozen other places, and lived on the buffalo by which he was surrounded. The white men could not starve him, but he could harass *them* constantly, and he did so. Finally the Department was compelled to abandon Forts Reno and Kearney, and gave up the country to Sitting Bull, by the treaty of 1868.

Five years later, in 1873, it was judged expedient to break that treaty and try a new line of operation, this time up the valley of the Yellowstone. This line possessed one and only one advantage ; while the Yellowstone was navigable, supplies, and even an expedition, could be sent up by steamer comparatively safe from the Indians. By land, as Stanley went, the

SITTING BULL'S DIARY.

A REGULAR DUEL.
COUNT'S COUP ON AN IRISHMAN.

SCALPS A TEAMSTER.
STEALS A DROVE OF HORSES.

Yellowstone route was as bad as the rest, except for provisions. It was very long, and did not stop the supplies of Sitting Bull. The only reason Stanley escaped serious disaster, was that he kept near the river and was able to use his artillery, while Sitting Bull was not as yet joined by any very formidable force of agency Indians. In the war of 1876 all this was to be changed, and Sitting Bull was to find himself in a perfect position, occupying interior lines, able to strike at his enemies wherever he pleased and beat them in details, and all the while able to draw his supplies and reinforcements from a number of concentrating lines, none of which his enemies were able to cut. Indians kept streaming in to his help from all the quarter circle of agencies, informing him of every step taken by his enemies, and bringing ammunition, guns, ponies and men by hundreds.

Of Sitting Bull* personally, not very much is known. It is many years since he attended a council, and he has been so long secluded from the whites that no portrait of him is extant. From the description of agency Indians and others, he is said to be a heavily built Indian, with a large, massive head, and (strange to say) *brown hair*, unlike most Indians. He is heavily marked with the small-pox. The events of his life have been recorded by himself, and fell into the hands of the whites by an accident soon after the Phil. Kearney massacre. A scout brought into one of the forts an old roster book, once belonging to the Thirteeenth United States Infantry, which Sitting Bull had captured, and in this was found a series of over a hundred little Indian pictures, describing the various exploits of the artist. In the first he is shown as a young warrior, naked and unadorned, taking his first scalp by charging a Crow Indian mounted. From the mouth of the young warrior goes a line which joins him to his "totem" or symbol, a buffalo bull sitting upon its haunches, which identified the book as the diary of Sitting Bull. This totem is found in all the pictures. Almost every picture represents the killing of a man or woman, or both, some Indians, some whites. A few represent Sitting Bull carrying off herds of horses. These pictures are in regular Indian style, such as a clever child, without teaching, might draw. There is no attempt at art, but there is no mistake as to what is meant. There are the men, the horses, the women,

---

* This account varies from the one given later and we cannot say which is correct at this writing. — ED

the Indian war bonnets, the white man's stove-pipe hat, in the true spirit of caricature, the salient features seized and fixed.

It was stated at one time that Sitting Bull, while hating the white Americans, and disdaining to speak their language, was yet very fond of the French Canadians; that he talked French, and that he had been converted to Christianity by a French Jesuit, named Father De Smet. How true this may be is uncertain, but probably there is some foundation for it.

One thing about Sitting Bull is certain ; he is an Indian of unusual powers of mind, and a warrior whose talent amounts to genius, while his stubborn heroism in defence of the last of his race is undeniable. Cruel he must be; that is from the instincts of his race; a general of the first natural order he must be, to set the United States at defiance, as he did for the last ten years. That he was able to do this so long was owing to his skilful use of two advantages, — a central position surrounded by " bad-lands," and the quarter circle of agencies from which he drew supplies and allies every campaign.

In the face of these advantages and of Sitting Bull's talents as a warrior, the government gave up the fight in 1868. In 1876 it was determined to try one more campaign against Sitting Bull. We shall see how it succeeded.

The Sioux war originated in injustice and cupidity, and especially in the lust of gold, excited by the famous Black Hills expedition. The rush of miners to the Black Hills was a direct consequence of the weakness of our government, and its lack of control over the turbulent frontier population. When, however, the Sioux formally resolved on war, it became absolutely necessary to attack them, to hinder them from attacking the frontier settlements, and prevent an indiscriminate massacre of innocent and guilty alike.

Three separate columns were, therefore, assembled in the Northwest. The first, under General Crook, was to strike north from Fort Fetterman ; the second, under General Gibbon, to march westwardly from Fort Ellis, in Montana, two hundred miles to the northeast; the third, under General Terry, was to march southwest from the little village of Bismarck, in the north of Dakota Territory. All three were to converge on the sources of the Yellowstone River. In this country it was reported that Sitting Bull, Crazy Horse, and the most turbulent of the Sioux chiefs had hidden their villages, and were preparing their forces

SITTING BULL'S DIARY.

STORMS A CROW ENCAMPMENT AND TAKES THIRTY SCALPS. KILLS A FRONTIERSMAN.
BAGS A BEARER OF DISPATCHES. KILLS A CROW WARRIOR.

25

for a grand raid. To prevent this raid was the object of the campaign.

Generals Terry and Gibbon joined forces near the mouth of the Tongue River, and took measures at once to ascertain the whereabouts of the Indians, who were supposed to be somewhere near the Little Big Horn. Gibbon was to march by one route and Custer by another, and attack the Indians at different points and at the same time. Custer left camp on the 22d, and early on the 25th of June, 1876, discovered what he was in search of, — the camp of Sitting Bull.

This cunning savage had for years baffled every effort of the government to chastise or persuade him and his band to come upon a reservation, and through his many successful raids and great popularity as a warrior, gathered under his leadership the most formidable savage horde that ever existed on this continent. They were not only armed with the latest improved weapons and well supplied with ammunition (for years of successful trade with the British posts had made them rich), but they were composed of the most skilful warriors of the savage Sioux bands, whose equal for ferocity as well as dexterity in the use of weapons and horses, the world has never produced.

Custer's sudden appearance on the bluffs overlooking the Little Big Horn was a complete surprise to the Indian village. The village was a very large one for a hostile band of Indians — it extended for three and a half miles up the valley, and is estimated to have contained at least five thousand people.

Custer, as had always been his custom, divided his command in three parts: one division under Major Reno, one under Captain Benteen, the third commanded by himself. Reno was ordered to charge the lower end of the village, Benteen to charge the centre on the opposite side, and he intended to strike the enemy on the upper end of the valley. He never dreamed that officers under his command would fail to obey him; but before he had reached the ford where he had intended to make his crossing and attack the Indians, Reno had retired out of danger, and with Benteen's wagon-train and packs, barricaded themselves on the top of a prominent hill. Custer, all unconscious of having been deserted by his subordinates, charged the Indians at the ford, and partly succeeded in crossing; but that portion of the Indians that Reno should have engaged, turned and massed themselves around Custer, mustering over two thousand warriors.

Custer's gallant little band was driven back across the stream, hotly pressed by the still gathering myriad of yelling savages, who, being dismounted, poured a steady hail of death from behind every obstacle which could conceal their supple bodies. Custer's mounted troops on the side of a ruggedly terraced hill, stood very little chance of lasting long in this uneven battle. We suppose, from the position of the dead bodies of Captain Calhoun's company, that they were deployed to check the advance of the Indians, while Custer and the rest of the command took the next higher terrace, in hopes that the General might see how fared the fight under his subalterns. Judge what must have been his thoughts when he heard nor saw nothing beyond the sea of savages which were gradually closing around him. Calhoun's company all dead, every man and officer's dead body found in line, shows that they fought kneeling — without hope — but not one flinched from his position among his dead and dying comrades.

On the next higher terrace Captain Keogh's company was ordered to dismount and hold the savages in check, while the General and the rest of the command took still higher ground and kept their flanks open.   Still no sound of the welcome rattle in the distance of Reno or Benteen's carbines.   The brave Keogh and his noble men followed the example set by Calhoun. No panic ; no group of tangled up mob. There they knelt in open order and fired at what they could see of the unmerciful foe that returned their fire from behind every crevice in the many ravines around them.

Keogh's company gone, and over them passed the exultant band of Big Cheyennes, side by side with Iron Horn's band of Sioux, led by the most desperate Indian of the whole Northwest (Rain-in-the-Face), who had sent Custer word a year before that he would take his scalp.

Custer gained the highest defensible point on the hill, and surveyed the valley down the stream, in the hopes of seeing Reno charge in the rear of his enemies. He glanced at the bluffs across the valley, from whence he expected Benteen hours ago. He heard no bugle notes of the charge rending the sulphurous battle air. Colonel Tom Custer (as gallant an officer as ever drew a sword, who had won his position from the ranks for personal bravery in action, and who wore upon his breast what no other officer in the service could boast of, two medals from Con-

CUSTER'S LAST FIGHT ON THE LITTLE BIG HORN.

gress for battle-flags taken from the enemy in the charge), Captain Yates, Captain Cook, his youngest brother, " Boston; " his nephew, "Autie" Reed, and Lieutenant Riley, and about thirty-five men were around the General.

The men had killed what few horses were left, and used their dead bodies for protection against the leaden rain that poured around them. They were out of ammunition. A prolonged yell rended the air, such as might have proceeded from the choir of hell. On rushed the now thickly crowded mass of savages, each intent upon the fiendish desire to bathe his hand in the blood of their defenceless victims. Fiercely rushed the leaders of the Cheyennes, with tomahawk and knife in hand. Rain-in-the-Face was well up with his rival braves, anxious not to be outdone in courage, and also to be revenged on the Custers.

Like a bayed lion, Custer sprang forward to meet them, sabre in hand — a few bright gleams of light shot from the sabre's blade, down went the foremost; another twinkling circle, and another brave went tottering back. A momentary hesitation pervaded the moving mass of men, a hundred guns were brought to bear upon Custer, but so close were they intermingled that they could not shoot. Another brave strode forward, with uplifted tomahawk, thinking to count " Coup," but the weapon was parried from his hand by the dextrous swordsman just as the steel entered his savage breast. Rain-in-the-Face, seeing the fate of three braves, raised his pistol and fired.

This ended the career of the greatest cavalry leader America ever saw. From the Canadian Indians we have this: " Rain-in-the-Face dropped his gun and sprang forward to claim his scalp, but the arms of the braves surrounding the corpse were extended to prevent the rash act, accompanied by a loud protest. Rain-in-the-Face sullenly relinquished his intention, and took his revenge by mutilating the body of poor Tom Custer."

The Indians consider the striking of an enemy with a hand weapon the highest mark of courage — this among the Indians of the Northwest counts " Coup," a stroke, and scores one in promotion of an Indian as a great warrior; that is why Custer was approached so near that he could use his sabre. They were all anxious to kill him with a hand weapon, — he having defended himself so courageously, and struck down three of their bravest warriors, they feared to take his scalp, having a superstition that the Great Spirit will wreak vengeance on the head of one who so dishonors himself.

Then the wounded Indians came streaming back into camp, saying: "We have killed them all; put up your lodges where they are."

There was no danger now to the Sioux, — Long Hair (Custer) was dead.*

The story, as told by the Crow scout who escaped during Custer's fight on the Little Big Horn, may justly be regarded with suspicion. He probably deserted at the commencement of the fight. He could scarcely have succeeded in making his way safely through the mass of Indians, who completely surrounded that gallant band, at any other time.

The following is Sitting Bull's account of that sad and terrible affair, as related to a reporter of a leading newspaper, and it is but another vindication of that brave man, General G. A. Custer, from aspersions of rashness made by self-interested parties: —

Through the intercession of Major Walsh, Sitting Bull was persuaded at nightfall to hold a special conference with me. It was explained to him that I was not his enemy, but that I was his good friend. He was told by Major Walsh that I was a great paper chief; one who talked with a million tongues to all the people in the world. Said the Major: "This man is a man of wonderful medicine; he speaks, and the people on this side and across the great water open their ears and hear him. He tells the truth; he does not lie. He wishes to make the world know what a great tribe is encamped here on the land owned by the White Mother. [This interview took place at Fort Walsh, on British Territory, and the "White Mother" here mentioned is Queen Victoria.] He wants it understood that her guests are mighty warriors. The Long-Haired Chief (alluding to General Custer) was his friend. He wants to hear from you how he fought and whether he met death like a brave."

"Agh-howgh!" (It is well) said Sitting Bull.

He finally agreed to come, after dark, to the quarters which had been assigned to me, on the condition that nobody should be present except myself, his interlocutor, Major Walsh, two

---

* A survey of the disastrous battle-ground disclosed a dreadful slaughter. Two hundred and seven men were buried in one place, and the total number of killed is estimated at three hundred and fifteen, including seventeen commissioned officers.

interpreters, and the stenographer I had employed for the occasion.

At the appointed time, half-past eight, the lamps were lighted, and the most mysterious Indian Chieftain who ever flourished in North America was ushered in by Major Walsh, who locked the door behind him. This was the first time that Sitting Bull had condescended, not merely to visit but to address a white man from the United States. During the long years of his domination he had withstood, with his hands, every attempt on the part of the United States government at a compromise of interests. He had refused all proffers, declined any treaty. He had never been beaten in a battle with United States troops; on the contrary, his warriors had been victorious over the pride of our army. Pressed hard, he had retreated, scorning the factions of his bands who accepted the terms offered them, with the same bitterness with which he scorned his white enemies.

Here he stood, his blanket rolled back, his head upreared, his right moccasin put forward, his right hand thrown across his chest.

I arose and approached him, holding out both hands. He grasped them cordially.

" How ! " said he.

" How ! "

And now let me attempt a better portrait of Sitting Bull. He is about five feet, ten inches high. He was clad in a black and white calico shirt, black cloth leggings and moccasins, magnificently embroidered with beads and porcupine quills. He held in his left hand a fox-skin cap, its brush drooping to his feet; with the dignity and grace of a natural gentleman he had removed it from his head at the threshold. His long, black hair hung far down his back, athwart his cheeks and in front of his shoulders. His eyes gleamed like black diamonds. His visage, devoid of paint, was noble and commanding; nay, it was something more. Besides the Indian character given to it by high cheek-bones, a broad, retreating forehead, a prominent, aquiline nose, and a jaw like a bull dog's, there was about the mouth something of beauty, but more of an expression of exquisite, cruel irony. Such a mouth and such eyes as this Indian's, if seen in the countenance of a white man, would appear to denote qualities similar to those which animated the career of Mazarin and inspired the pen of Machiævelli.

Yet there was something fearfully sweet in his smile as he extended to me his hands.

Such hands! They felt as small and soft as a maiden's, but when I pressed them I could feel the sinews beneath the flesh quivering hard, like a wild animal's. I led him to a seat, a lounge set against the wall, on which he sank with indolent grace. Major Walsh, brilliant in red uniform, sat beside him, and a poitable table was brought near. Two interpreters brought chairs and seated themselves, and at a neighboring desk the stenographer took his place. I afterward learned that two Sioux chiefs stood on guard outside the door, and that all the Indians in the fort had their arms ready to spring in case of a suspected treachery. On the previous night, two of the Indians had been taken suddenly ill, and their sickness had been ascribed by some warriors to poison. So restless and anxious were all the savages that nothing but the influence and tact of Major Walsh could have procured for me and for your readers the following valuable, indeed, historical, colloquy with the Sphinx of the Northwest.

I turned to the interpreter and said: —

"Explain again to Sitting Bull that he is with a friend."

The interpreter explained.

"Banee!" said the chief, holding out his hand again and pressing mine.

Major Walsh here said: "Sitting Bull is in the best mood now that you could possibly wish. Proceed with your questions, and make them as logical as you can. I will assist you, and trip you up occasionally if you are likely to irritate him."

Then the dialogue went on. I give it literally

"You are a great chief," said I to Sitting Bull, "but you live behind a cloud. Your face is dark, my people do not see it. Tell me, do you hate the Americans very much?"

A gleam as of fire shot across his face.

"I am no chief."

This was precisely what I expected. It will dissipate at once the erroneous idea which has prevailed, that Sitting Bull is either a chief or a warrior.

"What are you?"

"I am," said he, crossing both hands upon his chest, slightly nodding, and smiling satirically, "a man."

"What does he mean?" I inquired, turning to Major Walsh.

"He means," responded the Major, "to keep you in ignorance of his secret if he can. His position among his bands is anomalous. His own tribes, the Uncpapas, are not all in fealty to him. Parts of nearly twenty different tribes of Sioux, besides a remnant of the Uncpapas, abide with him. So far as I have learned, he rules over these fragments of tribes, which compose his camp of twenty-five hundred, including between eight hundred and nine hundred warriors, by sheer compelling force of intellect and will. I believe that he understands nothing particularly of war or military tactics, at least not enough to give him the skill or the right to command warriors in battle. He is supposed to have guided the fortunes of several battles, including the fight in which Custer fell. That supposition, as you will presently find, is partially erroneous. His word was always potent in the camp or in the field, but he has usually left to the war chiefs the duties appertaining to engagements. When the crisis came he gave his opinion, which was accepted as law."

"What was he then?" I inquired, continuing this momentary dialogue with Major Walsh. "Was he, is he, a mere medicine man?"

"Don't for the world," replied the Major, "intimate to him, in the questions you are about to ask him, that you have derived the idea from me, or from any one, that he is a mere medicine man. He would deem that to be a profound insult. In point of fact he is a medicine man, but a far greater, more influential medicine man than any savage I have ever known. He has constituted himself a ruler. He is a unique power among the Indians. To the warriors, his people, he speaks with the authority of a Robert Peel, to their chiefs with that of a Richelieu. This does not really express the extent of his influence ; for behind Peel and Richelieu there were traitors and in front of them were factions. Sitting Bull has no traitors in his camp; there are none to be jealous of him. He does not assert himself over strongly. He does not interfere with the rights or duties of others. His power consists in the universal confidence which is given to his judgment, which he seldom denotes until he is asked for an expression of it. It has been, so far, so accurate, it has guided his people so well, he has been caught in so few mistakes and he has saved even his ablest and oldest chiefs from so many evil consequences of their own misjudgment, that to-day his word among them all, is worth more than the united voices of the rest of the camp. He speaks. They listen and they obey. Now let us hear what his explanation will be."

"You say you are no chief?"

".. No!" with considerable hauteur.

"Are you a head soldier?"

"I am nothing — neither a chief nor a soldier."

"What? Nothing?"

"Nothing."

"What, then, makes the wariors of your camp, the great chiefs who are here along with you, look up to you so? Why do they think so much of you?"

Sitting Bull's lips curled with a proud smile.

"Oh, I used to be a kind of a chief; but the Americans made me go away from my father's hunting ground."

"You do not love the Americans?"

You should have seen this savage's lips.

"I saw to-day that all the warriors around you clapped their hands and cried out when you spoke. What you said appeared to please them. They liked you. They seemed to think that what you said was right for them to say. If you are not a great chief, why do these men think so much of you?

At this Sitting Bull, who had in the meantime been leaning back against the wall, assumed a posture of mingled toleration and disdain.

"Your people look up to men because they are rich; because they have much land, many lodges, many squaws?"

"Yes."

"Well, I suppose my people look up to me because I am poor. That is the difference."

In this answer was concentracted all the evasiveness natural to an Indian.

"What is your feeling toward the Americans now?"

He did not even deign an answer. He touched his hip, where his knife was.

I asked the interpreter to insist on an answer.

"Listen," said Sitting Bull, not changing his posture, but putting his right hand out upon my knee. "I told them to-day what my notions were — that I did not want to go back there.

Every time that I had any difficulty with them they struck me first. I want to live in peace."

" Have you an implacable enmity to the Americans? Would you live with them in peace if they allowed you to do so; or do you think that you can only obtain peace here?"

" The White Mother is good."

" Better than the Great Father?"

" Howgh!"

And then after a pause, Sitting Bull continued. " They asked me to-day to give them my horses. I bought my horses, and they are mine. I bought them from men who came up the Missouri in mackinaws. They do not belong to the Government, neither do the rifles. The rifles are also mine. I bought them; I paid for them. Why I should give them up I do not know. I will not give them up."

" Do you really think, do your people believe, that it is wise to reject the proffers that have been made to you by the United States Commissioners? Do not some of you feel as if you were destined to lose your old hunting grounds? Don't you see that you will probably have the same difficulty in Canada that you have had in the United States?"

" The White Mother does not lie."

" Do you expect to live here by hunting? Are there buffaloes enough? Can your people subsist on the game here?"

" I don't know; I hope so."

" If not, are any part of your people disposed to take up agriculture? Would any of them raise steers and go to farming?"

" I don't know."

" What will they do, then?"

" As long as there are buffaloes that is the way we will live."

" But the time will come when there will be no more buffaloes."

" Those are the words of an American."

" How long do you think the buffaloes will last?"

Sitting Bull arose. " We know," said he, extending his right hand with an impressive gesture, " that on the other side the buffaloes will not last very long. Why? Because the country there is poisoned with blood — a poison that kills all the buffaloes or drives them away. It is strange," he continued, with his peculiar smile, " that the Americans should complain that the Indians kill buffaloes. We kill buffaloes, as we kill other animals, for food and clothing, and to make our lodges warm. They kill buffaloes — for what? Go through your country. See the thousands of carcasses rotting on the Plains. Your young men shoot for pleasure. All they take from a dead buffalo is his tail, or his head, or his horns, perhaps, to show they have killed a buffalo. What is this? Is it robbery? You call us savages. What are they? The buffaloes have come North. We have come North to find them, and to get away from a place where the people tell lies."

To gain time, and not to dwell importunately on a single point, I asked Sitting Bull to tell me something of his early life. In the first place, where he was born?

"I was born on the Missouri River; at least I recollect that somebody told me so — I don't know who told me or where I was told of it."

"Of what tribe are you?"

"I am an Uncpapa."

"Of the Sioux?"

"Yes; of the great Sioux Nation."

"Who was your father?"

"My father is dead."

"Is your mother living?"

"My mother lives with me in my lodge."

"Great lies are told about you. White men say that you lived among them when you were young; that you went to school; that you learned to write and read from books; that you speak English; that you know how to talk French?"

"It is a lie."

"You are an Indian?"

(Proudly) "I am a Sioux."

Then, suddenly relaxing from his hauteur, Sitting Bull began to laugh. "I have heard," he said "of some of these stories. They are all strange lies. What I am I am," and here he leaned back and resumed his attitude and expression of barbaric grandeur.

"I am a man. I see. I know. I began to see when I was not yet born; when I was not in my mother's arms. It was then I began to study about my people. I studied about many things. I studied about the small-pox, that was killing my people — the great sickness that was killing the women and children. I was so interested that I turned over on my side. The God Almighty

KILLING BUFFALO FOR PLEASURE.

must have told me at that time [and here Sitting Bull unconsciously revealed his secret], that I would be the man to be the
judge of all the other Indians — a big man, to decide for them in
all their ways.''

"And you have since decided for them?''

" I speak. It is enough.''

" Could not your people, whom you love so well, get on with
the Americans?''

" No !''

" Why?''

"I never taught my people to trust Americans. I have told
them the truth — that the Americans are great liars. I have never
dealt with the Americans. Why should I? The land belonged
to my people. I say I never dealt with them — I mean I never
treated them in a way to surrender my people's rights. I
traded with them, but I always gave full value for what I got.
I never asked the United States Government to make me presents of blankets or cloth, or anything of that kind. The most I
did was to ask them to send me an honest trader that I could
trade with, and I proposed to give him buffalo robes and elk
skins, and other hides in exchange for what we wanted. I told
every trader who came to our camps that I did not want any
favors from him — that I wanted to trade with him fairly and
equally, giving him full value for what I got, but the traders
wanted me to trade with them on no such terms. They wanted to
give little and get much. They told me if I did not accept what
they give me in trade they would get the government to fight me.
I told them I did not want to fight.''

" But you fought?''

"At last, yes; but not until I had tried hard to prevent a
fight. At first my young men, when they began to talk bad,
stole five American horses. I took the horses away from them
and gave them back to the Americans. It did no good. By and
by we had to fight.''

It was at this juncture that I began to question the great savage before me in regard to the most disastrous, most mysterious
Indian battle of the century, — Custer's encounter with the
Sioux on the Big Horn — the Thermopylæ of the plains. Sitting Bull, the chief genius of his bands, has been supposed to
have commanded the Sioux forces when Custer fell.

That the reader may understand Sitting Bull's statements, it

26

will be necessary for him to read the following preliminary
sketch. It should be understood, moreover, that, inasmuch as
every white man with Custer perished, and no other white man,
save one or two scouts, had conferred carefully with Sitting
Bull or any of his chiefs since that awful day, this is the first
authentic story of the conflict which can possibly have appeared
out of the lips of a survivor. It has the more historical value,
since it comes from the chief among Custer's and Reno's foes.

Custer, on the 22d of June, started up the Rosebud, with the
following order from General Terry in his pocket: —

"*Lieutenant-Colonel Custer, Seventh Cavalry.*

" COLONEL: The brigadier-general commanding directs that as
soon as your regiment can be made ready for the march, you
proceed up the Rosebud in pursuit of the Indians whose trail
was discovered by Major Reno a few days since. It is, of
course, impossible to give any definite instructions in regard to
this movement, and, were it not impossible to do so, the department commander places too much confidence in your zeal, energy
and ability, to wish to impose upon you precise orders which
might hamper your action when nearly in contact with the
enemy. He will, however, indicate to you his own views of
what your action should be, and he desires that you should conform to them unless you shall see sufficient reason for departing
from them. He thinks that you should proceed up the Rosebud
until you ascertain definitely the direction in which the trail
above spoken of leads. Should it be found, as it appears to be
almost certain that it will be to turn toward the Little Big
Horn, he thinks that you should still proceed southward, perhaps
as far as the headquarters of the Tongue, and then turn toward the
Little Big Horn, feeling constantly, however, toward your left,
so as to preclude the possibility of the escape of the Indians to
the south or southeast by passing around your left flank. The
column of Colonel Gibbon is now in motion for the mouth
of the Big Horn. As soon as it reaches that point it will cross
the Yellowstone and move up at least as far as the parks of the
Big and Little Big Horn. Of course, its future movements
must be controlled by circumstances as they arise; but it is
hoped that the Indians, if upon the Little Big Horn, may be so
nearly inclosed by two columns that their escape will be impossible. The department commander desires that on your way

CROSSING THE ROSEBUD.

up the Rosebud you should thoroughly examine the upper part
of Tulloch's Creek, and that you should endeavor to send a
scout through to Colonel Gibbon's column with information
of the result of your examination. The lower part of this
creek will be examined by a detachment of Colonel Gibbon's
command. The supply steamer will be pushed up the Big Horn
as far as the forks of the river are found to be navigable for
that space, and the department commander, who will accompany
the column of Colonel Gibbon, desires you to report to him
there not later than the expiration of the time for which your
troops are rationed, unless in the meantime you receive further
orders.   Respectfully,

"E. W. SMITH,

Captain Eighteenth Infantry, Acting Assistant Adjutant-General."

With these tentative instructions, General Custer proceeded
on his way. Hearing of the Indians, he found that he had a
great opportunity to strike them. He touched their trail and
followed it. He laid his plans, with what lack of success we
know. But shall we not also inquire what was the real cause
of his untimely, unnecessary failure?

General Custer had been chided for a division of his troops.
In point of fact he never attacked an Indian camp when he had
more than a company, without so separating his command as to
encompass, bewilder and capture it. We shall presently see
whether it was the fault of his dispositions on this occasion
which lost him his last battle. Here is Reno's account of the
way in which the commands respectively, under Custer, himself
and Benteen, started into action: —

"The regiment left the camp at the mouth of Rosebud River,
after passing in review before the department commander, under
command of Brevet Major General G. A. Custer, Lieutenant-
Colonel, on the afternoon of the 22d of June, and marched up
the Rosebud twelve miles and encamped. On the 23d, marched
up the Rosebud, passing many old Indian camps, and following
a very large lodge-pole trail, but not fresh, making thirty-three
miles. On the 24th, the march was continued up the Rosebud,
the trail and signs freshening with every mile, until we had
made twenty-eight miles, and we then encamped and waited for
information from the scouts. At 9 : 25 P. M. Custer called the
officers together and informed us that, beyond a doubt, the

village was in the valley of the Little Big Horn, and that to reach it it was necessary to cross the divide between the Rosebud and Little Big Horn, and that it would be impossible to do so in the daytime without discovering our march to the Indians; that we would prepare to move at eleven P. M. This was done, the line of march turning from the Rosebud to the right, up one of its branches, which headed near the summit at the divide.

"About two P. M. of the 25th, the scouts told him that he could not cross the divide before daylight. We then made coffee and rested three hours, at the expiration of which time the march was resumed, the divide crossed, and about eight A. M., the command was in the valley of one of the branches of the Little Big Horn. By this time the Indians had been seen, and it was certain that we could not surprise them, and it was determined to move at once to the attack.

" Previous to this no division of the regiment had been made since the order was issued on the Yellowstone annulling wing and battalion organizations. General Custer informed me he would assign commands on the march. I was ordered by Lieut. W. W. Cook, adjutant, to assume command of Companies M, A, and G, Capt. Benteen of Companies H, D, and K, Custer retaining C, E, F, I and L under his immediate command, and Company B, Capt. McDougall, in rear of the pack train. I assumed command of the companies assigned to me, and without any definite orders moved forward with the rest of the column and well to its left. I saw Benteen moving further to the left, and as they passed he told me he had orders to move well to the left and sweep everything before him. I did not see him again until about half-past two P. M. The command moved down the creek toward the Little Big Horn Valley, Custer, and five companies, on the right bank, myself and three companies on the left bank, and Benteen further to the left and out of sight."

It appears to have been about the middle of the forenoon when Custer thus subdivided his column. Reno goes on to say that at half-past twelve Lieut. Cook, Custer's adjutant, came to him, told him that the village was only two miles away, and ordered him to move forward rapidly and charge it. Other evidence likewise shows that this order was given about that time, and that Reno was urged not to let up on the Indians. The Indian village, consisting of camps of Cheyennes, Ogallalas, Minneconjous and Uncpapas, was nearly three miles long. Reno crossed the Little

Big Horn, formed his first line just south of the crossing and charged, He says : —

" I deployed, and, with the Ree scouts at my left charged down the valley with great ease for about two and a half miles."

Reno, instead of holding the ground thus gained, retreated, being hard pressed. He made a temporary stand in a bunch of timber, but finally retreated back over the valley, and across the Little Big Horn and up the bluffs, on the summit of which he intrenched himself late in the afternoon.

Custer's march to the ford, where he attempted to cross the Little Big Horn and attack the Indians in their rear, was much longer than Reno's march, consequently Custer's assault was not made until after Reno's. Custer's intention was to sandwich, as it were, the main body of the Indians between Reno's and his own forces. He hoped by thus pressing them on two sides — Reno constantly fighting them and he himself constantly fighting them — to disconcert them and crush them at last. His plan is thus seen to have been that of a general. It relieves him from the aspersion of rashness. It must, in this connection, be remembered that Custer had fought Indians many times and had never been beaten by them, although on several occasions he had encountered more than three times the number of his own troops. He trusted in this instance to the fealty of his own officers, the bravery of his soldiers and his own genius to overcome the mere weight of numbers, as he had so often done before.

The testimony of Sitting Bull which I am about to give, is the more convincing and important from the very fact of the one erroneous impression he derived as to the identity of the officer in command of the forces which assailed his camp. He confounds Reno with Custer. He supposes that one and the same general crossed the Little Big Horn where Reno crossed, charged as Reno charged, retreated as Reno retreated back over the river, and then pursued the line of Custer's march, attacked as Custer attacked, and fell as Custer fell.

" Did you know the Long Haired Chief?" I asked Sitting

" No."

" What! Had you never seen him?"

" No. Many of the chiefs knew him."

" What do they think of him?"

" He was a great warrior."

" Was he brave? "

" He was a mighty chief."

" Now, tell me.   Here is something that I wish to know.   Big lies are told about the fight in which the Long Haired Chief was killed.   He was my friend.   No one has come back to tell the truth about him, or about that fight.   You were there; you know.   Your chiefs know.   I want to hear something that forked tongues do not tell — the truth."

" It is well."

Here I drew forth a map of the battle-field and spread it out across Sitting Bull's knees and explained to him the names and situations as represented on it, and he smiled.

" We thought we were whipped," he said.

" Ah!   Did you think the soldiers were too many for you? "

" Not at first ; but by-and-by, yes.   Afterwards, no."

" Tell me about the battle.   Where was the Indian camp first attacked? "

" Here " (pointing to Reno's crossing on the map).

"About what time in the day was that? "

" It was some two hours past the time when the sun is in the centre of the sky."

" What white chief was it who came over there against your warriors? "

" The Long Hair."

"Are you sure? "

" The Long Hair commanded."

" But you did not see him? "

" I have said that I never saw him."

" Did any of the chiefs see him? "

" Not here, but there," pointing to the place where Custer charged and was repulsed, on the north bank to the Little Big Horn.

" Why do you think it was the Long Hair who crossed first and charged you here at the right side of the map? "

"A chief leads his warriors."

" Was there a good fight here, on the right side of the map? Explain it to me? "

" It was so," said Sitting Bull, raising his hands.   " I was lying in my lodge.   Some young men ran into me and said: ' The Long Hair is in the camp.   Get up.   They are firing in the camp.' I said, all right, and jumped up and stepped out of my lodge.''

'' Where was your lodge.''

'' Here, with my people,'' answered Sitting Bull, pointing to the group of Uncpapa lodges, designated as '' abandoned lodges '' on the map.

'' So the first attack was made, then, on the right side of the map, and upon the lodges of the Uncpapas? ''

'' Yes.''

'' Here the lodges are said to have been deserted? ''

'' The old men, the squaws, and the children were hurried away.''

'' Toward the other end of the camp? ''

'' Yes. Some of the Minneconjou women and children also left their lodges when the attack began.''

'' Did you retreat at first? ''

'' Do you mean the warriors? ''

'' Yes, the fighting men.''

'' Oh, we fell back, but it was not what warriors call a retreat ; it was to gain time. It was the Long Hair who retreated. My people fought him here in the brush (designating the timber behind which the Indians pressed Reno) and he fell back across here (placing his finger on the line of Reno's retreat to the northern bluffs)

'' So you think that was the Long Hair whom your people fought in that timber and who fell back afterwards to those heights? ''

'' Of course.''

'' What occurred afterward? Was there any heavy fighting after the retreat of the soldiers to the bluffs? ''

'' Not then ; not there.''

'' Where, then? ''

'' Why, down here ; '' and Sitting Bull indicated with his finger the place where Custer approached and touched the river. '' That,'' said he, '' was where the big fight was fought a little later. After the Long Hair was driven back to the bluffs he took this road (tracing with his finger the line of Custer's march on the map), and went down to see if he could not beat us there.''

[Here the reader should pause to discern the extent of Sitting Bull's error, and to anticipate what will presently appear to be Reno's misconception or mistake. Sitting Bull, not identifying

Reno in the whole of this engagement, makes it seem that it was Custer who attacked, when Reno attacked in the first place, and afterward moved down to resume the assault from a new position. He thus involuntarily testifies to the fact that Reno's assault was a brief, ineffectual one before his retreat to the bluffs, and that Reno, after his retreat, ceased on the bluffs from aggressive fighting.]

"When the fight commenced here," I asked, pointing to the spot where Custer advanced behind the Little Big Horn, "what happened?"

"Hell!"

"You mean, I suppose, a fierce battle?"

"I mean a thousand devils."

"The village was by this time thoroughly aroused?"

"The squaws were like flying birds; the bullets were like humming bees."

"You say that when the first attack was made off here on the right of the map, the old men and squaws and children ran down the valley toward the left. What did they do when this second attack came from up here toward the left?"

"They ran back again to the right, here and there," answered Sitting Bull, placing his swarthy fingers on the words "Abandoned Lodges."

"And where did the warriors run?"

"They ran to the fight — the big fight."

"So that in the afternoon, after the first fight, on the right hand side of the map, was over, and after the big fight on the left hand side began, you say the squaws and children all returned to the right hand side, and that the warriors, the fighting men of all the Indian camps, ran to the place where the big fight was going on?'

"Yes."

"Why was that? Were not some of the warriors left in front of these intrenchments on the bluffs, near the right side of the map? Did not you think it necessary, — did not your war chiefs think it necessary, — to keep some of your young men there to fight the troops who had retreated to these intrenchments?"

"No."

"Why?"

"You have forgotten."

" How? "

" You forget that only a few soldiers were left by the Long Hair on those bluffs. He took the main body of his soldiers with him to make the big fight down here on the left."

" So there were no soldiers to make a fight left in the intrenchments on the right hand bluff? "

" I have spoken. It is enough. The squaws could deal with them. There were none but squaws and pappooses in front of them that afternoon."

This startling assertion of Sitting Bull involves the most terrible charge which has been brought against Reno. It amounts to an assertion, that Reno, having made his assault, been beaten and retreated, stayed there on the bluffs without renewing the attack for which Gen. Custer, who had by this time come down with his horsemen on the rear of the Sioux camp from the north, vainly awaited — how hopelessly !

" Well, then," I inquired of Sitting Bull, " did the cavalry, who came down and made the big fight, fight? "

Again Sitting Bull smiled.

" They fought. Many young men are missing from our lodges. But is there an American squaw who has her husband left? Were there any Americans left to tell the story of that day? "

" No.'

" How did they come on to the attack? "

" I have heard that there are trees which tremble.

" Do you mean the trees with trembling leaves? "

" Yes."

" They call them in some parts of the Western country Quaking Asps ; in the eastern part of the country they call them Silver Aspens."

" Hah? A great white chief, whom I met once, spoke these words, ' Silver Aspens,' trees that shake; these were the Long Hair's soldiers."

" You do not mean that they trembled before your people because they were afraid? "

" They were brave men. They were tired. They were too tired."

" How did they act? How did they behave themselves? "

At this Sitting Bull again arose. I also arose from my seat, as did the other persons in the room, except the stenographer

" Your people," said Sitting Bull, extending his right hand, " were killed. I tell no lies about dead men. These men who came with the Long Hair were as good men as ever fought. When they rode up their horses were tired and they were tired. When they got off from their horses they could not stand firmly on their feet, They swayed to and fro — so my young men have told me — like the limbs of cypresses in a great wind. Some of them staggered under the weight of their guns. But they begun to fight at once; but by this time, as I have said, our camps were aroused, and there were plenty of warriors to meet them. They fired with needle guns. We replied with magazine guns — repeating rifles. It was so (and here Sitting Bull illustrated by patting his palms together with the rapidity of a fusillade). Our young men rained lead across the river and drove the white braves back."

"And then?"

"And then they rushed across themselves."

"And then?"

"And then they found that they had a good deal to do."

" Was there at that time some doubt about the issue of the battle, whether you would whip the Long Hair or not?"

" There was so much doubt about it that I started down there (here again, pointing to the map) to tell the squaws to pack up the lodges and get ready to move away."

" You were on that expedition, then, after the big fight had fairly begun?"

" Yes."

" You did not personally witness the rest of the big fight? You were not engaged in it?"

" No; I have heard of it from the warriors."

" When the great crowds of your young men crossed the river in front of the Long Hair, what did they do? Did they attempt to assault him directly in his front?"

"At first they did, but afterward they found it better to try and get around him. They formed themselves on all sides of him, except just at his back."

" How long did it take them to put themselves around his flanks?"

"As long as it takes the sun to travel from here to here" (indicating some marks upon his arm, with which, apparently, he is used to gauge the progress of the shadow of his lodge across his arm, and probably meaning half an hour. An Indian has no more definite way than this to express the lapse of time).

" The trouble was with the soldiers," he continued; "they were so exhausted, and their horses bothered them so much, that they could not take good aim. Some of their horses broke away from them and left them to stand and drop and die. When the Long Hair, the General, found that he was so outnumbered and threatened on his flanks, he took the best course he could have taken. The bugle blew. It was an order to fall back. All the men fell back fighting and dropping. They could not fire fast enough, though. But from our side it was so," said Sitting Bull, and here he clapped his hands rapidly, twice a second, to express with what quickness and continuance the balls flew from the Henry and Winchester rifles wielded by the Indians. " They could not stand up under such a fire," he added.

" Were any military tactics shown? Did the Long Haired Chief make any disposition of his soldiers, or did it seem as though they retreated altogether, helter-skelter, fighting for their lives?"

" They kept in pretty good order. Some great chief must have commanded them all the while. They would fall back across a *coulie*, and make a fresh stand beyond, on higher ground. The map is pretty nearly right. It shows where the white men stopped and fought before they were all killed. I think that is right — down there to the left, just above the Little Big Horn. There was one party driven out there, away from the rest, and there a great many men were killed. The places marked on the map are pretty nearly the places where all were killed."

" Did the whole command keep on fighting until the last?"

" Every man, so far as my people could see. There were no cowards on either side."

Cowards! One would think not. The best testimony, from one who has examined the battle-field and the line of Custer's retreat, is as follows: —

" From this point [the north bank of the Little Big Horn, where Custer was forced back by overpowering numbers] he was driven back to make successive stands on the higher ground. His line of retreat stretches from the river to the spot indicated on the map as that where he fell. On the line of retreat, Calhoun's company seems to have been thrown across it to check the Indians. At a distance of about three-quarters of a mile from the river, the whole of Calhoun's company lay dead in an irregular line, Calhoun and Crittenden in place in the rear. About a mile beyond this, on the ridge parallel to the stream, still following the line of retreat indicated on the map, Keogh's company was slaughtered in position, his right resting on the hill where Custer fell, and which seems to have been held by Yates' company. On the most prominent part of the ridge Custer made his last desperate stand. Here, with Captain Yates, Colonel Cook, Captain Custer, Lieutenant Riley, and others, and thirty-two men of Yates' command, he went down, fighting heroically to the last, against the tremendous odds which assailed them on all sides. It is believed by some that, finding the situation a desperate one, they killed their horses for a barricade. From the point where Custer fell, the line of retreat again doubles back toward the river through a ravine, and along this line in the ravine twenty-three bodies of Smith's company were found. Where this terminates, near the river, are found the dead men and horses of Captain Custer's company, commingled with Smith's, and the situation of the dead indicates that some desperate attempt was made to make a stand near the river, or to gain the woods.

I inquired of Sitting Bull: "How long did this big fight continue?"

"The sun was there," he answered, pointing to within two hours of from the western horizon.

"You cannot certainly depend," here observed Maj. Walsh, "upon Sitting Bull's or any other Indian's statement in regard to time or numbers. But his answer — indeed, all his answers — exactly correspond with the replies to similar questions of my own. If you will proceed you will obtain from him in a few moments some important testimony."

I went on to interrogate Sitting Bull: —

"This big fight, then, extended through three hours?"

"Through most of the going forward of the sun."

"Where was the Long Hair the most of the time?"

"I have talked with my people; I cannot find one who saw the Long Hair until just before he died. He did not wear his hair long as he used to wear it. His hair was like yours," said Sitting Bull, playfully touching my forehead with his fingers. "It was short, but it was of the color of the grass when the frost comes."

' Did you hear from your people how he died? Did he die on horseback "

" No; none of them died on horseback."

"All were dismounted? "

" Yes."

"And Custer, the Long Hair? "

" Well, I have understood that there were a great many brave men in that fight, and that from time to time, while it was going on, they were shot down like pigs. They could not help themselves. One by one the officers fell. I believe the Long Hair rode across once from this place down here (meaning the place where Tom Custer's and Smith's companies were killed), to this place up here (indicating the spot on the map where Custer fell), but I am not sure about this. Any way it was said that up there where the last fight took place, where the last stand was made, the Long Hair stood like a sheaf of corn with all the ears fallen around him."

" Not wounded? "

" No."

" How many stood by him? "

"A few."

" When did he fall? "

" He killed a man when he fell. He laughed."

" You mean he cried out? "

" No, he laughed; he had fired his last shot.'

" From a carbine? "

" No, a pistol."

" Did he stand up after he first fell?"

" He rose up on his hands and tried another shot, but his pistol would not go off,"

" Was any one else standing up when he fell down? "

" One man was kneeling, that was all. But he died before the Long Hair. All this was far up on the bluffs, far away from the Sioux encampment. I did not see it. It was told to me. But it is true."

" The Long Hair was not scalped? '

" No; my people did not want his scalp."

" Why? "

" I have said he was a great chief."

" Did you at any time," I persisted, " during the progress of the fight, believe that your people would get the worst of it? "

"At one time, as I have told you, I started down to tell the squaws to strike the lodges. I was then on my way up to the right end of the camp, where the first attack was made upon us. But before I reached that end of the camp, where the Minneconjou and Uncpapa squaws and children were, and where some of the other squaws — Cheyennes and Ogallalas — had gone, I was overtaken by one of the young warriors, who had just come from the fight. He called out to me. He said: ' No use to leave camp; every white man is killed.' So I stopped and went no further. I turned back, and by-and-by I met the warriors returning."

" But in the meantime," I asked, " were there no warriors occupied up here at the right end of the camp? Was nobody left, except the squaws and the children and the old men, to take care of that end of the camp? Was nobody ready to defend it against the soldiers in those intrenchments up there?"

" Oh," replied Sitting Bull again, " there was no need to waste warriors in that direction. There were only a few soldiers in those intrenchments, and we knew they wouldn't dare to come out."

This finished the interview, and with a few more How! Hows, the wily chieftain withdrew.

George A. Custer, who wrote the major portion of this book, an account of whose tragic death we have just related, was born December 5, 1839, in a western village called New Rumley, in Ohio; and at the time of his death (June 25, 1876) was in the thirty-seventh year of his age. From his first entrance into public life he never suffered a reverse, and faults and merits alike seemed to conspire to befriend him on the road to success. After going through the common schools came his first piece of fortune. John A. Bingham, member from his district, sent him to West Point in 1857, and the rebellion broke out in 1861, just as he graduated into the army, with grade of second lieutenant of cavalry. By nature he was remarkably favored physically, being one of the handsomest of men — tall, slender, lithe, and very active; with a noble, knightly face surrounded by long, golden, curling locks. To him, West Point Academy was exceptionally irksome. He naively tells us, in a class of thirty-four members, *thirty-three* graduated above him; and almost on his very graduation day, his reckless romance of character cost him a court-

martial, which would have ruined any one not possessed of
" Custer's luck."

There is something peculiarly characteristic and interesting in
the story he tells of the boy officer of the guard, who, seeing
two cadets quarrelling, instead of arresting both, calls out to bystanders, " Stand back, boys; let's have a fair fight." It was
the key-note of his whole character. " Let's have a fair fight,"
was his motto then and to his death, and no man ever loved one
better. Surely, he had enough of fair fights the rest of his life.

The remains of General George A. Custer arrived in West
Point, New York, October 10, 1877, on steamer " Mary Powell."
Steamers " Hopkins " and " Henry Smith " also arrived from
New York with the Loyal League Commandery and Connec-
ticut Volunteer Cavalry Association on board. A detachment
of cavalry escorted the remains to the chapel, where a portion
of the Episcopal burial service was read. The remains were
then escorted to the cemetery, the band playing a funeral march.
At the grave the remainder of the burial service was read, and
the infantry fired a salute. There, beneath the green sod, sleeps
as brave a soldier as ever trod the field of battle, and as true a
heart as ever beat 'neath a soldier's uniform.

Captains Custer and Yates, and Lieutenants A. E. Smith and
D. McIntoch and James Calhoun, were reinterred at Fort Leavenworth, Kansas, August 3, 1877.

A granite shaft which is to mark the spot where Custer and
the seven companies of the Seventh United States Cavalry laid
down their lives, was shipped from Montello, Wis., to Montana,
July 2, 1883. The monument consists of a cube of Montello
granite, four and one-half by five and one-half feet, resting on
a base of the same material. It is inscribed with the names of
the slain.

27

XXIII.

James B. Hickok, better known as Wild Bill, was a native of Illinois. From childhood up, Wild Bill, as we shall call him, was passionately fond of fire-arms; and at twelve years of age could knock the eye out of a squirrel at almost every shot. Pistol practice was his favorite amusement, and all his childish efforts were bent on obtaining ammunition to pursue his beloved sport. He became as expert in the use of fire-arms as the present crack nines are with the base ball. In vain did his parents endeavor, by force and persuasion, to induce their boy to attend the country school, and there store his youthful mind with knowledge that would serve him well in after years; but all in vain. Bill's mind was otherwise inclined; and, consequently, his education was very limited.

Bill left home when about eighteen years of age, and made his way to the "Future Great City" (St. Louis), and from there proceeded by boat to Kansas, where he joined Jim Lane's famous jay-hawkers, or anti-slavery forces. In all trials of marksmanship in the regiment Bill came off victorious, and was often complimented by Colonel Jim Lane. It is said of him that, early one morning, just after reveille, a flock of wild geese were heard approaching, flying in the direction of the camp. Billy quickly seized his repeating rifle and secured three fine birds, before the flock could escape by rising higher in the air. They were estimated to be fully two hundred yards high.

We cannot follow this remarkable man in all his various ramblings, nor give a full account of his many daring deeds and hair-breadth escapes. His personal appearance is accurately described in Chapter IV. of this book.

Captain B—— relates the following adventure, which happened during one of their foraging expeditions to obtain fresh meat : —

"Early one morning, Bill came on the trail of a large band of elk, and soon afterwards we were in hot pursuit. The wind was in the right direction, and about three hours' riding, following carefully the trail, brought us in sight of the elk, who were en-

J. B. HICKOK. (WILD BILL.)

tirely unsuspicious of the slightest danger. Picketing our horses, we now commenced to stalk on foot, and the ground being favorable, got within forty yards of where they were making their midday halt. It would be difficult to imagine a more perfectly beautiful sight. I should fancy about eighty of these magnificent animals, of different ages, sexes, and sizes, were in the band. Some were lying down, and others quietly feeding. Our position was on the brow of a small, steep sand ridge, thickly covered with long grass at the top, through which we could watch quietly the movements of the band without a chance of being discovered. A good, stiff breeze, blowing directly from them to us, prevented the possibility of their getting our wind; and, there being no danger of anything alarming them, we lay for at least five minutes perfectly still, to admire so grand a sight, and get quite cool and collected after our stalk. How poor Landseer or Rosa Bonheur would have enjoyed such a sight! Of all animal creation, I consider the elk, beyond question, the handsomest. The bulls were full maned and almost black about the neck and muzzle. Some of the old ones had grand heads, but the greatest number were about one or two years old, and with antlers not fully grown. The cows were very handsome, and in splendid condition; and there were many this year's calves, all as graceful and pretty as they could well be.

" Picking out our favorites, we now got ready. I selected a fine bull, who was certainly not over fifty yards from where I lay, and taking a deliberate aim, sent a bullet directly through his heart. Bill's rifle missed fire, and Comstock knocked over a grand old bull, who was sent kicking to the ground. We then blazed away at the nearest elk, and knocked over three others. In the excitement of firing at the retreating elks, no attention was paid to those already down, and we were disgusted and surprised to see Comstock's first love, who was the finest of the lot, trotting steadily away and well out of range.

" Cutting the throats of the fallen ones as quickly as possible, we mounted and galloped after the band, who, having neither seen nor smelt us, were by no means greatly alarmed; and after a sharp spin of some four miles, keeping well to leeward and out of sight, again struck the herd. This time we got within about a hundred yards from where they were quietly feeding at a walk, and once more did considerable execution. It was now getting late; we had as much meat as the wagon could carry, and, though we might certainly have struck the band a third time, as they had never either seen or smelt us, we tempered mercy with prudence, and rode back to camp.

"It is surprising what a number of elk got off after having been apparently mortally wounded, and considered even beyond the assistance of another shot.

"Lieutenant K. once shot a fine bull who rolled over, like Comstock's had done, seemingly *in articulo mortis.* He had on the occasion a new knife, which he was most anxious to christen, and laying down his discharged rifle, he advanced to flesh his weapon. The elk, however, appeared to object to being operated on, and kicked lustily whenever he approached to put his charitable project into execution. Now, an elk's kick is worse than one from a Mexican mustang, and the lieutenant, being well aware of his danger, dodged about from side to side in a decidedly cautious and wary manner, trying in vain, to reach him safely. This game lasted over two minutes, at the end of which time the animal, apparently disgusted at the clumsy efforts being made to send him to the happy hunting-grounds, concluded to remain a little longer on this earth, and quietly jumping up, galloped off, and was seen no more."

A still more amusing incident happened to Wild Bill. He also one day knocked over a fine bull who fell apparently quite dead, as he pitched right over on getting the shot, with one of his forelegs entangled amid his branching antlers. Bill came up to cut his throat, and, to save the trouble of picketing his horse, tied the end of the lariat to the elk's hind leg, while he dragged the body round to a more convenient position for performing his execution. The movement cleared the entangled limb, and the elk, who was only " creased," *i.e.,* shot through the thick part of the neck and momentarily paralyzed, jumped up, and with the horse fastened to him, galloped off as strong and well as if he had never been touched. The sight was laughable in the extreme. Away went the elk, and following close after was the horse. Wild Bill raced after the pair, shouting, " Whoa, Jerry ! Whoa, Jerry ! " not daring to fire lest he should injure his horse

No one could tell how the race would end. Suddenly the elk turned round to fight the horse, whom he disliked following so close to his heels. This gave Bill the chance he wanted, and, whipping out his navy, he shot the lariat in two just where it was

WILD BILL AND THE ELK.

tied to the elk's leg, and with another shot laid the elk out on the grass.

The following appeared in *Harper's Weekly*. Captain Honesty was relating to Colonel N. an account of the duel between Wild Bill and Dave Tutt. I will give the story in his words: —

"They say Bill's wild. Now he isn't any sich thing. I've known him going on ter ten year, and he's as civil a disposed person as you'll find he-e-arabouts. But he won't be put upon.

"I'll tell yer how it happened. But come inter the office; thar's a good many round hy'ar as sides with Tutt — the man that's shot. But I tell you 'twas a fair fight. Take some whiskey? No? Well, I will if yer'l excuse me. You see," contined the captain, setting the empty glass on the table in an emphatic way, "Bill was up in his room a-playin seven up, or four hand, or some of them pesky games. Bill refused to play with Tutt, who was a professional gambler. Yer see, Bill was a scout on our side durin' the war, and Tutt was a reb scout. Bill had killed Dave Tutt's mate, and, atween one thing and another, there war an unusual hard feelin' atwixt 'em.

"Ever sin' Dave come back he had tried to pick a row with Bill; so Bill wouldn't play cards with him any more. But Dave stood over the man who was gambling with Bill and lent the fellow money. Bill won about two hundred dollars, which made Tutt spiteful mad, Bime-by, he says to Bill: —

"'Bill, you've got plenty of money; pay me that $40 yer owe me in that horse trade.'

"And Bill paid him. Then he said: —

"'Yer owe me $35 more; yer lost it playin' with me t'other night.'

"Dave's style was right provoking; but Bill answered him perfectly gentlemanly: —

"'I think yer wrong Dave. It's only $25. I have a memorandum of it in my pocket, downstairs. Ef it's $35 I'll give it yer.'

"Now, Bill's watch was lyin' on the table. Dave took up the watch , put it in his pocket, and said; 'I'll keep this yere watch till you pay me that $35.

"This made Bill shooting mad; fur don't yer see Colonel, it war a doubting his honor like, so he got up and looked Dave in the eyes, and said to him; 'I don't want ter make a row in this

house. It's a decent house, and I don't want ter injure the
keeper. You'd better put that watch back on the table.''

" But Dave grinned at Bill mighty ugly, and walked off with
the watch, and kept it several days. All this time Dave's friends
were spurring Bill onter fight; there was no end ter the talk.
They blackguarded him in an underhand sort of a way, and
tried ter get up a scriminage, and then they thought they could
lay him out. Yer see Bill had enemies all about. He's settled
the accounts of a heap of men who lived round here. This is
about the only place in Missouri whar a reb can come back and
live; and ter tell yer truth, Colonel'' — and the captain, with an
involuntary movement, hitched up his revolver belt as he said
with expressive significance, " they don't stay long round here.

Well, as I war saying, these rebs don't like to see a man
walkin' round town who they knew in the reb army as one of
their men, who they now know was on our side, all the time he
war sendin, us information, sometimes from Pap Price's own
headquarters. But they couldn't provoke Bill inter a row, for
he's afeard of hisself when he gets awful mad; and he allers left
his shootin' irons in his room when he went out. One day these
cusses drew their pistols on him and dared him to fight, and then
they told him that Tutt was a goin' ter pack that watch across the
squar' next day at noon.

" I heard of this, for everybody was talkin' about it on the
street, and so I went after Bill, and found him in his room,
cleaning and greasing and loading his revolvers.

" ' Now, Bill,' says I, ' you're goin' ter git inter a fight.'

" ' Don't you bother yerself, captain,' says he. ' It's not the
first time I have been in a fight; and these d —— d hounds have
put on me long enough. You don't want me ter give up my honor,
do yer?'

" ' No, Bill,' says I ' yer must keep yer honor.'

" Next day about noon, Bill went down on the squar.' He had
said that Dave Tutt shouldn't pack that watch across the squar',
unless dead men could walk.

" When Bill got onter the squar' he found a crowd stanin' on
the corner of the street by which he entered the squar', which is
from the south, yer know. In this crowd he saw a lot of Tutt's
friends; some were cousins of his'n, just back from the reb
army; and they jeered him, and boasted that Dave was a goin'
to pack that watch across the squar' as he promised.

" Then Bill saw Tutt stanin' near the court-house, which yer remember is on the west side, so that the crowd war behind Bill.

" Just then Tutt, who war alone, started from the court-house and walked out into the squar', and Bill moved away from the crowd toward the west side of the squar'. 'Bout fifteen paces brought them opposite to each other, and 'bout fifty yards apart. Tutt then showed his pistol. Bill had kept a sharp eye on him, and before Tutt could pint it Bill had his'n out.

"At that moment you could have heard a pin drop in that squar'. Both Tutt and Bill fired, but one discharge followed the other so quick that it's hard to say which went off first. Tutt was a famous shot, but he missed this time; the ball from his pistol went over Bill's head. The instant Bill fired, without waitin' ter see if he had hit Tutt, he wheeled on his heels and pointed his pistol at Tutt's friends, who had already drawn their weapons.

" ' Aren't ye satisfied, gentlemen?' cried Bill, as cool as an alligator. ' Put up your shootin' irons, or there'll be more dead men here.' And they put 'em up, and said it war a fair fight.

" ' What became of Tutt?' I asked of the Captain, who had stopped at this point of his story, and was very deliberately engaged in refilling his empty glass. ' Oh, Dave? He was as plucky a feller as ever drew a trigger; but, Lord bless yer! it was no use. Bill never shoots twice at the same man, and his ball went through Dave's heart. He stood stock still for a second or two, then raised his arm as if ter fire again, then he swayed a little, staggered three or four steps, and then fell dead. Bill and his friends wanted ter have the thing done regular, so we went up ter the justice, and Bill delivered himself up. A jury was drawn; Bill was tried and cleared the next day. It was proved that it was a case of self-defence. Don't yer see, Colonel?'

" I answered that I was afraid that I did not see that point very clearly.

" ' Well, well!' he replied, with an air of compassion; ' you haven't drunk any whiskey, that's what's the matter with you.' And then, putting his hand on my shoulder with a half-mysterious half-conscious look in his face, he muttered, in a whisper:—

" ' *The fact is thar was an undercurrent of a woman in that fight!*' "

Meeting Wild Bill one day in Springfield, I questioned him about the McKandlas affair.

"I don't like to talk about that McKandlas affair," said Bill, in answer to my question. "It gives me a queer shiver whenever I think of it, and somethimes I dream about it, and wake up in a cold sweat.

"You see this McKandlas was the captain of a gang of desperadoes, horse thieves, murderers, regular cut throats, who were the terror of every body on the border, and who kept us in the mountains in hot water whenever they were around. I knew them all in the mountains, when they pretended to be trapping, but they were hiding from the hangman. McKandlas was the biggest scoundrel and bully of them all, and was allers a braggin' of what he could do. One day I beat him shootin' at a mark, and then threw him at the back-holt. And I didn't drop him as soft as you would a baby, you may be sure. Well he got savage mad about it, and swore he would have his revenge on me sometime.

"This was just before the war broke out, and we were already takin' sides in the mountains either for the South or the Union. McKandlas and his gang were border ruffians in the Kansas row, and of course they went with the rebs. Bime-by he clar'd out, and I shouldn't have thought of the feller agin ef he hadn't crossed my path. It 'pears he didn't forget me.

"It was in 1861, when I guided a detachment of cavalry who were comin' in from Camp Floyd. We had nearly reached the Kansas line, and were in South Nebraska, when one afternoon I went out of camp to go to the cabin of an old friend of mine, a Mrs. Waltman. I took only one of my revolvers with me, for although the war had broke out, I didn't think it necessary to carry both my pistols, and in all or'nary scrimmages, one is better than a dozen, ef you shoot straight. I saw some wild turkeys on the road as I was goin' down and popped one of 'em over, thinkin' he'd be just the thing for supper.

"Well, I rode up to Mrs. Waltman's, jumped off my horse, and went into the cabin, which is like most of the cabins on the prarer, with only one room, and that had two doors, one openin' in front and tother on a yard like.

"'How are you, Mrs. Waltman?' I said, feeling as jolly as you please.

"'The minute she saw me she turned as white as a sheet, and

screamed: ' Is that you, Bill? Oh, my God! they will kill you! Run! Run! They will kill you!'

" ' Who's a goin' to kill me?' said I. ' There's two can play at that game.'

" ' It's McKandlas and his gang. There's ten of them, and you've no chance. They've jes' gone down the road to the corn-rack. They came up here only five minutes ago. McKandlas was draggin' poor Parson Shipley on the ground with a lariat round his neck. The preacher was most dead with choking and the horses stamping on him. McKandlas knows yer bringin' in that party of Yankee cavalry, and he swears he'll cut yer heart out. Run, Bill, run! — But it's too late; they're comin' up the lane.'

" While she was a talkin' I remembered I had but one revolver, and a load gone out of that. On the table there was a horn of powder and some little bars of lead. I poured some powder into the empty chamber and rammed the lead after it by hammering the barrel on the table, and had just capped the pistol when I heard McKandlas shout.

" ' There's that d —— d Yank, Wild Bill's horse; he's here; and we'll skin him alive!'

" If I had thought of runnin' before it was too late now, and the house was my best holt as sort of fortress, like. I never thought I should leave that room alive."

The scout stopped in his story, rose from his seat, and strode back and forward in a state of great excitement.

" I tell you what it is, Kernel," he resumed, after a while; " I don't mind a scrimmage with these fellows round here. Shoot one or two of them and the rest run away. But all of McKandlas's gang were reckless, blood-thirsty devils, who would fight as long as they had strength to pull a trigger. I have been in tight places, but that's one of the few times I said my prayers.

" ' Surround the house and give him no quarter!' yelled McKandlas. When I heard that I felt as quiet and as cool as if I was a-going to church. I looked round the room and saw a Hawkins rifle hanging over the bed.

" ' Is that loaded?' said I to Mrs. Waltman.

" ' Yes,' the poor thing whispered. She was so frightened she couldn't speak out loud.

" 'Are you sure?' said I, as I jumped to the bed and caught

it from its hooks.   Although my eye did not leave the door, yet I could see she nodded ' Yes,' again.   I put the revolver on the bed, and just then McKandlas poked his head inside the doorway, but jumped back when he saw me with a rifle in my hand.

" Come in here, you cowardly dog ! ' I shouted.   ' Come in here, and fight me ! '

" McKandlas was no coward, if he was a bully.   He jumped inside the room with his gun levelled to shoot; but he was not quick enough.   My rifle ball went through his heart.   He fell back outside the house, where he was found afterward holding tight to his rifle, which had fallen over his head.

" His disappearance was followed by a yell from his gang, and then there was a dead silence.   I put down the rifle and took the revolver, and I said to myself : ' Only six shots and nine men to kill.   Save you powder, Bill, for the death-hug's a-comin' ! '   I don't know why it was, Kernel,'' continued Bill, looking at me inquiringly, " but at that moment things seemed clear and sharp. I could think strong.

" There was a few seconds of that awful stillness, and then the ruffians came rushin' in at both doors.   How wild they looked with their red, drunken faces and inflamed eyes, shouting and cussing ! But I never aimed more deliberately in my life.

" One — two — three — four ; and four men fell dead.

" That didn't stop the rest.   Two of them fired their bird-guns at me.   And then I felt a sting run all over me.   The room was full of smoke.   Two got in close to me, their eyes glaring out of the clouds.   One I knocked down with my fist.   ' You are out of the way for a while,' I thought.   The second I shot dead.   The other three clutched me and crowded me on to the bed.   I fought hard.   I broke with my hand one man's arm. He had his fingers around my throat.   Before I could get to my feet I was struck across the breast with the stock of a rifle, and I felt the blood rushing out of my nose and mouth.   Then I got ugly, and I remember that I got hold of a knife, and then it was all cloudy like, and I was wild, and I struck savage blows, fol-lowing the devils up from one side to the other of the room and into the corners, striking and slashing until I knew that every-one was dead.

" All of a sudden it seemed as if my heart was on fire.   I was bleeding everywhere.   I rushed out to the well and drank from the bucket, and then tumbled down in a faint."

Breathless with the intense interest with which I had followed this strange story, all the more thrilling and weird when its hero, seeming to live over again the bloody events of that day, gave way to its terrible spirit with wild, savage gestures. I saw then — what my scrutiny of the morning had failed to discover — the tiger which lay concealed beneath that gentle exterior.

"You must have been hurt almost to death," I said.

"There was eleven buck-shot in me. I carry some of them now. I was cut in thirteen places. All of them bled enough to have let out the life of a man. But that blessed old Dr. Mills pulled me through it, after a bed siege of many a long week."

"That prayer of yours, Bill, may have been more potent for your safety than you think. You should thank God for your deliverance."

"To tell you the truth, Kernel," responded the scout, with a certain solemnity in his grave face, "I don't talk about such things ter the people round here, but I allers feel sort of thankful when I get out of a bad scrape."

"In all your wild perilous adventures," I asked him, "have you ever been afraid? Do you know what the sensation is? I am sure you will not misunderstand the question, for I take it we soldiers comprehend justly that there is no higher courage than that which shows itself when the consciousness of danger is keen, but where moral strength overcomes the weakness of the body."

"I think I know what you mean, sir, and I'm not ashamed to say that I have been so frightened that it 'peared as if all the strength and blood had gone out of my body, and my face was as white as chalk. It was at the Wilmecreek fight. I had fired more than fifty cartridges, and I think fetched my man every time. I was on the skirmish line, and was working up closer to the rebs, when all of a sudden a battery opened fire right in front of me, and it sounded as if fifty thousand guns were firing, and every shot and shell screeched within six inches of my head. It was the first time I was ever under artillery fire, and I was so frightened that I couldn't move for a minute or so, and when I did go back, the boys asked me if I had seen a ghost? They may shoot bullets at me by the dozen, and its rather exciting if I can shoot back; but I am always sort of nervous when the big guns go off."

"I would like to see you shoot."

" Would yer? " replied the scout, drawing his revolver; and approaching the window, he pointed to a letter O in a signboard which was fixed to the stone wall of a building on the other side of the way.

" That sign is more than fifty yards away. I will put these six balls into the inside of the circle which isn't bigger than a man's heart."

In an off-hand way, and without sighting the pistol with his eye, he discharged the six shots of his revolver. I afterwards saw that all the bullets had entered the circle.

As Bill proceeded to reload his pistol, he said to me, with a *naivete* of manner which was meant to be assuring: —

" Whenever you get into a row, be sure and not shoot too quick. Take time. I've known many a feller slip up for shootin' in a hurry."

It would be easy to fill a volume with the adventures of that remarkable man. My object here has been to make a slight record of one who was one of the best — perhaps the very best — example of a class who, more than any other, encountered perils and privations in defence of our frontier settlers.

Wild Bill's wife was as remarkable a woman as Bill was a man. She had two husbands, and both were assassinated by worthless characters. She married her first husband while a girl of fifteen; he being the well-known clown and showman, William Lake, who was famous all over the union in the early days of show business, before mammoth aggregations like Barnum's took the field.

She was financial manager of the concern, and, being a woman of natural parts and positive character, proved a very successful financier. August 21, 1869, while the circus was exhibiting at Granby, Newton County, Mo., a loafer named Jake Killian slipped in without paying. Lake noticed this, and, summoning a couple of men, ejected the deadhead, who armed himself, returned to the tent, paid his way in, and, seeking out Lake, shot him dead. The murderer escaped, but was tracked, captured, tried, convicted, and sentenced — to three and a half years' imprisonment in the penitentiary! After her husband's death Mrs. Lake took the management of the circus, which she conducted for three seasons, visiting all parts of the Union. She then sold off her menagerie, apparatus and stud, and settled in some Western city — Chicago, I think — whence in the winter of 1875-6 she proceeded so San Francisco. There she remained but a few weeks, coming to Cheyenne a year ago last April, where a little while afterwards she married again, her second husband being J. B. Hickok, so widely known as " Wild Bill."

Mrs. Lake certainly entertained a deep and lasting affection for Hickok, and Hickok as truly reciprocated her passion, as the following letter, written not long after their marriage, when he had gone to the Black Hills to seek fortune and adventure, will testify:—

" DEADWOOD, BLACK HILLS,
" DAKOTA TERRITORY, July 17, 1876.

" MY OWN DARLING WIFE AGNES: I have but a few moments left before this letter starts. I never was so well in my life. You would laugh to see me now. I have just got in from prospecting. Will go out again to-morrow. Will write again in the morning, but God knows when it (the letter) will start. My friend will take this to Cheyenne if he lives. I don't expect to hear from you; but it is all the same. I know my Agnes and only live to love her. Never mind, pet, we will have a home yet. Then we will be so happy. I am almost sure I will do well here. The man is hurrying me. Good by, dear wife. Love to Emma.

" J. B. HICKOK (Wild Bill)."

Such a letter, betraying the most lover-like aspirations and a strong vein of romance, was to be looked for from such a man as Custer had described and analyzed, though it will read oddly to any one at the East accustomed to regard the frontiersman of many brawls as of necessity a bully and a blackguard.

This was probably the last letter Wild Bill ever wrote, for his death ensued a fortnight later. No Sioux took his coveted scalp, no hero of the frontier " got the drop" on him. It might be said of him as of the Jewish warrior, " Died Abner as the fool dieth," or as Johnson wrote of Charles XII.:—

His fall was destined to a foreign strand,
A petty fortress and a dubious hand.

He does not appear to have set out on the prospecting tour to which he alludes in his letter, for August 1st he was still at Deadwood, where fate brought him to the same card-table with one Jack McCall, a gambling sharper and an ugly character. Of him Bill got the better at poker. On the last hand McCall bet

28

$10 and lost, and when he came to settle found that he had only $7.50. Bill, remarking, "You oughtn't to overbet your pile; that's no way to play cards," handed him back a $5 bill to pay for his lodging and breakfast, and the men parted. He thought no more of the matter, neither did any one else who knew of it. Next morning Bill was sitting with a number of card-players in the Senate saloon, when McCall came behind him noiselessly placed the muzzle of his revolver to the back of his head and crying, "Take that, damn you," fired. Wild Bill died, and never knew how, why, or by whom he was killed. The ball traversed the skull, came out under his right eye, and entered the arm of his opponent, a steamboat captain, disabling him for life. McCall, keeping his revolver cocked and pointed on the players, backed out of the room and escaped. A miners' court was formed, which acquitted him, mainly because of his declaration that Wild Bill had killed his brother in an affray, so that he was but the avenger of blood. California Joe, another of Custer's scouts, whom he describes at length in this book, however, approached him after the acquittal and said significantly, " I guess you had better leave Deadwood, it isn't a healthy place." McCall looked in his eye and left.

Deadwood was not a healthy place. A little while later California Joe was killed; not until he had assisted in a notable funeral accorded to the remains of Wild Bill, whom the people of Deadwood seem to have regretted sincerely. McCall went on to Custer City, and there could not keep from boasting that he had killed Wild Bill. A United States Marshall overheard him and arrested him, and on the 1st of March last the murderer of the second of Mrs. Lake's husbands was hanged in due course of law at Yankton. He died game. As Marshall Burdick was returning from the execution he received the following letter: —

" LOUISVILLE, KY., February 25, 1877.

" DEAR SIR: I saw in the morning papers a piece about the sentence of the murderer of ' Wild Bill,' Jack McCall. There was a young man of the name of John McCall left here about six years ago, who has not been heard from for the last three years. He has a father, mother, and three sisters living here in Louisville, who are very uneasy about him since they heard about the murder of ' Wild Bill.' If you can send us any information about him we will be very thankful to you. This John McCall

WILD BILL'S GRAVE.

is about twenty-five years old; has light hair, inclined to curl, and one eye crossed. I cannot say about his height, as he was not grown when he left here. Please write as soon as convenient, as we are very anxious to here from you.

    " Very respectfully,

                        " MARY A. McCALL."

It was the same John McCall who had left home six years before, a boy still at the growing age, who had turned gambler and ruffian, and had trodden the red path of murder to the scaffold.

XXIV.

Hon. W. F. Cody ("Buffalo Bill"), was born in Scott County, Iowa, from whence his father, Isaac Cody, emigrated a few years afterwards to the distant frontier Territory of Kansas, settling near Fort Leavenworth. While still a boy his father was killed in what is now known as the "Border War," and his youth was passed amid all the excitements and turmoil incident to the strife and discord of that unsettled community, where the embers of political contentions smouldered until they burst into the burning flame of civil war. This state of affairs among the white occupants of the territory, and the ingrained ferocity and hostility to encroachment from the native savage, created an atmosphere of adventure well calculated to educate one of his peculiar temperament to a familiarity with danger and self-reliance in the protective means for its avoidance.

From a child used to shooting and riding, he at an early age became a celebrated pony express rider, then the most dangerous occupation on the plains. He was known as a boy to be most fearless, and ready for any mission of danger, and respected by such men then engaged in the express service as Old Jule and the terrible Slade, whose correct finale is truthfully told in Mark Twain's "Roughing It." He accompanied General Albert Sidney Johnston on his Utah expedition, guided trains overland, hunted for a living, and gained his sobriquet by wresting the laurels as a buffalo hunter from all claimants — notably Comstock, in a contest with whom he killed sixty-nine buffaloes in one day to Comstock's forty-six — became scout and guide for the now celebrated Fifth Cavalry (of which Gen. E. A. Carr was major), and is thoroughly identified with that regiment's Western history; was chosen by the Kansas and Pacific Railroad to supply meat to the laborers while building the road, in one season killing four thousand eight hundred and sixty-two, besides deer and antelope; was chief of scouts in the department that protected

Hon. W. F. CODY. (Buffalo Bill.)

the building of the Union Pacific. In these various duties his encounters with the red men have been innumerable, and are well authenticated by army officers in every section of the country. In fact, wherever you meet an army officer, there you meet an admirer and indorser of Buffalo Bill. He is, in fact, the representative man of the frontiersmen of the past — that is, not the bar-room brawler or bully of the settlements, but a genuine specimen of Western manhood, — a child of the plains, who was raised there, and familiar with the country previous to railroads, and when it was known on our maps as the " Great American Desert," so graphically described by General Custer in the first chapter of this book. By the accident of birth and early association, a man who became insensibly inured to the hardships and dangers of primitive existence, and possessed of those qualities that afterward enabled him to hold positions of trust, and without his knowing or intending it, made him nationally famous.

Gen. Richard Irving Dodge, Gen. Sherman's chief of staff, correctly says : —

" The success of every expedition against Indians depends, to a degree, on the skill, fidelity, and intelligence of the men employed as scouts, for not only is the command habitually dependent on them for good routes and comfortable camps, but the officer in command must rely on them almost entirely for their knowledge of the position and movements of the enemy."

Therefore, besides mere personal bravery, a scout must possess the moral qualities associated with a good captain of a ship — full of self-reliance in his own ability to meet and overcome any unlooked-for difficulties, to be a thorough student of nature, a self-taught weather prophet, a geologist by experience, an astronomer by necessity, a naturalist, and thoroughly educated in the warfare, stratagems, trickery, and skill of his implacable Indian foe. Because in handling expeditions or leading troops, on him alone depends correctness of destination, avoidance of dangers, protection against sudden storms, the finding of game, grass, woods, and water, the lack of which, of course, is more fatal than the deadly bullet. In fact, more lives have been lost on the plains from incompetent guides than ever the Sioux or Pawnees destroyed.

Our best Indian-fighting officers are quick to recognize these traits in those claiming frontier lore, and to no one in the military history of the West has such deference been shown by them than to W. F. Cody, as is witnessed by the continuous years of service he has passed, the different commands he has served, the expeditions and campaigns he has been identified with, his repeated holding, when he desired, the position of " Chief of Scouts of United States Army," and the intimate associations and contact resulting from it with Gen. W. T. Sherman (with whom he was at the making of the Comanche and Kiowa treaty), Gen. Phil. Sheridan (who has often given him special recognition, and chosen him to organize expeditions, notably that of the Duke Alexis, related in a previous chapter of this work), old Gen. Harney, Gens. W. S. Hancock, Crook, Pope, Miles, Ord, Augur, Terry, McKenzie, Carr, Forsythe, Merritt, Brisbin, Emory, Gibbon, Royal, Hazen, Duncan, Palmer, Pembroke, and the late lamented Gen. Custer. His history, in fact, would be almost a history of the middle West, and, though younger, equalling in term of service and in personal adventure, Kit Carson, Old Jim Bridger, California Joe, Wild Bill, and the rest of his dead and gone associates.

As another evidence of the confidence placed in his frontiersmanship, it may suffice to mention the celebrities whose money and position most naturally sought the best protection the Western market could afford, and who chose to place their lives in his keeping: Sir Geoge Gore, Earl Dunraven, James Gordon Bennett, Duke Alexis, Gen. Custer, Lawrence Jerome, Remington, Professor Ward of Rochester, Professor Marsh of Yale College, Major J. G. Hecksher, Dr. Kingsley (Canon Kingsley's brother), and others of equal rank and distinction.

The following letter of his old commander and celebrated Indian fighter, Gen. E. A. Carr, written years ago relative to him, is a tribute as generous as any brave man has ever made to one of his position. " From his services with my command, steadily in the field, I am qualified to bear testimony as to his qualities and character.

" He was very modest and unassuming. He is a natural gentleman in his manners as well as in character, and has none of the roughness of the typical frontiersman. He can take his own part when required, but I have never heard of his using a knife or a pistol, or engaging in a quarrel when it could be avoided. His personal strength and activity are very great, and his temper and disposition are so good that no one has reason to quarrel with him.

BUFFALO BILL KILLS AN INDIAN.

" His eyesight is better than a good field-glass; he is the best trailer I ever heard of, and also the best judge of the ' lay of country' — that is, he is able to tell what kind of country is ahead, so as to know how to act. He is a perfect judge of distance, and always ready to tell correctly how many miles it is to water, or to any place, or how many miles have been marched. * * *

" Mr. Cody seemed never to tire, and always ready to go, in the darkest night or the worst weather, and usually volunteered, knowing what the emergency required. His trailing, when following Indians or looking for stray animals or game, is simply wonderful. He is a most extraordinary hunter.

" In a fight Mr. Cody is never noisy, obstreperous, or excited. In fact, I never hardly noticed him in a fight, unless I happened to want him, or he had something to report, when he was always in the right place, and his information was always valuable and reliable.

" During the winter of 1866 we encountered hardships and exposure in terrific snow storms, sleet, etc. On one occasion that winter Mr. Cody showed his quality by quietly offering to go with some dispatches to Gen. Sheridan across a dangerous region, where another principal scout was reluctant to risk himself. * * *

" Mr. Cody has since served with me as post guide and scout at Fort McPherson, where he frequently distinguished himself. * * *

" In the summer of 1876, Cody went with me to the Black Hills region, where he killed Yellow Hand. Afterward he was with the Big Horn and Yellowstone expedition. I consider that his services to the country and the army, by trailing, finding, and fighting Indians, and thus protecting the frontier settlers and by guiding commands over the best and most practicable routes, have been far beyond the compensation he has received."

Thus it will be seen that, notwithstanding it may sometimes be thought his fame rests upon the pen of the romancer and novelist, had they never been attracted to him (and they were solely by his sterling worth), W. F. Cody would none the less have been a character in American history. Having assisted in founding substantial peace in Nebraska, where he was honored by being elected to the Legislature (while away on a hunt), he has settled at North Platte, to enjoy its fruits and minister to the wants and advancements of the domestic circle with which he is blessed.

Buffalo Bill is, par excellence, the exemplar of the strong and unique traits that characterize a true American frontiersman.

The following is an account of Buffalo Bill's duel with Yellow Hand, mentioned by General Carr: —

The Indians had commenced hostilities in the Black Hills, and were murdering and scalping all whites who were unfortunate enough to fall into their hands. The military authorities ordered the Fifth Cavalry to scout the country at the foot of the Black Hills, and protect the whites as far as possible. The regiment operated for some two weeks on the South Fork of the Cheyenne, routing numbers of bands of roving hostiles, and were upon the point of returning, when news reached them of the massacre of brave General Custer and his band of heroes on the Little Big Horn. Orders were received to join General Crook in the Big Horn country.

The same evening news was received that a large band of Indians had left the Red Cloud agency and were in all probability heading for Sitting Bull's camp of hostiles.

Colonel Merritt at once decided to intercept them. He selected between four and six hundred picked troops, and made a forced march to War Bonnet Creek, as the Indians would have to cross that creek in order to reach their destination. They arrived there the next night, and scouts were sent out, who reported that no Indian trail could be seen. On the following morning, Buffalo Bill discovered a large body of Indians, which proved to be the Cheyennes.

Colonel Merritt concealed his forces, and with his scouts, kept a watchful eye upon the approaching hostiles. Presently a number of warriors, probably twenty, were seen to ride off in an opposite direction, and their manœuvres puzzled the Colonel for a moment; but by the aid of field-glasses two soldiers were seen approaching in the distance, evidently bearing dispatches, and the object of the Indians was to capture these men. Here was a dilemma — Colonel Merritt did not wish to uncover his ambuscade, neither could he stand still and see these men captured and probably murdered before his eyes. But Buffalo Bill suggested a way out of the dilemma that proved to be a good one, and was at once sanctioned by Colonel Merritt. Selecting fifteen men, he made a detour and took his station behind a neighboring hill,

BUFFALO BILL'S DUEL WITH YELLOW HAND.

quietly awaiting the orders of the Colonel. Bill's object was to cut off the scouting party from the main body of Indians, and at the same time rescue the two dispatch-bearers.

When the messengers had arrived within about five hundred yards of the command, with the Cheyennes two hundred yards in their rear, Colonel Merritt shouted : —

" Go in now, Cody, and be quick about it. They are going to charge on the couriers."

Bill and his picked men at once broke from their concealment and charged upon the Indians, driving them some distance and killing three of them; but gaining courage by the arrival of their main body, the Indians turned on the scouts, and a lively fight took place. During a lull in the discharge of fire-arms, one highly ornamented chief, with great bravado rode out in front of his party, and sang out in the Cheyenne tongue : —

" I know you, Pa-he-haska; if you want to fight, come and fight me."

Nothing delighted Buffalo Bill more than to encounter an Indian single-handed, and he at once accepted the challenge.

Bill and the Indian now advanced at full speed. When about fifty yards apart, Bill raised his Winchester and fired, killing the Indian's pony, and at the same time was violently thrown from his own horse, who had stepped into a hole. Both were now on foot, and about twenty-five yards apart. Bill was the first to raise his rifle, and instantly two reports rang out in quick succession. The Indian's bullet whistled harmlessly by Bill, but the scout's bullet struck the Indian in the breast, and he reeled and fell ; and in less than ten seconds, Cody had finished him with his hunting-knife, and deprived him of his scalp and war-bonnet.

The whole affair occupied but a few moments, and the Indians, seeing the fate of their chief, charged down upon Bill, who was some distance in advance of his command, in hopes of revenging their chief's death; but Colonel Merritt, who had silently witnessed the duel, ordered a company to rescue the brave scout. As the soldiers came up, Bill swung the chief's top-knot and bonnet in the air, and shouted: —

" *The first scalp for Custer!* "

Colonel Merritt, seeing that further concealment was useless, charged upon the Indians with his whole regiment, and drove them back to Red Cloud agency. Here it was learned that the

29

Indian chief whom Bill had killed bore the name of **Yellow Hand, and** was a son of old Cut-Nose, a leading chief **of the** Cheyennes.

W. F. Cody, although having established his right to the title of " Buffalo Bill " years before, had not had an opportunity to convince the Pawnees of the justice of the claim previous to the time of the following incident : A short while previously, a band of marauding redskin renegades from that nation, while on a stealing excursion near Ellsworth, had occasion to regret their temerity, and cause to remember him to the extent of three killed, which fact for a time resulted in an enmity that needed something out of the usual run to establish him in their favor. While on a military expedition under General E. A. Carr, upon the Republican, he met Major North and the Pawnee scouts. One day a herd of buffalo was discovered, and Cody desired to join the hunt. The Indians objected, telling the Major " the white talker would scare them away." Seventy-three Indians attacked the herd and succeeded in killing twenty-three.

Later in the day another herd was discovered, and Major North insisted that the white chief should have a chance to prove his skill. After much grumbling, and with ill-concealed smiles of derision, the Indians consented to become spectators for the time being. Judge of their surprise, when Cody charged the herd, and, single-handed and alone, fairly amazed them, by killing forty-eight buffalo in thirty minutes; thus forever gaining their admiration and friendship, that has since often accrued to his benefit.

Once, on the South Fork of the Solomon, Colonel Royal ordered Cody to kill some buffalo, that were in sight, to feed his men; but declined to send his wagons until assured of the game. Bill rounded the herd, and getting them in a line for camp, drove them in and killed seven near headquarters, the Colonel remarking that " that was furnishing grub and its own transportation."

The building of the Kansas Pacific Railroad through the heart **of the** Indian country was accomplished with much difficulty and **not** with out many exciting conflicts with the red skins. The contractors employed about twelve hundred men, who were boarded by Messrs. Goddard Brothers. One of this firm employed Cody to supply him with meat for his boarders. As it **required** about twelve buffaloes a day to meet their wants, the job

DANGERS ENCOUNTERED CONSTRUCTING THE RAILROAD.

was by no means an easy one. It was also attended with much danger, on account of the Indians.

But whoever knew Cody to flinch from danger? As the pay was large, Bill accepted and at once entered upon his duties. It was here he gained the sobriquet of " Buffalo Bill," which was given him by the road hands.

While supplying the Kansas Pacific hands with buffalo hams and humps, Bill met with some thrilling adventures, and narrowly escaped with his life on several occasions.

One day, having mounted his favorite horse Brigham, namesake of Brigham Young, Bill started for the Smoky Hill River in quest of buffalo. After a sharp ride of some fifteen miles he ascended an elevated piece of ground overlooking the valley, and cast his eye over the landscape in search of his favorite game. Instead of seeing " buffalo," he saw " Indians," and they spied Cody about the same time; and hastily mounting their horses, they started toward Bill. It was a ride now for life, and nobly did old Brigham do his duty.

One of the Indians, mounted upon a fine spotted horse and armed with a repeating rifle, succeeded in getting within a hundred yards of Bill and made it decidedly warm by his continual firing; often sending a bullet in close proximity to Cody's ear. Bill made up his mind to put a stop to this by-play, and suddenly wheeling his horse he took deliberate aim, and sent a bullet into the brain of the spotted steed, thus suddenly checking the headlong career of the Indian.

The hostiles chased Cody to within half a mile of a company of soldiers who were stationed at the end of the track to protect the workmen. Seeing the soldiers the Indians beat a hasty retreat.

Captain Nolan, of the Tenth Cavalry, now arrived, and learnwhat had happened, determined to pursue the Indians. Bill was furnished with a fresh horse, and was soon galloping after the flying Indians. Their horses being fresh, they soon gained upon the redskins, and succeeded in killing eight of them.

One stalwart savage, mounted upon a powerful bay, seeing he was about to be overtaken, turned suddenly upon Buffalo Bill and raised his battle-axe to cleave the brave scout's skull; but Bill was prepared for him, and drove his huge bowie-knife to the hilt in the breast of the warrior. The few incidents here narrated will give the reader an insight into the character of this

world-renowned scout.   He is now delighting thousands of
Americans by his exhibitions of prairie life throughout the
country, accompanied by that wonderful marksman, Dr. W. F.
Carver.

DR. CARVER. (EVIL SPIRIT OF THE PLAINS.)

XXV.

W. F. Carver ("the evil spirit of the plains"), whose renown as the most expert rifleman in the universe, and whose phenomenal skill is of such superlative excellence that his "form" is, by the shooting fraternity, practical hunters, and military experts of all nations, acknowledged to be the perfect acme of possible merit in its line, was born at Saratoga Springs, New York, in 1840. His history eclipses anything yet adduced in the most extravagant romance, covering as it does — and possibly in his case alone of all living men — the extremes that exist between the stolen emigrant boy of the uncivilized Western plains of America, living a captive among the savage red men, to the tribute of this continent of marksmen and the admiring patronage of the crowned occupants and the courts of the palaces of England and continental Europe — a fame so rarely achieved in any profession of art among one's fellow-men that it can only be expressed as universal — excelsior. His father, migrating in 1844 to the then far West, settled near the Falls of St. Anthony, in Minnesota, where now stands the populous city of Minneapolis. A raid of the Teton and Crow Sioux, in a short year afterwards, during the temporary absence of the father, resulted in the butchery of his mother and sister, burning of the settlement, and the captivity of the subject of our sketch. Through some unlooked for goodness in a chief called Red Wing, whom the little stranger's appearance pleased, the boy's life was spared, and he was adopted, and for years remained an accepted member of the tribe. Thrilling as his experiences in Indian life were, and as interesting as they may be, space prevents any lengthy relation of them, though the fact that thirteen years were passed with varying joys and sorrows will suffice to show how eventful it must have been. With all its regrets, however, the years spent in close alliance with primitive man in his nomadic life, outdoor sports, hunting, horsemanship, etc., laid the foundation of that now spendid physique and extraordinary skill that causes his present renown, and has gained for him, through his deadly aim, the title of "The Evil Spirit of the Plains."

The death of his patron, Red Wing, absolving him from his

debt of gratitude to the tribe, he joined at the first opportunity a trapper named Brewster, and, with the invading hunters, waged a war of unrelenting vengeance against the red devils, killing among others the noted chief Wolf Catcher, and became one of the best riders, sharpest shooters, expert hunters, and one of the most marked celebrities on the plains. Eventually his fame became widespread on the prairie, and falling in with Cody (Buffalo Bill), Omohundro (Texas Jack), Hickock (Wild Bill), and California Joe, they for years rode the plains together, hunting, trapping, and assisting civilization in its progress. Their coming East, and the encroachments of the settlers, caused his attention to be drawn to the possibilities of extending his fame; but, when first challenging the champions of the country and asserting his abilities, his offers were treated with derision and his feats on foot and horse were voted imaginary. Going to California, then sweeping the continent from ocean to ocean, this wizard rifleman convinced all doubters, became the season's wonder, and in his advent marked a new era in the history of American marksmanship. Nor was his skill more remarkable than the wonder of his endurance, he having, with a rifle, beaten the greatest shotgun score on record, by breaking, at Brooklyn, New York, July 13, 1878, 5,500 glass balls thrown in the air in seven hours and thirty-six minutes. During the feat he raised to his shoulder 62,120 pounds, or $31\frac{1}{8}$ tons in weight. In working the lever of the rifle he moved 248,480 pounds with the middle finger of his right hand, and withstood from the recoil an aggregate weight of 298,176 pounds, equal to 149 tons.

Accepted by America as its representative rifle chief, he thirsted for "new worlds to conquer." So, bravely carrying the "war into Europe," he landed in Britain, threw down the glove to that nation of experts, and in many a well contested struggle carried our banner to continuous victory, adding to our fame by the exhibition of those sturdy qualities that have long been our national pride. In over two hundred and seven matches he never was beaten on even terms, and won the title of "champion pigeon shooter of the world" in a grand tournament, among the contestants, being fourteen of the best men known to fame, Cholmondeley, Pennell, Turner-Turner, Haggert, Scott, Walter, Mass, our own Ira A. Paine, Graham, Bryden, and others, for the "Title," the Sportsman Champion Cup, valued at **£200 and £100** sweepstakes. This victory is justly considered the greatest ever achieved in trap shooting; and, although, foeman worthy of his steel had to be overcome, the London *Sportsman*, while paying his opponents earned compliments, says: "Not a particle of honor do we wish, however, to take from Carver; and when, in being presented with the magnificent trophy, he was pronounced the first *bona fide* champion shot we have ever had in this country, he had gained a title of which he may be justly proud."

His marvellous exhibitions caused his sojourn in England, and his visits to Ireland, Wales, France, Germany, Belgium, Holland, Hungary, and Austria to savor of a continual ovation from the admiring populace, and the no less astonished and delighted members of royalty. By special request, he exhibited at Sandringham before the Queen, Prince, and Princess of Wales, Duke and Duchess of Connaught, and the members of the royal household, receiving the very exceptional gift of the "Prince of Wales Feathers," and the "Princess of Wales Horseshoe," — an emblem of Denmark, — and received the plaudits of thirty thousand soldiers, who were assembled to witness his feats, under the command of General Sir Robert Steel, at Aldershot; was personally congratulated and decorated with valuable mementos by the Emperor Wilhelm of Germany, who titled him "Der Shutzen Kœnig;" the Crown Prince and Princess, others of the royal family, Von Bismarck, and the renowned soldier, Von Moltke, and his staff, whose special praise was more than enthusiastic. The Grand Duke Albert, of Austria, Count Wilzk (with whom he enjoyed a sixteen-days' chamois hunt in the Styrian Mountains), and the King of Saxony, also paid tribute to his skill.

In fact, no visiting scholar, soldier, or statesman that ever left American shores received more consideration in those countries, where the momentary possibilities of war's exigencies lends an absorbing interest in that deadly art, whose complete development is often a motive for desired peace.

Dr. Carver, a fine specimen of physical manhood, — six feet, two and a half inches in height, and built from "the ground up;" — is polished in manner, and of pleasing address; modest in demeanor; with all the accomplishments in flood and field of his Indian tutors; of undaunted nerve; is a pistol and bow-and-arrow expert, a perfect horseman; in fact, a model plainsman.

Frank North, as he is familiarly called upon the prairies, was the first man to enlist Indians in the United States service, he having organized a band of twenty-seven young Pawnee warriors and been made lieutenant over them.

Major North is a native of New York State, and was born in 1840; but his father moved to Nebraska, settling near Columbus, in the winter of 1856–57, and directly thereafter was frozen to death at Emigrant Crossing, on Big Pappillion Creek, while trying to secure wood for his suffering family.

Shortly after the death of his father, young North joined a party of trappers, — McMurray, Glass, and Messenger, — and began taking beaver and otter on the tributaries of Platte River; but meeting with indifferent success, returned to Columbus and engaged in anything that promised remuneration, as the family was almost entirely dependent on him for support.

In 1860, being now twenty years of age, Frank procured employment with Agent DePuy, at the Pawnee Indian Reservation. Here, while performing his other duties, he acquired such a thorough knowledge of the Pawnee language, that in the following year he was engaged as interpreter by the Indian Commissioner.

From the breaking out of the Sioux war, in 1864, Major North began to win a name for himself, as a man who had no superior for bravery, and whose abilities as a scouting officer were something wonderful, while his management of his Pawnee Indian scouts was perfect, he having them under better discipline and control than their own chiefs could gain over them.

Acting under orders from General Custer, Lieutenant North enlisted one hundred more Pawnee warriors, who were then equipped like the regular cavalry, and North was commissioned captain.

On the 13th of January, 1865, the company was mustered into service, the delay being due to difficulties regarding their acceptance by the government, but when regularly put on the muster rolls Captain North began active operations. Learning of depredations being made by the Sioux in the neighborhood of Julesburg, he took forty of his Pawnees and proceeded directly to the scene of trouble. On the route to Julesburg he was horrified to find the bodies of no less than fourteen white persons, pilgrims on their way to Pike's Peak, mutilated beyond recognition; their scalps torn off, tongues cut out, legs cut open, and bodies full of arrows. Julesburg had also been attacked, and the garrison was on the point of yielding when rescued.

MAJOR NORTH'S DUEL WITH THE CHEYENNE.

North now pushed after the Sioux with all possible speed, and‘ meeting with twenty-eight of the incarnate devils, he fell upon them with such irresistible force that not a single Sioux in the party escaped his vengeance.

The Indians, whom North had thus annihilated, were a predatory band from Red Cloud's forces, and had done an inestimable amount of damage through the section they had invaded. Only a few days previous to their disastrous meeting with Captain North this same party had suddenly attacked Lieutenant Collins, with fourteen men, and killed the entire party.

Shortly after this successful sortie, Captain North was ordered to pursue a body of twelve Cheyennes and punish them for atrocities committed in the neighborhood of Fort Sedgwick. Taking twenty of his Pawnees, he got on the Cheyenne trail, and, after following it about thirty miles, came up with the enemy, whom he found in line of battle. At the first volley, however, the Cheyennes fled, followed hard by Captain North. In this pursuit the Pawnees were unable to keep up with their captain, as their horses were too badly jaded to endure extra riding. Captain North, however, was mounted on a superior animal, and being full of desperate pluck, was determined to kill one Cheyenne at least. Looking back, at length, he saw his men fully a mile behind him, and several of them dismounted. Realizing the danger of his position, he took deliberate aim and fired at the Cheyennes, one of whom tumbled from his pony dead. At this, the other Indians turned on the captain, and he was compelled to flee for his life.

The Indians rode rapidly after him, shooting constantly, until a bullet struck the Captain's horse in the side, rendering him unfit for further travel. Leaping to the ground, Captain North used his horse for a breast-work, from which he fired until the position had become too dangerous. He then started to run, but after getting several yards was headed off by one warrior, who was in advance of his comrades, and who rode rapidly toward Captain North, and leaping from his pony advanced quite close with rifle to his shoulder, ready to send the fatal messenger of death to the Captain's heart, and then secure his scalp. The warrior, evidently believed that his intended victim had fired his last shot, or he would not have ventured so near, and the Captain by his movements, aided him in this belief. When within ten feet of each other Captain North suddenly raised his Winchester, and fired his last shot, killing the Indian instantly. His last shot being gone, he suddenly remembered the two holsters on the saddle, each containing a loaded revolver, and he boldly returned for them. With these pistols he fought the Cheyennes nearly half an hour longer, and until relieved by Lieutenant Small. This fight, one of the most daring ever made, is still spoken of, and the story frequently told over and over again among Western men, who almost reverence the name of Frank J. North.

In March following, while acting under the orders of General Augur, Captain North raised a battalion of two hundred Pawnees, who were divided into four companies and taken to Fort Kearney, where they were equipped for cavalry service. He was then given a major's commission, and, with his Indian soldiers, guarded construction trains on the Union Pacific Railroad until its completion to Ogden. In this service he was engaged almost constantly with depredating Sioux and Cheyennes, who descended on the construction trains at every opportunity. After the road had reached Utah, large shipments of silver were being made almost weekly, and as this precious metal was brought into stations in large bricks, which, for want of storage, was usually piled up on and about the platforms to await shipment, Major North's Indians had also to perform the duty of guarding the precious metal.

When the road was completed, Major North retired to a ranch on Dismal River, sixty-five miles north of North Platte, where he went into the cattle raising business. Buffalo Bill, after his first meeting with Major North at Fort McPherson, served with him on several campaigns, and in this service a very warm friendship sprang up between them, which led to the formation of a co-partnership in the cattle ranch on Dismal River. The firm of Cody & North is known among cattle men in every part of America; they now have seven thousand head of cattle and four hundred head of horses, and to every one who calls at their ranch there is a hearty, white man's welcome. Major North, aside from his reputation as an Indian fighter and brave man, is a gentleman of the most generous and noble instincts, popular with all classes, and a friend honest and honorable to the end.

In March, 1877, W. F. Cody (Buffalo Bill) and "Doc" Carver (Evil Spirit of the Plains), while returning from a successful hunting expedition, visited the camp of Texas Jack (J. B.

THE INDIANS FIRST VIEW OF A TRAIN.

30

Omohundro), and while seated around the camp-fire talking of
buffalo hunts old times, etc., Texas Jack says : —

" This reminds me of my first buffalo hunt with Indians. If I
don't get like the butcher's calf, and ' kind o' give out,' I'll try
and give an idea of one of the most exciting scenes I ever saw or
read of, not excepting my school-boy impression of Andy Jack-
son's hoo-doo at New Orleans. I thought I had seen fun in a
Texas cattle stampede, been astonished in a mustang chase ; but
it wasn't a marker, and it made me believe that Methuselah was
right when he suggested that the oldest could ' live and learn.'
It is a pity the old man didn't stick it out. He could have enjoyed this lesson.

"A few years ago I was deputized United States Agent, under
Major North, to accompany a party of Pawnee and Ponca
Indians. Although " blanket Indians " (living wild), they have
for a long time been friends of the Government, and have done
excellent service under command of the justly celebrated Major
Frank North, whose famed Pawnee scouts have always been a
terror to the Sioux nation. Owing to their hatred of each other
it is necessary to send an agent with them to prevent ' picnics '
and also to settle disputes with the white hunters. As Major
North was in poor health at that time, this delicate task fell to
me.

"As I don't like to be long-winded, I'll pass over the scenes
and incidents of wild Indian camp-life, the magnificent sight of
a moving village of ' nature's children,' looking like a long
rainbow in the bright colors of their blankets, beads, feathers,
war paint, etc., as it would keep us up all night. It required
eleven days to make the march from the Louis River Reservation
to Plum Creek, on the North Platte, where our runners reported.

" Early in the evening as we were about making camp, my
old friend, Baptiste, the interpreter, joyfully remarked: 'Jack,
the blanket is up three times, — fun and fresh meat to-morrow.'

" There was a great pow-vow that night, and all the warriors
were to turn out for the grand, buffalo surround,' leaving the
squaws and papooses in the village. Just before day break,
there was a general stir and bustle on all sides, giving evidence of
the complete preparations making for the coming event. As it
was dark, I busied myself in arranging my own outfit, thinking
of the grand sight soon to be witnessed, and wondering how I
would ' pan out ' in the view of my ' red brothers '. I had not

noticed the manner of their own arrangements in an important particular that I will hereafter allude to.

"At a given signal all started, and, when the first blue streaks of dawn allowed the moving column to be visible I had time to make an inspection of the strange cavalcade, and note peculiarities. I saw at once the 'white brother' placed at a disadvantage.

"I had started fully equipped — bridle, saddle, lariat, rifle, pistol, belt, etc. — and astride of my pony. They, with as near nothing in garments as Adam and Eve, only breech clout and moccasins, no saddle, no blanket, not even a bridle, only a small mouth rope, light bow and a few arrows in hand — in fact not an ounce of weight more than necessary, and, unlike myself, all scudding along at a marvellous rate, leading their fiery ponies, so as to reserve every energy for the grand event in prospect.

"Taking it all in at a glance, your 'humble servant,' quite abashed, let go all holts and slipped off his critter, feeling that the Broncho looked like a government pack mule. I at once mentally gave up the intention of paralyzing my light rigged side pards in the coming contest. As they were all walking, I thought the buffalo were quite near; but what was my surprise, as mile after mile was scored, that I gradually found myself dropping slowly but surely behind, and, so as not to get left, compelled every now and then to mount and lope to the front, there to perceive from the twinkling eyes of friend 'Lo' a smile that his otherwise stolid face gave no evidence of. How deep an Indian can think, and it not be surface plain, I believe has never been thoroughly measured. Just imagine this 'lick' kept up with apparent ease by them for ten or twelve miles, and you may get a partial idea of your friend Jack's tribulations.

"Fortunately, I kept up, but at what an expense of muscle, verging on a complete 'funk,' you can only appreciate by a similar spin.

"About this time a halt was made, and you bet I was mighty glad of it. Suddenly two or three scouts rode up. A hurried council was held, during which the pipe was passed. Everything seemed to be now arranged, and, after a little further advance, again a halt, when, amid great but suppressed excitement, every Indian mounted his now almost frantic steed, each eagerly seeking to edge his way without observation to the front.

"About two hundred horses almost abreast in the front line,

say one hundred and fifty wedging in half way between, formed a half second line, and one hundred struggling for place — a third line; the chiefs in front gesticulating, pantomiming, and, with slashing whips, keeping back the excited mass, whose plunging, panting ponies, as impatient as their masters, fretted, frothed, and foamed — both seemed moulded into one being, with only one thought, one feeling, one ambition, as with flashing eye they waited for the signal, ' Go,' to let their pent-up feelings speed on to the honors of the chase.

" Their prey is in fancied security, now quietly browsing to the windward in a low, open flat, some half a mile wide and two or three miles long, on top of a high divide, concealed from view by risings and breaks. Gradually they approach the knoll, their heads reach the level, the backs of the buffalo are seen, then a full view, when Pi-ta-ne-sha-a-du (Old Peter, the head chief) gives the word, drops the blanket, and they are ' off.'

" Whew! wheez! thunder and lightning! Jerome Parks, and Hippodromes! talk of tornadoes, whirlwinds, avalanches, waterspouts, prairie fires, Niagara, Mount Vesuvius (and I have seen them all except old Vesuv.) ; boil them all together, mix them well, and serve on one plate, and you will have a limited idea of the charge of this ' light brigade.' They fairly left a hole in the air. With a roar like Niagara, the speed of a whirlwind, like the sweep of a tornado, the rush of a snow-slide, the suddenness of a water-spout, the rumbling of Vesuvius, with the fire of death in their souls, they pounce on their prey, and in an instant, amid a cloud of dust, nothing is visible but a mingled mass of flying arrows, horses' heels, buffalos' tails, Indian heads, half of ponies, half of men, half of buffalo, until one thinks it a dream, or a heavy case of ' jim-jams.'

" I just anchored in astonishment. Where are they? Ah! there is one; there is another, a third, four, five. Over the plains in all directions they go, as the choice meat hunters cut them out, while in a jumbled mass, circling all around is the main body. The clouds of dust gradually rise as if a curtain was lifted, horses stop as buffalos drop, until there is a clear panoramic view of a busy scene, all quiet, everything still (save a few fleet ones in the distance); horses riderless, browsing proudly, conscious of success; the prairie dotted here, there, everywhere with dead bison; and happy, hungry hunters skinning, cutting, slashing the late proud monarch of the plains.

" I was so interested in the sight that I came near being left, when fortunately a lucky long-range shot (the only one fired during the day) at a stray heifer saved my reputation. In about two hours every pony was loaded, their packing being quite a study that would need a deserved and lengthy description. It was wonderful.

"As I had a heap of walk out, I proposed to ride in, so took a small cut of choice meat — a straight cut — for camp. Every pony was packed down only mine, seeing which ' Peter's Pappoose' (' the Sun Chief ') invited himself up behind. Talk of gall — an Indian has got more cheek than a government mule. He laughed at my objections, but as he had loaned me the pony I had to submit. He even directed the gait, and kept up a continual jabbering of ' Wisgoots, ugh! de-goinartsonse stak-ees, ugh ! ' which I afterward learned meant ' Hurry up ; I am tired, hungry, and dry — how ! ' "

An old '49er then related the following that happened when California Joe and he were trapping together. Joe and I had been meeting with good success and having no trouble with Indians. One night Joe was late in getting to camp, but when he did return he had plenty of Indian traps, ponies and game, and he gave me the following account of his adventure, but of course I cannot repeat his exact language, and so will relate it as best I can : —

Joe that afternoon ran across a fresh trail of what appeared to have been made by three Indians. Following the trail cautiously for a mile or more, Joe came to where the Indians had camped the night previous on the banks of a small stream. On the opposite side of the creek were tall bluffs covered with trees. Joe decided to secrete himself in the dense thicket until night, and await the return of the Indians to camp.

About sundown one buck, loaded with game, came in and commenced building a fire ; shortly after, two more made their appearance, and Joe could see that it was a small hunting party, armed with bows and arrows only. After enjoying their evening meal, and smoking and chatting for some time, the three Indians wrapped themselves in their blankets, and were soon sound asleep. Cautiously Joe now began to descend from his high perch, but the " best laid plans of mice and men gang aft aglee," and so it proved in this case ; for, as silently as death, Joe was easing himself down when he happened to place his foot on a

CALIFORNIA JOE IN CLOSE QUARTERS

dead limb, which broke with a snap that startled the three Indians from their slumber, and came near landing Joe within ten feet of them.

The wily Indians began at once to search for the cause of the noise, and, it being moonlight, they soon discovered Joe in the tree on the bluffs, and, in their Indian dialect, called upon him to come down at the same time they commenced advancing and discharging their arrows, whooping and yelling as only Indians can.

By the aid of the moon Joe fired at the nearest one, and had the pleasure of seeing him drop. Then climbing to the very top of the tallest tree, he prepared to reload his trusty rifle (this happened before the days of the Winchester or Remington), but the remaining two began rapidly to ascend, and soon were in dangerous proximity to the old scout, and the nearest one prepared to use his bow. The situation was becoming desperate, but Joe, nothing daunted, broke off a good sized club from a dead limb, and taking good aim, landed it fairly upon the head of the Indian, knocking him from his perch. In his fall, he struck his companion, and both of them fell into the creek bottom. One was instantly killed, and the other badly wounded.

Joe quickly descended and dispatched the wounded, and with three scalps and what plunder he could carry, hastened to his own camp.

XXVI.

CROOK'S CAMPAIGN.

General Crook was ordered to Silver City, Arizona, last fall, and arrived there on the 3d of September. He found the whole Apache country in a state of unrest, and on the point of an outbreak. His first step was to learn the true cause of the trouble, and endeavor to pacify the Indians. With this object in view, he went among them, and devoted his entire time and attention until December 1st to a settlement of the difficulties by personal conferences and assurances. His efforts as a " pacificator," backed by his well-known fighting qualities, proved eminently successful.

The predatory Chiricahuas, however, were out in Mexico, and he became satisfied that they were going to make a raid on Arizona. He tried last fall to get into communication with them, but did not succeed, as they had left their old haunts in Mexico which the peaceful Indians knew about.

After the raid that followed it was utterly impossible to catch the raiding party. You might as well try to catch a flock of crows with a company of cavalry. These Indians ride from fifty to sixty miles in a single night, and next morning disappear apparently from the face of the earth. They leave no trail, and it is impossible to find them. It now became necessary to go into Mexican territory after them. This General Crook decided to do, and also to secure the co-operation of Mexican troops.

General Crook left Silver Creek, Arizona, May 1, 1883, with one hundred and ninety-three Apache scouts under Crawford and Wood Mackey, with Chaffer's company of forty-two men of the Sixth Cavalry, and rations for two months, on mules. He started in on the San Bernardino River, and followed that stream up to the Bavispe, finding good water and good food for the stock all the way, there being Mexican ranches all along these streams.

After leaving the Bavispe he encountered a country of indescribable roughness. A number of pack-mules lost their footing, stepped from the trail, and, falling down the precipices, were killed.

The stronghold of the Chiricahuas was in the very heart of the Sierra Madras. The position is finely watered, and has a dense

474

GENERAL CROOK TRYING TO COMMUNICATE WITH THE CHIRICAHUAS.

growth of timber and plenty of rich and succulent grass. The hostiles had been camped for months near the head of Bavispe, occupying prominent elevated peaks affording a fine lookout for miles, rendering a surprise almost impossible, and leaving a safe and sure retreat open through the rough adjacent canyons. Crook was guided by an Apache called Nadoski, who was captured near San Carlos, just previous to the expedition. After fourteen days' hard marching, night and day, the Indian camps of Chato and Bonito were discovered in the heart of the Sierra Madres in an almost impregnable position. The Apaches did not dream of an attack, for entrance to the trenches was next to impossible. The warriors were principally out on a raid under Juh, only thirty-seven bucks being in camp with the women and children. The San Carlos scouts, under Captain Crawford and Lieutenants Atwood and Mackey, with Al Seball, McIntosh and Mickey Free, chiefs of the scouts, surrounded the camp before the hostiles were aware of their proximity, and advanced from different points, and were near before they were discovered. The scouts secreted themselves behind the rocks and commenced firing upon the camp, creating a perfect panic. A number succeeded in escaping, though nearly all surrendered. Seven were found dead in camp. Five Mexican women and a little girl were recaptured. They were taken from Carmen and Chihuahua, and are now with Crook in good health. Everything in the camp was burned or carried off by the scouts. Among the property captured were one hundred ponies and mules, forty being loaded with plunder, saddles, girdles, clothes, gold and silver watches, and several thousand dollars in gold and silver and greenbacks, showing they had been very successful in their raids. After the fight, most of those who escaped came in. Altogether, three hundred and eighty-three prisoners were taken. The chiefs captured were Chato, Bonito, Geronimo, Nachez, Loco and Nana. The two latter were long reported dead. The chiefs say an American boy, six years old, captured a month ago in New Mexico, is with the squaws in the mountains. He is, no doubt, Charlie McComas.

General Crook plainly told them that if they wanted any more fighting he would give it to them; that he had followed them all the way from across the Rio Grande to fight them for our people, and that he had the Mexicans to help him. He then told them that the Mexican Generals Guerra and Fuirra were guarding the eastern slope of the Sierra Madras, and the Sinaloa and Sonora troops under General Topeta were guarding the western slope, and the Talamora Indians (friendly) were guarding the south. In fact, they were completely surrounded, and if they tried to escape they would all be destroyed. They were thoroughly broken in spirit by his talk about the Mexicans, and began to come into his camp by dozens, and told General Crook to do with them as he thought best.

The captured Indians state that when the Chiricahuas discovered the Apache scouts were in the country they became greatly alarmed, and abandoned on the trail the three hundred head of cattle they were driving away from points in western Chihuahua. The cattle were afterwards picked up and driven off by a band of Mexicans. Before General Crook left the mountains the Indians promised to join him on the border if they could round up their women in time. Geronimo and Natchez went after them, and wanted Crook to wait until they returned, but his rations were getting low and he would not wait any longer.

One old squaw, who was the possessor three $50 bills, made inquiry of some one at Colonel Biddle's as to the value of her possessions; upon being informed that the notes were for $5 each she grunted and declined to negotiate, and pointed with her skinny finger to the naught after the five on each note. Quite a number of bucks had silver stars and other ornaments beaten out of Mexican dollars on their head-gear, and several of them American double eagles, made into necklaces. A rough estimate of the amount of wealth among them is fully $5,000, and probably more. The troops and packers of the command state that the place where the capture occurred is the prettiest spot on earth, and the road to it rougher than mortal man ever trod. Large numbers of the hostiles seem pleased with the situation, evidently expecting an immediate return to the " fleshpots " of San Carlos. The only complaint comes from some of the squaws, whose bucks are among those who escaped. The officers who were with the expedition state that Crook had surrounded the Indians before they knew of his presence; that if he had not done so it would have taken six months and all the men there were in Arizona to have gotten them.

The captives stated that the Chiricahuas, were unanimous for peace, and had already sent two messengers to try to reach San Carlos.

SURRENDERING MEXICAN WOMEN TO GENERAL COOK AND BURNING APACHE LODGES.

One squaw, who was quite communicative and spoke the English language tolerably well, says, that numbers of the raids made by the Apaches were headed by a white man som fifty years of age, who was married to a squaw of their tribe.

The man is supposed to be L. N. Streeter, who was wounded and captured near Hermosillo some days ago while heading an Apache foray.

Streeter is about fifty years of age, and was born in California, his father being captain of an English merchantman trading on the Pacific coast and his mother a native Californian. Of his boyhood or early manhood very little is known, he first coming into notice in Arizona by his connection as clerk with the San Carlos Agency during Governor Safford's administration in this Territory. While there he had some difficulty with the officials, caused, it is said, by his giving aid and comfort to hostile Apaches. He left there suddenly and went straight for the camp of Juh and Geronimo, which was then near Janos Pass, on the line between Sonoro and Chihuahua. It is stated that while he was at the agency he became enamored of a squaw belonging to the tribe, and it was this fact that induced his leaving civilization to cast his fortunes with the Apaches. Governor Safford offered a large reward for his apprehension, some stories placing the amount as high as $5,000. He was not apprehended, however, and has never returned to Arizona.

He is said by those knowing him intimately to be very intelligent and well educated, and a manuscript now in the hands of the writer, written while Streeter was at Grenados, goes to prove it. He speaks the Apache dialect fluently and is said to have great influence with them. His standing among the savages, by whom he is known as Don Cassamiro, may be seen when it is known that the eldest son of Chief Geronimo is named for him.

The white boy mentioned by General Crook is supposed to be Charles Ware McComas, whose father and mother were murdered by the Indians at Thompson's Canon, twenty five miles from Silver City, New Nexico, and the boy captured and carried into Mexican territory.

He is only six years old, though large for his age, tipping the scale at 100 pounds. He is a natural blond, and rather prepossessing in appearance.

His father, Judge H. C. McComas, was a well known lawyer of

31

St. Louis and a former partner of M. McKeighan, the style of the firm being McComas & McKeighan.

The Judge was visiting some mining property at the time he was killed by the Indians.

After the fight the command, with the prisoners, marched leisurely back to American soil. The entire command with the prisoners are encamped on Silver Creek, about sixty miles from Tombstone. Not one of Crook's command was lost during the campaign.

At the risk of repetition of a few minor details we submit a portion of General Crook's official report. He says: —

" We moved southeast down San Bernardino, the most northerly branch of the Zarjin, the largest river in Western Mexico. For three days we did not see a human being. The whole country had been laid waste by Apaches, and much land of value, and formerly cultivated, had grown up into jungle, cane and mesquite. We followed the trail which our guide, ' Peaches,' assured me had been made by hostile Chiricahuas. On the 6th of May we passed by the hamlets of Bavispe, San Miguel and Boreanca, whose inhabitants welcomed us with exuberant joy. The authorities of Bavispe offered to come to our assistance with every man if needed, and also offered the services of four guides conversant with the foot-hills of the Sierra Madres. These offers I did not accept for want of transportation and supplies, and not believing that any guides could be equal to those whom we had been following. On the 15th of May scouts discovered camps and Indians, which were afterwards found to be those of Chato and Bonito. In accordance with my careful instructions they would have been surrounded but for the fact that some scouts incautiously fired upon a buck and squaw.

The surprise was complete, and in the subsequent fight, which lasted several hours, the Indians were thoroughly beaten, camps and their contents captured, and five half-grown girls and young boys taken prisoners. Nine dead Indians were found afterward, that had been killed in the fight. The extremely rugged nature of the country, the camps being situated half way up the face of a precipitous mountain, gashed with ravines and arroyas, preventing any exact count being made without extreme danger from Indians who might be wounded or hidden in the rocks, and who could have killed at their will without exposing themselves. There was considerable property stolen from Americans and

SURRENDER OF CHIEFS NANA AND LOCO.

Mexicans found in the camp, and about forty horses and mules. Early on the 18th a Chiricahua entered my camp. He is not a chief, but one of the most prominent men of his tribe, noted for his intelligence and bravery. He said the country to which we had penetrated was looked upon as impregnable; that the Mexican troops had never succeeded in getting into it, but had always been met and driven back, with rocks as well as bullets, as soon as they had passed the foot-hills. He explained that the feeling of security was so great that a large number of men were then absent on raids in Sonora and Chihuahua. He told me where the different chiefs were raiding. It was also stated that with Chato's band was a small white boy, captured in New Mexico, and corresponding so closely in description to Charles McComas that I have no doubt it is he. He said in consequence of the attack the Chiricahuas had scattered to the mountains like so many quail, and that he would go back and gather them together and return. 'But,' said he, 'you have Apache soldiers with you, and my people will not respond to my smoke signals, because they'll be sure your scouts have made them.' He went on to say that the captive boy was alive and in good spirits, but had gone off with the squaws, who had broken away from the camp upon discovering that our scouts were closing in upon them.

"From that on Chiricahuas came in rapidly from all points of the compass — men, women and children. All the chiefs surrendered and gave themselves up. All chiefs at last fairly begged to be taken back to San Carlos. I replied they were asking a great deal; that I had no power to put them on the reservation, and that I could not close my eyes to the atrocities of which they had been guilty. Many of the Americans wanted their band routed out, and that if I took them to San Carlos no doubt a cry would be raised for their blood. They had not only to face Americans but Mexicans also, whose people they had murdered in so cruel a manner. They could not expect me to fight their battles or palliate their villainous conduct. The chiefs then said: 'We give ourselves up; do with us as you please.' They begged to remain where I was for a few days longer, and explained what scarcely needed explanation, that the country was so fearfully rough they could not gather up all their people at once, as they were so much scattered. To this I could not assent, the supply of rations for the command making such delay impossible. We had by this time 384 Chiricahuas Indians and six Mexican captives to feed, and it was about as much as we could do to get back to our base without starvation.

Hieronymo then said if we would go along slowly towards the boundary they could send their runners out to warn all those who had not yet come in. They would try and overtake us at San Bernardino, or if not successful in that, would move along the mountains until they reached San Carlos. I assented to their sending after the remainder of their people still hiding in the mountains, but refused to give them any written passes, telling them if they could not catch up with the troops they must take their chances of being killed by any Mexicans or Americans they might encounter. Let the Apache see that he has something to gain by proper behavior and something to lose by not falling in with the new order of things. Vengeance is just as much to be deprecated as a silly sentimentalism. To attempt to punish one or a dozen of tribes for deeds for which all were equally guilty, would be a gross act of tyranny, while to attempt to punish all after they had surrendered in good faith, would be not only perfidious, but would involve us in war with a small but desperate handful of men, who would then fight with the recklessness of buccaneers under the black flag. The chief is no more guilty than every member of his band, since he has often less influence than individual members, being merely the mouth-piece or spokesman. To punish individuals guilty of particular crime should be done, were it possible to get evidence, but from the nature of things this is impossible. The Chiricahuas will present no difficulty whatever in the work of subjecting them to peaceful restraint and good discipline. They were not deprived of their arms for the best of reasons. It is not advisable to let an Indian think you are afraid of him, even when fully armed. Show him that at his best he is powerless in your hands, when he will become your best friend and cheerfully obey all he may be instructed to do. It is unfair, too, to deprive him of the means of protecting his home and property against the white scoundrels, who, armed to the teeth, infest the border, and would consider nothing so worthy their prowess as to plunder ponies, or other property, from unarmed Indians just beginning to plant and raise stock. So long as white horse and cattle thieves roam the country, so long should the Indians at San Carlos be allowed to carry arms for their own protection. Further, it is not practicable to disarm the Indians. Their arms can never be taken from them

CHAS. WARE McCOMAS—APACHE PRISONER.

unless they are taken prisoners with their arms in their hands, while engaged in fighting, by sudden surprise or disabling wounds. When Indians first surrender, or come upon a reservation they anticipate being disarmed and make their arrangements in advance, concealing most of their best weapons and delivering up only the surplus and unserviceable. The disarming of Indians has, in almost every instance on record, been a farcical failure. I may add that the fact that the Indians left behind have not come in is a matter of no significance. The Indians have no idea of the value of time. Members of Loco's band, who came into San Carlos in May last, were sixty-six days in making the journey, though they had forty or fifty miles less distance to travel than those whom I left in the Sierra Madres.

[Signed.]   GEORGE CROOK,
         Brig. Gen. Commanding.

General Hatch, after reading an account of the capture of Nana and the Apaches, in speaking of General Crook says:

"The finest Indian fighter in the army is George Crook. Now, he *is* an Indian fighter, and there never was a better one. What are the qualifications of an Indian fighter? Well, I'll tell you: Pluck and endurance. He's got to know how to starve. A white man can starve an Indian every time. He can outlast him in everything. It is the men who can starve, who can do without meat and drink, that can fight Indians. Take that country that Crook's been over. The lava beds that were made famous during the Modoc campaign are lawns compared to it. The Apaches were in a country that the word rough doesn't give a faint idea of it. It is nothing but craters, the crests of which are of porphyry. Now, there's nothing so easy as to stick a gun through a crevice in the porphyry and fire away at any body of men that is approaching. I crossed over the crest of one of those craters once, and closed in with a body of Indians two thousand feet below. No, Crook took things easy. He went along slowly and rested at places with the idea of taking the Indians in without any fighting, and he accomplished it. He had a great many of my old scouts with him. It's a mistaken idea that Indians are treacherous. They are soldiers — born soldiers, and are loyal to whoever they fight for. When the Indians enlist with you they'll fight for you to the death. Iv'e seen them kill their own people, not because they had any bitter feelings for them, but because they were on my side. When their six months were out, though, then look out — they are with you no longer." Asked about Indian tactics, the General said: "They do not scatter and fight individually, as is generally supposed. They fight like soldiers, in a body, under a commander, and are military in every sense. They advance and retire, execute flank movements, and are up in all the evolutions. I'll never forget," said the General, with a laugh, "when I had a handful of soldiers with me, just after the war, in Texas — I believe it was in 1866. A large body of Indians came down on us, and from the appearance of things it was all up with us. We were armed with magazine guns — Spencer rifles, which the Indians had never seen or heard of. They had the common muzzle-loading guns, and when we massed ourselves together, we could see that they were coming the old Indian dodge on us, circling around, coming nearer and nearer, firing arrows at us, and, as they got closer, waiting the time when we should fire into them, when they would dash down upon us and get away with us before we could reload. I knew what their tactics were, and I awaited the result with the greatest enjoyment. When they got close up I gave my men the word to fire, and bang went the rifles. Then the Indians came at us as swift as the horses could carry them. I knew they were unconscious of the fact we had nine loads in each gun, and when at the word my boys fired again they were thunderstricken. They were still on the charge when we plumped into them again. At every fire their men dropped. Then, when we fired into them again without moving our rifles, they turned and ran and we put after them, still firing. Well, you never saw anything like the demoralization among them. They must have thought the devil was after them. We chased them as far as we could, but they were too fast for us and we gave it up. But to return to Crook's Indians. In the fall of 1876, the Chiricahua and Hot Springs Indians went on the war-path. I followed them into the country, and after a big fight defeated them. The next year the same Indians broke out again, and we whipped them once more. They have been fighting about once a year since. Every year we kill so many, and a process of extermination goes on which will finally wipe them out. They'll fight again, and their numbers will be again lessened. You can't prevent them from fighting, and the only thing you can do with them is to wipe them out."

XXVII.

Captain John Tobin, late of the U. S. A., is another veteran plainsman and mountaineer.

If his life and adventures were written up it would make a wonderfully thrilling and interesting book, and would read more like romance than reality, yet the facts can all be substantiated by indisputable authority. He is the sole survivor of the famous Gunnison massacre.

John Tobin was born in Dungarvan, County of Weatherford, Ireland. At the early age of fifteen he espoused the cause of Ireland, and attached himself to the " Young Ireland Party," and was engaged in the assault on the Cappoquin Barracks, in Weatherford county. Learning that a warrant had been issued for his arrest, he fled to England, and succeeded in boarding the ill-fated Tuscarora. During the voyage the captain gave orders to " smoke " the vessel (fumigate the ship by burning tar). Through the carelessness of one of the sailors the tar was ignited, and the vessel caught fire, and at one time total destruction seemed inevitable. The hatches were ordered battened down, and, by almost superhuman exertions, the crew succeeded in extinguishing the fire. When the vessel arrived near Cape May, the Captain, by some mistake, ran her upon a coral reef, where both ship and cargo proved a total loss. The passengers and crew were rescued by neighboring fishermen, aided by wreckers.

From here the brave lad made his way to Cape May, and thence to Philadelphia. Feeling that Ireland could never be free without trained military leaders, he determined upon entering the army as soon as he should reach the requisite age. We cannot follow the dauntless boy through all his varied and checkered life. We will, however, relate an incident in the Captain's fitful career that happened in 1855.

Young Tobin entered the army, as previously determined, and at the time we mention was stationed at Fort Lane, Oregon, and held the rank of sergeant of cavalry.

On the evening of the ninth of October, 1855, a messenger arrived, bringing word that the Rogue River Indians were upon the war path, and were committing all kinds of outrages against the white settlers. He further stated that a number of men, women, and children had been massacred and their wagon train

(491)

captured and carried away by the red-skins. All was now excitement among the troopers, and many and dire were the threats made against the savages. Major Fitzgerald, with one hundred and thirty men, including the company to which Tobin belonged, was ordered to proceed in the direction the hostiles were supposed to be, and afford what protection he could to the whites.

Leaving Fort Lane in the afternoon of the same day, the command rode rapidly toward the scene of slaughter. Night soon overtook the rescuing party, and it proved to be a dark and cloudy one. The route lay through a narrow tract of land skirted on both sides with heavy timber, and the troops found it difficult to proceed. To *see* was impossible, owing to the intense darkness of the night. It was also dangerous, as the command could be easily ambuscaded and totally annihilated. The brave band of troopers struggled manfully on, literally *feeling* their way through the intense blackness surrounding them. No thought of danger, no wish to delay, but all eager and anxious to meet the savage foe. Toward morning, while riding slowly along, Tobin's horse shied suddenly and refused to proceed. The sergeant dismounted, determined to ascertain the cause of his horse's strange action. His first thought was "Indians." Not daring to strike a light, he groped around in the dark and stumbled over something which, upon close inspection, proved to be a human body, entirely naked and horribly mutilated. The facts were reported to Major Fitzgerald, who at once ordered a halt and detailed eight or ten men to examine the ground.

What was the horror of this little band of soldiers to discover the remains of twenty dead and mutilated men, women and children, stripped of every vestige of covering, with huge gashes in their legs and sides; some were literally disemboweled.

The gray dawn of morn had by this time made its appearance, and the sight that presented itself to the troopers was horrible in the extreme. Scouts were immediately sent out to ascertain the whereabouts of the Indians.

The scouts soon returned, and reported the Indians encamped about four miles further on, in the midst of an open valley. They, evidently, were not dreaming of being attacked, as they were howling and boasting of their prowess, and dancing the scalp dance. Major Fitzgerald, after hearing the report, determined to start at once and ride rapidly to the Indian camp and begin the attack without delay.

THE ATTACK ON EMIGRANT WAGONS.

For once the red man and the white would be on an equal footing. The command arrived in the vicinity of the hostiles about sunrise; but, owing to the open nature of the ground, a complete surprise could not be effected. The troopers were all well mounted, and armed with carbines, pistols and sabres. As they emerged from the timber and appeared in view on the open plain, the savages quickly mounted their ponies and began to prepare for battle, crying, "choco-choco, Basson" (come on, come, you pale faces). Major Fitzgerald formed his men in line of battle, and rode rapidly to within easy range of the savages, obtaining a position that cut off the retreat to the timber in their rear. The savages, seeing their escape was next to impossible, prepared to make a desperate resistance.

The Indians outnumbered the troopers four to one. The latter opened upon them a brisk fire of bullet and buckshot that caused them to waver; they rallied, however, and returned the fire with a rapid discharge of small arms and arrows.

It was soon apparent to all that the Indians were adopting Siegel's tactics to "fight and retreat," and, by making a detour, reach the forest, some three-quarters of a mile in their rear. The commanding officer, divining their intentions, and without giving his troops time to reload, ordered them to draw sabre and charge. At the word of command, the men drew their sabres and fearlessly charged upon the horde of desperate and savage warriors.

The conflict now raged hand to hand, and was desperate and bloody in the extreme.

Take away all hope of escape from an Indian warrior, and let death stare him in the face, and he becomes a fiend incarnate. Such was the condition of the hostiles who opposed Major Fitzgerald's command. On the other hand, the horrible scene witnessed by the gallant cavalrymen the night previous cried for vengeance, and the recollection of the twenty innocent men, women and children murdered by these same red devils would continually arise, like Banquo's ghost, before their eyes, and spurred them on to heroic deeds of valor. Many and sanguinary were the hand-to-hand contests upon this hotly contested battle-ground, two opposed to three, and three to one; sabre against spear, and knife against tomahawk.

Before leaving Fort Lane, Sergeant Tobin had borrowed a six-shooter from Post Farrier Laughlin, and this, in all probability, saved his life. In the very commencement of the battle he was attacked by three stalwart savages, armed with spears and tomahawks, who made a most determined assault upon him. Tobin calmly awaited their attack, and, by reserving his fire until they were within a few feet of him, he succeeded in killing two of them instantly and badly wounding a third, who, in his dying struggle, gave a peculiar whoop that attracted the attention of three more savages, who came with flying leaps to the aid of their wounded comrade.

Again was Tobin in a desperate situation. He had still three loads left in his revolver, and determined to sell his life as dearly as possible. The foremost Indian came bounding forward, shouting the battle-cry, and when within ten feet of our hero, sent his battle-axe with terrible force directly at the head of Tobin. Fortunately it missed the brave trooper, although passing in uncomfortable proximity to his head. The next instant the savage lay writhing in death with a ball from Tobin's revolver through his brain. Quicker than our tardy pen can trace the facts, the second Indian fell to rise no more. The third was but a few feet behind his comrades, and, seeing their fate, he hesitated before attacking a man who had just slain five of the bravest warriors of the tribe.

The brave trooper had but one more shot left, and, although a man of iron nerve, and a splendid marksman, the terrific combat was telling upon him. Would he be as successful with the sixth red-skin as he had been with the others? was the question that flashed through his brain. With great care and deliberation the warrior took aim and hurled his spear directly at the head of John Tobin. It swerved in its course, and the long, heavy handle struck him a glancing blow on the side of the head that felled him to the ground. The savage instantly sprang forward to finish his victim, but the plucky trooper's time had not yet come. Recovering himself, he arose to a half-sitting, half-stooping position. The Indian was now within three feet of him, with scalping knife in hand, when Tobin's bullet pierced his brain, and he fell without a groan.

The battle lasted over two hours, and ranged over a space half a mile square. Five hundred streaked and painted savages lay dead and dying on the bloody field. One red-skin alone of all that band of savage warriors succeeded in eluding the troopers and reaching the timber, where he disappeared with a yell of defiance. All efforts to capture him proving futile.

A view of the battle ground presented a sickening sight. One savage had buried his knife to the hilt in the breast of a trooper, who had retaliated by thrusting his sabre through the body of the Indian. Both were dead, one lying across the other.

Now that the battle was ended, the troopers turned their attention to their wounded comrades, and to burying the dead. Twenty-three troopers had made their last charge, and sorrowing companions proceeded to give them decent burial.

Before the sad task was half finished a messenger arrived, attracted by the firing, who stated that the Indians had attacked Harris ranch, and unless aid was sent at once, the whites would all be murdered.

Sergeant Tobin, with a detail of twenty-five men, was ordered to proceed at once to the ranch and render the inmates what aid he could. A short ride of two hours brought them to within sight of the ranch. The place was in the hands of some fifty savages. The troopers formed in fours, and rode boldly in the direction of the Indians. The latter deeming discretion the better part of valor, discharged their arms at the troopers, and then fled precipitately to the woods. The troops returned the fire, but the distance being too great, no damage was done on either side. The troopers found Mr. Harris just breathing his last, while his wife and her fourteen-year-old daughter were tied to trees, and but for the timely arrival of Sergeant Tobin, would have been subjected to a fate worse than death. The daughter was wounded in the shoulder.

From these brave women Tobin learned that the Indians had attacked the house some two hours before, and the inmates had made a determined resistance. Mr. Harris was shot early in the fight, and lay upon the floor in a dying condition. The heroic mother had taken her stand at a port hole, and kept the Indians at bay. The women were possessed of two rifles. The young girl did the loading and the mother did the shooting. Four Indians were killed by this brave woman, and several more were wounded. It was by a combined attack from front and rear that the Indians finally succeeded in gaining an entrance and making captives of the inmates.

This was but the beginning of a series of Indian outrages that lasted over two years, and cost the Government many valuable lives and a large amount of money.

32

Capt. John Tobin was the veteran mountaineer who saved the entire Mormon hand-cart trains from destruction by risking his life in crossing the Rocky Mountains in winter to obtain aid from Gov. Brigham Young for the starving and snow-bound emigrants in the winter of 1856.

He corroborates John D. Lee's confession of the Mountain Meadows massacre, an account of which we give in the following pages.

In order that the reader may understand the following extract, taken from "Mormonism Unveiled," we will state that a large emigrant train of eighteen wagons, five hundred head of cattle, the property of some thirty families, consisting of one hundred and twenty men, women and children, guided by Captain Fancher, were on their way to California to find homes. On the 22d day of September, 1857, the emigrants were attacked at Mountain Meadows, Washington County, M. T., by Indians and Mormons, and the entire party slain. John D. Lee, nearly twenty years afterwards, was arrested, tried, convicted, and executed for his part in this infamous transaction. The following is a part of his confession after he found there was no hope for him : —

About the 7th of September, 1857, I went to Cedar City from my home at Harmony, by order of President Haight. I did not know what he wanted of me, but he had ordered me to visit him and I obeyed. If I remember correctly, it was on Sunday evening that I went there. When I got to Cedar City, I met Isaac C. Haight on the public square of the town. Haight was then President of that State of Zion, and the highest man in the Mormon priesthood in that country, and next to Wm. H. Dame in all of Southern Utah, and as Lieutenant-Colonel he was second to Dame in the command of the Iron Military District. The word and command of Isaac C. Haight were *the law* in Cedar City, at that time, and to disobey his orders was certain death; be they right or wrong, no Saint was permitted to question them, their duty was obedience or death.

When I met Haight, I asked him what he wanted with me. He said he wanted to have a long talk with me on private and particular business. We took some blankets and went over to the old Iron Works, and lay there that night, so that we could talk in private and in safety. After we got to the Iron Works, Haight told me all about the train of emigrants. He said (and I then believed every word that he spoke, for I believed it was an impossible thing for one so high in the Priesthood as he was, to be guilty of falsehood) that the emigrants were a rough and abusive set of men. That they had, while travelling through Utah, been very abusive to all the Mormons they met. That they had insulted, outraged, and ravished many of the Mormon women. That the abuses heaped upon the people by the emigrants during their trip from Provo to Cedar City, had been constant and shameful; that they had burned fences and destroyed growing crops; that at many points on the road they had poisoned the water, so that all people and stock that drank of the water became sick, and many had died from the effects of poison. That these vile Gentiles publicly proclaimed that they had the very pistol with which the Prophet, Joseph Smith, was murdered and had threatened to kill Brigham Young and all of the Apostles. That when in Cedar City they said they would have friends in Utah who would hang Brigham Young by the neck until he was dead, before snow fell again in the Territory. They also said that Johnston was coming, with his army, from the East, and they were going to return from California with soldiers, as soon as possible, and would then desolate the land, and kill every d — d Mormon man, woman and child that they could find in Utah. That they violated the ordinances of the town of Cedar, and had, by armed force, resisted the officers who tried to arrest them for violating the law. That after leaving Cedar City the emigrants camped by the company, or co-operative field, just below Cedar City, and burned a large portion of the fencing, leaving the crops open to the large herds of stock in the surrounding country. Also that they had given poisoned meat to the Corn Creek tribe of Indians, which had killed several of them, and their Chief, Konosh, was on the trail of the emigrants, and would soon attack them. All of these things, and much more of a like kind, Haight told me as we lay in the dark at the old Iron Works. I believed all that he said, and, thinking that he had full right to do all that he wanted to do, I was easily induced to follow his instructions.

Haight said that unless something was done to prevent it, the emigrants would carry out their threats and rob every one of the outlying settlements in the South, and that the whole Mormon people were liable to be butchered by the troops that the emigrants would bring back with them from California. I was then told that the Council had held a meeting that day, to consider the matter, and that it was decided by the authorities to arm the Indians, give them provisions and ammunition, and send them after the emigrants, and have the Indians give them a *brush*, and if they killed part or all of them, so much the better.

I said, " Brother Haight, who is your authority for acting in this way?"

He replied, " It is the *will of all in authority*. The emigrants have no pass from any one to go through the country, and they are liable to be killed as common enemies, for the country is at war now. No man has a right to go through this county without a written pass."

We lay there and talked much of the night, and during that time Haight gave me very full instructions what to do, and how to proceed in the whole affair. He said he had consulted with Colonel Dame, and every one agreed to let the Indians use up the whole train if they could. Haight then said : —

" I expect you to carry out your orders."

I knew I had to obey or die. I had no wish to disobey, for I then thought that my superiors in the Church were the mouthpieces of Heaven, and that it was an act of godliness for me to obey any and all orders given by them to me, without my asking any questions.

My orders were to go home to Harmony, and see Carl Shirts, my son-in-law, an Indian interpreter, and send him to the Indians in the South, to notify them that the Mormons and Indians were at war with the " *Mericats* " (as the Indians called all whites that were not Mormons) and bring all the Southern Indians up and have them join with those from the North, so that their force would be sufficient to make a successful attack on the emigrants.

It was agreed that Haight would send Nephi Johnson, another Indian interpreter, to *stir up* all the other Indians that he could find, in order to have a large enough force of Indians to give the emigrants a good *hush*. He said, " These are the orders that have been agreed upon by the Council, and it is in accordance with the feelings of the *entire people*."

I asked him if it would not have been better to first send to Brigham Young for instructions, and find out what he thought about the matter.

" No," said Haight, " that is unnecessary, *we are acting by orders*. Some of the Indians are now on the war-path, and all of them must be sent out; all must go, so as to make the thing a success."

It was then intended that the Indians should kill the emigrants, and make it *an Indian massacre*, and not have any whites interfere with them. No whites were to be known in the matter, it was to be all done by the Indians, so that it could be laid to them, if any questions were ever asked about it. I said to Haight: —

"You know what the Indians are. They will kill all the party, women and children, as well as the men, and you know we are sworn not to shed innncent blood."

"Oh h — l!" said he, "there will not be one drop of *innocent* blood shed, if every one of the d — d pack are killed, for they are the worse lot of out-laws and ruffians that I ever saw in my life."

We agreed upon the whole thing, how each one should act, and then left the iron works, and went to Haight's house and got breakfast.

After breakfast I got ready to start, and Haight said to me :—

"Go, Brother Lee, and see that the instructions of those in authority are obeyed, and as you are dutiful in this, so shall your reward be in the kingdom of God, for God will bless those who willingly obey counsel, and make all things fit for the people in these last days."

I left Cedar City for my home at Harmony, to carry out the instructions that I had received from my superior.

I then believed that he acted by the direct order and command of William H. Dame, and others even higher in authority than Colonel Dame. One reason for thinking so was from a talk I had only a few days before, with Apostle George A. Smith, and he had just then seen Haight, and talked with him, and I knew that George A. Smith never talked of things that Brigham Young had not talked over with him beforehand. Then the Mormons were at war with the United States, and the orders to the Mormons had been all the time to kill and waste away our enemies, but lose none of our people. These emigrants were from the section of the country most hostile to our people, and I believed then as I do now, that it was the will of every true Mormon in Utah, at that time, that the enemies of the church should be killed as fast as possible, and as this lot of people had men amongst them that were supposed to have helped kill the prophets in the Carthage jail, the killing of all of them would be keeping our oaths and avenging the blood of the prophets.

In justice to myself I will give the facts of my talk with George A. Smith.

In the latter part of the month of August, 1857, about ten days before the company of Captain Fancher, who met their doom at Mountain Meadows, arrived at that place, General George A. Smith called on me at one of my homes at Washington City, Washington county, Utah Territory, and wished me to take him round by Fort Clara, via Pinto settlements, to Hamilton Fort, or Cedar City. He said : —

" I have been sent down here by the old Boss, Brigham Young, to instruct the brethren of the different settlements not to sell any of their grain to our enemies. And to tell them not to feed it to their animals, for it will all be needed by ourselves. I am also to instruct the brethren to prepare for a *big fight*, for the enemy is coming in large force to attempt our destruction. But Johnston's army will not be allowed to approach our settlements from the east. God is on our side and will fight our battles for us, and deliver our enemies into our hands. Brigham Young has received revelations from God, giving him the right and the power to call down the curse of God on all our enemies who attempt to invade our territory. *Our greatest danger* lies in the people of California — a class of reckless miners who are strangers to God and his righteousness. They are likely to come upon us from the south and destroy the small settlements. But we will try and outwit them before we suffer much damage. The people of the United States who oppose our Church and people are a mob, from the President down, and as such it is impossible for their armies to prevail against the Saints who have gathered here in the mountains."

He continued this kind of talk for some hours to me and my friends who were with me.

General George A. Smith held high rank as a military leader. He was one of the twelve apostles of the Church of Jesus Christ of Latter Day Saints, and as such he was considered by me to be an inspired man. His orders were to me sacred commands, which I considered it my duty to obey, without question or hesitation.

I took my horses and carriage and drove with him to either Hamilton Fort or Cedar City, visiting the settlements with him, as he had requested. I did not go to hear him preach at any of our stopping places, nor did I pay attention to what he said to the leaders in the settlements.

The day we left Fort Clara, which was then the headquarters of the Indian missionaries under the presidency of Jacob Hamblin, we stopped to noon at the Clara River. While there the Indians gathered around us in large numbers and were quite saucy and impudent. Their chiefs asked me where I was going and who I had with me. I told them that he was a big captain.

" Is he a Mericat captain? "

" No," I said, " he is a Mormon."

The Indians then wanted to know more. They wanted to have a talk.

The General told me to tell the Indians that the Mormons were their friends, and that the Americans were their enemies, and the enemies of the Mormons, too; that he wanted the Indians to remain the fast friends of the Mormons, for the Mormons were all friends to the Indians; that the Americans had a large army just east of the mountains, and intended to come over the mountains into Utah and kill all of the Mormons and Indians in Utah Territory ; that the Indians must get ready and keep ready for war against all of the Americans, and keep friendly with the Mormons and obey what the Mormons told them to do — that this was the will of the Great Spirit; that if the Indians were true to the Mormons and would help them against their enemies, then the Mormons would always keep them from want and sickness and give them guns and ammunition to hunt and kill game with, and would also help the Indians against their enemies when they went into war.

This talk pleased the Indians, and they agreed to all that I asked them to do.

I saw that my friend Smith was a little nervous and fearful of the Indians, notwithstanding their promises of friendship. To relieve him of his anxiety I hitched up and started on our way, as soon as I could do so without rousing the suspicions of the Indians.

We had ridden along about a mile or so when General Smith said : —

" Those are savage looking fellows. I think they would make it lively for an emigrant train if one should come this way."

I said I thought they would attack any train that would come in their way. Then the General was in a deep study for some time, when he said:

" Suppose an emigrant train should come along through this

southern country, making threats against our people and bragging of the part they took in helping kill our prophets, what do you think the brethren would do with them? Would they be permitted to go their way, or would the brethren pitch into them and give them a good drubbing?"

I reflected a few moments, and then said: —

"You know the brethren are now under the influence of the late reformation, and are still red-hot for the gospel. The brethren believe the government wishes to destroy them. I really believe that any train of emigrants that may come through here will be attacked, and probably all destroyed. I am sure they would be wiped out if they had been making threats against our people. Unless emigrants have a pass from Brigham Young, or some one in authority, they will certainly never get safely through this country.

My reply pleased him very much, and he laughed heartily, and then said: —

"Do you really believe the brethren would make it lively for such a train?"

I said: "Yes, sir; I know they will, unless they are protected by a pass, and I wish to inform you that unless *you want every train captured* that comes through here, you must inform Governor Young that if he wants emigrants to pass without being molested, he must send orders to that effect to Colonel Wm. H. Dame or Major Isaac C. Haight, so that they can give passes to the emigrants, for *their passes will insure safety*, but nothing else will, except the positive orders of Governor Young, as the people are all bitter against the Gentiles, and full of religious zeal, and anxious to avenge the blood of the Prophets."

The only reply he made was to the effect that on his way down from Salt Lake City he had had a long talk with Major Haight on the same subject, and that Haight had assured him, and given him to understand that emigrants who came along without a pass from Governor Young could not escape from the Territory.

We then rode along in silence for some distance, when he again turned to me and said: —

"Brother Lee, I am satisfied that the brethren are under the full influence of the reformation, and I believe they will do just as you say they will with the wicked emigrants that come through the country making threats and abusing our people."

I repeated my views to him, but at much greater length, giving my reasons in full for thinking that Governor Young should give orders to protect all the emigrants that he did not wish destroyed. I went into a full statement of the wrongs of our people, and told him that the people were under the blaze of the reformation, full of wild fire and fanaticism, and that to shed the blood of those who would *dare to speak* against the Mormon Church or its leaders, they would consider doing the will of God, and that the people would do it as willingly and cheerfully as they would any other duty That the apostle Paul, when he started forth to persecute the followers of Christ, was not any more sincere than every Mormon was then, who lived in Southern Utah.

My words served to cheer up the General very much; he was greatly delighted and said: —

" I am glad to hear so good an account of our people. God will bless them for all that they do to build up His Kingdom in the last days."

General Smith did not say one word to me, or intimate to me, that he wished *any emigrants* to pass in safety through the Territory. But he led me to believe then, as I believe now, that he did want, and expected every emigrant to be killed that undertook to pass through the Territory while we were at war with the Government. I thought it was his *mission* to prepare the people for the bloody work.

I have always believed, since that day, that General George A. Smith was then visiting Southern Utah to prepare the people for the work of exterminating Captain Fancher's train of emigrants, and I now believe that he was sent for that purpose by the direct command of Brigham Young.

I have been told by Joseph Wood, Thomas T. Willis, and many others, that they heard George A. Smith preach at Cedar City during that trip, and that he told the people of Cedar City that the emigrants were coming, and he told them that they must not sell that company *any grain or provisions* of any kind, for they were a mob of villains and outlaws, and the enemies of God and the Mormon people.

Sidney Littlefield, of Panguitch, has told me that he was knowing to the fact of Colonel Wm. H. Dame sending orders from Parowan to Major Haight, at Cedar City, to *exterminate the Francher outfit,* and to kill every emigrant without fail.

Littlefield then lived at Parowan, and Dame was the **Presiding Bishop**. Dame still has all the wives he wants, and is a great friend of Brigham Young.

The knowledge of how George A. Smith felt toward the emigrants, and his telling me that he had a long talk with Haight on the subject, made me certain that it was the wish of the *Church authorities* that Fancher and his train should be *wiped out*, and knowing all this, I did not doubt then, and I do not doubt it now, either, that Haight was acting by full authority from the Church leaders, and that the orders he gave to me were just the orders that he had been directed to give, when he ordered me to raise the Indians and have them attack the emigrants.

I acted through the whole matter in a way that I considered it my religious duty to act, and if what I did was a crime, it was a crime of the Mormon Church, and not a crime for which I feel individually responsible.

I must here state that Klingensmith was not in Cedar City that Sunday night. Haight said he had sent Klingensmith and others over towards Pinto, and around there, to stir up the Indians and force them to attack the emigrants.

On my way from Cedar City to my home at Harmony, I came up with a large band of Indians under Moquetas and Big Bill, two Cedar City chiefs; they were in their war paint, and fully equipped for battle. They halted when I came up and said they had had a big talk with Haight, Higby and Klingensmith, and had got orders from them to follow up the emigrants and kill them all, and take their property as the spoil of their enemies.

These Indians wanted me to go with them and command their forces. I told them that I could not go with them that evening, that I had orders from Haight, the *big Captain*, to send other Indians on the war-path to help them kill the emigrants, and that I must attend to that first; that I wanted them to go on near where the emigrants were and camp until the other Indians joined them; that I would meet them the next day and lead them.

This satisfied them, but they wanted me to send my little Indian boy, Clem with them. After some time I consented to let Clem go with them, and I returned home.

When I got home I told Carl Shirts what the orders were that Haight had sent to him. Carl was naturally cowardly and was not willing to go, but I told him the orders must be obeyed. He then started off that night, or early next morning, to stir up the Indians of the South, and lead them against the emigrants. The emigrants were then camped at Mountain Meadows.

The Indians did not obey my instructions. They met, several hundred strong, at the Meadows, and attacked the emigrants Tuesday morning, just before daylight, and at the first fire, as I afterwards learned, they killed seven and wounded sixteen of the emigrants. The latter fought bravely, and repulsed the Indians, killing some of them and breaking the knees of two war chiefs, who afterwards died.

The news of the battle was carried all over the country by Indian runners, and the excitement was great in all the small settlements. I was notified of what had taken place, early Tuesday morning, by an Indian who came to my house and gave me a full account of all that had been done. The Indian said it was the wish of all the Indians that I should lead them, and that I must go back with him to the camp.

I started at once, and by taking the Indian trail over the mountain, I reached the camp in about twelve miles from Harmony. To go round by the wagon road it would have been between forty and fifty miles.

When I reached the camp I found the Indians in a frenzy of excitement. They threatened to kill me unless I agreed to lead them against the emigrants, and help them kill them. They also said they had been told that they could kill the emigrants without danger to themselves, but they had lost some of their braves, and others were wounded, and unless they could kill all the " Mericats," as they called them, they would declare war against the Mormons and kill every one in the settlements.

I did as well as I could under the circumstances. I was the only white man there, with a wild and excited band of several hundred Indians. I tried to persuade them that all would be well, that I was their friend and would see that they had their revenge, if I found out that they were entitled to revenge.

My talk only served to increase their excitement, and being afraid that they would kill me if I undertook to leave them, and I would not lead them against the emigrants, so I told them that I would go south and meet their friends, and hurry them up to help them. I intended to put a stop to the carnage if I had the power, for I believed that the emigrants had been sufficiently punished for what they had done, and I felt then, and always have felt that such wholesale murdering was wrong.

At first the Indians would not consent for me to leave them, but they finally said I might go and meet their friends.

I then got on my horse and left the Meadows, and went south.

I had gone about sixteen miles, when I met Carl Shirts with about one hundred Indians, and a number of Mormons from the southern settlements. They were going to the scene of the conflict. How they learned of the emigrants being at the Meadows I never knew, but they did know it, and were there fully armed, and determined to obey *orders*.

Amongst those whom I remember to have met there, were Samuel Knight, Oscar Hamblin, William Young, Carl Shirts, Harrison Pearce, James Pearce, John W. Clark, William Slade, Sr., James Matthews, Dudley Leavitt, William Hawley (now a resident of Filmore, Utah Territory), William Slade, Jr., and two others whose names I have forgotten. I think they were George W. Adair and John Hawley. I know they were at the meadows at the time of the massacre, and I think I met them that night south of the Meadows, with Samuel Knight and the others.

The whites camped there that night with me, but most of the Indians rushed on to their friends at the camp on the Meadows.

I reported to the whites all that had taken place at the Meadows, but none of them were surprised in the least. They all seemed to know that the attack was to be made, and all about it. I spent one of the most miserable nights there that I ever passed in my life. I spent much of the night in tears and at prayer. I wrestled with God for wisdom to guide me. I asked for some sign, some evidence that would satisfy me that my mission was of heaven, but I got no satisfaction from my God.

In the morning we all agreed to go on together to Mountain Meadows, and camp there, and then send a messenger to Haight, giving him full instructions of what had been done, and to ask him for further instructions. We knew that the original plan was for the Indians to do all the work, and the whites to do nothing, only to stay back and plan for them, and encourage them to do the work. Now, we knew the Indians could not do the work, and we were in a sad fix.

I did not then know that a messenger had been sent to Brigham Young for instructions. Haight had not mentioned it to me.

I now think that James Haslem was sent to Brigham Young, as a sharp play on the part of the authorities to protect themselves, if trouble ever grew out of the matter.

We went to the Meadows and camped at the springs, about half a mile from the emigrant camp. There was a larger number of Indians there then, fully three hundred, and I think as many as four hundred of them. The two chiefs who were shot in the knee were in a bad fix. The Indians had killed a number of the emigrants' horses, and about sixty or seventy head of cattle were lying dead on the Meadows, which the Indians had killed for spite and revenge.

Our company killed a small beef for dinner, and after eating a hearty meal of it we held a council and decided to send a messenger to Haight. I said to the messenger who was either Edwards or Adair (I cannot now remember which it was), "Tell Haight, for my sake, for the people's sake, for God's sake, send me help to protect and save these emigrants, and pacify the Indians."

The messenger started from Cedar City for our camp on the Meadows, about 2 o'clock P. M.

We all staid on the field, and I tried to quiet and pacify the Indians, by telling them that I had sent to Haight, the Big Captain, for orders, and when he sent his order I would know what to do. This appeared to satisfy the Indians, for said they:

"The Big Captain will send you word to kill all the Mericats."

Along towards evening, the Indians again attacked the emigrants. This was Wednesday. I heard the report of their guns, and the screams of the women and children in the corral.

This was more than I could stand. So I ran with William Young and John Magnum, to where the Indians were, to stop the fight. While on the way to them they fired a volley, and three balls from their guns cut my clothing. One ball went through my hat and cut my hair on the side of my head. One ball went through my shirt and leaded my shoulder, the other cut my pants across my bowels. I thought this was rather warm work, but I kept on until I reached the place were the Indians were in force. When I got to them, I told them the Great Spirit would be mad at them if they killed the women and children. I talked to them some time, and cried with sorrow when I saw that I could not pacify the savages.

When the Indians saw me in tears, they called me "Yaw

Guts,'' which in the Indian language means '' cry baby,'' and
to this day they call me by that name, and consider me a
coward.

Oscar Hamblin was a fine interpreter, and he came to my aid
and helped me to induce the Indians to stop the attack. By his
help we got the Indians to agree to be quiet until word was returned from Haight. (I do not know now but what the messenger started for Cedar City, after this night of attack, but I was
so worried and perplexed at that time, and so much has happened to distract my thoughts since then, that my mind is not
clear on that subject.)

On Thursday, about noon, several men came to us from Cedar
City. I cannot remember the order in which all the people came
to the Meadows, but I do recollect that at this time and in this
company Joel White, William C. Stewart, Benjamin Arthur,
Alexander Wilden, Charles Hopkins and —— Tate, came to us
at the camp at the springs. These men said but little, but every
man seemed to know just what he was there for. As our messenger had gone for further orders, we moved our camp about
four hundred yards further up the valley on to a hill, where we
made camp as long as we staid there.

I soon learned that the whites were as wicked at heart as the
Indians, for every little while during that day I saw white men
taking aim and shooting at the emigrants' wagons. They said
they were doing it to keep in practice and to *help pass off the
time.*

I remember one man that was shooting, that rather amused
me, for he was shooting at a mark over a quarter of a mile off,
and his gun would not carry a ball two hundred yards. That
man was Alexander Wilden. He took pains to fix up a seat
under the shade of a tree, where he continued to load and shoot
until he got tired. Many of the others acted just as wild and
foolish as Wilden did.

The wagons were corraled after the Indians had made the first
attack. On the second day after our arrival the emigrants drew
their wagons near each other and chained the wheels one to the
other. While they were doing this there was no shooting going
on. Their camp was about one hundred yards above and north
of the spring. They generally got their water from the spring
at night.

Thursday morning I saw two men start from the corral with

buckets, and run to the spring and fill their buckets with water, and go back again. The bullets flew around them thick and fast, but they got into their corral in safety.

The Indians had agreed to keep quiet until orders returned from Haight, but they did not keep their word. They made a determined attack on the train on Thursday morning about daylight. At this attack the Clara Indians had one brave killed and three wounded. This so enraged that band that they left for home that day and drove off quite a number of cattle with them. During the day I said to John Mangum,

" I will cross over the valley and go up on the other side, on the hills to the west of the corral, and take a look at the situation."

I did go. As I was crossing the valley I was seen by the emigrants, and as soon as they saw that I was a white man they ran up a *white* flag in the middle of their corral, or camp. They then sent two little boys from the camp to talk to me, but I could not talk to them at that time, for I did not know what orders Haight would send back to me, and until I did know his orders I did not know how to act. I hid, to keep away from the children. They came to the place where they had last seen me and hunted all around for me, but being unable to find me, they turned and went back to the camp in safety.

While the boys were looking for me several Indians came to me and asked for ammunition with which to kill them. I told them they must not hurt the children — that if they did I would kill the first one that made the attempt to injure them. By this act I was able to save the boys.

It is all false that has been told about little girls being dressed in white and sent out to me. There never was anything of the kind done.

I staid on the west side of the valley for about two hours, looking down into the emigrant camp, and feeling all the torture of mind that it is possible for a man to suffer who feels merciful, and yet knows, as I then knew, what was in store for that unfortunate company if the Indians were successful in their bloody designs.

While I was standing on the hill looking down into the corral, I saw two men leave the corral and go outside to cut some wood; the Indians and whites kept up a steady fire on them all the time, but they paid no attention to danger, and kept right along at their work until they had it done, and then they went back into camp. The men all acted so bravely that it was impossible to keep from respecting them.

After staying there and looking down into the camp until I was nearly dead from grief, I returned to the company at camp. I was worn out with trouble and grief; I was nearly wild waiting for word from the authorities at Cedar City. I prayed for word to come that would enable me to save that band of suffering people, but no such word came. It never was to come.

On Thursday evening John M. Higbee, Major of the Iron Militia, and Philip K. Smith, as he is called generally, but whose name is Klingensmith, Bishop of Cedar City, came to our camp with two or three wagons, and a number of men all well armed. I can remember the following as a portion of the men who came to take part in the work of death which was so soon to follow, viz.: John M. Higbee, Major and commander of the Iron Militia, and also first counsellor to Isaac C. Haight; Philip Klingensmith, Bishop of Cedar City; Ira Allen, of the High Council; Robert Wiley, of the High Council; Richard Harrison, of Pinto, also a member of the High Counsel; Samuel McMurdy, one of the Counsellors of Klingensmith; Charles Hopkins, of the City Council of Cedar City; Samuel Pollock; Daniel McFarland, a son-in-law of Isaac C. Haight, and acting as Adjutant under Major Higbee; John Ure, of the City Council; George Hunter, of the City Council; and I honestly believe that John McFarland, now an attorney-at-law at St. George, Utah, was there — I am not positive that he was, but my best impression is that he was there, Samuel Jukes; Nephi Johnson, with a number of Indians under his command; Irvin Jacobs; John Jacobs; E. Curtis, a Captain of Ten; Thomas Cartwright of the City Council and High Council; William Bateman, who afterwards carried the flag of truce to the emigrant camp; Anthony Stratton; A. Loveridge; Joseph Clews; Jabez Durfey; Columbus Freeman, and some others whose names I cannot remember. I know that our total force was fifty-four whites and over three hundred Indians.

As soon as these persons gathered around the camp, I demanded of Major Higbee what orders he had brought. I then stated fully all that had happened at the Meadows, so that every person might understand the situation.

Major Higbee reported as follows: " It is the orders of the

President, that all the emigrants must be *put out of the way.* President Haight has counselled with Colonel Dame, or has had orders from him to put all of the emigrants out of the way; none who are old enough to talk are to be spared."

He then went on and said substantially that the emigrants had come through the country as our enemies, and as the enemies of the Church of Jesus Christ of Latter Day Saints. That they had no pass from any one in authority to permit them to leave the Territory. That none but friends were permitted to leave the Territory, and that as these were our sworn enemies, they must be killed. That they were nothing but a portion of Johnston's army. That if they were allowed to go on to California, they would raise the war cloud in the West, and bring certain destruction upon all the settlements in Utah. That the only safety for the people was in the utter destruction of the whole rascally lot.

I then told them that God would have to change my heart before I could consent to such a wicked thing as the wholesale killing of that people. I attempted to reason with Higbee and the brethren. I told them how strongly the emigrants were fortified, and how wicked it was to kill the women and children. I was ordered to be silent. Higbee said I was resisting authority.

He then said, " Brother Lee is afraid of shedding innocent blood. Why, brethren there is not a drop of innocent blood in that entire camp of Gentile outlaws; they are a set of cut-throats, robbers and assassins; they are a part of the people who drove the Saints from Missouri, and who aided to shed the blood of our Prophets, Joseph and Hyrum, and it is our orders from all in authority, to get the emigrants from their stronghold, and help the Indians kill them."

I then said that Joseph Smith had told us never to betray any one. That we could not get the emigrants out of their corral unless we used treachery, and I was opposed to that.

I was interrupted by Higbee, Klingensmith and Hopkins, who said it was the orders of President Isaac C. Haight to us, and that Haight had his orders from Colonel Dame and the authorities at Parowan, and that all in authority were of one mind, and that they had been sent by the Council at Cedar City to the Meadows to counsel and direct the way and manner that the company of emigrants should be disposed of.

The men then in council, I must here state, now knelt down in

33

a prayer circle and prayed, invoking the Spirit of God to direct them how to act in the matter.

After prayer, Major Higbee said, "Here are the orders," and handed me a paper from Haight. It was in substance that it was the orders of Haight to *decoy* the emigrants from their position, and kill all of them that could talk. This order was in writing. Higbee handed it to me and I read it, and then dropped it on the ground, saying.

"I cannot do this."

The substance of the orders were that the emigrants should be *decoyed* from their stronghold, and all exterminated, so that no one would be left to tell the tale, and then the authorities could say it was done by the Indians.

The words *decoy* and *exterminate* were used in that message or order, and these orders came to us as the orders from the Council at Cedar City, and as the orders of our military superior, that we were bound to obey. The order was signed by Haight as commander of the troops at Cedar City.

Haight told me the next day after the massacre, while on the Meadows, that he got his orders from Colonel Dame.

I then left the Council, and went away to myself, and bowed myself in prayer before God, and asked Him to overrule the decision of that Council. I shed many bitter tears, and my tortured soul was wrung nearly from the body by my great suffering. I will here say, calling upon Heaven, angels, and the spirits of just men to witness what I say, that if I could then have had a thousand worlds to command, I would have given them freely to save that company from death.

While in bitter anguish, lamenting the sad condition of myself and others, Charles Hopkins, a man that I had great confidence in, came to me from the Council, and tried to comfort me by saying that he believed it was all right, for the brethren in the *Priesthood* were all united in the thing, and it would not be well for me to oppose them.

I told him the Lord must change my heart before I could ever do such an act willingly. I will further state that there was a reign of terror in Utah and many a man had been put out of the way, on short notice, for disobedience and I had made some narrow escapes.

At the earnest solicitation of Brother Hopkins, I returned with him to the Council. When I got back, the Council again prayed for aid. The Council was called The City Counsellors, the Church or High Counsellors; and all in authority, together with the private citizens, then formed a circle, and kneeling down, so that elbows would touch each other, several of the brethren prayed for Divine instructions.

After prayer, Major Higbee said, " I have the evidence of God's approval of our mission. It is God's will that we carry out our instructions to the letter."

I said, " My God! this is more than I can do. I must and do refuse to take part in this matter."

Higbee then said to me, " Brother Lee, I am ordered by President Haight to inform you that you shall receive a crown of Celestial glory for your faithfulness, and your eternal joy shall be complete." I was much shaken by this offer, for I had full faith in the power of the Priesthood to bestow such rewards and blessings; but I was anxious to save the people. I then proposed that we give the Indians all of the stock of the emigrants, except sufficient to haul their wagons, and let them go. To this proposition all the leading men objected. No man there raised his voice or hand to favor the saving of life, except myself.

The meeting was then addressed by some one in authority, I do not remember who it was. He spoke in about this language : " Brethren, we have been sent here to perform a duty. It is a duty that we owe to God, and to our Church and people. The orders of those in authority are that all the emigrants *must* die. Our leaders speak with inspired tongues, and their orders come from the God of Heaven. We have no right to question what they have commanded us to do; it is our duty to obey. If we wished to act as some of our weak-kneed brethren desire us to do, it would be impossible; the thing has gone too far to allow us to stop now. The emigrants know that we have aided the Indians, and if we let them go they will bring certain destruction upon us. It is a fact that on Wednesday night two of the emigrants got out of camp and started back to Cedar City for assistance to withstand the Indian attacks; they had reached Richards' Springs when they met William C. Stewart, Joel White and Benjamin Arthur, three of our brethren from Cedar City. The men stated their business to the brethren, and as their horses were drinking at the Spring, Brother Stewart, feeling *unusually* full of zeal for the glory of God and the upbuilding of the Kingdom of God on earth, shot and killed one of the emigrants, a young man by the name of Aden. When Aden fell from his horse, Joel White shot and wounded the other Gentile; but he unfortunately got away, and returned to his camp and reported that the Mormons were helping the Indians in all that they were doing against the emigrants. Now, the emigrants will report these facts in California if we let them go. We must kill them all, and our orders are to get them out by treachery, if no other thing can be done to get them into our power.''

Many of the brethren spoke in the same way, all arguing that the orders must be carried out.

I was then told the plan of action that had been agreed upon, and it was this: The emigrants were to be decoyed from their stronghold under a promise of protection. Brother William Bateman was to carry a flag of truce and demand a parley, and then I was to go and arrange the terms of the surrender. I was to demand that all the children who were so young they could not talk should be put into a wagon, and the wounded were also to be put into a wagon. Then all the arms and ammunition of the emigrants should be put into a wagon, and I was to agree that the Mormons would protect the emigrants from the Indians, and conduct them to Cedar City in safety, where they should be protected until an opportunity came for sending them to California.

It was agreed that when I had made the full agreement and treaty, as the brethren called it, the wagons should start for Hamblin's Ranch with the arms, the wounded and the children. The women were to march on foot and follow the wagons in single file; the men were to follow behind the women, they also to march in single file. Major John M. Higbee was to stand with his militia company about two hundred yards from the camp, and stand in double file, open order, with about twenty feet space between the files, so that the wagons could pass between them. The drivers were to keep right along, and not stop at the troops. The women were not to stop there, but to follow the wagons. The troops were to halt the men for a few minutes, until the women were some distance ahead, out into the cedars, where the Indians were hid in ambush. Then the march was to be resumed, the troops to form in single file, each soldier to walk by an emigrant, and on the right-hand side of his man, and the soldier was to carry his gun on his left arm, ready for instant use. The march was to continue until the wagons had passed beyond the ambush of the Indians, and until the women were right in the midst of the Indians. Higbee was then to give the orders and words, " Do Your Duty." At this the troops were to shoot down the men ; the Indians were to kill all of the women and larger children, and the drivers of the wagons and I were to kill the wounded and sick men that were in the wagons. Two men were to be placed on horses near by, to overtake and kill any of the emigrants that might escape from the first assault. The Indians were to kill the women and large children, so that it would be certain that no Mormon would be guilty of shedding *innocent blood* — if it should happen that there was any innocent blood in the company that were to die. Our leading men all said that there was no innocent blood in the whole company.

The council broke up a little after daylight on Friday morning. All the horses, except two for the men to ride to overtake those who might escape, and one for Dan McFarland to ride as Adjutant, so that he could carry orders from one part of the field to another, were turned out on the range. Then breakfast was eaten, and the brethren prepared for the work in hand.

I was now satisfied that it was the wish of all of the Mormon priesthood to have the thing done. One reason for thinking so was that it was in keeping with the teachings of the leaders, and as Utah was then at war with the United States we believed all the Gentiles were to be killed as a war measure, and that the Mormons, as God's chosen people, were to hold and inhabit the earth and rule and govern the globe. Another, and one of my strongest reasons for believing that the leaders wished the thing done, was on account of the talk that I had with George A. Smith, which I have given in full in this statement. I was satisfied that Smith had passed the emigrants while on his way from Salt Lake City, and I then knew this was the train that he meant when he spoke of a *train* that would make threats and ill-treat our people, etc.

The people were in the full blaze of the reformation, and anxious to do some act that would add to their reputation as zealous churchmen.

I, therefore, taking all things into consideration, and believing, as I then did, that my superiors were *inspired* men, who could not go wrong in any matter relating to the church or the duty of its members, concluded to be obedient to the wishes of those in authority. I took up my cross and prepared to do my duty.

Soon after breakfast Major Higbee ordered the two Indian interpreters, Carl Shirts and Nephi Johnson, to inform the Indians of the plan of operations, and to place the Indians in ambush, so that they could not be seen by the emigrants until the work of death should commence.

This was done in order to make the emigrants believe that we had sent the Indians away, and that we were acting honestly and in good faith, when we agreed to protect them from the savages.

The orders were obeyed, and in five minutes not an Indian could be seen on the whole Meadows. They secreted themselves and lay still as logs of wood, until the order was given for them to rush out and kill the women.

Major Higbee then called all the people to order, and directed me to explain the whole plan to them. I did so, explaining just how every person was expected to act during the whole performance.

Major Higbee then gave the order for his men to advance. They marched to the spot agreed upon, and halted there. William Bateman was then selected to carry a flag of truce to the emigrants and demand their surrender, and I was ordered to go and make the treaty after some one had replied to our flag of truce. (The emigrants had kept a white flag flying in their camp ever since they saw me cross the valley.)

Bateman took a white flag and started for the emigrant camp. When he got about half way to the corral, he was met by one of the emigrants, that I afterwards learned was named Hamilton. They talked some time, but I never knew what was said between them.

Brother Bateman returned to the command and said that the emigrants would accept our terms, and surrender as we required them to do.

I was then ordered by Major Higbee to go to the corral and negotiate the treaty, and superintend the whole matter. I was again ordered to be certain and get all the arms and ammunition into the wagons. Also to put the children and the sick and wounded in the wagons, as had been agreed upon in council. Then Major Higbee said to me : —

" Brother Lee, we expect you to faithfully carry out all the instructions that have been given you by our council."

Samuel McMurdy and Samuel Knight were then ordered to drive their teams and follow me to the corral to haul off the children, arms, etc.

The troops formed in two lines, as had been agreed upon, and were standing in that way with arms at rest, when I left them.

I walked ahead of the wagons up to the corral. When I reached there I met Mr. Hamilton on the outside of the camp. He loosened the chains from some of their wagons, and moved one wagon out of the way, so that our teams could drive inside of the corral and into their camp. It was then noon, or a little after.

I found that the emigrants were strongly fortified; their wagons were chained to each other in a circle. In the centre was a rifle-pit, large enough to contain the entire company. This had served to shield them from the constant fire of their enemy, which had been poured into them from both sides of the valley, from a rocky range that served as a breastwork for their assailants. The valley at this point was not more than five hundred yards wide, and the emigrants had their camp near the centre of the valley. On the east and west there was a low range of rugged, rocky mountains, affording a splendid place for the protection of the Indians and Mormons, and leaving them in comparative safety while they fired upon the emigrants. The valley at this place runs nearly due north and south.

When I entered the corral, I found the emigrants engaged in burying two men of note among them, who had died but a short time before from the effect of wounds received by them from the Indians at the time of the first attack on Tuesday morning. They wrapped the bodies up in buffalo robes, and buried them in a grave inside the corral. I was then told by some of the men that seven men were killed and seventeen others were wounded at the first attack by the Indians, and that three of the wounded men had since died, making ten of their number killed during the siege.

As I entered the fortifications, men, women and children gathered around me in wild consternation. Some felt that the time of their happy deliverance had come, while others, though in deep distress, and all in tears, looked upon me with doubt, distrust and terror. My feelings at this time may be imagined (but I doubt the power of man being equal to even imagine how wretched I felt). No language can describe my feelings. My position was painful, trying and awful; my brain seemed to be on fire; my nerves were for a moment unstrung; humanity was overpowered, as I thought of the cruel, unmanly part that I was acting. Tears of bitter anguish fell in streams from my eyes; my tongue refused its office; my faculties were dormant, stupefied and deadened by grief. I wished that the earth would open and swallow me where I stood. God knows my suffering was great. I cannot describe my feelings. I knew that I was acting a cruel part and doing a damnable deed. Yet my faith in the godliness of my leaders was such that it forced me to think that I was not sufficiently spiritual to act the important part I was commanded to perform. My hesitation was only momentary. Then feeling that duty compelled *obedience to orders*, I laid aside my weakness and my humanity, and became an instrument in the hands of my superiors and my leaders. I delivered my message and told the people that they must put their arms in the wagon, so as not to arouse the animosity of the Indians. I ordered the children and wounded, some clothing and arms, to be put into the wagons. Their guns were mostly Kentucky rifles of the muzzle-loading style. Their ammunition was about all gone — I do not think there were twenty loads left in the whole camp. If the emigrants had had a good supply of ammunition they never would have surrendered, and I do not think we could have captured them without great loss, for they were brave men and very resolute and determined.

Just as the wagons were loaded, Dan. McFarland came riding into the corral and said that Major Higbee had ordered great haste to be made, for he was afraid that the Indians would return and renew the attack before he could get the emigrants to a place of safety.

I hurried up the people and started the wagons off towards Cedar City. As we went out of the corral I ordered the wagons to turn to the left, so as to leave the troops to the right of us. Dan. McFarland rode before the women and led them right up to the troops, where they still stood in open order as I left them. The women and larger children were walking ahead, as directed, and the men following them. The foremost man was about fifty yards behind the hindmost woman.

The women and children were hurried right on by the troops. When the men came up they cheered the soldiers as if they believed that they were acting honestly. Higbee then gave the orders for his men to form in single file and take their places as ordered before, that is at the right of the emigrants.

I saw this much, but about this time our wagons passed out of sight of the troops, over the hill. I had disobeyed orders in part by turning off as I did, for I was anxious to be out of sight of the bloody deed that I knew was to follow. I knew that I had much to do yet that was of a cruel and unnatural character. It was my duty, with the two drivers, to kill the sick and wounded who were in the wagons, and to do so when we heard the guns of the troops fire. I was walking between the wagons: the horses were going in a fast walk, and we were fully half a mile from Major Higbee and his men, when we heard the firing. As we heard the guns, I ordered a halt and we proceeded to do our part.

I here pause in the recital of this horrid story of man's inhumanity, and ask myself the question, Is it honest in me, and can I clear my conscience before my God, if I screen myself while I accuse others? No, never! Heaven forbid that I should put a burden upon others' shoulders that I am unwilling to bear my just portion of. I am not a traitor to my people, nor to my former friends and comrades who were with me on that dark day when the work of death was carried on in God's name, by a lot of deluded and religious fanatics. It is my duty to tell facts as they exist, and I will do so.

I have said that all of the small children were put into the wagons; that was wrong, for one little child, about six months old, was carried in his father's arms, and it was killed by the same bullet that entered its father's breast; it was shot through the head. I was told by Haight afterwards that the child was killed by accident, but I cannot say whether that is a fact or not. I saw it lying dead when I returned to the place of slaughter.

When we had got out of sight, as I said before, and just as we were coming into the main road, I heard a volley of guns at the place where I knew the troops and emigrants were. Our teams were then going at a fast walk. I first heard one gun, then a volley at once followed.

McMurdy and Knight stopped their teams at once, for they were ordered by Higbee, the same as I was, to help kill all the sick and wounded who were in the wagons, and to do it as soon as they heard the guns of the troops. McMurdy was in front; his wagon was mostly loaded with the arms and small children. McMurdy and Knight got out of their wagons; each one had a rifle. McMurdy went up to Knight's wagon, where the sick and wounded were, and raising his rifle to his shoulder, said: "O

Lord, my God, receive their spirits; it is for thy Kingdom that I do this.'' He then shot a man who was lying with his head on another man's breast; the ball killed both men.

I also went up to the wagon, intending to do my part of the killing. I drew my pistol and cocked it, but somehow it went off prematurely, and I shot McMurdy across the thigh, my pistol ball cutting his buck-skin pants. McMurdy turned to me and said:

"Brother Lee, keep cool; you are excited; you came very near killing me. Keep cool, there is no reason for being excited."

Knight then shot a man with his rifle; he shot the man in the head. Knight also brained a boy that was about fourteen years old. The boy came running up to our wagons, and Knight struck him on the head with the butt end of his gun, and crushed his skull. By this time many Indians reached our wagons, and all of the sick and wounded were killed almost instantly. I saw an Indian from Cedar City, called Joe, run up to the wagon and catch a man by the hair, and raise his head up and look into his face; the man shut his eyes, and Joe shot him in the head. The Indians then examined all of the wounded in the wagons, and all of the bodies, to see if any were alive, and all that showed signs of life were at once shot through the head. I did not kill any one there, but it was an accident that kept me from it, for I fully intended to do my part of the killing, but by the time I got over the excitement of coming so near killing McMurdy, the whole of the killing of the wounded was done. There is no truth in the statement of Nephi Johnson, where he says I cut a man's throat.

Just after the wounded were all killed, I saw a girl, some ten or eleven years old, running towards us from the direction where the troops had attacked the main body of emigrants; she was covered with blood. An Indian shot her before she got within sixty yards of us. That was the last person that I saw killed on that occasion.

About this time an Indian rushed to the front wagon, and grabbed a little boy, and was going to kill him. The lad got away from the Indian and ran to me, and caught me by the knees; and begged me to save him, and not let the Indian kill him. The Indian had hurt the little fellow's chin on the wagon-bed when he first caught hold of him. I told the Indian to let

THE MOUNTAIN MEADOWS MASSACRE.

the boy alone. I took the child up in my arms, and put him back in the wagon, and saved his life. This little boy said his name was Charley Fancher, and that his father was Captain of the train. He was a bright boy. I afterwards adopted him and gave him to Caroline. She kept him until Dr. Forney took all the children East. I believe that William Sloan, alias Idaho Bill, is the same boy.

After all the parties were dead, I ordered Knight to drive out on one side, and throw out the dead bodies. He did so, and threw them out of his wagon at a place about one hundred yards from the road, and then came back to where I was standing. I then ordered Knight and McMurdy to take the children that were saved alive (sixteen was the number, some say seventeen, I say sixteen), and drive on to Hamblin's ranch. They did as I ordered them to do. Before the wagons started, Nephi Johnson came up in company with the Indians that were under his command, and Carl Shirts I think came up too, but I know that I then considered that Carl Shirts was a coward, and I afterwards made him suffer for being a coward. Several white men came up too, but I cannot tell their names, as I have forgotten who they were.

Knight lied when he said I went to the ranch and ordered him to go to the field with his team. I never knew anything of his team, or heard of it, until he came with a load of armed men in his wagon, on the evening of Thursday. If anyone ordered him to go to the Meadows, it was Higbee. Every witness that claims that he went to the Meadows without knowing what he was going to do, has lied, for they all knew, as well as Haight or any one else did, and they all voted, every man of them, in the council, on Friday morning, a little before daylight, to kill all the emigrants.

After the wagons with the children, had started for Hamblin's ranch, I turned and walked back to where the brethren were. Nephi Johnson lies when he says he was on horseback, and met me, or that I gave him orders to go to guard the wagons. He is a perjured wretch, and has sworn to everything he could to injure me. God knows what I did do was bad enough, but he has lied to suit the leaders of the Church, who want me out of the way.

While going back to the brethren, I passed the bodies of several women. In one place I saw six or seven bodies near each

other; they were stripped perfectly naked, and all of their clothing was torn from their bodies by the Indians.

I walked along the line where the emigrants had been killed,
and saw many bodies lying dead and naked on the field, near by
where the women lay. I saw ten children; they had been killed
close to each other; they were from ten to sixteen years of age.
The bodies of the women and children were scattered along the
ground for quite a distance before I came to where the men were
killed.

I do not know how many were killed, but I thought then that
there were some fifteen women, about ten children, and about
forty men killed, but the statement of others that I have since
talked with about the massacre, makes me think there were fully
one hundred and ten killed that day on the Mountain Meadows
and that the ten who had died in the corral, and young Aden killed
by Stewart at Richards' Springs, would make the total number one
hundred and twenty-one.

When I reached the place where the dead men lay, I was told
how the orders had been obeyed. Major Higbee said: " The
boys have acted admirably, they took good aim, and all of the
d — d Gentiles but two or three fell at the *first fire*."

He said that three or four got away some distance, but the
men on horses soon overtook them and cut their throats. Higbee
said the Indians did their part of the work well, that it did not
take over a minute to finish up when they got fairly started. I
found that the first orders had been carried out to the letter.

Three of the emigrants did get away, but the Indians were
put on their trail and they overtook and killed them before they
reached the settlements in California. But it would take more
time than I have to spare to give the details of their chase and
capture. I may do so in my writings hereafter, but not now.

I found Major Higbee, Klingensmith, and most of the brethren
standing near by where the largest number of the dead men lay.
When I went up to the brethren, Major Higbee said: —

" We must now examine the bodies for valuables."

I said I did not wish to do any such work.

Higbee then said, " Well, you hold my hat and I will examine
the bodies, and put what valuables I get into the hat."

The bodies were all searched by Higbee, Klingensmith and
Wm. C. Stewart. I did hold the hat a while, but I soon got so
sick that I had to give it to some other person, as I was unable

to stand for a few minutes. The search resulted in getting a little money and a few watches, but there was not much money. Higbee and Klingensmith kept the property, I suppose, for I never knew what became of it, unless they did keep it. I think they kept it all.

After the dead were searched, as I have just said, the brethren were called up, and Higbee and Klingensmith, as well as myself, made speeches, and *ordered* the people to keep the matter a secret from the *entire* world. Not to tell their wives, or their most intimate friends, and we pledged ourselves to keep everything relating to the affair a secret during life. We also took the most binding oaths to stand by each other, and to always insist that the massacre was committed by Indians alone. This was the advice of Brigham Young, too, as I will show hereafter.

The men were mostly ordered to camp there on the field for that night, but Higbee and Klingensmith went with me to Hamblin's ranch, where we got something to eat, and staid there all night. I was nearly dead for rest and sleep; in fact, I had rested but little since the Saturday night before. I took my saddle-blanket and spread it on the ground soon after I had eaten my supper, and lay down on the saddle-blanket, using my saddle for a pillow, and slept soundly until next morning.

I was awakened in the morning by loud talking between Isaac C. Haight and William H. Dame. They were very much excited, and quarreling with each other. I got up at once, but was unable to hear what they were quarreling about, for they cooled down as soon as they saw that others were paying attention to them.

I soon learned that Col. Dame, Judge Lewis of Parowan, and Isaac C. Haight, with several others, had arrived at the Hamblin ranch in the night, but I do not know what time they got there.

After breakfast we all went back in a body to the Meadows to bury the dead and take care of the property that was left there.

When we reached the Meadows we all rode up to that part of the field where the women were lying dead. The bodies of men, women and children had been stripped entirely naked, making the scene one of the most loathsome and ghastly that can be imagined.

Knowing that Dame and Haight had quarreled at Hamblin's that morning, I wanted to know how they would act in sight of the dead, who lay there as the result of their orders. I was greatly interested to know what Dame had to say, so I kept close to them, without appearing to be watching them.

Colonel Dame was silent for some time. He looked all over the field, and was quite pale, and looked uneasy and frightened. I thought then that he was just finding out the difference between giving and executing orders for wholesale killing. He spoke to Haight, and said : —

" I must report this matter to the authorities.'

" How will you report it ? " said Haight.

Dame said, " I will report it just as it is."

" Yes, I suppose so, and implicate yourself with the rest ? " said Haight.

" No," said Dame. " I will not implicate myself, for I had nothing to do with it."

Haight then said, " That will not do, for you know a d—d sight better. You ordered it done. Nothing has been done except by your orders, and it is too late in the day for you to order things done and then go back on it, and go back on the men who have carried out your orders. You cannot *sow pig* on me, and I will be d—d if I will stand it. You are as much to blame as any one, and you know that we have done nothing except what you ordered done. I know that I have obeyed orders, and by G — d I will not be lied on."

Colonel Dame was much excited. He choked up, and would have gone away, but he knew Haight was a man of determination, and would not stand any foolishness.

As soon as Colonel Dame could collect himself, he said: —

" *I did not think there were so many of them, or I would not have had anything to do with it.*"

Colonel Dame was perfectly cowed. He did not offer to deny it again.

*   *   *   *   *   *   *   *   *   *

After the dead were covered up or buried, the brethren were called together and all took a most solemn oath, binding themselves under the most dreadful and awful penalties, to keep the whole matter secret from every human being, as long as they should live.

XXVIII.

THE MESSIAH CRAZE.

Chapter XXII of this volume contains a thrilling account of the massacre, on the Little Big Horn River, of the gallant Custer and his brave command ; not a living soul from among his followers escaping to tell the story. When the fight was ended, the warriors who were engaged in it did not wait for the certain coming of an avenging army, but under the guidance and advice of the medicine man, Sitting Bull, made their way into the British posessions. There they found a safe refuge among the tribes of kindred blood who are under the protection of the English. There they remained for several years, until, as the result of negotiations and pledges given by the government at Washington, they returned to their former hunting grounds. A large territory was assigned them as a reservation, and an Indian agency established at Pine Ridge, in South Dakota. This agency became the rallying point for the settlement of those scattered bands of Sioux who still looked to Sitting Bull for counsel, and his permanent residence, if an Indian can be said to have such a possession, was but a few miles away, on the banks of the Grand River. Supported in idleness by the government, or encouraged to make some effort at self-support by cattle raising or agriculture, these war-loving tribes found little to satisfy their inborn cravings for excitement. Since the almost total extinction of the buffalo the chase of that grand animal was no longer possible, and the only substitute they could find for its flesh and the excitement of procuring it, was that offered by the issue of live beef rations. On the days when such issue is to take place, the men of the tribe, with their families and tepees, camp in the vicinity of the agency, and, mounted on their ponies, appear at the corral. They climb the fence and inspect the herd ; selecting, as far as they are permitted, the particular beef they desire ; cracking jokes and making merry, in their solemn fashion, over the expected feast and excitement. When an animal has been assigned to them, they do not take it away to a suitable place and butcher it in a civilized fashion. They drive it out on the plains and proceed to excite and frighten it as much as possible, until it is reduced to the condi-

RATION DAY AT PINE RIDGE.

tion of a wild animal. Then, mounted on fleet ponies, they pursue it as in former years they did the buffalo, often using the bow and arrow in preference to the rifle.

In this same and uninspiring fashion their time has been spent until during the eventful year 1890 ; a new impulse took possession of them, and the strange Messiah craze introduced a new element into their lives. They became possessed with the belief that to the Indian a Messiah was about to come who should destroy the white man utterly, raise from the dead Indians who should believe in him, and restore the buffalo and fill the earth with abundance of game, and put all in the possession of the Red Man.

This belief was not confined to the tribes of the Sioux. It does not appear to have originated with them. It seems to have begun in a very interesting and harmless way among the tribes who dwell in the mountains west of the Mormon settlements in Utah and Idaho. An Indian of an unusually gentle disposition, who had been converted to Christianity and had been taught something of the story of the Bible, endeavored in his own way to carry the tidings of the Prince of Peace to his red brethren. He specially exerted himself to teach the doctrine of peace, and became known among his fellows as "The Peacemaker." A letter to Gen. Nelson A. Miles from an army officer stationed at Los Angeles, Cal., enables this strange character to tell his own story. The letter bears date Nov. 28, 1890. The letter says :

" I know it will be surprising when I say to you that I have found the Messiah, and the story of my finding is as follows : Last spring an Indian called and said he would like to speak to the commanding general. The messenger introduced him to me, and I turned him over to another officer for that purpose. But in a few moments he was turned over to me again. I took him into the room, and he gave me a history of himself. He said his name was Johnson Sides; that he was known as the Peacemaker among all Indians and the whites of Nevada, where he lived.

" To substantiate his statement he showed me a medal which he carried strung around his neck, on which was a legend to the effect that he was presented with the medal by some Christian society for his efforts toward doing good to his fellow men, whether white or red. He could talk very good English, was

GEN NELSON A. MILES, U. S. A.

dressed like an ordinary laborer, but had the Indian's way of wearing his hair. He told me he read or knew the Bible; that he was desirous of making peace with everyone, and that was why he was named Peacemaker. He said that Indians had come from afar off to see him, and he pulled out a pipe, such as are made by Northern Indians, which pipe was recognized as having come from either Montana or Dakota. Johnson Sides said it came from Dakota, and the kind of clay of which it was made could not be found in Nevada, and that the stem was of a peculiar wood not found in Nevada or California. He mentioned the names of the Indians who had visited him, and the tribes they belonged to; also gave the time they had called.

"I firmly believe that this is the good-natured Indian that has caused all this trouble; that he has taught the members of his tribe the story of Christ, or the Messiah, and the time when He will once more visit this earth, as it has been taught him by the Christian people interested in his welfare. He has told these visiting Indians of the paradise in store for all people when the Son shall once more visit the earth; and the Indian's paradise is whatever his imagination may lead him to believe, the same as the white man's. He has no doubt delivered the story in its true light, and the Indians in retelling the story have warped and woven it according to their understanding.

"Johnson Sides is well known to all people living along the line of the Central Pacific Railroad, in the vicinity of Reno and Winnemuca, Nev."

Sitting Bull returned from his refuge among the northern Indian tribes and took up his residence among the tribes who had formerly been so much influenced by him. But his power was greatly broken, and for more than a decade nothing occurred to call into play that genius for intrigue and diplomacy which he possessed and by which, without being himself a warrior, he had made himself so powerful among a race of warriors. His people were well fed and sufficiently clad; there was but little discontent among them. The advice he had formerly given had not resulted in any permanent benefit, but in loss and chagrin. The massacre of Custer, and the defeat of Reno were well enough as subjects of savage boasting; no real benefits had followed them however, but much suffering and loss. Now, in the pursuit of peace they realized the folly of it all, and the wiser and older chieftains

WAR DANCE OF THE SIOUX INDIANS OF NORTH AMERICA.

avoided the man who had been their leader in that great blunder.

While affairs were thus shaping themselves, the wily old medicine man bided his time, watching for an opportunity to restore his former prestige. Now he saw his opportunity. Traveling Indians visiting his tepee called up the vague traditions which have always existed among the Indian tribes of a coming deliverer, and whispers were passed along that a Messiah would shortly come. Was not he, Sitting Bull a great Medicine? A religious teacher? And shall he not lead his people in this?

Three years ago a Crow Indian in Montana, taught that the Messiah would make the Indians impervious to bullets; two years ago a medicine man named Swohalle, claimed that the Messiah was coming to wreak vengeance upon the pale-faces for their wrongs to the Indians, and now Sitting Bull actually claims to have seen the Messiah, and that his coming is near at hand.

Mr. Zook, a Montana ranchman, gives the following interesting account of the visit of the Messiah, as related to him:

"Sitting Bull was hunting one day near the Sheshone Mountains, and as night came on he was seized with a strange feeling, and at first involuntarily, but finally with alacrity, he followed a star which moved westward through the sky. All night the star guided him, and near morning he met the Messiah, clad in a white robe. His hair flowed upon his shoulders, his beard was long, and around his head shone a bright halo. When Sitting Bull beheld this wonderful apparition, he fainted and had a strange dream. A band of Cheyennes and Arapahoes, who had lond since been dead, appeared to him and danced, inviting him to join them. Presently he was restored to his senses, and the Messiah spoke to him. He asked him if the Indians would not rejoice to see their dead kindred and the buffalo restored to life: and Sitting Bull assured him that they would be deeply gratified. Then the Messiah told him that he had come to save the white men, but that they had persecuted him; and now he had come to rescue the long-tormented Indian. He showed him the holes in his hands, made by the nails when he was crucified, to convince him that he was the same Christ who had appeared 1,900 years ago. All day Christ instructed him and gave him evidence of his power. He said that the white men had come to take him, but as they approached the soil became quicksand, and the men and horses sank. As evening came on, he bade Sitting

Bull depart; and although he had been hunting away from his tepee for ten sleeps, he came to it in a very few minutes. He told his people his story and sent others to verify his statements, and they told the same tales."

When the Indians heard of this wonderful vision, they came in swarms to see Sitting Bull and pitched their tepees around him. There they inaugurated the "worship dances," and forming a ring to the number of 3,000 people, they danced around Sitting Bull and his chiefs whilst chanting a monotonous accompaniment of weird strains. Thus they danced all night until they dropped down from sheer exhaustion, when others would take their place.

Sitting Bull praised their zeal and bade them to depart to their winter quarters and there await the Messiah, who was to come in the spring-time. He likewise urged them to leave the pale-faces unmolested, as the Messiah would move them across the ocean, and they would torment the Indians no more. Following his advice they took down their tepees and departed to their homes.

Kicking Horse, a Sioux, who claims to have just returned from a visit to heaven, tells the following curious story: He says that he entered heaven through a hole in the sky, and that he saw the Great Spirit, who told him that the Indians had suffered long enough, and that the time had come for their deliverance. They were to occupy the earth once more, which had been taken from them by the whites, but they were not to kill or molest them. The Great Spirit told him that the earth was getting full of holes, and many places were rotten. He would gradually send a wave of earth 20 feet or more over the country, and that it would move slowly. The Indian must keep dancing so as to be on top, and when the wave passed all the pale-faces would be buried underneath and the Indians would be on top. All the dead Indians would be restored to life again, and the buffaloes, horses, game, and their old hunting grounds would be as they were hundreds of years ago, and the Indians would for all time in the future own and occupy the earth. All Indians who would not listen to the words of the prophet and keep dancing would be turned into fishes and dwell in the rivers and streams.

He said, that whilst talking to the Great Spirit the devil came to them. He describes the devil as being very tall, with immense knee-joints, a monster mouth and long teeth. He was covered all over with coarse hair. He asked for half of the people, meaning the Indians, but the Great Spirit refused to grant his request. He asked again, but the Great Spirit replied: "You can have none of my chosen Indian children, but you can have all the whites."

And now still greater excitement prevails on account of the appearance of a squaw who has come recently from Canada, and who claims to be the mother of the expected Messiah. She glories in the euphonious name of Walutawin (Scarlet woman), and is the wife of Tiksoga, a member of Watoksi's band of

WALUTAWIN (SCARLET WOMAN).

Sioux, but it is said that she is not a native, as she belongs to a band of Indians across the Manitoba line. She is of a commanding figure, and when she appeared in court, in answer to the charges brought against her of inciting the Indians to revolt, she seemed to be entirely at her ease, and spoke in a low voice with intense earnestness. She proclaimed herself as the mother of Christ, who was now upon the earth making preparations to rebuild it for His chosen people. Great herds of buffalo were to wander about as in the days of long ago, and the Indians who now sleep in death were to rise again, and forevermore wander over the earth. In those days there will be no more reservation;

no messenger from the great father to say to the Indians, come back here, stay on your reservation. Thus she expatiated upon the rosy-tinted dawning of the Indian millenium, and painted a glowing word-picture of their future freedom in the land.

No trouble is feared among the Indians at present, though they remain restless and are exciting themselves by frequent war dances, and are still looking for the coming of the Messiah, who is to exterminate the white man. The failure of the Messiah to appear, however, on certain specified dates has somewhat dampened their fervor, and when the next failure occurs the belief of the Indians in their so-called prophets will be badly shaken, if not entirely destroyed.

But this belief in a coming Messiah who is to rescue the Indians prevails not only among the Sioux Indians, but in many other tribes. Do we not all know the well-known poem of "Hiawatha?" which relates his dwelling among men until he took his departure:

> To the Islands of the Blessed,
> To the kingdom of Ponemah,
> To the land of the Hereafter!

He told them that he was going on a long and distant journey, and that many moons and many winters would vanish ere he came to see them again. But he promised to return to them some day, and bade them patiently await his coming.

As Hiawatha was the great deliverer of the Iroquois, so was Manabozho among the Chippewas. He was regarded as the messenger of the Great Spirit sent down to them as a prophet endowed with miraculous power. He lived among the people, learning their mode of life, and with them suffered joys and sorrows, hunger and want, joining in their war songs and dances. He was regarded as the spirit of the Northwest tempests, and as a divine benefactor. He affected to be influenced by the spirit of a god, but from his love of mischief he seemed at times inspired with the malignity of a devil. His voice was at one moment deep and sonorous as a thunder-clap, and at another it was soft as a woman's voice can be. He evinced the sagacity, cunning, perseverance and heroic courage which constitute the admiration of the Indian, yet there was nothing too low or trivial for him to attempt when upon mischief bent. The period of his labors upon earth having expired, he withdrew to dwell with his brother in the North, where he directs the storms. It is believed that he will return again to this earth and exercise an important power in the final disposition of the human race.

Similar in character to Hiawatha and Manabozho, is the Algon-

CALLING THE INDIANS TO THE GHOST DANCE.

quin hero, Glooskap. His name means the liar, because he promised when he left the earth to return once more, and he has not done so yet. He is represented as a giant whose head touches the stars, and whilst he is fearful to encounter as a foe, yet at home he is gentle, though full of mischief, but sympathetic withal.   According to the Indians of Maine, Glooskap created the world, and made the first men from the ash tree, and they were "devoid of sense" till he gave it to them.

He came first into this country through Nova Scotia, Maine and Canada, into the land of the Wabanaki, next to sunrise.   There were only wild Indians there in those days.   Then he created the small elves—little men, dwellers in hills, and in this way he peopled the land.   He made all the animals and they were under his control.

Now, many years ago, far in the North, whilst the Indians were assembled at a certain place, there was a great earthquake, and the ground heaved and rumbled.   The rocks shook and fell down, and the Indians were filled with consternation.   Presently Glooskap stood before them and said :   "I go away now, but I shall return again ; when you feel the ground tremble, then know it is I."

So they will know when the last day is near at hand, for Glooskap will shake the ground beneath his mighty tread, the earth will shudder at his approach.   In that day a great battle will take place between the frost giants, stone giants and other powers of evil, and great hills will be dashed together, and mighty trees will tremble and fall to the ground.   All the wild animals shall flee in terror to the uttermost limits of the earth, and the Indian will be overcome with terror.

Before Glooskap left the world he freed it from the mighty monsters of olden times, chased the giants out of the wildernesses, and appeased the dreaded Chenoo of the North ; whilst evil beasts, devils and serpents were no longer allowed to roam at will.   He did all in his power to make his chosen people happy.

But the white man came, and with ruthless hand
Cleared the forests and sowed the land,
And drove from their haunts by the sunny shore
Micmac and moose forevermore.
And Glooskap, saddened and sore distressed,
Took his way to the unknown West,
And the Micmac kindled his wigwam fire
Far from the grave of his child and his sire;
Where now, as he weaves his basket gay,
And paddles his birch canoe away,
He dreams of the happy time for men
When Glooskap shall come to his tribe again.

Glooskap is now making arrows and preparing for a great

battle, and he is to come forth at the new twilight of the gods and exterminate the Iglesmani, establishing an eternally happy hunting ground.

The following account of the last day was obtained from an old Passamaquaddy Indian by Mrs. W. Wallace Brown of Calais, Me.:

"Is Glooskap living yet?"

"Yes, far away—no one knows where. Some say he sailed away in his stone canoe beyond the sea to the East, but he will return in it one day. Others say that he went to the West. One story tells that while he was alive those who went to him and found him could have their wishes given to them. But there is a story that if one travels long, and is not afraid, he may still find the great Sagamore. Yes, he lives in a very great, a very long wigwam. He is always making arrows. One side of the lodge is full of arrows. They are as thick as that. When it is quite full he will come forth and make war. He never allows anyone to enter the wigwam while he is making these arrows."

"And on whom will he make war?"

"He will make war on all—kill all. There will be no more world—world all gone. Dunno how quick—mebbe long time. All be dead then, mebbe—guess it will be a long time."

"Are any to be saved by anyone?"

THE PINE RIDGE AGENCY

TRADING POST.

AGENCY BUILDINGS.

Govt. Indian School.

542 LIFE ON THE PLAINS.

"Dunno. Me hear how some say world all burn up some day, water all boil, all fire; some good ones be taken up in good heavens, but me dunno—me just hear that. Only hear so."

The excitement caused by the spread of these reports and the hopes thus inspired in the Indian hearts offered the opportunity which Sitting Bull and other medicine men waited for. Nor are we to believe they were entirely insincere in their belief.

"Hope springs eternal in the human breast."

Many believe it true because they wish it so.

Among all savage people exercises which for want of a better term we call dances, are used to express great spiritual or devotional exercises. As soon as the Indians became possessed of the Messiah idea, they organized the Messiah or Ghost Dance, and this was taken in charge by the medicine men.

One man was appointed "High Priest," to have entire control of the ceremonies. His four assistants were likewise invested with power to start or stop the dance at will. They were given authority to punish any person who should refuse to obey their commands.

While the priests are employed in their prayers, the squaws make a good-sized sweat-house. Poles are stuck in the ground and the tops bent together and securely tied. These saplings are strong enough to bear the weight of several hundred pounds. Over the framework are heaped blankets and robes to such a thickness that no smoke or steam can pass from the interior. A fire is started in a hole in the ground several feet from the small entrance to the sweat-lodge, and twenty or thirty good-sized stones are placed therein to be heated. When these rocks have become sufficiently hot, the young men who are to partake of the bath, strip, with the exception of the breech-clout, and crawl through the door. They seat themselves in a circle, with their feet toward the center and their backs against the sides of the lodge. The attendant shoves some of the hot stones inside, and the young men pour water from a hide-bucket upon the little stone heap. Steam and vapor arise, completely filling the enclosure. The attendant has meanwhile covered the opening so that no air from the outside may penetrate. As the vapor condenses, the attendant thrusts more stones within, and thus the operation is continued as long as the youths can stand the confinement. The pipe is also smoked during the sweat. When the young men issue from their bath, the perspiration is fairly streaming from every pore. If it is not cold weather they plunge into a pool in the creek near by, but if it be chilly they wrap blankets about their bodies. None of the whites and half-breeds, who have witnessed these things ever saw a Sioux rub himself after issuing from the bath.

Several sweat-houses are erected in order to prepare the young men for the dance. When a good number of young men, say fifty or sixty, have thus prepared themselves, the high-priest and his assistants come forward. The high-priest wears eagle-feathers in his hair, and a short skirt reaches from his waist nearly to his knees. The dancers wear no ornaments whatever, and enter the circle without their blankets, many of them wearing only their ordinary clothes.

That Indians should lay aside all ornaments and finery, and dance without the trappings which they so dearly love, proves conclusively that some powerful religious influence is at work. In their other dances, the Omaha, the Old Woman, the Sun, and War Dances, feathers and bangles, weapons, herbs or painted and plaited grasses, porcupine quills, horses' tails, and bits of fur-skins, necklaces, bells, silver disks, etc., are worn in great profusion.

The candidates for "conversion" do not fast, as has been stated by several writers who have not thoroughly investigated this subject. After they have come forth from the sweat-house they are ready to enter the sacred circle. The high-priest runs quickly from the village to the open space of ground, five or six hundred yards distant, and, stationing himself near the sacred tree, begins his chant as follows:

"Hear, hear you all persons!

"Come, hurry up and dance, and when you have finished running the circle, tell these people what you have seen in the spirit land.

"I myself have been in the spirit land and have seen many strange and beautiful things, all of which great Wakantanka rules over and which my eyes tell me are good and true."

As the speaker proceeds, the men and woman leave their tepees and crowd to the dance-ground. They form two or three circles, according to the number of persons who wish to participate, and, grasping hands with fingers interlocked ("Indian grip"), the

SIOUX GHOST DANCE. (Drawn from Sketch Made on the Spot.)

544

circles begin to move around toward the left. They rub their palms in dust or sand to prevent slipping, for it is considered unlucky for one to break connections.

The sacred tree needs a few words of explanation. It is a nearly straight sapling thirty or forty feet high, trimmed of branches to a height of several feet. To the topmost twigs is actached a small white flag or canvass strip, supposed to be an emblem of purity, together with some of colors. The base of the tree is wrapped with rushes and flags to a thickness of about five feet. Between the reeds the dancers from time to time thrust little gifts or peace-offerings. These offerings are supposed to allay the anger of the Great Spirit, and are given in perfectly good faith by the poor natives. They consist of small pieces of calico, bags of tobacco, or pipes.

As the circle moves toward the left, the priest and his assistants cry out loudly for the dancers to stop a moment. As they pause he raises his hands toward the west, and, upon all the people acting similarly, begins the following remarkable prayer:

"Great Spirit, look at us now. Grandfather and Grandmother have come. All these good people are going to see Wakantanka, but they will be brought safely back to earth. Everything that is good you will see there, and you can have all these things by going there. All things that you hear there will be holy and true, and when you return you can tell your friends how spiritual it is."

As he prays, the dancers cry aloud with all the fervor of religious fanatics. They moan and sob, many of them exclaiming: "Great Father, I want you to have pity upon me!"

The breasts of the worshippers heave with emotion; they groan and cry as if they were suffering great agony; and as the priest begs them to ask great Wakantanka to forgive their sins, such a cry of despair and anguish arises as to deeply affect even the whites present.

After prayer and weeping, and offerings have been made to the sacred pole, the dance is started again. The dancers go rather slowly at first, and as the priests in the center begin to shout and leap about, the dancers partake of the enthusiasm. Instead of moving with a regular step, each person jumps backward and forward, up and down, as hard as he or she can without relinquising their hold upon their neighbor's hand.

One by one the dancers fall out of the ranks, some staggering like drunken men, others wildly rushing here and there almost bereft of reason. Many fall upon the earth to writhe about as if possessed of demons, while blinded women throw their clothes over their heads and run through brush or against trees. The priests are kept busy waving eagle-feathers in the faces of the most violent worshipers. The feather is considered sacred, and its use, together with the mesmeric glance and motion of the priest, soon causes the victim to fall into a trance or deep sleep.

When the "converts" come out of the trance they frequently claim to have seen glorious visions, to have visited heaven, and to have talked with the Messiah. An Indian named Little Wound relates his experience as follows:

"When I fell in the trance a great and grand eagle came and carried me over a great hill, where there was a village such as we used to have before the whites came into the country. The tepees were all of buffalo hides, and we made use of the bow and arrow, there being nothing of white man's manufacture in the beautiful land. Nor were any whites permitted to live there. The broad and fertile lands stretched in every direction, and were most pleasing to my eyes.

"I was taken into the presence of the great Messiah, and he spoke to me these words:

"'My child, I am glad to see you. Do you want to see your children and relations who are dead?'"

"I replied: 'Yes, I would like to see my relations who have been dead a long time.' The God then called my friends to come up to where I was. They appeared, riding the finest horses I ever saw, dressed in superb and most brilliant garments, and seeming very happy. As they approached, I recognized the playmates of my childhood, and I ran forward to embrace them while the tears of joy ran down my cheeks.

"We all went together to another village, where there were very large lodges of buffalo-hide, and there held a long talk with the great Wakantanka. Then he had some squaws prepare us a meal of many herbs, meat, and wild fruits and 'wasna' (pounded beef and choke-cherries). After we had eaten, the Great Spirit prayed for our people upon the earth, and then we all took a smoke out of a fine pipe ornamented with the most beautiful feathers and porcupine quills. Then we left the city and looked into a great valley where there were thousands of buffalo, deer, and elk feeding.

"After seeing the valley, we returned to the city, the Great

SIOUX MEDICINE CHIEF.

Spirit speaking meanwhile. He told me that the earth was now *bad* and *worn out;* that we needed a new dwelling-place where the rascally whites could not disturb us. He further instructed me to return to my people, the Sioux, and say to them that if they would be constant in the dance and pay no attention to the whites he would shortly come to their aid. If the high-priests would make for the dancers medicine-shirts and pray over them, no harm could come to the wearer; that the bullets of any whites that desired to stop the Messiah Dance would fall to the ground without doing anyone harm, and the person firing such shots would drop dead. He said that he had prepared a hole in the ground filled with hot water and fire for the reception of all white men and non-believers. With these parting words I was commanded to return to earth.''

One of the visions seen by a young woman, when under the influence of the trance, varied somewhat from the others. She said:

'' I was carried into the beautiful land as others have been, and there I saw a small but well-made lodge constructed entirely of rushes and reeds. These were woven closely together and resembled the fine basket-work that many of our squaws make during the winter. The tepee was provided with a stone wall, which was composed of small, flat stones laid up against the walls to the height of three or four feet. In this lodge the great Wakantanka dwelt and would issue forth at noon. Promptly at the time when the sun was above me the lodge trembled violently and then began its descent toward the earth. It landed near the dance-ground, and there stepped forth a man clothed in a blanket of rabbit-hides. This was the Messiah, and he had come to save us.''

The vision of Little Horse is still more remarkable. Through the Weasel he said:

'' Two holy eagles transported me to the Happy Hunting Grounds. They showed me the Great Messiah there, and as I looked upon his fair countenance I wept, for there were nail-prints in his hands and feet where the cruel whites had once fastened him to a large cross. There was a small wound in his side also, but as he kept himself covered with a beautiful mantle of feathers this wound only could be seen when he shifted his blanket. He insisted that we continue the dance, and promised me that no whites should enter his city nor partake of the good things he had prepared for the Indians. The earth, he said, was now worn out and it should be repeopled.

'' He had a long beard and long hair and was the most handsome man I ever looked upon.''

A SIOUX VILLAGE.

It is impossible to follow with unprejudiced mind the development of this strange movement among the Indians and not be impressed with the strong undercurrent of truly religious feeling among them.   The address of the old chief Two Lance at the great council held on Wounded Knee Creek, in the Spring of 1890, reveals a state of mind and heart of which the savage red man has not often been suspected.   It was at this meeting that the head chiefs gave countenance to the new faith.

Runners announced that a great council would be held upon Wounded Knee Creek, in which an old man would deliver a special message from Great Wakantanka to the Sioux nation, and requested all men and women interested in the welfare of the nation to be present.   The meeting was held at night upon a spot of ground near No Water's camp.   Probably four or five hundred men and six hundred women were present.   Two Lance, the old man selected to speak, rose slowly to his feet, advanced to a point near the great bonfire around which the people were seated in several circles, and spoke the following words :

"Brothers, if you listen to my words attentively you will profit thereby.   We have returned from the country of the Utes bringing good news for the Dakotas.   Many, many winters ago the Great Spirit sent His Son upon the earth to teach men to do right—to be good.   Instead of listening to the words of the holy Visitor, the wicked white men killed Him.   He has appeared to a good and righteous man in the land of the Utes, and told him that he would soon come upon earth again ; but this time for the salvation of the Indians, and not the whites. The whites are to be overwhelmed, so the Messiah said, by a great earthquake or storm.   In the terrible convulsion of the earth, all Indians who are not prepared to welcome their Lord will meet with the same fate as the whites.   Therefore, O my people, I exhort, nay, command you to do all that the good man says, in order that you may not suffer the death of our despised enemies.

"The holy Teacher further says that the overpowering of those who have oppressed us is not to be accomplished by force of arms, that no weapons are to be used.   We are simply to pray and trust in the Messiah, and dance as he shall command.   This is to us a very strange doctrine, as you will admit.   We have been accustomed to fight, not to pray.   Therefore we must be all the more careful to obey every command of the new Saviour, or we will displease him.

"In conclusion, I have but to urge upon you to watch very carefully every motion of the dance which we are about to execute for you, and, when you have learned the songs and the movements, join in with us. Be repentant for your sins, pray the Great Wakantanka to look down upon you in pity, to give you food and clothing. Be sincere, be earnest, and He will hear our prayers."

A SIOUX TOMB.

Filled with the strange new hope inspired by such language, and despairing of finding truth or help in the white man, the Indians eagerly adopted the new doctrine and the now famous "Messiah Craze" reached its fullest development. In a succeeding chapter will be related the tragic events to which it has led, together with some reflections on the policy which has led to so frightful a cost in suffering and death.

THE LAST STAND.

552

CHAPTER XXIX.

THE SIOUX OUTBREAK.

In 1889 Congress, without consulting the tribes of the Sioux, appointed a commission, of which Ex-Gov. Foster, of Ohio, and Gen. Geo. A. Crook were distinguished members, for the purpose of "buying" an enormous tract of land belonging to what was then their reservation. Again and again the Indians who were the responsible leaders of the tribe refused to consent, but the commissioners, by securing the signatures of Indians of all grades, obtained an apparent consent of the majority of the tribe.

ONE OF ST. CASEY'S SCOUTS.

The Sioux have no written proof of the promise made them two years ago by Ex-Governor Foster and his colleagues, but they have the testimony of many witnesses who heard the words of the whites, which were forgotten by the speakers almost as soon as uttered. Among other things, the commissioners promised that the one million pounds of beef per year which had been struck out of the annuity list should be returned; that thirty school-houses should be erected upon the reservation; that they would do all in their power to have more flour, cloth, wagons and utensils issued annually; and that the whites should be prohibited from entering the bounds of the reservation. General Crook took a strong position against the errors committed by the others in making hasty promises that signatures to the bill might be secured. Against the integrity and personal character of the commissioners nothing can be said. It is their ignorance of Indian nature and their frivolous and careless methods in the consideration of a measure of the greatest importance to the Sioux which must be condemned.

WINTER CAMP OF CASEY'S SCOUTS.

The commissioners were satisfied with the result. They had secured from the Sioux several million acres of land. In their anxiety to attain this end, they did not pause in their work to make inquiries as to the right of any man to sign the bill. Let it be remembered, to their shame, that they received the signature of the squaw-man notorious upon the reservation as a political trickster, who had resided but a few years at Pine Ridge, had left his former Indian wife because she no longer pleased him, and was living with another; and this man they listed as a " full-blooded Ogalalla " ! An honest and faithful German employee, filled with righteous indignation on seeing the name of the impostor on the bill (a copy of which is in the possession of Chief Red Cloud), denounced the " Ogalalla " in the most bitter terms. Strange as it may appear to lovers of justice and honor, this scoundrel was recently appointed to a government position, while the manly German who had the courage to denounce him was cautioned to " keep a civil tongue in his head, or he would lose his situation."

Can we wonder that a proud people, compelled to render obedience to such men, should cry out, with all the fervor of a race in bondage, to the great Messiah to come to their aid? They had tried the Government at Washington, and found it a broken reed; to whom could they turn next save to Him who said, " I will repay " ?

The Sioux waited patiently for thirty-four weeks in the vain hope of receiving more rations and the fulfilment of the commission's promises. A great council was held. Agent Galagher was appealed to. The agent went to Washington and consulted with such of the officials as he could find at their post of duty. He insisted that the million pounds of beef withdrawn from the yearly annuities should be returned or he would not be responsible for the action of the Indians under his charge. He claimed that the Indians were suffering from a lack of sufficient food, and knew of a certainty that several children had died from starvation.

How did the Commissioner of Indian Affairs receive the agent's report? Did he endeavor to have the million pounds of beef re-entered in the annuities? By no means. He concluded the reports of Mr. Galagher were somewhat exaggerated, and gave the matter no further thought.

The winter of 1889 set in, and still there was no evidence that the promises would be fulfilled. Fortunately it was a mild winter, and the Sioux did not suffer more than during the summer. Mr. Sweeny, one of the school-teachers upon Medicine Root Creek, relates that the children under his instruction brought their dinners in little beaded sacks. Out of curiosity he opened several of these " lunch baskets, " and examined their contents. None of them contained more than a small piece of jerked beef and a hastily prepared heavy biscuit. No bread, cake, pie, or vegetable was found in any of those examined. He told me further that the children would get very hungry on the colder days, and during recess would dig out chipmunks and prairie dogs, which they cooked and ate without seasoning. The teacher fed many of the hungry little ones at his own home, using

LIEUTENANT CASEY.

a considerable part of his slender salary in this charitable work.

The report of Agent Galagher, submitted to the Indian Bureau upon his resignation in favor of Agent Royer, showed a number of cattle smaller by one-third than was reported by Mr. McGillicuddy. It had taken the Sioux ten or twelve years to accumulate the herds of horses and cattle which the documents show were ranging upon the reservation in the summer of 1889. What has become of the five thousand missing steers? Did thieves steal them? The deputy marshals say they have not arrested more than forty cattle-thieves upon the reserve during the past two years, and these offenders never secured more than one or two head before capture. Is it probable the Sioux would deliberately kill the herds of

CAMP OF FRIENDLY SIOUX.

which they were so proud, unless forced to do so by hunger?

When the rations were reduced one million pounds they asked that a discrimination be made between summer and winter weight of steers. They said : " If you give us four hundred steers every other Wednesday during the summer and list them as weighing twelve hundred pounds each, you should list the same number during the winter as weighing nine hundred pounds each. Your cattle are not stable-fed ; they range about in the winter snows searching for grass. They find but a small quantity ; therefore they cannot fatten, but, on the contrary, grow poor. The shrinkage is not in bone and sinew, but in the most tender portions. Write to the Great Father and say we cannot live upon the few cattle he gives us."

The Great Father, of course, took no notice of this request, and the Indians were compelled to slaughter their own herds. One by one the cattle disappeared, until at last but few remained upon the government ranges. The agent, seeing the work of years vanishing in weeks, made another frantic appeal to Washington. But his letter was pigeon-holed along with those of other agents. The authorities could not understand why Indians should suffer. Did they not fare sumptuously every day at the expense of a rich and generous government? Why, then, should they harass the commissioner by frequent appeals for aid? It was evident that all these Indians were liars seeking to defraud a government which had already been too liberal. And so the bureau did nothing, and the Sioux continued to kill their cattle.

Such was the situation and such the state of mind among the tribes of the Sioux when the startling message of Two Lance was delivered at the great council on Wounded Knee Creek.

In a few days the whole nation was infatuated with the new craze. They danced, and prayed, and pleaded with such earnestness as can scarcely be imagined. But their God heard not. He saw not their gifts thrust into the matting about the Sacred Tree. He regarded no song of appeal for aid. He heeded not the tears nor the sobs of anguish for sin.

In their affliction they turned their gaze to the stars, to the moon above, during the long and weary hours of the night dance. The heavenly bodies seemed to look down with pity and compassion upon the supplicating throng beneath, but their cries met no response.

On and on they danced, dragging weary limbs about the circle.

TEPEE CAMP OF A HEAD CHIEF.

hoping, trusting that He who lived beyond the stars would take pity upon them. The hoot of the owls in the great cotton-wood trees, or the yelp of a coyote upon the plain, mocked the sanctity of the song, and these sounds were the only answers to their pleadings.

As time passed and the Messiah failed to appear, there came a change in the minds of the worshipers. Some of the more sceptical advocated a cessation of the ceremonies, but they en-countered the most bitter denunciation on the part of those still firm in the faith. The trouble between the two factions reached its height during Agent Galagher's visit to No Water's camp upon Wounded Knee Creek. Those who had lost faith in the Messiah attempted to dissuade the others from driving the agent back to Pine Ridge; but the latter were strongest and carried the day, compelling Mr. Galagher to return to the agency more hastily than he set out.

A few weeks afterward Dr. Royer entered upon his duties at Pine Ridge. With the new administration came an order to all Indians not believers in the new Messiah to locate near the agency. The Indian police were kept very busy for several weeks notify-ing the distant camps of this command, and assisting those who were unable to travel. Early in November all the anti-Messiah-ists were encamped near the agency, under the surveillance of the military. The converts to the new doctrine encamped on several creeks twenty miles from the agency until the middle of November, and then, becoming alarmed at the presence of so many troops, fled into the Bad Lands.

For two miles in every direction around the agency were the tepees of the friendlies. Ten years ago nearly all the Sioux were living in hide or canvas lodges. Now the most of them live in good, substantial houses, many of which are decorated with pic-tures and ornaments. Every Dakota owns a tepee, but uses it only during summer hunting excursions. The youngest children were born in log houses, and even the older persons are so ac-customed to a good dwelling that they feel ill at ease in a canvas lodge. Consider therefore, the sufferings of these people, crowded together in frail tents, with insufficient clothing, with no fuel to be had nearer than the timber-covered bluffs eight miles away, and the half-starved ponies able to haul but small quantities of this.

WINTER CAMP OF U. S TROOPS.

They pleaded in vain with the agent to allow them to return to their log houses. The children were sick with colds, many had diphtheria, and several died. Fortune smiled upon them by giving a month of the most beautiful weather in the fall, but fearful storms have since swept down upon them with scarcely an hour's warning. Blizzards may spring up inside of thirty minutes; the thermometer has been known to fall fifty-eight degrees inside of an hour upon the reservation. Even the most stoical man must be moved when he contemplates the terrible suffering, not to mention the loss of life and property, that must needs accompany a Dakota storm.

The anti-Messiahists were perfectly aware of the danger that threatened them. Not long ago the wife of one of the greatest chiefs said:

"Why are we detained here? My husband, my brother, my cousin are not going to join the dancers in the Bad Lands. There is not a family in this large camp" (of one hundred and ninety-five tepees) "that does not watch over at least one sick child. The coughing and crying of poor distressed babes keeps us all awake at night. It is two miles from here to the government buildings, and, should a great blizzard swoop down upon us, many women and children would perish before the men could get us into the Great Father's warm houses.

"Look about you! You see a much-patched lodge. There are holes in every strip of canvas on the poles, through which the chilly blast penetrates. Our little fire is not large enough to keep the children warm, and were it made greater, the smoke would be so dense we could scarcely remain inside. We cannot haul much wood in our wagons, for the distance to the bluffs where the pines grow is eight miles, and our horses are not strong.

"Oh! why are we kept here? The hostiles should be made to suffer, not us. They caused all this trouble. Why do the innocent suffer while the guilty go unpunished?"

And here the poor woman broke down sobbing. Her lord looked on in silence, bearing, with all the impassiveness of his race, the troubles brought down upon his home by the action of the dancers.

The answer to such appeals was the announcement that at the call of the agent, alarmed at his inability to secure obedience to

INTERIOR OF OFFICERS' TENT

his mandate that the dance cease; more troops were coming. Meanwhile, correspondents of eastern newspapers anxious to secure sensational items with which to regale their readers, spread false reports as to the character of the Messiah dance, and in all direction added to the alarm.

The Indians, who had not lost faith in the promised Messiah, and who were not conscious of any breach of law or right in their worship of Him, resented the presence of the troops and fled to the Bad Lands, not because they wanted to fight, but because they desired to worship their Great Spirit and be ready to welcome the Messiah, undisturbed by the white man.

No effort was spared to carry out the policy of repression and control which the goverment had inaugurated, and to secure the collection of all the Indians under the guns of the agency. It was recognized on all sides that the most powerful influence was that exerted by Sitting Bull. It was determined that he should be brought to the agency and every influence that could be brought to bear was put forth to this end. The report of Indian Agent McLaughlin reveals the nature of such efforts, and throws a flood of light on the character of him who was, perhaps, the greatest Indian since the days of Tecumseh.

The document is addressed to Commissioner of Indian Affairs Morgan, and reads in full as follows:

"Having just returned from Grand River district, and, referring to my former communication regarding the ghost dance craze among the Indians, I have the honor to report that on Saturday evening last I learned that such a dance was in progress in Sitting Bull's camp, and that a large number of Indians of the Grand River settlements were participators. Sitting Bull's camp is on the Grand River, forty miles southwest from the agency, in a section of country outside of the line of travel, only visited by those connected with the Indian service, and was, therefore, a secluded place for these scenes.

"I concluded to take them by surprise, and on Saturday morning left for that settlement, accompanied by Louis Primeau, arriving there about 3 P. M., and, having left the road usually traveled by me in visiting the settlement, we got upon them unexpectedly and found a ghost dance at its height.

"There were about forty-five men, twenty-five women, twenty-five boys, and ten girls participating (a majority of the boys and girls, until a few weeks ago, pupils of the day schools of the Grand River settlement), and approximating 200 with lookers-on, most of whom had their families with them and encamped in the neighborhood. I did not attempt to stop the dance then going on, as, in their crazed condition, under the excitement, it would have been useless to attempt it, but after remaining some time talking with a number of the spectators, I went on to the house of Henry Bullhead, three miles distant, where I remained over night, and returned to Sitting Bull's house next morning, where I had a long talk with Sitting Bull and a number of his followers.

INDIAN POLICE.

"I spoke very plainly to them, pointing out what had been

done by the government for the Sioux people, and how this faction, by their present conduct, were abusing the confidence that had been reposed in them by the government in its magnanimity in granting them full amnesty for all past offences when, from destitution and imminent starvation, they were compelled to surrender as prisoners of war in 1880 and 1881, and I dwelt at length upon what was being done in the way of education of their children and for their own industrial advancement, and assured them of what this absurd chase would lead to and the result that would certainly follow.

"I spoke with feeling and earnestness, and my task was well received, and I am convinced that it had a good effect. Sitting Bull, while being very obstinate and at first inclined to assume the role of big chief before his followers, finally admitted the truths of my reasoning, and said that he believed me to be a friend to the Indians as a people, but that I did not like him personally, but that when in doubt in any matter in following my advice he had always found it well, and that now he had a proposition to make to me which, if I agreed to and would carry out, it would allay all further excitement among the Sioux over the ghost dance, or else convince me of the truth of the belief of the Indians in their new doctrine.

"He then stated his proposition, which was that I should accompany him on a journey to trace from the beginning the story of the Indian Messiah, and when he reached the last tribe, or where it originated, if they could not produce the man who started the story, and we did not find the new Messiah, as described, upon the earth, together with the dead Indians returning to reinhabit this country, he would return convinced that they (the Indians) had been too credulous and imposed upon, which report from him would satisfy the Sioux, and all practices of the ghost societies would cease; but if we found the Messiah, they be permitted to continue their medicine practices, and organize as they are now endeavoring to do.

"I told him that this proposition was a novel one, but that the attempt to carry it out would be similar to an attempt to catch up with the wind that blew last year, but that I wished him to come to my house, where I would give him a whole night or a day and night, in which time I thought I could convince him of the absurdity of this foolish craze, and the fact of his making me the proposition that he did was a convincing proof that he did not fully believe in what he was professing and he tried so hard to make others believe.

" He did not, however, promise fully to come into the agency to discuss the matter, but said he would consider my talk and decide after deliberation. I consumed three days in making this trip, and feel well repaid for what I accomplished, as my presence in their midst encouraged the weaker and doubting, and set those who are believers to thinking of the advisability of discontinuing the nonsensical practices. I also found that the active members in the dance were not more than half the number of the earlier dancers, and I believe that it is losing ground among the Indians, and while there are many who half-believe, I am satisfied that I can keep the dance confined to the Grand River district.

" Desiring to use every reasonable means to bring Sitting Bull and his followers to abandon this dance, and to look upon its practice as detrimental to their individual interest and the welfare of their children, I made the trip herein reported to ascertain the extent of the disaffection and the best means of effecting its discontinuance. From close observation I am convinced that the dance can be broken up ; and after due reflection would respectfully suggest that in case my visit to Sitting Bull fails to bring him to regard the matter as he ought to do, all Indians living on Grand River be notified that those wishing to be known as opposed to the ghost doctrine, friendly to the government, desiring the support provided in the treaty, must report to the agency for such enrollment and be required to camp near the agency for a few weeks, and those selecting their medicine practices, a violation of department orders, to remain on Grand River. Something looking towards breaking up this craze must be done, and now that cold weather is approaching is the proper time. Such a step as here suggested would leave but a few followers, as most would report for enrollment, and thus he would be forced in himself.

" There are not many frauds among these Indians, still there are a few, and they have been used to turn in all their arms and get a memorandum or report for the same. Knowing the Indians as I do, I am confident that I can by such a course settle the Messiah craze at this agency, and also thus break up the

DEATH OF SITTING BULL.

power of Sitting Bull without trouble, and with but little excitement. This will be sustained by public sentiment, and conform to the discipline approved by the good-disposed Indians. It is true that it would unsettle the Indians in that district in their home life for a few weeks, but after which all worry and uneasiness would cease, while, with the ghost practices continued, all the participants being Indians regularly rationed by the government without any appearance of withdrawal of this support, anxiety among well disposed, and the greater temptation for others to join is increased."

When it was found that cajolery and threats were alike thrown away on Sitting Bull, his arrest was determined on. It was held that his failure to send his children to the agency school, and to report in person was a sufficient breach of peace to justify such a step. A band of Indian police led by a brave "faithful" named Bull Head was detailed for the purpose. Cautiously but rapidly approaching the old man's camp, they succeeded in reaching his house or tepee before the alarm was given. As soon, however, as their errand was understood, it became evident that his followers would resist. It will perhaps never be known how the melee commenced, but Bull Head, understanding that his mission was the removal of this prisoner alive or dead, promptly shot him, himself being immediately mortally wounded.

Bull Head, lieutenant of police, came to Sitting Bull's house with a warrant for his arrest. No one but the old chief and his two sons were there. Sitting Bull opened the door and his son seeing the house surrounded by police, gave the cry of alarm. Without hesitating a moment Bull Head fired at Sitting Bull, the ball striking the breast over the left nipple, killing him almost instantly. While reeling Sitting Bull managed to draw a revolver, which exploded just as he fell, the bullet entering Bull Head's thigh. Bull Head died two days later from the effects. A terrific hand-to-hand fight ensued. Sitting Bull's followers swarmed around the police and guns were clubbed. The ground was strewn with broken stocks and bent barrels. The police, numbering thirty, were getting the worst of it and retreated into Sitting Bull's house. The hostiles retired to ambush, having learned of the soldiers' coming. The dead and wounded were carried back to the post. The bodies were frightfully mutilated, one Indian policeman lifting Sitting Bull's scalp.

The old chief's body was a sickening sight. An Indian battered his face into jelly with a plank. After tiring of this devilish sport, he balanced the plank on his nose, and left it there with maniacal glee. The few remaining hairs in his head were clipped off, his moccasins and most of his clothing carried away for relics. Among his personal effects were found letters from Mrs. Weldon of New York warning him to flee from the agency, as the government was about to have him killed. Sitting Bull was prepared to depart when surprised by the Indian police.

The event leading up to the killing of Sitting Bull, and that tragic and ill advised occurrence itself, at once threw the tribes of the Sioux into the wildest excitement. From all sides came reports that they were gathering under other leaders and rendezvousing in the inaccessible hills of the country called the Bad Lands. Hundreds of young warriors who had remained near the agency, and who were considered "friendlies," stole away during the night and joined their friends in the war dance. Into the camp which they had formed no white man save one was permitted to enter. This man was a pious Catholic priest, known as father Juby, known to many of them for his sincere goodness and friendship toward their race. But although they received him kindly and heard his message, they refused to be influenced by it.

The first reliable information regarding the location of the camp of the hostiles was brought in by Louis Shangraux, one of the bravest fellows that ever left Pine Ridge Agency. The mission of peace attempted by the thirty-two Indians headed by this half-breed (part French part Indian) was one of the most dangerous and exciting expeditions ever carried out in the history of border warfare in this country.

At noon Monday, the 15th of December, there appeared a sight never to be forgotten. Over the hill, a quarter of a mile to the northwest of the agency came riding at full speed thirty-two men, sixteen abreast. Their horses were covered with foam from a long and rapid ride, and as they advanced they chanted in loud tones their song of victory, heralding their exploits. As the cavalcade drew near the song became louder. Louis Shangraux rode at the head, with No Neck immediately behind him.

Every man was superbly mounted and well armed. Six-shooters were strapped to their sides, while the gun-case (in many instances neatly beaded and ornamented) was strapped to the saddle, only the butts of trusty Winchesters being visible. The ponies seemed to partake of the joy of the men, for they pranced about and champed their bits, while their eyes snapped with vivacity. They drew up in front of the general's (Brooke) headquarters,

LOUIS SHANGRAUX, THE HALF-BREED SCOUT.

and as the last notes of the song died away leaped from the animals' backs. The general himself welcomed them with words of commendation, for he thoroughly appreciated the efforts of the "friendlies" in the desire to prevent bloodshed. The Indians remained closeted with the officers for some time, and then left to return to their several tepees.

The account given by Shangraux, itself intensely dramatic, reveals most clearly the mental condition of those whom the policy of the government had driven into the attitude of "hostiles." The account is given as nearly as possible in his own words:

Louis was given the power to select his party, and accordingly chose some good, true men who he knew could be depended upon in case of trouble. No white men went with them, for it was believed the hostiles would kill any one not an Indian who should venture near the camp. From subsequent events this was found to be true.

Bright and early the "friendlies" set out, with several days' provisions and plenty of ammunition. They rode at a good pace, and reached a high point of land about five miles from the hostiles at sundown — there went into camp near a small stream. The fire which they started to prepare coffee was seen by the hostiles, and at sunrise twenty Sioux, armed to the teeth, rode into the friendlies' camping-ground, and demanded:

"What do you want here? Have you come to spy on us? Speak quick, or we will shoot you."

The scouts did not appear frightened, but advanced without arms to meet the hostiles. Louis assured them that they had come on a mission of peace to hold a great council and talk over matters. He said that his men were not warriors, but talkers. After some parley, the hostiles agreed to escort the band into the Bad Lands camp. So, as soon as the ponies were caught and saddled up, the entire outfit moved toward Short Bull's great fort.

The country through which they rode presents a similar appearance to a volcanic region. Great fissures yawn on all sides, peaks of gray-colored earth, or a dirty whitish limestone bluff towers here and a precipice extends there. The trees become stunted as one advances, and the grass disappears. Finally all vegetation vanishes, and there remains naught but a series of peaks, of deep valleys, of horrible pits suggestive of the road to the infernal regions! Truly, a more fitting place for an Indian massacre could not be found in the United States. Occasional broader valleys afford a stunted growth of grass for ponies, but these fertile spots are great distances apart and of limited extent.

ON GUARD.

In prehistoric times eruptions of the submerged volcanoes, or shrinkages in the earth's crust, have caused the irregularities which everywhere exist. The scout says that the country affords splendid places for ambuscades—little amphitheatres, as it were, with but one entrance, the sides of which are so irregular as to form good hiding-places for lurking savages. The hostiles' fort cannot be approached except through about five miles of such land. May God have mercy on any army that attemps to enter such a place without two or three hundred good scouts in advance to thoroughly investigate every nook and corner!

One mile from the fort the entire party was halted, and Short Bull himself advanced for a few words regarding Shangraux's mission. The scout says nothing of importance transpired until all were within the fort; then he had time to look about, and note particularly the inside and outside of the stronghold.

The camp is placed upon a plateau one hundred and thirty feet above the surrounding valleys. There is only one place where men can enter it, and that place is but twenty feet wide. The peaks tower higher than the little plateau on which lies the fort, but these hills, being perpendicular and terminating in points, would afford no advantage to troops. The road, or shelving-rock layer, leading into the fort is broad at the base, but narrow as one approaches the top, and slopes at an angle of about twenty-one degrees. It would be extremely difficult for soldiers to charge up this shelving rock, and, even did they reach the summit, the breastwork thrown across the entrance would effectually check them.

Trenches are everywhere to be seen, and near the entrance exceed ten feet in depth and are very wide. On the farther side from the entrance there are two places where the hill slopes at an angle of thirty-eight or forty degrees. Of course, it would be out of the question for one to climb up such an incline, but the Indians might slide down safely in case they were compelled to retreat. All other sides of the plateau are perpendicular. Some rifle-pits have been excavated on the hills near at hand, and the Sioux, taking advantage of these, might harrass the soldiers should the latter gain access to the camp.

Taken altogether, Shangraux says the fortress is the most impregnable place he ever saw, and in his opinion the two hundred and fifty men who are now in it, and who assert their intention

FORTIFIED CAMP OF HOSTILES, BAD LANDS, SOUTH DAKOTA.

to die there before they will leave it, will be able to kill many hundred soldiers before they are whipped. He claims that the only way properly to assault the spot is by cannon. The Sioux have never fought a command armed with Hotchkiss guns and howitzers, and if cannon can be brought near, so that shells can be thrown into the fort, he thinks the Indians will not be able to hold it.

In corners, or under cover of little caves dug into the banks, were tons of jerked beef. Every warrior had three cartridge belts full of ammunition. They had loading tools by means of which they could reload old shells. There are two good springs of water inside the fort, and stunted cedars in a valley a mile distant. In case the fort was surrounded he thinks the wood supply could be cut off and the hostiles brought to terms. They would be able to raid cattle ranches south of their stronghold unless sufficient troops were sent to completely surround them.

The camp was thoroughly organized to withstand a prolonged siege, and was admirably chosen as a rally point for a long and desperate campaign.

Louis gave a very graphic description of the ghost dance as he beheld it executed in the camp:

"When we entered there were about two hundred and sixty-two lodges present. One hundred and seventeen of these remained and one hundred and forty-five returned with us to the agency. The squaws and men came forward to greet us, and all seemed very friendly. They supposed at first that we had come to join them, but when they learned our true mission they seemed very suspicious, and refused for some time to have anything to do with us. Just before we began the council, which lasted the greater part of four days, the high-priest and his helpers came forward and announced that there would be a ghost dance. They formed a circle about the Sacred Tree and began their chant.

"Of all the wild dancing I saw on Wounded Knee, this beat the 'shooting-match.' People went into trances by the dozen, and the priests were kept busy relating the experiences of the fainters. Several remained in trances as long as twelve hours, and gave evidences of utter exhaustion when the directors roused them.

"Short Bull said: 'I see the Messiah coming from the West. He is riding in a plain-wagon drawn by two mules, and looks very much like a black man. If he is our Messiah, we are greatly fooled. Now I see him again, and he is an Indian. Ah! wait; I see him the third time, and he is a white man. He tells me to send my children to school, to make large farms, and not to fight any more. Do not fight my children, unless the soldiers first fire upon you.'

"People were so excited they trembled all over, their eyes rolled, and the muscles of their faces twitched. They were the most crazy Indians I ever beheld."

SIOUX BOYS.

The dancing continued for nearly thirty hours; then there was an intermission of several hours, during which a council was held in order to give audience to the peace commission. Short Bull and Two Strike (his real name is Nompagahpa, and a literal translation is, "Knocks down Two"), aided by Crow Dog, championed the cause of the hostiles, while No Neck and Louis Shangraux spoke on behalf of the friendlies. Louis does not remember what he said in the first council, but the substance of his remarks could be put into one sentence:

37

"The agent will forgive you if you will return now, give you more rations, but not permit you to dance."

Short Bull's (Tatankaptecelan) reply was so forcible as to remain in Louis's memory in the exact words of the speaker.

The speech of Tatankaptecelan ran as follows:

"I have risen to-day to tell you something of importance. You have heard the words of the brothers from the agency camps, and if you have done as myself, you have weighed them carefully. If the Great Father would permit us to continue the dance, would give more rations, and quit taking away portions of the reservation, I would be in favor of returning. But even if you (turning to Louis) say that he will, how can we discern whether you are telling the truth? We have been lied to so many times that we will not believe any words that your agent sends to us. If we return he will take away our guns and ponies, put some of us in jail for stealing cattle and plundering houses. We prefer to stay here and die if necessary, to loss of liberty. We are free now and have plenty of beef, can dance all the time in obedience to the command of Great Wakantanka. We tell you to return to your agent and say to him that the Dakotas in the Bad Lands are not going to come in."

No Neck rejoined:

"Think, my people, how foolish is this action! Do come in, and all will be well; remain out here, and you will be killed."

Short Bull added:

"It is better to die here as brave men, and in obedience to the commands of the Good Spirit, than to live like cowards at the agency on scanty rations, disarmed, without horses and guns. No, we will not return! If we dance, our Good Spirit will protect us, and when all dancers are sincere, the bullets of the soldiers will harmlessly fall to the ground without power to hurt. There is no army so powerful that it can contend with Wakantanka; therefore we are not afraid to remain here."

The gathering broke up, and nearly every one continued in the ghost dance. For two days the hostiles would not have further words with the friendly scouts. Friday and Saturday, the 12th and 13th, the last council was held. The scenes accompanying the closing of this gathering, Saturday afternoon, were very thrilling, and for a space of two hours it seemed as if a general

battle would ensue between those who desired to return to the
agency and the hostiles.

About noon, Saturday, Two Strike — who had been one of
the leaders in the dance — arose and announced his intention to
return to the agency with the scouts, accompanied by about one
hundred and forty-five lodges. Crow Dog (Kangi Sunka, the
Indian who killed Spotted Tail about ten years ago) also announced his intention of returning. At this declaration from
two such prominent men, Short Bull sprang to his feet and cried
out, angrily:

"At such a time as this we should all stick together like brothers.
Do not leave; remain with us. These men from the agency are
not telling us the truth; they will conduct you back to the
agency and they will place you in jail there. Louis is at the
bottom of this affair. *I know he is a traitor; kill him, kill
him!*"

And, running to the place where the guns were stacked, Short
Bull grasped his gun and, followed by many of his young men,
surrounded Shangraux. Louis' situation was desperate. He
knew these furious men might kill him at the slightest resistance, so he laughed as good-naturedly as possible under the
circumstances and told them to put up their guns, as he was
their friend instead of their enemy.

"No, do not let the friendlies return!" cried the young men;
"kill them or compel them to remain with us. They will tell
the agent all they have seen, and the soldiers will know how to
enter our camp."

With clubbed guns many of the desperate youths rushed upon
the friendlies and scouts; others cocked their Winchesters, and
for a few moments it looked as if poor Louis and No Neck,
Two Strike and Crow Dog would lose their lives. Crow Dog
sat upon the ground and drew his blanket over his head. He
told your correspondent afterward that he expected to be struck
and killed any moment, and that he did not wish to know the
person who ·should commit the dastardly act — murdering a
brother Dakota.

The wiser heads prevailed, however, and after a great hub-
bub, in which several young men were knocked down, order was
restored. One of the horses and several of the dogs of the
friendlies were shot during the *melee*. When the one hundred

and forty-five lodges started from the camp, another difficulty arose. It was during this trouble that Crow Dog made his famous short speech:

"I am going back to White Clay (the location of the agency); you can kill me if you want to, now, and prevent my starting. The agent's words are true, and it is better to return than to stay here. I am not afraid to die."

Imagine the surprise of the friendlies when, upon looking back from the top of a ridge two miles distant, they saw the one hundred and seventeen lodges of hostiles coming after them. They halted to wait for Short Bull to catch up, and then the entire outfit moved toward the agency, all happy in the prospect of peace and forgiveness.

But the hopes of the friendlies were short-lived, for Short Bull became scared after having proceeded four miles farther, and, together with his band, left the rear of the column and returned to the Bad Lands.

Sunday and Monday morning, the Indians moved along the trail, reaching Red Cloud's camp, in sight of the agency headquarters just before noon. Monday. Louis and the scouts had ridden ahead and reached the general's presence as narrated in the fore-part of this article.

By this time it had become clearly evident that if the policy of force was to be made effective it would be necessary to concentrate a powerful military body in the land of the Dakotas. General Miles, one of the most successful and experienced of our army in dealing with the Indian was fortunately in command. From his headquarters in Chicago he directed the concentration of troops at Pine Ridge under the immediate command of Colonel Forsythe, of the Seventh Cavalry regiment. General Miles had already by the publication of an able article in the *North American Review* defined his position with regard to the treatment of the Indians, and the country expected of him a degree of temperance and patience and good judgment which could only result in great good. In so far as human foresight could control events this expectation was not disappoinied, and if it had been possible for officers and men to have caught the spirit of forbearance and self-control of their commander, the whole sad affair might and probably would have been brought to a close without the distressing and bloody events with which this story must close.

WINTER CAMP AT PINE RIDGE.

581

Under General Miles' direction, steps were taken to assure the Indians of the intention of the government to deal justly by them, although there would be no flinching from the stern and inflexible administration of the law toward those who remained hostile. It was perhaps a mistake that the old Seventh Cavalry, whose gallant leader, General Custer, and so many of their comrades had beens lain by this very tribe should have been among the soldiers detailed to this duty. Among them, "Remember Custer!" has been their battle-cry, and common report has credited them with an inflexible determination to revenge his death and that of their comrades.

Each day brought conflicting reports, but it was evident that the influence of the "Medicine man" was waning and that the tribe was recovering from its alleged frenzy. Little by little the bands of hostiles approached the agency, urged forward by the good generalship of Miles, who had so disposed of his forces that the bands were surrounded on all sides, save that towards the government station. It had been determined to secure a surrender of the hostiles and that their guns should be taken from them. Of all requirements this is the hardest for an Indian. His gun is next to his life. Without it he is as nothing. For it he will risk everything.

In this manner time dragged along until December 27th; on that day Big Foot's band was discovered shortly before noon by Little Bat, one of the Indian scouts. The hostile camp was eight miles northwest of Major Whiteside's camp on Wounded Knee. When this was reported to Major Whiteside he ordered four troops of the Seventh Cavalry into the saddle and marched to the point indicated by the scout. As the military approached the hostiles formed in a long line of battle 150 strong, armed with guns and knives, the latter stuck in their belts of cartridges, which were strapped outside their blankets.

Major Whiteside brought the men up in battle line, and when they came within about rifle-shot reach, one of the hostiles, an Indian, who was later recognized as Big Foot, came forward on foot and unarmed and signalled that he wanted to speak with the Major. Dismounting, the latter walked out and met the chief. As they came forward Big Foot extended his hand in token of peace.

"I am sick. My people here want peace and—"

Major Whiteside cut him short with: "I won't talk, nor will I have any parleying at all. It is either unconditional surrender or fight. What is your answer?"

"We surrender," said the chief. "We would have done so before, but we could not find you, and I did not find any soldiers to surrender to."

CAPT. WALLACE, TROOP K, 7TH CAVALRY.
KILLED AT WOUNDED KNEE CREEK, DECEMBER 28th, 1890.

Then at a signal his warriors raised a white flag. In less time than it takes to write it, the military had their prisoners surrounded and a courier was hastened into Pine Ridge Agency for the other four troops of the Seventh Cavalry and Lieutenant Taylor's scouts to help guard and disarm the party. There were 150 warriors, all perfectly armed, and 250 squaws, together with many chil-

dren. They seemed to be all well fixed for war, except that
some of them were without ponies. Major Whiteside had 2,500
soldiers.

Sunday, December 28th, at eight o'clock, they were ordered to
be in readiness to move. At that hour the cavalry and dismounted troops were massed about the Indian village, the Hotchkiss guns overlooking the camp not fifty yards away. Colonel
Forsythe ordered all the Indians to come forward away from the
tents. They came and sat in a half-circle until counted. The
dismounted troops where then thrown around them. Company
K, Captain Wallace, and Company B, Captain Varnum. The
order was then given to twenty Indians to go and get their guns.
Upon returning it was seen that only two guns were had. A
detachment at once began to search the village, resulting in thirty-
eight guns being found.

As this task was about completed, the Indians surrounded by
companies K and B began to move.

As was afterward learned the medicine man who accompanied
the band had made a last effort to reassert his power. He had
assured those who would believe in him that to the believer in the
Messiah who wore a " Ghost shirt," a garment provided for the
dancers, which had been "medicined" by him, no harm could
come, and the bullets of the soldiers, turned harmless from them,
would only kill white men. With blind faith they trusted him.
Standing in their midst he took a handful of dust from the ground
and threw it into the air, the Indian signal of battle. From
under their blankets the waiting warriors drew their Winchesters
and began firing rapidly at the troops not twenty feet away.

Nothing can describe the surprise and just anger of the soldiers at this act of unspeakable folly and treachery. The
deluded savages had just surrendered "at discretion." They
were almost surrounded by four or five times their own number of
soldiers and under the lips of the Hotchkiss guns, whose terrible
power they were to be the first Indians to feel. Nothing but
the blindest and most fanatical faith in the power of their medicine can account for their conduct; this, or the feeling that they
would rather die than part with their guns. The evidence, as we
shall see, points to the former as the key to their conduct. In
a moment the space of a few square rods was like the crater of
a volcano. More than thirty soldiers fell under the murderous

fire delivered literally in their faces. Nor could it be at once returned without extreme danger that friends would suffer quite as much as enemies. Indians whose guns had been taken, seized knives and tomahawks and began an attack, hand-to-hand. One of these standing near the gallant Capt. Wallace, had evidently selected him for a victim and buried a hatchet in his brain. With the nerve of the true American soldier, recovering from their surprise, and forming their ranks so that the danger of mutual destruction was reduced, a vengeful fire was poured into the group of nearly two hundred Indians. In an instant they realized the extent of their delusion when they saw that the "ghost shirt" formed an armor no more impregnable than their naked skins. Those who had not fallen in the first mad tumult, turned and fled toward the south, where the ground, broken into ravines, offered some shelter from the leaden storm. Women carrying papooses, half-grown children, and old men and warriors wearing the ghost shirt, could not in the smoke and dust be easily distinguished. Into the fleeing mass was poured an exterminating fire. So soon as the body of fleeing Indians had separated itself so that there was no danger to the cavalrymen, the Hotchkiss guns began their frightful work. Out of their steel lips there poured a stream of death-dealing missiles recaching after their fleeing victims far beyond the range of the cavalryman's carbine.

When the smoke of conflict cleared away, a sad sight revealed itself. The dead and dying were everywhere. Where the insane conflict had begun, friend and enemy lay side by side, some grappled in a death embrace. Among the tepees and away toward the south, and even under the shadow of the ravines, where the bullets from the far-reaching machine guns had reached them, men and women, and even little babes, lay in death, or with wounds, many of which would result in death. It was the saddest, apparently the most senseless of all the tragedies connected with the dealings of this nation with its "wards." Big Foot and his "band" were fairly obliterated.

Many occurrences illustrated how desperate was the fanaticism of the deluded red man, and how bitter his disappointment at the failure of the object of his faith. One young buck, one of the stongest and bravest, and who fell almost at the first fire, lay mortally wounded. When nurses of the Red Cross Society

GEN. MILES AND STAFF.

came to him and saw his condition, he asked as a dying request that they would lay him beside the body of the medicine man who had given the signal for the fight. His request was granted. He raised himself a moment to glance in the face of the dead prophet with a look of hatred, and then seizing his knife with what strength remained to him, plunged it two or three times in the dead body before he could be seized and prevented. When an explanation was asked, he told of the false promises which had been made and the lying prophecy about the "ghost shirt" and the "medicine." He believed now in the utter folly of it, and ere he died wished in his brutal way a brute's revenge.

Meanwhile, the news of the fight spread in all directions. Settlers fled to the forts and near towns. Friendly Indians flocked nearer to the agencies, while unfriendly ones fled to the hills.

Under cover of night, it is estimated that more than 2,500 young warriors who had camped at the agency, fled away toward the Bad Lands.

When the smoke of battle cleared away, when the terrible war-song of the Hotchkiss guns became silent, the anger of the soldiers, so natural at the treachery which had been practiced on them, gave place to sorrow and pity. Over the field of battle, searching the ravines and places of concealment, but always on the watch for that vindictive spirit that prompts a savage to spend his dying strength in killing a foe, the soldiers sought for the wounded, the non-combatants and for prisoners. So as time cleared away the uncertainty and secrecy of the movements of Big Foot's band, there came to light facts which had led many to feel that while its destruction was frightful, shocking the entire country, it was, perhaps, providential. The confessions of prisoners and the boasting of dying Indians has led even Gen. Miles to the conviction that a deep-laid plot existed wherein the Indians of Big Foot's band were to go through the form of a surrender and be taken to the agency. There, on an agreed signal, a night attack was to be made by all the warriors at the agency whose secrecy could be relied on. It was hoped and expected by them that by such a blow they would be able to strike terror into the heart of the white man, and that all the discontented tribes of the northwest, to the number of nearly a hundred thousand, would rise and join them in the greatest Indian war of history. Whether the leaders were sincere in their professed

Messianic belief, or merely used it as a means of controlling their followers, can never be determined ; of the sincerity of the rank and file there can be little doubt.

On receipt of the news of the Wounded Knee fight, Gen. Miles went at once to the scene of action. Hitherto he had remained at his headquarters, in Chicago, and directed the disposition of the troops by telegraph. He now assumed command in person.

While the desperate zealots of Big Foot's band were putting to such disastrous test the virtue of the Messiah medicine, an allied band were putting to another test the skill and discipline of a band of army adjuncts in the shape of teamsters and a force of " cow-boy" guards. A supply train was waylaid. The men in charge were not men inured to methods of Indian warfare and attack. It has been more than a dozen years since the employees of the government have had practical experience in it, and it was feared that the new men might fail if put to a severe test. But the wonderful American adaptibility displayed itself. Promptly, as though they were drilled veterans, they drew their wagons into the corral form, the horses within, and shielding their bodies behind a fortress extemporized from bales and boxes, they poured a murderous fire on their circling enemies. Chagrined by their failure, the Indians withdrew, carrying away their dead, as is their custom.

These two conflicts comprise all the real fighting in that which has passed into history as the great Sioux outbreak. It has been seldom in the history of the conflict of the red man with his white " brother" that an uprising of the Indian tribes has in its beginning exhibited such portentous promise. Stung by the oft-repeated breaches of treaty on the part of the government, driven by the prospect of hunger and suffering, and welded together by a religious frenzy, it promised at one time to involve all the tribes of the northwest, and extend its devastating terrors from the Missouri to the Pacific. It is thought by such excellent judges as General Miles and others equally well-posted, that the master mind of Sitting Bull had thought out the chances for the red man in such a conflict, in which the small number of our army, called on to protect so wide a territory, would have frittered away its strength and discipline in the presence of the best armed and equipped, and practically numberless, bands of barba-

GUARDING THE WAGON TRAIN.

rians the world has ever seen. But forces were found at work with which the Indian has not been hitherto called on to contend. The telegraph and the railroad have not hitherto counted as important factors. In this contest, the click of the operator's instrument almost mingled with the rattle of the rifle shots. The railway whistle could almost be heard from the field of battle. The resources of the most powerful nation on earth were available in a few days. Machine guns and artillery carried an unaccustomed terror to savage hearts.

There is little more to tell. As soon as the Indians could be made to understand that the way of surrender was open to them, they began to make their way to the headquarters which General Miles had established at the Pine Ridge Agency. They saw that the conflict was hopeless. The Messiah, which the warlike had hoped, as did the Jews of old, would come as a destroying angel, sweeping the white man from the earth and raising the Indian and buffalo from the dead, came not. The ghost shirt, which the medicine man had subjected to his incantations, was as pervious to the white man's bullets as the veriest cotton rag. Others remembered that in all the best messages which they had received from the Messiah, as for example, those from Johnson Sides, the Ute prophet, they had been told not to fight, and they realized that, in spirit and in fact, they had disobeyed these messages. Whatever had been the injustice and provocation by the white man, they had allowed themselves to be drawn into an attitude of bloodshed and rebellion. Under the impulse of these feelings, sincerely grieved over the loss of their friends and humiliated by their crushing defeat, they surrendered their cherished guns and submitted themselves and their fate to the Great Chief Miles.

Outside of the causes which led to it, and outside the murder of Sitting Bull, for the killing of that chief can hardly be described in any other word, there has never been a great Indian campaign more admirably conducted. Had it not been for the insane folly of Big Foot's band of zealots, which caused the fight at Wounded Knee, there would have remained but little for adverse criticism.

When the surrender had been completed, a " grand review " was held in order that the conquered tribes might be impressed, one would think, with the ease with which their extermination

THE INDIAN'S SLAUGHTER-HOUSE.

591

could have been effected. In the snow and cold of a Dakota winter, the infantry regiments, the battallions of cavalry, and the squadrons of light artillery countermarched in the presence of their commander. The Indians stood in grim silence, looking on. The next day occurred a scene which in its grim humor surpasses any occurrence recorded in the history of Indian warfare· Imitating the whites, the Indians marshaled their broken forces, hitched their lean and half-starved ponies to their wagons, loaded in their wives and children, and in silence filed in a forlorn review in the presence of their captain. It was as if they wished to show what a poor and weak remnant it was over which the white man boasted his power.

Twenty-five or thirty of the leading chiefs have been taken on to Washington to visit the Great Father and lay before him the grievance of their people. The sense of justice latent in this nation has been aroused in the Indian's behalf. Let us hope that while it does not lead to a false and childish sentimentalism in his treatment, it may secure such changes in the method of treatment as will secure truth and uprightness in carrying out the promises made.

THE END.